All Military Vehicles of the United States in WW II

DOGMA

All Military Vehicles of the United States in WW II

ISBN/EAN: 9783954540853

Auflage: 1

Erscheinungsjahr: 2012

Erscheinungsort: Bremen, Deutschland

© DOGMA in Europäischer Hochschulverlag GmbH & Co KG, Fahrenheitstr. 1, 28359 Bremen (www.dogma.de). Alle Rechte beim Verlag und bei den jeweiligen Lizenzgebern.

All Military Vehicles of the United States in WW II

DOGMA

This manual supersedes those portions of TM 9–2800, 27 October 1947, that pertain to Ordnance Corps vehicles, and TB 9–2800–2, 8 March 1948, including C1, 16 January 1950

Section I. INTRODUCTION

1. Scope

a. This manual covers the Army military vehicles for which the Ordnance Corps has the responsibility of storage and issue. Chassis that the Ordnance Corps supplies to other technical services for mounting bodies and special equipment peculiar to those services are also included.

b. A halftone illustration and dimensioned line sketch of each vehicle is shown, followed by tabulated data. These data include classification, purpose, characteristics, and performance of each vehicle. Data and illustrations have been obtained from the most reliable sources available at time of publication. These sources include vehicle manufacturers and responsible agencies of the Ordnance Corps. Further information is given in the technical manuals and supply catalogs listed for each vehicle.

c. Section II contains the vehicles arranged alphabetically. Within the alphabetical arrangement, the transport vehicles are listed by increasing capacities and the combat vehicles are listed by increasing caliber of the major armament. In the index, however, the vehicles are grouped by types.

d. Matériel which has been declared obsolete since publication of the superseded edition, 27 October 1947, has not been included in the revision.

e. The appendix contains a list of references to other pertinent publications.

2. Explanation of Terminology

a. Classification. Vehicles are classified from the standpoint of suitability for use as follows:

  (1) *Standard.* Standard vehicles are the most advanced and satisfactory that have been adopted, and are those which are preferred for procurement.

  (2) *Substitute standard.* Substitute standard vehicles are those that do not have as satisfactory military characteristics as standard vehicles, but are usable substitutes for standard vehicles and, when necessary, may be procured to supplement the supply of standard vehicles.

  (3) *Limited standard.* Limited standard vehicles are those that do not have as satisfactory military characteristics as standard vehicles, but are usable substitutes for standard vehicles, and are either in use or available for issue to meet supply demands. Complete vehicles will not be procured, but component parts, even though they may be limited-procurement articles, may be procured if necessary to maintain these vehicles in serviceable condition throughout a reasonable life expectancy.

  (4) *Nonclassified.* Vehicles to which no classification is assigned.

b. Technical Data.

  (1) *Wheels.* Where such data as "6 x 4" and "4 x 4" appear in vehicular nomenclature, the first figure indicates total number of wheels, and the second figure indicates number of driving wheels. Dual wheels are considered as one wheel.

  (2) *Net weight.* Weight of fully equipped vehicle in operating condition with fuel, lubricants, and water, but without crew or payload, unless otherwise specified.

    Note. It is emphasized that weights given in this manual are for tactical use only, and are not intended as official shipping weights for use in shipment by commercial carriers, due to variations between vehicles, variations resulting from changes in stowage, etc. Official vehicular shipping weights are contained in TB9–OSSC–G.

  (3) *Payload.* Weight of cargo or passengers, including crew, which may be safely imposed on vehicle.

  (4) *On-highway payload.*

    (a) Permissible payload for a tactical transport vehicle operated on highways only is based upon the maximum load capacity of the vehicle's tires.

    Caution: Payload and maximum gross weight for unrestricted operation will not exceed those shown on the vehicle data plate.

1

(b) Tactical vehicles for which the permissible on-highway loading is not given in this manual, nor on the vehicle data plate, will be reported by the using organization to the Office, Chief of Ordnance for determination of allowable loading.

(5) *Gross weight or fighting weight.* Weight of vehicle fully equipped and serviced for operation, including crew, plus maximum allowable payload of cargo or passengers.

(6) *Shipping dimensions.* Minimum dimensions to which a completely assembled vehicle may be reduced by lowering cab, top, or windshield, removing body bows, gun mounts, etc.

(7) *Ground clearance.* Minimum clearance under lowest point of chassis.

(8) *Computed grade ability.* The grade (slope), measured in percent, that a vehicle will ascend with given load and in specified gear or range, as calculated by standard formula. Percent of grade is defined as the ratio between the vertical rise and the horizontal distance traveled, expressed in percent. Examples of grades measured in terms of degree of angle and percent follow:

Degree of angle	Percent of grade
0	0
10	17. 633
30	57. 735
45	100

(9) *Turning radius.* Radius of minimum circle withing which vehicle can negotiate a complete turn.

(10) *Fording depth.* Depth of water through which vehicle can be successfully operated at slowest speed.

(11) *Cruising range.* Average distance vehicle will travel on one filling of fuel at rated fuel consumption.

(12) *Communications equipment.* The type numbers of communications equipment listed for combat vehicles have the following meanings:

AN/ARC-3	Radio Set
AN/GRC-3	Radio Set
AN/GRC-4	Radio Set
AN/GRC-5	Radio Set
AN/GRC-6	Radio Set
AN/GRC-7	Radio Set
AN/GRC-8	Radio Set
AN/GRC-9	Radio Set
AN/GRR-5	Radio Set
AN/PRC-9	Radio Set
AN/U1C-1	Auxiliary Interphone Equipment
AN/V1A-1	Auxiliary Interphone Equipment
AN/VRC-3	Radio Set
AN/VRC-5	Radio Set
AN/VRC-7	Radio Set
AN/VRC-8	Radio Set
AN/VRC-9	Radio Set
AN/VRC-10	Radio Set
AN/VRC-13	Radio Set
AN/VRC-14	Radio Set
AN/VRC-15	Radio Set
AN/VRQ-1	Radio Set
AN/VRQ-2	Radio Set
AN/VRQ-3	Radio Set
BC-667	Interphone Amplifier
NAVY TCS	Radio Set
RC-99	Interphone Equipment
RC-298	Interphone Extension Kit
SCR-52B	Radio Set
SCR-193S	Radio Set
SCR-193T	Radio Set
SCR-245	Radio Set
SCR-499	Radio Set
SCR-506	Radio Set
SCR-507	Radio Set
SCR-508	Radio Set
SCR-510	Radio Set
SCR-528	Radio Set
SCR-542	Radio Set
SCR-593	Radio Set
SCR-608	Radio Set
SCR-608B	Radio Set
SCR-610	Radio Set
SCR-619	Radio Set
SCR-628	Radio Set
SCR-694C	Radio Set

3. Definition of Vehicles

Vehicles are defined in AR 700–105. These definitions cover *vehicles* and *motor vehicles*, which are divided into *tactical* and *administrative vehicles.* Further groupings are *general-purpose vehicles, special-equipment vehicles, special-purpose vehicles, combat vehicles, trailers,* and *semitrailers.*

4. Responsibility

For each type of vehicle stored and issued by each technical service and the Air Force, the technical service responsible for design and development; preparation of specifications; purchase and inspection (including spare parts); storage and issue of spare parts for organizational, field, and depot maintenance; and performance of depot maintenance is given in SR 700–110–1 (AFR 65–17).

5. Excessive Weights and Dimensions

The weights and dimensions of some vehicles included in this manual exceed the permissible limits given in AR 700–105. SR 700–105–10 lists these vehicles and explains wherein they exceed the limitations.

6. Winterization and Deep-Water Fording Kits

a. Winterization kits available for vehicles are listed in SB 9–16.

b. Deep-water fording kits available for vehicles are listed in TM 9–2853.

7. Different Voltages

The commercial-type vehicles and the older tactical vehicles have 6-volt electrical systems. Many of the newer tactical vehicles have 24-volt electrical systems. There are also some vehicles with 12-volt electrical systems. Damage is almost certain to result from connecting the electrical systems of two or more vehicles, such as trucks and trailers, having different voltages. Therefore, using organizations are cautioned against connecting the electrical systems of vehicles having different voltages, unless one vehicle has been modified to accomodate the voltage of the other.

AMBULANCE, METROPOLITAN, ¾-TON, 4-LITTER
(Cadillac-Miller, Model 50–86 and Cadillac-Superior, Model 51–86, 1951)

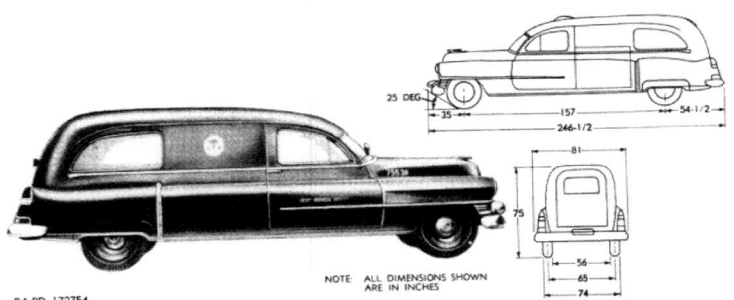

RA PD 172754

NOTE: ALL DIMENSIONS SHOWN ARE IN INCHES

Vehicle illustrated: Model 51–86.
Classification: Standard.

Purpose: To transport sick and wounded personnel.

GENERAL DATA

Crew..2; Passengers (including crew) 12
Weight (lb)..Net 5,720
   Payload..1,500
   Gross...7,220
Rear-axle gear ratio...4.27:1
Axle load (lb):
   Empty....................................front 2,740; rear 2,980
   Loaded...................................front 3,000; rear 4,220
Tires:
   Ply 6; Size 8.90 x 15..............Pressure (psi) front 24, rear 30
   Tread, center-to-center, front............................(in.) 59
Shipping dimensions, uncrated...............(cu ft) 867; (sq ft) 139
Ground clearance...(in.) 9
Electrical system..(volts) 6
   No. of batteries..1
   Type of ground......................................negative
Fuel octane rating..80
Capacities:
   Fuel..(gal) 20
   Cooling system (qt)...............w/o heater 18; w/heater 19
   Crankcase, refill.......................................(qt) 5
   Transmission..(qt) 3¾
   Rear axle...(qt) 2½
Brakes:
   Manufacturer; Bendix...........................Type; hydraulic
   Parking brake, type.................................rear-wheel
Transmission forward speeds.....................................3
   Gear ratio........................High 1:1; Low 2.393:1

PERFORMANCE

Computed grade ability in lowest gear, loaded.................(percent) 25
Turning radius...(ft) 29
Fording depth..(in.) 9¾
Fuel consumption, loaded....................................(mpg) 8
Cruising range, loaded.....................................(mi) 160
Allowable speed, recommended............................(mph) 65

ENGINE

Manufacturer: Cadillac....................................Model 1951
Type..................4-cycle, valve-in-head; No. of cylinders (90-deg V) 8
Displacement...(cu in.) 331
Bore...(in.) 3¹³⁄₁₆
Stroke...(in.) 3¾
Compression ratio...7.5:1
Governed speed..not governed
Brake horsepower (max w/std accessories)...............141 at (rpm) 3,400
Torque (max w/std accessories)...................297 lb-ft at (rpm) 1,800

ADDITIONAL DATA

Rear axle, type..hypoid, semi-floating
Transmission, type...synchromesh

AMBULANCE, METROPOLITAN, ¾-TON, 4-LITTER

(Cadillac-Superior, Models 62, 1942; V–8, 1948; and 4986, 1949)

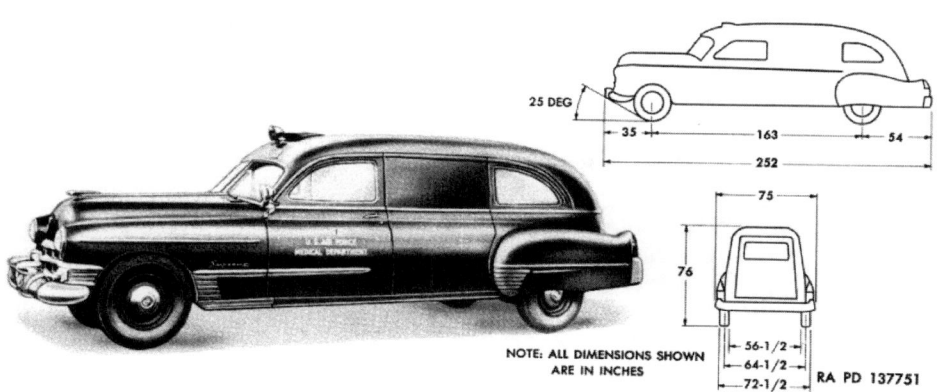

25 DEG

35 ← 163 → 54

252

75

76

NOTE: ALL DIMENSIONS SHOWN
ARE IN INCHES

56-1/2
64-1/2
72-1/2

RA PD 137751

Vehicle illustrated: Model 4986, 1949.
Classification: Standard.

Purpose: To transport sick and wounded personnel.

GENERAL DATA

Crew..2; Passengers (including crew) 12
Weight (lb) ....Net 5,530; Payload 1,500; Gross 7,030
Rear-axle gear ratio...3.77:1
Axle load (lb):
   Empty....................................front 2,660; rear 2,870
   Loaded..................................front 2,920; rear 4,110
Tires:
   Ply 6; Size 8.90 x 15; Pressure (psi).............front 24; rear 30
   Tread, center-to-center, front...........................(in.) 59
Shipping dimensions, uncrated....................(cu ft) 836; (sq ft) 132
Ground clearance..(in.) 9
Electrical system...(volts) 6
   No. of batteries..1
   Type of ground..negative
Fuel octane rating...88
Capacities:
   Fuel...(gal) 20
   Cooling system (qt).....................w/o heater 18; w/heater 19
   Crankcase, refill..(qt) 5
   Transmission..(qt) 1¾
   Rear axle...(qt) 2½
Brakes:
   Manufacturer; Bendix..........................Type; hydraulic
   Parking brake, type.....................................rear-wheel
Transmission forward speeds..3
   Gear ratio............................High 1:1; low 2.39:1

PERFORMANCE

Computed grade ability in lowest gear, loaded.............(percent) 25
Turning radius...(ft) 28½
Fording depth...(in.) 9¾
Fuel consumption, loaded................................(mpg) 8
Cruising range, loaded..................................(mi) 160
Allowable speed, recommended............................(mph) 65

ENGINE

Manufacturer: Cadillac..................................Model 1949
Type: Valve-in-head, 4-cycle............No. of cylinders (90-deg V) 8
Displacement..(cu in.) 331
Bore...(in.) 3¹³⁄₁₆
Stroke..(in.) 3⅝
Compression ratio...7.50:1
Governed speed......................................not governed
Brake horsepower (max w/std accessories)............141 at (rpm) 3,400
Torque (max w/std accessories).........297 lb-ft at (rpm) 1,800

ADDITIONAL DATA

Transmission, type..synchromesh
Rear axle, type..............................hypoid, semi-floating

AMBULANCE, METROPOLITAN, ¾-TON, 4-LITTER

(Packard-Henney, Models 4294 HDA, 1942 and 2213–9, 1949)

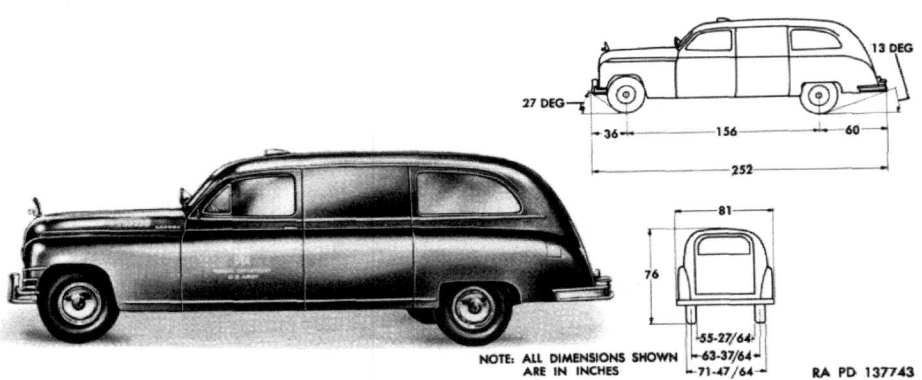

NOTE: ALL DIMENSIONS SHOWN ARE IN INCHES   RA PD 137743

Vehicle illustrated: Model 2213–9, 1949.
Classification: Standard.

Purpose: To transport sick and wounded personnel.

GENERAL DATA

Crew	2; Passengers (including crew) 12
Weight (lb)	Net 6,223; Payload 1,500; Gross 7,723
Rear-axle gear ratio	4.54:1
Axle load (lb):	
Empty	front 3,295; rear 2,928
Loaded	front 3,540; rear 4,183
Tires:	
Ply 6; Size 7.50 x 16; Pressure (psi)	front 30, rear 40
Tread, center-to-center, front	(in.) 59¹⁹⁄₃₂
Shipping dimensions, uncrated	(cu ft) 900; (sq ft) 142
Vehicle dimensions:	
Ground clearance	(in.) 9
Loading height, empty	(in.) 24½
Electrical system	(volts) 6
No. of batteries	1
Type of ground	positive
Fuel octane rating	80
Capacities:	
Fuel	(gal) 20
Cooling system (qt)	w/o heater 19; w/heater 19½
Crankcase, refill	(qt) 7
Transmission	(qt) 1
Rear axle	(qt) 3
Brakes:	
Manufacturer: Packard	Type: hydraulic
Parking brake, type	rear-wheel
Transmission forward speeds	3
Gear ratio	High 1:1; Low 2.43:1

PERFORMANCE

Computed grade ability in lowest gear, loaded	(percent) 28
Turning radius	(ft) 28
Fording depth	(in.) 9
Fuel consumption, loaded	(mpg) 10
Cruising range, loaded	(mi) 200
Allowable speed, governed	(mph) 60

ENGINE

Manufacturer: Packard	Model 2213
Type	L-head, 4-cycle; No. of cylinders (in line) 8
Displacement	(cu. in.) 356
Bore	(in.) 3½
Stroke	(in.) 4⅝
Compression ratio	7.00:1
Governed speed	(rpm) 3,600
Brake horsepower (max w/std accessories)	144 at (rpm) 3,600
Torque (max)	282 lb-ft at (rpm) 2,000

ADDITIONAL DATA

Transmission, type	synchromesh
Rear axle, type	hypoid, semifloating

AMBULANCE, METROPOLITAN, 1½-TON, 12-LITTER, M423

(Linn Coach and Truck Division)

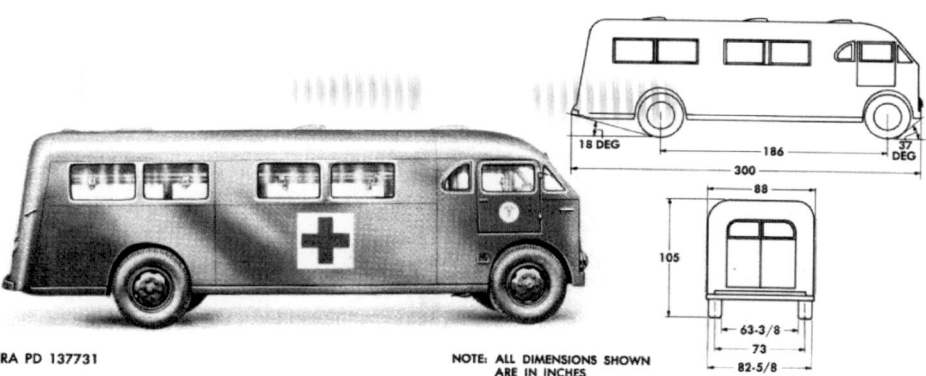

RA PD 137731

NOTE: ALL DIMENSIONS SHOWN
ARE IN INCHES

Classification: Standard.

Purpose: To transport sick and wounded personnel.

GENERAL DATA

Crew..................................2; Passengers (including crew) 14
Weight (lb)......................Net 6,500; Payload 3,000; Gross 9,500
Front-axle gear ratio...6.6:1
Axle load (lb):
  Empty.................................front 4,000; rear 2,500
  Loaded................................front 5,000; rear 4,500
Tires:
  Ply 10; Size 9.00 x 20...............Pressure (psi) front 60; rear 55
  Tread, center-to-center, front......................(in.) 64¼
Shipping dimensions, uncrated................(cu ft) 1,530; (sq ft) 180
Ground clearance......................................(in.) 10
Electrical system.....................................(volts) 12
  No. of batteries...1
  Type of ground..positive
Fuel octane rating..70
Capacities:
  Fuel...(gal) 29
  Cooling system (qt)..........w/o heater 17; w/heater 18½
  Crankcase, refill.................................(qt) 5
  Transmission......................................(qt) 2¾
  Transfer..(qt) 3
  Front axle..(qt) 2½
Brakes:
  Manufacturer; Wagner Electric..............Type; hydraulic
  Parking brake, type.........................transmission
Transmission forward speeds....................................4
  Gear ratio.........................High 1:1; Low 6.4:1
Transfer speeds..1
  Gear ratio...1:1

PERFORMANCE

Computed grade ability in lowest gear, loaded...........(percent) 42
Turning radius.......................................(ft) 32
Fuel consumption, loaded.............................(mpg) 8
Cruising range, loaded...............................(mi) 232
Allowable speed, governed............................(mph) 50

ENGINE

Manufacturer: Dodge.......................................Model T-214
Type: L-head, 4-cycle...................No. of cylinders (in line) 6
Displacement......................................(cu in.) 230.2
Bore..(in.) 3¼
Stroke..(in.) 4⅜
Compression ratio...................................6.7:1
Governed speed......................................(rpm) 3,200
Brake horsepower (max w/std accessories)............94 at (rpm) 3,500
Torque (max)..........................175 lb-ft at (rpm) 1,300

ADDITIONAL DATA

Front-wheel drive only
Floodlight over rear door

AUTOMOBILE, LIMOUSINE, HEAVY, 7-PASSENGER, 4 x 2

(Chrysler, Crown Imperial)

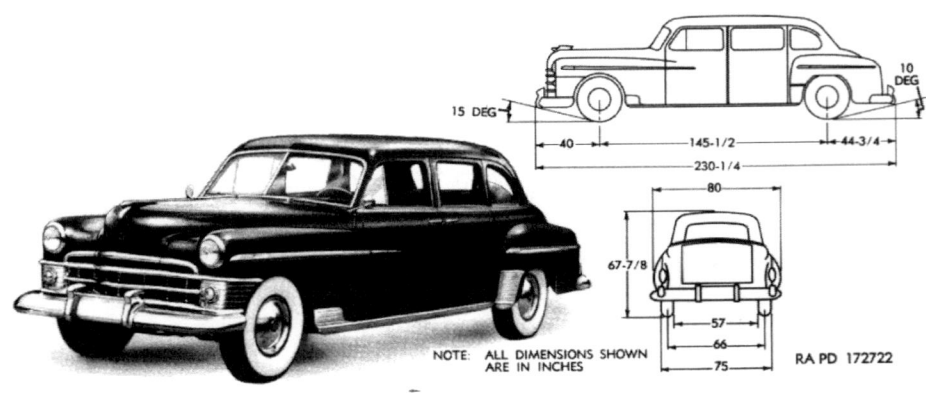

NOTE: ALL DIMENSIONS SHOWN ARE IN INCHES   RA PD 172722

Classification: Nonclassified.

Purpose: To transport personnel.

GENERAL DATA

Crew	1; Passengers (including crew) 7
Weight (lb)	Net 5,491
Payload	1,225
Gross	6,716
Rear-axle gear ratio	3.58:1
Axle load (lb):	
Empty	front 2,880; rear 2,611
Loaded	front 3,190; rear 3,526
Tires:	
Ply 6; Size 8.90 x 15; Pressure	(psi) 24
Tread, center-to-center, front	(in.) 57½
Shipping dimensions, uncrated:	(cu ft) 725;(sq ft) 128
Ground clearance	(in.) 6⅞
Electrical system	(volts) 6
No. of batteries	1
Type of ground	positive
Fuel octane rating	72
Capacities:	
Fuel	(gal) 20
Cooling system	(qt) 21
Crankcase, refill	(qt) 5
Transmission	(qt) 1½
Rear axle	(qt) 2½
Brakes:	
Manufacturer; Chrysler	Type; hydraulic
Parking brake, type	transmission
Transmission forward speeds	4
Gear ratio: High 1:1	Low 3.57:1

PERFORMANCE

Computed grade ability in lowest gear, loaded	(percent) 32
Fuel consumption, loaded	(mpg) 14
Cruising range, loaded	(mi) 280
Allowable speed, recommended	(mph) 70

ENGINE

Manufacturer: Chrysler	Model C–50
Type: 4-cycle, valve-in-head	No. of cylinders (90-deg V) 8
Displacement	(cu in.) 331
Bore	(in.) 3¹³⁄₁₆
Stroke	(in.) 3⅝
Compression ratio	7.5:1
Governed speed	not governed
Brake horsepower, gross	180 at (rpm) 4,000
Torque, maximum gross	312 lb-ft at (rpm) 2,000

ADDITIONAL DATA

Rear axle, type	hypoid, semifloating
Transmission, type	hydraulic, prestomatic

AUTOMOBILE, SEDAN, LIGHT, 5-PASSENGER

(Chevrolet, Models KB, 1940; 1503–AG, 1941; 1503–BG, 1942; 1553–GJ, 1949; and 1503–GJ, 1949)

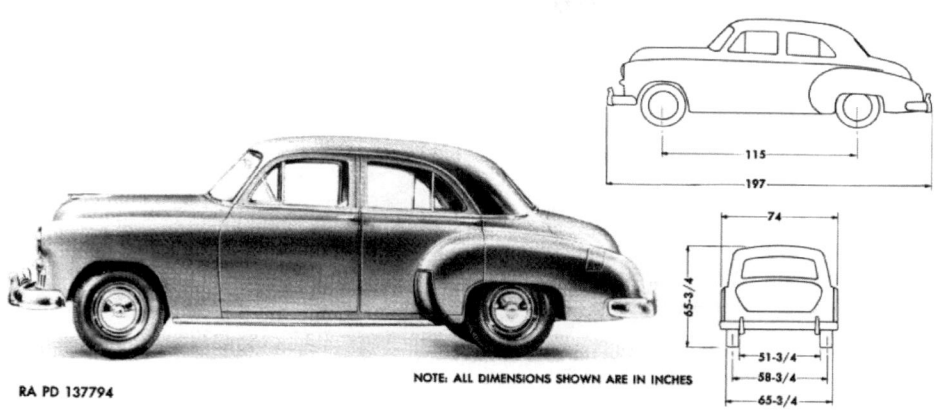

RA PD 137794

NOTE: ALL DIMENSIONS SHOWN ARE IN INCHES

Vehicle illustrated: Model 1503–GJ, 1949.
Classification: Standard.

Purpose: To transport personnel.

GENERAL DATA

Crew	1; Passengers (including crew) 5
Weight (lb)	Net 3,220; Payload 800; Gross 4,020
Rear-axle gear ratio	4.11:1
Axle load (lb):	
Empty	front 1,740; rear 1,480
Loaded	front 2,010; rear 2,010
Tires:	
Ply 4; Size 6.70x15; Pressure	(psi) 24
Tread, center-to-center, front	(in.) 57
Shipping dimensions, uncrated	(cu ft) 550; (sq ft) 100
Ground clearance	(in.) 8½
Electrical system	(volts) 6
No. of batteries	1
Type of ground	negative
Fuel octane rating	72
Capacities:	
Fuel	(gal) 16
Cooling system (qt)	w/o heater 15; w/heater 16
Crankcase, refill	(qt) 5
Transmission	(qt) ¾
Rear axle	(qt) 1¾
Brakes:	
Manufacturer; Chevrolet	Type; hydraulic
Parking brake, type	rear-wheel
Transmission forward speeds	3
Gear ratio	High 1:1; Low 2.94:1

PERFORMANCE

Computed grade ability in lowest gear, loaded	(percent) 35
Turning radius (ft)	right 19; left 20
Fording depth	(in.) 15
Fuel consumption, loaded	(mpg) 14
Cruising range, loaded	(mi) 224
Allowable speed, recommended	(mph) 70

ENGINE

Manufacturer: Chevrolet	Model GAA or GAM 1001 up
Type: Valve-in-head, 4-cycle	No. of cylinders (in line) 6
Displacement	(cu in.) 216.5
Bore	(in.) 3½
Stroke	(in.) 3¾
Compression ratio	6.6:1
Governed speed	not governed
Brake horsepower (max w/std accessories)	83 at (rpm) 3,200
Torque (max w/std accessories)	168 lb-ft at (rpm) 1,100

ADDITIONAL DATA

Transmission, type	synchromesh
Rear axle, type	hypoid, semifloating

Differences in data for Models KB, 1940; 1503–AG, 1941; and 1503–BG, 1942 are as follows:

Tires:	
Ply 4; Size 6.00x16; Pressure	(psi) front 28; rear 30
Tread, center-to-center, front	(in.) 57¾
Engine	Model 2AA or 2AC or BA 1001 up

AUTOMOBILE, SEDAN, LIGHT, 5-PASSENGER

(Ford, Models 01A, 8-cyl, 112-in WB, 1940; 1GA73A, B, and C, 6-cyl, 114-in WB, 1941;
11A73A, B, and C (11AS73C), 8-cyl, 114-in WB, 1941; 2GA73A, B, and C, 6-cyl,
114-in WB, 1942; 21A73A, B, and C, 8-cyl, 114-in WB, 1942; 79A, 1947; and 98HA,
1949)

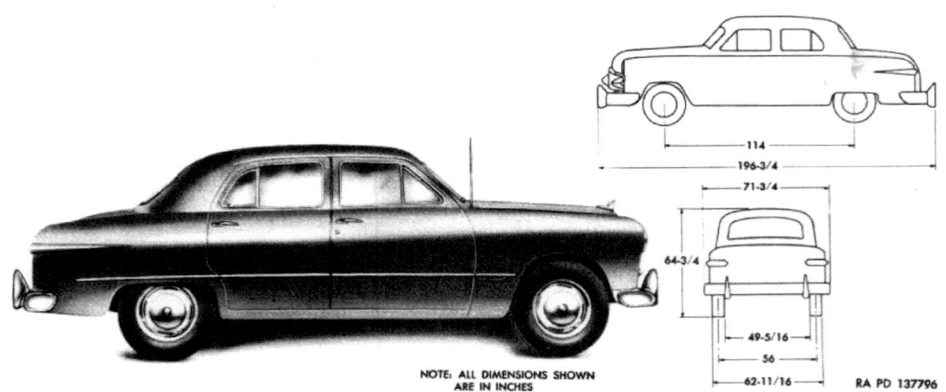

NOTE: ALL DIMENSIONS SHOWN
ARE IN INCHES   RA PD 137796

Technical Manual: 10-1375; Supply Catalog: SNL G-522.

Vehicle illustrated: Model 98HA, 1949.
Classification: Standard.

Purpose: To transport personnel.

GENERAL DATA

Crew	1; Passengers (including crew) 5
Weight (lb)	Net 3,395; Payload 775; Gross 4,170
Rear-axle gear ratio	3.78:1
Axle load (lb):	
Empty	front 1,765; rear 1,630
Loaded	front 1,967; rear 2,203
Tires:	
Ply 6; Size 6.00 x 16; Pressure	(psi) 35
Tread, center-to-center, front	(in.) 58
Shipping dimensions, uncrated	(cu ft) 560; (sq ft) 99
Ground clearance	(in.) 7¾
Electrical system	(volts) 6
No. of batteries	1
Type of ground	positive
Fuel octane rating	72
Capacities:	
Fuel	(gal) 17
Cooling system	(qt) 15
Crankcase, refill	(qt) 5
Transmission	(qt) 1¾
Rear axle	(qt) 1¾
Brakes:	
Manufacturer; Ford-Wagner	Type; hydraulic
Parking brake, type	rear-wheel
Transmission forward speeds	3
Gear ratio: High 1:1	Low 3.11:1

PERFORMANCE

Computed grade ability in lowest gear, loaded	(percent) 36
Turning radius	(ft) 20¾
Fording depth	(in.) 18¾
Fuel consumption, loaded	(mpg) 13
Cruising range, loaded	(mi) 221
Allowable speed, (recommended)	(mph) 70

ENGINE

Manufacturer: Ford	Part No. (6-cyl) FM-2GA-6005
	(8-cyl, 100-hp) FM-59A-6005
	(8-cyl, 90-hp) FM-01A-6005
	FM-21A-6005
	FM-41A-6011B
Type: L-head, 4-cycle	No. of cylinders (in line) 6; (90-deg V) 8
Displacement: (cu in)	(6-cyl) 226
	(8-cyl, 100-hp) 239.4
	(8 cyl, 90-hp) 221
Bore: (in.)	(6-cyl) 3.3
	(8-cyl, 100-hp) 3¹⁄₁₆
	(8-cyl, 90-hp) 3¹⁄₁₆
Stroke: (in.)	(6-cyl) 4.4
	(8-cyl, 100-hp) 3¾
	(8-cyl, 90-hp) 3¾
Compression ratio	(6-cyl) 7.6:1
	(8-cyl, 100-hp) 6.4:1
	(8-cyl, 90-hp) 6.2:1
Governed speed	not governed
Brake horsepower (max w/std accessories)	(6-cyl) 90
	(8-cyl) 90 and 100
Torque (max) (lb,-ft):	
(6 cyl)	180 at (rpm) 1,200
(8-cyl, 100-hp)	176 at (rpm) 2,000
(8-cyl, 90-hp)	156 at (rpm) 2,200

ADDITIONAL DATA

Transmission, type	synchromesh
Rear axle, type:	
(late models)	hypoid, semifloating
(early models)	spiral-bevel, semifloating

AUTOMOBILE, SEDAN, LIGHT, 5-PASSENGER

(Ford, Model 1HA, 1951)

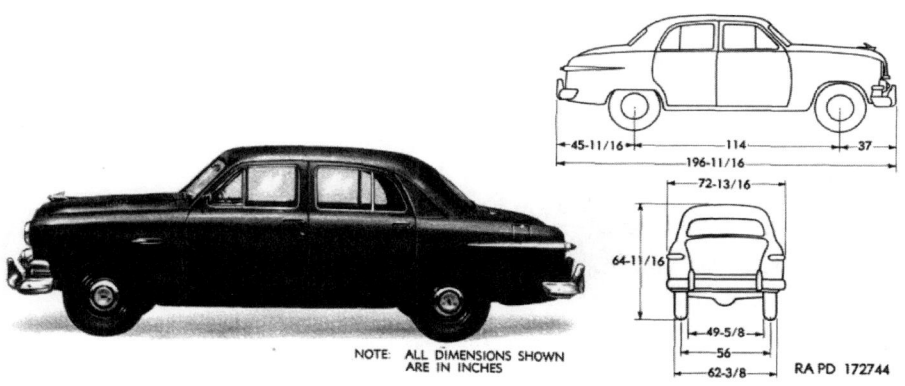

NOTE: ALL DIMENSIONS SHOWN ARE IN INCHES

RA PD 172744

Classification: Standard.

Purpose: To transport personnel.

GENERAL DATA

Crew..1; Passengers (including crew) 5
Weight (lb)..Net 3,200
    Payload...775
    Gross...3,975
Rear-axle gear ratio...3.73:1
Axle-load (lb):
    Empty.................................front 1,660; rear 1,540
    Loaded...............................front 1,795; rear 2,180
Tires:
    Ply 4; Size 6.00 x 16; Pressure (psi) front 28, rear 25.
    Tread, center-to-center, front...........................(in.) 56
Shipping dimensions, uncrated: (cu ft) 535.............(sq ft) 98
Vehicle dimensions:
    Ground clearance......................................(in.) 6⅞
Electrical system..(volts) 6
    No. of batteries...1
    Type of ground.......................................positive
Fuel octane rating...72
Capacities:
    Fuel..(gal) 16
    Cooling system.......................................(qt) 16
    Crankcase, refill......................................(qt) 5
    Transmission..(qt) 1¾
    Rear axle...(qt) 1¾
Brakes:
    Manufacturer; Ford..........................Type; hydraulic
    Parking brake, type................................rear-wheel
Transmission forward speeds...................................3
    Gear ratio: High 1:1...........................Low 2.819:1

PERFORMANCE

Computed grade ability in lowest gear, loaded...............(percent) 36
Turning radius...(ft) 20
Fording depth..(in.)18
Fuel consumption, loaded....................................(mpg) 17
Cruising range, loaded..(mi) 272
Allowable speed, recommended................................(mph) 70

ENGINE

Manufacturer: Ford...............................Model Series H
Type: 4-cycle, L-head...................No. of cylinders (in line) 6
Displacement.......................................(cu in.) 226
Bore..(in.) 3.3
Stroke..(in.) 4.4
Compression ratio....................................6.8:1
Governed speed....................................not governed
Brake horsepower (max w/std accessories)...............95 at (rpm) 3,300
Torque (max w/std accessories)................180 lb-ft at (rpm) 1,200

ADDITIONAL DATA

Rear axle, type...............................hypoid, semifloating
Transmission, type....................................synchromesh

AUTOMOBILE, SEDAN, LIGHT, 5-PASSENGER

(Plymouth, Models P9, 1940; P11, 1941; P14, 1942; P15S, 1947–48; and P18, 1949)

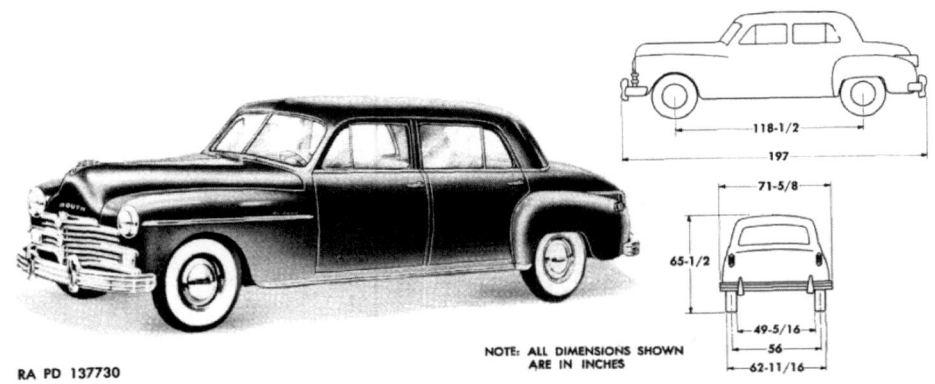

NOTE: ALL DIMENSIONS SHOWN
ARE IN INCHES

RA PD 137730

Technical Manuals: 10-1151; (Model P9) 10-1149 (Model P11): Supply Catalog: SNL G-521 (Models P11 and P14).

Vehicle illustrated: Model P18, 1949.
Classification: Standard.

Purpose: To transport personnel.

GENERAL DATA

Crew..1; Passengers (including crew) 5
Weight (lb)........................Net 3,175; Payload 750; Gross 3,925
Rear-axle gear ratio..3.9:1
Axle load (lb):
    Empty..................................front 1,705; rear 1,470
    Loaded................................front 1,934; rear 1,991
Tires:
    Ply 4; Size 6.00 x 16; Pressure............................(psi) 28
    Tread, center-to-center, front...........................(in.) 57
Shipping dimensions, uncrated..........(cu ft) 556; (sq ft) 100
Ground clearance......................................(in.) 8½
Electrical system.....................................(volts) 6
    No. of batteries..1
    Type of ground..positive
Fuel octane rating..72
Capacities:
    Fuel..(gal) 17
    Cooling system...(qt) 15
    Crankcase, refill.......................................(qt) 5
    Transmission...(qt) 13½
    Rear axle...(qt) 1¾
Brakes:
    Manufacturer: Chrysler..................Type: hydraulic
    Parking brake, type..............................transmission
Transmission forward speeds.................................3
    Gear ratio.............................High 1:1; Low 2.57:1

PERFORMANCE

Computed grade ability in lowest gear, loaded.............(percent) 35
Turning radius...(ft) 20
Fuel consumption, loaded.................................(mpg) 17
Cruising range, loaded....................................(mi) 280
Allowable speed, recommended.............................(mph) 70

ENGINE

Manufacturer...Chrysler
Type...............L-head, 4-cycle; No. of cylinders (in line) 6
Displacement...(cu in.) 217.8
Bore..(in.) 3¼
Stroke..(in.) 4⅜
Compression ratio...6.6:1
Governed speed......................................not governed
Brake horsepower (max w/std accessories)..........95 at (rpm) 3,600
Torque (max)...........................172 lb-ft at (rpm) 1,200

ADDITIONAL DATA

Transmission, type....................................synchromesh
Rear axle, type.........................hypoid, semifloating
    Differences in data for Model P18, 1949.
Tires:
    Ply 4; Size 6.70 x 15; Pressure..........................(psi) 24
    Tread, center-to-center, front...........................(in.) 55
Compression ratio..7:1
Brake horsepower (max w/std accessories)..........97 at (rpm) 3,600
Torque (max w/std accessories)............175 lb-ft at (rpm) 1,200

AUTOMOBILE, SEDAN, MEDIUM, 5-PASSENGER
(Buick, Model 41, 1948 and Model 41, 1950)

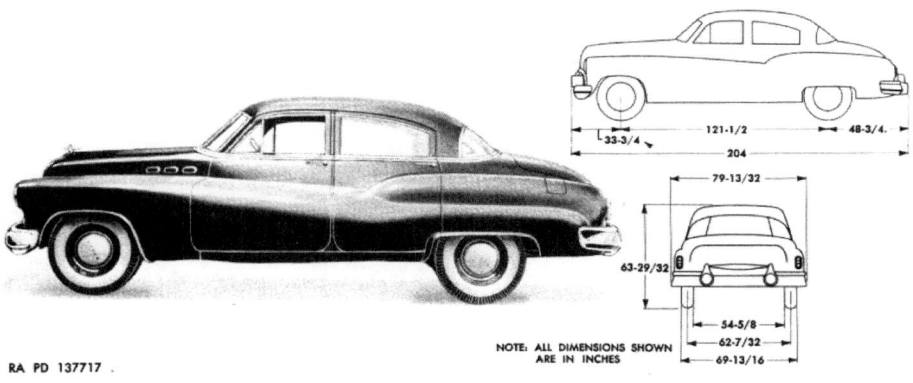

RA PD 137717 .

Vehicle illustrated: Model 41, 1950.
Classification: Standard.

Purpose: To transport personnel.

GENERAL DATA

Crew........................1; Passengers (including crew) 5
Weight (lb)....................Net 3,786; Payload 750; Gross 4,536
Rear-axle gear ratio..4.1:1
Axle load (lb):
  Empty..front 1,986; rear 1,800
  Loaded (5 pass)........................front 2,185; rear 2,351
Tires:
  Ply 4; Size 7.60 x 15; Pressure..........................(psi) 24
  Tread, front, center-to-center......................(in.) 59⅛
Shipping dimensions, uncrated....................(cu ft) 596; (sq ft) 112
Ground clearance....................................(in.) 6⅞
Electrical system..(volts) 6
  No. of batteries.....................................1
  Type of ground....................................negative
Fuel octane rating....................................72
Capacities:
  Fuel...(gal) 19
  Cooling system..............(qt) w/o heater 13; w/heater 14¾
  Crankcase, refill..................................(qt) 4½
  Transmission.......................................(qt) ⅞
  Rear axle...(qt) 2
Brakes:
  Manufacturer; Bendix or Delco....................Type; hydraulic
  Parking brake, type.............................rear-wheel
Transmission forward speeds....................................3
  Gear ratio.........................High 1:1; Low 2.67:1

PERFORMANCE

Computed grade ability in lowest gear, loaded...............(percent) 48
Turning radius..(ft) 20
Fuel consumption, loaded..............................(mpg) 17
Cruising range, loaded................................(mi) 320
Allowable speed, recommended.........................(mph) 70

ENGINE

Manufacturer: Buick....................................Model 1950-41
Type: Valve-in-head, 4-cycle..............No. of cylinders (in line) 8
Displacement......................................(cu in.) 248.1
Bore...(in.) 3⁵⁄₃₂
Stroke...(in.) 4⅛
Compression ratio....................................6.6:1
Governed speed....................................not governed
Brake horsepower (max w/std accessories)..............110 at (rpm) 3,600
Torque (max)........................212 lb-ft at (rpm) 2,000

ADDITIONAL DATA

Transmission, type....................................synchromesh
Rear axle, type.........................hypoid, semifloating

AUTOMOBILE, SEDAN, MEDIUM, 5-PASSENGER

(Packard, Models 1803, 1940; 1903, 1941; 2003, 1942)

RA PD 137770

NOTE: ALL DIMENSIONS SHOWN
ARE IN INCHES

Supply Catalogue: SNL G-644.

Vehicle illustrated: Model 2003, 1942.
Classification: Standard.

Purpose: To transport personnel.

GENERAL DATA

Crew	1 Passengers (including crew) 6
Weight (lb)	Net 3,560; Payload 850; Gross 4,410
Rear-axle gear ratio	4. 1:1
Axle load (lb):	
Empty	front 1,873; rear 1,687
Loaded	front 2,078; rear 2,332
Tires:	
Ply 4; Size 6.50x15; Pressure	(psi) 28
Tread, center-to-center, front	(in.) 59¼
Shipping dimensions, uncrated	(cu ft) 597; (sq ft) 106
Ground clearance	(in.) 8¹⁄₁₆
Electrical system	(volts) 6
No. of batteries	1
Type of ground	positive
Fuel octane rating	70
Capacities:	
Fuel	(gal) 17
Cooling system	(qt) 17
Crankcase, refill	(qt) 5½
Transmission	(qt) 1
Rear axle	(qt) 2½
Brakes:	
Manufacturer; Packard	Type; hydraulic
Parking brake, type	rear-wheel
Transmission forward speeds	3
Gear ratio	High 1:1; Low 2.43:1

PERFORMANCE

Computed grade ability in lowest gear, loaded	(percent) 33
Turning radius	(ft) 21
Fording depth	(in.) 18¾
Fuel consumption, loaded	(mpg) 13
Cruising range, loaded	(mi) 220
Allowable speed, recommended	(mph) 70

ENGINE

Manufacturer: Packard	Model 2001
Type: L-head, 4-cycle	No. of cylinders (in line) 8
Displacement	(cu in.) 282
Bore	(in.) 3¼
Stroke	(in.) 4¼
Compression ratio	6. 85:1
Governed speed	not governed
Brake horsepower (max w/std accessories)	125 at (rpm) 3,600
Torque (max)	230 lb-ft at (rpm) 2,000

ADDITIONAL DATA

Transmission, type	synchromesh
Rear axle, type	hypoid, semifloating

AUTOMOBILE, SEDAN, MEDIUM, 5-PASSENGER

(Pontiac, Chieftain, 6-cyl, 1949 and 8-cyl, 1949)

RA PD 137728

NOTE: ALL DIMENSIONS SHOWN
ARE IN INCHES

Classification: Standard.

Purpose: To transport personnel.

GENERAL DATA

Crew..1; Passengers (including crew) 5
Weight (lb)..........................Net 3,440; Payload 850; Gross 4,290
Rear-axle gear ratio..4.1:1
Axle load (lb):
   Empty................................front 1,870; rear 1,570
   Loaded...............................front 2,075; rear 2,215
Tires:
   Ply 4; Size 7.10 x 15; Pressure..........................(psi) 24
   Tread, center-to-center, front............................(in.) 58
Shipping dimensions, uncrated...............(cu ft) 562; (sq ft) 107
Ground clearance.....................................(in.) 6⅞
Electrical system.......................................(volts) 6
   No. of batteries...1
   Type of ground......................................negative
Fuel octane rating...75
Capacities:
   Fuel...(gal) 17½
   Cooling system (qt).............w/o heater 18¼; w/heater 19¾
   Crankcase, refill..(qt) 5
   Transmission...(qt) ⅞
   Rear axle...(qt) 1⅜
Brakes:
   Manufacturer; Bendix.........................Type; hydraulic
   Parking brake, type.................................rear-wheel
Transmission forward speeds....................................3
   Gear ratio..............................High 1:1; Low 2.67:1

PERFORMANCE

Computed grade ability in lowest gear, loaded.............(percent) 32
Turning radius...(ft) 20
Fuel consumption, loaded...................................(mpg) 16
Cruising range..(mi) 280
Allowable speed, recommended..............................(mph) 70

ENGINE

Manufacturer: Pontiac...............................Model; none
Type: L-head, 4-cycle.....................No. of cylinders (in line) 6
Displacement...................................(cu in.) 239.2
Bore..(in.) 3⁹⁄₁₆
Stroke..(in.) 4
Compression ratio..................................6.5:1
Governed speed...............................not governed
Brake horsepower, (max w/std accessories)............90 at (rpm) 3,400
Torque (max).......................178 lb-ft at (rpm) 1,200

ADDITIONAL DATA

Rear axle, type.......................hypoid, semi-floating
Transmission, type....................................synchromesh
   Data given for 6-cyl model. Changes in data for 8-cyl engine are as
   follows:
No. of cylinders...................................(in line) 8
Displacement......................................(cu in.) 248.9
Bore...(in.) 3¼
Stroke...(in.) 3¾
Brake horsepower (gross)....................104 at (rpm) 3,800
Torque (max gross).................190 lb-ft at (rpm) 2,200

AUTOMOBILE, SEDAN, HEAVY, 5-PASSENGER

(Cadillac, Model 75, 1948)

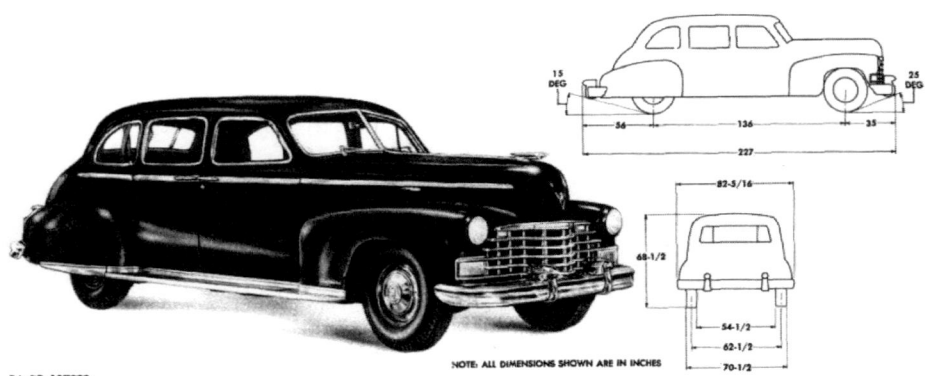

RA PD 137800

NOTE: ALL DIMENSIONS SHOWN ARE IN INCHES

Classification: Nonclassified.

Purpose: To transport personnel.

GENERAL DATA

Crew...1; Passengers (including crew) 5
Weight (lb)...........................Net 5,047; Payload 900; Gross 5,947
Rear-axle gear ratio...................Standard 4.22:1; Hydramatic 3.77:1
Axle load (lb):
    Empty..front 2,410; rear 2,637
    Loaded...front 2,660; rear 3,287
Tires:
    Ply 6; Size 7.50 x 16; Pressure.....................(psi) front 24; rear 32
    Tread, center-to-center...............................(in.) 58½
Shipping dimensions, uncrated.....................(cu ft) 737; (sq ft) 130
Ground clearance....................................(in.) 9
Electrical system....................................(volts) 6
    No. of batteries..1
    Type of ground.......................................negative
Fuel octane rating....................................80
Capacities:
    Fuel...(gal) 24
    Cooling system (qt)...............w/o heater 25; w/heater 26
    Crankcase, refill...................................(qt) 7
    Transmission.......................................(qt) 1¾
    Rear axle..(qt) 2½
Brakes:
    Manufacturer; Bendix.........................Type; hydraulic
    Parking brake, type..............................rear-wheel
Transmission forward speeds..............Standard 3; Hydramatic 4
    Gear ratio:
        Standard....................................High 1:1; Low 2.39:1
        Hydramatic.................................High 1:1; Low 3.819:1

PERFORMANCE

Computed grade ability in lowest gear, loaded................(percent) 31
Turning radius.......................................(ft) 23
Fording depth..(in.) 9
Fuel consumption, loaded.............................(mpg)12
Cruising range, loaded...............................(mi) 288
Allowable speed, recommended..........................(mph) 70

ENGINE

Manufacturer: Cadillac............................. Model 1948
Type: L-head, 4-cycle.................No. of cylinders (90-deg V) 8
Displacement.......................................(cu in.) 346
Bore...(in.) 3½
Stroke...(in.) 4½
Compression ratio.................................7.25:1
Governed speed.................................not governed
Brake horsepower (max w/std accessories)...........130 at (rpm) 3,200
Torque (max).......................272 lb-ft at (rpm) 1,800

ADDITIONAL DATA

Transmission, type.....................synchromesh or hydramatic
Rear axle, type......................................full-floating

BICYCLE, MILITARY, MEN'S, M305, AND BICYCLE, MILITARY, MEN'S

(Westfield, Columbia, Series MF and MG, 1942–43)

NOTE: ALL DIMENSIONS SHOWN
ARE IN INCHES

44-1/4

72

22

41-1/2

RA PD 137779

Supply Catalog: SNL G–519.

Vehicle illustrated: M305.
Classification: Standard.

Purpose: To transport personnel for messenger or dispatch service.

GENERAL DATA

Crew 1
Weight (lb) ....Net 55; Payload 200
Shipping dimensions, uncrated ....(cu ft) 40; (sq ft) 12
Tires ....Ply 2; Size 26 x 2.125; Pressure (psi) 22
Type of drive ....chain

ADDITIONAL DATA

BICYCLE, MILITARY, WOMEN'S, M306, AND BICYCLE, MILITARY, WOMEN'S

(Westfield, Columbia, Series MF and MG, 1942–43)

NOTE: ALL DIMENSIONS SHOWN ARE IN INCHES

72

44-1/4

22

41-1/2

RA PD 137780

Technical Manual: 10–1481; Supply Catalog: SNL G–519.

Classification: Standard.

Purpose: To transport personnel for messenger or dispatch service.

GENERAL DATA

Crew..1
Weight (lb)..Net 52; Payload 175
Shipping dimensions, uncrated.........................(cu ft) 40; (sq ft) 12
Tires...................................Ply 2; Size 26 x 2.125; Pressure (psi) 22
Type of drive..chain

ADDITIONAL DATA

BULLDOZER, TANK-MOUNTING, M1 AND M1A1

(Mounted on medium tank M4 series)

RA PD 338362

Technical Manual: 9-719; Supply Catalog: SNL G-228.

Bulldozer illustrated: M1A1 (mounted on medium tank, M4A3).
Classification: Limited Standard.

Purpose: To be mounted on medium tanks of the M4 series for moving earth. The M1 is applicable to those having standard vertical volute suspension; the M1A1 is applicable to all tanks of this series.

GENERAL DATA

Weight (net increase to vehicle weight, including oil) (lb)........M1 7,100; M1A1 7,400
Moldboard length (in.)....................................M1 124; M1A1 138
Moldboard height..(in.) 48
Relation of moldboard cutting edge to ground:
　Highest position above (in)..............................M1 30; M1A1 42
　Lowest position below................................(in.) 18

PERFORMANCE

Lift load (on blade) (lb)...............................M1 4,000; M1A1 5,000

ADDITIONAL DATA

Blade can be jettisoned from inside of tank.

BULLDOZER, TANK-MOUNTING, M2
(Mounted on medium tank M4A3)

RA PD 355062

Technicl Manual: 9-722; Supply Catalog: SNL G-228.

Classification: Standard.

Purpose: To be mounted on Medium Tank, M4A3, 76-mm Gun for moving earth.

GENERAL DATA

Weight (net increase to vehicle weight, including oil)............(lb) 6,000
Moldboard length...(in.) 124
Moldboard height...(in.) 36¾
Reversible moldboard cutting edge.....................(in.) 124 x 8 x ¾
Angle of moldboard cutting edge (with horizontal):
  At ground level...(deg) 58
  At lowest position..(deg) 65
Relation of moldboard cutting edge to ground:
  Carrying position, above...................................(in.) 29
  Highest position, above...................................(in.) 30½
  Lowest position, below....................................(in.) 12¼
Vehicle angle of approach:
  Blade in carrying position.................................(deg) 24
  Blade in highest position..................................(deg) 25

PERFORMANCE

Rate of lift:
  Vehicle engine at 1,500 rpm.........................(in. per sec) 5.83
  Vehicle engine at 2,100 rpm.........................(in. per sec) 7.26
Forward speed of vehicle while bulldozing (vehicle in low gear with engine
  at 1,500 rpm)..(mph) 1 to 3
Recommended maximum speed of vehicle with bulldozer attached
                                          (mph) 15

ADDITIONAL DATA

BULLDOZER, TANK-MOUNTING, M3

(Mounted on medium tank M46)

Technical Manual: 9-723; Supply Catalog: SNL G-246.

Classification: Standard.

Purpose: To be mounted on Medium Tank, M46 for moving earth.

GENERAL DATA

Weight (net increase to vehicle weight, including oil) .... (lb) 6,000
Moldboard length .... (in.) 124
Moldboard height .... (in.) 36¾
Reversible moldboard cutting edge .... (in.) 146 x 8 x ¾
Angle of moldboard cutting edge (with horizontal):
    At ground level .... (deg) 58
    At lowest position .... (deg) 60
Relation of moldboard cutting edge to ground:
    Carrying position, above .... (in.) 29
    Highest position, above .... (in.) 30½
    Lowest position, below .... (in.) 9
Vehicle angle of approach:
    Blade in carrying position .... (deg) 21
    Blade in highest position .... (deg) 25

PERFORMANCE

Rate of lift:
    Vehicle engine at 1,500 rpm .... (in. per sec) 5.50
    Vehicle engine at 2,100 rpm .... (in. per sec) 7.75
Forward speed of vehicle while bulldozing (vehicle in low gear with engine
    at 1,500 rpm) .... (mph) 1 to 2
Recommended maximum speed of vehicle with bulldozer attached
    (mph) 15

ADDITIONAL DATA

BUS, AMBULANCE, 18-LITTER, 4 x 2
(ACF-Brill)

NOTE: ALL DIMENSIONS SHOWN ARE IN INCHES

RA PD 172740

Classification: Nonclassified.

Purpose: To transport sick and wounded personnel.

GENERAL DATA

Crew..2; Passengers (including crew) 20
Weight (lb) ....Net 18,080
Rear-axle gear ratio.......................................5. 143:1
Axle load (lb):
  Empty, front 7,600...rear 10,480
Tires:
  Ply 12; Size 11.00 x 20; Pressure ....(psi) 70
  Tread, center-to-center, front.......................(in.) 80¼
Shipping dimensions, uncrated.....................(cu ft) 2,800; (sq ft) 280
Vehicle dimensions:
  Ground clearance................................(in.) 8¼
  Step height, empty................................(in.) 15¾
Electrical system..(volts) 12
  No. of batteries..1
  Type of ground...positive
Fuel octane rating...75
Capacities:
  Fuel...(gal) 107
  Cooling system, w/heater................................(qt) 80
  Crankcase, refill...(qt) 24
  Transmission...(qt) 10
  Rear axle...(qt) 13
Brakes:
Manufacturer;-Timken-Bendix.......................Type; air
  Parking brake, type....................................transmission
Transmission forward speeds.......................................3
  Gear ratio.........................High 1:1; Low 3.32:1

PERFORMANCE

Computed grade ability in lowest gear, loaded.................(percent) 16
Turning radius (ft).............................right 41; left 39½
Fuel consumption, loaded...............................(mpg) 4
Cruising range, loaded...................................(mi) 428
Allowable speed, governed...............................(mph) 51

ENGINE

Manufacturer: Hall-Scott...............................Model 180
Type................................4-cycle, valve-in-head
No. of cylinders........................(horizontal, in line) 6
Displacement.......................................(cu in.) 707
Bore..(in.) 5
Stroke..(in.) 6
Compression ratio.....................................6:1
Governed speed..................................(rpm) 2,200
Brake horsepower (max w/std accessories).............208 at (rpm) 2,200
Torque (max w/std accessories) ....540 lb-ft at (rpm) 1,200

ADDITIONAL DATA

Rear axle, type.........................spiral-bevel, full-floating
Transmission, type.....................................synchromesh

22

BUS, BODY ON CHASSIS, 29-PASSENGER, 4 x 2
(Ford, Model F–5)

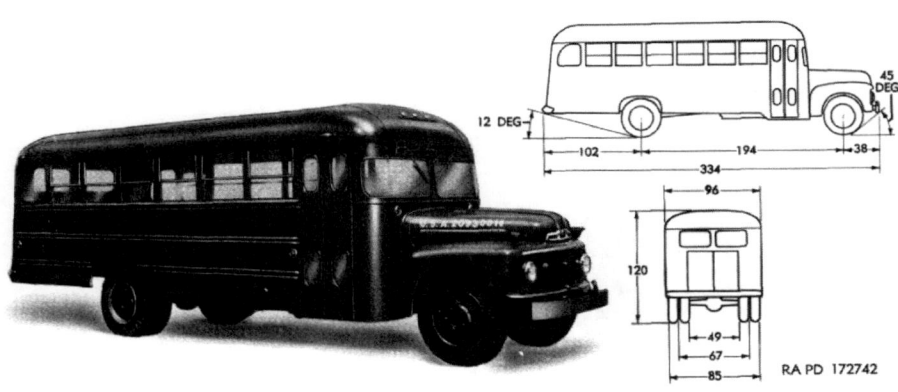

RA PD 172742

Classification: Nonclassified.

Purpose: To transport personnel.

GENERAL DATA

Crew...1; Passengers (including crew) 30
Weight (lb)...Net 9,750
    Payload..5,250
    Gross...15,000
Rear-axle gear ratio (two-speed).................High 5.83:1; Low 8.11:1
Axle load (lb):
    Empty...front 3,200; rear 6,550
    Loaded.......................................front, 4,050; rear 10,950
Tires:
    Ply 10.............................Size 8.25 x 20; Pressure (psi) 65
    Tread, center-to-center, front..........................(in.) 58½
Shipping dimensions, uncrated...............(cu ft) 2,220; (sq ft) 222
Vehicle dimensions:
    Ground clearance......................................(in.) 10¾
    Step height, empty.....................................(in.) 16
Electrical system..(volts) 6
    No. of batteries...1
    Type of ground..positive
Fuel octane rating..71
Capacities:
    Fuel..(gal) 30
    Cooling system, w/o heater.............................(qt) 18
    Crankcase, refill......................................(qt) 5
    Transmission..(qt) 4
    Rear axle..(qt) 7½
Brakes:
    Manufacturer; Ford...........................Type; hydrovac
    Parking brake, type...........................transmission
Transmission forward speeds....................................4
    Gear ratio: High 1:1...............................Low 6.4:1

PERFORMANCE

Computed grade ability in lowest gear, loaded.............(percent) 38
Turning radius..(ft) 32
Fording depth...(in.) 24
Fuel consumption, loaded.................................(mpg) 8
Cruising range, loaded...................................(mi) 240
Allowable speed, governed...............................(mph) 60

ENGINE

Manufacturer: Ford...................................Model 8 MTH
Type.....................4-cycle, L-head; No. of cylinders (in line) 6
Displacement..(cu in.) 254
Bore..(in.) 3.5
Stroke..(in.) 4.4
Compression ratio..6.8:1
Governed speed.......................................(rpm) 3,200
Brake horsepower (max w/std accessories).........110 at (rpm) 3,150
Torque, maximum gross....................212 lb-ft at (rpm) 1,200

ADDITIONAL DATA

Rear axle, type....................2-speed, spiral-bevel, full-floating
Transmission, type....................................synchromesh

BUS, BODY ON CHASSIS, 37-PASENGER, 4 x 2

(General Motors Corp., Model HCS–57)

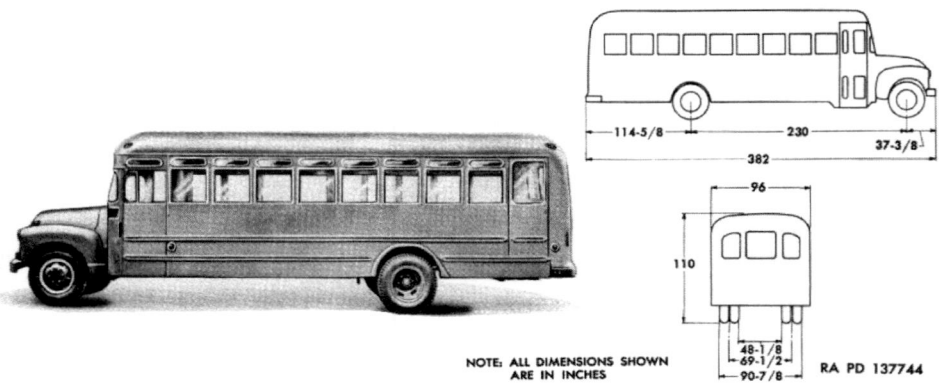

NOTE: ALL DIMENSIONS SHOWN ARE IN INCHES

RA PD 137744

Classification: Nonclassified.

Purpose: To transport personnel.

GENERAL DATA

Crew..............................1; Passengers (including crew) 38
Weight (lb)....................Net 11,985; Payload 6,000; Gross 17,985
Rear-axle gear ratio....................High 6.67:1; Low 8.85:1
Axle load (lb):
  Empty....................................front 4,430; rear 7,565
  Loaded...................................front 4,806; rear 13,179
Tires:
  Ply 10....................Size 9.00 x 20; Pressure (psi) 65
  Tread, center-to-center, front.................(in.) 61¾
Shipping dimensions, uncrated............(cu ft) 2,340; (sq ft) 255
Ground clearance...(in.) 10⅝
Electrical system...(volts) 6
  No. of batteries..1
  Type of ground...negative
Fuel octane rating..72
Capacities:
  Fuel...(gal) 30
  Cooling system......................................(qt) 18
  Crankcase, refill....................................(qt) 10½
  Transmission...(qt) 6
  Rear axle..(qt) 13
Brakes:
  Manufacturer; GMC........................Type; hydrovac
  Parking brake, type.........................transmission
Transmission forward speeds...............................5
  Gear ratio............High 1:1; Fourth 1.72:1; Low 7.58:1

PERFORMANCE

Computed grade ability in lowest gear, loaded..............(percent) 41
Turning radius..(ft) 38
Fording depth..(in.) 12
Fuel consumption, loaded....................................(mpg) 5
Cruising range, loaded......................................(mi) 150
Allowable speed, governed...................................(mph) 56

ENGINE

Manufacturer: GMC...Model 270
Type.....................Valve-in-head, 4-cycle; No. of cylinders (in line) 6
Displacement...(cu in.) 269.5
Bore..(in.) 3²⁵⁄₃₂
Stroke...(in.) 4
Compression ratio..6.75:1
Governed speed..(rpm) 3,200
Brake horsepower (max w/std accessories)..............106 at (rpm) 3,200
Torque (max w/std accessories)...............216 lb-ft at (rpm) 1,100

ADDITIONAL DATA

Transmission, type....................................synchromesh
Rear axle, type..............................hypoid, full-floating

BUS, 29-PASSENGER, 4 x 2

(International Harvester, Model L–163)

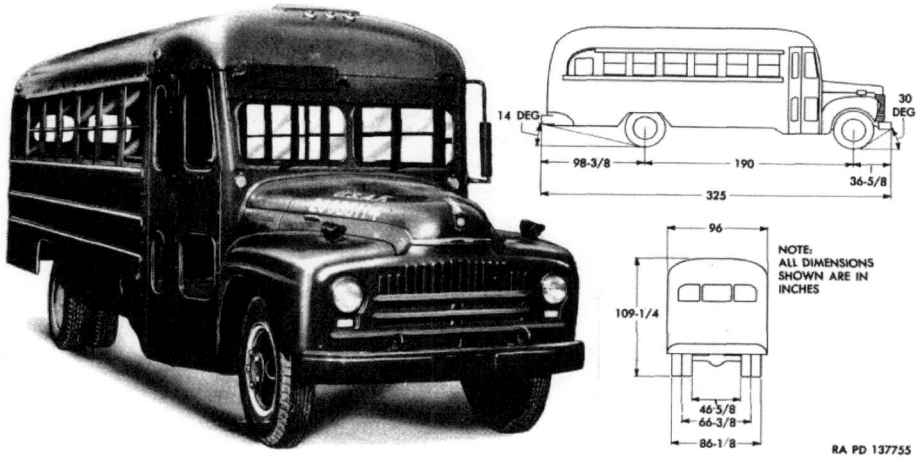

NOTE:
ALL DIMENSIONS
SHOWN ARE IN
INCHES

RA PD 137755

Classification: Nonclassified.

Purpose: To transport personnel.

GENERAL DATA

Crew..1; Passengers (including crew) 30
Weight (lb)......................Net 10,500; Payload 5,000; Gross 15,500
Rear-axle gear ratio..6.666:1
Axle load (lb):
    Empty..front 3,495; rear 7,005
    Loaded.......................................front 4,145; rear 11,355
Tires:
    Ply 10...............................Size 8.25 x 20; Pressure (psi) 65
    Tread, center-to-center, front.............................(in.) 63
Shipping dimensions, uncrated......................(cu ft) 1,980; (sq ft) 217
Vehicle dimensions:
    Ground clearance...(in.) 10 5/16
    Step height..(in.) 15
Electrical system..(volts) 6
    No. of batteries...1
    Type of ground..negative
Fuel octane rating..72
Capacities:
    Fuel..(gal) 30
    Cooling system..(qt) 17½
    Crankcase, refill..(qt) 7
    Transmission..(qt) 4
    Rear axle...(qt) 4
Brakes:
    Manufacturer; Wagner............................Type; hydraulic
    Parking brake, type...................................transmission
Transmission forward speeds..4
    Gear ration: High 1:1.................................Low 6.4:1

PERFORMANCE

Computed grade ability in lowest gear, loaded...................(percent) 27
Turning radius..(ft) 32¾
Fording depth..(in.) 24
Fuel consumption, loaded.....................................(mpg) 5
Cruising range, loaded.......................................(mi) 150
Allowable speed, governed....................................(mph) 55

ENGINE

Manufacturer: International Harvester.....................Model SD–240
Type....................Valve-in-head, 4-cycle; No. of cylinders (in line) 6
Displacement...(cu in.) 240.3
Bore...(in.) 3 9/16
Stroke...(in.) 4 9/16
Compression ratio..6.5:1
Governed speed...(rpm) 3,400
Brake horsepower (max w/std accessories)...............93 at (rpm) 3,400
Torque (max)................................186 lb ft at (rpm) 1,100

ADDITIONAL DATA

Transmission, type...synchromesh

25

BUS, 37-PASSENGER, 4 x 2
(Southern Coach, Model S–36–M)

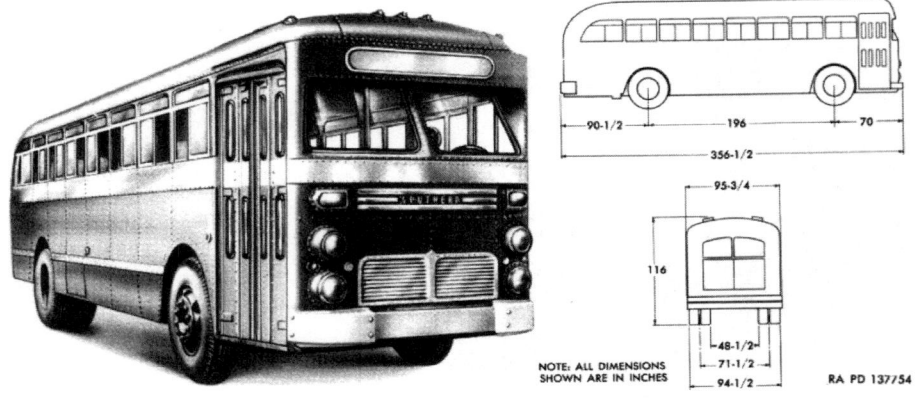

NOTE: ALL DIMENSIONS SHOWN ARE IN INCHES

RA PD 137754

Classification: Nonclassified.

Purpose: To transport personnel.

GENERAL DATA

Crew..1; Passengers (including crew) 38
Weight (lb)......................Net 15,825; Payload 6,610; Gross 22,435
Rear-axle gear ratio...5:28:1
Axle load (lb):
    Empty..front, 6905; rear 8,920
    Loaded..front 9,400; rear 13,035
Tires:
    Ply 12..Size 10:10 x 20; Pressure (psi) 70
    Tread, center-to-center, front.................................(in.) 80¼
Shipping dimensions, uncrated.................(cu ft) 2,300; (sq ft) 238
Vehicle dimensions:
    Ground clearance...(in.) 13
    Step height, empty..(in.) 17⅝
Electrical system..(volts) 12
    No. of batteries..1
    Type of ground..positive
Fuel octane rating...75
Capacities:
    Fuel ....(gal) 75
    Cooling system...(qt) 64
    Crankcase, refill...(qt) 13
    Transmission..(qt) 11½
    Rear axle..(qt) 11½
Brakes:
    Manufacturer; Timken..Type; air
    Parking brake, type.......................................transmission
Transmission forward speeds...4
    Gear ratio...High 1:1; Low 4.67:1

PERFORMANCE

Computed grade ability in lowest gear, loaded.................(percent) 24
Turning radius..(ft) 34
Fording depth..(in.) 12
Fuel consumption, loaded..(mpg 5)
Cruising range, loaded...(mi) 375
Allowable speed, governed..(mph) 60

ENGINE

Manufacturer: Waukesha.................................Model 140–G K B–33
Type........................Valve-in-head, 4-cycle; No. of cylinders (in line) 6
Displacement...(cu in.) 525
Bore..(in.) 4½
Stroke..(in.) 5½
Compression ratio...6.4:1
Governed speed...(rpm) 2,700
Brake horsepower (max w/std accessories)..............173 at (rpm) 2,700
Torque (max w/std accessories)........................425 lb-ft at (rpm) 800

ADDITIONAL DATA

Transmission, type..synchromesh
Rear axle, type....................................spiral-bevel, full-floating

BUS, 37-PASSENGER, 2½-TON, 4 x 2
(International Harvester, Models K7 and KS7 w/two-speed axle)

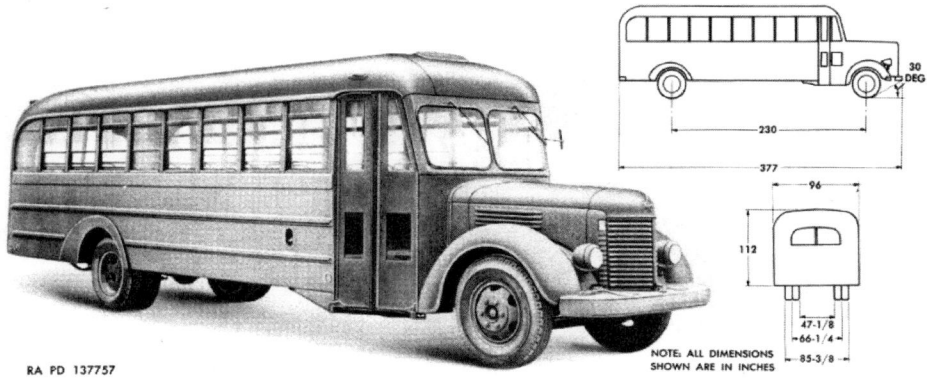

RA PD 137757

NOTE: ALL DIMENSIONS SHOWN ARE IN INCHES

Technical Manuals: 9–822; 9–1822; 9–1825A; 9–1826C; 9–1827B; 9–1827C; 9–1828A; Supply Catalog: SNL G–541.

Classification: Nonclassified.

Purpose: To transport personnel.

GENERAL DATA

Crew..1; Passengers (including crew) 38
Weight (lb).........................Net 12,387; Payload 6,650; Gross 19,037
Rear-axle gear ratio:
  K7...7.16:1
  KS7..High 6.143:1; Low 8.52:1
Axle load (lb):
  Empty...front 4,581; rear 7,806
  Loaded..front 5,587; rear 13,450
Tires:
  Ply 10; Size 8.25 x 20; Pressure..............................(psi) 60
  Tread, center-to-center, front....................................(in.) 65¾
Shipping dimensions, uncrated.....................(cu ft) 2,346; (sq ft) 252
Ground clearance..(in.) 9⅝
Electrical system...(volts) 6
  No. of batteries..1
  Type of ground...negative
Fuel octane rating..70
Capacities:
  Fuel...(gal) 31
  Cooling system..(qt) 20½
  Crankcase, refill..(qt) 7
  Transmission..(qt) 4¾
  Rear axle...(qt) 3½
Brakes:
  Manufacturer; Wagner.........................Type; hydraulic
  Parking brake, type......................................transmission
Transmission forward speeds...5
  Gear ratio...................High 0.823:1; Fourth 1:1; Low 6.525:1

PERFORMANCE

Computed grade ability in lowest gear, loaded (percent)...K7, 29; KS7, 34
Turning radius...(ft) 37½
Fording depth...(in.) 30
Fuel consumption, loaded......................................(mpg) 8
Cruising range, loaded..(mi) 248
Allowable speed, governed....................................(mph) 45

ENGINE

Manufacturer: International Harvester....................Model, BLD–269
Type....................Valve-in-head, 4-cycle; No. of cylinders (in line) 6
Displacement..(cu in.) 269.1
Bore...(in.) 3⁹⁄₁₆
Stroke..(in.) 4½
Compression ratio..6.3:1
Governed speed..(rpm) 2,500
Brake horsepower (max w/std accessories)............87.5 at (rpm) 2,500
Torque (max)..........................216.5 lb-ft at (rpm) 1,000

ADDITIONAL DATA

Transmission, type...sliding-gear
Rear axle, type:
  K7..................................spiral-bevel, full-floating
  KS7...................two-speed spiral-bevel, full-floating

BUS, INTEGRAL, 37-PASSENGER, 4 x 2

(ACF-Brill, Model C–37)

NOTE: ALL DIMENSIONS SHOWN ARE IN INCHES   RA PD 172741

Classification: Nonclassified.

Purpose: To transport personnel.

GENERAL DATA

Crew	1; Passengers (including crew) 38
Weight (lb)	Net 14,000
Payload	8,700
Gross	22,700
Rear-axle gear ratio	5.286:1
Axle load (lb):	
Empty	front 4,730; rear 9,270
Loaded	front 8,100; rear 14,600
Tires:	
Ply 10	Size 9.00 x 20; Pressure (psi) 65
Tread, center-to-center, front	(in.) 81¼
Shipping dimensions, uncrated	(cu ft) 2,290; (sq ft) 239
Vehicle dimensions:	
Ground clearance	(in.) 10
Step height, empty	(in.) 16
Electrical system	(volts) 12
No. of batteries	1
Type of ground	positive
Fuel octane rating	72
Capacities:	
Fuel	(gal) 75
Cooling system (qt)	w/heater 36
Crankcase, refill	(qt) 10
Transmission	(qt) 4
Rear axle	(qt) 6½
Brakes:	
Manufacturer; Bendix-Westinghouse	Type; air
Parking brake, type	transmission
Transmission forward speeds	3
Gear ratio	High 1.04:1; Low 4.06:1

PERFORMANCE

Computed grade ability in lowest gear, loaded	(percent) 17
Turning radius (ft)	Right 37; Left 36
Fording depth	(in.) 20
Fuel consumption, loaded	(mpg) 4
Cruising range, loaded	(mi) 300
Allowable speed, governed	(mph) 60

ENGINE

Manufacturer: International	Model RD–450
Type	4-cycle, valve-in-head; No. of cylinders (in line) 6
Displacement	(cu in.) 450
Bore	(in.) 4¾
Stroke	(in.) 5
Compression ratio	6.3:1
Governed speed	(rpm) 2,600
Brake horsepower (max w/std accessories)	146 at (rpm) 2,600
Torque (max w/std accessories)	354 lb-ft at (rpm) 1,000

ADDITIONAL DATA

Live axle, type	full-floating, spiral-bevel
Transmission, type	synchromesh

BUS, INTEGRAL, 37-PASSENGER, 4 x 2
(ACF-Brill, Model 37RC)

NOTE: ALL DIMENSIONS SHOWN
ARE IN INCHES

RA PD 172703

Classification: Nonclassified.

Purpose: To transport personnel.

GENERAL DATA

Crew..............................1; Passengers (including crew) 38
Weight (lb)...Net 16,300
    Payload..8,700
    Gross...25,000
Rear-axle gear ratio......................................5.286:1
Axle load (lb):
    Empty........................front 5,000; rear 11,300
    Loaded.......................front 8,500; rear 16,500
Tires:
    Ply 12........................Size 10.00 x 20; Pressure (psi) 70
    Tread, center-to-center, front..................(in.) 79½
Shipping dimensions, uncrated...........(cu ft) 2,740; (sq ft) 274
Vehicle dimensions:
    Ground clearance.................................(in.) 10
    Step height, empty..............................(in.) 16
Electrical system......................................(volts) 12
    No. of batteries....................................1
    Type of ground..................................positive
Fuel octane rating..72
Capacities:
    Fuel...(gal) 75
    Cooling system (qt).........................w/heater 36
    Crankcase, refill.................................(qt) 10
    Transmission......................................(qt) 6
    Rear axle..(qt) 11½
Brakes:
    Manufacturer; Bendix-Westinghouse.............Type; air
    Parking brake, type..........................transmission
Transmission forward speeds.................................4
    Gear ratio.......................High 0.96:1; low 4.44:1

PERFORMANCE

Computed grade ability in lowest gear, loaded.......(percent) 20
Turning radius..(ft) 41
Fording depth...(in.) 20
Fuel consumption, loaded...............................(mpg) 4
Cruising range, loaded.................................(mi) 300
Allowable speed, governed..............................(mph) 60

ENGINE

Manufacturer: Hercules.............................Model TDXC
Type...................4-cycle, L-head; No. of cylinders (in line) 6
Displacement.......................................(cu in.) 501
Bore..(in.) 4½
Stroke..(in.) 5¼
Compression ratio.......................................6.5:1
Governed speed.....................................(rpm) 2,630
Brake horsepower, gross.....................173 at (rpm) 2,800
Torque, maximum, gross......................388 at (rpm) 1,425

ADDITIONAL DATA

Rear axle, type.......................spiral-bevel, full-floating
Transmission, type.................................synchromesh

BUS, INTEGRAL, 37-PASSENGER, 4 x 2
(Twin Coach, Utility Convertible, Model F32F)

NOTE: ALL DIMENSIONS SHOWN ARE IN INCHES   RA PD 172715

Classification: Nonclassified.

Purpose: To transport personnel; convertible to cargo carrier or ambulance.

GENERAL DATA

Crew...1; Passengers (including crew) 37
Weight (lb)..Net 14,620
    Payload...9,700
    Gross..24,320
Rear-axle gear ratio...4.857:1
Axle load (lb):
    Empty.................................front 6,150; rear 8,470
    Loaded..............................front 9,630; rear 14,690
Tires:
    Ply 12....................Size 10.00 x 20; Pressure (psi) front 70; rear 50
    Tread, center-to-center, front.............................(in.) 79¾
Shipping dimensions, uncrated...............(cu ft) 2,715; (sq ft) 261
Vehicle dimensions:
    Ground clearance...(in.) 10
    Loading height, empty......................................(in.) 40
    Step height, empty...(in.) 16
Electrical system..(volts) 12
    No. of batteries...1
    Type of ground..positive
Fuel octane rating...72
Capacities:
    Fuel...(gal) 8¹
    Cooling system (gal)..............w/o heater 9¾; w/heater 11
    Crankcase, refill...(qt) 12
    Transmission..(qt) 6
    Rear axle...(qt) 8
Brakes:
    Manufacturer; Eaton.................................Type; air
    Parking brake, type.............................transmission
Transmission forward speeds....................................4
    Gear ratio...........................High 1:1; Low 4.88:1

PERFORMANCE

Computed grade ability in lowest gear, loaded.................(percent) 17
Turning radius...(ft) 75½
Fording depth...(in.) 16
Fuel consumption, loaded....................................(mpg) 6
Cruising range, loaded.....................................(mi) 480
Allowable speed, governed...................................(mph) 60

ENGINE

Manufacturer: Fageol.............................Model FTC 210-21
Type..................................4-cycle, valve-in-head
No. of cylinders.........................(horizontal, in line) 6
Displacement...............................(cu in.) 477
Bore.....................................(in.) 4½
Stroke...................................(in.) 5
Compression ratio............................7.1:1
Governed speed..........................(rpm) 2,800
Brake horsepower (max w/std accessories).............210 at (rpm) 2,800
Torque (max w/std accessories)...............480 lb-ft at (rpm) 1,600

ADDITIONAL DATA

Engine radiator coolant filler neck extends 1 inch beyond over-all width. Seats are removable. Vehicle can be converted to an ambulance.
Rear axle, type..hypoid, full-floating
Transmission, type..constant-mesh

BUS, INTEGRAL, 2½-TON, 4 x 2
(GMC Model PGA 3301)

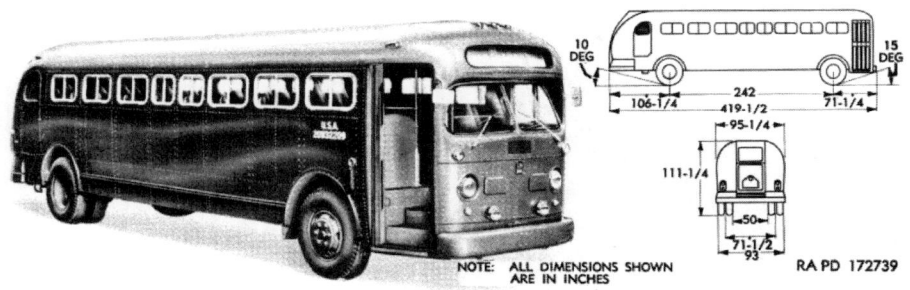

NOTE: ALL DIMENSIONS SHOWN ARE IN INCHES

RA PD 172739

Classification: Nonclassified.

Purpose: To transport personnel.

GENERAL DATA

Crew..1; Passengers (including crew) 38
Weight (lb)..Net 15,190
    Payload..8,700
    Gross..23,890
Rear-axle gear ratio..5.286:1
Axle load (lb):
    Empty..front 4,590; rear 10,600
    Loaded..front 7,730; rear 16,160
Tires:
    Ply 12..Size 10.00 x 20; Pressure (psi) 70
    Tread, center-to-center, front..(in.) 80½
Shipping dimensions, uncrated..(cu ft) 2,550; (sq ft) 277
Vehicle dimensions:
    Ground clearance..(in.) 10
    Step height, empty..(in.) 17⅛
Electrical system..(volts) 12
    No. of batteries..1
    Type of ground..positive
Fuel octane rating..72
Capacities:
    Fuel..(gal) 75
    Cooling system (qt)..................................w/o heater 16½; w/heater 30
    Crankcase, refill..(qt) 9
    Transmission..(qt) 6
    Rear axle..(qt) 11½
Brakes:
    Manufacturer; Bendix-Westinghouse..................................Type; air
    Parking brake, type..transmission
Transmission forward speeds..4
    Gear ratio..High 1:1; Low 4.88:1

PERFORMANCE

Computed grade ability in lowest gear, loaded..................(percent) 22
Turning radius..(ft) 43½
Fording depth..(in.) 20
Fuel consumption, loaded..(mpg) 4
Cruising range, loaded..(mi) 300
Allowable speed, governed..(mph) 62

ENGINE

Manufacturer: GMC..Model 503
Type..................................4-cycle, valve-in-head; No. of cylinders (in line) 6
Displacement..(cu in.) 502.7
Bore..(in.) 4⅛₆
Stroke..(in.) 5⅛
Compression ratio..6.5:1
Governed speed..(rpm) 2,800
Brake horsepower (max w/std accessories)..................175 at (rpm) 2,800
Torque (max w/std accessories)..................412 lb-ft at (rpm) 1,200

ADDITIONAL DATA

Rear axle, type..hypoid, full-floating
Transmission, type..constant-mesh

BUS, 37-PASSENGER, 5- TO 6-TON, 4 x 2

(Mack, Model EH)

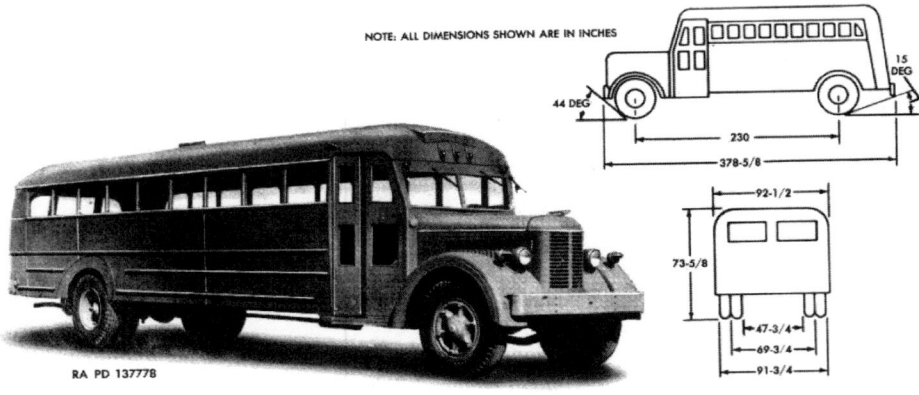

NOTE: ALL DIMENSIONS SHOWN ARE IN INCHES

RA PD 137778

Technical Manual: 10-1681

Classification: Nonclassified.

Purpose: To transport personnel.

GENERAL DATA

Crew.................................1; Passengers (including crew) 38
Weight (lb)....................Net 14,900; Payload 10,500; Gross 25,400
Rear-axle gear ratio..8.59:1
Axle load (lb):
    Empty.................................front 8,050; rear 6,850
    Loaded...............................front 8,290; rear 17,110
Tires:
    Ply 12..................Size 10.00 x 20; Pressure (psi) 70
    Tread, center-to-center, front.....................(in.) 69½
Shipping dimensions, uncrated...........(cu ft) 1,500; (sq ft) 243
Ground clearance.......................................(in.) 10
Electrical system......................................(volts) 6
    No. of batteries...1
    Type of ground......................................negative
Fuel octane rating..70
Capacities:
    Fuel..(gal) 50
    Cooling system....................................(qt) 31
    Crankcase, refill.................................(qt) 11
    Transmission.....................................(qt) 10½
    Rear axle..(qt) 14
Brakes:
    Manufacturer; Bendix-Westinghouse.............Type; air
    Parking brake, type.........................transmission
Transmission forward speeds................................5
    Gear ratio.............High 1 : 1; Fourth 1.45 : 1; Low 8.05 : 1

PERFORMANCE

Computed grade ability in lowest gear, loaded...............(percent) 28
Turning radius..(ft) 42
Fording depth...(in.) 45
Fuel consumption, loaded..............................(mpg) 5.5
Cruising range, loaded................................(mi) 275
Allowable speed, governed.............................(mph) 35

ENGINE

Manufacturer; Mack...............................Model EN 354
Type.................L-head, 4-cycle; No. of cylinders (in line) 6
Displacement...(cu in.) 354
Bore...(in.) 3¾
Stroke...(in.) 5
Compression ratio....................................5.5:1
Governed speed.......................................(rpm) 2,620
Brake horsepower (max w/std accessories)...........110 at (rpm) 2,620
Torque (max)...................255 lb-ft at (rpm) 1,200

ADDITIONAL DATA

Transmission, type...................................synchromesh
Rear axle, type................double-reduction, full-floating

CAR, ARMORED, LIGHT, M8

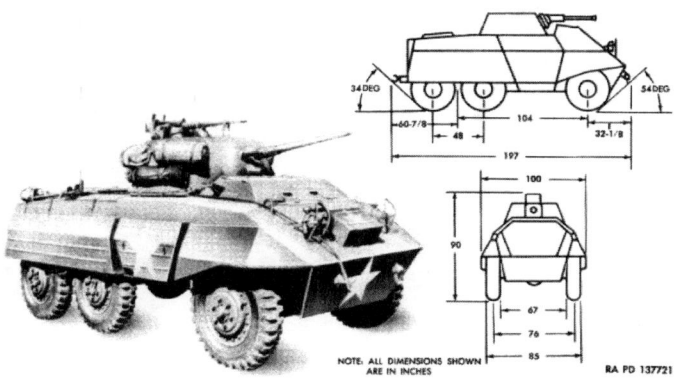

NOTE: ALL DIMENSIONS SHOWN ARE IN INCHES   RA PD 137721

Technical Manuals: 9-743, 9-1743, 9-1825B, 9-1826C, 9-1827C, 9-1928A, 9-1832A; **Supply Catalog:** SNL G-136.

Classification: Limited Standard.

Armament: 1 gun, 37-mm, M6; 1 gun, machine cal. .30, M1919A4 (flexible), mounted coaxially; 1 gun, machine cal. .50; M2, heavy barrel (flexible), pedestal mounted on top of turret.

Ammunition: 80 rounds, 37-mm for vehicles having 64-round ammunition racks, 50 rounds for vehicles having 34-round racks; 400 rounds, cal. .30 for carbine M1; 1,575 rounds, cal. .30 (machine gun); 420 rounds cal. .50; 12 hand grenades; 4 pots, smoke, M1 or M2; 6 mines, antitank, w/fuze; 15 signal ground (assorted).

Fire Control and Vision Devices: Telescope, M70D (sight).

Communications: (SCR–506 or SCR–193T or AN/ GRC–9) or (SCR–506 or SCR–193T or SCR–608B or RC–99); or (SCR–506 or SCR–193T or An/GRC–9 or SCR–694C) and SCR–619 or SCR–610) and (RC–99; or SCR–619 or SCR–610) and (RC–99).

GENERAL DATA

Crew	4
Weight (lb)	Net 14,500; Payload 2,700; Gross 17,200
Axle gear ratio	6.66:1

Axle load (lb):

Empty	front 5,010; rear (each) 4,745
Loaded	front 6,360; rear (each) 5,420

Tires:

Ply 12; Size 9.00 x 20; Pressure (psi)	front 60; rear 50
Tread, center-to-center, front	(in.) 76

Vehicle dimensions:

Ground clearance	(in.) 11½
Pintle height	(in.) 26
Shipping dimensions, uncrated	(cu ft) 1,030; (sq ft) 137
Electrical system	(volts) 12
No. of batteries	1
Type of ground	negative
Fuel octane rating	72

Purpose: To provide high-speed mobility, defense firepower and crew protection for reconnaissance.

GENERAL DATA—Continued

Capacities:

Fuel	(gal) 54
Cooling system	(qt) 23½
Crankcase, refill	(qt) 7
Transfer	(qt) 2¾
Transmission	(qt) 4½
Axles (qt)	front 2¾; rear (each) 2¾

Brakes:

Manufacturer: Bendix	Type; hydrovac
Parking brake, type	transfer
Transmission forward speeds	4
Gear ratio	High 1:1; Low 6.499:1
Transfer speeds	2
Gear ratio	High 1:1; Low 1.956:1

PERFORMANCE

Computed grade ability in lowest gear, loaded	(percent) 60
Turning radius	(ft) 28
Fording depth	(in.) 32
Fuel consumption, loaded	(mpg) 5
Cruising range, loaded	(mi) 250
Allowable speed, recommended	(mph) 56

ENGINE

Manufacturer: Hercules	Model JXD
Type	L-head, 4-cycle; No. of cylinders (in line) 6
Displacement	(cu in.) 320
Bore	(in.) 4
Stroke	(in.) 4¼
Governed speed	not governed
Compression ratio	6.5:1
Brake horsepower (max w/std accessories)	86 at (rpm) 2,800
Torque (max)	200 lb-ft at (rpm) 1,150

ADDITIONAL DATA

Transmission, type	sliding-gear
Rear axle, type	spiral-bevel, full-floating

CAR, ARMORED, UTILITY, M20

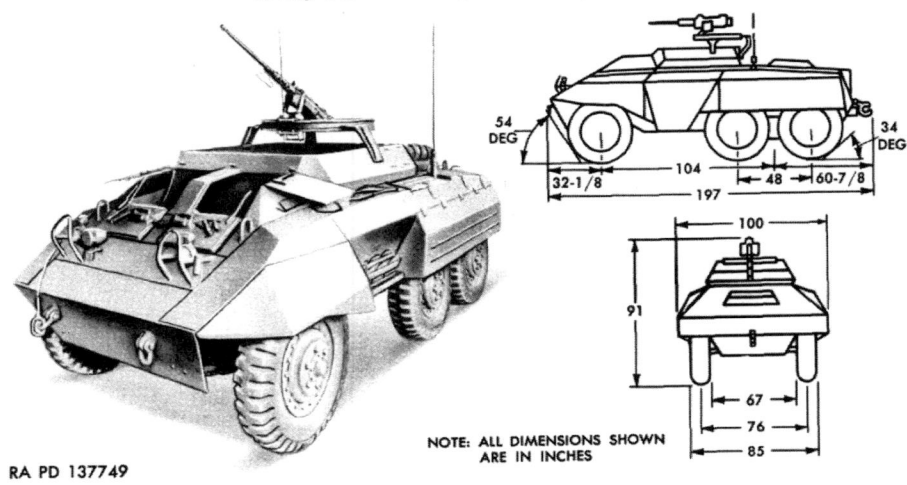

RA PD 137749

NOTE: ALL DIMENSIONS SHOWN ARE IN INCHES

Technical Manuals: 9-743, 9-1743, 9-1825B, 9-1826C, 9-1827C, 9-1828A, 9-1832A; Supply Catalog: SNL G-176.

Classification: Standard.

Armmament: One gun, machine, cal. .50, M2, heavy barrel (flexible) ring mounted.

GENERAL DATA

Crew	6
Weight (lb)	Net 12,250; Payload 3,400; Gross 15,650
Axle gear ratio	6.66:1
Axle load (lb):	
Empty	front 3,900; rear (each) 4,175
Loaded	front 5,600; rear (each) 5,025
Tires (combat):	
Ply 12; Size 9.00 x 20; Pressure (psi)	front 60; rear 50
Tread, center-to-center, front	(in.) 76
Shipping dimensions, uncrated	(cu ft) 1,038; (sq ft) 137
Vehicle dimensions:	
Ground clearance	(in.) 11½
Pintle height	(in.) 26
Electrical system	(volts) 12
No. of batteries	1
Type of ground	negative
Fuel octane rating	72
Capacities:	
Fuel	(gal) 54
Cooling system	(qt) 23½
Crankcase, refill	(qt) 7
Transfer	(qt) 2¾
Transmission	(qt) 4½
Axles (qt)	front 2¾; rear (each) 2¾
Brakes:	
Manufacturer; Bendix	Type; hydrovac
Parking brake, type	transfer
Transmission forward speeds	4
Gear ratio	High 1:1; Low 6.499:1
Transfer speeds	2
Gear ratio	High 1:1; Low 1.956:1

Ammunition: 500 rounds cal. .30 for carbine M1; 1,050 rounds cal. .50; 12 hand grenades; 4 pots, smoke; 3 mines, antitank w/fuze; 10 rockets for launcher, rocket, 2.36-in., M9A1; 36 signal, ground (assorted).

Communications: (SCR-506 or AN/GRC-9 or SCR-694C) and (SCR-506 or SCR-608 or SCR-510 or SCR-619 or SCR-610); or (AN/VRC-3); or (AN/GRC-3, -4, -5, -6, -7, or -8) and (SCR-506).

Purpose: To provide a highly mobile armored personnel and cargo carrier or field commander's car.

PERFORMANCE

Computed grade ability in lowest gear, loaded	(percent) 60
Turning radius	(ft) 28
Fording depth	(in.) 32
Fuel consumption, loaded	(mpg) 5
Cruising range, loaded	(mi) 250
Allowable speed, recommended	(mph) 56

ENGINE

Manufacturer: Hercules	Model JXD
Type	L-head, 4-cycle; No. of cylinders (in line) 6
Displacement	(cu in.) 320
Bore	(in.) 4
Stroke	(in.) 4¼
Compression ratio	6.5:1
Governed speed	not governed
Brake horsepower (max w/std accessories)	86 at (rpm) 2,800
Torque (max)	200 lb-ft at (rpm) 1,150

ADDITIONAL DATA

Transmission, type	sliding-gear
Rear axle, type	spiral-bevel, full-floating

CAR, HALF-TRACK, M2A1

RA PD 137768

NOTE: ALL DIMENSIONS SHOWN ARE IN INCHES

Technical Manuals: 9-710, 9-1710, 9-1710C, 9-1711, 9-1825A, 9-1826B, 9-1828A; **Supply Catalog:** SNL G-102.

Classification: Limited Standard.

Armament: 1 gun, machine, cal. .50, M2, heavy barrel (flexible) ring mounted on front of driver's compartment; 1 gun, machine, cal. .30, M1919A4 (flexible) pintle mounted on right side or rear of body.

Ammunition 700 rounds, cal. .50; 7,750 rounds, cal. .30; 540 rounds, cal. .45 for submachine gun; 10 hand grenades; 14 mines, antitank w/fuze.

Communications: (SCR-508 or SCR-528).

Purpose: To transport cargo and personnel in combat zone.

GENERAL DATA

Crew	10
Weight (lb)	Net 14,600; Payload 5,000; Gross 19,600
Front-axle gear ratio	6.8:1
Rear-axle (jackshaft) gear ratio	4.44:1
Axle load (lb):	
Empty	front 5,250; rear (each track) 4,675
Loaded	front 7,100; rear (each track) 6,250
Tires: (combat):	
Ply 12	Size 8.25 x 20; Pressure (psi) 55
Tread, center-to-center, front	(in.) 63¹³⁄₁₆
Track ground pressure (loaded)	(psi) 11
Shipping dimensions, uncrated	(cu ft) 1,191; (sq ft) 143
Vehicle dimensions:	
Ground clearance	(in.) 11³⁄₁₆
Pintle height (loaded)	(in.) 28
Electrical system	(volts) 12
No. of batteries	1
Type of ground	negative
Fuel octane rating	72
Capacities:	
Fuel	(gal) 60
Cooling system	(qt) 26
Crankcase, refill	(qt) 10½
Transfer and transmission (qt) 7½	PTO 8
Axles (qt)	front 3½; rear 6
Winch:	
Load capacity	(lb) 10,000
Oil capacity	(qt) 2
Brakes: Manufacturer; Bendix	Type; hydrovac
Parking brake, type	transfer
Transmission forward speeds	4
Gear ratio	High 1:1; Low 4.92:1
Transfer speeds	2
Gear ratio	High 1:1; Low 2.48:1

PERFORMANCE

Computed grade ability in lowest gear, loaded	(percent) 60
Turning radius	(ft) 29½
Fording depth	(in.) 32
Fuel consumption, loaded	(mpg) 3½
Cruising range, loaded	(mi) 210
Allowable speed, recommended	(mph) 45
Maximum recommended towed load, gross	off highway (lb) 4,500

ENGINE

Manufacturer: White	Model 160AX
Type	L-head, 4-cycle; No. of cylinders (in line) 6
Displacement	(cu in.) 386
Bore	(in.)4
Stroke	(in.) 5⅛
Compression ratio	6.44:1
Governed speed	not governed
Brake horsepower (max w/std accessories)	127 at (rpm) 3,000
Torque (max)	325 lb-ft at (rpm) 1,200

ADDITIONAL DATA

Data given for vehicle w/o winch and w/front roller. For vehicle w/winch and w/o front roller, changes in data are as follows: Weight (lb): Net 15,100; Payload 4,500. Axle load (lb): Empty, front 5,587, rear (each track) 4,757; Loaded, front 7,252, rear (each track) 6,174. Shipping dimensions uncrated: (cu ft) 1,242; (sq ft) 149. Over-all length (in) 241¾.

Angle of approach (deg) 33.

Equipped w/controller for trailer electric brakes.

Transmission, type	constant-mesh
Live axles, type	spiral-bevel, full-floating

CARRIAGE, MOTOR, MULTIPLE GUN, M16

RA PD 137724

NOTE: ALL DIMENSIONS SHOWN
ARE IN INCHES

Technical Manuals: 9-710, 9-1710, 9-1710C, 9-1711, 9-1825A, 9-1826B, 9-1828A, 9-1829A; Supply Catalog: SNL G-102.

Classification: Substitute Standard.
Armament: 4 guns, machine, cal. .50, Browning, M2, heavy barrel, turret type, turret mounted.
Ammunition: 5,000 rounds, cal. .50; 420 rounds, cal. .45 for submachine gun; 26 hand grenades; 10 rifle grenades.

Fire Control and Vision Devices: Sight, reflex, M18, or sight, illuminating, MK 9, Mod 1.
Communications: (SCR-52B) and (SCR-593); or (AN/VAC-13, -14, or -15) and (SCR-593 or AN/GRR-5).
Purpose: To provide mobility for machine guns.

GENERAL DATA

Crew	5
Weight (lb)	Net 18,640; Payload 3,000; Gross 21,640
Front-axle gear ratio	6.8:1
Rear-axle (jackshaft) gear ratio	4.44:1
Axle load (lb):	
Empty	front 7,224; rear (each track) 5,708
Loaded	front 7,824; rear (each track) 6,908
Tires (combat):	
Ply 12	Size 8.25 x 20; Pressure (psi) 55
Tread, center-to-center, front	(in.) 64½
Track ground pressure (loaded)	(psi) 11.2
Shipping dimensions, uncrated	(cu ft) 1,072; (sq ft) 146
Vehicle dimensions:	
Ground clearance	(in.) 17¼
Pintle height (loaded)	(in.) 28
Electrical system	(volts) 12
No. of batteries	1
Type of ground	negative
Fuel octane rating	72
Capacities:	
Fuel	(gal) 60
Cooling system	(qt) 26
Crankcase, refill	(qt) 10½
Transmission and transfer w/PTO	(qt) 9
Axles (qt)	front 3½; rear 6
Winch:	
Load capacity	(lb) 10,000
Oil capacity	(qt) 2
Brakes:	
Manufacturer; Bendix	Type; hydrovac
Parking brake, type	transfer
Transmission forward speeds	4
Gear ratio	High 1:1; Low 4.92:1
Transfer speeds	2
Gear ratio	High 1:1; Low 2.48:1

PERFORMANCE

Maximum grade ability	(percent) 60
Turning radius	(ft) 30
Fording depth	(in.) 32
Fuel consumption, loaded	(mpg) 3½
Cruising range, loaded	(mi) 210
Allowable speed, recommended	(mph) 45
Maximum recommended towed load, gross, off highway	(lb) 4,500

ENGINE

Manufacturer: White	Model 160AX
Type	L-head, 4-cycle; No. of cylinders (in line) 6
Displacement	(cu in.) 386
Bore	(in.) 4
Stroke	(in.) 5⅛
Compression ratio	6.44:1
Governed speed	not governed
Brake horsepower (max w/std accessories)	127 at (rpm) 3,000
Torque (max w/std accessories)	325 lb-ft at (rpm) 1,300

ADDITIONAL DATA

Equipped w/controller for trailer electric brakes.

Live axles, type	spiral-bebel, full-floating
Transmission, type	constant mesh

36

CARRIAGE, MOTOR, COMBINATION GUN, M15A1

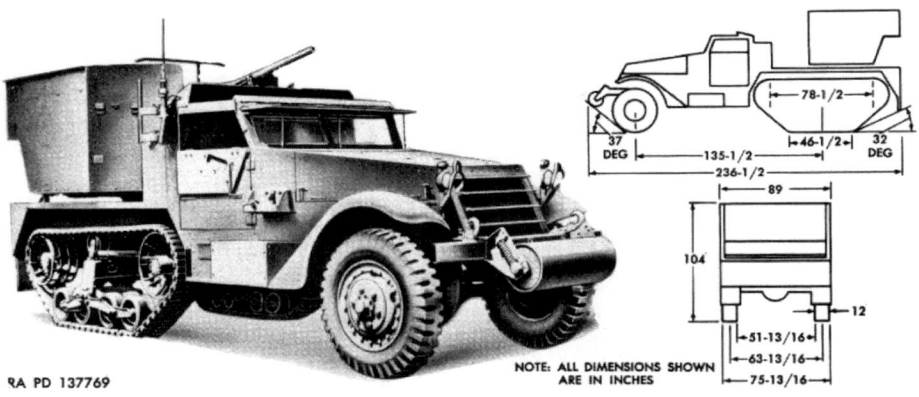

RA PD 137769

NOTE: ALL DIMENSIONS SHOWN ARE IN INCHES

Technical Manuals: 9-710, 9-1710, 9-1710C, 9-1711, 9-1825A, 9-1826B, 9-1828A, 9-1829A; Supply Catalog: SNL G-102.

Classification: Limited Standard.

Armament: 1 gun, automatic, 37-mm, M1A2, turret mounted; 2 guns, machine, cal. .50, Browning, M2, heavy barrel, mounted coaxially.

Ammunition: 200 rounds, 37-mm; 1,200 rounds, cal. .50-
Fire Control and Vision Devices: Sight, computing, M14.
Communications: (SCR-528).
Purpose: To provide a highly mobile antiaircraft weapon.

GENERAL DATA

Crew	7
Weight (lb)	Net 18,385; Payload 2,415; Gross 20,800
Front-axle gear ratio	6.8:1
Rear-axle (jackshaft) gear ratio	4.44:1
Axle load (lb):	
Empty	front 5,760; rear (each track) 6,313
Loaded	front 7,624; rear (each track) 6,588
Tires (combat):	
Ply 12; Size 8.25 x 20; Pressure	(psi) 55
Tread, center-to-center front	(in.) 63¹³⁄₁₆
Track ground pressure (loaded)	(psi) 11.6
Shipping dimensions, uncrated	(cu ft) 1,400; (sq ft) 162
Vehicle dimensions:	
Ground clearance	(in.) 17⅛
Pintle height (loaded)	(in.) 28
Electrical system	(volts) 12
No. of batteries	1
Type of ground	negative
Fuel octane rating	72
Capacities:	
Fuel	(gal) 60
Cooling system	(qt) 26
Crankcase, refill	(qt) 10½
Transfer and transmission	(qt) 7½
Axles (qt)	front 3½; rear 6
Brakes:	
Manufacturer; Bendix	Type; hydrovac
Parking brake, type	transfer
Transmission forward speeds	4
Gear ratio	High 1:1; Low 4.92:1
Transfer speeds	2
Gear ratio	High 1:1; Low 2.48:1

PERFORMANCE

Maximum grade ability	(percent) 60
Turning radius	(ft) 29½
Fording depth	(in.) 32
Fuel consumption, loaded	(mpg) 3½
Cruising range, loaded	(mi) 210
Allowable speed, recommended	(mph) 40
Maximum recommended towed load, gross, off highway	(lb) 4,500

ENGINE

Manufacturer: White......................Model 160AX

Type	L-head, 4-cycle; No. of cylinders (in line) 6
Displacement	(cu in.) 386
Bore	(in.) 4
Stroke	(in.) 5⅛
Compression ratio	6.44:1
Governed speed	not governed
Brake horsepower (max w/std accessories)	127 at (rpm) 3,000
Torque (max)	325 lb-ft at (rpm) 1,200

ADDITIONAL DATA

Equipped w/controller for trailer electric brakes.

Live axles, type	spiral-bevel, full-floating
Transmission, type	constant-mesh

CARRIAGE, MOTOR, TWIN 40-MM GUN, M19A1

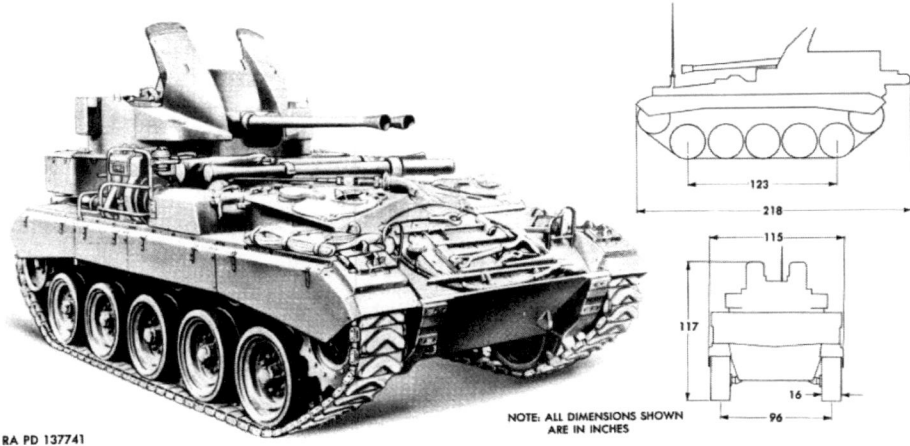

NOTE: ALL DIMENSIONS SHOWN
ARE IN INCHES

RA PD 137741

Technical Manuals: 9-761, 9-1718C, 9-1727K, 9-1729A, 9-1729B, 9-1726C, 9-1731D, 9-1825A, 9-1826A, 9-1828A; Supply Catalog: SNL G-248.

Classification: Standard.

Armament: Gun, dual, automatic, 40-mm, M2, turret mounted.

Ammunition: 350 rounds, 40-mm; 480 rounds, cal. .45, for submachine gun; 900 rounds, cal. .30 for carbines; 10 rifle grenades w/cartridge for carbine; 12 hand grenades.

Fire Control and Vision Devices: Periscope M13 or M6 (drivers); quadrant, gunner's M1; sight, computing, M13; system, local control, M16A1, or M16.

Communications: (AN/VRC-5) and (SCR-593 or AN/GRR-5); or (AN/VRC-8 or -9) and (AN/UIC-1) and (SCR-593 or AN/GRR-5).

Purpose: To provide a mobile anti-aircraft weapon.

GENERAL DATA

Crew	6
Weight, fighting	(lb) 41,165
Shipping dimensions, uncrated	(cu ft) 1,705; (sq ft) 175
Ground pressure	(psi) 10.1
Ground clearance	(in.) 16½
Pintle height, unloaded	(in.) 18½
Electrical system	(volts) 24
No. of batteries	(6-volt) 4
Type of ground	negative
Fuel octane rating	70
Capacities:	
Fuel	(gal) 110
Cooling system (2 systems)	(each) (qt) 40
Crankcase, refill (each engine)	(qt) 8
Auxiliary-engine crankcase, refill	(qt) 3½
Transmission	(each) (qt) 15
Differential	(qt) 20
Transfer	(qt) 4½
Final drive	(each) (qt) 2
Brakes	mechanical, controlled-differential
Parking brake, type	locking knobs on steering-brake levers
Transmission forward speeds	4
Gear ratio	High 1:1; 3d 1.55:1; Low 3.92:1
Transfer speeds	forward 2; reverse 1
Gear ratio	High 1.03:1; Low 2.34:1; Reverse 2.44:1
Differential-drive gear ratio	2.62:1
Final-drive gear ratio	2.94:1
Hull construction	welded homogeneous armor plate
Armor, Turret: Welded homogeneous armor plate.	

PERFORMANCE

Maximum grade ability	(percent) 60
Turning radius	(ft) 50
Fording depth	(in.) 42
Maximum width of ditch vehicle can cross	(in.) 88
Maximum vertical obstacle vehicle can climb	(in.) 32
Fuel consumption (average conditions)	(mpg) ¾
Cruising range (average conditions)	(mi) 85
Allowable speed, recommended	(mph) 30
Maximum allowable towed load, gross	(lb) 10,000

ENGINE

Manufacturer: Cadillac	No. used 2; Model 44T24
Type	L-head, 4-cycle, No. of cylinders (90-deg V) 8
Displacement	(cu in.) 349
Bore	(in.) 3½
Stroke	(in.) 4½
Compression ratio	7.06:1
Governed speed	not governed
Brake horsepower (max w/std accessories)	110 at (rpm) 3,400
Torque (max w/std accessories)	240 lb-ft at (rpm) 1,200
Type of ignition	distributor

ADDITIONAL DATA

Auxiliary-generator engine .... Wisconsin Model TFG
Manual and power traversing and elevating mechanism.

Data given for vehicle equipped w/track, steel, T72. Track steel T72E1 is interchangeable. Track, rubber, T85E1 also applicable w/changed sprocket.

CARRIAGE, MOTOR, 76-MM GUN, M18

NOTE: ALL DIMENSIONS SHOWN ARE IN INCHES

¹ RA PD 137739

Technical Manuals: 9–755, 9–1725, 9–1731D, 9–1731G, 9–1731K, 9–1750D, 9–1755A, 9–1755B, 9–1826B, 9–1828A, 9–1829A; Supply Catalog: SNL G–163.

Classification: Standard.

Armament: 1 gun, 76-mm, M1A1C or M1A2, turret mounted; 1 gun, machine, cal. .50, Browning, M2, heavy barrel (flexible mounted on revolving ring on top of turret).

Ammunition: 45 rounds, 76-mm; 840 rounds, cal. .50; 450 rounds, cal. .30, carbine; 12 hand grenades; 4 smoke pots; 18 signals, aircraft.

Purpose: To provide mobility for 76-mm gun and crew protection.

Fire Control and Vision Devices: Periscope, M4A1 w/telescope, M47A2 (vision); periscope, M13, or M13B1, or M6 (vision); quadrant, elevation, M9; quadrant, gunner's M1; telescope, M76C (sight).

Communications: (SCR–619 or SCR–610) and (RC–99); or (SCR–619 or SCR–610) and (RC–99) and (AN/VRC–3).

GENERAL DATA

Crew... 5
Weight, fighting...(lb) 37, 557
Over-all length w/gun in traveling position.............(in.) 254
Shipping dimensions, uncrated...............(cu ft) 1,550; (sq ft) 199
Ground clearance...(in.) 14¼
Pintle height, loaded.......................................(in.) 25½
Ground pressure..(psi) 11.9
Electrical system..(volts) 24
  No. of batteries..(12-volt) 2
  Type of ground...negative
Fuel octane rating.. 80
Capacities:
  Fuel...(gal) 170
  Transmission and cooler.................................(qt) 48
  Differential and transfer, including cooler.............(qt) 20
  Final drives...(each) (qt) 5
  Engine oil tank..(qt) 48
Brakes.....................mechanical, controlled-differential
  Parking brake, type.........pedal for locking steering brakes
Transmission forward speeds....................................... 3
  Gear ratio.............................High 1:1; Low 2.286:1
Transfer speeds... 1
  Gear ratio.. 1:1
Final-drive gear ratio......................................2.176:1
Differential-drive gear ratio...............................3.133:1
Hull construction................welded homogeneous armor plate
Turret construction..................................casting and plate
Turret race diameter......................................(in.) 81

PERFORMANCE

Maximum grade ability.................................(percent) 60
Turning radius..(ft) 33
Fording depth..(in.) 48
Maximum width of ditch vehicle can cross................(in.) 74
Maximum vertical obstacle vehicle can climb.............(in.) 36
Fuel consumption (average conditions)..................(mpg) 0.6
Cruising range (average conditions)....................(mi) 105
Allowable speed, governed..............................(mph) 45
Maximum allowable towed load, gross...................(lb) 10,000

ENGINE

Manufacturer.......Continental Model R975C4—from serial No. 1351 up
Type.....................4-cycle, radial, air-cooled; No. of cylinders 9
Displacement.......................................(cu in.) 973
Bore..(in.) 5
Stroke...(in.) 5½
Compression ratio.....................................5.7:1
Governed speed....................................(rpm) 2,400
Brake horsepower (max w/std accessories)...........400 at (rpm) 2,400
Torque (max w/std accessories)...........940 lb-ft at (rpm) 1,700
Type of ignition...magneto

ADDITIONAL DATA

This vehicle from Serial Nos. 1 through 1350 uses Engine Model R975C1; changes in data are as follows:

Brake horsepower (max w/std accessories)...............350 at (rpm) 2,400
Torque (max w/std accessories)...........840 lb-ft at (rpm) 1,800

  Engines R975C1 and R975C4 are interchangeable.

  Data given for vehicle equipped w/track, steel T69. Track, rubber, T85E1, also applicable w/changed sprocket.

  Manual and power turret-traversing mechanism.

Auxiliary generator...........................Homelite model HRUH–28

CARRIAGE, MOTOR, 90-MM GUN, M36

RA PD 137737

NOTE: ALL DIMENSIONS SHOWN
ARE IN INCHES

Technical Manuals: 9–758, 9–1731B, 9–1731D, 9–1731G, 9–1731K, 9–1750A, 9–1750B, 9–1750L, 9–1825A, 9–1825B, 9–1826B, 9–1828A, 9–1829A; Supply Catalog:
SNL G–210.

Classification: Standard.
Armament: 1 gun, 90-mm, M3, turret mounted; 1 gun, machine, cal. .50, Browning, M2 heavy barrel (flexible), pedestal mounted on top of turret bustle.
Ammunition: 47 rounds, 90-mm; 1,050 rounds, cal. .50; 450 rounds, cal. .30, carbine; 12 hand grenades; 4 smoke pots; 18 signal, pyrotechnic.

Purpose: To provide mobility for 90-mm gun and crew protection in offensive combat.
Fire Control and · Vision Devices: Periscope, M13, or M13B1, or M6 (vision); quadrant, elevation, M9; quadrant, gunner's, M1; telescope, M83C or M76F, or M71C; telescope, panoramic, M12 (sight); indicator, azimuth, M18.
Communications: (SCR–619 or SCR–610) and (RC–99); or (SCR–619 or SCR–610) and (RC–99) and (AN/VRC–3).

GENERAL DATA

Crew..5
Weight, fighting...(lb) 61,000
Overall length w/gun in traveling position...............(in.) 254
Shipping dimensions, uncrated..........(cu ft) 2,200; (sq ft) 240
Ground clearance..(in.) 17¾
Pintle height, loaded...(in.) 27⅛
Ground pressure..(psi) 12.6
Electrical system...(volts) 24
    No. of batteries..(12-volt) 2
    Type of ground...negative
Fuel octane rating...80
Capacities:
    Fuel...(gal) 192
    Cooling system...(qt) 68
    Crankcase, refill..(qt) 32
    Transmission, differential, and final drives:
        Three-piece, round-nose.........................(qt) 152
        One-piece, sharp-nose.............................(qt) 164
Brakes..........................mechanical, controlled-differential
    Parking brake, type..............pedal for locking steering brake
Transmission forward speeds..5
    Gear ratio............High 0.73:1; Fourth 1:1; Low 7.56:1
Differential-drive gear ratio....................................3.53:1
Final-drive gear ratio..2.84:1
Hull construction.................welded homogeneous armor plate
Armor, Turret: Welded, armor plate.

PERFORMANCE

Maximum grade ability.......................................(percent) 60
Turning radius...(ft) 31
Fording depth...(in.) 36
Maximum width of ditch vehicle can cross.....................(in.) 89
Maximum vertical obstacle vehicle can climb..................(in.) 18
Fuel consumption (mpg): Off ·highway 0.6...........On highway 0.8
Cruising range (mi): Off highway 110................On highway 155
Allowable speed, governed.....................................(mpg) 26
Maximum allowable towed load, gross.....................(lb) 10,000

ENGINE

Manufacturer: Ford..Model GAA
Type...............4-cycle, valve-in-head; No. of cylinders (60-deg V) 8
Displacement...(cu in.) 1,100
Bore...(in.) 5.4
Stroke...(in.) 6
Governed speed...(rpm) 2,600
Brake horsepower (max w/std accessories)............450 at (rpm) 2,600
Torque (max w/std accessories)..............950 lb-ft at (rpm) 2,100
Type of ignition...magneto

ADDITIONAL DATA

One-piece or three-piece differential housing used on this vehicle.
Data given w/track, rubber, T51. Track, rubber, T48; tracks, steel T49 and T54E1; track, rubber-backed steel, T74 are interchangeable.
Manual and power turret-traversing mechanism.
Auxiliary generator: Homelite Model HRUH–28.
Early models equipped w/hand brake on rear of transmission.

CARRIAGE, MOTOR, 90-MM GUN, M36B1

RA PD 137735

NOTE: ALL DIMENSIONS SHOWN ARE IN INCHES

Technical Manuals: 9-748, 9-1731B, 9-1731D, 9-1731G, 9-1731K, 9-1750D, 9-1750K, 9-1825A, 9-1825B, 9-1826D, 9-1828A, 9-1829A; **Supply Catalog:** SNL G-233.

Classification: Substitute Standard.

Armament: 1 gun, 90-mm, M3, turret mounted; 1 gun, machine cal. .50, Browning, M2, heavy barrel (flexible), pedestal mounted on top of turret bustle; 1 gun, machine, cal. .30, Browning, M1919A4, ball mounted at right front of hull.

Ammunition: 47 rounds, 90-mm; 1,000 rounds, cal. .50; 2,000 rounds, cal. .30, machine gun; 450 rounds, cal. .30, carbine; 12 hand grenades; 4 pots, smoke.

Purpose: To provide mobility for 90-mm gun and crew protection in offensive combat.

Fire Control and Vision Devices: Periscope, M13 or M13B1 or M6 (vision); quadrant, elevation, M9: quadrant, gunner's, M1; telescope, M83C or M76F or M71C; telescope panoramic, M12 (sight); azunytgm ubducatir M20.

Communications: (SCR-619 or SCR-610) and (RC-99); or (SCR-619 or SCR-610) and (RC-99) and (AN/VRC-3).

GENERAL DATA

Crew..5
Weight, fighting...(lb) 68,000
Shipping dimensions, uncrated.................(cu ft) 1,180; (sq ft) 208
Vehicle dimensions:
    Over-all length w/gun in traveling position............(in.) 286
    Ground clearance...(in.) 17⅛
    Pintle height, loaded......................................(in.) 27⅛
Ground pressure..(psi) 14.1
Electrical system...(volts) 24
    No. of batteries...(12-volt) 2
    Type of ground...negative
Fuel octane rating...80
Capacities:
    Fuel...(gal) 168
    Cooling system...(qt) 56
    Crankcase, refill..(qt) 32
    Transmission, differential, and final drives:
        Three-piece, round-nose.............................(qt) 152
        One-piece, sharp-nose...............................(qt) 164
Brakes...........................mechanical, controlled-differential
    Parking brake, type..........pedal for locking steering brakes
Transmission forward speeds...5
    Gear ratio........................High 0.73:1; Fourth 1:1; Low 7.56:1
Differential-drive gear ratio.....................................3.53:1
Final-drive gear ratio..2.84:1
Hull construction..................welded homogeneous armor plate
Armor, Turret: Welded homogeneous armor plate.

PERFORMANCE

Maximum grade ability.................................(percent) 60
Turning radius...(ft) 31
Fording depth..(in.) 36
Maximum width of ditch vehicle can cross.............(in.) 90
Maximum vertical obstacle vehicle can climb.........(in.) 24
Fuel consumption (average conditions)..................(mpg) 0.7
Cruising range (average conditions)....................(mi) 115
Allowable speed, governed............................(mph) 26
Maximum allowable towed load, gross...............(lb) 10,000

ENGINE

Manufacturer: Ford.....................................Model GAA
Type...........4-cycle, valve-in-head; No. of cylinders (60-deg V) 8
Displacement..(cu in.) 1,100
Bore..(in.) 5.4
Stroke...(in.) 6
Compression ratio..7.5:1
Governed speed...(rpm) 2,800
Brake horsepower (max w/std accessories).........450 at (rpm) 2,600
Torque (max w/std accessories)..........950 lb-ft at (rpm) 2,100
Type of ignition..magneto

ADDITIONAL DATA

Data given for vehicle equipped w/track, steel, T54E1, Tracks, rubber, T48 and T51; track, steel, T49; track, rubber-backed-steel, T74, are interchangeable.

One-piece or three-piece differential housing used on this vehicle.

Manual and power turret-traversing mechanism.

Auxiliary generator: Homelite model HRUH-28.

CARRIAGE, MOTOR, 90-MM GUN, M36B2

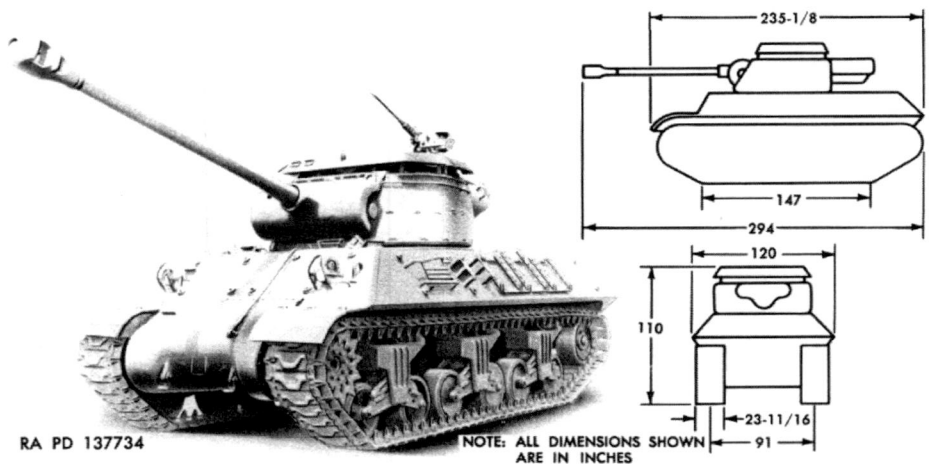

RA PD 137734

NOTE: ALL DIMENSIONS SHOWN ARE IN INCHES

Technical Manuals: 9–745, 9–1731D, 9–1731G, 9–1731K, 9–1750A, 9–1750B, 9–1750G, 9–1750L, 9–1825A, 9–1829A; Supply Catalog: SNL G–237.

Classification: Substitute Standard.

Armament: 1 gun, 90-mm, M3, turret mounted; 1 gun, cal. .50, Browning, heavy barrel, M2 (flexible) pedestal mounted on top of turret bustle.

Ammunition: 47 rounds, 90-mm; 1,000 rounds, cal. .50; 450 rounds cal. .30, carbine; 12 hand grenades; 4 pots, smoke; 18 signals, pyrotechnic.

Purpose: To provide mobility for 90-mm gun, and protection for crew.

Fire Control and Vision Devices: Periscope, M13, or M13B1, or M6 (vision); quadrant elevation, M9; quadrant, gunner's, M1; telescope, M83C, M76F, or M71C (sight); telescope, panoramic, M12 (sight).

Communications: (SCR–619 or SCR–610) and (RC–99); or (SCR–619 or SCR–610) and RC–(99) and (AN/VRC–3).

GENERAL DATA

Crew	5
Weight, fighting	(lb) 66,000
Over-all length w/gun in traveling position	(in.) 254
Shipping dimensions, uncrated	(cu ft) 1,950; (sq ft) 212
Ground clearance	(in.) 18¾
Pintle height, loaded	(in.) 24
Ground pressure	(psi) 9.5
Electrical system	(volts) 24
No. of batteries	(12-volt) 2
Type of ground	negative
Fuel octane rating	(Diesel fuel oil) 40
Capacities:	
Fuel	(gal) 165
Cooling system	(qt) 120
Crankcase, refill	(each engine) (qt) 28
Transmission, differential, and final drives:	
Three-piece, round-nose	(qt) 152
One-piece, sharp-nose	(qt) 164
Transfer	(qt) 2½
Oil tank (dry-sump engine only) (each tank)	(qt) 32
Brakes	mechanical, controlled-differential
Parking brake, type	pedal lock on steering brakes
Transmission forward speeds	5
Gear ratio	High 0.73:1; Fourth 1:1; Low 7.56:1
Transfer speeds	1
Gear ratio	1.37:1
Differential-drive gear ratio	3.53:1
Final-drive gear ratio	2.84:1
Hull construction	welded homogeneous armor plate

Armor, Turret: Cast homogeneous armor w/removable armor-plate top.

PERFORMANCE

Maximum grade ability	(percent) 50
Turning radius	(ft) 31
Fording depth	(in.) 42
Maximum width of ditch vehicle can cross	(in.) 90
Maximum vertical obstacle vehicle can climb	(in.) 19
Fuel consumption (average conditions)	(mpg) 0.7
Cruising range (average conditions)	(mi) 115
Allowable speed, governed	(mph) 25
Maximum allowable towed load, gross	(lb) 10,000

ENGINE

Manufacturer: GMC	Model 6046 or 6046D
Type	Twin Diesel, 2-cycle; No. of cylinders 12
Displacement	(cu in.) 850
Bore	(in.) 4¼
Stroke	(in.) 5
Compression ratio	16:1
Governed speed	(rpm) 2,100
Brake horsepower (max w/std accessories)	375 at (rpm) 2,100
Torque (max w/std accessories)	855 lb-ft at (rpm) 1,300
Type of ignition	compression

ADDITIONAL DATA

One-piece or three-piece differential housing used on this vehicle.

Manual and power turret-traversing mechanism.

Auxiliary generator: Homelite model HRUH–28.

Data given for vehicle equipped w/track, rubber, T54E1, w/extended end connectors.

CARRIAGE, MOTOR, 105-MM HOWITZER, M7

RA PD 137782

NOTE: ALL DIMENSIONS SHOWN
ARE IN INCHES

Technical Manuals: 9-731E, 9-1725, 9-1750A, 9-1750B, 9-1750C, 9-1750D, 9-1750K, 9-1751, 9-1825A, 9-1825B, 9-1826B, 9-1828A, 9-1829A; Supply Catalog: SNL G-128.

Classification: Substitute Standard.
Armament: 1 howitzer, 105-mm, M2A1, flexibly mounted in front end of fighting compartment; 1 gun, machine, cal. .50, Browning, M2, heavy barrel (flexible) ring mounted on machine gun turret at right side of hull.
Ammunition: 73 rounds, 105-mm; 600 rounds, cal. .50; 180 rounds, cal. .45, for submachine guns; 8 hand grenades.

Purpose: To provide mobility for 105-mm howitzer and crew protection.
Fire Control and Vision Devices: Quadrant, range, M4A1 or M4; quadrant, gunner's, M1; telescope, elbow, M16A1C (sight); telescope, panoramic, M12A2 (sight).
Communications: (RC–99).

GENERAL DATA

Crew..7
Weight, fighting..(lb) 52,000
Shipping dimensions, uncrated.............(cu ft) 1,650; (sq ft) 190
Ground pressure...(psi) 10.7
Ground clearance...(in.) 17⅛
Pintle height, loaded.......................................(in.) 25¼
Electrical system..(volts) 24
   No. of batteries..(12-volt) 2
   Type of ground..negative
Fuel octane rating..80
Capacities:
   Fuel..(gal) 176
   Engine oil tank:
      Early models...(qt) 32
      Late models..(qt) 52
   Transmission, differential, and final drives:
      Three-piece, round-nose.............................(qt) 152
      One-piece, sharp-nose...............................(qt) 164
Brakes.......................mechanical, controlled-differential
   Parking brake, type............pedal lock on steering brakes
Transmission forward speeds..5
   Gear ratio.................High 0.73:1; Fourth 1:1; Low 7.56:1
Final-drive gear ratio..2.84:1
Differential-drive gear ratio.................................3.53:1
Hull construction............welded homogeneous armor plate

PERFORMANCE

Maximum grade ability....................................(percent) 60
Turning radius..(ft) 31
Fording depth...(in.) 42
Maximum width of ditch vehicle can cross.....................(in.) 90
Maximum vertical obstacle vehicle can climb..................(in.) 24
Fuel consumption (average conditions)......................(mpg) 0.5
Cruising range (average conditions)..........................(mi) 85
Allowable speed, governed...................................(mph) 24
Maximum allowable towed load, gross......................(lb) 10,000

ENGINE

Manufacturer: Continental......................Model R-975-C-1
Type...................4-cycle, radial, air-cooled; No. of cylinders 9
Displacement...(cu in.) 973
Bore...(in.) 5
Stroke...(in.) 5½
Compression ratio...5.7:1
Governed speed..(rpm) 2,400
Brake horsepower (max w/std accessories)...........350 at (rpm) 2,400
Torque (max w/std accessories)............840 lb-ft at (rpm) 1,800
Type of ignition..magneto

ADDITIONAL DATA

One-piece or three-piece final drive used.
Parking brake, early model: Rear of transmission.
Engine is interchangeable with model R-975-C-4.
   Data given w/track, rubber, T51. Tracks, rubber, T48 and T51E1; tracks, steel, T49 and T54E1; tracks, rubber-backed steel, T74 and T80, are interchangeable.

43

CARRIAGE, MOTOR, 105-MM HOWITZER, M7B1

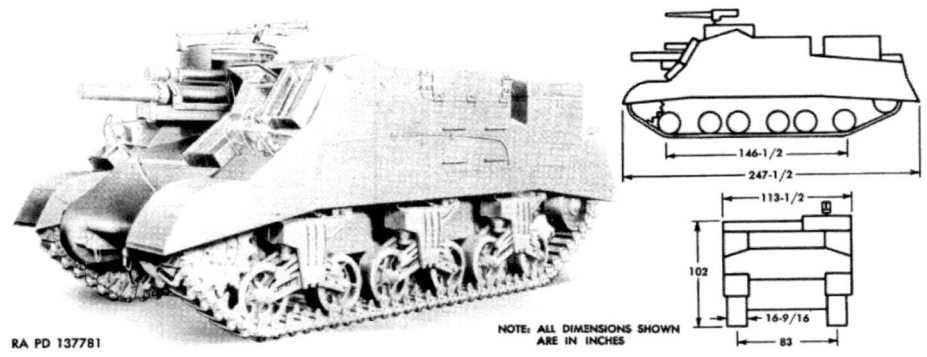

RA PD 137781

NOTE: ALL DIMENSIONS SHOWN ARE IN INCHES

Technical Manuals: 9–749, 9–1731B, 9–1750A, 9–1750B, 9–1750K, 9–1825A, 9–1825B, 9–1826B, 9–1828A, 9–1829A: **Supply Catalog:** SNL G–199.

Classification: Substitute Standard.

Armament: 1 howitzer, 105-mm, M2A1, flexibly mounted in forward end of fighting compartment; 1 gun, machine, cal. .50, Browning, M2, heavy barrel (flexible) ring mounted at right front of vehicle.

Ammunition: 73 rounds, 105-mm; 630 rounds, cal. .50; 180 rounds, cal. .45, for submachine gun; 540 rounds cal. .30, carbine; 8 hand grenades.

Purpose: To provide mobility for 105-mm howitzer and crew protection in offensive combat.

Fire Control and Vision Devices: Quadrant, gunner's M1; quadrant range, M4A1 or M4; telescope, elbow, M16A1C (sight); telescope, panoramic, M12A2, (sight).

Communications: (RC–99).

GENERAL DATA

Crew	7
Weight, fighting	(lb) 50,000
Shipping dimensions, uncrated	(cu ft) 1,695; (sq ft) 195
Ground pressure	(psi) 10.9
Ground clearance	(in.) 17½
Pintle height, loaded	(in.) 25¼
Electrical system	(volts) 24
No. of batteries	(12-volt) 2
Type of ground	negative
Fuel octane rating	80
Capacities:	
Fuel	(gal) 168
Cooling system	(qt) 56
Crankcase, refill	(qt) 32
Transmission, differential, and final drives:	
Three-piece, round-nose	(qt) 152
One-piece, sharp-nose	(qt) 164
Brakes	mechanical, controlled-differential
Parking brake type:	
Early models (round-nose)	rear of transmission
Late models (sharp-nose)	pedal for locking steering brakes
Transmission forward speeds	5
Gear ratio	High 0.73:1; Fourth 1:1; Low 7.56:1
Final-drive gear ratio	2.84:1
Differential-drive gear ratio	3.53:1
Hull construction	welded homogeneous armor plate

PERFORMANCE

Maximum grade ability	(percent) 60
Turning radius	(ft) 31
Fording depth	(ft) 36
Maximum width of ditch vehicle can cross	(in.) 90
Maximum vertical obstacle vehicle can climb	(in.) 24
Fuel consumption (average conditions)	(mpg) 0.7
Cruising range (average conditions)	(mi) 125
Allowable speed, governed	(mph) 26
Maximum allowable towed load, gross	(lb) 10,000

ENGINE

Manufacturer: Ford	Model GAA
Type	4-cycle, valve-in-head; No. of cylinders (60-deg V) 8
Displacement	(cu in.) 1,100
Bore	(in.) 5.4
Stroke	(in.) 6
Compression ratio	7.5:1
Governed speed	(rpm) 2,600
Brake horsepower (max w/std accessories)	450 at (rpm) 2,600
Torque (max w/std accessories)	950 lb-ft at (rpm) 2,100
Type of ignition	magneto

ADDITIONAL DATA

Data given for vehicle, equipped w/track, rubber, T15. Tracks, rubber, T48 and T51E; tracks, steel, T49 and T54E1 are interchangeable.

CARRIAGE, MOTOR, 105-MM, HOWITZER, M37

NOTE: ALL DIMENSIONS SHOWN ARE IN INCHES

RA PD 137748

Technical Manuals: 9-717, 9-1729A, 9-1729B, 9-1729C, 9-1825A, 9-1826A, 9-1828A, 9-1829A; **Supply Catalog:** SNL G-238.

Classification: Standard.

Armament: Howitzer, 105-mm, M4, flexibly mounted in front of fighting compartment. Gun, machine, cal. .50, Browning, M2, heavy barrel (flexible) ring mounted at right front of vehicle.

Ammunition: 126 rounds, 105-mm; 990 rounds, cal. .50; 750 rounds cal. .45 for submachine gun; 8 hand grenades.

GENERAL DATA

Crew	7
Weight, fighting	(lb) 46,000
Shipping dimensions, uncrated	(cu ft) 1,400; (sq ft) 177
Ground pressure	(psi) 11.7
Ground clearance	(in.) 18⅜
Pintle height, unloaded	(in.) 26½
Electrical system	(volts) 24
No. of batteries	(6-volt) 4
Type of ground	negative
Fuel octane rating	70
Capacities:	
Fuel	(gal) 110
Cooling system	(each) (qt) 40
Crankcase, refill	(each engine) (qt) 8
Transmission (hydramatic)	(each) (qt) 15
Differential	(qt) 20
Transfer	(qt) 4½
Final drive	(each) (qt) 2
Brakes	mechanical, controlled-differential
Parking brake, type	lever locks on steering brakes
Transmission (hydramatic) forward speeds	4
Gear ratio	High 1:1; Third 1.55:1; Low 3.92:1
Transfer speeds	(2 forward; 1 reverse) 3
Gear ratio	High 1.03:1; Low 2.34:1; Reverse 2.44:1
Final-drive gear ratio	2.94:1
Differential-drive gear ratio	2.62:1
Hull construction	welded homogeneous armor plate

Purpose: To provide mobility for 105-mm howitzer and crew protection in offensive combat.

Fire Control and Vision Devices: Periscope, M13 or M6 (vision); quadrant, elevation, M12; quadrant, gunner's M1; telescope, M76G; telescope, panoramic, M12 or M12A2 (sight).

Communications: (SCR-510) and (RC-99).

PERFORMANCE

Maximum grade ability	(percent) 60
Turning radius	(ft) 18
Fording depth	(in.) 42
Maximum width of ditch vehicle can cross	(in.) 108
Maximum vertical obstacle vehicle can climb	(in.) 36
Fuel consumption (average conditions)	(mpg) 9
Cruising range (average conditions)	(mi) 100
Allowable speed, recommended	(mph) 30
Maximum allowable towed load, gross	(lb) 10,000

ENGINE

Manufacturer: Cadillac	No. used 2; Model 44T24
Type	4-cycle, L-head; No. of cylinders (90-deg V) 8
Displacement	(cu in.) 349
Bore	(in.) 3½
Stroke	(in.) 4½
Compression ratio	7.06:1
Governed speed	not governed
Brake horsepower (max w/std accessories)	110 at (rpm) 3,400
Torque (max w/std accessories)	240 lb-ft at (rpm) 1,200
Type of ignition	distributor

ADDITIONAL DATA

Data given for vehicle equipped w/track, steel, T72. Track, steel, T72E1 interchangeable. Track, rubber, T85E1 applicable w/changed sprocket.

CARRIAGE, MOTOR, 105-MM RIFLE, T106

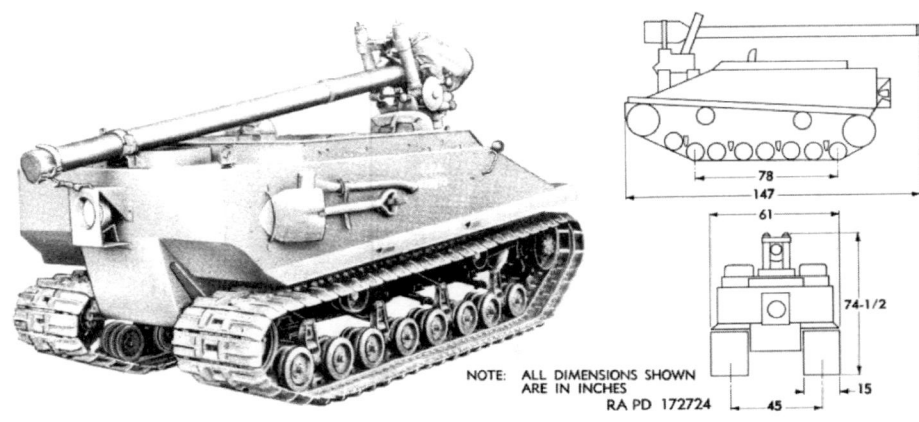

NOTE: ALL DIMENSIONS SHOWN ARE IN INCHES
RA PD 172724

Technical Manuals: (installation of rifle and mount): 9–329 (for basic vehicle): 9–772, 9–1772; **Supply Catalog:** (for rifle): S N L C–77 (for vehicle): S N L G–179.

Armament: 1 gun, 105-mm, recoilless, M27 flexibly mounted in gun compartment.
Ammunition: 4 rounds, 105-mm, M3A3.
Fire-control and vision devices:
    telescope, M90C (sight).
    telescope, elbow, M62 (sight).

Purpose: To provide mobility for 105-mm recoilless gun over swampy and rough terrain.
Communications:
    (SCR–506 or SCR–1935) and (SCR–508 or SCR–528 or SCR–608 or SCR–510 or SCR–619 or SCR–610);
    or (AN/GRC–9 or SCR–694C) and (SCR–510 or SCR–619 or SCR–610).

GENERAL DATA

Crew	2 to 4
Weight, fighting	(lb) 4,731
Over-all length (gun in traveling position)	(in.) 145
Shipping dimensions, uncrated	(cu ft) 381; (sq ft) 61.4
Ground pressure	(psi) 2.2
Ground clearance	(in.) 11
Pintle height, loaded	(in.) 27¼
Electrical system	(volts) 12
No. of batteries	(12-volt) 1 or (6-volt) 2
Type of ground	negative
Fuel octane rating	72
Capacities:	
Fuel	(gal) 35
Cooling system	(qt) 12¾
Crankcase, refill	(qt) 5
Transmission	(qt) 1
Differential and axle transmission	(qt) 6
Brakes	mechanical, controlled-differential
Parking brake, type:	
Early models	none
Late models	rear of axle transmission
Transmission forward speeds	3
Gear ratio	High 1:1; Low 2.66:1
Axle transmission speeds	2
Gear ratio	High 0.866:1; Low 2.74:1
Differential-drive gear ratio	4.87:1
Hull construction	welded sheet steel

PERFORMANCE

Maximum grade ability	(percent) 65
Turning radius	(ft) 12
Fording depth	will float
Maximum width of ditch vehicle can cross	(in.) 36
Maximum vertical obstacle vehicle can climb	(in.) 24
Fuel consumption (average conditions)	(mpg) 5
Cruising range (average conditions)	(mi) 175
Allowable speed, recommended	(mph) 36
Maximum allowable towed load, gross	(lb) 3,800

ENGINE

Manufacturer: Studebaker	Model: Champion
Type	4-cycle, L-head; No. of cylinders (in line) 6
Displacement	(cu in.) 170
Bore	(in.) 3
Stroke	(in.) 4
Compression ratio	7:1
Governed speed	not governed
Brake horsepower (max w/std accessories)	65 at (rpm) 3,600
Torque (max w/std accessories)	130 lb-ft at (rpm) 1,800
Type of ignition	distributor

ADDITIONAL DATA

Data given for vehicle equipped with track, endless-rubber-band with riveted steel shoes, T76.

Track, endless-rubber-band with riveted steel shoes, T76E1 also applicable with changed suspension. Changes in data for vehicle equipped with track, T76E1 are as follows:

Track width	(in.) 20
Shipping dimensions	(cu ft) 443; (sq ft) 71.5
Over-all width	(in.) 71
Ground pressure	(psi) 1.75

CARRIAGE, MOTOR, 155-MM GUN, M40

RA PD 137715

NOTE: ALL DIMENSIONS SHOWN ARE IN INCHES

Technical Manuals: 9-747, 9-1725, 9-1747, 9-1750B, 9-1750C, 9-1750D, 9-1751, 9-1825A, 9-1825B, 9-1826B, 9-1828A. 9-1829A; Supply Catalog: SNL G-232.

Classification: Standard.
Armament: Gun, 155-mm, M2, flexibly mounted at rear of fighting compartment.
Ammunition: 20 rounds, 155-mm; 12 hand grenades; 10 rifle grenades.

Purpose: To provide mobility for 155-mm gun and crew protection in offensive combat.
Fire Control and Vision Devices: Periscope M13 or M6 (vision); quadrant gunner's M1; telescope, M69F (sight); telescope, elbow, MA161F (sight); telescope, panoramic, M12 (sight).
Communications: (SCR-619 or SCR-610) and (RC-99).

GENERAL DATA

Crew	8
Weight, fighting	(lb) 81,000
Shipping dimensions, uncrated	(cu ft) 3,320; (sq ft) 307
Ground pressure	(psi) 10.7
Ground clearance	(in.) 19¼
Pintle height, unloaded	(in.) 21½
Electrical system	(volts) 24
No. of batteries	(12-volt) 2
Type of ground	negative
Fuel octane rating	80
Capacities:	
Fuel	(gal) 215
Engine oil tank	(qt) 52
Transmission, differential, and final drives	(qt) 152
Brakes	mechanical, controlled-differential
Parking brake, type	pedal for locking steering brakes
Transmission forward speeds	5
Gear ratio	High 0.73 :1; Fourth 1:1; Low 7.56 :1
Differential-drive gear ratio	3.53 :1
Final-drive gear ratio	2.84 :1
Hull construction	welded homogeneous armor plate

PERFORMANCE

Maximum grade ability	(percent) 60
Turning radius	(ft) 41½
Fording depth	(in.) 36
Maximum width of ditch vehicle can cross	(in.) 92
Maximum vertical obstacle vehicle can climb	(in.) 34
Fuel consumption (average conditions)	(mpg) 0.5
Cruising range (average conditions)	(mi) 107
Allowable speed, governed	(mph) 24
Maximum allowable towed load, gross	(lb) 10,000

ENGINE

Manufacturer: Continental	Model R975-C4
Type	4-cycle, radial, air-cooled; No. of cylinders 9
Displacement	(cu in.) 973
Bore	(in.) 5
Stroke	(in.) 5½
Compression ratio	5.7 :1
Governed speed	(rpm) 2,400
Brake horsepower (max w/std accessories)	400 at (rpm) 2,400
Torque (max w/std accessories)	900 lb-ft at (rpm) 1,700
Type of ignition	magneto

ADDITIONAL DATA

Data given for vehicle equipped w/track, steel, T66. Track, rubber-backed steel, T80 and track, rubber, T84 are interchangeable.

CARRIAGE, MOTOR, 155-MM HOWITZER, M41

RA PD 137746

NOTE: ALL DIMENSIONS SHOWN
ARE IN INCHES

Technical Manuals: 9-744, 9-1729A, 9-1729B, 9-1729C, 9-1825A, 9-1826A, 9-1828A, 9-1829A; **Supply Catalog:** SNL G-236.

Classification: Standard.

Armament: Howitzer, 155-mm, M1, flexibly mounted at rear of fighting compartment.

Ammunition: 22 rounds, 155-mm; 420 rounds, cal. .45 for submachine-gun; 480 rounds, cal. .30, carbine; 12 hand grenades.

Purpose: To provide mobility for 155-mm howitzer and crew protection in offensive combat.

Fire Control and Vision Devices: Periscope, M13 or M6 (vision); quadrant gunner's, M1; telescope, panoramic, M12A6.

Communications: (SCR–619 or SCR–610 or SCR–510) and (RC–99).

GENERAL DATA

Crew	12
Weight, fighting	(lb) 42,500
Shipping dimensions, uncrated	(cu ft) 1,430; (sq ft) 179
Ground pressure	(psi) 10.8
Ground clearance	(in.) 17¾
Pintle height, unloaded	(in.) 19¾
Electrical system	(volts) 24
No. of batteries	(12-volt) 2
Type of ground	negative
Fuel octane rating	70
Capacities:	
Fuel	(gal) 110
Cooling system	(each) (qt) 40
Crankcase, refill	(each) (qt) 8
Transmission	(each) (qt) 15
Transfer	(qt) 4½
Differential	(qt) 20
Final drive	(each) (qt) 2
Brakes	mechanical, controlled-differential
Parking brake, type	depressor knobs for locking steering brakes
Transmission forward speeds	4
Gear ratio	High 1:1; Third 1.55:1; Low 3.92:1
Transfer speeds	(2 forward; 1 reverse) 3
Gear ratio	High 1.03:1; low 2.34:1; reverse 2.44:1
Differential-drive gear ratio	2.62:1
Final-drive gear ratio	2.94:1
Hull construction	welded homogeneous armor plate

PERFORMANCE

Computed maximum grade ability	(percent) 60
Turning radius	(ft) 18
Fording depth	(in.) 42
Maximum width of ditch vehicle can cross	(in.) 108
Maximum vertical obstacle vehicle can climb	(in.) 40
Fuel consumption (average conditions)	(mpg) 0.9
Cruising range (average conditions)	(mi) 96
Allowable speed, recommended	(mph) 30
Maximum allowable towed load, gross	(lb) 10,000

ENGINE

Manufacturer: Cadillac	No. used 2; Model 42
Type	4-cycle, L-head; No. of cylinders (90-deg V) 8
Displacement	(cu in.) 346
Bore	(in.) 3½
Stroke	(in.) 4½
Compression ratio	7.06:1
Governed speed	not governed
Brake horsepower (max w/std accessories)	110 at (rpm) 3,400
Torque (max w/std accessories)	240 lb-ft at (rpm) 1,200
Type of ignition	distributor

ADDITIONAL DATA

Manual and power traversing and elevating mechanism.

Data given for vehicle equipped w/track, steel, T72. Track, steel, T72E1 interchangeable. Track, rubber, T85E1 applicable w/changed sprocket.

CARRIAGE, MOTOR, 8-INCH HOWITZER, M43

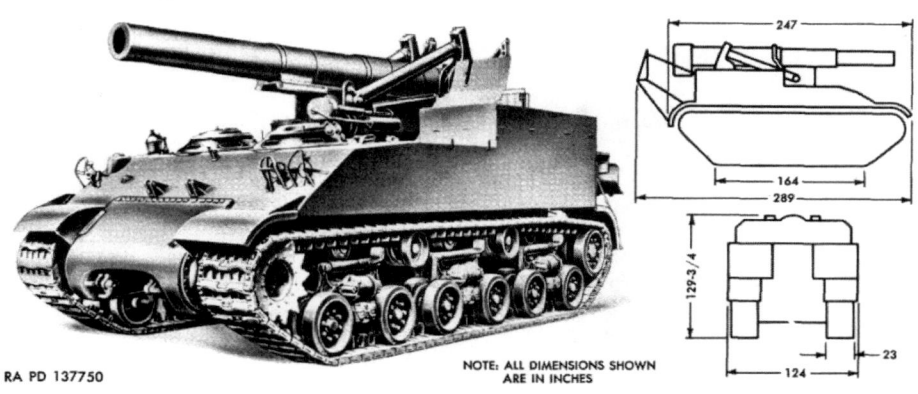

RA PD 137750

NOTE: ALL DIMENSIONS SHOWN
ARE IN INCHES

Technical Manuals: 9–747, 9–1725, 9–1747, 9–1750B, 9–1750C, 9–1750D, 9–1751, 9–1825A, 9–1825B, 9–1826B, 9–1828A, 9–1829A; Supply Catalog: SNL G–232.

Classification: Standard.

Armament: Howitzer, 8 in, M2, flexibly mounted at rear of fighting compartment.
Ammunition: 12 rounds, 8 in; 12 hand grenades; 10 rifle grenades.

Purpose: To provide mobility for 8-in. howitzer and crew protection in offensive combat.

Fire Control and Vision Devices: Periscope, M13 or M6 (vision); quadrant, gunner's, M1; telescope, M69G (sight); telescope, elbow, M16A1G (sight); telescope, panoramic, M12 (sight).
Communications: (SCR–619 or SCR–610) and (RC–99)

GENERAL DATA

Crew..8
Weight, fighting..(lb) 80,000
Shipping dimensions, uncrated............(cu ft) 2,690; (sq ft) 249
Ground clearance...(in.) 19¾
Pintle height, unloaded....................................(in.) 21½
Ground pressure...(psi) 10.2
Electrical system...(volts) 24
   No. of batteries.......................................(12-volt) 2
   Type of ground...negative
Fuel octane rating..80
Capacities:
   Fuel..(gal) 215
   Transmission, differential, and final drives.............(qt) 152
   Engine oil tank..(qt) 52
Brakes...........................mechanical, controlled-differential
   Parking brake, type..........pedal for locking steering brakes
Transmission forward speeds...................................5
   Gear ratio...............High 0.73:1; Fourth 1:1; Low 7.56:1
Differential-drive gear ratio...............................3.53:1
Final-drive gear ratio......................................2.84:1
Hull construction...................welded homogeneous armor plate

PERFORMANCE

Maximum grade ability....................................(percent) 60
Turning radius...(ft) 41½
Fording depth..(in.) 36
Maximum width of ditch vehicle can cross...................(in.) 92
Maximum vertical obstacle vehicle can climb................(in.) 34
Fuel consumption (average conditions).......................(mpg) .5
Cruising range (average conditions).......................(mi) 107
Allowable speed, governed..................................(mph) 24
Maximum allowable towed load, gross......................(lb) 10,000

ENGINE

Manufacturer: Continental...........................Model R975-C4
Type...................4-cycle, radial, air cooled; No. of cylinders 9
Displacement..(cu in.) 973
Bore...(in.) 5
Stroke..(in.) 5½
Compression ratio..5.7:1
Governed speed...(rpm) 2,400
Brake horsepower (max w/std accessories).............400 at (rpm) 2,400
Torque (max w/std accessories)................940 lb-ft at (rpm) 1,700

ADDITIONAL DATA

Data given for vehicle equipped w/track, steel T66. Track, rubber-backed steel, T80 and Track, rubber, T84 are interchangeable.

CARRIER, CARGO, M29

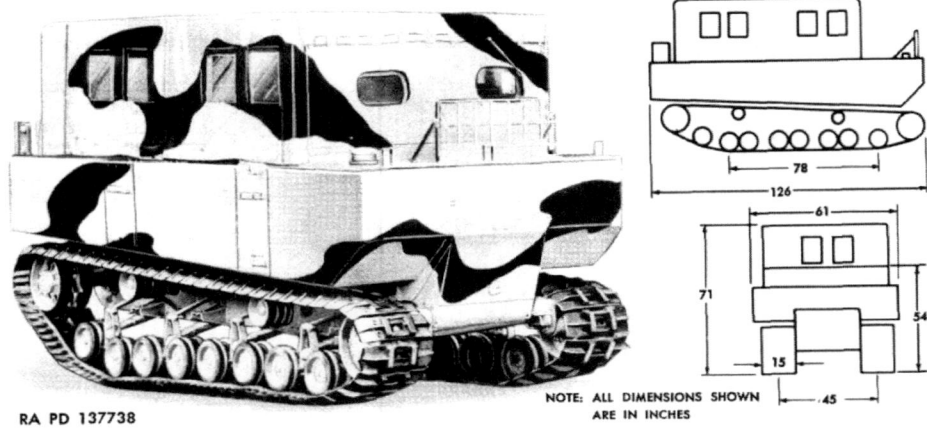

RA PD 137738

NOTE: ALL DIMENSIONS SHOWN
ARE IN INCHES

Technical Manuals: 9-772, 9-1772, 9-1825B, 9-1826A, 9-1828A; Supply Catalog: SNL G-179.

Classification: Standard.

Communications: (SCR-506 or SCR-193S) and (SCR-508 or SCR-528 or SCR-608 or SCR-510 or SCR-619 or SCR-610); or (AN/GRC-9 or SCR-694C) and (SCR-510 or SCR-619 or SCR-610).

Purpose: To transport personnel or cargo over snow and ice or difficult terrain.

GENERAL DATA

Crew	2 to 4
Weight (lb)	Net 3,725; Crew and Equipment 1,200; Gross 4,925
Shipping dimensions, uncrated	(cu ft) 242; (sq ft) 54
Ground clearance	(in.) 11
Ground pressure	(psi) 2.1
Pintle height, loaded	(in.) 27⅛
Electrical system	(volts) 12
No. of batteries	one 12-volt or two 6-volt
Type of ground	negative
Fuel octane rating	72
Capacities:	
Fuel	(gal) 35
Cooling system	(qt) 12¾
Crankcase, refill	(qt) 5
Transmission	(qt) 1
Differential and axle transmission	(qt) 6
Brakes	mechanical, controlled-differential
Parking brakes:	
Early models	none
Late models	rear of axle transmission
Transmission forward speeds	3
Gear ratio	High 1:1; Low 2.66:1
Axle-transmission speeds	2
Gear ratio	High 0.866:1; Low 2.74:1
Differential-drive gear ratio	4.87:1
Hull construction	welded sheet steel

PERFORMANCE

Maximum grade ability	(percent) 65
Turning radius	(ft) 12
Fording depth	will float

PERFORMANCE—Continued

Maximum width of ditch vehicle can cross	(in.) 36
Maximum vertical obstacle vehicle can climb	(in. 24)
Fuel consumption (average conditions)	(mpg) 5
Cruising range (average conditions)	(mi) 175
Allowable speed, recommended	(mph) 36
Maximum allowable towed load, gross	(lb) 3,800

ENGINE

Manufacturer: Studebaker	Model Champion
Type	4-cycle, L-head; No. of cylinders (in line) 6
Displacement	(cu in.) 170
Bore	(in.) 3
Stroke	(in.) 4
Compression ratio	7:1
Governed speed	not governed
Brake horsepower (max w/std accessories)	65 at (rpm) 3,600
Torque (max w/std accessories)	130 lb-ft at (rpm) 1,800
Type of ignition	distributor

ADDITIONAL DATA

Above data is for early-production vehicles having 15-in. track.

For later-production vehicles having 20-in. track, data is as follows:

Weight (lb)	Net 4,077; Crew and equipment 1,200; Gross 5,277
Shipping dimensions, uncrated	(cu ft) 261; (sq ft) 58
Over-all width	(in.) 66
Ground pressure	(psi) 1.6

Data given for vehicle equipped w/15-in. track, steel, endless rubber band, T76. Track, 20-in., steel, endless rubber band, T76E1 applicable w/changed suspension.

CARRIER, CARGO, AMPHIBIAN, M29C

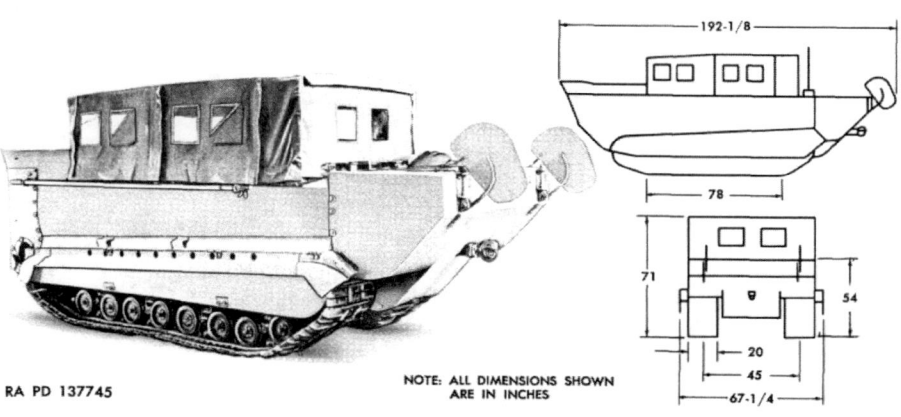

RA PD 137745

NOTE: ALL DIMENSIONS SHOWN
ARE IN INCHES

Technical Manuals: 9-772, 9-1772, 9-1825B, 9-1826A, 9-1828A; Supply Catalog: SNL G-179.

Classification: Standard.

Communications: (SCR-506 or SCR-193S) and (SCR-508 or SCR-528 or SCR-608 or SCR-510 or SCR-619 or SCR-610); or (AN/GRC-9 or SCR-694C) and (SCR-510 or SCR-619 or SCR-610).

Purpose: To transport personnel or light cargo on land or water.

GENERAL DATA

Crew	2 to 4
Weight (lb)	Net 4,778; Crew and equipment 1,200; Gross 5,971
Shipping dimensions, uncrated	(cu ft) 403; (sq ft) 90
Freeboard at gross weight:	
Bow	(in.) 10½
Stern	(in.) 8
Ground clearance	(in.) 11
Pintle height, loaded	(in.) 27½
Ground pressure	(psi) 1.91
Electrical system	(volts) 12
No. of batteries	(12-volt) 1 or (6-volt) 2
Type of ground	negative
Fuel octane rating	72
Capacities:	
Fuel	(gal) 35
Cooling system	(qt) 12¾
Crankcase, refill	(qt) 5
Transmission	(qt) 1
Differential and axle transmission	(qt) 6
Capstan	(qt) 1
Brakes	mechanical, controlled-differential
Parking brakes:	
Early models	none
Late models	rear of axle transmission
Transmission forward speeds	3
Gear ratio	High 1:1; Low 2.66:1
Axle-transmission speeds	2
Gear ratio	High 0.866:1; Low 2.74:1
Differential-drive gear ratio	4.87:1
Hull construction	welded sheet steel

PERFORMANCE

Maximum grade ability	(percent) 65
Turning radius (on land)	(ft) 12
Fording depth	will float
Maximum width of ditch vehicle can cross	(in.) 36
Maximum vertical obstacle vehicle can climb	(in.) 10
Fuel consumption (average conditions)	(mpg) 5
Fuel consumption on water:	
(2,000 rpm, wide-open throttle)	(gph) 2.5 to 2.7
Cruising range (average conditions)	(mi) 175
Allowable speed, recommended	(mph) 36
Maximum allowable towed load, gross	(lb) 3,800

ENGINE

Manufacturer: Studebaker	Model Champion
Type	4-cycle, L-head; No. of cylinders (in line) 6
Displacement	(cu in.) 170
Bore	(in.) 3
Stroke	(in.) 4
Compression ratio	7:1
Governed speed	not governed
Brake horsepower (max w/std accessories)	65 at (rpm) 3,600
Torque (max w/std accessories)	130 lb-ft at (rpm) 1,800
Type of ignition	distributor

ADDITIONAL DATA

Data given for vehicle equipped w/track, steel, endless rubber band, T76E1.

CARRIER, CARGO, AMPHIBIOUS, T46E1

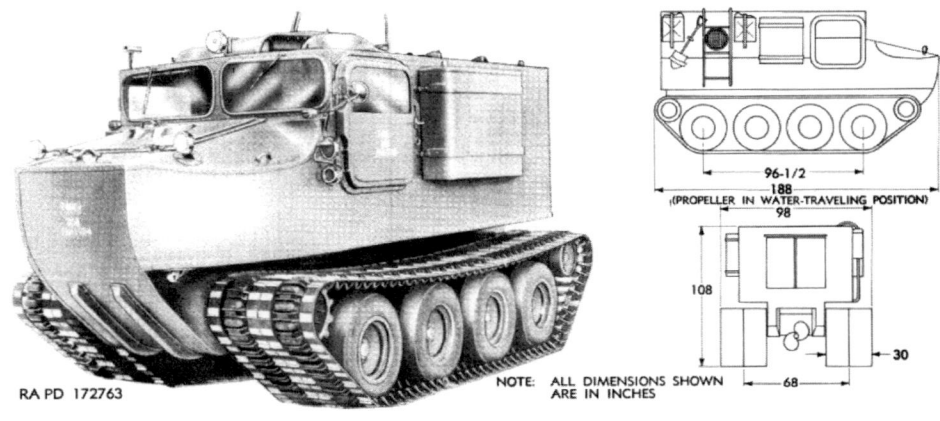

RA PD 172763

NOTE: ALL DIMENSIONS SHOWN ARE IN INCHES

96-1/2
188
(PROPELLER IN WATER-TRAVELING POSITION)
98
108
30
68

Technical Manuals: 9-1825A, 9-1825C, 9-1825E, 9-1828A.

Purpose: To transport general cargo and personnel on land or water.

GENERAL DATA

Crew	2
Weight, fighting	(lb) 12,162
Shipping dimensions, uncrated	(cu ft) 1,180; (sq ft) 132
Ground pressure	(psi) 2.1
Vehicle dimensions:	
Ground clearance	(in.) 16¾
Pintle height, loaded	(in.) 39¾
Cargo-compartment inside dimensions (in.):	
Length 91	Width 68; Height 58
Cargo space	(cu ft) 208
Electrical system	(volts) 24
No. of batteries	(12-volt) 2
Type of ground	negative
Fuel octane rating	80
Capacities:	
Fuel	(gal) 60
Crankcase, refill	(qt) 16
Transmission, cross-drive	(qt) 21
Brakes:	
Hand-lever-controlled, hydraulic, multiple-disk steering brakes. Pedal operates them as service brakes.	
Parking brake: Latch locks on steering brakes.	
Transmission ranges (high, low, and reverse)	3
Overall maximum useable ratio:	
High range	18.494
Low range	42.277
Torque-converter stall ratio	4.5:1
Final-drive gear ratio	4.11:1
Hull construction	riveted aluminum-alloy sheet

PERFORMANCE

Maximum grade ability	(percent) 60
Turning radius	pivots in place
Maximum width of ditch vehicle can cross	(in.) 60
Maximum vertical obstacle vehicle can climb	(in.) 18
Fuel consumpion (average conditions)	(on land) (mpg) 2.3
	(on water) (gph) 12
Cruising range (average conditions)	(on land) (mi) 140
	(on water) (hrs) 5
Allowable speed, governed	(mph) 28
Maximum allowable towed load, gross	(lb) 6,000

ENGINE

Manufacturer: Continental	Model AO-268-3A
Type	4-cycle, valve-in-head, air-cooled
No. of cylinders	(opposed) 4
Displacement	(cu in.) 269
Bore	(in.) 4⅝
Stroke	(in.) 4
Compression ratio	6.9:1
Governed speed	(rpm) 3,200
Brake horsepower (max w/std accessories)	127 at (rpm) 3,200
Torque (max w/std accessories)	225 lb-ft at (rpm) 2,600
Type of ignition	magneto

ADDITIONAL DATA

Over-all length w/propeller in land traveling position .... (in.) 193

CARRIER, PERSONNEL, HALF-TRACK, M3

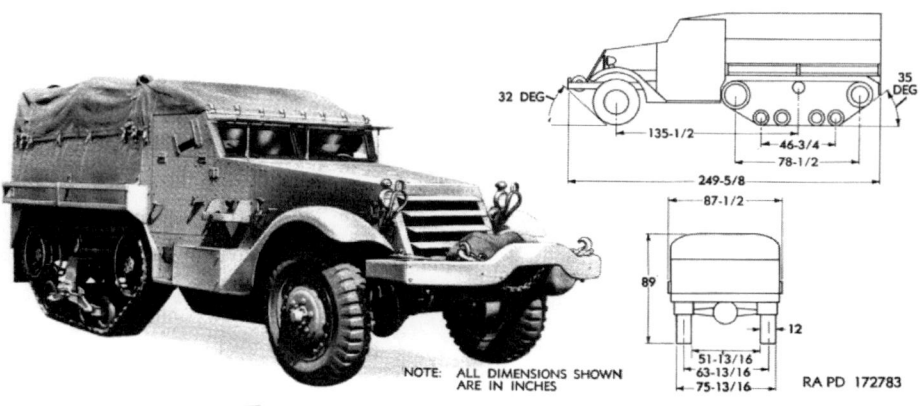

NOTE: ALL DIMENSIONS SHOWN ARE IN INCHES

RA PD 172783

Technical Manuals: 9-710, 9-1710, 9-1710C, 9-1711, 9-1827B, 9-1827C, 9-1828A, 9-1829A; **Supply Catalog:** SNL G-102.

Classification: Limited Standard.

Armament: 1 gun, machine, cal. .30, Browning, M1919A4 (flexible) pedestal mounted behind center seat of driver's compartment.

Ammunition: 4,000 rounds, cal. .30; 540 rounds, cal. .45, for sub-machine-gun; 22 hand grenades; 24 mines, antitank w/fuze.

Purpose: To transport cargo and personnel in combat zone.

Communications: (SCR-193 or SCR-245 or SCR-506 or SCR-508 or SCR-510).

GENERAL DATA

Crew	13
Weight (lb)	Net 15,500; Payload 4,500; Gross 20,000
Front-axle gear ratio	6.8:1
Rear-axle (jackshaft) gear ratio	4.44:1
Axle load (lb):	
Empty	front 5,735; rear (each track) 4,883
Loaded	front 7,400; rear (each track) 6,300
Tires (combat):	
Ply 12; Size 8.25 x 20; Pressure	(psi) 55
Tread, center-to-center, front	(in.) $63^{13}\!/_{16}$
Track ground pressure (loaded)	(psi) 11.3
Shipping dimensions, uncrated	(cu ft) 1,127; (sq ft) 152
Vehicle dimensions:	
Ground clearance	(in.) $17\frac{1}{8}$
Pintle height (loaded)	(in.) 28
Electrical system	(volts) 12
No. of batteries	1
Type of ground	negative
Fuel octane rating	72
Capacities:	
Fuel	(gal) 60
Cooling system	(qt) 26
Crankcase, refill	(qt) $10\frac{1}{2}$
Transfer and transmission (qt)	w/o PTO $7\frac{1}{2}$; w/PTO 9
Axles (qt)	front $3\frac{1}{2}$; rear 6
Winch:	
Load capacity	(lb) 10,000
Oil capacity	(qt) 2
Brakes:	
Manufacturer: Bendix or Wagner	Type; hydrovac
Parking brake, type	transfer
Transmission forward speeds	4
Gear ratio	High 1:1; Low 4.92:1
Transfer speeds	2
Gear ratio	High 1:1; Low 2.48:1

PERFORMANCE

Maximum grade ability	(percent) 60
Turning radius	(ft) $29\frac{1}{2}$
Fording depth	(in.) 32
Fuel consumption, loaded	(mpg) $3\frac{1}{2}$
Cruising range, loaded	(mi) 210
Allowable speed, recommended	(mph) 45
Maximum recommended towed load, gross, off highway	(lb) 4,500

ENGINE

Manufacturer: White	Model 160AX
Type	L-head, 4-cycle; No. of cylinders (in line) 6
Displacement	(cu in.) 386
Bore	(in.) 4
Stroke	(in.) $5\frac{1}{4}$
Compression ratio	6.44:1
Governed speed	not governed
Brake horsepower (max w/std accessories)	127 at (rpm) 3,000
Torque (max)	325 lb-ft at (rpm) 1,200

ADDITIONAL DATA

Data given for vehicle w/winch. For vehicle w/o winch and w/front roller, changes in data are as follows: Net weight (lb): 15,000; Payload 5,000. Axle load (lb): Loaded, front 6,900; rear (each track) 6,550; Empty, front 5,175; rear (each track) 4,913. Over-all length (in.) $243\frac{1}{2}$; Shipping dimensions, uncrated: (cu ft) 1,100; (sq ft) 148. Angle of approach (deg) 37. Equipped w/controller for trailer electric brakes.

Live axles, type	spiral-bevel, full-floating
Transmission, type	constant-mesh

53

CARRIER, PERSONNEL, HALF-TRACK, M3A1

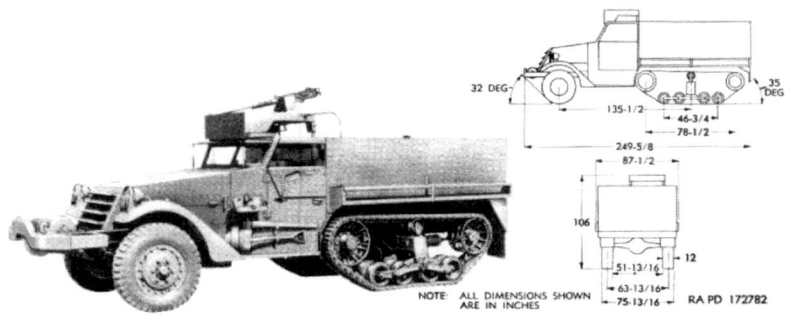

NOTE: ALL DIMENSIONS SHOWN ARE IN INCHES   RA PD 172782

Technical Manuals: 9-710, 9-1710, 9-1710C, 9-1711, 9-1827B, 9-1827C, 9-1828A; **Supply Catalog:** SNL G-102.

Classification: Limited Standard.

Armament: 1 machine gun, cal. .50, Browning, heavy barrel, M2 (flexible) ring mounted at top right side of driver's compartment; 1 machine gun, cal. .30, Browning, M1919A4 (flexible), pintle mounted on either side or rear of vehicle.

Ammunition: 700 rounds, cal. .50; 7,750 rounds, cal. .30; 540 rounds, cal. .45, for submachine gun; 22 hand grenades; 24 mines, antitank, w/fuze.

Purpose: To transport cargo and personnel in combat zone.

Communications: (SCR-499 or SCR-542); or (SCR-507 or SCR-193T) and (SCR-508 or SCR-608 or SCR-510 or SCR-619 or SCR-610); or (SCR-506 or SCR-193T) and (SCR-508 or SCR-528) and (AN/VRC-3); or (SCR-508 or SCR-528 or SCR-510) and (AN/VRC-3); or (SCR-508 or SCR-528) and (SCR-593); or (SCR-508) and (SCR-593) and (AN/GRC-9 or SCR-694C); or (SCR-506 or SCR-508) and (SCR-593 or SCR-499); or (SCR-508) and (SCR-510); or (AN/GRC-3, -4, -5, -6, -7, or -8 or AN/VRQ-1, -2, or -3 or AN/VRC-8, -9, or -10) and (SCR-506 or AN/GRC-9 or SCR-694C or SCR-593 or AN/GRC-5).

GENERAL DATA

Crew	13
Weight (lb)	Net 15,300; Payload 5,200; Gross 20,500
Front-axle gear ratio	6.8 :1
Rear-axle (jackshaft) gear ratio	4.44 :1
Axle load (lb):	
Empty	front 5,661; rear (each track) 4,820
Loaded	front 7,585; rear (each track) 6,458
Tires (combat):	
Ply 12	size 8.25 x 20; Pressure (psi) 55
Tread, center-to-center, front	(in.) 63¹³⁄₁₆
Track ground pressure (loaded)	(psi) 11.6
Shipping dimensions, uncrated	(cu ft) 1,340; (sq ft) 152
Vehicle dimensions:	
Ground clearance	(in.) 11¾₆
Pintle height (loaded)	(in.) 28
Electrical system	(volts) 12
No. of batteries	1
Type of ground	negative
Fuel octane rating	72
Capacities:	
Fuel	(gal) 60
Cooling system	(qt) 26
Crankcase, refill	(qt) 10½
Transmission and transfer (qt)	w/o PTO 7½; w/PTO 9
Axles (qt)	front 3½; rear 6
Winch:	
Load capacity	(lb) 10,000
Oil capacity	(qt) 2
Brakes:	
Manufacturer; Bendix or Wagner	Type; hydrovac
Parking brake, type	transfer
Transmission forward speeds	4
Gear ratio	High 1:1; Low 4.92 :1
Transfer speeds	2
Gear ratio	High 1:1; Low 2.48 :1

PERFORMANCE

Maximum grade ability	(percent) 60
Turning radius	(ft) 29½
Fording depth	(in.) 32
Fuel consumption, loaded	(mpg) 3½
Cruising range, loaded	(mi) 210
Allowable speed, recommended	(mph) 45
Maximum recommended towed load, gross, off highway	(lb) 4,500

ENGINE

Manufacturer: White	Model 160AX
Type	L-head, 4-cycle; No. of cylinders (in line) 6
Displacement	(cu in.) 386
Bore	(in.) 4
Stroke	(in.) 5⅛
Compression ratio	6.44 :1
Governed speed	not governed
Brake horsepower (max w/std accessories)	127 at (rpm) 3,000
Torque (max)	325 lb-ft at (rpm) 1,200

ADDITIONAL DATA

Data given for vehicle w/winch. For vehicle w/o winch and w/front roller, changes in data are as follows: Weight (lb): Net 14,800; Payload 5,700. Axle load (lb): Empty, front 5,106, rear (each track) 4,847; Loaded, front 7,073; rear (each track) 6,714.

Over-all length (in.) 242½. Shipping dimensions, uncrated: (cu ft) 1,306; (sq ft) 148. Angle of approach (deg) 37.

Equipped w/controller for trailer electric brakes.

Live axles, type	spiral-bevel, full-floating
Transmission, type	constant-mesh

CARRIER, 81-MM MORTAR, HALF-TRACK, M4

RA PD 137727

NOTE: ALL DIMENSIONS SHOWN ARE IN INCHES

Technical Manuals: 9-710, 9-1710, 9-1710C, 9-1711, 9-1827B, 9-1827C, 9-1828A, 9-1829A; **Supply Catalog:** SNL G-102.

Classification: Limited Standard.

Armament: 1 gun, machine, cal. .50, Browning, M2, heavy barrel (flexible) and 1 gun, machine, cal. .30, Browning, M1919A4 (flexible) both skate mounted on gun ring running completely around inside of body. One mortar, 81-mm, M1, mounted on floor at rear of vehicle.

Purpose: To provide mobility for 81-mm mortar and protection for crew.

Ammunition: 96 rounds, 81-mm; 750 rounds, cal. .50; 540 rounds, cal. .45 for submachine gun; 2,000 rounds, cal. .30; 10 hand grenades; 14 mines, antitank, w/fuze.

Fire Control and Vision Devices: Sight, M4.

GENERAL DATA

Crew..8
Weight (lb)......................Net 14,430; Payload 3,420; Gross 17,850
Front-axle gear ratio...6.8:1
Rear-axle (jackshaft) gear ratio..................................4.44:1
Axle load (lb):
    Empty.................................front 5,339; rear (each track) 4,545
    Loaded................................front 5,630; rear (each track) 6,110
Tires (combat):
    Ply 12...............................Size 8.25 x 20; Pressure (psi) 55
    Tread, center-to-center, front....................(in.) 63¹³⁄₁₆
Track ground pressure (loaded)..............................(psi) 10.9
Shipping dimensions, uncrated..............(cu ft) 1,005; (sq ft) 135
Vehicle dimensions:
    Ground clearances..(in.) 17¼
    Pintle height (loaded)......................................(in.) 28
Electrical system...(volts) 12
    No. of batteries..1
    Type of ground...negative
Fuel octane rating..72
Capacities:
    Fuel...(gal) 60
    Cooling system......................................(qt) 26
    Crankcase, refill.................................(qt) 10½
    Transmission and transfer...........(qt) w/o PTO 7½; w/PTO 9
    Axles.....................................(qt) front 3½; rear 6
Winch:
        Load capacity..(lb) 10,000
        Oil capacity..(qt) 2
Brakes: Manufacturer; Bendix...........................Type; hydrovac
    Parking brake, type...................................transfer
Transmission for ward speeds....................................4
    Gear ratio..High 1:1; Low 4.92:1
Transfer speeds..2
    Gear ratio..High 1:1; Low 2.48:1

PERFORMANCE

Maximum grade ability.......................................(percent) 60
Turning radius..(ft) 30
Fording depth...(in.) 32
Fuel consumption, loaded......................................(mpg) 3½
Cruising range, loaded..(mi) 210
Allowable speed, recommended................................(mph) 45
Maximum recommended towed load, gross, off highway........(lb) 4,500

ENGINE

Manufacturer: White.......................................Model 160AX
Type.............................L-head, 4-cycle; No. of cylinders (in line) 6
Displacement...(cu in.) 386
Bore...(in.) 4
Stroke...(in.) 5⅛
Compression ratio...6.44:1
Governed speed...not governed
Brake horsepower (max w/std accessories)..........127 at (rpm) 3,000
Torque (max)....................................325 lb-ft at (rpm) 1,200

ADDITIONAL DATA

Data given for vehicle w/winch. Data changes for vehicle w/o winch and w/roller are as follows: Weight (lb): Net 14,000, Payload 3,850, Axle load (lb): Empty, front 4,329; rear (each track) 5,050, Loaded, front 5,200; rear (each track) 6,325. Over-all length (in.) 243¾. Shipping dimensions, (cu ft) 978; (sq ft) 134. Angle of approach (deg) 37.

Equipped w/controller for trailer electric brakes.

Live axles, type...spiral-bevel, full-floating
Transmission, type...constant-mesh

55

CARRIER, 81-MM MORTAR, HALF-TRACK, M4A1

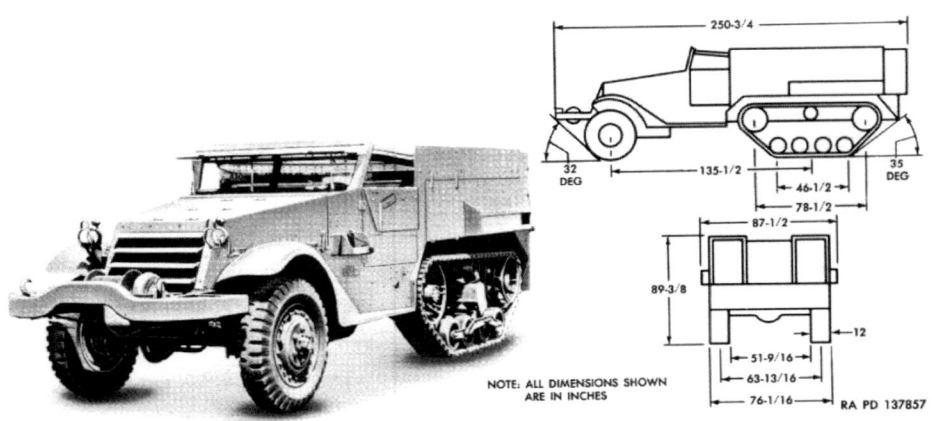

NOTE: ALL DIMENSIONS SHOWN ARE IN INCHES

RA PD 137857

Technical Manuals: 9–710, 9–1710, 9–1710C, 9–1711, 9–1827B, 9–1827C, 9–1828A, 9–1829A; Supply Catalog: SNL G–102

Classification: Limited standard.

Armament: 1 mortar, 81-mm, mounted on floor at rear of vehicle; 1 gun, machine, cal. .30, Browning, M1919A4 (flexible) skate mounted on gun ring running completely around inside of body.

Purpose: To provide mobility for 81-mm mortar, and protection for crew.

Ammunition: 96 rounds, 81-mm, 2,000 rounds, cal. .30; 540 rounds cal. .45, for submachine gun; 10 hand grenades; 14 mines, antitank w/fuze.

Fire Control and Vision Devices: Sight, M6.

GENERAL DATA

Crew	8
Weight (lb)	Net 15,750; Payload 4,390; Gross 20,140
Front-axle gear ratio	6.8 : 1
Rear-axle (jackshaft) gear ratio	4.44 : 1
Axle load (lb):	
Empty	front 5,830; rear (each track) 4,960
Loaded	front 7,460; rear (each track) 6,340
Tires (combat):	
Ply 12	Size 8.25 x 20; Pressure (psi) 55
Tread, center-to-center, front	(in.) 63³¹⁄₁₆
Track ground pressure (loaded)	(psi) 11.4
Shipping dimensions, uncrated	(cu ft) 1,140; (sq ft) 153
Vehicle dimensions:	
Ground clearance	(in.) 17⅛
Pintle height (loaded)	(in.) 28
Electrical system	(volts) 12
No. of batteries	1
Type of ground	negative
Fuel octane rating	72
Capacities:	
Fuel	(gal) 60
Cooling system	(qt) 26
Crankcase, refill	(qt) 10½
Transmission and transfer (qt)	w/o PTO 7½; w/PTO 9
Axles (qt)	front 3½; rear 6
Winch:	
Load capacity	(lb) 10,000
Oil capacity	(qt) 2
Brakes: Manufacturer; Bendix	Type; hydrovac
Parking brake, type	transfer
Transmission forward speeds	4
Gear ratio	High 1:1; Low 4.92 : 1
Transfer speeds	2
Gear ratio	High 1:1; Low 2.48 : 1

PERFORMANCE

Maximum grade ability	(percent) 60
Turning radius	(ft) 30
Fording depth	(in.) 32
Fuel consumption, loaded	(mpg) 3½
Cruising range, loaded	(mi) 210
Allowable speed, recommended	(mph) 45
Maximum recommended towed load, gross, off highway	(lb) 4,500

ENGINE

Manufacturer: White	Model 160AX
Type	L-head, 4-cycle; No. of cylinders (in line) 6
Displacement	(cu in.) 386
Bore	(in.) 4
Stroke	(in.) 5⅛
Compression ratio	6.44 : 1
Governed speed	not governed
Brake horsepower (max w/std accessories)	127 at (rpm) 3,000
Torque (max)	325 lb-ft at (rpm) 1,200

ADDITIONAL DATA

Data given for vehicle w/winch. Data changes for vehicles w/o winch and w/roller are as follows: Weight (lb): Net 15,320; Payload 4,820. Axle load (lb): Empty, front 4,596, rear (each track) 5,362; Loaded, front 6,150, rear (each track) ..,995. Over-all length (in.) 243¾. Shipping dimensions (cu ft) 1,103, (sq ft) 148. Angle of approach (deg) 37.

Equipped w/controller for trailer electric brakes.

Live axles, type	spiral-bevel, full-floating
Transmission, type	constant-mesh

CARRIER, 81-MM MORTAR, HALF-TRACK, M21

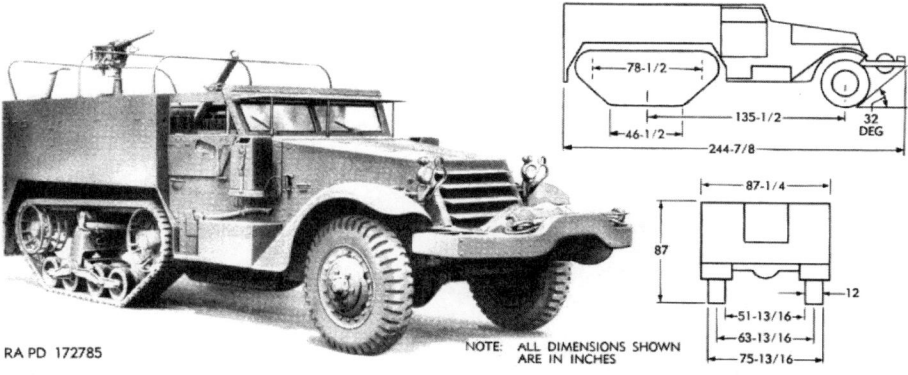

RA PD 172785

NOTE: ALL DIMENSIONS SHOWN ARE IN INCHES

Technical Manuals: 9-710, 9-1710, 9-1710C, 9-1711, 9-1827B, 9-1827C, 9-1828A, 9-1829A; **Supply Catalog:** SNL G-102

Classification: Standard.

Armament: 1 mortar, 81-mm, M1, mounted on floor at center of body (forward firing only); 1 gun, machine, cal. .50, Browning, M2, heavy barrel (flexible), pedestal mounted at rear of body.

GENERAL DATA

Crew	6
Weight (lb)	Net 15,500; Payload 4,500; Gross 20,000
Front-axle gear ratio	6. 8:1
Rear-axle (jackshaft) gear ratio	4. 44:1
Axle load (lb):	
Empty	front 5,735; rear (each track) 4,883
Loaded	front 6,900; rear (each track) 6,550
Tires (combat):	
Ply 12	Size 8.25 x 20; Pressure (psi) 55
Tread, center-to-center, front	(in.) 63¹³⁄₁₆
Track ground pressure (loaded)	(psi) 11. 7
Shipping dimensions, uncrated	(cu ft) 1,100; (sq ft) 152
Vehicle dimensions:	
Ground clearance	(in.) 17¼
Pintle height (loaded)	(in.) 28
Electrical system	(volts) 12
No. of batteries	1
Type of ground	negative
Fuel octane rating	72
Capacities:	
Fuel	(gal) 60
Cooling system	(qt) 26
Crankcase, refill	(qt) 10½
Transfer and transmission	(qt) 9
Axles (qt)	front 3½; rear 6
Winch:	
Load capacity	(lb) 10,000
Oil capacity	(qt) 2
Brakes:	
Manufacturer; Bendix	Type; hydrovac
Parking brake, type	transfer
Transmission forward speeds	4
Gear ratio	High 1:1; Low 4. 92:1
Transfer speeds	2
Gear ratio	High 1:1; Low 2. 48:1

Purpose: To provide a self-propelled mount for 81-mm mortar.

Ammunition: 97 rounds, 81-mm; 400 rounds, cal. .50; 600 rounds, cal. .45, for submachine gun; 12 hand grenades; 12 mines, antitank w/fuze.

Fire-Control and Vision Devices: Sight, M6.

Communications: (SCR-510) and (SCR-509); or (AN/VRC-8, -9, or -10).

PERFORMANCE

Computed grade ability in lowest gear, loaded	(percent) 60
Turning radius	(ft) 30
Fording depth	(in.) 32
Fuel consumption, loaded	(mpg) 3½
Cruising range, loaded	(mi) 210
Allowable speed, recommended	(mph) 45
Maximum recommended towed load, gross, off highway	(lb) 4,500

ENGINE

Manufacturer: White	Model 160AX
Type	L-head, 4-cycle; No. of cylinders (in line) 6
Displacement	(cu in.) 386
Bore	(in.) 4
Stroke	(in.) 5½
Compression ratio	6. 44:1
Governed speed	not governed
Brake horsepower (max w/std accessories)	127 at (rpm) 3,000
Torque (max)	325 lb-ft at (rpm) 1,200

ADDITIONAL DATA

Equipped w/controller for trailer electric brakes.

Live axles, type	spiral-bevel, full floating
Transmission, type	constant-mesh

CARRIER, UNIVERSAL, T16
(Universal Bren Carrier)

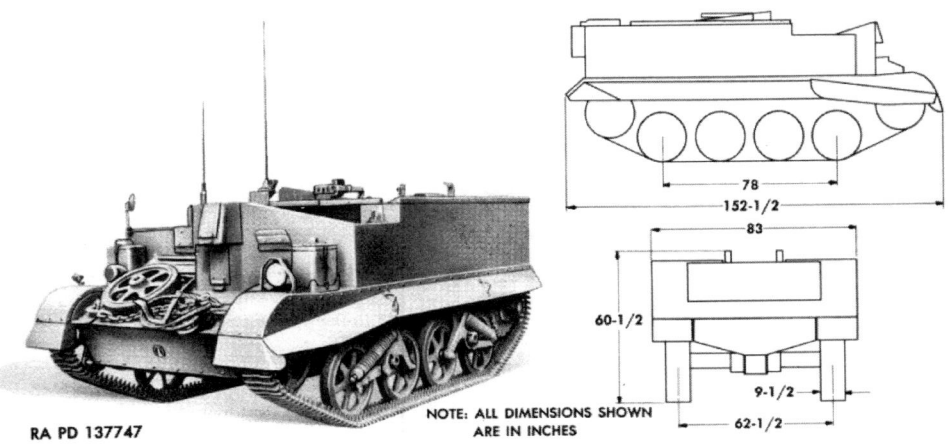

RA PD 137747

NOTE: ALL DIMENSIONS SHOWN ARE IN INCHES

Technical Manuals: 9–746, 9–1746A, 9–1746B, 9–1825B, 9–1828A, 9–1829A; Supply Catalog: SNL G–166.

Classification: Nonclassified.

Purpose: To transport personnel or cargo and provide crew protection.

GENERAL DATA

Crew...4
Weight (lb)..............Net 7,756; Crew and equipment 1,684; Gross 9,440
Shipping dimensions, uncrated........................(cu ft) 445; (sq ft) 88
Ground pressure...(psi) 6.4
Ground clearance...(in.) 11⅛
Electrical system...(volts) 12
   No. of batteries..(12-volt) 1
   Type of ground...negative
Fuel octane rating..70
Capacities:
   Fuel...(gal) 24
   Cooling system..(qt) 24½
   Crankcase, refill (including cooler)....................(qt) 6
   Transmission..(qt) 2½
   Differential (including oil reservoir and cooler)........(qt) 7
Brakes:
   Mechanical differential steering brakes, hand-lever controlled. Also mechanical sprocket-hub brakes, both pedal and hand-lever controlled.
   Parking brake, type.............lever for locking sprocket-hub brakes
Transmission forward speeds.......................................4
   Gear ratio.......................High 1:1; Third 1.69:1; Low 6.4:1
Differential-drive gear ratio...................................5.83:1
Hull construction....................................watertight welded

PERFORMANCE

Maximum grade ability......................................(percent) 60
Turning radius..(ft) 17
Fording depth...(in.) 36
Maximum width of ditch vehicle can cross........................(in.) 36
Maximum vertical obstacle vehicle can climb....................(in.) 24
Fuel consumption (average conditions)..........................(mpg) 5
Cruising range (average conditions)............................(mi) 120
Allowable speed, governed.....................................(mph) 33

ENGINE

Manufacturer: Ford...Model 29W
Type....................4-cycle, L-head; No. of cylinders (90-deg V) 8
Displacement...(cu in.) 239
Bore..(in.) 3⅛
Stroke...(in.) 3¾
Compression ratio...6.4:1
Governed speed...(rpm) 3,800
Brake horsepower (max w/std accessories)...............100 at (rpm) 3,800
Torque (max w/std accessories)...................176 lb-ft at (rpm) 2,000
Type of ignition...distributor

ADDITIONAL DATA

Differences among models: The universal carrier T16 is equipped with four bogie wheels on each side, while the previous Canadian carriers were equipped with three bogie wheels on each side.
   Right-hand drive.
Transmission, type....................................selective sliding-gear

CRANE, TRUCK MOUNTED, M2
(Thew Shovel, Model MC 6 x 6)
Used w/TRAILER, 3-Ton, 2-Wheel, Clamshell, M16

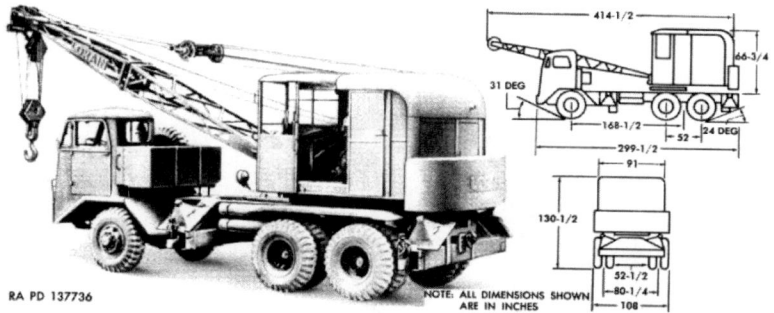

RA PD 137736

NOTE: ALL DIMENSIONS SHOWN ARE IN INCHES

Technical Manuals: 9-771, 9-1825A, 9-1826C, 9-1827A, 9-1828A, 9-1829A; Supply Catalog: SNL G-172.

Classification: Standard.

Purpose: To provide ·mobility for crane equipment·

GENERAL DATA

Crew..2
Weight (lb)..Gross 53,500
Axle gear ratio..8.43:1
Axle load (lb): Loaded...............front 8800; rear (each) 22,350
Tires:
    Ply 14.............................Size 12.00 x 20; Pressure (psi) 85
    Tread, center-to-center, front..........................(in.) 75
Shipping dimensions, uncrated...................(cu ft) 3,382; (sq ft) 311
Vehicle dimensions:
    Ground clearance...(in.) 11
    Pintle height, loaded....................................(in.) 33
Electrical system..(volts) 12
    No. of batteries.......................................(6-volt) 2
Fuel octane rating..70
Capacities:
    Fuel...(gal) 100
    Cooling system...(qt) 64
    Crankcase, refill..(qt) 16
    Transfer..(qt) 4
    Transmission...(qt) 11
    Axles (each)...(qt) 10
Brakes:
    Manufacturer; Bendix-Westinghouse................Type, air
    Parking brake, type................................transfer
Transmission forward speeds....................................4
    Gear ratio............................High 1:1; Low 6.54:1
Transfer speeds..2
    Gear ratio............................High 1:1; Low 2.55:1

PERFORMANCE

Computed grade ability in lowest gear, loaded.............(percent) 60
Turning radius (ft)............................right 45; left 47½
Fording depth..(in.) 30
Fuel consumption, loaded..................................(mpg) 2
Cruising range, loaded....................................(mi) 200
Allowable speed, governed................................(mph) 30
Maximum recommended towed load, gross............(lb) 24,000

ENGINE

Manufacturer: Hercules..........................Model HXC
Type.....................L-head, 4-cycle; No. of cylinders (in line) 6
Displacement..(cu in.) 779
Bore...(in.) 5¼
Stroke...(in.) 6
Compression ratio.....................................5.69:1
Governed speed......................................(rpm) 2,100
Brake horsepower (max w/std accessories)...........179 at (rpm) 2,100
Torque (max w/std accessories).................555 lb-ft at (rpm) 900

ADDITIONAL DATA

Turntable engine:
    Manufacturer: Waukesha..........................Model MZR
    Type.....................4-cycle, L-head; No. of cylinders (in line) 6
    Displacement................(cu in.) 404; Bore 4¼; Stroke 4¾
    Governed speed......................................(rpm) 1,375
    Brake horsepower (max w/std accessories)........70 at (rpm) 1,375
    Torque (max w/std accessories)..........270 lb-ft at (rpm) 1,375
Capacities:
    Fuel tank..(gal) 50
    Cooling system...(qt) 32
    Crankcase..(qt) 11
Electrical system..(volts) 6
    No. of batteries..1
Turntable assembly:
    Counterweight over-all width............................(in.) 94
    Cab width..(in.) 91
    Tail swing (center of rotation to rear of counterweight)........(in.) 107
    Boom foot pin to ground.................................(in.) 70½
    Boom foot pin to center of rotation.......................(in.) 27
    Swing speed..(rpm) 4.19
    Hoist speed (rope speed)...............................(fpm) 149.8
    Boom hoisting time, from horizontal to 10-ft radius..........(sec) 45
Lifting capacity:

Boom radius	Outriggers extended	Outriggers retracted
11 ft	40,000 lb	21,850 lb
12 ft	36,680 lb	19,350 lb
15 ft	29,050 lb	14,350 lb
18 ft	24,000 lb	11,350 lb
20 ft	21,500 lb	9,950 lb

For trailer data, see page 130.

59

DOLLY, TRAILER CONVERTER, LIGHT DUTY, 3-TON 2-WHEEL, M363

(Fruehauf, Model DC3)

NOTE: ALL DIMENSIONS SHOWN
ARE IN INCHES

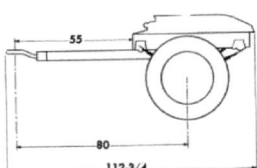

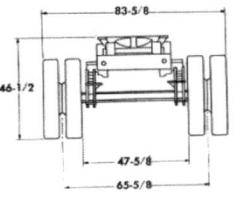

RA PD 137823

Supply Catalog: SNL G-708.

Classification: Standard.

Purpose: To convert semitrailers up to 15,000 lb gross weight to full trailers.

<table>
<tr><td colspan="2">**GENERAL DATA**</td></tr>
<tr><td>Weight (lb)</td><td>Net 1,765; Payload 7,000; Gross 8,765</td></tr>
<tr><td>Weight distribution (lb):</td><td></td></tr>
<tr><td>Empty</td><td>axle 1,715; lunette 50</td></tr>
<tr><td>Loaded</td><td>axle 8,715; lunette 50</td></tr>
<tr><td>Tires</td><td>Ply 8; Size 7.50 x 20; Pressure (psi) 55</td></tr>
<tr><td>Shipping dimensions, uncrated</td><td>(cu ft) 251; (sq ft) 65</td></tr>
<tr><td>Vehicle dimensions:</td><td></td></tr>
<tr><td>Ground clearance</td><td>(in.) 13⅛</td></tr>
<tr><td>Center of fifth wheel to center of axle</td><td>(in.) 2</td></tr>
<tr><td>Height to center of fifth wheel</td><td>(in.) 46¾</td></tr>
<tr><td>Fifth wheel</td><td>Size (in.) 33; Type: rigid semi-automatic</td></tr>
<tr><td>Brakes, service</td><td>none</td></tr>
<tr><td>Parking brake</td><td>none</td></tr>
<tr><td>Towing vehicle to be used</td><td>truck, 1½-ton, 4 x 2</td></tr>
</table>

ADDITIONAL DATA

DOLLY, TRAILER CONVERTER, 6-TON, 2-WHEEL, M364

(Heil, Model D2)

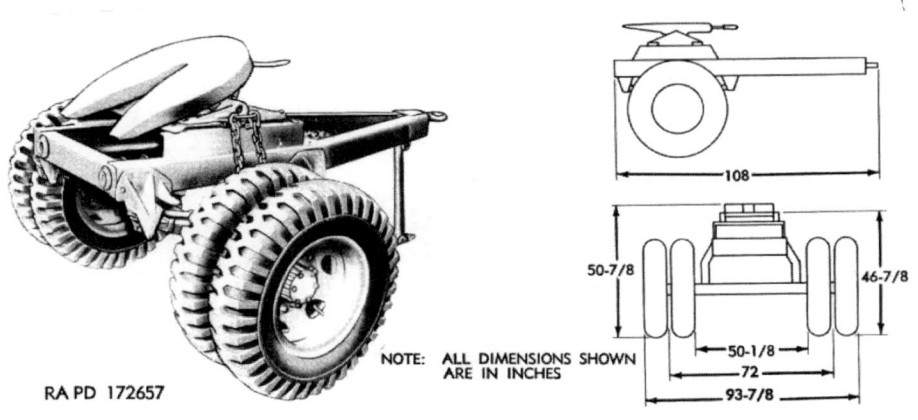

RA PD 172657

NOTE: ALL DIMENSIONS SHOWN ARE IN INCHES

Technical Manual: 9–846; Supply Catalog: SNL G–745.

Classification: Standard.

Purpose: To convert semitrailer to full trailer.

GENERAL DATA

Weight (lb)............................Net 2,000; Payload 9,000; Gross 11,000
Tires...............................Ply 10; Size 9 x 20; Pressure (psi) 65
Shipping dimensions, uncrated..........................(cu ft) 300; (sq ft) 71
Vehicle dimensions:
    Ground clearance..(in.) 16⅜
    Fifth wheel.........................Size (in.) 30; Type: semiautomatic
Brakes...none
Minimum towing vehicle to be used.....................Truck, 2½-ton, 4 x 2

ADDITIONAL DATA

DOLLY, TRAILER CONVERTER, 8-TON, 2-WHEEL

(Fruehauf; Signal Corps Models K83 and K83A)

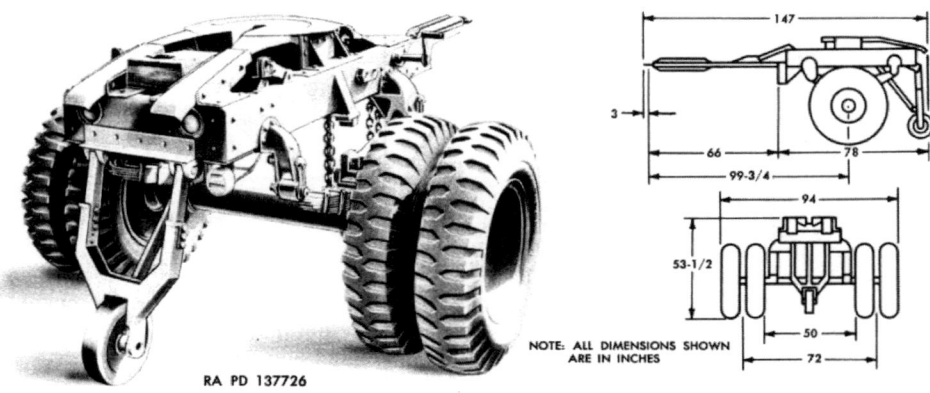

RA PD 137726

NOTE: ALL DIMENSIONS SHOWN ARE IN INCHES

Technical Manual: 9–846; Supply Catalog: SNL G–695.

Classification: Standard.

Purpose: To convert Signal Corps semitrailers, Models K78A and K78B to full trailers.

GENERAL DATA

Weight (lb)..........................Net 3,000; Payload 15,000; Gross 18,000
Fifth wheel..........................Size (in.) 30; Type, rigid, semiautomatic
Tires................................Ply 10; Size 9.00 x 20; Pressure (psi) 65
Shipping dimensions, uncrated (drawbar removed)...(cu ft) 299; (sq ft) 52
Ground clearance.......................................(in.) 15⅜
Brakes...none
Towing vehicle to be used..........................truck, 2½-ton, 4 x 2

ADDITIONAL DATA

Hinged drawbar—optional hinge height, 40 or 32 inches. Lock provides rigid drawbar for transporting dolly with vehicle having 18-, 29-, or 4-inch pintle height. Equipped with taillights for protection when towed. Over-all length given with drawbar in horizontal position, and landing gear down.

DOLLY, TRAILER CONVERTER, 10-TON, 2-WHEEL, M365

(Springfield Auto Works, Production Engineering)

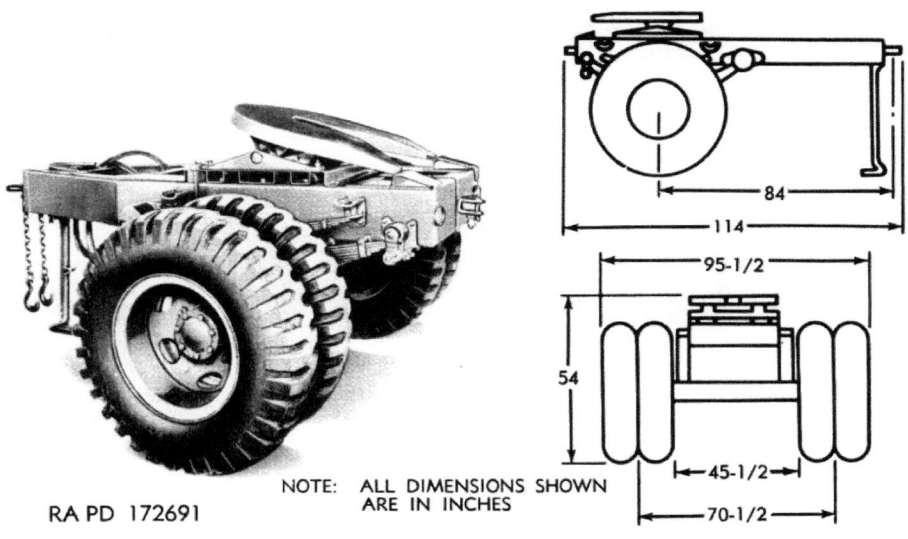

RA PD 172691

NOTE: ALL DIMENSIONS SHOWN ARE IN INCHES

Technical Manuals: 9-892, 9-846; Supply Catalog: SNL G-676.

Classification: Standard.

Purpose: To convert semitrailer, cargo, 10-ton, to full trailer.

GENERAL DATA

Weight (lb)............................	Net 3,380; Payload 12,520; Gross 15,900
Fifth wheel..............................	Size (in.) 30; Type, Semiautomatic
Tires....................................	Ply 14; Size 11.00 x 20; Pressure (psi) 80
Shipping dimensions, uncrated...........................	(cu ft) 340; (sq ft) 76
Ground clearance..	(in.) 16
Brakes...	none
Towing vehicle to be used.............................	truck, 4- to 5-ton, 4 x 4

ADDITIONAL DATA

GUN, TWIN 40-MM, SELF-PROPELLED, T141

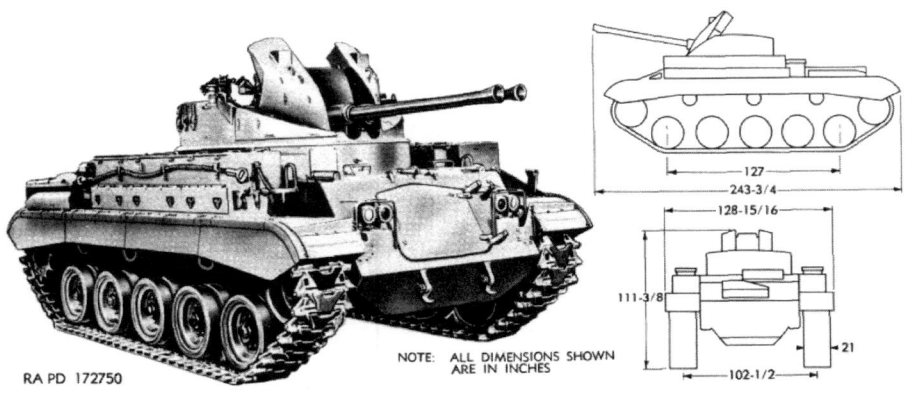

NOTE: ALL DIMENSIONS SHOWN ARE IN INCHES

RA PD 172750

Technical Manuals: 9-1730B, 9-1730F, 9-1825C, 9-1826B, 9-1828A, 9-1829A; **Supply Catalog:** SNL G-253.

Armament: Gun, dual automatic, 40MM, M2A1, turret mounted; 1 gun, machine, cal. .30, Browning, M1919A4 (flexible) pedestal mounted at rear of turret.

Ammunition: 480 rounds, 40-MM; 1,750 rounds, cal. .30, machine gun; 360 rounds, cal. .30, carbine; 8 hand grenades; 4 rockets.

Purpose: To provide a mobile antiaircraft weapon.

Fire-Control and Vision Devices: Periscope, M13 (vision and commander's); quadrant, gunner's, M1; sight, computing, T154; sight, reflex, M24C.

Communications: (AN/VRC-6 and AN/GRR-5 and AN/UIC-1).

GENERAL DATA

Crew..6

Weight, fighting...(lb) 43,000

Shipping dimensions...........................(cu ft) 1,900; (sq ft) 205

Ground pressure..(psi) 8

Ground clearance..(in.) 17 9/16

Pintle height, loaded.....................................(in.) 30 3/4

Electrical system...(volts) 24
No. of batteries..4
Type of ground..negative

Fuel octane rating...80

Capacities:
Fuel..(gal) 140
Crankcase, refill...(qt) 44
Transmission...(qt) 32

Brakes:
Hand-lever controlled, hydraulic, multiple-disk steering brakes.
Pedal operates them as service brakes.
Parking brake, type....................Lever for locking service brakes

No. of ranges (high, low, and reverse).........................3

Ratio from engine output shaft to torque-converter input shaft.......0.769:1

Torque-converter stall ratio..............................4:1

Ratio from torque-converter output shaft to final-drive flange:
High range 1.4:1; Low range 5.34:1

Final-drive gear ratio.................................4.25:1

Turret ring inside diameter.............................(in.) 31

PERFORMANCE

Maximum grade ability..............................(percent) 60
Turning radius (ft)...........................pivots in place
Fording depth......................................(in.) 48
Maximum width of ditch vehicle can cross............(in.) 72
Maximum vertical obstacle vehicle can climb........(in.) 28
Fuel consumption (average conditions)..............(mpg) 0.7
Cruising range (average conditions).................(mi) 100
Maximum speed.....................................(mph) 45
Maximum allowable towed load, gross................(lb) 5,000

ENGINE

Manufacturer: Continental..................Model AOS-895-3
Type.........................4-cycle, valve-in-head, air-cooled
No. of cylinders.......................(horizontal opposed) 6
Displacement...................................(cu in.) 895
Bore..(in.) 5 3/4
Stroke..(in.) 5 3/4
Compression ratio.................................5.5:1
Governed speed..................................(rpm) 2,800
Brake horsepower (max w/std accessories)............446 at (rpm) 2,400
Torque (max w/std accessories)..........890 lb-ft at (rpm) 2,200
Type of ignition...................................magneto

ADDITIONAL DATA

Equipped with manual and power traversing and elevating mechanism.
Data given for vehicle equipped with track, rubber-backed-steel, T91E3 w/detachable rubber grousers.

Auxiliary generator set: Engine, GMC model A41-1; generator, Delco, model GM-A-8585.

GUN, 155-MM, SELF-PROPELLED, T97

NOTE: ALL DIMENSIONS SHOWN ARE IN INCHES

RA PD 172707

Technical Manuals: 9-1718F, 9-1730F, 9-1825C, 9-1825E, 9-1826B, 9-1828A, 9-1829A; Supply Catalog: SNL G-259.

Armament: 1 gun, 155-mm, T8D; 1 gun, machine, cal. .50, Browning, M2, heavy barrel (flexible) mounted on top of turret.

Ammunition: 20 rounds, 155-mm; 945 rounds, cal. .50; 180 rounds, cal. .45 submachine gun; 1,050 rounds, cal. .30 carbine; 8 hand grenades.

Purpose: To provide mobility for 155-mm gun, and crew protection in offensive combat.

Fire-Control and Vision Devices: Periscope, M17 (vision); periscope, M15 (commander's); telescope, T159 (sight); telescope, panoramic, T149 (sight).

Communications: (SCR–619 or AN/PRC–9) and (RC–99).

GENERAL DATA

Crew	6
Weight, fighting	(lb) 90,000
Shipping dimensions, uncrated	(cu ft) 4,550; (sq ft) 390
Ground pressure	(psi) 10.6
Ground clearance	(in.) 18½
Pintle height, loaded	(in.) 25
Electrical system	(volts) 24
No. of batteries	(12-volt) 4
Type of ground	negative
Fuel octane rating	80

Capacities:

Fuel	(gal) 350
Crankcase, refill	(qt) 104
Transmission, cross-drive (including cooler)	(qt) 96
Final drive	(each) (qt) 5

Brakes:

Hand-lever controlled, hydraulic, multiple-disk steering brakes. Pedal operates them as service brakes.

Parking brake, type	Lever for locking service brakes
Ratio from engine output shaft to torque converter input shaft	1.162:1
Ratio from torque converter output shaft to final drive flange	High range 1.4:1; Low range 4.93:1
No. of ranges (High, low and reverse)	3
Torque converter stall ratio	4:1
Final-drive gear ratio	5.0769:1
Hull construction	Welded homogeneous armor plates and castings
Turret-ring inside diameter	(in.) 67⅝

PERFORMANCE

Maximum grade ability	(percent) 60
Turning radius (ft)	Pivots in place
Fording depth	(in.) 48
Maximum width of ditch vehicle can cross	(in.) 96
Maximum vertical obstacle vehicle can climb	(in.) 48
Fuel consumption (average conditions)	(mpg) 0.4
Cruising range (average conditions)	(mi) 150
Allowable speed, recommended	(mph) 35
Maximum allowable towed load, gross	(lb) 5,000

ENGINE

Manufacturer: Continental	Model AV-1790-5B

Type:

4-cycle, valve-in-head, air-cooled No. of cylinders	(90-deg V) 12
Displacement	(cu in.) 1,790
Bore	(in.) 5¾
Stroke	(in.) 5¾
Compression ratio	6.5:1
Governed speed	(rpm) 2,950
Brake horsepower (max w/std accessories)	810 at (rpm) 2,800
Torque (max w/std accessories)	1,560 lb-ft at (rpm) 2,400
Type of ignition	magneto

ADDITIONAL DATA

Auxiliary generator set: Engine, GMC model A41-1; Generator, Delco, Model GM-A-8585.

Data given for vehicle equipped with track, steel, T80E6.

Track, rubber T84E1 is interchangeable.

HEARSE, ¾-TON, 4 x 2

(Watson Automotive; Cadillac Model 4876 w/Superior Hearse Body, 1948)

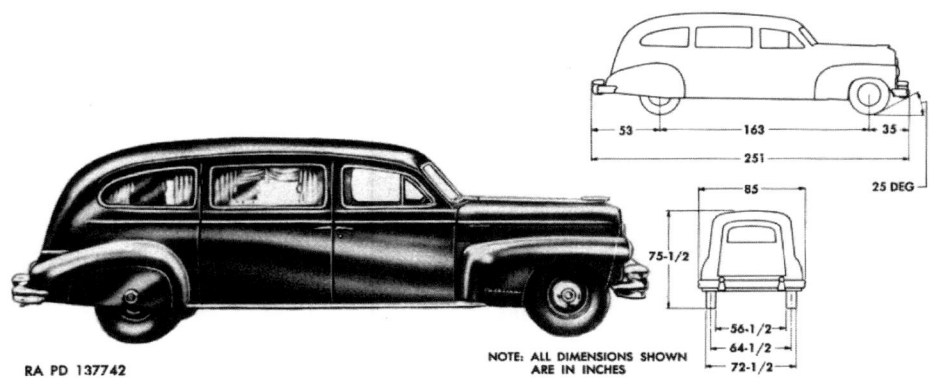

RA PD 137742

NOTE: ALL DIMENSIONS SHOWN ARE IN INCHES

Classification: Standard.

Purpose: To transport deceased personnel.

GENERAL DATA

Crew.. 2
Weight (lb)........................Net 5,750; Pay load 1,500; Gross 7,250
Rear-axle gear ratio....................Standard 4.27:1; Hydramatic 3.77:1
Axle load (lb):
    Empty.......................................front 2,775; rear 2,975
    Loaded......................................front 3,425; rear 3,825
Tires:
    Ply 6.......................Size 7.50 x 16; Pressure (psi) front 34; rear 36
    Tread, center-to-center, front.......................(in.) 58½
Shipping dimensions, uncrated.......................(cu ft) 933; (sq ft) 149
Ground clearance...(in.) 9
Electrical system......................................(volts) 6
    No. of batteries...1
    Type of ground...negative
Fuel octane rating... 80
Capacities:
    Fuel...(gal) 24
    Cooling system (qt)................w/o heater 25; w/heater 26
    Crankcase, refill..(qt) 7
    Transmission..(qt) 1¾
    Axle..(qt) 2½
Brakes:
    Manufacturer; Bendix..........................Type; hydraulic
    Parking brake, type.....................................rear-wheel
Transmission forward speeds..................Standard 3; Hydramatic 4
    Gear ratio:
        Standard...........................High 1:1; Low 2.39:1
        Hydramatic...........................High 1:1; Low 3.819:1

PERFORMANCE

Computed grade ability in lowest gear, loaded.................(percent) 25
Turning radius...(ft) 28½
Fording depth..(in.) 9
Fuel consumption, loaded...................................(mpg) 8
Cruising range, loaded.....................................(mi) 192
Allowable speed, recommended...............................(mph) 70

ENGINE

Manufacturer: Cadillac...................................Model 1948
Type......................L-head, 4-cycle; No. of cylinders (90-deg V) 8
Displacement..(cu in.) 346
Bore...(in.) 3½
Stroke...(in.) 4½
Compression ratio.......................................7.25:1
Governed speed......................................not governed
Brake horsepower (max w/std accessories)..............130 at (rpm) 3,200
Torque (max)..272 lb-ft at (rpm) 1,800

ADDITIONAL DATA

HEARSE, ¾-TON, 4 x 2

(Watson Automotive, Chrysler Model C38 w/Superior Body, 1948–49)

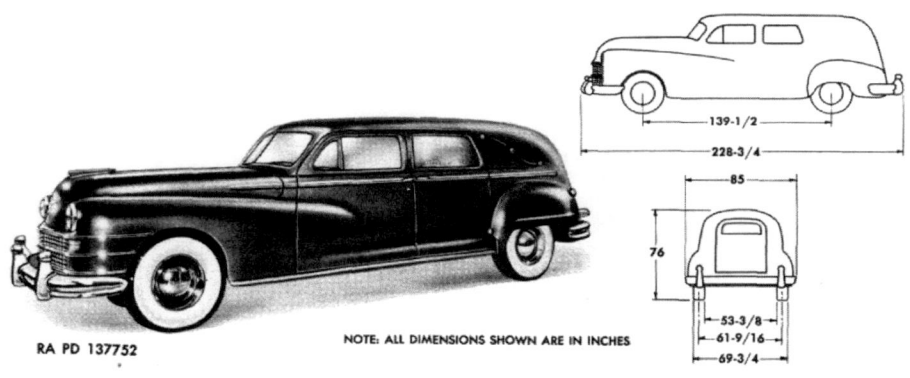

RA PD 137752

NOTE: ALL DIMENSIONS SHOWN ARE IN INCHES

Classification: Nonclassified.

Purpose: To transport deceased personnel.

GENERAL DATA

Crew..1
Weight (lb)...........................Net 4,330; Payload 1,000; Gross 5,330
Rear-axle gear ratio...3.73
Axle load (lb):
    Empty......................................front 2,205; rear 2,125
    Loaded.....................................front 2,605; rear 2,725
Tires:
    Ply 4..............................Size 7.60 x 15; Pressure (psi) 24
    Tread, center-to-center, front.....................(in.) 57 13/16
Shipping dimensions, uncrated....................(cu ft) 855; (sq ft) 135
Ground clearance...(in.) 9⅜
Electrical system...(volts) 6
    No. of batteries...1
    Type of ground...positive
Fuel octane rating...75
Capacities:
    Fuel...(gal) 20
    Cooling system (qt)...............w/o heater 17; w/heater 18
    Crankcase, refill...(qt) 5
    Transmission..(qt) 1½
    Rear axle...(qt) 1⅝
Brakes:
    Manufacturer; Chrysler.........................Type; hydraulic
    Parking brake, type...................................transmission
Transmission forward speeds.......................................4
    Gear ratio...........................High 1:1; Low 3.57:1

PERFORMANCE

Computed grade ability in lowest gear, loaded.............(percent) 31
Turning radius...(ft) 23
Fuel consumption, loaded..(mpg) 13
Cruising range, loaded...(mi) 260
Allowable speed, recommended.................................(mph) 70

ENGINE

Manufacturer: Chrysler..................................Model C38
Type.........................L-head, 4-cycle; No. of cylinders (in line) 6
Displacement..(cu in.) 250.6
Bore..(in.) 3⅜
Stroke...(in.) 4½
Compression ratio..6.6:1
Governed speed..................................not governed
Brake horsepower (max w/std accessories)............114 at (rpm) 3,600
Torque (max)..........................204 lb-ft at (rpm) 1,200

ADDITIONAL DATA

HOWITZER, 155-MM, SELF-PROPELLED, T99E1

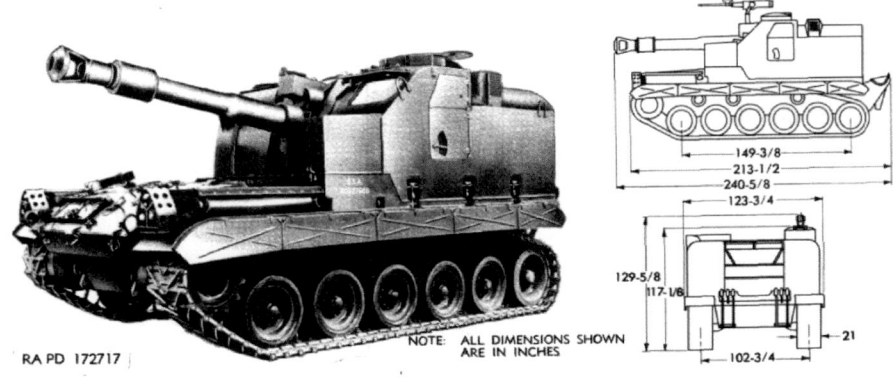

NOTE: ALL DIMENSIONS SHOWN ARE IN INCHES

RA PD 172717

Technical Manuals: 9-1730B, 9-1730F, 9-1825C, 9-1825E, 9-1826B, 9-1826A; Supply Catalog: SNL G-257.

Armament: 1 Howitzer, 155-mm, T97E1, turret mounted; 1 gun, machine, cal. .50, Browning, M2, heavy barrel (flexible) pedestal mounted on top of turret.

Ammunition: 30 rounds, 155-mm; 945 rounds, cal. .50; 180 rounds, cal. .45 for sub-machine-gun; 840 rounds, cal. .30 carbine; 8 hand grenades.

Purpose: To provide high mobility for 155-mm howitzer to give close support to rapidly moving armored or infantry columns.

Fire-Control and Vision Devices: Periscope, M17 (vision); periscope, M15A1 (commander's); telescope, T153 (sight); telescope, panoramic, T149E1 (sight).

Communications: (SCR-610 or SCR-619) and (AN/VIA-1).

GENERAL DATA

Crew	5
Weight, fighting	(lb) 60,000
Shipping dimensions, uncrated	(cu ft) 2,130; (sq ft) 219
Ground pressure	(psi) 9.5
Ground clearance	(in.) 18⅝₆
Pintle height, loaded	(in.) 23¾₆
Electrical system	(volts) 24
No. of batteries	4
Type of ground	negative
Fuel octane rating	80
Capacities:	
Fuel	(gal) 152
Crankcase, refill	(qt) 44
Auxiliary-engine crankcase	(qt) 3½
Transmission, cross-drive (including cooler)	(qt) 72
Final drive	(each) (qt) 5

Brakes:
Hand-lever-controlled, hydraulic, multiple-disk steering brakes. Pedal operates them as service brakes.
Parking brake, type .... Lever for locking service brakes

Ratio from torque converter output shaft to final drive flange: High range 1.41:1; Low range 5.34:1	
No. of ranges (high, low, and reverse)	3
Ratio from engine output shaft to torque converter input shaft	0.769:1
Torque-converter stall ratio	3.8:1
Final-drive gear ratio	4.25:1
Hull construction	welded homogeneous armor plate

PERFORMANCE

Maximum grade ability	(percent) 60
Turning radius (ft)	pivots in place
Fording depth	(in.) 48
Maximum width of ditch vehicle can cross	(in.) 72
Maximum vertical obstacle vehicle can climb	(in.) 30
Fuel consumption (average conditions)	(mpg) 0.5
Cruising range (average conditions)	(mi) 80
Maximum speed	(mph) 35
Maximum allowable to wed load, gross	(lb) 5,000

ENGINE

Manufacturer: Continental	Model AOS-895-3
Type	4-cycle, valve-in-head, air cooled
No. of cylinders	(opposed) 6
Displacement	(cu in.) 895
Bore	(in.) 5¾
Stroke	(in.) 5¾
Compression ratio	5.5:1
Governed speed	(rpm) 2,800
Brake horsepower (max w/std accessories)	440 at (rpm) 2,800
Torque (max w/std accessories)	900 lb-ft at (rpm) 2,100
Type of ignition	magneto

ADDITIONAL DATA

Data given for vehicle equipped with track, rubber-backed-steel, T91E3 w/detachable rubber grousers.

Auxiliary generator set: Engine, GMC Model A41-1; generator, Delco Model GM-A-8585.

Manual and power turret-traversing mechanism.

Howitzer equipped with bore evacuator and muzzle brake.

LANDING VEHICLE, TRACKED, MK 4, LVT (4)

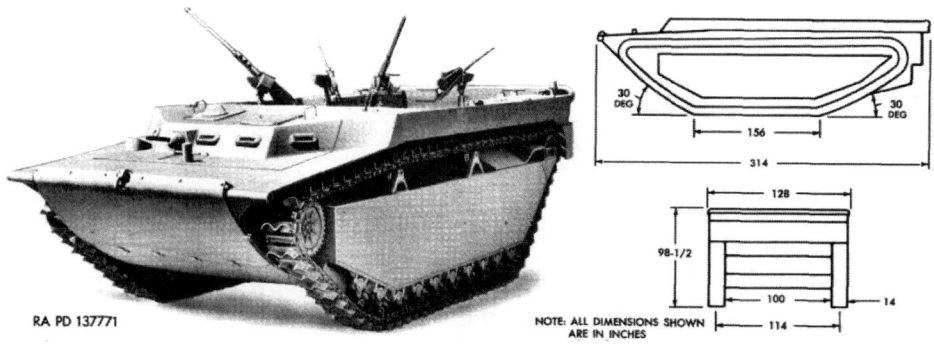

RA PD 137771

NOTE: ALL DIMENSIONS SHOWN ARE IN INCHES

Technical Manuals: 9-775, 9-1726A, 9-1726C, 9-1728, 9-1775, 9-1825A, 9-1826B, 9-1829A; **Supply Catalog:** SNL G-209.

Classification: Standard.

Armament: 2 guns, machine, cal. .50, Browning, M2, heavy barrel (flexible), pintle mounted at front of crew compartment; 3 guns, machine, cal. .30, Browning, M1919A4 (flexible), 1 ball mounted at right front of hull, 2 pintle mounted on sides of crew compartment.

Ammunition: 5,000 round, Cal. .30; 2,000 rounds, cal. .50; 450 rounds, cal. .45, for submachine guns; 24 hand grenades.

Purpose: To land personnel and cargo and transport it on rough terrain, swamp land, and water.

Fire-Control and Vision Devices: Periscope, M12 or M6 (vision).

Communications: (SCR–508 or AN/GRC–3, –4, –5, –6, –7, or –8) and (AN/GRC–9 or NAVY TCS); or (SCR–528 or AN/GRC–3, –4, –5, –6, –7, or –8) and (two AN/GRC–9 or two NAVY TCS).

GENERAL DATA

Crew	2 to 7
Weight (lb)	Payload 9,000; Fighting 36,400
Shipping dimensions, uncrated	(cu ft) 2,290; (sq ft) 279
Ground pressure	(psi) 8.5
Ground clearance (in.)	18; (on soft ground) 15¼
Loaded waterline length	(in.) 296
Loaded freeboard (min)	(in.) 42
Loaded draft (in.)	Front 35¼; Rear 31
Cargo space to top of coaming	(in.) 63¾
Electrical system	(volts) 12
No. of batteries	(6-volt) 2
Type of ground	negative
Fuel octane rating	80
Capacities:	
Fuel	(gal) 140
Transmission and differential	(qt) 24
Engine oil tank	(qt) 23
Final drives	(each) (qt) 3
Brakes	mechanical, controlled-differential
Parking brake, type	ratchet locks on steering brakes
Transmission forward speeds	5
Gear ratio	High 2.29:1; Low 5.37:1
Differential-drive gear ratio	2.76:1
Final-drive gear ratio	3.15:1
Hull construction	welded sheet steel

PERFORMANCE

Maximum grade ability	(percent) 60
Turning radius (ft)	Water 48; Land 30
Fording depth	floats
Maximum width of ditch vehicle can cross	(in.) 60
Maximum vertical obstacle vehicle can climb	(in.) 36
Fuel consumption (average conditions)	(mpg) water 0.6; land 0.9
Cruising range (average conditions)	(mi) water 100; land 150
Allowable speed, governed	(mph) water 7; land 15

ENGINE

Manufacturer: Continental	Model W670-9A
Type	4-cycle, radial, air-cooled; No. of cylinders 7
Displacement	(cu in.) 667.86
Bore	(in.) 5⅛
Stroke	(in.) 4⅝
Compression ratio	6.1:1
Governed speed	(rpm) 2,400
Brake horsepower (max w/std accessories)	250 at (rpm) 2,400
Torque (max w/std accessories)	578 lb-ft at (rpm) 1,600
Type of ignition	magneto

ADDITIONAL DATA

69

LANDING VEHICLE, TRACKED, (ARMORED), MK 4, LVT (A) (4) AND MK 5, LVT (A) (5)

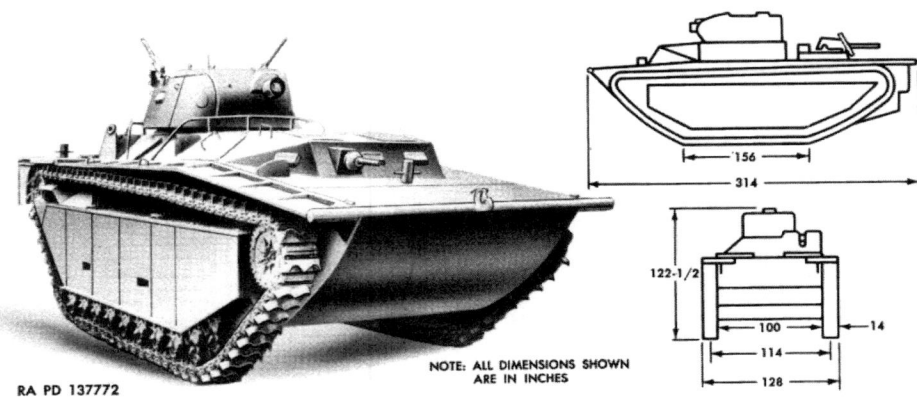

NOTE: ALL DIMENSIONS SHOWN ARE IN INCHES

RA PD 137772

Technical Manuals: 9-775, 9-1726A, 9-1726C, 9-1727K, 9-1728, 9-1775, 9-1825A, 9-1826B, 9-1829A; Supply Catalog: SNL G-214.

Classification: Limited Standard.

Armament: One 75-mm howitzer, M2 or M2A1, turret mounted; 3 guns, machine, cal. .30, Browning-M1919A4 (flexible), 1 ball mounted at right front of vehicle, 2 pintle mounted on sides of turret.

Ammunition: 75 rounds, 75-mm; 6,000 rounds cal. .30, for machine gun; 32 rounds, cal. .30 carbines; 1,440 rounds, cal. .45 for sub-machine-guns; 24 rockets, 4.5 in.; 6 rifle grenades; 24 hand grenades.

Fire-Control and Vision Devices: Periscope, M12 or M6 (vision); quadrant, gunner's, M1; telescope, M70C (sight); telescope, panoramic, M12A5 (sight).

Purpose: To land cargo and personnel in combat and for transport on swampy or rough terrain and water.

Communications: (SCR-508 or SCR-608B or AN/GRC-3, -4, -5, -6, -7, or -8) and (AN/GRC-9 or Navy-TCS); or (SCR-508 or SCR-528 or SCR-608B) and (AN/VRC-3); or (SCR-506 or (RC-99); or (SCR-619 or SCR-610) and (RC-99); or (SCR-506) and (SCR-508 or SCR-528 or SCR-608B or AN/GRC-3, -4, -5, -6, -7, or -8).

GENERAL DATA

Crew	6
Weight, fighting	(lb) 40,000
Shipping dimensions, uncrated	(cu ft) 2,850; (sq ft) 279
Ground clearance (in.)	18; (on soft ground) 14¾
Ground pressure	(psi) 9.9
Loaded waterline length	(in.) 279
Loaded freeboard (minimum)	(in.) 27
Loaded draft (in.)	front 21¾; rear 37¼
Cargo space to top of coaming	(in.) 52
Electrical system	(volts) 12
No. of batteries	(6-volt) 2
Type of ground	negative
Fuel octane rating	80
Capacities:	
Fuel	(gal) 140
Auxiliary-generator fuel tank	(gal) 12
Transmission and differential	(qt) 24
Engine oil tank	(qt) 23
Final drive	(each) (qt) 3
Brakes	mechanical, controlled-differential
Parking brake, type	ratchet locks on steering brakes
Transmission forward speeds	5
Gear ratio	High 2.29:1; Low 5.37:1
Differential-drive gear ratio	2.76:1
Final-drive gear ratio	3.15:1
Hull construction	welded homogeneous armor plate

PERFORMANCE

Maximum grade ability	(percent) 60
Turning radius (ft)	Water 48; Land 30
Fording depth	floats
Maximum width of ditch vehicle can cross	(in.) 60
Maximum vertical obstacle vehicle can climb	(in.) 36
Fuel consumption (average conditions) (mpg)	Water 0.7; Land 1
Cruising range (average conditions) (mi)	Water 100; Land 150
Allowable speed, governed (mph)	Water 7; Land 15

ENGINE

Manufacturer: Continental	Model W670-9A
Type	4-cycle, radial, air-cooled; No. of cylinders 7
Displacement	(cu in.) 667.86
Bore	(in.) 5⅛
Stroke	(in.) 4⅝
Compression ratio	6.1:1
Governed speed	(rpm) 2,400
Brake horsepower (max w/std accessories)	250 at (rpm) 2,400
Torque (max w/std accessories)	578 lb-ft at (rpm) 1,600
Type of ignition	magneto

ADDITIONAL DATA

Both models have hand turret traverse. Mk. 5, LVT (A) (5) has power turret-traversing mechanism and elevation stabilizer.

Auxiliary generator: Delco Model 7-B-12.

MOTORCYCLE, SOLO, CHAIN DRIVE
(Harley-Davidson, Models 40 WLA, 41 WLA, 42 WLA)

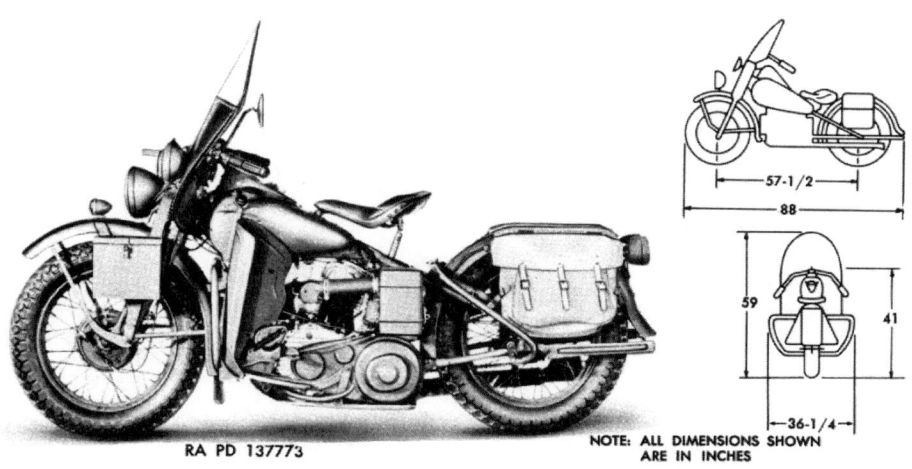

RA PD 137773

NOTE: ALL DIMENSIONS SHOWN
ARE IN INCHES

Technical Manuals: 9–879; 9–1879; Supply Catalog: SNL G–523.

Vehicle illustrated: Model 42 WLA.
Classification: Standard.

Purpose: To transport personnel for reconnaissance, messenger service, police operations, and convoy control.

GENERAL DATA

Crew..1
Weight (lb)....................................Net 513; Payload 250; Gross 763
Axle load (lb):
 Empty...front 245; rear 268
 Loaded..front 370; rear 393
Tires.....................Ply 4; Size 4.00 x 18; Pressure (psi) front 18; rear 2⁰
Shipping dimensions, uncrated...........................(cu fr) 76; (sq ft) 23
Ground clearance..(in.) 4
Electrical system:...(volts) 6
 No. of batteries...1
 Type of ground...negative
Fuel octane rating...72
Capacities:
 Fuel..(gal) 3¾
 Cooling system...air
 Oil tank...(qt) 4½
 Transmission...(qt) ¾
Brakes: Manufacturer; Harley-Davidson.............Type, mechanical
Transmission forward speeds...3
 Engine-to-wheel ratio....................High 4.59 : 1; Low 11.34 : 1

PERFORMANCE

Computed grade ability in lowest gear, loaded................(percent) 32
Turning radius (ft)..................................right 7; left 7½
Fording depth...(in.) 16
Fuel consumption, loaded....................................(mpg) 37
Cruising range, loaded......................................(mi) 124
Allowable speed, recommended................................(mph) 70

ENGINE

Manufacturer: Harley-Davidson..........................Model WLA
Type........................L-head, 4-cycle; No. of cylinders (45-deg V) 2
Displacement...(cu in.) 45.124
Bore..(in.) 2¾
Stroke...(in.) 3¹³/₁₆
Compression ratio....................................4.32 : 1
Governed speed.......................................not governed
Brake horsepower (max w/std accessories)...............23 at (rpm) 4,600
Torque (max)..........................28 lb-ft at (rpm) 3,000

ADDITIONAL DATA

Data given for Model 42 WLA.
Changes in data for Model 40 WLA are as follows:
Shipping dimensions, uncrated..........................(cu ft) 73; (sq ft) 21
Capacities:
 Oil tank...(qt) 1

ENGINE

Model..40 WLA
 Compression ratio....................................4.3 : 1
Changes in data for Model 41 WLA are as follows:
Shipping dimensions, uncrated..........................(cu ft) 84; (sq ft) 23
Capacities:
 Oil tank...(qt) 4

ENGINE

Model..41 WLA
 Compression ratio....................................4.75 : 1
Torque (max)..........................24 lb-ft at (rpm) 4,000

71

MOTORCYCLE, SOLO, CHAIN DRIVE
(Harley-Davidson, Model WL45)

RA PD 137729

NOTE: ALL DIMENSIONS SHOWN
ARE IN INCHES

Classification: Standard.

Purpose: To transport personnel for reconnaissance messenger service police operations, and convoy control.

GENERAL DATA

Crew..1
Weight (lb)...............................Net 477; Payload 250; Gross 727
Axle load (lb):
    Empty...front 229; rear 248
    Loaded..front 354; rear 373
Tires: Ply 4; Size 4.00 x 18; Pressure (psi)..............front 18; rear 20
Shipping dimensions, uncrated..........................(cu ft) 75; (sq ft) 22
Ground clearance..(in.) 4½
Electrical system..(volts) 6
    No. of batteries...1
    Type of ground..negative
Fuel octane rating..72
Capacities:
    Fuel...(gal) 3¾
    Cooling system..air
    Oil tank...(qt) 3½
    Transmission...(qt) ¾
Brakes: Manufacturer; Harley-Davidson.............Type; mechanical
Transmission forward speeds..3
    Engine-to-wheel ratio.......................High 4.74:1; Low 11.72:1

PERFORMANCE

Computed grade ability in lowest gear, loaded...................(percent) 29
Turning radius...(ft) 7¼
Fording depth...(in.) 16
Fuel consumption, loaded.....................................(mpg) 37
Cruising range, loaded..(mi) 125
Allowable speed, recommended..................................(mph) 70

ENGINE

Manufacturer: Harley-Davidson..............................Model WL
Type.....................L-head, 4-cycle; No. of cylinders (45 deg V) 2
Displacement..(cu in.) 45
Bore...(in.) 2¾
Stroke...(in.) 3¹¹⁄₁₆
Compression ratio...6:1
Governed speed...not governed
Brake horsepower (max w/std accessories)...............23 at (rpm) 4,600
Torque (max).............................27½ lb-ft at (rpm) 4,000

ADDITIONAL DATA

MOTORCYCLE, SOLO, CHAIN DRIVE

(Harley-Davidson, Model 50 WLA)

NOTE: ALL DIMENSIONS SHOWN ARE IN INCHES

RA PD 172659

Classification: Standard.

Purpose: To transport personnel for reconnaissance, messenger service, police operations, and convoy control.

GENERAL DATA

Crew..1
Weight (lb)...........................Net 562; Payload 250; Gross 812
Axle load (lb):
    Empty...front 241; rear 321
    Loaded..front 366; rear 446
Tires.....................Ply 4; Size 18 x 4; Pressure (psi) front 16; rear 18
Shipping dimensions, uncrated........................(cu ft) 115; (sq ft) 23
Vehicle dimensions: Ground clearance..............................(in.) 4
Electrical system...(volts) 6
    No. of batteries...1
    Type of ground...negative
Fuel octane rating...72
Capacities:
    Fuel...(gal) 3⅜
    Oil tank, refill...(qt) 4½
    Transmission...(qt) ¾
Brakes: Manufacturer: Harley-Davidson..............Type; mechanical
Transmission forward speeds..3
Engine to wheel ratio...........................High 4.59:1; Low 11.34:1

PERFORMANCE

Computed grade ability in lowest gear, loaded.................(percent) 30
Turning radius..(ft) 8
Fording depth...(in.) 16
Fuel consumption, loaded...................................(mpg) 35
Cruising range, loaded.......................................(ml) 120
Allowable speed, recommended................................(mph) 65

ENGINE

Manufacturer: Harley-Davidson..............................Model WLA
Type.........................4-cycle, L-head; No. of cylinders (45-deg V) 2
Displacement...(cu in.) 45
Bore..(in.) 2¾
Stroke...(in.) 3¹³⁄₁₆
Compression ratio...5:1
Governed speed..not governed
Brake horsepower (max w/std accessories).............23 at (rpm) 4,600
Torque (max w/std accessories)..............28 lb-ft at (rpm) 3,000

ADDITIONAL DATA

MOTORCYCLE, SOLO, EXTRA LIGHT

(Indian, Model 149M, T3)

NOTE: ALL DIMENSIONS SHOWN
ARE IN INCHES   RA PD 172695

Classification: Standard.

Purpose: Airborne.

GENERAL DATA

Crew	1
Weight (lb)	Net 310; Payload 200; Gross 510
Axle load (lb):	
Empty	front 144; rear 164
Loaded	front 247; rear 263
Tires	Ply 4; Size 3¼ x 18; Pressure (psi) 2_0
Shipping dimensions, uncrated	(cu ft) 55; (sq ft) 17
Ground clearance	(in.) 5
Electrical system	magneto and generator
No. of batteries	(6-volt) 1
Type of ground	negative
Fuel octane rating	72
Capacities:	
Fuel	(gal) 3¾
Oil tank	(qt) 1½
Transmission	(qt) ¾
Primary drive	(qt) ¾
Type of drive	chain
Cooling system	air
Brakes: Manufacturer; Indian	Type; mechanical

PERFORMANCE

Computed grade ability in lowest gear, loaded	(percent) 30
Turning radius	(ft) 6¾
Fording depth	(in.) 12
Fuel consumption, loaded	(mpg) 80
Cruising range, loaded	(mi) 300
Maximum speed, recommended	(mph) 60
No. of forward speeds	4
Engine-to-wheel ratio	High 6:12:1; Low 17:01:1

ENGINE

Manufacturer: Indian	Model 149M
Type	Vertical, 4-cycle; No. of cylinders 1
Displacement	(cu in.) 13.3
Bore	(in.) 2¾
Stroke	(in.) 3
Compression ratio	7:1
Brake horsepower (max w/std accessories)	9 at (rpm) 6,000
Torque (max)	9.8 lb-ft at (rpm) 3,800

ADDITIONAL DATA

Equipped with parachute attaching rings.

MOTORCYCLE, SOLO, EXTRA LIGHT, M1

(Indian, Model 148)

RA PD 137774

NOTE: ALL DIMENSIONS SHOWN ARE IN INCHES

Classification: Standard.

Purpose: Airborne.

GENERAL DATA

Crew..1
Weight (lb)................................Net 250; Payload 225; Gross 475
Axle load (lb):
    Empty...front 110; rear 140
    Loaded..front 222; rear 253
Tires........................Ply 4; Size 3 x 18; Pressure (psi) 20
Shipping dimensions, uncrated........................(cu ft) 46 (sq ft) 15
Ground clearance...(in.) 5½
Electrical system..magneto and generator
    No. of batteries...(6-volt) 1
    Type of ground...negative
Fuel octane rating...72
Capacities:
    Fuel...(gal) 2¾
    Oil tank...(qt) 1½
    Transmission...(qt) ¾
    Primary drive...(qt) ⅜
Type of drive..chain
Cooling system..air
Brakes: Manufacturer; Indian...........................Type; mechanical

PERFORMANCE

Computed grade ability in lowest gear, loaded.................(percent) 25
Turning radius...(ft) 5½
Fording depth...(in.) 12
Fuel consumption, loaded..(mpg) 90
Cruising range, loaded...(mi) 250
Maximum speed, recommended.......................................(mph) 45
No. of forward speeds...3
    Engine-to-wheel ratio....................High 6.4:1; Low 18.2:1

ENGINE

Manufacturer: Indian...Model 1
Type.................................Vertical, 4-cycle; No. of cylinders 1
Displacement..(cu in.) 13.5
Bore...(in.) 2½
Stroke..(in.) 2¾
Compression ratio..4.75:1
Brake horsepower (max w/std accessories).............6.3 at (rpm) 4,800
Torque (max)...............................8.1 lb-ft at (rpm) 3,600

ADDITIONAL DATA

Equipped with parachute attaching rings.

MOTORCYCLE, SOLO, 3-WHEEL
(Harley-Davidson, Model G, 1950)

NOTE: ALL DIMENSIONS SHOWN ARE IN INCHES

RA PD 172660

Classification: Nonclassified.

GENERAL DATA

Crew..1
Weight (lb)...........................Net 500; Payload 500; Gross 1,395
Tires...................Ply 4; Size 5.00 x 16; Pressure (psi) front 12; rear 16
Shipping dimensions, uncrated....................(cu ft) 167; (sq ft) 39
Vehicle dimensions:
    Ground clearance...(in.) 4½
Electrical system...(volts) 6
    No. of batteries...1
    Type of ground...negative
Fuel octane rating...72
Capacities:
    Fuel...(gal) 3¾
    Oil tank, refill...(qt) 3½
    Transmission...(qt) ¼
Brakes: Manufacturer; Harley-Davidson.............Type; mechanical
Transmission forward speeds...3
    Engine-to-wheel ratio................High 5.85:1; Low 14.4:1

Purpose: To provide transportation for messenger service, convoy control, and police operations.

PERFORMANCE

Turning radius...(ft) 8
Fording depth...(in.) 16
Fuel consumption, loaded............................(mpg) 35
Cruising range, loaded................................(mi) 120
Allowable speed..(mph) 45

ENGINE

Manufacturer: Harley-Davidson.....................Model G
Type...............4-cycle, L-head; No. of cylinders (45-deg V) 2
Displacement...(cu in.) 45
Bore...(in.) 2¾
Stroke..(in.) 3¹³⁄₁₆
Compression ratio..4.75:1
Governed speed...not governed
Brake horsepower (max w/std accessories)...........23 at (rpm) 4,600
Torque (max w/std accessories)......................28 at (rpm) 3,000

ADDITIONAL DATA

SCOOTER, MOTOR, AIRBORNE, 2-WHEEL

(Cushman, Model 53)

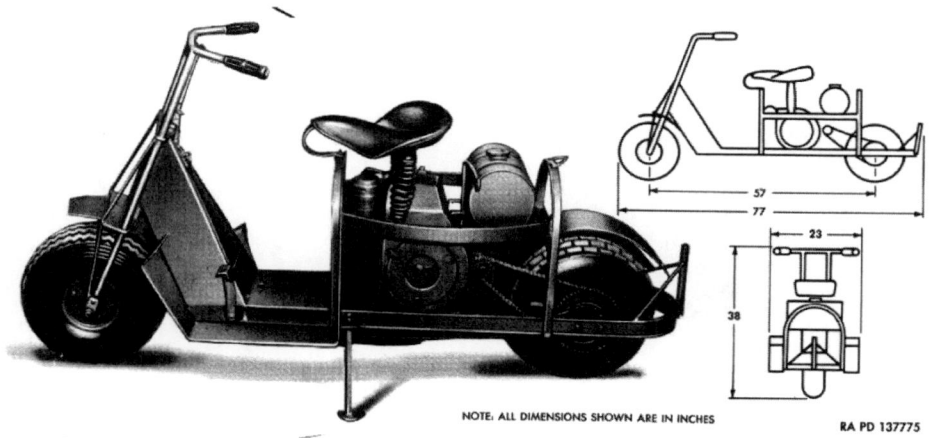

NOTE: ALL DIMENSIONS SHOWN ARE IN INCHES

RA PD 137775

Technical Manual: 9-876; Supply Catalog: SNL G-683.

Classification: Limited Standard.

Purpose: To transport one person.

GENERAL DATA

Crew..1
Weight (lb)..............................Net 260; Payload 225; Gross 485
Axle load (lb):
  Empty..front 100; rear 160
  Loaded...front 195; rear 290
Tires..........................Ply 4; Size 6.00 x 6; Pressure (psi) 15
Shipping dimensions, uncrated.........................(cu ft) 39; (sq ft) 12
Ground clearance...(in.) 6¾
Electrical system: ignition..................................magneto
Fuel octane rating...70
Capacities:
  Fuel...(gal) 2
  Crankcase...(qt) 1¾
  Transmission..(qt) ¼
  Cooling system..air
Brakes:
  Manufacturer; Cushman...........................Type; mechanical
  Parking brake...none
Type of drive...chain
Transmission forward speeds....................................2
  Engine-to-wheel ratio..................High 5.03:1; Low 14.99:1

PERFORMANCE

Computed grade ability in lowest gear, loaded..............(percent) 25
Turning radius..(ft) 6¾
Fording depth..(in.) 12
Fuel consumption, loaded....................................(mpg) 50
Cruising range, loaded......................................(mi) 100
Maximum speed...(mph) 40

ENGINE

Manufacturer: Cushman....................................Model 16M71
Type.........................Vertical, 4-cycle; No. of cylinders 1
Displacement...(cu in.) 14.89
Bore...(in.) 2⅝
Stroke...(in.) 2¾
Compression ratio..5.4:1
Brake horsepower (max w/std accessories)..............4.6 at (rpm) 3,600
Torque (max)........................7.5 lb-ft at (rpm) 2,600

ADDITIONAL DATA

SCOOTER, MOTOR, 3-WHEEL, W/SIDE CAR

(Cushman, Model 32)

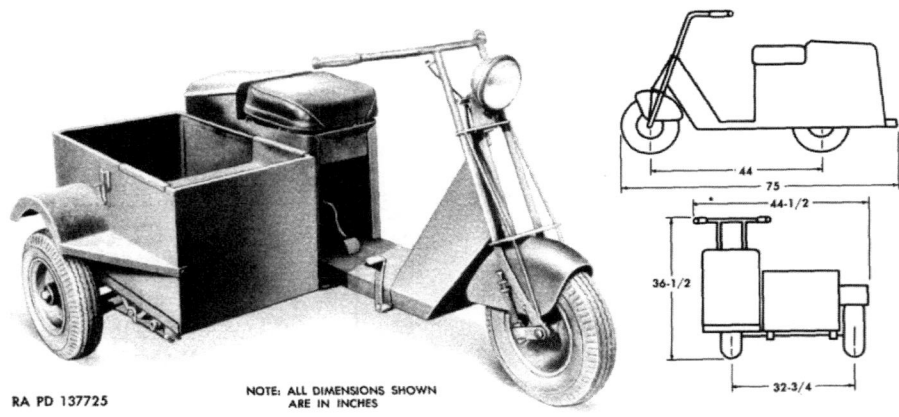

RA PD 137725

NOTE: ALL DIMENSIONS SHOWN
ARE IN INCHES

Technical Manual: 10–1399.

Classification: Limited Standard.

Purpose: For light delivery and messenger service.

GENERAL DATA

Crew..1
Weight (lb)...................Net 325; Payload 325; Gross 650
Axle load (lb):
    Empty...front 100; rear 225
    Loaded.......................................front 220; rear 430
Shipping dimensions uncrated.........(cu ft) 71; (sq ft) 23.1
Tires........................Ply 4; Size 4.00 x 8; Pressure (psi) 30
Vehicle dimensions:
    Ground clearance..(in.) 4
    Side car inside dimensions (in.)........Length 30; Width 18; Height 16
    Cargo space..(cu ft) 5
Electrical system...(volts) 6
    No. of batteries..none
Fuel octane rating...70
Capacities:
    Fuel..(gal) 1¾
    Crankcase...(qt) 1¾
    Cooling system..air
Brakes:
    Manufacturer; Cushman...........................Type; mechanical
    Parking brake...none
Type of drive...chain
Transmission speeds..no transmission
    Engine-to-wheel ratio: 5:1 w/60-tooth rear-wheel sprocket, 4.41:1
    w/53-tooth rear-wheel sprocket.

PERFORMANCE

Computed grade ability, loaded......................(percent) 4
Turning radius (ft)...........................left 5¾; right 6¾
Fording depth..(in.) 10
Fuel consumption, loaded...................................(mpg) 42
Cruising range, loaded.......................................(mi) 50
Maximum speed...(mph) 35

ENGINE

Manufacturer: Cushman............................Model 15M71
Type...........................Vertical, 4-cycle; No. of cylinders 1
Displacement..(cu in.) 14.89
Bore...(in.) 2¾
Stroke...(in.) 2¾
Compression ratio...5.4:1
Brake horsepower (max w/std accessories)...............4.6 at (rpm) 3,600
Torque (max)..........................7.5 lb-ft at (rpm) 2,600

ADDITIONAL DATA

78

SCOOTER, MOTOR, PACKAGE DELIVERY, 3-WHEEL

(Cushman Package Kar, Model 39)

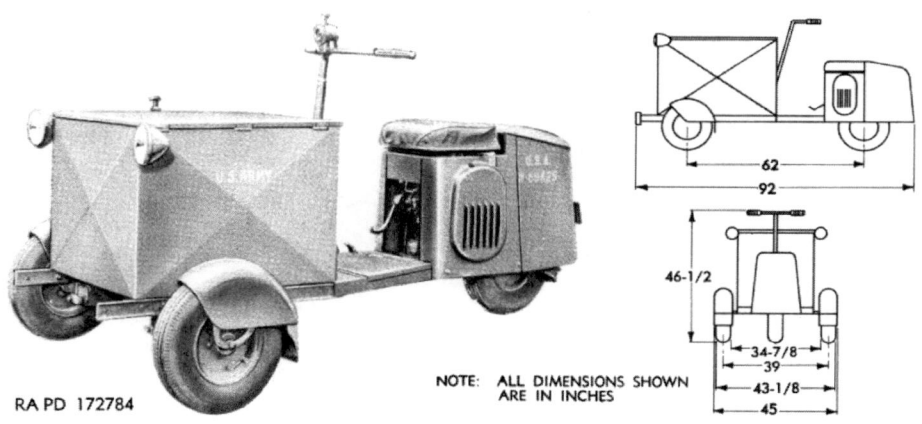

RA PD 172784

NOTE: ALL DIMENSIONS SHOWN ARE IN INCHES

Supply Catalog: SNL G-672.

Classification: Substitute Standard.

Purpose: For light delivery and messenger service.

GENERAL DATA

Crew..1
Weight (lb)............................Net 415; Payload 350; Gross 765
Axle load (lb):
  Empty..front 235; rear 180
  Loaded...front 410; rear 355
Shipping dimensions, uncrated.................(cu ft) 112; (sq ft) 28.8
Tires:
  Ply 4..................................Size 4.00 x 8; Pressure (psi) 30
  Tread...................................center-to-center, front (in.) 39
Vehicle dimensions:
  Ground clearance..(in.) 5½
  Package compartment inside dimensions (in.):
    Length 28.........................Width 22; Height 21
  Cargo space...(cu ft) 7½
Electrical system...(volts) 6
  No. of batteries..none
Fuel octane rating...70
Capacities:
  Fuel...(gal) 1⅝
  Crankcase..(qt) 1¾
  Transmission...(qt) ¼
  Cooling system..air
Brakes:
  Manufacturer; Cushman.......................Type; mechanical
  Parking brake.............................lock on service brake pedal
Type of drive...chain
Transmission forward speeds..2
  Engine-to-wheel ratio................High 6.48:1; Low 13.43:1

PERFORMANCE

Computed grade ability in lowest gear, loaded................(percent) 12
Turning radius...(ft) 11
Fording depth...(in.) 6
Fuel consumption, loaded...(mpg) 42
Cruising range, loaded...(mi) 50
Maximum speed ....(mph) 30

ENGINE

Manufacturer: Cushman.......................................Model 10M70
Type.................................Vertical, 4-cycle; No. of cylinders 1
Displacement..(cu in.) 14.89
Bore..(in.) 2⅞
Stroke...(in.) 2¾
Compression ratio...5.4:1
Brake horsepower (max w/std accessories)................4 at (rpm) 3,600
Torque (max)................................7.5 lb-ft at (rpm) 2,600

ADDITIONAL DATA

79

SEMITRAILER, 32-PASSENGER BUS CHASSIS, 3-TON, 2-WHEEL

(Fruehauf, Model 220DDF–SP)

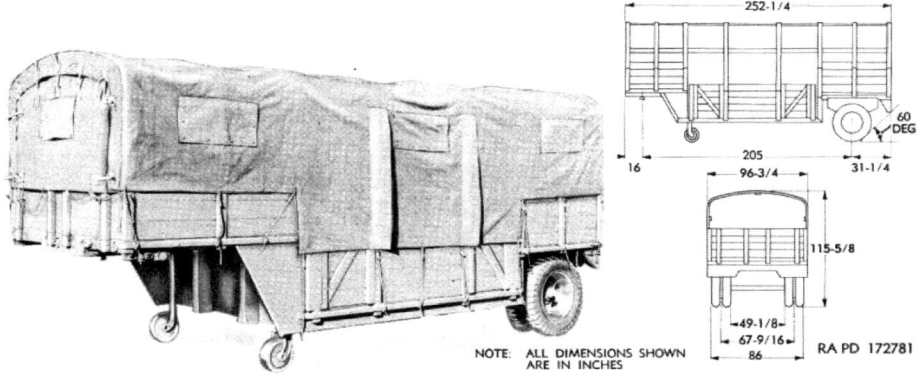

NOTE: ALL DIMENSIONS SHOWN ARE IN INCHES

RA PD 172781

Supply Catalog: SNL G–701.

Classification: Nonclassified.

Purpose: To transport personnel.

GENERAL DATA

Weight (lb)..........................Net 6,790; Payload 6,480; Gross 13,270
Weight distribution (lb):
    Empty.................................fifth wheel 3,010; axle 3,780
    Loaded................................fifth wheel 6,480; axle 6,790
Tires..............................Ply 8; Size 7.50 x 20; Pressure (psi) 55
Shipping dimensions uncrated......................(cu ft) 1,640; (sq ft) 170
Vehicle dimensions:
    Ground clearance................................(in.) 15½
    Step height, empty..............................(in.) 24⅝
    Height of fifth wheel, landing gear down.........................(in.) 44
    Body inside dimensions (in.):
        Length 246............................Width 90; Height: front 61¾
                                      center 90
                                      rear 72
Brakes: Manufacturer; Borg-Warner.......................Type; electric
    Parking brake, type..............................mechanical
Minimum towing vehicle to be used..........truck, tractor, 1½-ton, 4 x 2

ADDITIONAL DATA

SEMITRAILER, VAN, 3-TON, 2-WHEEL

(Black, Diamond, Model T118, 1942–43; Carolina, Model M2A, 1943–44; Checker, Model CC3; Highway, Models SKD 1742A, 1941, SKD 2043, SKD 2269, steel, SKD 2316, wood, SKD 2353 WKD; Kingham, Model H30S, 1942–43; Steel Products, Model ASV, 1943; Strick, Models 300, 300–18, 1942–1943; Truck Engineering, Model 2SF, 1943)

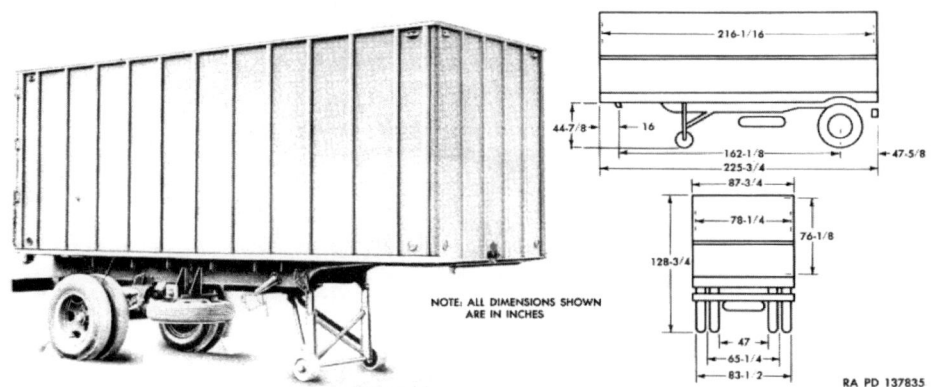

NOTE: ALL DIMENSIONS SHOWN ARE IN INCHES

RA PD 137835

Technical Manuals: 10-1168, 10-1363, 10-1675; **Supply Catalogs:** SNL G-530; Carolina, SNL G-570; Checker, SNL G-560; Highway, SNL G-579; Kingham, SNL G-565; Steel Products, SNL G-571; Strick, SNL G-582; Truck Engineering, SNL G-566.

Vehicle illustrated: Black Diamond.
Classification: Standard.

Purpose: To transport general cargo.

GENERAL DATA

Weight (lb) Net	5,870
Payload	on inferior roads 6,000; on highway 10,000
Gross	on inferior roads 11,870; on highway 15,870
Weight distribution (lb):	
Empty	fifth wheel 1,860; axle 4,010
Loaded:	
On inferior roads	fifth wheel 4,512; axle 7,358
On highway	fifth wheel 6,280; axle 9,590
Tires	Ply 8; Size 7.50 x 20; Pressure (psi) 55
Shipping dimensions, uncrated	(cu ft) 1,468; (sq ft) 138
Vehicle dimensions:	
Ground clearance	(in.) 13¼
Loading height	(in.) 49¾
Height of fifth wheel, landing gear down	(in.) 44¾
Cargo space	(cu ft) 744
Brakes:	
Manufacturer; Warner	Type; electric
Parking brake	none
Minimum towing vehicle to be used	Truck, tractor, 1½-ton, 4 x 2

ADDITIONAL DATA

Some models equipped with wood bodies; others with steel bodies.

SEMITRAILER, STAKE AND PLATFORM, 3½-TON, 2-WHEEL

(Black Diamond, Models T118 and T118A; Checker, Model CC4; Dorsey, Model D8; Highway, Model SKD 2267; Hobbs, Models 5DF and DF18, 1942; Kingham, Model H30S, 1942–43; Strick, Models 300 and 300–18, 1942–43; Utility, Model G–SW2)

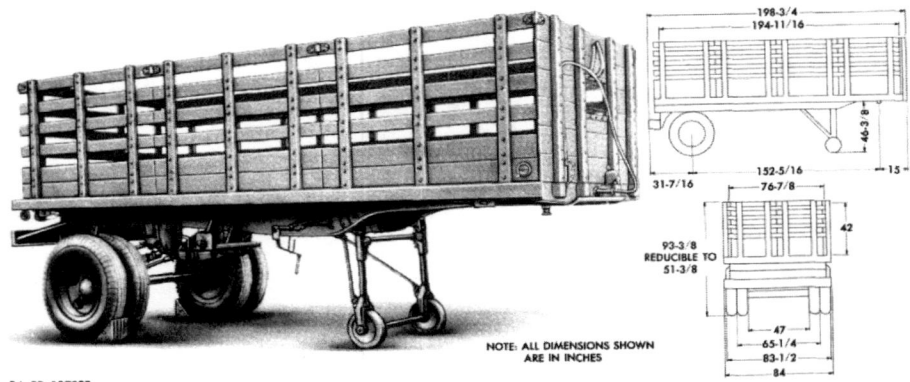

NOTE: ALL DIMENSIONS SHOWN ARE IN INCHES

RA PD 137802

Technical Manual: 10-1363; **Supply Catalogs:** Black Diamond, SNL G–530; Checker, SNL G–560; Dorsey, SNL G–563; Highway, SNL G–579; Hobbs, SNL G–564; Kingham, SNL G–565; Strick, SNL G–582; Utility, SNL G–567.

Vehicle Illustrated: Highway.
Classification: Standard.

Purpose: To transport general cargo.

GENERAL DATA

ADDITIONAL DATA

Weight (lb) Net 4,700
  Payload .... on inferior roads 7,000; on highway 12,600
  Gross .... on inferior roads 11,700; on highway 17,300
Weight distribution (lb):
  Empty .... fifth wheel 1,890; axle 2,810
  Loaded:
    On inferior roads .... fifth wheel 5,160; axle 6,540
    On highway .... fifth wheel 7,780; axle 9,520
Tires .... Ply 8; Size 7.50 x 20; Pressure (psi) 55
Shipping dimensions, uncrated .... (cu ft) 906; (sq ft) 116
Vehicle dimensions:
  Ground clearance .... (in.) 13¼
  Loading height, empty .... (in.) 51¾
  Height of fifth wheel landing gear down .... (in.) 46¾
  Cargo space .... (cu ft) 364
Brakes:
  Manufacturerurer; Warner .... Type; electric
  Parking brake .... none
Minimum towing vehicle to be used .... truck, tractor, 1½-ton, 4 x 2

SEMITRAILER, STAKE AND PLATFORM, 5-TON, 2-WHEEL
(Olson, Trailmobile, Truck Engineering, Model 516)

RA PD 172635

NOTE: ALL DIMENSIONS SHOWN ARE IN INCHES

Technical Manual: 9–890; Supply Catalog: SNL G–675.

Classification: Standard.

Purpose: To transport general cargo.

GENERAL DATA

Weight (lb) Net..6,640
    Payload......................on inferior roads 10,000; on highway 15,000
    Gross..........................on inferior roads 16,640; on highway 21,640
Weight distribution (lb):
    Empty.............................fifth wheel 2,275; axle 4,365
    Loaded:
        On inferior roads......................fifth wheel 7,000; axle 9,640
        On highway.........................fifth wheel 9,365; axle 12,275
Tires.............................Ply 10; Size 9.00 x 20; Pressure (psi) 65
Shipping dimensions, uncrated.....................(cu ft) 1,167; (sq ft) 135
Vehicle dimensions:
    Ground clearance..(in.) 16⅝
    Loading height, empty......................................(in.) 52⅜
    Height of fifth wheel, landing gear down.....................(in.) 43¾
    Cargo space...(cu ft) 515
Brakes:
    Manufacturer; Bendix-Westinghouse.......................Type; air
    Parking brake, type.....................................mechanical
Minimum towing vehicle to be used.............truck, tractor, 5-ton, 4 x 2

ADDITIONAL DATA

SEMITRAILER, ANIMAL AND CARGO, 6-TON, 2-WHEEL
(Highway, Model SKD 1815)

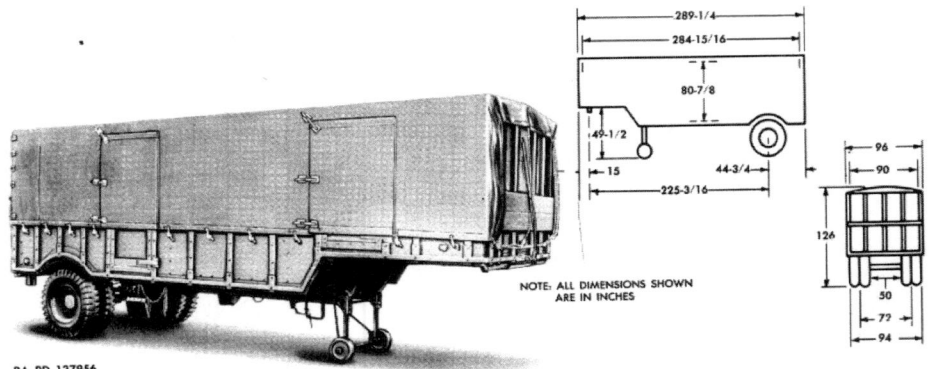

RA PD 137856

Technical Manual: 10–1372; **Supply Catalog:** SNL G–525.

Classification: Standard.

Purpose: To transport 8 men and 8 horses and equipment for both, including rifles and saddles.

GENERAL DATA

Weight (lb) _____Net 8,809; Payload 12,000; Gross 20,809
Weight distribution (lb):
    Empty_____fifth wheel 2,849; axle 5,960
    Loaded_____fifth wheel 7,809; axle 13,000
Tires_____Ply 10; Size 9.00 x 20; Pressure (psi) 65
Shipping dimensions, uncrated_____(cu ft) 2,025; (sq ft) 193
Vehicle dimensions:
    Ground clearance_____(in.) 14
    Loading height, empty_____(in.) 38
    Height of fifth wheel, landing gear down_____(in.) 49¾
    Cargo space_____(cu ft) 1,055
Brakes:
    Manufacturer; Bendix-Westinghouse_____Type; air
    Parking brake_____none
Minimum towing vehicle to be used_____truck, tractor, 2½-ton, 4 x 2

ADDITIONAL DATA

This model equipped with differential dual wheels.

SEMITRAILER, ANIMAL AND CARGO, 6-TON, 2-WHEEL

(Trailer Co. of America, Model TD, 32G, 1940–41)

RA PD 172628

NOTE: ALL DIMENSIONS SHOWN
ARE IN INCHES

Technical Manual: 10-1110; Supply Catalog: SNL G-580.

Classification: Standard.

Purpose: To transport 8 men and 8 horses and equipment for both, including rifles and saddles.

GENERAL DATA

Weight (lb) ....Net 8,580
   Payload.......................on inferior roads 12,000; on highway 16,020
   Gross....................on inferior roads 20,580; on highway 24,600
Weight distribution (lb):
   Empty...fifth wheel 3,710; axle 4,870
   Loaded:
      On inferior roads........................fifth wheel 8,930; axle 11,650
      On highway............................fifth wheel 10,800; axle 13,800
Tires...............................Ply 10; Size 9.00 x 20; Pressure (psi) 65
Shipping dimensions, uncrated.....................(cu ft) 2,070; (sq ft) 197
Vehicle dimensions:
   Ground clearance...(in.) 14¾
   Loading height, empty...(in.) 45¼
   Height of fifth wheel, landing gear down......................(in.) 49½
   Cargo space...(cu ft) 1,064
Brakes:
   Manufacturer; Bendix-Westinghouse.........................Type; air
   Parking brake, type..none
Minimum towing vehicle to be used..........truck, tractor, 2½-ton, 4 x 2

ADDITIONAL DATA

Equipped w/differential dual wheels.

SEMITRAILER, GASOLINE TANK, 6-TON, 2-WHEEL, 2,000-GAL., M30
(Davis Welding, Heil, Lufkin, Keystone, Krieger Steel, Independent, Progress, Model ST62M)

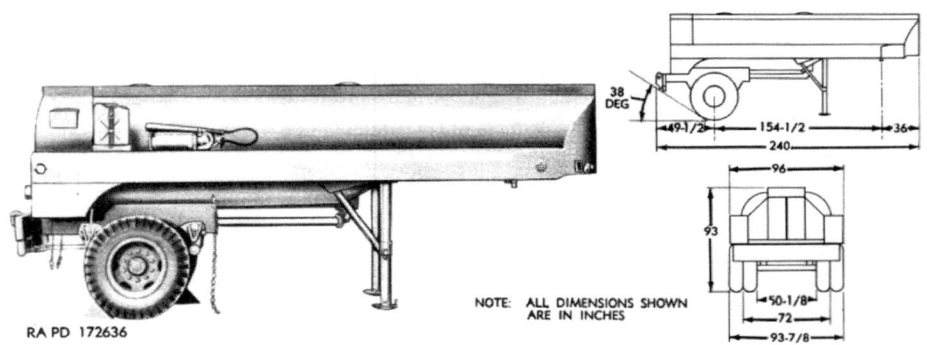

RA PD 172636

NOTE: ALL DIMENSIONS SHOWN ARE IN INCHES

Technical Manual: 9-891; **Supply Catalog:** SNL G-678.

Classification: Substitute Standard.

Purpose: To transport and dispense gasoline.

GENERAL DATA

Weight (lb) .... Net 6,750; Payload 12,200; Gross 18,950
  Weight distribution (lb):
    Empty..fifth wheel 2,750; axle 4,000
    Loaded......................................fifth wheel 7,750; axle 11,200
Tires........................Ply 12; Size 9.00 x 20; Pressure (psi) 65
Shipping dimensions, uncrated......................(cu ft) 1,790; (sq ft) 161
Vehicle dimensions:
  Ground clearance...(in.) 19½
  Pintle height, empty..(in.) 36
  Height of fifth wheel, landing gear down.......................(in.) 49¾
Brakes:
  Manufacturer; Bendix-Westinghouse.........................Type; air
  Parking brake, type...none
Minimum towing vehicle to be used.........truck, tractor, 4- to 5-ton, 4 x 4

ADDITIONAL DATA

20 gpm pump is powered by Briggs and Stratton air-cooled engine.

SEMITRAILER, STAKE AND PLATFORM, 6-TON, 2-WHEEL

(Fruehauf, Models WLS220S, 1941; WLS222, 1942; WLS223, 1942; WLS224, 1942–43; WLS224S, 1942; WLS225, 1942; WLS226, 1943; WLS226S, 1943; WLS227, 1943; WLS228S, 1943; WLS229, 1943; WLS230S, 1943, and Springfield, Model 939, 1943)

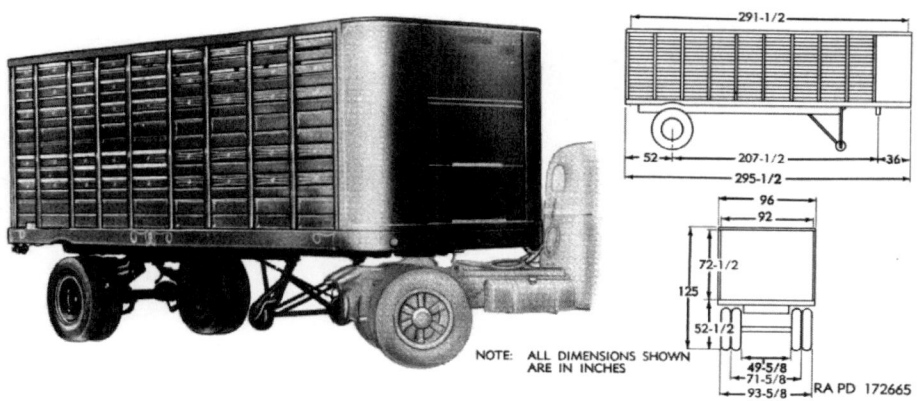

NOTE: ALL DIMENSIONS SHOWN ARE IN INCHES

RA PD 172665

Technical Manual: 10-1294; Supply Catalog: SNL G-581.

Vehicle illustrated: Fruehauf Model WLS226.

Classification: Nonclassified.

Purpose: To transport general cargo.

<table>
<tr><td>

GENERAL DATA

Weight (lb) Net..8,170
  Payload......................on inferior roads 12,000; on highway 17,780
  Gross.......................on inferior roads 20,170; on highway 25,950
Weight distribution (lb):
  Empty...............................fifth wheel 2,800; axle 5,370
  Loaded:
    On inferior roads...................fifth wheel 9,389; axle 10,881
    On highway.........................fifth wheel 12,144; axle 13,800
Tires...........................Ply 10; Size 9.00 x 20; Pressure (psi) 65
Shipping dimensions, uncrated....................(cu ft) 2,060; (sq ft) 197
Vehicle dimensions:
  Ground clearance..(in.) 15⅝
  Loading height, empty......................................(in.) 52½
  Height of fifth wheel, landing gear down...................(in.) 49¾
  Cargo space..(cu ft) 1,130
Brakes:
  Manufacturer; Fruehauf...................................Type; air
  Parking brake, type..none
Minimum towing vehicle to be used.........truck, tractor, 4- to 5-ton, 4 x 4

</td><td>

ADDITIONAL DATA

</td></tr>
</table>

SEMITRAILER, VAN, 6-TON, 2-WHEEL

(American Body, Model DF233V; Carter, Model C15935A; Dorsey, Model E14; Kentucky, Model 1—ORD; Olson, Model KV10; Strick, Model 400W; Timpte, Model T8D; Utility, Model GSW4 (KD), 1943)

RA PD 172637

Technical Manual: 9-888; Supply Catalog: SNLG-665.

Classification: Standard.

Purpose: To transport general cargo.

GENERAL DATA

Weight (lb) _____Net 7,200
    Payload_____on inferior roads 12,000; on highway 18,500
    Gross_____on inferior roads 19,200; on highway 25,700
Weight distribution (lb):
    Empty_____fifth wheel 3,350; axle 3,850
    Loaded:
        On inferior roads_____fifth wheel 8,900; axle 10,300
        On highway_____fifth wheel 11,900; axle 13,800
Tires_____Ply 10; Size 9.00 x 20; Pressure (psi) 70
Shipping dimensions, uncrated_____(cu ft) 1,780; (sq ft) 165
Vehicle dimensions:
    Ground clearance_____(in.) 15⅞
    Loading height, empty_____(in.) 46⅞
    Height of fifth wheel, landing gear down_____(in.) 50
    Body inside dimensions (in.)_____Length 240; Width 88¼; Height 78
    Cargo space_____(cu ft) 875
Brakes:
    Manufacturer; Bendix-Westinghouse_____Type; air
    Parking brake, type_____none
Minimum towing vehicle to be used_____truck, tractor, 4- to 5-ton, 4 x 4

ADDITIONAL DATA.

Bodies are knock-down type.

SEMITRAILER, VAN, 6-TON, 2-WHEEL

(Gerstenslager, Model W8125, 1942)

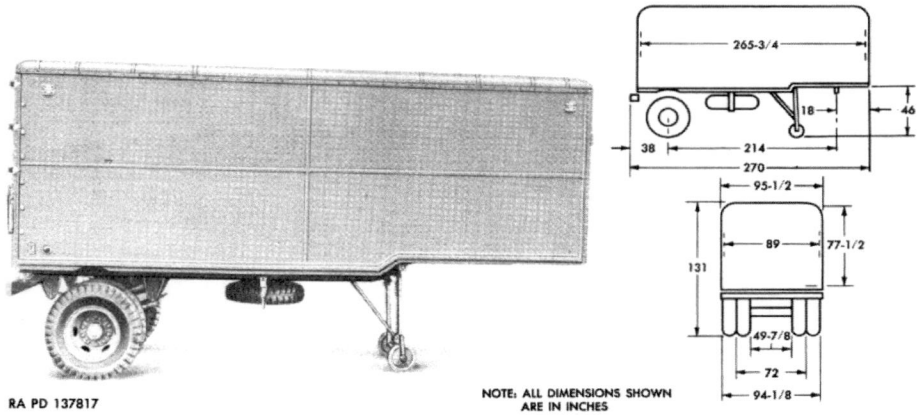

RA PD 137817

NOTE: ALL DIMENSIONS SHOWN
ARE IN INCHES

Technical Manual: 10-1315; Supply Catalog: SNL G-664.

Classification: Standard.

Purpose: To transport general cargo.

GENERAL DATA

Weight (lb)--Net 7,500
    Payload------------------on inferior roads 12,000; on highway 13,600
    Gross----------------------on inferior roads 19,500; on highway 21,100
Weight distribution (lb):
    Empty------------------------------fifth wheel 2,310; axle 5,190
    Loaded:
        On inferior roads------------------fifth wheel 6,740; axle 12,760
        On highway------------------------fifth wheel 7,330; axle 13,770
Tires--------------------------Ply 10; Size 9.00 x 20;, (Pressure (psi) 65
Shipping dimensions, uncrated------------------(cu ft) 1,819; (sq ft) 166
Vehicle dimensions:
    Ground clearance----------------------------------(in.) 13
    Loading height--------------------------------------(in.) 50¾
    Height of fifth wheel, landing gear down----------(in.) 48¾
    Cargo space----------------------------------(cu ft) 1,060
Brakes:
    Manufacturer; Bendix-Westinghouse------------------Type; air
    Parking brake--none
Minimum towing vehicle to be used----------truck, tractor, 2½ ton, 4 x 2

PERFORMANCE

Procured with wood bodies and steel bodies. Steel body increases net and gross weights 500 lb.

SEMITRAILER, VAN, 6-TON, 2-WHEEL

(Gramm, Model DF–75)

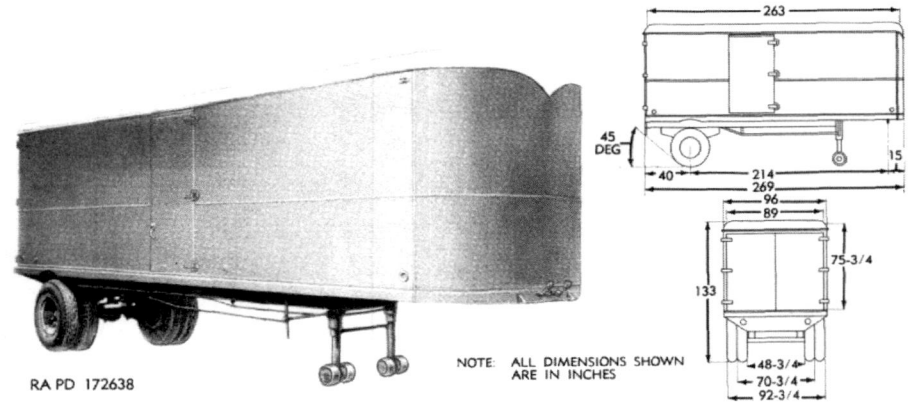

NOTE: ALL DIMENSIONS SHOWN
ARE IN INCHES

RA PD 172638

Technical Manual: 10-1217; **Supply Catalog:** SNL G-584.

Classification: Standard.

Purpose: To transport general cargo.

GENERAL DATA

Weight (lb) ....Net 8,000
   Payload....................on inferior roads 12,000; on highway 13,870
   Gross...........................on inferior roads 20,000; on highway 21,870
Weight distribution (lb):
   Empty...fifth wheel 2,960; axle 5,040
   Loaded:
     On inferior roads.......................fifth wheel 7,380; axle 12,620
     On highway..............................fifth wheel 8,070; axle 13,800
Tires......................................Ply 10; Size 9.00 x 20; Pressure (psi) 65
Shipping dimensions, uncrated......................(cu ft) 1,990; (sq ft) 179
Vehicle dimensions:
   Ground clearance...(in.) 14
   Loading height, empty...(in.) 49
   Height of fifth wheel, landing gear down.......................(in.) 49¾
   Cargo space...(cu ft) 1,020
Brakes:
   Manufacturer; Bendix-Westinghouse...........................Type: air
   Parking brake, type...none
Minimum towing vehicle to be used..........truck, tractor, 2½ ton, 4 x 2

ADDITIONAL DATA

SEMITRAILER, VAN, 6-TON, 2-WHEEL

(Gramm, Checker, American Bantam, Carolina, Model STV620)

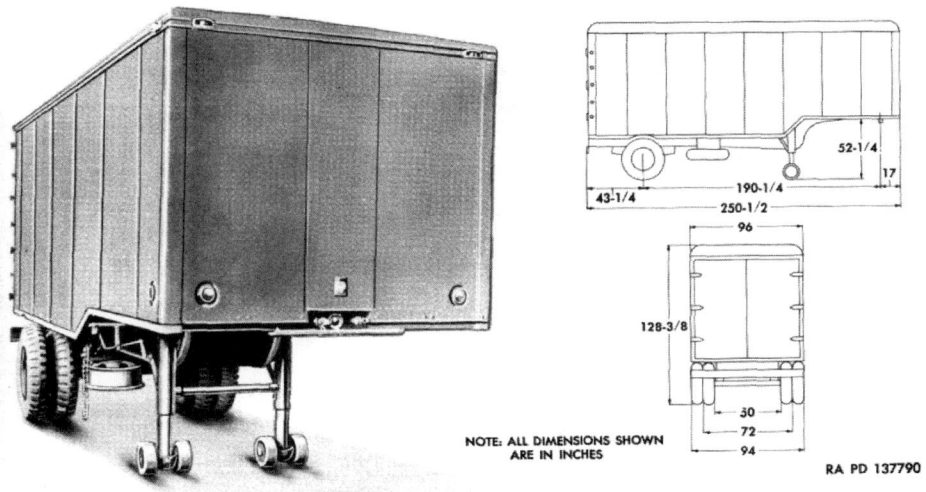

NOTE: ALL DIMENSIONS SHOWN
ARE IN INCHES

RA PD 137790

Technical Manual: 9-888; **Supply Catalog:** SNL G-707.

Classification: Standard.

Purpose: To transport general cargo.

GENERAL DATA

Weight (lb) _____Net 7,400
    Payload_____on inferior roads 12,000; on highway 13,000
    Gross_____on inferior roads 19,400; on highway 22,400
Weight distribution (lb):
    Empty_____fifth wheel 2,400; axle 5,000
    Loaded:
        On inferior roads_____fifth wheel 7,500; axle 5,000
        On highway _____fifth wheel 8,800; axle 13,600
Tires_____Ply 10; Size 9.00 x 20; Pressure (psi) 65
Shipping dimensions, uncrated_____(cu ft) 1,795; (sq ft) 167
Vehicle dimensions:
    Ground clearance_____(in.) 17
    Loading height, empty_____(in.) 48⅛
    Body inside dimensions (in.)
        Length 240_____Width 88; Height: rear 78, front 68¾
    Cargo space_____(cu ft) 899
    Height to fifth wheel with landing gear down_____(in.) 52¼
Brakes:
    Manufacturer; Bendix-Westinghouse_____Type: air
    Parking brake_____none
Minimum towing vehicle to be used_____truck, tractor, 2½-ton, 4 x 2

ADDITIONAL DATA

SEMITRAILER, VAN, 6-TON, 2-WHEEL

(Highway, Model SKD 2181)

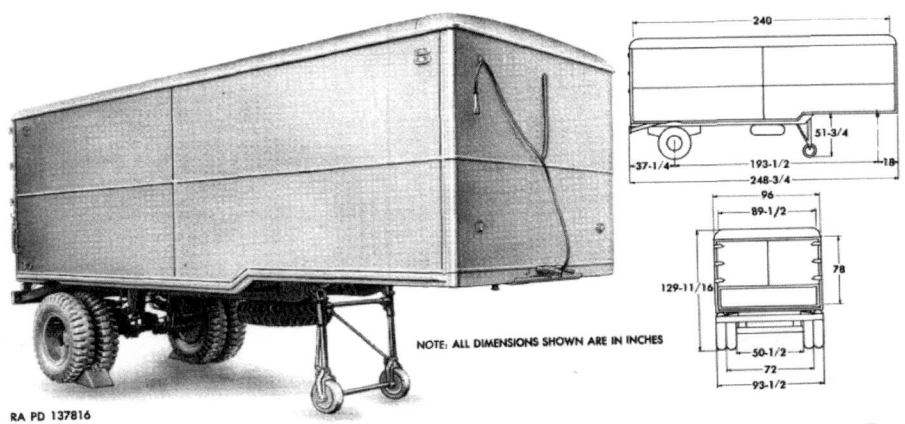

NOTE: ALL DIMENSIONS SHOWN ARE IN INCHES

RA PD 137816

Technical Manual: 10-1169; Supply Catalog: SNL G-594.

Classification: Standard.

Purpose: To transport general cargo.

GENERAL DATA

Weight (lb) Net..7,170
     Payload.....................on inferior roads 12,000; on highway 16,000
     Gross...........................on inferior roads 19,170; on highway 23,170
Weight distribution (lb):
     Empty....................................fifth wheel 2,090; axle 5,080
     Loaded:
          On inferior roads......................fifth wheel 7,706; axle 11,464
          On highway...............................fifth wheel 9,580; axle 13,590
Tires..............................Ply 10; Size 9.00 x 20; Pressure (psi) 65
Shipping dimensions, uncrated..........................(cu ft) 1,797; (sq ft) 166
Vehicle dimensions:
     Ground clearance...(in.) 14¾
     Loading height, empty...(in.) 50⅞
     Height of fifth wheel, landing gear down.........................(in.) 51¾
     Cargo space...(cu ft) 970
Brakes:
     Manufacturer; Bendix-Westinghouse..........................Type; air
     Parking brake...none
Minimum towing vehicle to be used........truck, tractor, 2½-ton, 4 x 2

ADDITIONAL DATA

SEMITRAILER, VAN, 6-TON, 2-WHEEL
(Highway, Model SKD 2215)

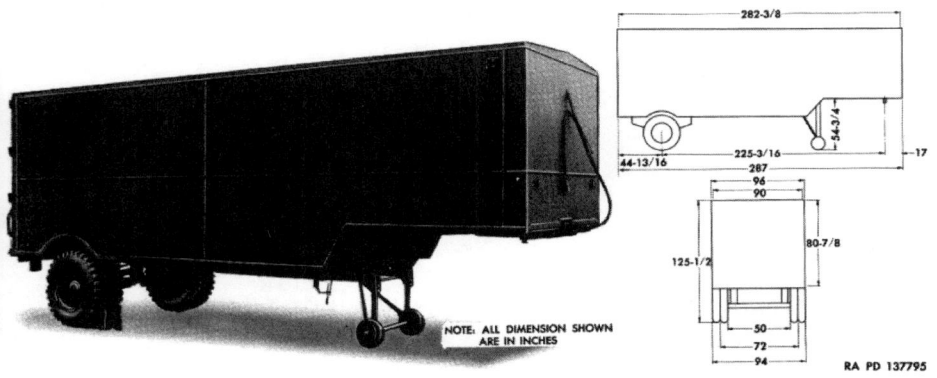

NOTE: ALL DIMENSION SHOWN ARE IN INCHES

RA PD 137795

Technical Manual: 10-1171; **Supply Catalog:** SNL G-525.

Classification: Standard.

Purpose: To transport general cargo.

GENERAL DATA

Weight (lb) Net...8,580
    Payload......................on inferior roads 12,000; on highway 13,500
    Gross.........................on inferior roads 20,580; on highway 22,080
Weight distribution (lb):
    Empty......................................fifth wheel 2,760; axle 5,820
    Loaded:
        On inferior roads......................fifth wheel 7,720; axle 12,860
        On highway..........................fifth wheel 8,350; axle 13,730
Tires...................................Ply 10; Size 9.00 x 20; Pressure (psi) 65
Shipping dimensions, uncrated......................(cu ft) 2,016; (sq ft) 192
Vehicle dimensions:
    Ground clearance...(in.) 14¾
    Loading height, empty..(in.) 40¾
    Height of fifth wheel, landing gear down.......................(in.) 49¼
    Cargo space...(cu ft) 1,190
Brakes:
    Manufacturer; Bendix-Westinghouse.......................Type; air
    Parking brake...none
Minimum towing vehicle to be used........truck, tractor, 2½-ton, 4 x 2

ADDITIONAL DATA

This semitrailer equipped with differential dual wheels.

SEMITRAILER, VAN, 6-TON, 2-WHEEL
(Highway, Model SKD 2270)

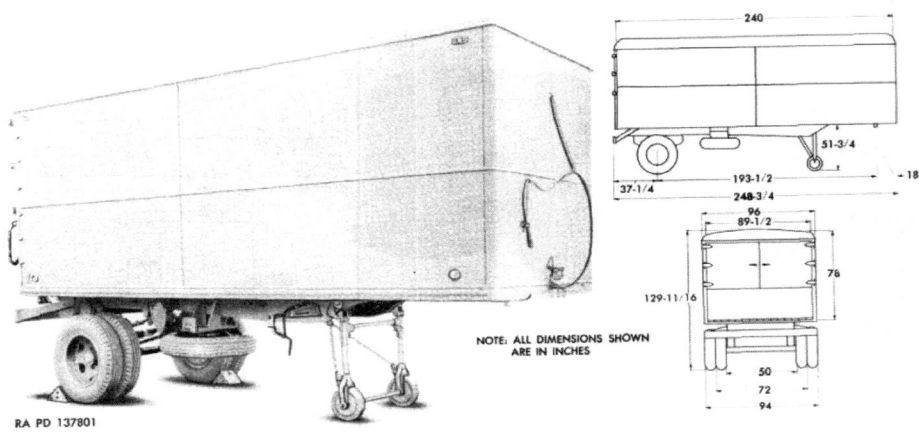

RA PD 137801

NOTE: ALL DIMENSIONS SHOWN
ARE IN INCHES

Technical Manual: 10–1381; **Supply Catalog:** SNL G–594.

Classification: Standard.

Purpose: To transport general cargo.

GENERAL DATA

Weight (lb) Net..7,267
    Payload.......................on inferior roads 12,000; on highway 16,000
    Gross...........................on inferior roads 19,267; on highway 23,267
Weight distribution (lb):
    Empty...fifth wheel 2,067; axle 5,200
    Loaded:
      On inferior roads.......................fifth wheel 7,683; axle 11,584
      On highway............................fifth wheel 9,557; axle 13,710
Tires......................Ply 10; Size 9.00 x 20; Pressure (psi) 65
Shipping dimensions, uncrated.....................(cu ft) 1,797; (sq ft) 166
Vehicle dimensions:
    Ground clearance...(in.) 14¾
    Loading height, empty...(in.) 50⅝
    Height of fifth wheel, landing gear down......................(in.) 51¾
    Cargo space..(cu ft) 970
Brakes:
    Manufacturer; Bendix-Westinghouse..........................Type: air
    Parking brake..none
Minimum towing vehicle to be used...........truck, tractor, 2½-ton, 4 x 2

ADDITIONAL DATA

SEMITRAILER, VAN, 6-TON, 2-WHEEL
(Olson, Model LV 10)

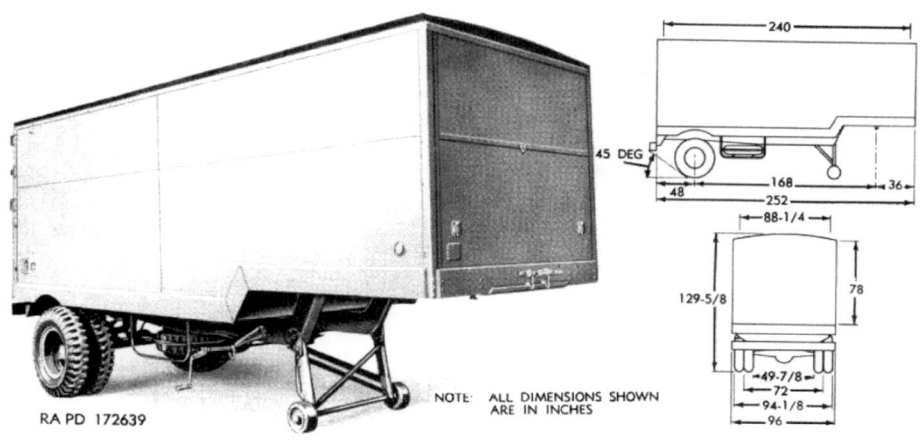

RA PD 172639

NOTE: ALL DIMENSIONS SHOWN ARE IN INCHES

Technical Manual: 9–888; Supply Catalog: SNL G–545.

Classification: Standard.

Purpose: To transport general cargo.

GENERAL DATA

Weight (lb) Net..7,970
    Payload.....................on inferior roads 12,000; on highway 17,830
    Gross.........................on inferior roads 19,970; on highway 25,800
Weight distribution (lb):
    Empty...............................fifth wheel 3,720; axle 4,250
    Loaded:
        On inferior roads....................fifth wheel 9,270; axle 10,700
        On highway..........................fifth wheel 12,000; axle 13,800
Tires.............................Ply 10; Size 9.00 x 20; Pressure (psi) 70
Shipping dimensions, uncrated.....................(cu ft) 1,815; (sq ft) 168
Vehicle dimensions:
    Ground clearance...(in.) 14⅞
    Loading height, empty...(in.) 48½
    Height of fifth wheel, landing gear down.........................(in.) 49½
    Body inside dimensions (in.)........Length 240; Width 88¼; Height 78
    Cargo space...(cu ft) 875
Brakes:
    Manufacturer; Bendix-Westinghouse........................Type: air
    Parking brake, type...none
Minimum towing vehicle to be used.......truck, tractor, 4- to 5-ton, 4 x 4

ADDITIONAL DATA

SEMITRAILER, VAN, 6-TON, 2-WHEEL

(Trailmobile, Model B34H, 1941–42)

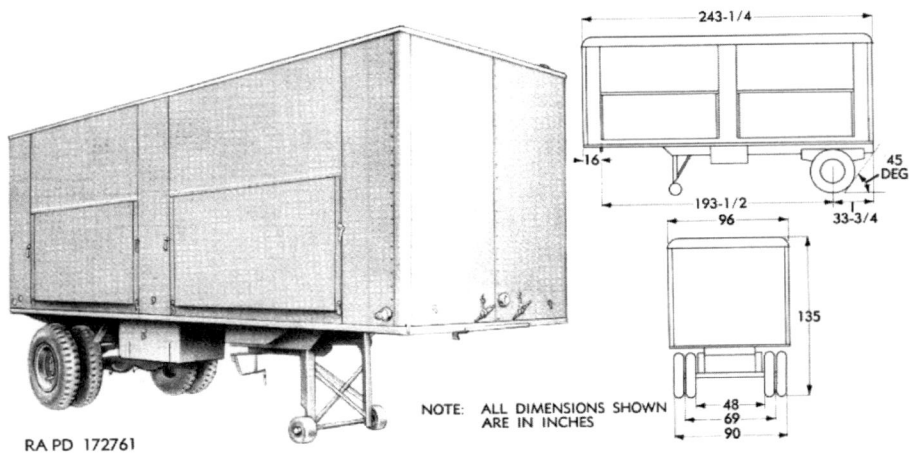

NOTE: ALL DIMENSIONS SHOWN ARE IN INCHES

RA PD 172761

Supply Catalog: SNL G-592.

Classification: Standard.

Purpose: To transport general cargo.

<table>
<tr><td colspan="2">

GENERAL DATA

</td><td>

ADDITIONAL DATA

</td></tr>
</table>

Weight (lb)..Net 7,050
  Payload...................on inferior roads 12,000; on highway 16,800
  Gross.......................on inferior roads 19,050; on highway 23,850
Weight distribution (lb):
  Empty...............................fifth wheel 2,260; axle 4,790
  Loaded:
    On inferior roads....................fifth wheel 7,860; axle 11,190
    On highway.........................fifth wheel 10,050; axle 13,800
Tires.............................Ply 10; Size 9.00 x 20; Pressure (psi) 65
Shipping dimensions, uncrated.......................(cu ft) 1,820; (sq ft) 162
Vehicle dimensions:
  Ground clearance.......................................(in.) 17
  Loading height, empty...................................(in.) 48
  Height of fifth wheel, landing gear down.......................(in.) 45⅜
  Body inside dimensions (in.):
    Length 240............................Width 89¾; Height 78½
  Cargo space.......................................(cu ft) 980
Brakes:
  Manufacturer; Bendix-Westinghouse.........................Type; air
  Parking brake, type..................................wheel chocks
Minimum towing vehicle to be used.........Truck, tractor 2½-ton, 4 x 2

SEMITRAILER, VAN, 6-TON, 2-WHEEL

(Utility, Model G–SW4)

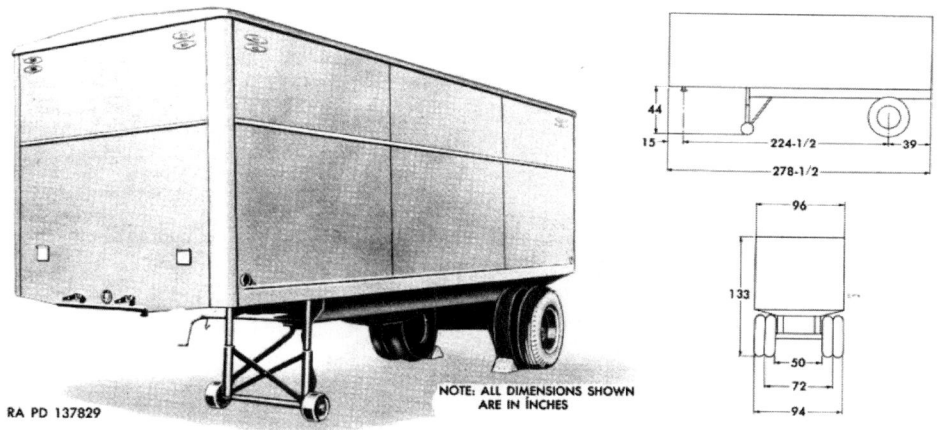

RA PD 137829

NOTE: ALL DIMENSIONS SHOWN
ARE IN INCHES

Technical Manual: 9–888; Supply Catalog: SNL G–588.

Classification: Standard.

Purpose: To transport general cargo.

<table>
<tr><td colspan="2">

GENERAL DATA

Weight (lb)..Net 7,550
   Payload...................on inferior roads 12,450; on highway 18,000
   Gross.........................on inferior roads 20,000; on highway 25,550
Weight distribution (lb):
   Empty..................................fifth wheel 2,800; axle 4,750
   Loaded:
      On inferior roads.....................fifth wheel 9,025; axle 10,975
      On highway...........................fifth wheel 11,800; axle 13,750
Tires..............................Ply 10; Size 9.00 x 20; Pressure (psi) 65
Shipping dimensions, uncrated.........................(cu ft) 2,060; (sq ft) 186
Vehicle dimensions:
   Ground clearance...................................(in.) 15
   Loading height, empty..............................(in.) 51½
   Body inside dimensions (in.):
      Length 270....................Width 89¾; Height 78
   Cargo space...................................(cu ft) 1,096
   Height of fifth wheel, landing gear down.........................(in.) 44
Brakes:
   Manufacturer; Timken...............................Type; air
   Parking brake, type..none
Towing vehicle to be used.................truck, tractor, 4- to 5-ton, 4 x 4

</td><td>

ADDITIONAL DATA

</td></tr>
</table>

SEMITRAILER, VAN, 7-TON, 4-WHEEL, M26

(Fruehauf, w/DOLLY, 7-ton, 2-wheel, trailer converter, Model C2); (Signal Corps Model V9/MPC–1)

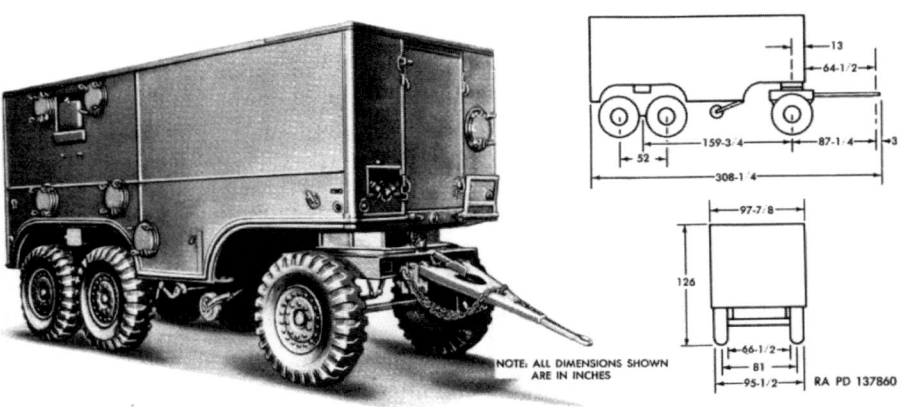

NOTE: ALL DIMENSIONS SHOWN ARE IN INCHES

RA PD 137860

Technical Manual: 9-884; Supply Catalog: SNL G-713.

Classification: Standard.

Purpose: To transport gun computer M8N and M8P.

GENERAL DATA

Weight (lb):
  As semitrailer.................Net 13,030; Payload 14,000; Gross 27,030
  W/dolly.....................Net 15,500; Payload 14,000; Gross 29,500
Weight distribution (lb):
  As semitrailer.................fifth wheel 7,200; bogie axle (each) 9,915
  W/dolly.....................dolly axle 9,670; bogie axle (each) 9,915
Tires...........................Ply 12; Size 14.00 x 20; Pressure (psi) 90
Shipping dimensions, uncrated......................(cu ft) 2,210 ;(sq ft) 210
Vehicle dimensions:
  Ground clearance..(in.) 14
  Loading height..(in.) 35
  Pintle height...(in.) 24
  Height of fifth wheel, landing gear down......................(in.) $48\frac{5}{8}$
  Body inside dimensions (in.):
    Length $227\frac{7}{8}$..........................Width $90\frac{1}{2}$; Height $84\frac{3}{4}$
  Cargo space...(cu ft) 1,010
Brakes:
  Manufacturer; Fruehauf..Type; air
  Parking brake...none
Minimum towing vehicles to be used
    truck, tractor, 4- to 5-ton, 4 x 4; truck, 4-ton, 6 x 6

ADDITIONAL DATA

Van body watertight for amphibious operations.
Weight of dolly 2,470 lb.

SEMITRAILER, STAKE AND PLATFORM, 10-TON, 2-WHEEL

(A. J. Miller, American Body, Carter, Coleman, Dorsey, Fruehauf, Highway, Keystone, Kreiger Steel, Omaha Std Body, Oneida, Pike, Queen City Trailer, Springfield Trailer, Strick, Timpte, Trailer Co of America, Utility, Winter-Weiss, Models 1025 and SKD 2361)

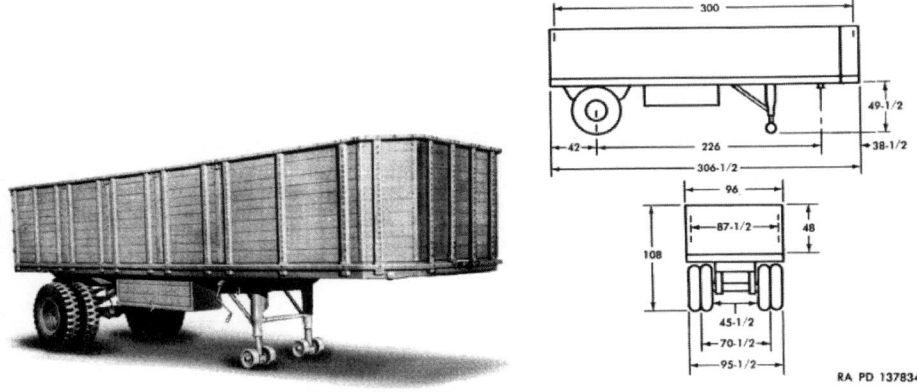

RA PD 137834

Technical Manual: 9-892; Supply Catalog: SNL G-676.

Vehicle illustrated: Highway Trailer Co.
Classification: Standard.

Purpose: Used by Transportation Corps and Ordnance to transport general cargo.

GENERAL DATA

Weight (lb): Net..9,430
    Payload.......................on inferior roads 20,000; on highway 22,000
    Gross.........................on inferior roads 29,430; on highway 31,430
Weight distribution (lb):
    Empty...............................fifth wheel 3,390; axle 6,040
    Loaded:
        On inferior roads..................fifth wheel 12,520; axle 16,910
        On highway........................fifth wheel 13,450; axle 17,980
Tires......................Ply 14; Size 11.00 x 20; Pressure (psi) 80
Shipping dimensions, uncrated......................(cu ft) 1,785; (sq ft) 204
Vehicle dimensions:
    Ground clearance..(in.) 16
    Loading height..(in.) 53½
    Height of fifth wheel, landing gear down.......................(in.) 52¾
    Cargo space...(cu ft) 730
Brakes:
    Manufacturer; Timken..Type; air
    Parking brakes...none
Minimum towing vehicle to be used..........truck, tractor, 5-ton, 4 x 2

ADDITIONAL DATA

SEMITRAILER, VAN, 11-TON, 2-WHEEL

(Black Diamond, Model SC728 (28 ft) 1944; Fruehauf, Model FF22BL (28 ft); Kentucky, Model C; Omaha Standard Body, Model F16 (28 ft) 1944; Reliance, Model STV1128; Trailer Co. of America, Model B34H15 (28 ft) 1944)

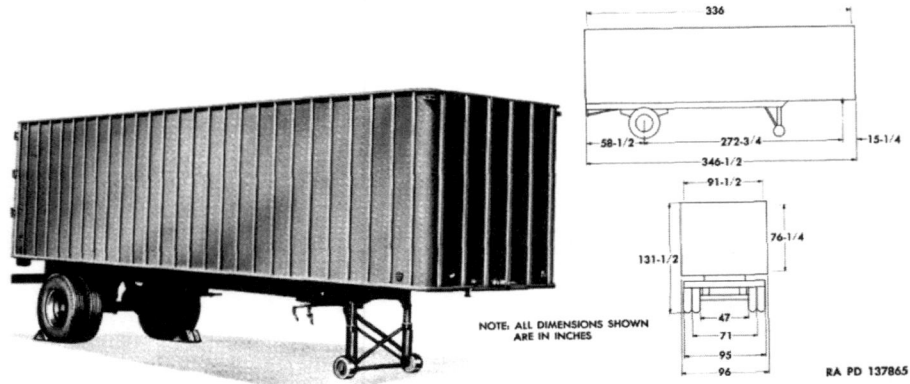

NOTE: ALL DIMENSIONS SHOWN ARE IN INCHES

RA PD 137865

Technical Manuals: 9-894, 9-896; Supply Catalogs: Black Diamond: SNL G-682; Fruehauf: SNL G-723; Kentucky: SNL G-706; Omaha Standard Body: SNL G-677; Reliance: SNL-G712; Trailer Co. of America: SNL G-681.

Vehicle illustrated: Black Diamond.　　　　　**Purpose:** To transport general cargo.
Classification: Standard.

GENERAL DATA	ADDITIONAL DATA

GENERAL DATA

Weight (lb):
　　Net..8,830
　　Payload..............................on highway 22,000; Gross 30,830
Weight distribution (lb):
　　Empty............................fifth wheel 2,740; axle 6,090
　　Loaded; on highway....................fifth wheel 13,070; axle 17,760
Tires....................Ply 12; Size 10.00 x 20; Pressure (psi) 70
Shipping dimensions, uncrated......................(cu ft) 2,532; (sq ft) 252
Vehicle dimensions:
　　Ground clearance....................................(in.) 16½
　　Loading height, empty..............................(in.) 51¾
　　Height of fifth wheel, landing gear down...............(in.) 49¾
　　Cargo space...(cu ft) 1,355
Brakes:
　　Manufacturer; Bendix-Westinghouse.......................Type; air
　　Parking brake...none
Minimum towing vehicle to be used........truck, tractor, 4- to 5-ton, 4 x 4

SEMITRAILER, TRANSPORTER, 40-TON, 8-WHEEL, M—15

(Used w/TRUCK, 12-ton, 6 x 6, tractor, M26 or M26A1 as component of TRUCK-TRAILER, 40-ton, tank recovery, M25)

RA PD 137723

Technical Manuals: 9-767, 9-1767E; Supply Catalog: SNL G-160.

Classification: Limited Standard.

Purpose: To recover and transport damaged tanks and matériel up to 80,000 pounds.

GENERAL DATA

Weight (lb)..........................Net 42,370; Payload 80,000; Gross 122,370
Weight distribution (lb):
    Empty: fifth wheel 14,170..........................8 rear wheels 28,200
    Loaded: fifth wheel 52,670..........................8 rear wheels 69,700
Tires.....................................Ply 20; Size 14.00 x 24; Pressure (psi) 90
Shipping dimensions, uncrated.......................(cu ft) 3,490; (sq ft) 398
Vehicle dimensions:
    Ground clearance..(in.) 28
    Loading height..(in.) 40½
    Height of fifth wheel, landing gear down........................(in.) 67¾
Brakes:
    Manufacturer; Fruehauf......................................Type; air
    Parking brake..none
Towing vehicle to be used..................truck, tractor, M26 or M26A1

ADDITIONAL DATA

Rear wheels retractable to reduce vehicle width from 150 to 124 in. for shipment.

SEMITRAILER, TRANSPORTER, 45-TON, 8-WHEEL, M15A1
(Used w/TRUCK, 12-ton, 6 x 6, tractor, M26 or M26A1 as component of TRUCK-TRAILER, 40-ton, tank recovery, M25)

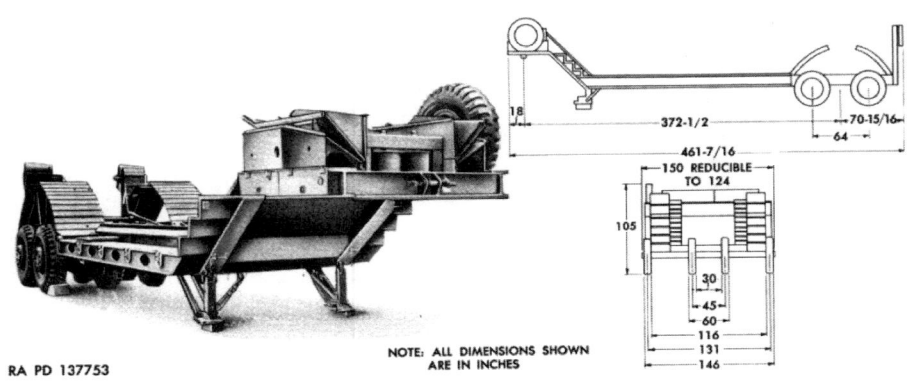

RA PD 137753

NOTE: ALL DIMENSIONS SHOWN
ARE IN INCHES

Technical Manuals: 9–767, 9–1767E; Supply Catalog: SNL G–160.

Classification: Substitute Standard.

Purpose: To recover and transport damaged tanks and matériel up to 90,000 pounds.

GENERAL DATA

Weight (lb)......................Net 42,370; Payload 90,000; Gross 132,370
Weight distribution (lb):
    Empty.....................fifth wheel 14,170; 8 rear wheels 28,200
    Loaded....................fifth wheel 57,500; 8 rear wheels 74,870
Tires........................Ply 20; Size 14.00 x 24; Pressure (psi) 90
Shipping dimensions, uncrated....................(cu ft) 3,490; (sq ft) 398
Vehicle dimensions:
    Ground clearance.....................................(in.) 28
    Loading height ....(in.) 40½
    Height of fifth wheel, landing gear down................(in.) 67¾
Brakes:
    Manufacturer; Fruehauf..............................Type; air
    Parking brake.......................................none
Towing vehicle to be used...................truck, tractor, M26 or M26A1

ADDITIONAL DATA

Rear wheels retractable to reduce width from 150 to 124 in. for shipment.

SLED, CARGO, 1-TON, M1

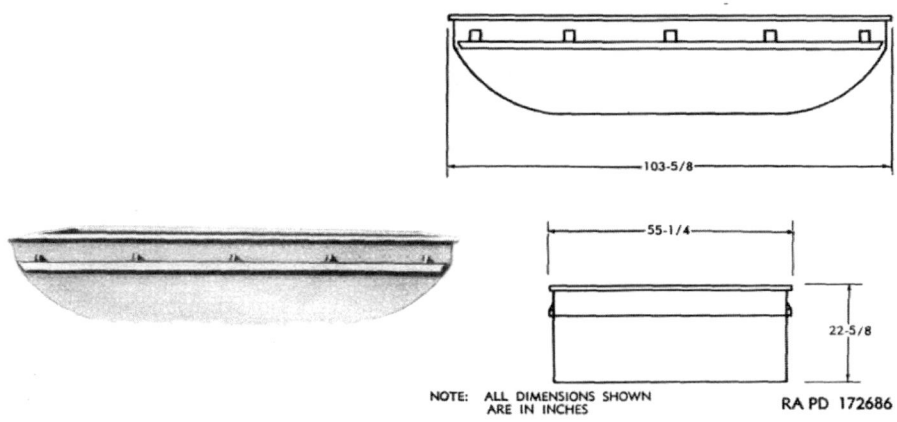

103-5/8

55-1/4

22-5/8

NOTE: ALL DIMENSIONS SHOWN
ARE IN INCHES

RA PD 172686

Supply Catalog: SNL G-721.

Classification: Substitute Standard.

Purpose: To transport cargo over snow and ice.

GENERAL DATA

Weight (lb)..........................Net 500; Payload 2,000; Gross 2,500
Shipping dimensions, uncrated..........................(cu ft) 75; (sq ft) 40
Vehicle dimensions:
  Loading height, empty..........................(in.) 22⅝
  Body inside dimensions (in.):
    Length 101..........................Width 53; Height 20
  Cargo space..........................(cu ft) 62
Towing vehicle to be used..Any vehicle equipped with a pintle and trac-
              tion devices.

ADDITIONAL DATA

SLED, CARGO, 1-TON, M1A1

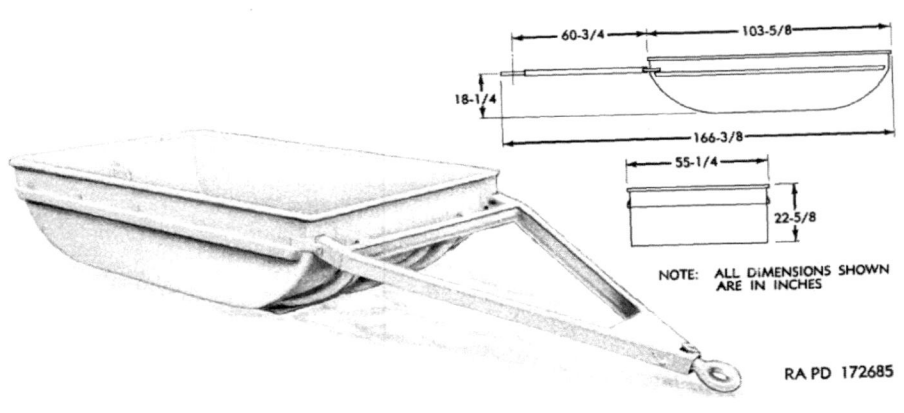

NOTE: ALL DIMENSIONS SHOWN ARE IN INCHES

RA PD 172685

Supply Catalog: SNL G-737.

Classification: Standard.

Purpose: To transport cargo over snow and ice.

GENERAL DATA

Weight (lb)............................Net 560; Payload 2,000; Gross 2,560
Shipping dimensions, uncrated (w/drawbar removed)...(cu ft) 75; (sq ft) 40
Vehicle dimensions:
    Loading height, empty.......................................(in.) 22⅝
    Body inside dimensions (in.):
        Length 10!......................................Width 53; Height 20
    Cargo space...(cu ft) 62
Towing vehicle to be used..Any vehicle equipped with a pintle and traction devices.

ADDITIONAL DATA

SLED, CARGO, 1-TON, M14

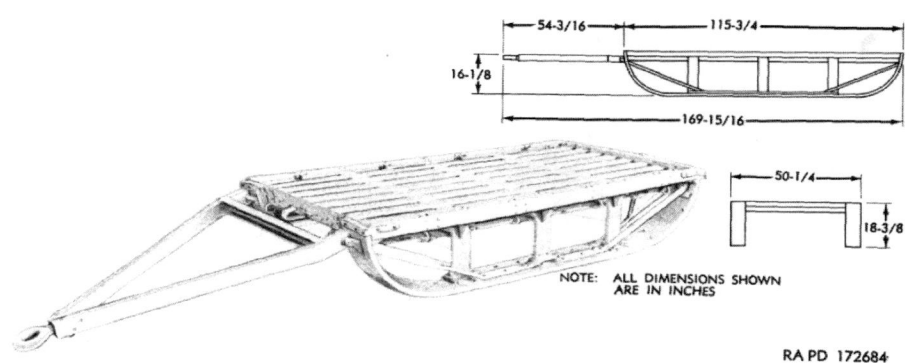

NOTE: ALL DIMENSIONS SHOWN ARE IN INCHES

RA PD 172684

Supply Catalog: SNL G-738.

Classification: Substitute Standard.

Purpose: To transport cargo over snow and ice.

GENERAL DATA

Weight (lb)..............................Net 610; Payload 2,000; Gross 2,610
Shipping dimensions, uncrated (w/drawbar removed).(cu ft) 62; (sq ft) 41
Vehicle dimensions:
    Loading height, empty.............................(in.) 18⅝
    Cargo space...(cu ft) none
Towing vehicle to be used.....................Any vehicle equipped with
  a pintle and traction devices.

ADDITIONAL DATA

SLED, CARGO, 1-TON, M14A1

NOTE: ALL DIMENSIONS SHOWN ARE IN INCHES

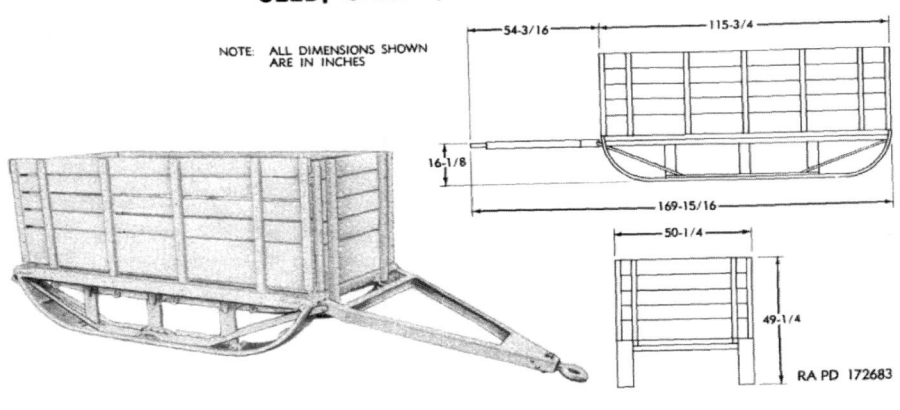

RA PD 172683

Supply Catalog: SNL G-739.

Classification: Standard.

Purpose: To transport cargo over snow and ice.

GENERAL DATA

Weight (lb)...............................Net 600; Payload 2,000; Gross 2,610
Shipping dimensions, uncrated (w/draw bar removed). (cu ft) 169; (sq ft) 41
Vehicle dimensions:
  Loading height, empty..(in.) 18¾
  Body inside dimensions (in.):
    Length 110................................Width 48; Height 20¼
  Cargo space...(cu ft) 61
Towing vehicle to be used.................Any vehicle equipped with
  a pintle and traction devices.

ADDITIONAL DATA

STATION WAGON, 7-PASSENGER, 4 x 2

(Willys, Models 4–63, 1948–49; 4–73–SW, 1950)

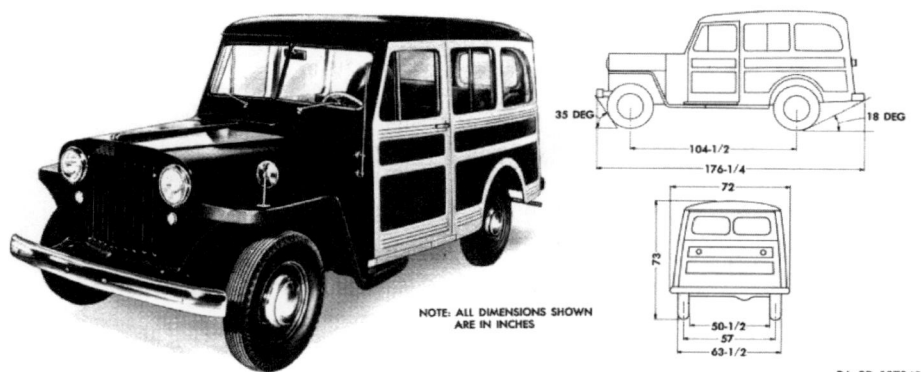

NOTE: ALL DIMENSIONS SHOWN
ARE IN INCHES

35 DEG
18 DEG
104-1/2
176-1/4
72
73
50-1/2
57
63-1/2

RA PD 137845

Vehicle illustrated: Model 4–73–SW, 1950.
Classification: Nonclassified.

Purpose: To transport personnel.

GENERAL DATA

Crew................................1; Passengers (including crew) 7
Weight (lb)....................Net 2,943; Payload 1,057; Gross 4,000
Rear-axle gear ratio.................................5.38:1
Axle load (lb):
   Empty.............................front 1,293; rear 1,650
   Loaded.............................front 1,600; rear 2,600
Tires:
   Ply 4; Size 6.70 x 15; Pressure....................(psi) front 20; rear 24
   Tread, center-to-center, front......................(in.) 55¼
Shipping dimensions, uncrated..............(cu ft) 535; (sq ft) 88
Ground clearance......................................(in.) 8¾
Electrical system...................................(volts) 6
   No. of batteries...1
   Type of ground...................................negative
Fuel octane rating......................................70
Capacities:
   Fuel...(gal) 15
   Cooling system (qt)................w/o heater 11; w/heater 12
   Crankcase, refill...................................(qt) 4
   Transmission.......................................(qt) ¾
   Rear axle..(qt) 1
Brakes:
   Manufacturer; Bendix......................Type; hydraulic
   Parking brake, type...........................rear-wheel
Transmission forward speeds............................3
   Gear ratio...........................High 1:1; Low 2.6:1

PERFORMANCE

Computed grade ability in lowest gear, loaded.................(percent) 22
Turning radius...(ft) 17½
Fording depth..(in.) 18
Fuel consumption, loaded......................................(mpg) 20
Cruising range, loaded..(mi) 300
Allowable speed, recommended.................................(mph) 65

ENGINE

Manufacturer: Willys.......................................Model 473
Type...................F-head, 4-cycle; No. of cylinders (in line) 4
Displacement...(cu in.) 134.2
Bore...(in.) 3⅛
Stroke...(in.) 4⅜
Compression ratio...7.4:1
Governed speed..not governed
Brake horsepower (max w/std accessories)................64 at (rpm) 4,000
Torque (max).........................114 lb-ft at (rpm) 2,000

ADDITIONAL DATA

Rear axle, type..hypoid, semifloating
Transmission, type...synchromesh

STATION WAGON, 8-PASSENGER, 4 x 2

(Chevrolet, Model 2109, 1949)

NOTE: ALL DIMENSIONS SHOWN
ARE IN INCHES

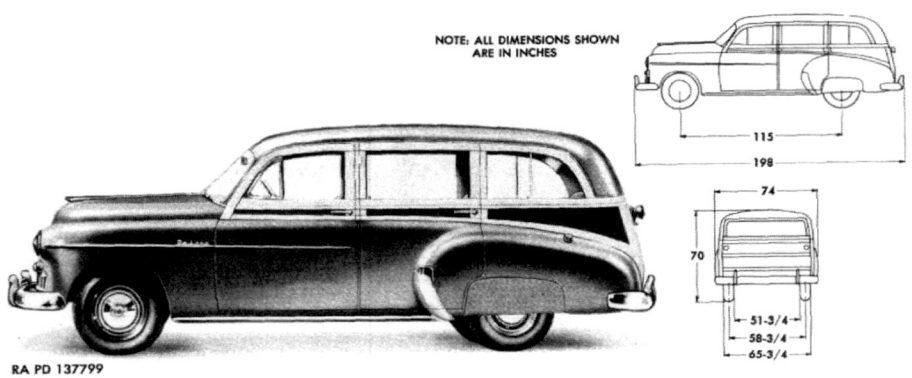

RA PD 137799

Classification: Nonclassified.

Purpose: To transport personnel.

GENERAL DATA

Crew..1; Passengers (including crew) 8
Weight (lb)....................Net 3,615; Payload 1,280; Gross 4,895
Rear-axle gear ratio...4. 11:1
Axle load (lb):
    Empty......................................front 1,725; rear 1,890
    Loaded.....................................front 1,968; rear 2,927
Tires:
    Ply 6...................Size 6.70 x 15; Pressure (psi) front 24; rear 30
    Tread, center-to-center, front...........................(in.) 57
Shipping dimensions, uncrated....................(cu ft) 605; (sq ft) 102
Ground clearance...(in.) 8½
Electrical system..(volts) 6
    No. of batteries..1
    Type of ground...negative
Fuel octane rating..72
Capacities:
    Fuel...(gal) 16
    Cooling system (qt)..................w/heater 16; w/o heater 15
    Crankcase, refill..(qt) 5
    Transmission...(qt) 3¼
    Rear axle...(qt) 1¾
Brakes:
    Manufacturer; Chevrolet........................Type; hydraulic
    Parking brake, type....................................rear-wheel
Transmission forward speeds.....................................3
    Gear ratio.............................High 1:1; Low 2.94:1

PERFORMANCE

Computed grade ability in lowest gear, loaded................(percent) 30
Turning radius (ft).............................right 19¼; left 19¾
Fording depth..(in.) 15
Fuel consumption, loaded....................................(mpg) 14
Cruising range, recommended................................(mi) 224
Allowable speed, recommended..............................(mph) 65

ENGINE

Manufacturer: Chevrolet......................Model GAA or GAM 1001 up
Type....................Valve-in-head, 4-cycle; No. of cylinders (in line) 6
Displacement..(cu in.) 216. 5
Bore...(in.) 3½
Stroke..(in.) 3¾
Compression ratio...6. 6:1
Governed speed..not governed
Brake horsepower (max w/std accessories).............83 at (rpm) 3,200
Torque (max)...........................168 lb-ft at (rpm) 1,100

ADDITIONAL DATA

Rear axle, type.............................hypoid, semifloating
Transmission, type....................................synchromesh

STATION WAGON, 8-PASSENGER, 4 x 2

(Chevrolet, Model 2119)

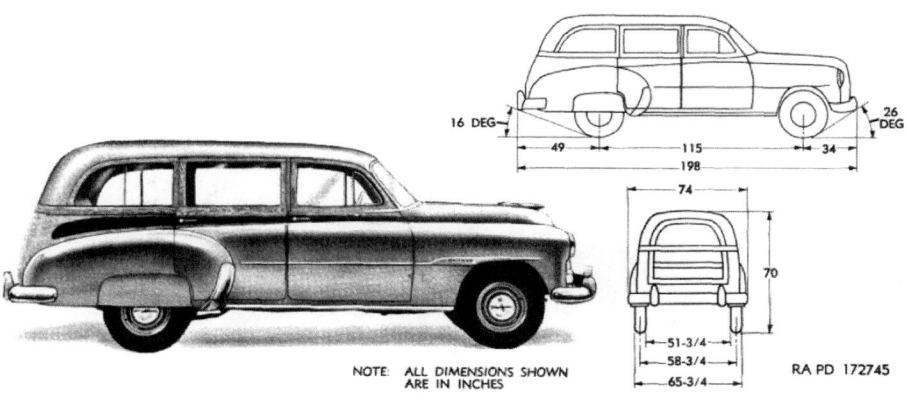

16 DEG · 49 · 115 · 198 · 34 · 26 DEG

74 · 70 · 51-3/4 · 58-3/4 · 65-3/4

NOTE: ALL DIMENSIONS SHOWN ARE IN INCHES

RA PD 172745

Classification: Standard.

Purpose: To transport personnel.

GENERAL DATA

Crew..1; No. Passengers (including crew) 8
Weight (lb)..Net 3,580
    Payload..1,400
    Gross..4,980
Rear-axle gear ratio..4.11:1
Axle load (lb):
    Empty..front 1,715; rear 1,865
    Loaded..front 1,905; rear 3,075
Tires:
    Ply 6; Size 6.70 x 15; Pressure..(psi) front 26; rear 30
    Tread, center-to-center, front..(in.) 56¾₆
Shipping dimensions, uncrated..(cu ft) 593; (sq ft) 102
Ground clearance..(in.) 8
Electrical system..(volts) 6
    No. of batteries..1
    Type of ground..negative
Fuel octane rating..72
Capacities:
    Fuel..(gal) 16
    Cooling system (qt)..w/o heater 15; w/heater 16
    Crankcase, refill..(qt) 5
    Transmission..(qt) ¾
    Rear axle..(qt) 1¾
Brakes:
    Manufacturer; Chevrolet..Type; hydraulic
    Parking brake, type..rear-wheel
Transmission forward speeds..3
    Gear ratio..High 1:1; Low 2.94:1

PERFORMANCE

Computed grade ability in lowest gear, loaded..(percent) 30
Turning radius (ft)..Right 18½; Left 19
Fording depth..(in.) 13
Fuel consumption, loaded..(mpg) 12
Cruising range, loaded..(mi) 192
Allowable speed, recommended..(mph) 65

ENGINE

Manufacturer: Chevrolet..Model HA or JA
Type..4-cycle, valve-in-head; No. of cylinders (in line) 6
Displacement..(cu in.) 216.5
Bore..(in.) 3½
Stroke..(in.) 3¾
Compression ratio..6.6:1
Governed speed..not governed
Brake horsepower (max w/std accessories)..85 at (rpm) 3,300
Torque (max w/std accessories)..170 lb-ft at (rpm) 1,000–2,000

ADDITIONAL DATA

Rear axle, type..semifloating hypoid
Transmission, type..synchromesh

STATION WAGON, 8-PASSENGER, 4 x 2

(Plymouth, Model P15S, 1948)

NOTE: ALL DIMENSIONS SHOWN
ARE IN INCHES

RA PD 137797

Classification: Standard.

Purpose: To transport personnel.

GENERAL DATA

Crew..1; Passengers (including crew) 8
Weight (lb)............................Net 3,525; Payload 1,200; Gross 4,725
Rear-axle gear ratio...4.1:1
Axle load (lb):
    Empty..front 1,735; rear 1,790
    Loaded.......................................front 2,076; rear 2,649
Tires:
    Ply 4............................Size 6.00 x 16; Pressure (psi) 28
    Tread, center-to-center, front...........................(in.) 57
Shipping dimensions, uncrated...................(cu ft) 615; (sq ft) 105
Ground clearance...(in.) 8¾
Electrical system...(volts) 6
    No. of batteries...1
    Type of ground..positive
Fuel octane rating..72
Capacities:
    Fuel..(gal) 17
    Cooling system (qt)....................w/heater 16; w/o heater 15
    Crankcase, refill...(qt) 5
    Transmission...(qt) 1¾
    Rear axle...(qt) 1¾
Brakes:
    Manufacturer; Chrysler.........................Type; hydraulic
    Parking brake, type.......................................transmission
Transmission forward speeds...3
    Gear ratio.........................High 1:1; Low 2.57:1

PERFORMANCE

Computed grade ability in lowest gear, loaded..................(percent) 32
Turning radius..(ft) 39

ENGINE

Manufacturer: Chrysler..........................Model Plymouth P15
Type...................L-head, 4-cycle; No. of cylinders (in line) 6
Displacement...................................(cu in.) 217.8
Bore..(in.) 3¼
Stroke..(in.) 4¾
Compression ratio.................................6.6:1
Governed speed.............................not governed
Brake horsepower (max w/std accessories)...............95 at (rpm) 3,600
Torque (max).............................176 lb-ft at (rpm) 1,200

ADDITIONAL DATA

Rear axle, type.............................hyphoid, semi-floating
Transmission, type...synchromesh

TANK, LIGHT, M24

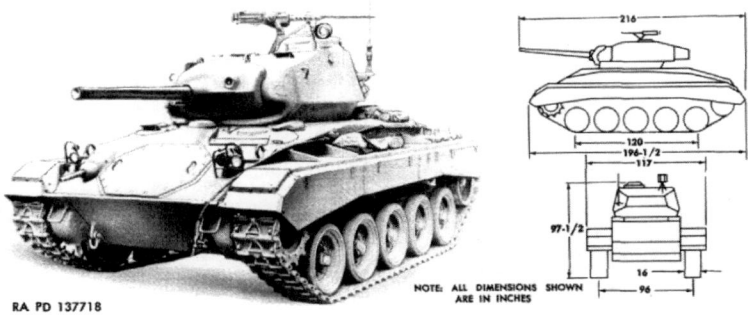

NOTE: ALL DIMENSIONS SHOWN ARE IN INCHES

RA PD 137718

Technical Manuals: 9–729, 9–1727K, 9–1729A, 9–1729B, 9–1729C. 9–1731D, 9–1825A, 9–1826A, 9–1828A, 9–1829A; **Supply Catalog:** SNL G–200.

Classification: Standard.

Armament: 1 gun, 75-mm, M6, turret mounted; 2 guns, machine, cal. .30, Browning, M1919A4 (flexible); 1 mounted coaxially with main armament, 1 ball mounted at right front of hull; 1 gun, machine, cal. .50, Browning, M2, heavy barrel (flexible) pintle mounted on top of turret.

Ammunition: 48 rounds, 75-mm; 420 rounds, cal. .50; 180 rounds cal. .45 for sub-machine-gun; 4,125 rounds cal. .30; 90 rounds cal. .30, carbine; 8 hand grenades; 12 ground signals.

GENERAL DATA

Crew..5
Weight, fighting..(lb) 40,500
Shipping dimensions, uncrated..........(cu ft) 1,310; (sq ft) 161
Ground pressure..(psi) 11
Ground clearance..(in.) 18
Pintle height, loaded..(in.) 20
Electrical system..(volts) 24
    No. of batteries..(6-volt) 4
    Type of ground..negative
Fuel octane rating..80
Capacities:
    Fuel..(gal) 110
    Cooling system......................................(each) (qt) 40
    Crankcase, refill..................................(each) (qt) 9
    Transmission (hydramatic)..................(each) (qt) 15
    Differential..(qt) 20
    Transfer..(qt) 4½
    Final drive......................................(each) (qt) 2
Brakes......................................mechanical, controlled-differential
    Parking brake, type....Depressor knobs for locking steering brakes
Transmission forward speeds..4
    Gear ratio..........High 1:1; Third 1.55 :1; Low 3.92 :1
Transfer speeds..................................Forward 2; Reverse 1
    Gear ratio..................High 1.03 :1; Low 2.34 :1; Reverse 2.44 :1
Differential-drive gear ratio..2.62 :1
Final-drive gear ratio..2.94 :1
Hull construction..................welded homogeneous armor plate

Purpose: To provide mobile fire power and crew protection in offensive combat.

Fire Control and Vision Devices: Periscope, M10P or periscope M4A1 w/telescope, M77G or M38A2 (gunner's); periscope, M13 or M13B1 or M6 or periscope, M15 or M15A1 (vision); quadrant, elevation, M9; quadrant, gunner's M1; telescope, M83F or M71K (sight); indicator, azimuth, M19.

Communications: (SCR–508 or SCR–528 or SCR–608 or SCR–628 or RC–99) and (RC–298) and (AN/VRC–3); or (SCR–508 or SCR–528 or AN/GRC–3, –4, –5, –6, –7, or –8).

PERFORMANCE

Maximum grade ability......................................(percent) 60
Turning radius..(ft) 23
Fording depth..(in.) 40
Maximum width of ditch vehicle can cross......................(in.) 96
Maximum vertical obstacle vehicle can climb......................(in.) 36
Fuel consumption (average conditions)......................(mpg) ⅞
Cruising range (average conditions)......................(mi) 100
Allowable speed, recommended..........................(mph) 34
Maximum allowable towed load, gross......................(lb) 10000

ENGINE

Manufacturer; Cadillac......................No. used 2; Model 44T24
Type..................4-cycle, L-head; No. of cylinders (90-deg V) 8
Displacement..(cu in.) 349
Bore..(in.) 3¼
Stroke..(in.) 4¼
Compression ratio..7.06 :1
Brake horsepower (max w/std accessories)..............110 at (rpm) 3,400
Torque (max w/std accessories)..................240 lb-ft at (rpm) 1,200
Type of ignition..distributor

ADDITIONAL DATA

Data given for vehicle equipped with track, steel, T72. Track, steel, T72E1 is interchangeable. Track, rubber, T85E1 applicable with changed sprocket.
Equipped with elevation stabilizer.
Manual and power turret-traversing mechanism.

TANK, MEDIUM, M4A1, 75-MM GUN

NOTE: ALL DIMENSIONS SHOWN ARE IN INCHES

RA PD 137776

Technical Manuals: 9-731A, 9-731AA, 9-1725, 9-1731G, 9-1731K, 9-1750A, 9-1750B, 9-1750C, 9-1750D, 9-1750K, 9-1825B, 9-1826B, 9-1828A, 9-1829A; Supply Catalog: SNL G-104.

Classification: Limited Standard.

Armament: 1 gun, 75-mm, M3, turret mounted; 2 guns, machine, cal. .30, Browning, M1919A4 (flexible), 1 mounted coaxially with main armament, 1 ball mounted at right front of hull; 1 gun, machine, cal. .50, Browning, M2, heavy barrel (flexible), mounted on revolving hatch on top of turret.

Ammunition: 90 rounds, 75-mm; 300 rounds, cal. .50; 4,750 rounds, cal. .30; 900 rounds, cal. .45 for submachine gun; 12 hand grenades; 12 2-inch smoke bombs.

Communications: (SCR-508 or SCR-608 or SCR-528 or AN/GRC-3, -4, -5, -6, -7, or -8) and (RC-298); or (SCR-508 or SCR-528) and (RC-298) and (AN/VRC-3); or (AN/VRC-3) and (RC-99) and (RC-298).

GENERAL DATA

Crew..5
Weight, fighting...(lb) 67,700
Shipping dimensions, uncrated.........(cu ft) 1,605; (sq ft) 175
Ground pressure..(psi) 13.9
Ground clearance..(in.) 17¼
Pintle height, loaded....................................(in.) 21¼
Electrical system...(volts) 24
    No. of batteries.....................................(12-volt) 2
    Type of ground......................................negative
Fuel octane rating..80
Capacities:
    Fuel...(gal) 175
    Auxiliary-engine fuel tank............................(gal) 5
    Engine oil tank..(qt) 36
    Transmission, differential, and final drives (qt):
        Three-piece, round-nose..........................152
        One-piece, sharp-nose............................164
Brakes........................mechanical, controlled-differential
    Parking brake, type:
        Early models.......................rear of transmission
        Late models.......pedal for locking steering brakes
Transmission forward speeds...................................5
    Gear ratio..............High 0.73:1; Fourth 1:1; Low 7.56:1
Differential-drive gear ratio..........................3.53:1
Final-drive gear ratio..................................2.84:1
Hull construction.........welded homogeneous cast and plate armor
Armor, turret............................cast homogeneous

Purpose: To provide mobile fire power and crew protection for offensive combat.

Fire Control and Vision Devices: Periscope, M10C or periscope, M4A1 w/telescope, M38A2 (gunner's); periscope, M13 or M13B1 or M6 (vision); quadrant, elevation, M9; quadrant, gunner's, M1; telescope, M83F or M71K (sight); indicator, azimuth, M19.

PERFORMANCE

Maximum grade ability..................................(percent) 60
Turning radius...(ft) 31
Fording depth..(in.) 36
Maximum width of ditch vehicle can cross..............(in.) 90
Maximum vertical obstacle vehicle can climb............(in.) 24
Fuel consumption (average conditions)..................(mpg) 0.6
Cruising range (average conditions)...................(mi) 100
Allowable speed, governed..............................(mph) 24
Maximum allowable towed load, gross................(lb) 10,000

ENGINE

Manufacturer: Continental...........................Model R975-C1
Type..........................4-cycle, radial, air-cooled; No. of cylinders 9
Displacement...(cu in.) 973
Bore..(in.) 5
Stroke...(in.) 5½
Compression ratio...5.7:1
Governed speed..(rpm) 2,400
Brake horsepower (max w/std accessories)..........350 at (rpm) 2,400
Torque (max w/std accessories)............840 lb-ft at (rpm) 1,800
Type of ignition..magneto

ADDITIONAL DATA

Data given for vehicle equipped with track, rubber, T48. Track, rubber, T51; tracks, steel, T49 and T54E1; and track, rubber-backed-steel, T74 are interchangeable.

Data given for vehicle equipped with vertical volute spring suspension.

Auxiliary generator Homelite Model HRUH-28.

Manual and power turret-traversing mechanism.

One-piece or three-piece differential housing used on this vehicle.

Continental engine R975-C4 is interchangeable. Changes in data are as follows:

Brake horsepower (max w/std accessories)..............400 at (rpm) 2,400
Torque (max w/std accessories)....................940 lb-ft at (rpm) 1,700

TANK, MEDIUM, M4A3, 75-MM GUN

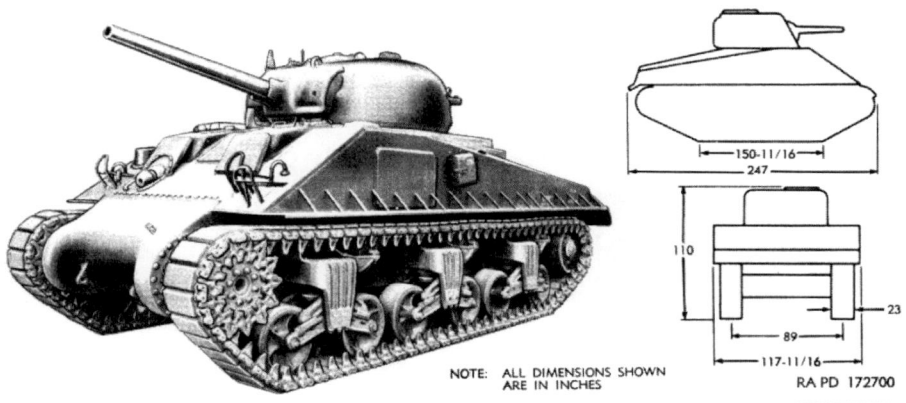

NOTE: ALL DIMENSIONS SHOWN
ARE IN INCHES

RA PD 172700

Technical Manuals: 9–759, 9–1731B, 9–1731G, 9–1731K, 9–1750B, 9–1750K, 9–1825A, 9–1825B, 9–1826B, 9–1828A, 9–1829A; **Supply Catalog:** SNL G–204.

Classification: Limited Standard.

Armament: 1 gun, 75-mm, M3, turret mounted; 2 guns, machine, cal. .30, Browning, M1919A4 (flexible), 1 mounted coaxially with main armament, 1 ball mounted at right front of hull; 1 gun, machine, cal. .50, Browning, M2, heavy barrel (flexible) mounted on revolving hatch on top of turret.

Fire Control and Vision Devices: Periscope, M10C or M4A1 w/telescope, M38A2 (Commander, gunner); periscope, M6 or M13 or M13B1 (vision); quadrant, elevation, M9; quadrant, gunner's M1; telescope, M10F (for tanks with combination gun mount M34A1) (sight); indicator, azimuth, M20.

GENERAL DATA

Crew	5
Weight, fighting	(lb) 69,565
Shipping dimensions, uncrated	(cu ft) 1,840; (sq ft) 201
Ground pressure	(psi) 10.1
Ground clearance	(in.) 17⅛
Pintle height, loaded	(in.) 28
Electrical system	(volts) 24
No. of batteries	(12-volt) 2
Type of ground	negative
Fuel octane rating	80
Capacities:	
Fuel	(gal) 168
Cooling system	(qt) 56
Crankcase, refill	(qt) 32
Transmission, differential, and final drives (qt):	
Three-piece, round-nose	152
One-piece, sharp-nose	164
Brakes	mechanical, controlled-differential
Parking brake, type:	
Early models	rear of transmission
Late models	pedal for locking steering brakes
Transmission forward speeds	5
Gear ratio	High 0.73:1; Fourth 1:1; Low 7.56:1
Differential-drive gear ratio	3.53:1
Final-drive gear ratio	2.84:1
Hull construction	welded homogeneous armor plate
Turret construction	cast homogeneous armor

Purpose: To provide mobile fire power and crew protection for offensive combat.

Ammunition: 104 rounds, 75-mm; 6,250 rounds, cal. .30 machine gun; 630 rounds, cal. .50; 900 rounds, cal. .45 for submachine gun; 12 hand grenades; 12 ground signals.

Communications: (SCR–508 or SCR–608 or SCR–528 or AN/GRC–3, –4, –5, –6, –7, or –8) and (RC–298); or (SCR–508 or SCR–528) and (RC–298) and (AN/VRC–3); or (AN/VRC–3) and (RC–99) and (RC–298).

PERFORMANCE

Maximum grade ability	(percent) 60
Turning radius	(ft) 31
Fording depth	(in.) 36
Maximum width of ditch vehicle can cross	(in.) 90
Maximum vertical obstacle vehicle can climb	(in.) 24
Fuel consumption (average conditions)	(mpg) 0.6
Cruising range (average conditions)	(mi) 100
Allowable speed, governed	(mph) 26
Maximum allowable towed load, gross	(lb) 10,000

ENGINE

Manufacturer: Ford	Model GAA
Type	4-cycle, valve-in-head; No. of cylinders (60-deg V) 8
Displacement	(cu in.) 1,100
Bore	(in.) 5.4
Stroke	(in.) 6
Compression ratio	7.5:1
Governed speed	(rpm) 2,600
Brake horsepower (max w/std accessories)	450 at (rpm) 2,600
Torque (max w/std accessories)	950 lb-ft at (rpm) 2,100
Type of ignition	magneto

ADDITIONAL DATA

One-piece or three-piece differential housing used on this vehicle.
Auxiliary engine: Homelite Model H RUH–28.
Manual and power turret-traversing mechanism.
Horizontal volute spring suspension.
Data given for vehicle equipped with track, steel, T66. Track, rubber-backed-steel, T80 and track, rubber, T84 are interchangeable.

113

TANK, 76-MM GUN, T41E1

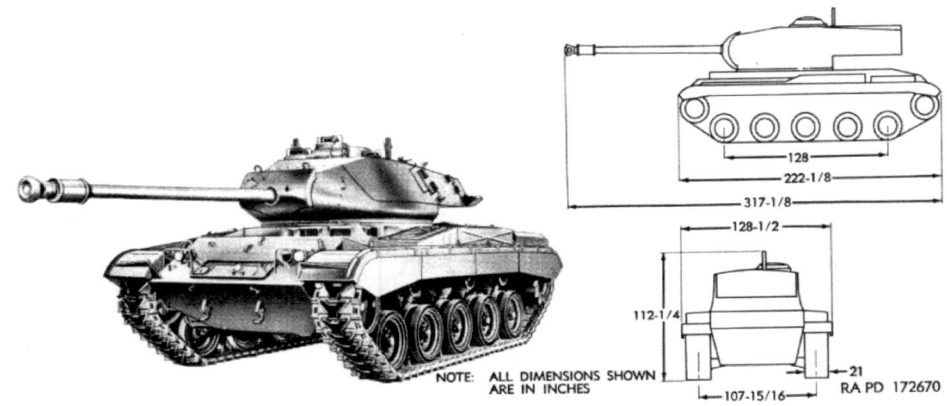

NOTE: ALL DIMENSIONS SHOWN ARE IN INCHES

RA PD 172670

Technical Manuals: 9–730, 9–1730B, 9–1730F, 9–1825C, 9–1825E, 9–1826B, 9–1828A, 9–1829A; Supply Catalog: SNL G–251.

Armament: 1 gun, 76-mm, T91E3, turret mounted; 1 gun, machine, cal. .50, Browning, M2, heavy barrel, turret type, mounted coaxially with main armament; 1 gun, machine, cal. .50, Browning, M2, heavy barrel (flexible) pintle mounted on top of turret.

Ammunition: 60 rounds 76-mm; 4,630 rounds cal. .50; 18 rounds cal. .45 for submachine gun; 90 rounds cal. .30 carbine; 8 hand grenades; 12 ground signals.

Purpose: To provide mobile fire power and crew protection in offensive combat. Suitable for airborne use.

Fire Control and Vision Devices: Finder, range, T37; periscope, M15 (vision); periscope, T32 (commander, gunner); quadrant, elevation, M9; quadrant, gunner's, M1; drive, ballistic, T23; indicator, azimuth, T24.

Communications: (SCR–508 or SCR–528) and (AN/VIA–1); or (AN/GRC–3, –4, –5, –6, –7, or –8) and (AN/VIA–1).

GENERAL DATA

Crew..4
Weight, fighting..(lb) 50,789
Over-all length (gun in traveling position)................(in.) 273¾₆
Shipping dimensions, uncrated............(cu ft) 2,290; (sq ft) 245
Ground pressure..(psi) 9.5
Ground clearance..(in.) 17¼
Pintle height, loaded.......................................(in.) 30
Electrical system..(volts) 24
   No. of batteries......................................(6-volt) 4
   Type of ground...negative
Fuel octane rating..80
Capacities:
   Fuel...(gal) 140
   Crankcase, refill.......................................(qt) 56
   Auxiliary engine crankcase.............................(qt) 3½
   Transmission, cross-drive (including cooler)...........(qt) 64
   Final drive......................................(each) (qt) 3
Brakes:
   Hand-lever controlled, hydraulic, multiple-disk steering brakes. Pedal operates them as service brakes.
   Parking brake, type: Park position on transmission selector lever.
Ratio from engine output to torque converter input.........0.715:1
Torque converter stall ratio................................3.8:1
Ratio from torque converter output shaft to final-drive flange:
   High range.............................1.4:1; Low range 5.34:1
No. of ranges (high, low, and reverse)..........................3
Final-drive gear ratio......................................4.25:1
Hull construction....................welded homogeneous armor plate
Turret construction.............................welded steel plat·

PERFORMANCE

Maximum grade ability....................................(percent) 60
Turning radius (ft).................................pivots in place
Fording depth...(in.) 48
Maximum width of ditch vehicle can cross....................(in.) 72
Maximum vertical obstacle vehicle can climb.................(in.) 28
Fuel consumption (average conditions)......................(mpg) 1.2
Cruising range (average conditions)........................(mi) 120
Maximum allowable speed, governed..........................(mph) 40
Maximum allowable towed load, gross......................(lb) 10,000

ENGINE

Manufacturer; Continental........................Model AOS 895-3
Type.......................4-cycle, valve-in-head, air-cooled
No. of cylinders....................................(opposed) 6
Displacement..(cu in.) 895
Bore..(in.) 5¾
Stroke..(in.) 5¾
Compression ratio..5.5:1
Governed speed.......................................(rpm) 2,800
Brake horsepower, gross.......................500 at (rpm) 2,800
Torque, gross...........................960 lb-ft at (rpm) 2,400
Type of ignition...magneto

ADDITIONAL DATA

Auxiliary Generator Set: Engine GMC Model A41–1; Generator, Delco model GM-A-8585.

Manual and power turret-traversing mechanism.

Gun equipped with bore evacuator and muzzle brake.

Data given for vehicle equipped with track, rubber-backed-steel, T87. Track, rubber, T88E1 is interchangeable.

TANK, MEDIUM, M4A1, 76-MM GUN

RA PD 137714

NOTE: ALL DIMENSIONS SHOWN ARE IN INCHES

Technical Manuals: 9-731AA, 9-1725, 9-1731G, 9-1731K, 9-1750A, 9-1750B, 9-1750C, 9-1750D, 9-1750K, 9-1825A, 9-1825B, 9-1826B, 9-1828A, 9-1829A; **Supply Catalog:** SNL G-207.

Classification: Limited Standard.

Armament: 1 gun, 76-mm, M1A1C or M1A2, turret mounted; 2 guns, machine, cal. .30, Browning, M1919A4 (flexible), 1 mounted coaxially with main armament, 1 ball mounted at right front of hull; 1 gun, machine, cal. .50, Browning, M2, heavy barrel (flexible) mounted on revolving hatch door on top of turret.

Ammunition: 86 rounds, 76-mm; 630 rounds, cal. .50; 180 rounds, cal. .45 for submachine gun; 6,875 rounds, cal. .30; 90 rounds, cal. .30, carbine; 12 hand grenades; 12 ground signals.

GENERAL DATA

Crew..5
Weight, fighting...(lb) 73,595
Overall length w/gun in traveling position................(in.) 293⅝₆
Shipping dimensions, uncrated............(cu ft) 2,360; (sq ft) 240
Ground pressure...(psi) 10.6
Ground clearance..(in.) 18⅜
Pintle height, loaded..(in.) 22
Electrical system...(volts) 24
   No. of batteries....................................(12-volt) 2
   Type of ground.......................................negative
Fuel octane rating...80
Capacities:
   Fuel...(gal) 172
   Auxiliary-engine fuel tank...........................(gal) 6
   Engine oil tank..(qt) 36
   Transmission, differential, and final drives (qt):
     Three-piece, round-nose.........................152
     One-piece, sharp-nose...........................164
Brakes..........................mechanical, controlled-differential
   Parking brake, type..............pedal for locking steering brakes
Transmission:
   Forward speeds...5
   Gear ratio........................High 0.73:1; Fourth 1:1; Low 7.56:1
Differential-drive gear ratio...............................3.53:1
Final-drive gear ratio......................................2.84:1
Hull construction...........welded homogeneous armor casting and plates
Armor, turret...................................cast homogeneous armor

Purpose: To provide mobile fire power and crew protection for offensive combat.

Fire Control and Vision Devices: Periscope, M10G (gunner's); periscope, M8A1, w/telescope, M39A2 or periscope, M4A1, w/telescope, M47A2 (commander's); periscope, M13 or M13B1 or M6 (vision); quadrant, elevation, M9; quadrant, gunner's, M1; telescope, M83D, or M71D (sight); indicator, azimuth, M19.

Communications: (SCR-508 or SCR-608 or SCR-528 or AN/GRC-3, -4, -5, -6, -7, or -8) and (RC-298); or (SCR-508 or SCR-528) and (RC-298) and (AN/VRC-3); or (AN/VRC-3) and (RC-99) and (RC-298).

PERFORMANCE

Maximum grade ability.......................................(percent) 60
Turning radius..(ft) 31
Fording depth..(in.) 42
Maximum width of ditch vehicle can cross...................(in.) 90
Maximum vertical obstacle vehicle can climb................(in.) 24
Fuel consumption (average conditions)......................(mpg) 0.6
Cruising range (average conditions)........................(mi) 100
Allowable speed, governed....................................(mph) 24
Maximum allowable towed load, gross........................(lb) 10,000

ENGINE

Manufacturer: Continental.......................Model R975-C4
Type.................4-cycle, radial, air-cooled; No. of cylinders 9
Displacement..(cu in.) 973
Bore..(in.) 5
Stroke..(in.) 5½
Compression ratio..5.7:1
Governed speed..(rpm) 2,400
Brake horsepower (max w/std accessories)...........400 at (rpm) 2,400
Torque (max w/std accessories)..............940 lb-ft at (rpm) 1,700
Type of ignition...magneto

ADDITIONAL DATA

One-piece or three-piece differential housing used on this vehicle.
Manual and power turret-traversing mechanism.
Equipped with elevation stabilizer.
Auxiliary generator Homelite Model HRUH-28.
Data given for vehicle equipped with track, steel, T66. Track, rubber-backed-steel, T80, and track, rubber, T84 are interchangeable.

115

TANK, MEDIUM, M4A3, 76-MM GUN

RA PD 137720

NOTE: ALL DIMENSIONS SHOWN ARE IN INCHES

Technical Manuals: 9-759, 9-1731B, 9-1731G, 9-1731K, 9-1750A, 9-1750B, 9-1750K, 9-1825A, 9-1825B, 9-1826B, 9-1828A, 9-1829A; Supply Catalog: SNL G-205.

Classification: Substitute Standard.

Armament: 1 gun, 76-mm, M1A2 or M1A1C, turret mounted; 2 guns, machine, cal. .30, Browning, M1919A4 (flexible), 1 mounted coaxially with main armament, 1 ball mounted at right front of hull; 1 gun, machine, cal. .50, Browning, M2, heavy barrel (flexible) mounted on revolving hatch on top of turret.

Ammunition: 86 rounds, 76-mm; 6,875 rounds, cal. .30; 630 rounds, cal. .50; 180 rounds, cal. .45 for submachine-gun; 90 rounds, cal. .30, carbine; 12 ground signals; 12 hand grenades.

Purpose: To provide mobile fire power and crew protection for offensive combat.

Fire Control and Vision Devices: Periscope, M10G, and periscope, M8A1 w/telescope, M39A2, or periscope, M4A1 w/telescope, M47A2 (gunner's); periscope, M13 or M13B1 or M6 (vision); quadrant, elevation, M9; quadrant gunner's, M1; telescope, M83D, or M71D (sight).

Communications: (SCR-508 or SCR-608 or SCR-528 or AN/GRC-3, -4, -5, -6, -7, or -8) and (RC-298); or (SCR-508 or SCR-528) and (RC-298) and (AN/VRC-3); or (AN/VRC-3) and (RC-99) and (RC-298).

GENERAL DATA

Crew 5
Weight, fighting .... (lb) 74,125
Over-all length (gun in traveling position) .... (in.) 296
Shipping dimensions, uncrated .... (cu ft) 2,370; (sq ft) 242
Ground pressure .... (psi) 10.7
Ground clearance .... (in.) 18¾
Pintle height, loaded .... (in.) 28
Electrical system .... (volts) 24
   No. of batteries .... (12-volt) 2
   Type of ground .... negative
Fuel octane rating 80
Capacities:
   Fuel .... (gal) 168
   Cooling system .... (qt) 56
   Crankcase, refill .... (qt) 32
   Transmission, differential, and final drives (qt):
      Three-piece, round-nose 152
      One-piece, sharp-nose 164
Brakes .... mechanical, controlled-differential
   Parking brake, type:
      Early models .... rear of transmission
      Late models .... pedal for locking steering brakes
Transmission forward speeds 5
   Gear ratio .... High 0.73:1; Fourth 1:1; Low 7.56:1
Differential-drive gear ratio 3.53:1
Final-drive gear ratio 2.84:1
Hull construction .... welded homogeneous armor plate
Turret construction .... cast homogeneous armor

PERFORMANCE

Maximum grade ability .... (percent) 60
Turning radius .... (ft) 31
Fording depth .... (in.) 36
Maximum width of ditch vehicle can cross .... (in.) 90
Maximum vertical obstacle vehicle can climb .... (in.) 24
Fuel consumption (average conditions) .... (mpg) 0.6
Cruising range (average conditions) .... (mi) 100
Allowable speed, governed .... (mph) 26
Maximum allowable towed load, gross .... (lb) 10,000

ENGINE

Manufacturer: Ford .... Model GAA
Type .... 4-cycle, valve-in-head; No. of cylinders (60-deg V) 8
Displacement .... (cu in.) 1,100
Bore .... (in.) 5.4
Stroke .... (in.) 6
Compression ratio 7.5:1
Governed speed .... (rpm) 2,800
Brake horsepower (max w/std accessories) .... 450 at (rpm) 2,600
Torque (max w/std accessories) .... 950 lb-ft at (rpm) 2,100
Type of ignition .... magneto

ADDITIONAL DATA

Auxiliary engine: Homelite model HRUH-28.
Data given for vehicle equipped with track, steel, T66. Track, rubber-backed-steel, and track, rubber, T84 are interchangeable.
One-piece or three-piece differential housing used on this vehicle.
Manual and power turret-traversing mechanism.

TANK, MEDIUM, M26 AND M26A1

NOTE: ALL DIMENSIONS SHOWN
ARE IN INCHES

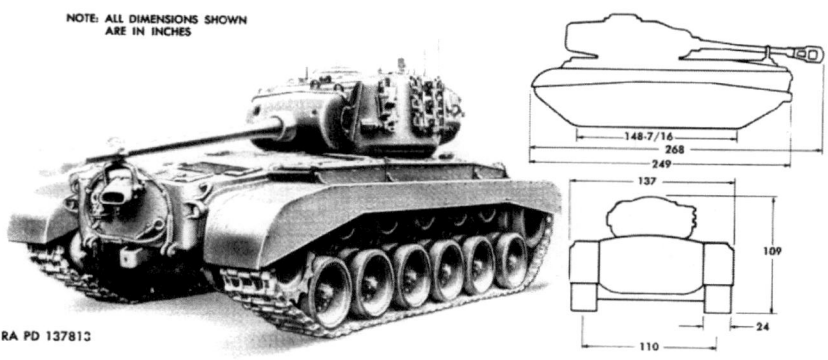

RA PD 137813

Technical Manuals: 9–735, 9–1731B, 9–1731G, 9–1735A, 9–1735B, 9–1735C, 9–1826B, 9–1826C, 9–1828A, 9–1829A; Supply Catalog: SNL G–226.

Vehicle illustrated: M26.

Classification: Limited Standard.

Armament: 1 gun, 90-mm, M3, turret mounted; 2 gun, machine, cal. .30, Browning. M1919A4 (flexible); 1 ball mounted at right front of hull, 1 mounted co-axially with main armament; 1 gun, machine, cal. .50, Browning, M2, heavy barrel (flexible) pintle mounted on top of turret.

Ammunition: 70 rounds 90-mm; 5,000 rounds cal.. 30; 550 rounds cal. .50; 12 hand grenades.

Communications: (SCR–508 or SCR–608 or SCR–528) and (RC–298); or (SCR 508 or SCR–528) and (RC–298) and (AN/VRC–3); (AN/VRC–3) and (RC–99) and (RC–298).

GENERAL DATA

Crew..5
Weight, fighting...(lb) 92,000
Shipping dimensions, uncrated.............(cu ft) 2,340; (sq ft) 257
Ground pressure...(psi) 12.7
Ground clearance..(in.) 17¼
Pintle height, loaded..(in.) 28
Electrical system...(volts) 24
  No. of batteries..(12-volt) 2
  Type of ground..negative
Fuel octane rating...80
Capacities:
  Fuel..(gal) 191
  Cooling system...(qt) 88
  Crankcase, refill..(qt) 32
  Auxiliary-engine crankcase.....................................(qt) 3
  Transmission (including cooler).............................(qt) 54½
  Differential...(qt) 72
Final drive...(each) (qt) 7
Brakes.................................mechanical, controlled-differential
  Parking brake, type.............hand-lever locks on steering brakes
Transmission (torqmatic):
  Forward speeds...3
  Gear ratio.............................High 0.336:1; Low 1.377:1
Differential-drive gear ratio..3.41:1
Final-drive gear ratio..3.95:1
Hull construction......welded castings and plate; turret cast homogeneous

Purpose: To provide mobile fire power and crew protection for offensive combat.

Fire Control and Vision Devices: Periscope, M13 or M13B1 or M6 (vision); periscope, M15 or M13 or M13B1 or M6 (vision); periscope, M16 or M10F or periscope, M4A1 w/telescope M77F or M77H (gunner); quadrant, elevation, M9; quadrant gunner's, M1; telescope, M83C, or M71N, or M71C (sight); indicator, azimuth, M20.

PERFORMANCE

Maximum grade ability......................................(percent) 60
Turning radius...(ft) 31
Fording depth..(in.) 48
Maximum width of ditch vehicle can cross..................(in.) 95
Maximum vertical obstacle vehicle can climb................(in.) 46
Fuel consumption (average conditions)....................(mpg) 0. 5
Cruising range (average conditions)......................(mi) 92
Allowable speed, governed................................(mph) 30
Maximum allowable towed load, gross.....................(lb) 1,000

ENGINE

Manufacturer: Ford..Model GAF
Type................4-cycle, valve-in-head; No. of cylinders (60-deg V) 8
Displacement..(cu in.) 1,000
Bore..(in.) 5. 4
Stroke...(in.) 6
Compression ratio...7. 5:1
Governed speed...(rpm) 2,600
Brake horsepower (max w/std accessories).........500 at (rpm) 2,600
Torque (max w/std accessories)................950 lb-ft at (rpm) 2,100
Type of ignition...magneto

ADDITIONAL DATA

Variable torque multiplicating through torque converter.
Stall ratio 4.04:1.
Manual and hydraulic turret-traversing mechanism. Elevation stabilizer.
Auxiliary engine: Waukesha, Model G-TGU.
Length of ground contact (wheelbase) on right side (in.) 152¾.
Data given for vehicle equipped with Steel Track, T81.
Rubber-backed-steel track, T80E1 and rubber track, T84E1 are also applicable with changed sprockets and final drive assemblies.
M26A1 equipped with Gun, 90-mm M3A1 and Mount, combination gun, M67A1.

TANK, MEDIUM, M46 AND M46A1

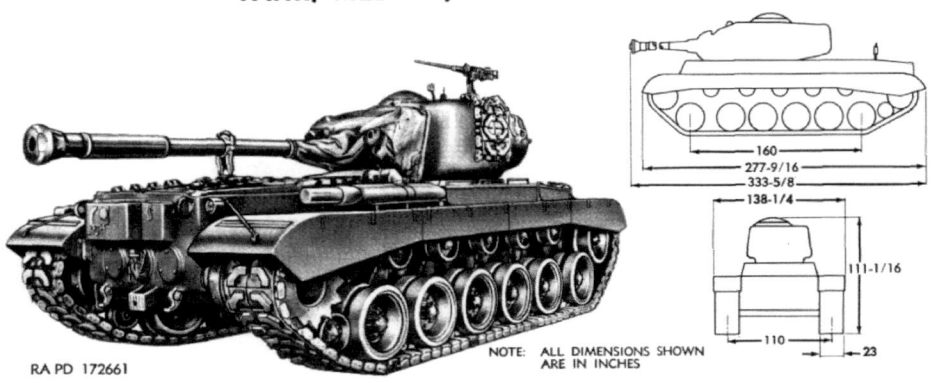

RA PD 172661

NOTE: ALL DIMENSIONS SHOWN ARE IN INCHES

Technical Manuals: 9–718, 9–1718A, 9–1718B, 9–1718C, 9–1718D, 9–1718E, 9–1718F, 9–1825A, 9–1825C, 9–1825D, 9–1825E, 9–1826B, 9–1828A, 9–1829A; Supply Catalog: SNL G–244.

Vehicle illustrated: M46.

Classification: Substitute Standard.

Purpose: To provide mobile fire power and crew protection for offensive combat.

Armament: 1 gun, 90-mm, M3A1, turret mounted: 1 gun, machine cal. .50, Browning, M2, heavy barrel (flexible) pedestal mounted on top of turret; 2 guns, machine, cal. .30, Browning, M1919A4 (flexible), 1 ball mounted at right front of hull, 1 mounted coaxially with main armament.

Ammunition: 70 rounds, 90-mm; 525 rounds, cal. .50; 5,500 cal. .30 machine gun, 90 rounds, cal. .30 carbine; 12 hand grenades; 12 ground signals.

GENERAL DATA

Crew	5
Weight, fighting	(lb) 97,000
Over-all length, gun in traveling position	(in.) 304¹³⁄₁₆
Shipping dimensions, uncrated	(cu ft) 2,700, (sq ft) 291
Ground pressure	(psi) 13.2
Ground clearance	(in.) 19¼
Pintle height, unloaded	(in.) 28½
Electrical system	(volts) 24
No. of batteries	(12-volt) 4
Type of ground	negative
Fuel octane rating	80
Capacities:	
Fuel	(gal) 233
Crankcase, refill	(qt) 72
Auxiliary engine crankcase	(qt) 3½
Transmission, cross-drive (including cooler)	(qt) 92
Final drive	(each) (qt) 8
Brakes:	

Hand-lever-controlled, hydraulic, multiple disk steering brakes. Pedal operates them as service brakes.

Parking brake, type .... lever for locking service brakes

No. of ranges (high, low, and reverse)	3
Ratio from engine output to torque converter input	1.162:1
Torque-converter stall ratio	4:1
Ratio from torque converter output shaft to final drive flange:	
High range	1.4:1
Low range	4.93:1
Final-drive gear ratio	3.95:1
Hull construction	welded homogeneous armor plate

Fire Control and Vision Devices: Periscope, M16C (commander's); periscope, M13 or M13B1 or M6 (vision); periscope, M16C or M10F (gunner's); quadrant, M9; quadrant, gunner's M1; telescope, M71E5C or T152 (sight); indicator, azimuth, M20.

Communications: (SCR–508 or SCR–528 or SCR–608B) and (AN/VIA–1); or (SCR–508 or SCR–528 or SCR–608B) and (AN/VRC–3) and (AN/VIA–1); or (AN/VRC–3) and (RC–99) and (AN/VIA–1 or AN/GRC–3, –4, –5, –6, –7, or –8) and (AN/VIA–1); or (AN/VRC–7) and (AN/VIA–1).

PERFORMANCE

Maximum grade ability	(percent) 60
Turning radius	pivots in place
Fording depth	(in.) 48
Maximum width of ditch vehicle can cross	(in.) 102
Maximum vertical obstacle vehicle can climb	(in.) 36
Fuel consumption (average conditions)	(mpg) ⅓
Cruising range (average conditions)	(mi) 70
Allowable speed, recommended	(mph) 30
Maximum allowable towed load, gross	(lb) 10,000

ENGINE

Manufacturer: Continental	Model AV–1790–5A (M46)
	AV–1790–5B (M46A1)
Type: 4-cycle, valve-in-head	air cooled
No. of cylinders	(90-deg V) 12
Displacement	(cu in.) 1,790
Bore	(in.) 5¾
Stroke	(in.) 5¾
Compression ratio	6.5:1
Governed speed	(rpm) 2,950
Brake horsepower (max w/std accessories)	810 at (rpm) 2,800
Torque (max w/std accessories)	1,560 lb-ft at (rpm) 2,400
Type of ignition	magneto

ADDITIONAL DATA

Manual and power turret-traversing mechanism.

Gun equipped with bore evacuator and muzzle brake.

Auxiliary engine: Wisconsin Model TFT.

Data given for vehicle equipped with track, rubber-backed-steel, T80E1. Track, rubber-backed-steel, T-80E4 and track, rubber, T84-E1 are interchangeable.

TANK, 90-MM GUN, M47

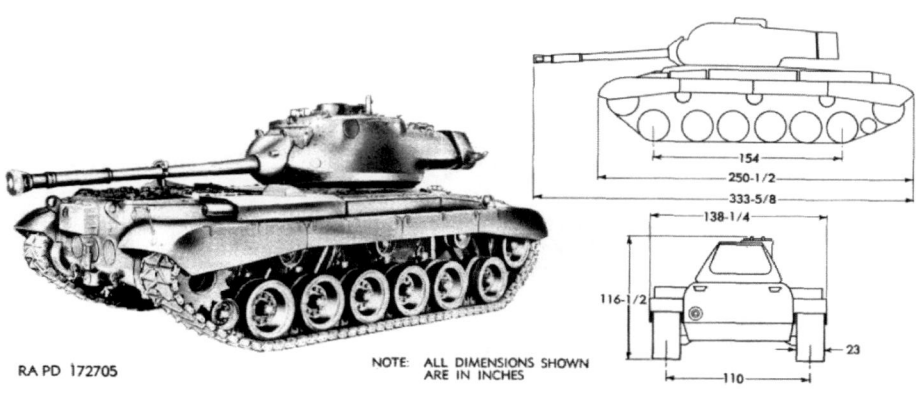

NOTE: ALL DIMENSIONS SHOWN ARE IN INCHES

RA PD 172705

Technical Manuals: 9-1718A, 9-1718F, 9-1730F, 9-1825C, 9-1825E, 9-1826B, 9-1828A, 9-1829A; Supply Catalog: SNL G-262.

Classification: Standard.

Armament: 1 gun, 90-mm, T119, turret mounted; 1 gun, machine, cal. .50, Browning, M2, heavy barrel, turret type, mounted coaxially with main armament; 1 gun, machine, cal. .50, Browning, heavy barrel (flexible) mounted on revolving hatch on top of turret; 1 gun, machine, cal. .30, Browning, M1919A4 (flexible) ball mounted at right front of hull.

Ammunition: 71 rounds, 90-mm; 3,440 rounds, cal. .50; 180 rounds, cal. .45, sub-machine gun; 4,125 rounds, cal. .30 machine gun; 90 rounds, cal. .30 carbine; 8 smoke grenades; 12 ground signals.

Purpose: To provide mobile fire power and crew protection for offensive combat.

Fire Control and Vision Devices: Drive, ballistic, T23E1; finder, range, T41; indicator, azimuth, T24; periscope, M6 M13, or M13B1 (vision); periscope, T35 (commander, gunner); quadrant, gunner's M1; quadrant, elevation, T21.

Communications: (AN/GRC-3, -4, -5, -6, -7, or -8) and (AN/VIA-1).

GENERAL DATA

Crew	5
Weight, fighting	(lb) 97,200
Over-all length, gun in traveling position	(in.) 279½
Shipping dimensions, uncrated	(cu ft) 2,610; (sq ft) 269
Ground pressure	(psi) 13.7
Ground clearance	(in.) 19¾
Pintle height, loaded	(in.) 28.6
Electrical system	(volts) 24
No. of batteries	4
Type of ground	negative
Fuel octane rating	80
Capacities:-	
Fuel	(gal) 233
Crankcase, refill	(qt) 64
Auxiliary engine crankcase	(qt) 3½
Transmission, cross-drive (including cooler)	(qt) 92
Final drive	(each) (qt) 8
Brakes:	
Hand-lever controlled, hydraulic, multiple-disk steering brakes. Pedal operates them as service brakes.	
Parking brake, type	Lever for locking service brakes.
No. of ranges (high, low, and reverse)	3
Ratio from engine output to torque converter input	1.162:1
Torque-converter stall ratio	4:1
Ratio from torque converter output shaft to final drive flange:	
High range 1.4:1; Low range 4.93:1	
Final-drive gear ratio	4.47:1
Hull construction	Welded homogeneous armor plate and castings
Turret-ring inside diameter	(in.) 73

PERFORMANCE

Maximum grade ability	(percent) 60
Turning radius (ft)	Pivots in place
Fording depth	(in.) 48
Maximum width of ditch vehicle can cross	(in.) 102
Maximum vertical obstacle vehicle can climb	(in.) 36
Fuel consumption (average conditions)	(mpg) 0.4
Cruising range (average conditions)	(mi) 100
Allowable speed, recommended	(mph) 37
Maximum allowable towed load, gross	(lb) 10,000

ENGINE

Manufacturer: Continental	Model AV-1790-5B
Type	4-cycle, valve-in-head; air-cooled
No. of cylinders	(90-deg V) 12
Displacement	(cu in.) 1,790
Bore	(in.) 5¾
Stroke	(in.) 5¾
Compression ratio	6.5:1
Governed speed	(rpm) 2,950
Brake horsepower (max w/std accessories)	810 at (rpm) 2,800
Torque (max w/std accessories)	1,560 lb-ft at (rpm) 2,400
Type of ignition	magneto

ADDITIONAL DATA

Manual and power traversing and elevating mechanism.
Gun equipped with bore evacuator and muzzle brake.
Auxiliary generator: Wisconsin Model TFT.
Data given for vehicle equipped w/track, steel, T80E6. Track, rubber T84E1 is interchangeable.

TANK, MEDIUM, M4, 105-MM HOWITZER

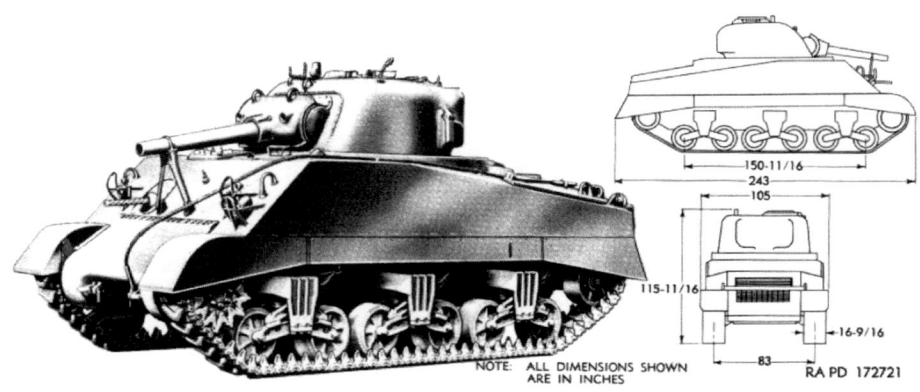

NOTE: ALL DIMENSIONS SHOWN ARE IN INCHES
RA PD 172721

Technical Manuals: 9-731AA, 9-1725, 9-1731G, 9-1731K, 9-1750A, 9-1750B, 9-1750C, 9-1750D, 9-1750K, 9-1825A, 9-1825B, 9-1826B, 9-1828A, 9-1829A; Supply Catalog: SNL G-104.

Classification: Limited Standard.

Armament: 1 howitzer, 105-mm, M4, turret mounted; 2 guns, machine, cal. .30, Browning, M1919A4 (flexible), 1 mounted coaxially with main armament, 1 ball mounted at right front of hull; 1 gun machine, cal. .50, Browning, M2, heavy barrel (flexible) mounted on revolving hatch on top of turret.

Ammunition: 66 rounds 105-mm; 630 rounds cal. .50; 180 rounds cal. .45 for sub-machine-gun; 4,400 rounds cal. .30; 90 rounds cal. .30, carbine; 12 hand grenades; 12 ground signals.

Purpose: To provide mobile fire power and crew protection for offensive combat.

Fire Control and Vision Devices: Periscope, M4A1 w/telescope M77C (commander's); periscope, M10D (gunner's); periscope, M6, M13, or M13B1 (vision); quadrant, elevation, M9; quadrant, gunner's, M1; telescope, M768 (sight); indicator, azimuth, M19.

Communications: (SCR–528 or AN/GRC–3, –4, –5, –6, –7, or –8 and RC 298); or (SCR–508 or SCR–528) and (RC–298) and (AN/VRC–3); or (AN/VRC–3) and (RC–99) and (RC–298).

GENERAL DATA

Crew...5
Weight, fighting...(lb) 69,385
Shipping dimensions, uncrated................(cu ft) 1,715; (sq ft) 178
Ground pressure...(psi) 13.9
Ground clearance......................................(in.) 18⅞
Pintle height, loaded.................................(in.) 24½
Electrical system..(volts) 24
    No. of batteries.................................(12-volt) 2
    Type of ground.................................negative
Fuel octane rating.......................................80
Capacities:
    Fuel...(gal) 172
    Auxiliary-engine fuel tank......................(gal) 6
    Engine oil tank.................................(qt) 36
    Transmission, differential, and final drives (qt):
        Three-piece, round-nose..................152
        One-piece, sharp-nose....................164
Brakes...........................mechanical, controlled-differential[1]
    Parking brake, type............pedal for locking steering brakes
Transmission:
    Forward speeds.................................5
    Gear ratio.............High 0.73:1; Fourth 1:1; Low 7.56:1
Differential-drive gear ratio............................3.53:1
Final-drive gear ratio..................................2.84:1
Hull construction................welded homogeneous armor plate
Armor, turret.......................cast homogeneous armor

PERFORMANCE

Maximum grade ability...............................(percent) 60
Turning radius...(ft) 31
Fording depth...(in.) 36
Maximum width of ditch vehicle can cross..............(in.) 90
Maximum vertical obstacle vehicle can climb...........(in.) 24
Fuel consumption (average conditions)................(mpg) 0.6
Cruising range (average conditions)...................(mi) 100
Allowable speed, governed.............................(mph) 24
Maximum allowable towed load, gross..................(lb) 10,000

ENGINE

Manufacturer: Continental.........................Model R975–C4
Type.................4-cycle, radial, air-cooled; No. of cylinders 9
Displacement...(cu in.) 973
Bore..(in.) 5
Stroke...(in.) 5.5
Compression ratio.......................................5.7:1
Governed speed...(rpm) 2,400
Brake horsepower (max w/std accessories)........400 at (rpm) 2,400
Torque (max w/std accessories)...........940 lb-ft at (rpm) 1,700
Type of ignition..magneto

ADDITIONAL DATA

Auxiliary generator, Homelite Model HRUH-28.
Data given for vehicle equipped with track, rubber, T48.
Track, rubber, T51; tracks, steel, T49 and T54E1; and track, rubber-backed-steel, T74, are interchangeable.
Manual turret-traversing mechanism.

TANK, MEDIUM, M4A3, 105-MM HOWITZER

RA PD 137719

NOTE: ALL DIMENSIONS SHOWN
ARE IN INCHES

Technical Manuals: 9-759, 9-1731B, 9-1731G, 9-1731K, 9-1750A, 9-1750B, 9-1750K, 9-1825A, 9-1825B, 9-1826B, 9-1828A, 9-1829A; Supply Catalog: SNL G-104.

Classification: Limited Standard.

Armament: 1 howitzer, 105-mm, M4, turret mounted; 1 gun machine cal. .30, Browning, M1919A4 (flexible) coaxially mounted w/main armament; 1 gun, machine cal. .50, Browning, M2, heavy barrel (flexible) pedestal mounted on top of turret.

Communications: (SCR-528 or AN/GRC-3, -4, -5, -6, -7, or -8) and (RC-298); or (SCR-508 or SCR-528) and (RC-298) and (AN/VRC-3); or (AN/VRC-3) and (RC-99) and (RC-298).

Purpose: To provide mobile fire power and crew protection for offensive combat.

Ammunition: 66 rounds, 105-mm; 4,000 rounds, cal. .30; 630 rounds, cal. .50; 900 rounds, cal. .45 for submachine gun; 12 hand grenades; 12 ground signals.

Fire Control and Vision Devices: Periscope, M4A1 w/telescope M77C (gunner); periscope, M10D (commander); periscope, M13 or M13B1 or M6 (vision); quadrant elevation, M9; quadrant gunner's, M1; telescope, M76G (sight).

GENERAL DATA

Crew	5
Weight, fighting	(lb) 72,865
Shipping dimensions, uncrated	(cu ft) 1,850; (sq ft) 202
Ground pressure	(psi) 10.5
Ground clearance	(in.) 17½
Pintle height, loaded	(in.) 28
Electrical system	(volts) 24
No. of batteries	(12-volts) 2
Type of ground	negative
Fuel octane rating	80
Capacities:	
Fuel	(gal) 168
Cooling system	(qt) 56
Crankcase, refill	(qt) 32
Transmission, differential, and final drives (qt):	
Three-piece, round-nose	152
One-piece, sharp-nose	164
Brakes	mechanical, controlled-differential
Parking brake, type:	
Early models	rear of transmission
Late models	pedal for locking steering brakes
Transmission forward speeds	5
Gear ratio	High 0.73:1; Fourth 1:1; Low 7.56:1
Differential-drive gear ratio	3.53:1
Final-drive gear ratio	2.84:1
Hull construction	welded homogeneous armor plate
Turret	cast homogeneous armor

PERFORMANCE

Maximum grade ability	(percent) 60
Turning radius	(ft) 31
Fording depth	(in.) 36
Maximum width of ditch vehicle can cross	(in.) 90
Maximum vertical obstacle vehicle can climb	(in.) 24
Fuel consumption (average conditions)	(mpg) 0.6
Cruising range (average conditions)	(mi) 100
Allowable speed, governed	(mph) 26
Maximum allowable towed load, gross	(lb) 1,000

ENGINE

Manufacturer: Ford	Model GAA
Type	4-cycle, valve-in-head; No. of cylinders (60-deg V) 8
Displacement	(cu. in.) 1,100
Bore	(in.) 5.4
Stroke	(in.) 6
Compression ratio	7.5:1
Governed speed	(rpm) 2,600
Brake horsepower (max w/std accessories)	450 at (rpm) 2,600
Torque (max w/std accessories)	950 lb-ft at (rpm) 2,100
Type of ignition	magneto

ADDITIONAL DATA

One-piece or three-piece differential housing used on this vehicle.
Auxiliary engine: Homelite model HRUH-28.
Manual turret-traversing mechanism.
Data computed for vehicle equipped w/track, steel, T-66.
Track, rubber-backed-steel, T80, and track, rubber, T84 are interchangeable.

TANK, MEDIUM, M45

152-1/4
252
138
109
23
110

NOTE: ALL DIMENSIONS SHOWN ARE IN INCHES

RA PD 137732

Technical Manuals: 9-735, 9-1731B, 9-1731D, 9-1731G, 9-1735A, 9-1735B, 9-1735C, 9-1825B, 9-1826B, 9-1826C, 9-1828A, 9-1829A; Supply Catalog: SNL G-226.

Classification: Standard.

Armament: 1 Howitzer, 105-mm, M4, turret mounted; 2 guns, machine, cal. .30, Browning, M1919A4 (flexible), 1 mounted coaxially with main armament, 1 ball mounted at right front of hull; 1 gun, machine, cal. .50, Browning, M2, heavy barrel (flexible), pedestal mounted on top of turret.

Ammunition: 74 rounds, 105-mm; 5,000 rounds, cal. .30; 550 rounds, cal. .50; 900 rounds, cal. .45, for submachine-gun; 12 hand grenades.

Purpose: To provide mobile fire power and crew protection for offensive combat.

Fire Control and Vision Devices: Periscope, M6, M13, or M13B1 (vision); periscope, M15 (gunner's); periscope, M18C or M10D (commander's); quadrant, elevation, M9; quadrant, gunner's, M1; telescope, M76G (sight); telescope, elbow, M62 (sight); indicator, azimuth, M20.

Communications: (SCR–528 or SCR–608 or AN/GRC–3, –4, –5, –6, –7, or –8) and (RC–298); or (SCR–508 or SCR–528) and (RC–298) and (AN/VRC–3); or (AN/VRC–3) and (RC–99) and (RC–298).

GENERAL DATA

Crew	5
Weight, fighting	(lb) 92,500
Shipping dimensions, uncrated	(cu ft) 2,190; (sq ft) 242
Ground pressure	(psi) 13.4
Ground clearance	(in.) 17¾
Pintle height, loaded	(in.) 28
Electrical system	(volts) 24
No. of batteries	(12-volt) 2
Type of ground	negative
Fuel octane rating	80
Capacities:	
Fuel	(gal) 191
Cooling system	(qt) 88
Crankcase, refill	(qt) 32
Auxiliary engine crankcase	(qt) 3
Transmission (including cooler)	(qt) 54½
Differential	(qt) 72
Final drives	(each) (qt) 7
Brakes	mechanical, controlled-differential
Parking brake, type	hand-lever locks on steering brakes
Transmission (torqmatic):	
forward speeds	3
Gear ratio	High 0.336:1; Low 1.377:1
Differential-drive gear ratio	3.41:1
Final-drive gear ratio	3.95:1
Hull construction	cast homogeneous armor and welded armor plate

PERFORMANCE

Maximum grade ability	(percent) 60
Turning radius	(ft) 31
Fording depth	(in.) 48
Maximum width of ditch vehicle can cross	(in.) 95
Maximum vertical obstacle vehicle can climb	(in.) 46
Fuel consumption (average conditions)	(mpg) 0.5
Cruising range (average conditions)	(mi) 100
Allowable speed, governed	(mph) 30
Maximum allowable towed load, gross	(lb) 10,000

ENGINE

Manufacturer: Ford	Model GAF
Type	4-cycle, valve-in-head; No. of cylinders (60-deg V) 8
Displacement	(cu in.) 1,100
Bore	(in.) 5.4
Stroke	(in.) 6
Compression ratio	7.5:1
Governed speed	(rpm) 2,800
Brake horsepower (max w/std accessories)	500 at (rpm) 2,600
Torque (max w/std accessories)	950 lb-ft at (rpm) 2,100
Type of ignition	magneto

ADDITIONAL DATA

Auxiliary engine: Waukeshau, Model G-TGU.
Data given for vehicle equipped with track, rubber-backed-steel, T80E1.
Track, rubber, T84E1 is interchangeable.
Manual and power turret-traversing mechanism.
Equipped with elevation stabilizer.

TRACTOR, CARGO, M8E2

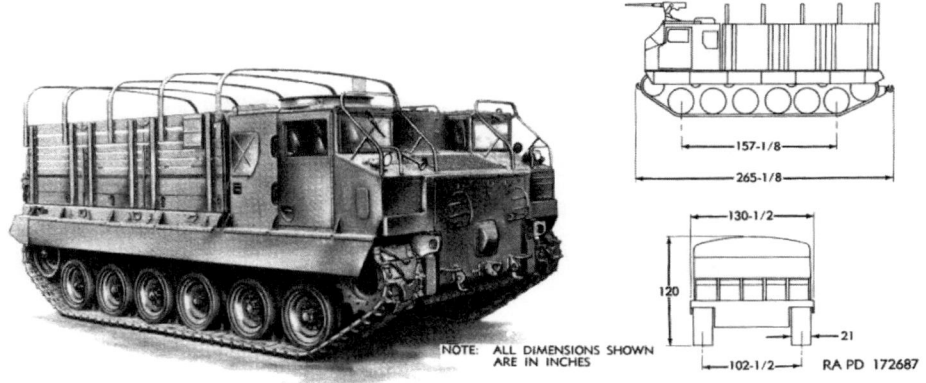

NOTE: ALL DIMENSIONS SHOWN ARE IN INCHES

RA PD 172687

Technical Manuals: 9-1730B, 9-1828A, 9-1829A; Supply Catalog: SNL G-252.

Classification: Standard.
Armament: 1 ring mount M-68 at top of cab.
Ammunition: 525 rounds cal. .50; 360 rounds cal. .30 carbine; 10 rockets.

Purpose: To tow heavy artillery, transport personnel, cargo, or ammunition over all types of terrain.

GENERAL DATA

Crew	2
Weight (lb)	Net 37,500; Payload 17,500; Gross 55,000
Shipping dimensions, uncrated	(cu ft) 2,420; (sq ft) 242
Ground pressure	(psi) 8.3
Vehicle dimensions:	
Ground clearance	(in.) 19⁵⁄₁₆
Pintle height, loaded	(in.) 30
Loading height, empty	(in.) 57¾
Body inside dimensions (in.):	
Length 157	Width 114½; Height 62¼
Cargo space	(cu ft) 650
Electrical system	(volts) 24
No. of batteries	2
Type of ground	negative
Fuel octane rating	80
Capacities:	
Fuel	(gal) 225
Crankcase, refill	(qt) 44
Transmission, cross-drive (including cooler)	(qt) 72
Power take-off	(qt) 1
Winch:	
Oil	(qt) 336
Transmission	(qt) 6
Load	(lb) 45,000
Final drive (each)	(qt) 5

Brakes:
Hand-lever controlled, hydraulic, multiple-disk steering brakes. Pedal operates them as service brakes.

Parking brake, type	Lever for locking service brakes
Ratio from engine output to torque converter input	0.715 : 1
Torque-converter stall ratio	3.8 : 1
No. of ranges (high, low, and reverse)	3
Ratio from torque converter output shaft to final drive flange	High range 1.4 : 1; Low range 5.34 : 1
Final-drive gear ratio	4.75 : 1
Hull construction	welded sheet steel

PERFORMANCE

Maximum grade ability	(percent) 60
Turning radius (ft)	pivots in place
Fording depth	(in.) 42
Maximum width of ditch vehicle can cross	forward (in.) 84
	reverse (in.) 80
Maximum vertical obstacle vehicle can climb	(in.) 30
Fuel consumption (average conditions)	(mpg) 0.8
Cruising range (average conditions)	(mi) 180
Maximum speed	(mph) 40
Maximum allowable towed load, gross	(lb) 39,000

ENGINE

Manufacturer: Continental	Model AOS 895-3
Type	4-cycle, valve-in-head, air cooled; No. of cylinders (opposed) 6
Displacement	(cu in.) 895
Bore	(in.) 5¾
Stroke	(in.) 5¾
Compression ratio	5.5 : 1
Governed speed	(rpm) 2,800
Brake horsepower (max w/std accessories)	363 at (rpm) 2,800
Torque (max w/std accessories)	760 lb-ft at (rpm) 2,060
Type of ignition	magneto

ADDITIONAL DATA

Data given for vehicle equipped with track, rubber-backed-steel, T91E3 w/detachable rubber grousers.

123

TRACTOR, HIGH-SPEED, 13-TON, M5

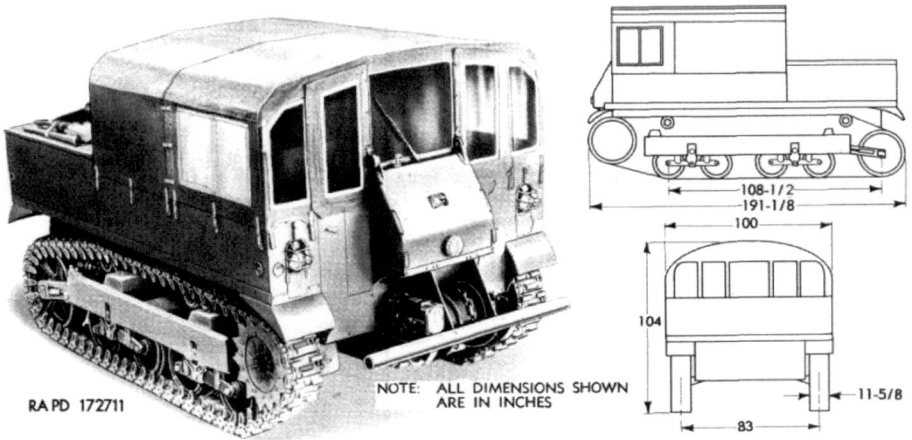

RA PD 172711

NOTE: ALL DIMENSIONS SHOWN ARE IN INCHES

Technical Manuals: 9-786, 9-1785A, 9-1786B, 9-1825A, 9-1826A, 9-1826C, 9-1828A, 9-1829A; Supply Catalog: SNL G-162.

Classification: Standard.
Armament: See Additional Data.
Ammunition: 56 rounds, 105-mm or 24 rounds, 155-mm with extra primers and fuzes; 550 rounds cal. .50.

Purpose: To tow heavy artillery over rough terrain, and transport gun crews and ammunition.

GENERAL DATA

Crew	9
Weight, fighting	(lb) 28,572
Shipping dimensions, uncrated	(cu ft) 1,150; (sq ft) 133
Ground pressure	(psi) 11.3
Ground clearance	(in.) 19¾
Pintle height, loaded	(in.) 28⅝
Electrical system	(volts) 12
No. of batteries	1
Type of ground	negative
Fuel octane rating	70
Capacities:	
Fuel	(gal) 100
Cooling system	(qt) 100
Crankcase, refill	(qt) 22
Winch:	
Oil capacity	(pt) 1¼
Load capacity	(lb) 15,000
Clutch-reduction-gear case	(pt) 3¼
Clutch selector unit	(pt) 3
Transmission and differential	(qt) 48
Final drive	(each) (qt) 3
Brakes	mechanical, controlled-differential
Parking brake, type	buttons for locking steering levers
Clutch gear-reduction unit:	
Speeds	2
Gear ratio	High 1:1; Low 1.71:1
Transmission:	
Forward speeds	4
Gear ratio	High 1:1; Low 5.43:1
Differential-drive gear ratio	2.6:1
Final-drive gear ratio	2.353:1

PERFORMANCE

Maximum grade ability	(percent) 50
Turning radius	(ft) 20
Fording depth	(in.) 53
Maximum width of ditch vehicle can cross	(in.) 66
Maximum vertical obstacle vehicle can climb	(in.) 18
Fuel consumption (average conditions)	(mpg) 1¼
Cruising range (average conditions)	(mi) 150
Maximum allowable speed, recommended	(mph) 30
Maximum allowable towed load, gross	(lb) 20,000

ENGINE

Manufacturer: Continental	Model R6572
Type	4-cycle, valve-in-head, No. of cylinders (in line) 6
Displacement	(cu in.) 572
Bore	(in.) 4¾
Stroke	(in.) 5¾
Compression ratio	6.5:1
Governed speed	not governed
Brake horsepower (max w/std accessories)	207 at (rpm) 2,900
Torque (max w/std accessories)	455 lb-ft at (rpm) 1,600
Type of ignition	distributor

ADDITIONAL DATA

Provided with electric- and air-brake systems for use with trailers.

Some vehicles provided with ring mount for cal. .50 machine gun, all others may be converted.

Data given for vehicle equipped with track, rubber, T16. Tracks, steel, T36E6 and T54E1, and track, rubber, T44 are interchangeable.

TRACTOR, HIGH-SPEED, 13-TON, M5A1

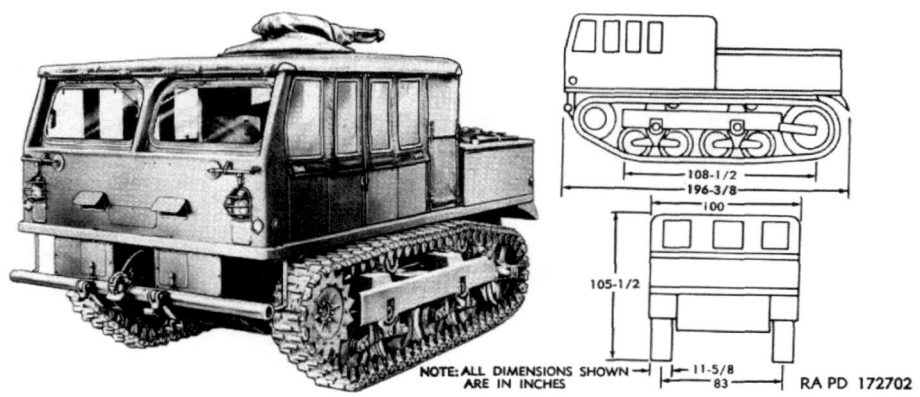

NOTE: ALL DIMENSIONS SHOWN
ARE IN INCHES

RA PD 172702

Technical Manuals: 9-786, 9-1786A, 9-1786B, 9-1825A, 9-1826A, 9-1826C, 9-1828A, 9-1829A; Supply Catalog: SNL G-162.

Classification: Substitute Standard.

Armament: Ring mount for gun, machine, cal. .50, Browning, M2, heavy barrel (flexible).

Ammunition: 56 rounds, 105-mm or 24 rounds, 155-mm with extra fuzes and primers; 550 rounds cal. .50.

Purpose: To tow heavy artillery over rough terrain, and transport gun crews and ammunition.

GENERAL DATA

Crew	11
Weight, fighting	(lb) 30,405
Shipping dimensions, uncrated	(cu ft) 1,200; (sq ft) 137
Ground pressure	(psi) 12.1
Ground clearance	(in.) 19¾
Pintle height, loaded	(in.) 28½
Electrical system	(volts) 12
No. of batteries	1
Type of ground	negative
Fuel octane rating	70
Capacities:	
Fuel	(gal) 100
Cooling system	(qt) 100
Crankcase, refill	(qt) 22
Winch:	
Oil capacity	(pt) 1¾
Load capacity	(lb) 15,000
Clutch-reduction-gear case	(pt) 3¼
Clutch-selector unit	(pt) 3
Transmission and differential	(qt) 48
Final drive	(each) (qt) 3
Brakes	mechanical, controlled-differential
Parking brake, type	buttons for locking steering levers
Clutch gear-reduction-unit:	
Speeds	2
Gear ratio	High 1:1; Low 1.71 :1
Transmission:	
Forward speeds	4
Gear ratio	High 1:1; Low 5.43 :1
Differential-drive gear ratio	2.6 :1
Final-drive gear ratio	2.353 :1

PERFORMANCE

Maximum grade ability	(percent) 50
Turning radius	(ft) 20
Fording depth	(in.) 53
Maximum width of ditch vehicle can cross	(in.) 66
Maximum vertical obstacle vehicle can climb	(in.) 18
Fuel consumption (average conditions)	(mpg) 1½
Cruising range (average conditions)	(mi) 150
Allowable speed, recommended	(mph) 30
Maximum allowable towed load, gross	(lb) 20,000

ENGINE

Manufacturer: Continental........Model R6572

Type	4-cycle, valve-in-head; No. of cylinders (in line) 6
Displacement	(cu in.) 572
Bore	(in.) 4¾
Stroke	(in.) 5¾
Compression ratio	6.5 :1
Governed speed	not governed
Brake horsepower (max w/std accessories)	207 at (rpm) 2,900
Torque (max w/std accessories)	455 lb-ft at (rpm) 1,600
Type of ignition	distributor

ADDITIONAL DATA

Provided with electric- and air-brake systems for use with trailers.

Data given for vehicle equipped with track, rubber, T16. Tracks, steel, T36E6 and T55E1, and track, rubber, T44 are interchangeable.

TRACTOR, HIGH-SPEED, 13-TON, M5A2

NOTE: ALL DIMENSIONS SHOWN
ARE IN INCHES
RA PD 172718

Technical Manuals: 9-786, 9-1786A, 9-1786B, 9-1825A, 9-1826A, 9-1826C, 9-1828A, 9-1829A; Supply Catalog: SNL G-162.

Classification: Substitute Standard.
Armament: See Additional Data.
Ammunition: 56 rounds, 105-mm, or 24 rounds, 155-mm with extra fuzes and primers; 550 rounds cal. .50.

Purpose: To tow heavy artillery over rough terrain, and transport gun crews and ammunition.

GENERAL DATA

Crew	9
Weight, fighting	(lb) 26,149
Shipping dimensions, uncrated	(cu ft) 1,315; (sq ft) 152
Ground pressure	(psi) 5.7
Ground clearance	(in.) 19¾
Pintle height, loaded	(in.) 28½
Electrical system	(volts) 12
No. of batteries	1
Type of ground	negative
Fuel octane rating	70
Capacities:	
Fuel	(gal) 100
Cooling system	(qt) 100
Crankcase, refill	(qt) 22
Winch:	
Oil capacity	(pt) 1¼
Load capacity	(lb) 15,000
Clutch reduction-gear case	(pt) 3¼
Clutch selector unit	(pt) 3
Transmission and differential	(qt) 48
Final drive	(each) (qt) 3
Brakes	mechanical, controlled-differential
Parking brake, type	buttons for locking steering brakes
Clutch gear-reduction unit:	
Speeds	2
Gear ratio	High 1:1; Low 1.71:1
Transmission:	
Forward speeds	4
Gear ratio	High 1:1; Low 5.43:1
Differential-drive gear ratio	2.6:1
Final-drive gear ratio	2.53:1

PERFORMANCE

Maximum grade ability	(percent) 50
Turning radius	(ft) 20
Fording depth	(in.) 53
Maximum width of ditch vehicle can cross	(in.) 66
Maximum vertical obstacle vehicle can climb	(in.) 18
Fuel consumption (average conditions)	(mpg) 1½
Cruising range (average conditions)	(mi) 150
Allowable speed, recommended	(mph) 30
Maximum allowable towed load, gross	(lb) 20,000

ENGINE

Manufacturer: Continental	Model: R6572
Type	4-cycle, valve-in-head; No. of cylinders (in line) 6
Displacement	(cu in.) 572
Bore	(in.) 4¾
Stroke	(in.) 5¾
Compression ratio	6.5:1
Governed speed	not governed
Brake horsepower (max w/std accessories)	207 at (rpm) 2,900
Torque (max w/std accessories)	455 lb-ft at (rpm) 1,600
Type of ignition	distributor

ADDITIONAL DATA

Provided with electric- and air-brake systems for use with trailers.
Some vehicles equipped with ring mount for cal. .50 machine gun, others can be converted.
Data given for vehicle equipped with track, steel, T82.

TRACTOR, HIGH-SPEED, 13-TON, M5A3

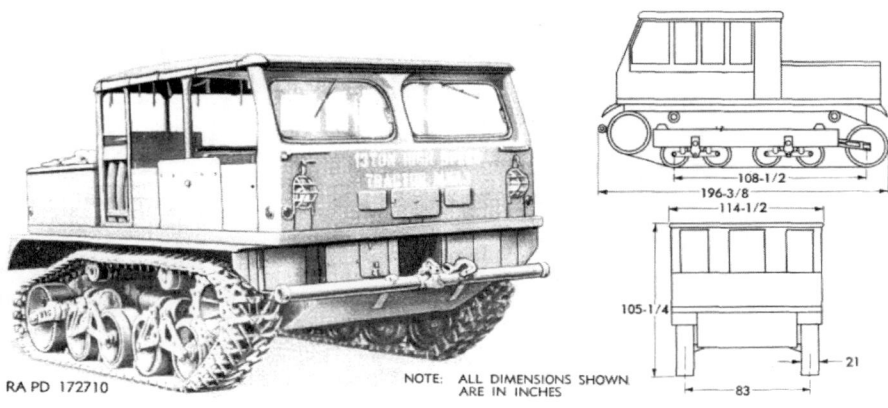

RA PD 172710

NOTE: ALL DIMENSIONS SHOWN
ARE IN INCHES

Technical Manuals: 9-786, 9-1786A, 9-1786B, 9-1825A, 9-1826A, 9-1826C, 9-1828A, 9-1829A; Supply Catalog: SNL G-162.

Classification: Standard.
Armament: Ring mount for gun, machine, cal. .50, Browning, M2, heavy barrel (flexible).
Ammunition: 56 rounds, 105-mm or 24 rounds, 155-mm with extra fuzes and primers; 550 rounds cal. .50.

Purpose: To tow heavy artillery over rough terrain, and transport gun crews and ammunition.

GENERAL DATA

Crew	11
Weight, fighting	(lb) 30,350
Shipping dimensions, uncrated	(cu ft) 1,375; (sq ft) 157
Ground pressure	(psi) 6.7
Ground clearance	(in.) 19¾
Pintle height, loaded	(in.) 28½
Electrical system	(volts) 12
No. of batteries	1
Type of ground	negative
Fuel octane rating	70
Capacities:	
Fuel	(gal) 100
Cooling system	(qt) 100
Crankcase, refill	(qt) 22
Winch:	
Oil capacity	(pt) 1¾
Load capacity	(lb) 15,000
Clutch-reduction-gear case	(pt) 3¼
Clutch selector unit	(pt) 3
Transmission and differential	(qt) 48
Final drive	(each) (qt) 3
Brakes	mechanical, controlled-differential
Parking brake, type	buttons for locking steering levers
Clutch gear-reduction unit:	
Speeds	2
Gear ratio	High 1:1; Low 1.71:1
Differential-drive gear ratio	2.6:1
Final-drive gear ratio	2.353:1
Transmission:	
Forward speeds	4
Gear ratio	High 1:1; Low 5.43:1

PERFORMANCE

Maximum grade ability	(percent) 50
Turning radius	(ft) 20
Fording depth	(in.) 53
Maximum width of ditch vehicle can cross	(in.) 66
Maximum vertical obstacle vehicle can climb	(in.) 18
Fuel consumption (average conditions)	(mpg) 1½
Cruising range (average conditions)	(mi) 150
Allowable speed, recommended	(mph) 30
Maximum allowable towed load, gross	(lb) 20,000

ENGINE

Manufacturer: Continental	Model; R6572
Type	4-cycle, valve-in-head; No. of cylinders (in line) 6
Displacement	(cu in.) 572
Bore	(in.) 4¾
Stroke	(in.) 5⅜
Compression ratio	6.5:1
Governed speed	not governed
Brake horsepower (max w/std accessories)	207 at (rpm) 2,900
Torque (max w/std accessories)	455 lb-ft at (rpm) 1,600
Type of ignition	distributor

ADDITIONAL DATA

Provided with electric- and air-brake systems for use with trailers. Data given for vehicle equipped with track, steel, T82.

TRACTOR, HIGH-SPEED, 18-TON, M4, M4A1, M4C, AND M4A1C

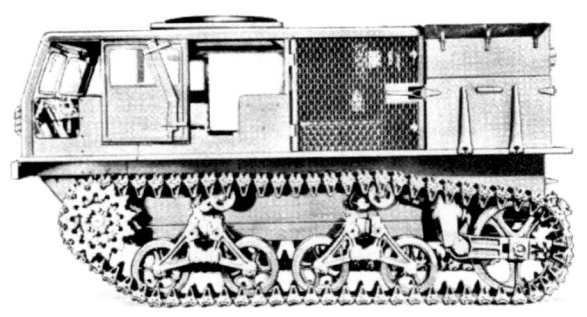

RA PD 172748

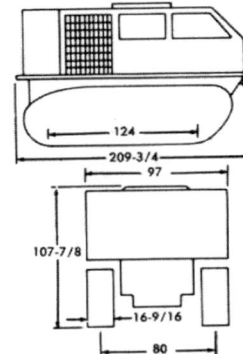

NOTE: ALL DIMENSIONS SHOWN ARE IN INCHES

Technical Manuals: 9-785, 9-1785A, 9-1785B, 9-1825A, 9-1826C, 9-1827A, 9-1828A, 9-1829A; **Supply Catalog:** SNL G-150.

Vehicle illustrated: M4.

Classification: Limited Standard.

Armament: Ring mount on top of cab for 1 gun, machine, cal. .50, Browning, M2, heavy barrel (flexible), or 1 gun, machine, cal. .30, Browning, M1919A4 (flexible).

Purpose: To tow heavy artillery over rough terrain and transport gun crews and ammunition.

Ammunition: 54 rounds, 90-mm or 105-mm; 550 rounds, cal. .50.

GENERAL DATA

Crew..11
Weight, fighting...................................(lb) 31,400
Shipping dimensions, uncrated..........(cu ft) 1,270; (sq ft) 141
Ground pressure....................................(psi) 7.6
Ground clearance..................................(in.) 20⅝
Pintle height, loaded..............................(in.) 29
Electrical system.................................(volts) 12
   No. of batteries.....................................1
   Type of ground................................negative
Fuel octane rating.....................................70
Capacities:
   Fuel...(gal) 125
   Cooling system....................................(qt) 72
   Crankcase, refill..................................(qt) 18
   Winch:
      Oil capacity....................................(qt) 3
      Load capacity.............................(lb) 30,000
   Torque-converter-pump-drive housing..............(qt) 1
   Torque converter..................................(qt) 34
   Fan-drive gear housing...........................(qt) ⅞
   Fan-drive housing.................................(qt) ⅓
   Transmission and differential.....................(qt) 28
   Final drive...............................(each) (qt) 10
Brakes.................mechanical, controlled-differential
   Parking brake, type...........knobs for locking steering brakes
Torque-converter stall ratio.........................4.8:1
Transmission:
   Forward speeds.......................................3
   Gear ratio..........High 0.438:1, Low 1.56:1; Creeper gear 2.16:1
Differential-drive gear ratio.....................2.682:1
Final-drive gear ratio............................2.764:1

PERFORMANCE

Maximum grade ability..........................(percent) 30
Turning radius...................................(ft) 18½
Fording depth....................................(in.) 41

PERFORMANCE—Continued

Maximum width of ditch vehicle can cross..........(in.) 60
Maximum vertical obstacle vehicle can climb.......(in.) 29
Fuel consumption (average conditions)............(mpg) 0.8
Cruising range (average conditions)...............(mi) 100
Allowable speed, governed........................(mph) 35
Maximum allowable towed load, gross............(lb) 38,700

ENGINE

Manufacturer Waukesha.......................Model 145GZ
Type.............4-cycle, valve-in-head; No. of cylinders (in line) 6
Displacement....................................(cu in.) 817
Bore..(in.) 5⅞
Stroke...(in.) 6
Compression ratio..............................5.95:1
Governed speed..................................(rpm) 2,100
Brake horsepower (max w/std accessories)........190 at (rpm) 2,100
Torque (max w/std accessories)............600 lb-ft at (rpm) 1,200
Type of ignition.............................distributor

ADDITIONAL DATA

Provided with electric- and air-brakes systems for use with trailers.

Data given for vehicle equipped with track, rubber, T48. Tracks, steel, T49 and T54E1 are interchangeable.

Above data are for M4. Changes for others are as follows: M4C carries 30 rounds, 155-mm or 12 rounds, 240-mm and 550 rounds cal. .50.

M4A1 carries 30 rounds, 155-mm or 12 rounds, 240-mm and 550 rounds cal. .50. A hoist is provided for handling the shells.

Changes in data for M4A1:

Tracks used: Track, rubber, T48 with extended end connectors, tracks, steel, T49 and T54E1 with extended end connectors.
Over-all width....................................(in.) 111
Ground pressure....................................(psi) 5.4
Shipping dimensions, uncrated.........(cu ft) 1,450; (sq ft) 162

M4A1C is the same as M4A1, except the M4A1C has provision for stowage of shells in the rear crew compartment.

TRACTOR, HIGH-SPEED, 38-TON, M6

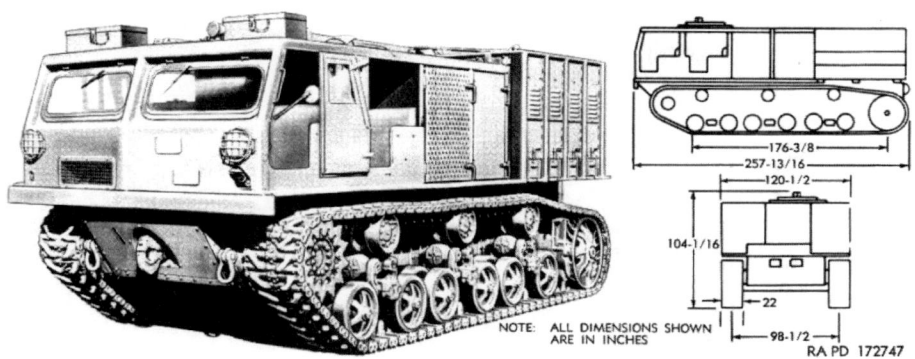

NOTE: ALL DIMENSIONS SHOWN ARE IN INCHES

RA PD 172747

Technical Manuals: 9–788, 9–1785A, 9–1788, 9–1825A, 9–1826C, 9–1827A, 9–1828A, 9–1829A; **Supply Catalog:** SNL G–184.

Classification: Standard.

Armament: Ring mount on top of cab for gun, machine, cal. .50, Browning, M2, heavy barrel (flexible).

Ammunition: 14 rounds, 240-mm, or 14 rounds, 8-inch, or 32 rounds, 120-mm; extra fuzes and primers; 550, rounds cal. .50.

Purpose: To tow heavy artillery and transport gun crews and ammunition.

GENERAL DATA

Crew	11
Weight, gross	(lb) 76,000
Shipping dimensions, uncrated	(cu ft) 1,870; (sq ft) 215
Ground pressure	(psi) 9.8
Ground clearance	(in.) 21½
Pintle height, loaded	(in.) 30
Electrical system	(volts) 12
No. of batteries	(12-volt) 2
Type of ground	negative
Fuel octane rating	70
Capacities:	
Fuel	(gal) 300
Cooling system	(each) (qt) 72
Crankcase, refill	(each) (qt) 26
Winch:	
Oil capacity	(qt) 4
Load capacity	(lb) 55,000
Torque-converter-pump-drive housing	(each) (qt) 1
Torque converter	(each) (qt) 38
Fan-drive-gear housing	(each) (qt) 1¼
Transmission and differential	(qt) 88
Final drive	(each) (qt) 25
Brakes	mechanical, controlled-differential
Parking brake, type	knobs for locking steering brakes
Transmission:	
Forward speeds	2
Gear ratio	High 0.695:1; Low 2.12:1
Torque-converter stall ratio	4.8:1
Differential-drive gear ratio	2.682:1
Final-drive gear ratio	3.06:1

PERFORMANCE

Maximum grade ability	(percent) 60
Turning radius	(ft) 26½
Fording depth	(in.) 54
Maximum width of ditch vehicle can cross:	
Forward	(in.) 102
Reverse	(in.) 96
Maximum vertical obstacle vehicle can climb	(in.) 30
Fuel consumption (average conditions)	(mpg) 0.3
Cruising range (average conditions)	(mi) 100
Maximum speed	(mph) 21
Maximum allowable towed load, gross	(lb) 50,000

ENGINE

Manufacturer: Waukesha	No. used 2; Model 145GZ
Type	4-cycle, valve-in-head; No. of cylinders (in line) 6
Displacement	(cu in.) 817
Bore	(in.) 5⅜
Stroke	(in.) 6
Compression ratio	5.95:1
Governed speed	(rpm) 2,100
Brake horsepower (max w/std accessories)	190 at (rpm) 2,100
Torque (max w/std accessories)	600 lb-ft at (rpm) 1,200
Type of ignition	distributor

ADDITIONAL DATA

Provided with electric- and air-brake systems for use with trailers.

Data given for vehicle equipped with track, steel, T73. Track rubber-backed-steel, T80E2, and track, rubber, T84E2 are applicable with spaced-out sprockets.

TRAILER, CARGO, ¼-TON, 2-WHEEL

(American Bantam, Model T3, 1942–43; Willys, Model MBT, Amphibian; Converto; Fruehauf; Gemco; Pacific Car; Springfield; A Black; Checker Cab; Strick; Transportation Equipment; Utility)

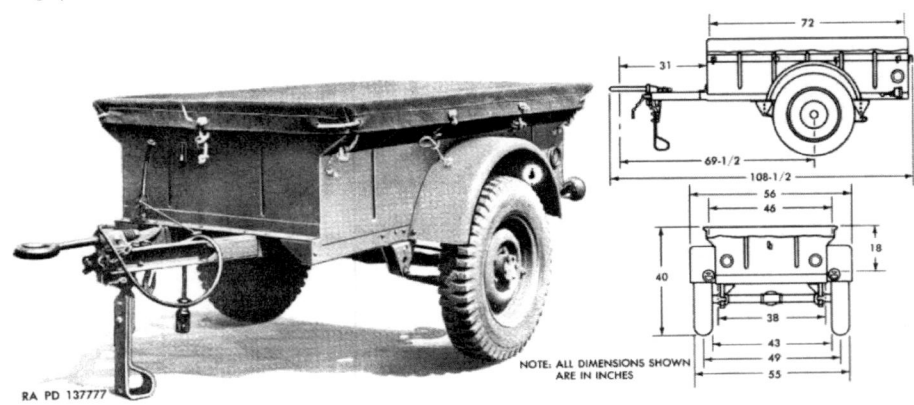

RA PD 137777

NOTE: ALL DIMENSIONS SHOWN ARE IN INCHES

Technical Manual: 10–1281; Supply Catalog: SNL G–529.

Vehicle illustrated: Willys.
Classification: Standard.

Purpose: To transport general cargo on land or water.

GENERAL DATA

Weight (lb): Net..550
    Payload............................off highway 500; on highway 1,000
    Gross..............................off highway 1,050; on highway 1,550
Weight distribution (lb):
    Empty...lunette 80; axle 470
    Loaded:
        Off highway.................................lunette 153; axle 897
        On highway...............................lunette 226; axle 1,324
Tires...............................Ply 6; Size 6.00 x 16; Pressure (psi) 30
Shipping dimensions, uncrated.......................(cu ft) 116; (sq ft) 42
Vehicle dimensions:
    Ground clearance..(in.) 12½
    Lunette height, empty.......................................(in.) 22
    Cargo space...(cu ft) 29
Parking brake, type....................................mechanical
Towing vehicles to be used:
    Any land vehicle or amphibian equipped with pintle hook

ADDITIONAL DATA

Trailer will float with 500-pound payload, with 6 inches freeboard.

TRAILER, CARGO, ¼-TON, 2-WHEEL, M100

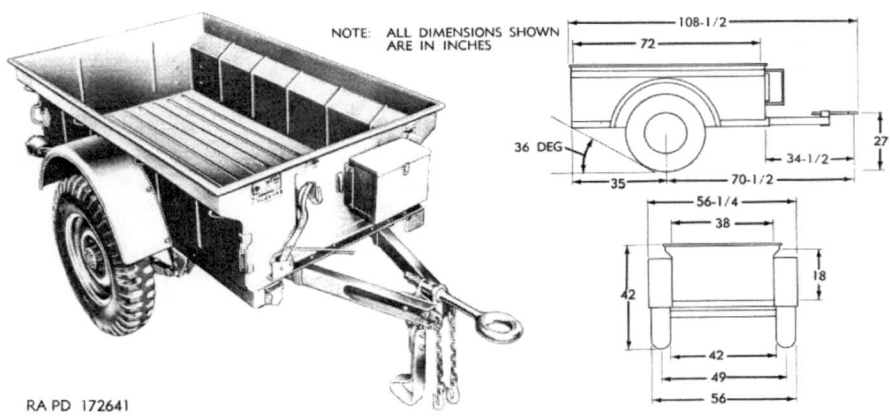

NOTE: ALL DIMENSIONS SHOWN ARE IN INCHES

108-1/2
72
36 DEG
35
34-1/2
70-1/2
27
56-1/4
38
42
18
42
49
56

RA PD 172641

Technical Manual: 9-871A; Supply Catalog: SNL G-747.

Classification: Standard.

Purpose: To transport general cargo on land or water.

GENERAL DATA

Weight (lb): Net	56^5
Payload	off highway 500; on highway 75^0
Gross	off highway 1,065; on highway 1,315
Weight distribution (lb):	
Empty	lunette 85; axle 480
Loaded:	
Off highway	lunette 100; axle 965
On highway	lunette 120; axle 1,195
Tires	Ply 6; Size 7.00 x 16; Pressure (psi) 35
Shipping dimensions, uncrated	(cu ft) 149; (sq ft) 43
Vehicle dimensions:	
Ground clearance	(in.) 13½
Loading height, empty	(in.) 42
Body inside dimensions (in):	
Length 72	Width 38; Height 18
Cargo space	(cu ft) 28½
Parking brake, type	mechanical
Towing vehicle to be used:	
Any land or amphibious vehicle equipped with pintle hook.	

ADDITIONAL DATA

Trailer will float with 500-lb payload.

TRAILER, CARGO, ¾-TON, 2-WHEEL, M101

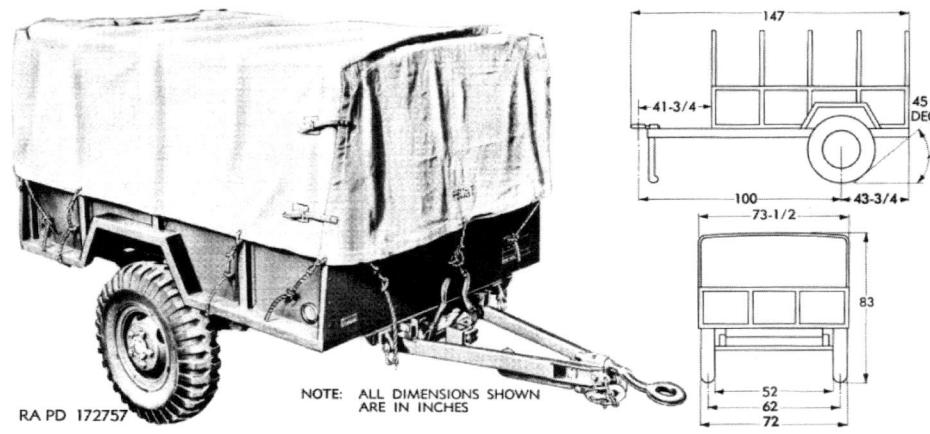

RA PD 172757

NOTE: ALL DIMENSIONS SHOWN
ARE IN INCHES

Purpose: To transport general cargo.

GENERAL DATA

Weight (lb)..Net 1,340
   Payload..........................off highway 1,500; on highway 2,250
   Gross.............................off highway 2,840; on highway 3,590
Weight distribution (lb):
   Empty...............................lunette 115; axle 1,225
   Loaded:
      Off highway..................................lunette 200; axle 2,640
      On highway..................................lunette 230; axle 3,360
Tires..............................Ply 8; Size 9.00 x 16; Pressure (psi) 40
Shipping dimensions, uncrated..........................(cu ft) 520; (sq ft) 75
Vehicle dimensions:
   Ground clearance...................................(in.) 14
   Loading height, empty..............................(in.) 35
   Lunette height w/body horizontal...................(in.) 21⅜
   Body inside dimensions (in.):
      Length 96............................Width 65½; Height 48
   Cargo space..(cu ft) 175
Parking brake, type...mechanical
Minimum towing vehicle to be used.....................truck, ¾-ton, 4 x 4

ADDITIONAL DATA

TRAILER, CARGO, 1-TON, 2-WHEEL
(American Bantam, T6; Ben Hur 41–33, 41–120; etc. See Additional Data)

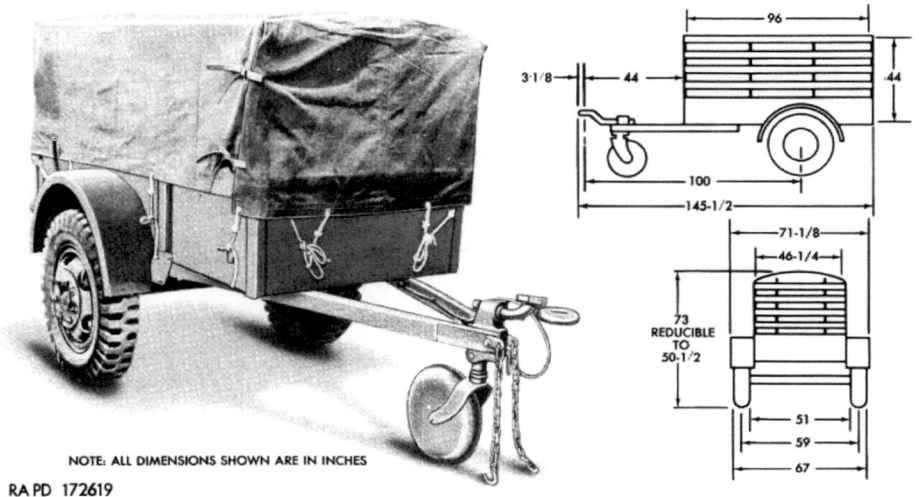

NOTE: ALL DIMENSIONS SHOWN ARE IN INCHES

RA PD 172619

Technical Manual: 9–883; Supply Catalog: SNL G–518.

Vehicle illustrated: Ben Hur.
Classification: Standard.

Purpose: To transport general cargo.

GENERAL DATA

Weight (lb)	Net 1,300
Payload	off highway 2,000; on highway 3,000
Gross	off highway 3,300; on highway 4,300
Weight distribution (lb):	
Empty	lunette 150; axle 1,150
Loaded:	
Off highway	lunette 260; axle 3,040
On highway	lunette 315; axle 3,985
Tires	Ply 8; Size 7.50 x 20; Pressure (psi) 55
Shipping dimensions, uncrated	(cu ft) 437; (sq ft) 72
Vehicle dimensions:	
Ground clearance	(in.) 15
Loading height	(in.) 37¾
Cargo space	(cu ft) 113
Brakes	hand parking only
Towing vehicles to be used	truck, ¼-ton, 4 x 4; ½-ton, 4 x 2

ADDITIONAL DATA

Similar vehicles manufactured by Century Boat works, T6; Checker, CC5, CC5A; Dorsey, T6; Gerstenslager, A; Henney, H1; Hercules Body, T6; Highland Body and Trailer, T6; Hobbs, 0901D; Hyde, L1; Mifflinburg Body, T6; Nabors, 3GC; Nash Kelvinator. A; Omaha Std Body, TW2; Pike, T6; Queen City, T6; Redman, T6; Steel Products, AC; Strick, US; Transportation Equip, T6; Truck Eng Corp, T6; Willys Overland, TW6; Winter-Weiss, T6; Baker; Covered Wagon; Keystone; Streich, M1.

Weight data for wood body; steel body 1,490 lb net, 3,490 lb gross off highway, 4,300 lb gross on highway.

Height of lunette (in.) High position 31; Low position 26

133

TRAILER, TIRE REPAIR, 1-TON, 2-WHEEL, LOAD A, M25
(TRAILER, 1-ton, 2-wheel, cargo, w/equipment installed by Kreiger)

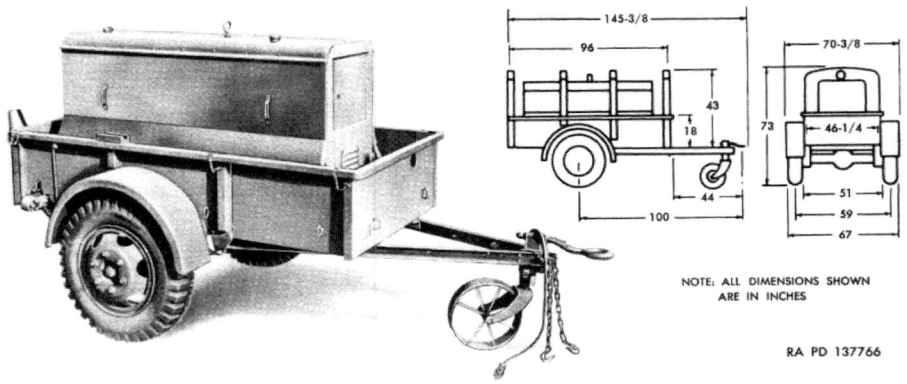

NOTE: ALL DIMENSIONS SHOWN
ARE IN INCHES

RA PD 137766

Technical Manual: 9-883; Supply Catalog No: SNL G-234.

Classification: Standard.

Purpose: To transport 25-kw generator to supply power for mobile tire-repair unit.

GENERAL DATA

Weight (lb) .... Net 1,300; Payload 2,500; Gross 3,800
Weight distribution (lb):
    Empty..lunette 150; axle 1,150
    Loaded...lunette 280; axle 3,520
Tires....................................Ply 8; Size 7.50 x 20; Pressure (psi) 55
Shipping dimensions, uncrated...........................(cu ft) 432; (sq ft) 71
Vehicle dimensions:
    Ground clearance..(in.) 15
    Loading height...(in.) 31¼
Brakes..hand parking only
Towing vehicle to be used..........truck, 2½-ton, tire repair, load A, M32

ADDITIONAL DATA

TRAILER, TIRE REPAIR, 1-TON, 2-WHEEL, LOAD B, M25
(TRAILER, cargo, 1-ton, 2-wheel, w/equipment installed by Kreiger)

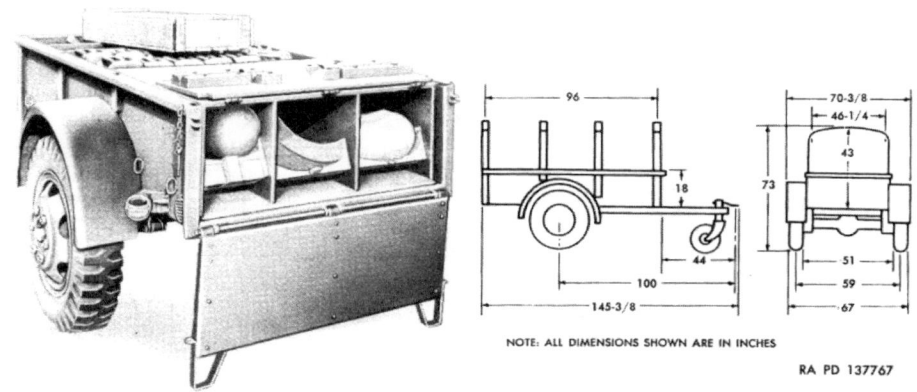

NOTE: ALL DIMENSIONS SHOWN ARE IN INCHES

RA PD 137767

Technical Manual: 9-883; Supply Catalog: SNL G-234.

Classification: Standard.

Purpose: To transport tire buffers, extra large matrices, head plate, and bags for mobile tire-repair unit, and water and gasoline in 5-gallon cans for servicing power unit in trailer carrying load A.

GENERAL DATA

Weight (lb)..........................Net 1,300; Payload 1,050; Gross 2,350
Weight distribution (lb):
    Empty...lunette 150; axle 1,150
    Loaded.......................................lunette 220; axle 2,130
Tires..........................Ply 8; Size 7.50 x 20; Pressure (psi) 55
Shipping dimensions, uncrated......................(cu ft) 432; (sq ft) 71
Vehicle dimensions:
    Ground clearance...(in.) 15
    Loading height...(in.) 31¼
Brakes..hand parking only
Towing vehicle to be used...truck, 2½ ton, 6 x 6, tire repair, load B, M32

ADDITIONAL DATA

TRAILER, WATER TANK, 1-TON, 2-WHEEL, 250-GAL

(Ben Hur, Model KWT; Checker, Models CC1, CC1A, CC1B, CC1C; Springfield Wagon and Trailer, Model SWT (T1–250); City Tank; Davis Welding; Fayette, Model 25; Lavine, Model KWT)

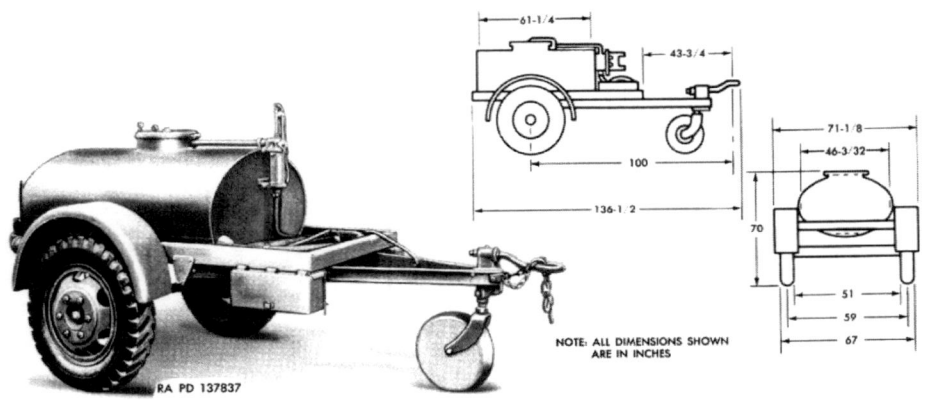

NOTE: ALL DIMENSIONS SHOWN ARE IN INCHES

RA PD 137837

Technical Manual: 9-883; Supply Catalog: SNL G-527.

Vehicle illustrated: Ben Hur.
Classification: Standard.

Purpose: To transport, store, and dispense drinking water.

GENERAL DATA

Weight (lb):
    Steel tank.........................Net 1,500; Payload 2,000; Gross 3,500
    Aluminum tank..................Net 1,350; Payload 2,000; Gross 3,350
Weight distribution (w/steel tank) (lb):
    Empty...lunette, 225; axle 1,275
    Loaded...lunette 270; axle 3,230
Tires.................................Ply 8; Size 7.50 x 20; Pressure (psi) 55
Shipping dimensions, uncrated.....................(cu ft); 347 (sq ft) 68
Ground clearance...(in.) 15
Brakes..parking; mechanical
Towing vehicles to be used................truck, ¼-ton, 4 x 4; ½-ton, 4 x 2

ADDITIONAL DATA

Height of lunette (in.).....................High position 31; Low position 26

TRAILER, CARGO, 1½-TON, 2-WHEEL, M104

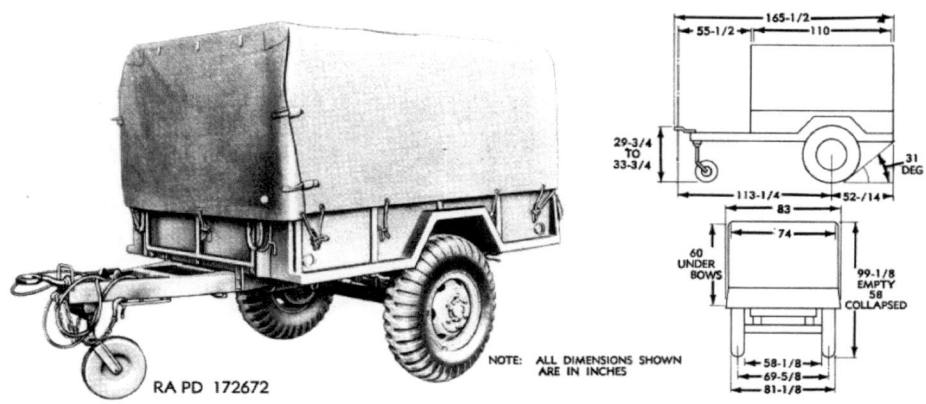

RA PD 172672

NOTE: ALL DIMENSIONS SHOWN ARE IN INCHES

Technical Manual: 9-875B; **Supply Catalog:** SNL G-754.

Classification: Standard.

Purpose: To transport general cargo.

GENERAL DATA

Weight (lb): Net..2,400
    Payload.............................off highway 3,000; on highway 5,500
    Gross.................................off highway 5,400; on highway 7,900
Weight distribution (lb):
    Empty..lunette 200; axle 2,200
    Loaded:
        Off highway.....................................lunette 370; axle 5,030
        On highway......................................lunette 510; axle 7,390
Tires: Ply 12; Size 11.00 x 20; Pressure (psi):
    On highway..50
    Cross country..35
Shipping dimensions, uncrated......................(cu ft) 462; (sq ft) 96
Vehicle dimensions:
    Ground clearance..(in.) 19½
    Loading height, empty..(in.) 40
    Body inside dimensions (in.):
        Length 110...........................Width 74; Height 60
        Cargo space.......................................(cu ft) 283
Brakes:
    Manufacturer; Timken-Detroit...................Type; air-hydraulic
    Parking brake, type.....................................mechanical
Minimum towing vehicle to be used...................truck, 2½-ton, 6 x 6

ADDITIONAL DATA

This trailer can be used only with a towing vehicle having an air supply such as the M34.

TRAILER, WATER TANK, 1½-TON, 2-WHEEL, M106

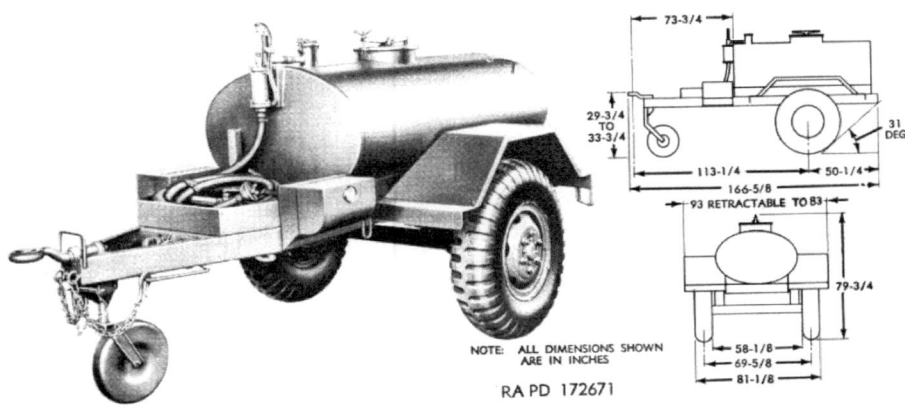

NOTE: ALL DIMENSIONS SHOWN ARE IN INCHES

RA PD 172671

Technical Manual: 9-875B; Supply Catalog: SNL G-754.

Classification: Standard.

Purpose: To transport, store, and dispense drinking water.

GENERAL DATA

Weight (lb) .... Net 2,280; Payload 3,335; Gross 5,615
Weight distribution (lb):
    Empty..lunette 280; axle 2,000
    Loaded...lunette 280; axle 5,335
Tires: Ply 12; Size 11.00 x 20; Pressure (psi):
    On highway...50
    Cross country...35
Shipping dimensions, uncrated........................(cu ft) 700; (sq ft) 105
Vehicle dimensions:
    Ground clearance...(in.) 19½
    Capacity..(gal) 400
    Fording depth.....................................complete submergence
Brakes:
    Manufacturer: Timken-Detroit.....................Type: air-hydraulic
    Parking brake, type....................................mechanical
Minimum towing vehicle to be used...................truck, 2½-ton, 6 x 6

ADDITIONAL DATA

Can be used only with a towing vehicle having an air supply, such as the M34.

Equipped with hand pump and 25-ft suction hose for filling and faucets for dispensing. Also filler hatch and manhole with hinged cover.

TRAILER, DIRECTOR, 2-TON, 4-WHEEL, M13
(Brill)

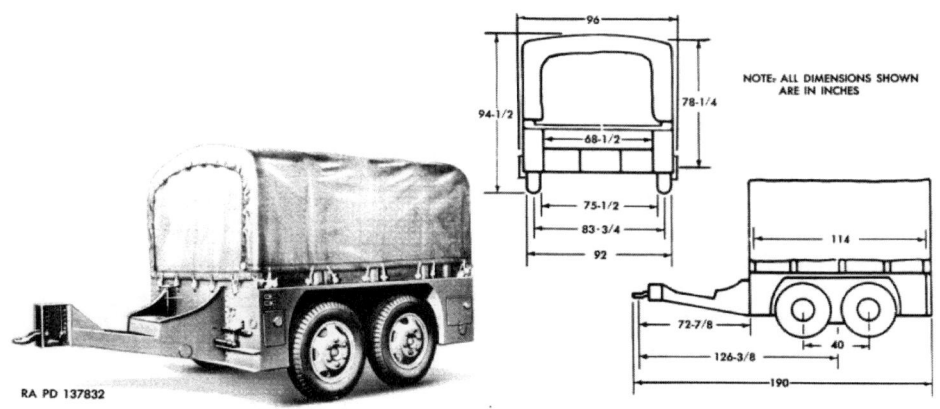

NOTE: ALL DIMENSIONS SHOWN ARE IN INCHES

RA PD 137832

Technical Manual: 9-881; Supply Catalog: SNL G-221.

Classification: Limited Standard.

Purpose: To carry directors, M9 and M10.

GENERAL DATA

Weight (lb)..Net 4,400; Gross 7,850
Weight distribution (lb):
    Empty....................................front axle 2,200; rear axle 2,200
    Loaded....................................front axle 3,925; rear axle 3,925
Tires....................................Ply 12; Size 7.50 x 20; Pressure (psi) 55
Shipping dimensions, uncrated......................(cu ft) 1,029; (sq ft) 126
Vehicle dimensions:
    Ground clearance..(in.) 4½
    Loading height..(in.) 17¾
Brakes:
    Manufacturer: Warner.................................Type: electric
    Parking brake.................manually operates the service brakes
Minimum towing vehicle to be used....................truck, ¾-ton, 4 x 4

ADDITIONAL DATA

TRAILER, DIRECTOR, 2-TON, 4-WHEEL, M14 AND M22
(Brill, Fruehauf)

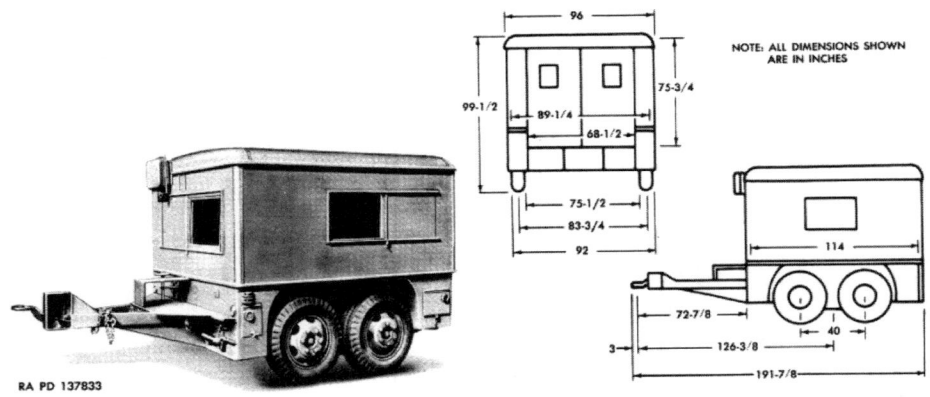

NOTE: ALL DIMENSIONS SHOWN
ARE IN INCHES

RA PD 137833

Technical Manual: 9-881; Supply Catalog: SNL G-221.

Vehicle illustrated: Fruehauf.
Classification: M14 Limited Standard; M22 Standard.

Purpose: To carry directors, M9 and M10.

GENERAL DATA

Weight w/director (lb)...................................Gross 8,900
Axle load (lb)..................................front, 4,450; rear 4,450
Tires.............................Ply 12; Size 7.50 x 20; Pressure (psi) 55
Shipping dimensions, uncrated.....................(cu ft) 1,060; (sq ft) 128
Ground clearance...(in.) 9¾
Brakes:
    Manufacturer; Warner....................................Type; electric
    Parking brake, type......................................handwheel operated
Minimum towing vehicle to be used..................truck, 1½-ton, 4 x 2

ADDITIONAL DATA

Height of lunette adjustable from 24¼ in. to 32¼ in.

TRAILER, GENERATOR, 2-TON, 4-WHEEL, M7
(Brill, Fruehauf, Kreiger)

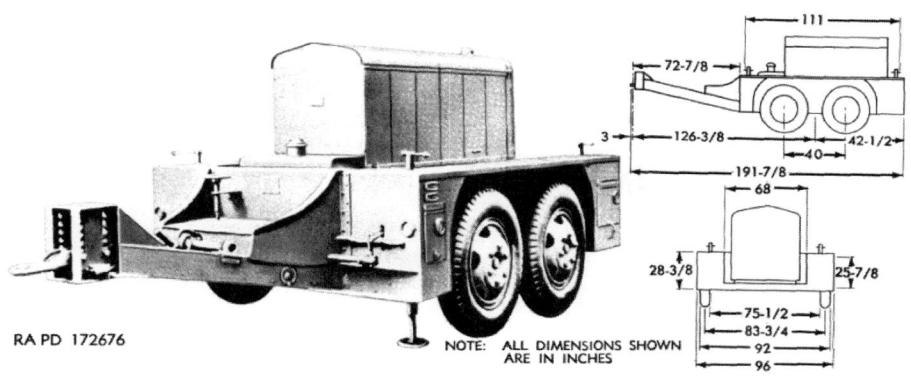

RA PD 172676

NOTE: ALL DIMENSIONS SHOWN ARE IN INCHES

Technical Manual: 9-881; Supply Catalog: SNL G-221.

Vehicle illustrated: Brill, with generator unit.
Classification: Standard.

Purpose: To transport generating units M7, M7A1, M15, M15A1 and M18.

GENERAL DATA

Weight (lb)..........................Net 4,150; Payload 4,298; Gross 8,448
Axle load (lb):
    Empty...front 2,075; rear 2,075
    Loaded..front 4,224; rear 4,224
Tires........................Ply 12; Size 7.50 x 20; Pressure (psi) 55
Shipping dimensions, uncrated.......................(cu ft) 470; (sq ft) 128
Vehicle dimensions:
    Ground clearance...(in.) 9¾
    Loading height...(in.) 17¾
    Body inside dimensions (in.):
        Length 111....................................Width 68; Height 25⅞
Brakes:
    Manufacturer; Warner........ ....Type; electric
    Parking brake, type.................................handwheel operated
Towing vehicle to be used.............................truck, 2½-ton, 6 x 6

ADDITIONAL DATA

TRAILER, GENERATOR, 2-TON, 4-WHEEL, M18

(Fruehauf, Kreiger)

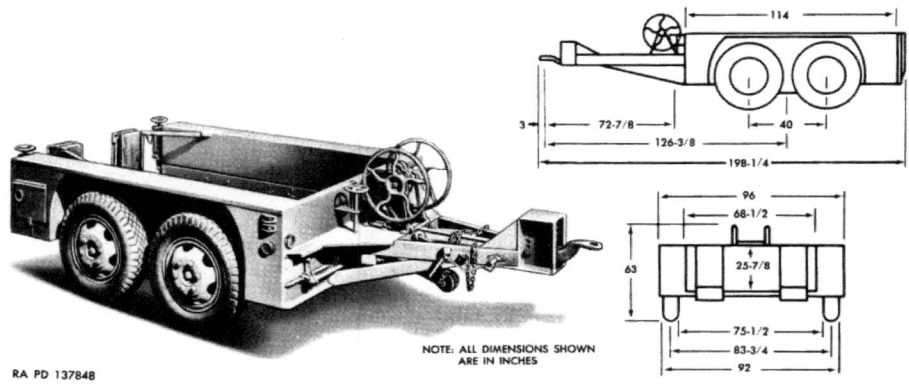

RA PD 137848

NOTE: ALL DIMENSIONS SHOWN
ARE IN INCHES

Technical Manual: 9-881; Supply Catalog: SNL G-221.

Vehicle illustrated: Fruehauf.
Classification: Standard.

Purpose: To transport generating units.

GENERAL DATA

Weight (lb)............................Net 4,000; Payload 4,194; Gross 8,194
Axle load (lb):
  Empty...front 2,000; rear 2,000
  Loaded..front 4,097; rear 4,097
Tires.........................Ply 12; Size 7.50 x 20; Pressure (psi) 55
Shipping dimensions, uncrated.......................(cu ft) 694; (sq ft) 132
Vehicle dimensions:
  Ground clearance..(in.) 9¾
  Loading height..(in.) 17¾
Brakes:
  Manufacturer: Warner............................Type; electric
  Parking brake, type..........................handwheel operated
Towing vehicle to be used...........................truck, 2½-ton, 6 x 6

ADDITIONAL DATA

Lunette height (in.)................................Adjustable from 24¾ to 32¾

TRAILER, BOMB, 2½-TON, 3-WHEEL, M5
(American Seating, Oneida, Saginaw, Electric Wheel)

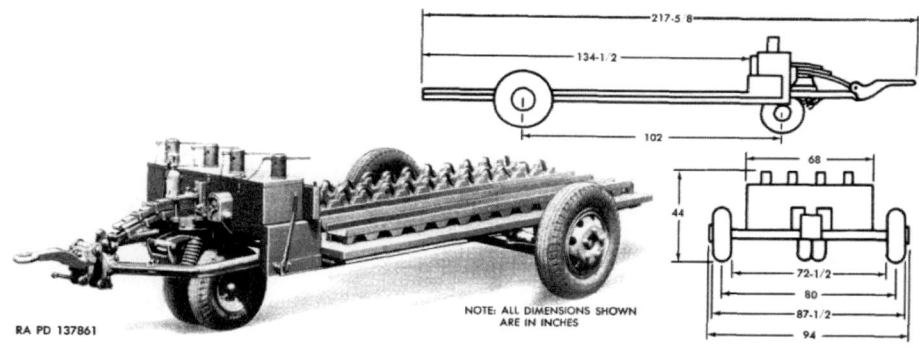

RA PD 137861

NOTE: ALL DIMENSIONS SHOWN ARE IN INCHES

Technical Manual: 9-760; Supply Catalog: SNL G-74.

Classification: Standard.

Purpose: Used by AF to transport bombs.

GENERAL DATA

Weight (lb) ....Net 3,200; Payload 5,000; Gross 8,200
Axle load (lb):
   Empty..front 1,066; rear 2,134
   Loaded.......................................front 2,400; rear 5,800
Vehicle dimensions:
   Ground clearance (rear axle)........................(in.) 9½
   Loading height....................................(in.) 21½
Tires:
   Ply.....................front 6; rear 8; Size front 6.50 x 10; rear 7.50 x 18
   Pressure (psi)...............................front 45; rear 55
   Tread, center-to-center, front........................(in.) 10¾
Shipping dimensions, uncrated...................(cu ft) 519; (sq ft) 142
Pintle height..(in.) 20½
Brakes: Manufacturer: Warner.............................Type: electric
Minimum towing vehicle to be used..................truck, 1½-ton, 4 x 2

ADDITIONAL DATA

Front of hitch yoke has reversible lunette to attach to rear pintle of another trailer, or to a prime mover, so that it can be towed in trains at speeds up to 45 mph on highways.

TRAILER, CLAMSHELL, 3-TON, 2-WHEEL, M16
(Gramm)
Used w/CRANE, Truck Mounted, M2

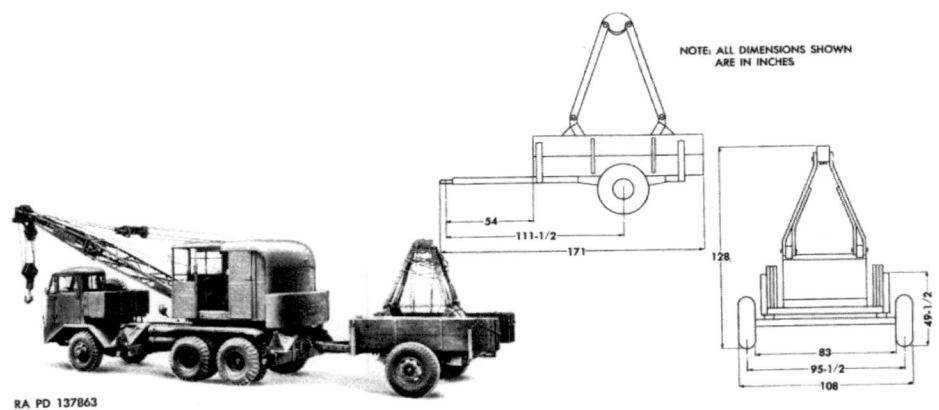

NOTE: ALL DIMENSIONS SHOWN
ARE IN INCHES

RA PD 137863

Technical Manual: 9-771; **Supply Catalog:** SNL G-172.

Classification: Standard.

Purpose: Equipment for Truck-Mounted Crane, M2.

GENERAL DATA

Weight (lb)........................Net 2,425; Payload 5,815; Gross 8,240
Weight distribution (lb)......................Loaded lunette, 725; axle 7,515
Tires....................................Ply 14; Size 12.00 x 20; Pressure (psi) 75
Shipping dimensions, uncrated:
   Loaded w/clamshell and 10-ft mats................(cu ft) 1,370; (sq ft) 128
Vehicle dimensions:
   Ground clearance...(in.) 15
   Loading height, empty..(in.) 49½
Brakes..none
Minimum towing vehicle to be used............Crane, Truck Mounted, M2

ADDITIONAL DATA

Lunette height...(in.) 33¼

TRAILER, AMMUNITION, 4-TON, 2-WHEEL, M21

(Oneida, Trailmobile)

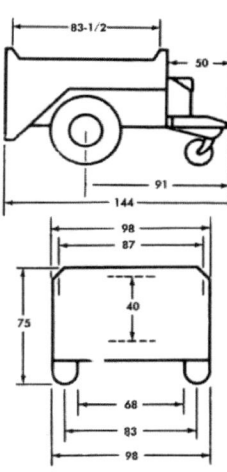

NOTE: ALL DIMENSIONS SHOWN
ARE IN INCHES

RA PD 172629

Technical Manuals: 9-792, 9-1827A; Supply Catalog: SNL G-213.

Classification: Limited Standard.

Purpose: To transport 72 rounds of 155-mm howitzer ammunition including powder charges, fuzes, and primers.

GENERAL DATA

Weight (lb)..............................Net 5,300; Payload 8,000; Gross 13,300
Weight distribution (lb):
   Empty..lunette 150; axle 5,150
   Loaded..lunette 275; axle 13,025
Tires............................Ply 18; Size 14.00 x 20; Pressure (psi) 75
Shipping dimensions, uncrated.......................(cu ft) 610; (sq ft) 98
Vehicle dimensions:
   Ground clearance..(in.) 12⅞
   Loading height...(in.) 35
   Height of lunette, trailer level......................................(in.) 27
Brakes:
   Manufacturer; Timken-Detroit...............................Type; air
   Parking brake, type...mechanical
Minimum towing vehicle to be used...................Truck, 4-ton, 6 x 6

ADDITIONAL DATA

TRAILER, CARGO, 6-TON, TRACKED

(Athey, Model BT898–1)

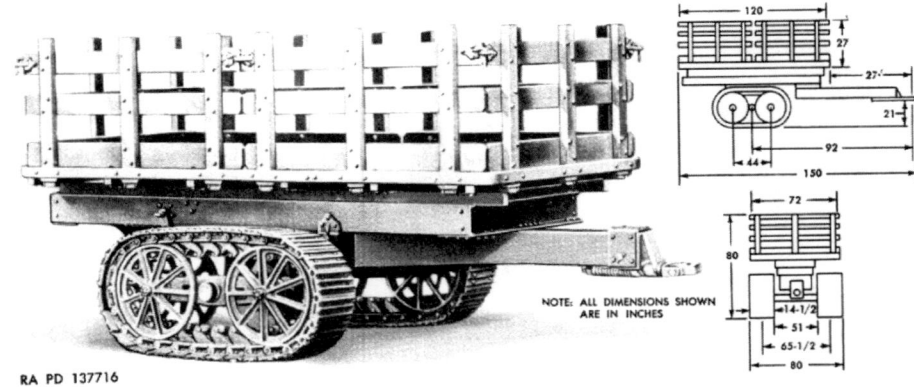

RA PD 137716

NOTE: ALL DIMENSIONS SHOWN ARE IN INCHES

Technical Manuals: 9–790A, 9–1790A; Supply Catalog: SNL G-123.

Classification: Nonclassified.

Purpose: To transport general cargo over soft or rough terrain.

GENERAL DATA

Body type...stake
Weight (lb)......................Net 6,300; Payload 12,000; Gross 18,300
Weight distribution (lb):
   Empty......................................lunette 440; axle 5,860
   Loaded...................................lunette 1,220; axle 17,080
Ground pressure...(psi) 13.3
Shipping dimensions, uncrated.................(cu ft) 565; (sq ft) 83
Vehicle dimensions:
   Body inside dimensions (in.):
     Length 120....................Width 72; Height, side rack 27
   Cargo space...(cu ft) 135
   Ground clearance.......................................(in.) 15
   Loading height...(in.) 40
   Pintle height..(in.) 21
Turning radius..(ft) 11
Towing vehicle to be used..................................tractor

ADDITIONAL DATA

After serial No. 3611, loading height is 52 inches. Body inside height, under bows 72 inches. Cargo space 371 cubic feet.

After serial No. 3440, over-all length is 172 inches. Wheel base 110 inches. Serial Nos. 3216 to 3611, inside body height 32 inches and cargo space 160 cubic feet.

Spring-cushioned or rigid lunette used.

Rear coupler or pintle hook used.

146

TRAILER, CARGO, 6-TON, TRACKED

(Athey, Model BT898–4)

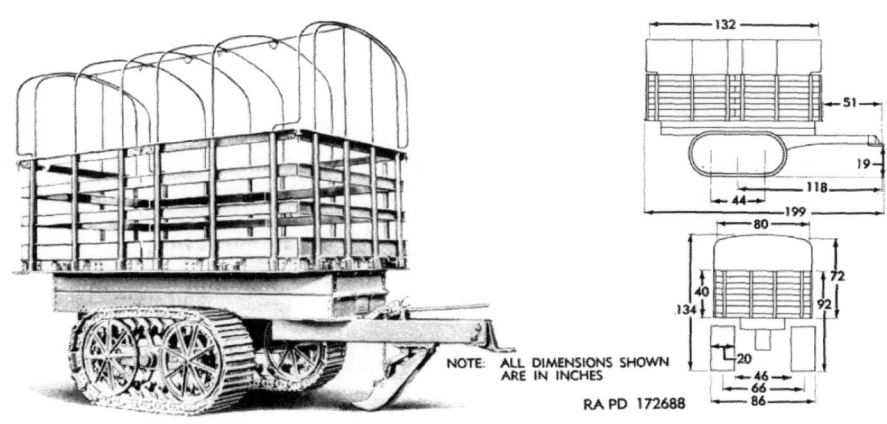

NOTE: ALL DIMENSIONS SHOWN
ARE IN INCHES

RA PD 172688

Technical Manuals: 9-790A, 9-1790A; Supply Catalog: SNL G-123.

Classification: Nonclassified.

Purpose: To transport general cargo over soft or rough terrain.

GENERAL DATA

Body type..stake
Weight (lb)............................Net 8,540; Payload 12,000; Gross 20,540
Weight distribution (lb):
    Empty..lunette 260; axle 8,280
    Loaded...lunette 260; axle 20,280
Ground pressure..(psi) 11.6
Shipping dimensions, uncrated.....................(cu ft) 895; (sq ft) 119
Vehicle dimensions:
    Body inside dimensions (in.):
        Length 132.....................Width 80; Height, under bows 72
                                 side rack 40
    Cargo space..(cu ft) 440
    Ground clearance...(in.) 15
    Loading height..(in.) 52
    Pintle height...(in.) 19
Turning radius...(ft) 12
Towing vehicle to be used......................................tractor

ADDITIONAL DATA

Rigid or spring-cushioned lunette used.
Spring-cushioned pintles used on serial Nos. below 3469.

TRAILER, AMMUNITION, 8-TON, 4-WHEEL, M23

(Utility)

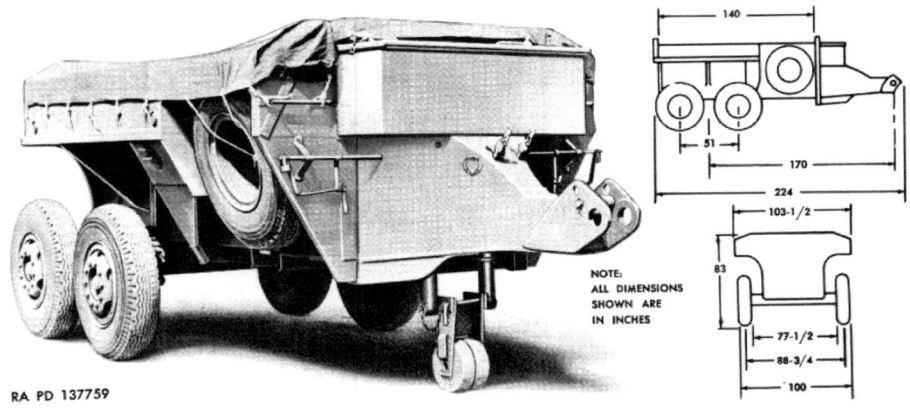

RA PD 137759

NOTE:
ALL DIMENSIONS
SHOWN ARE
IN INCHES

Technical Manuals: 9-793, 9-1827A; Supply Catalog: SNL G-216.

Classification: Standard.

Purpose: To transport ammunition; 96 rounds 155-mm or 60 rounds 8-in or 32 rounds 240-mm.

GENERAL DATA

Weight (lb)........................Net 10,000; Payload 16,000; Gross 26,000
Weight distribution (lb):
    Empty............................connecting eye 2,400; axle (each) 3,800
    Loaded.........................connecting eye 6,000; axle (each) 10,000
Tires...........................Ply 12; Size 11.00 x 20; Pressure (psi) 70
Shipping dimensions, uncrated....................(cu ft) 1,599; (sq ft) 186
Vehicle dimensions (in.):
    Ground clearance...13½
    Loading height...34
    Height to connecting eye, loaded..................................40 1/16
    Pintle height..18
Brakes: Manufacturer; Westinghouse...........................Type; air
Towing vehicles to be used: Attached directly to 7½-ton prime mover or towed by truck, 4- to 5-ton, 4 x 4, or greater capacity, with front of trailer supported on Heavy Carriage Limber, M5.

ADDITIONAL DATA

TRAILER, CARGO, 20-TON, TRACKED

(Athey, Model ET1076-1)

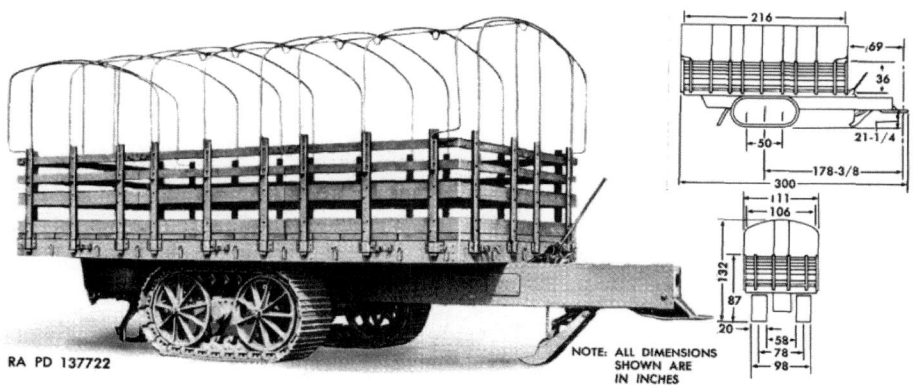

RA PD 137722

NOTE: ALL DIMENSIONS
SHOWN ARE
IN INCHES

Technical Manuals: 9-790B, 9-1790A; Supply Catalog: SNL G-123.

Classification: Nonclassified.

Purpose: To transport general cargo over soft or rough terrain.

GENERAL DATA

Body type	stake
Weight (lb)	Net 14,700; Payload 40,000; Gross 54,700
Weight distribution (lb):	
Empty	Lunette 340; axle 14,360
Loaded	Lunette 340; axle 54,360
Ground pressure	(psi) 27.1
Shipping dimensions, uncrated	(cu ft) 1,680; (sq ft) 231
Vehicle dimensions:	
Body inside dimensions (in.):	
Length	216
Width	106
Height	under bows 72; side rack 36
Cargo space	(cu ft) 960
Ground clearance	(in.) 17
Loading height	(in.) 53
Pintle height	(in.) 21¼
Turning radius	(ft) 21
Towing vehicle to be used	tractor

ADDITIONAL DATA

TRAILER, TRANSPORTER, 45-TON, 12-WHEEL, M9

(Pointer-Willamette, Model D45LF1; Checker Cab, Model D45LF1; Rogers Brothers, Model D45LF1; Winter-Weiss, Model D45LF1; Fruehauf Model CPT45SP)

Used w/TRUCK, 12-ton, 6 x 4, prime mover, M20, as component of TRUCK-TRAILER, 45-ton, tank transporter, M19

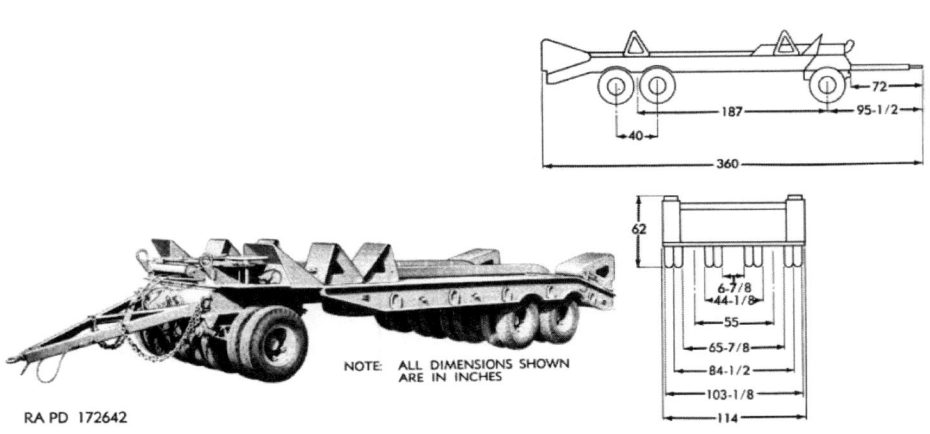

NOTE: ALL DIMENSIONS SHOWN ARE IN INCHES

RA PD 172642

Technical Manuals: 9-768, 9-1768C; Supply Catalog: SNL G-159.

Vehicle illustrated: Fruehauf.
Classification: Substitute Standard.

Purpose: To recover and transport damaged tanks and matériel weighing up to 90,000 pounds.

GENERAL DATA

Weight (lb) .... Net 20,150; Payload 90,000; Gross 110,150
Weight distribution (lb):
    Empty .... lunette 165; axle, front 6,550; rear (each) 6,718
    Loaded .... lunette 165; axle, front 36,550; rear (each) 36,718
Tires .... Ply 14; Size 8.25 x 15; Pressure (psi) 100
Shipping dimensions, uncrated .... (cu ft) 1,475; (sq ft) 285
Vehicle dimensions:
    Ground clearance .... (in.) 12
    Loading height .... (in.) 41
Brakes:
    Manufacturer; Fruehauf .... Type; air
    Parking brake, type .... mechanical
Towing vehicle to be used .... truck, 12-ton, 6 x 4, prime mover, M20

ADDITIONAL DATA

TRUCK, COMMAND RECONNAISSANCE, ¼-TON, 4 x 4
(Ford, Model GPW; Willys, Model MB)

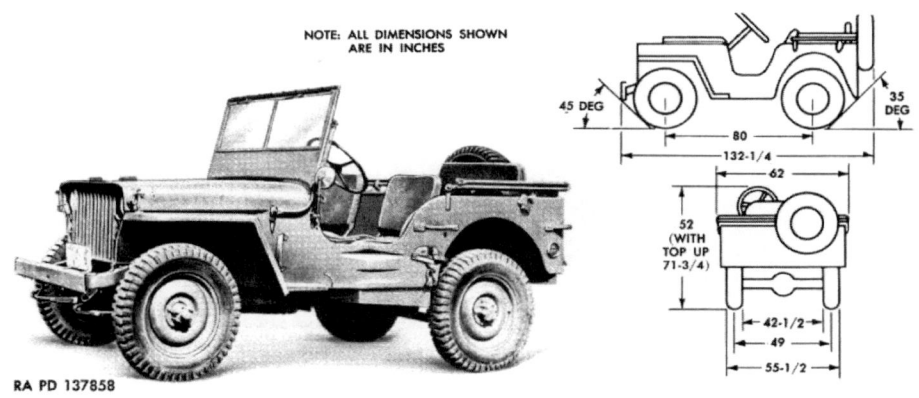

NOTE: ALL DIMENSIONS SHOWN ARE IN INCHES

RA PD 137858

Technical Manuals: 9-803, 9-1803A, 9-1803B, 9-1825B, 9-1826A, 9-1827C, 9-1828A: Supply Catalog: SNL G-503.

Classification: Standard.

Purpose: To transport command and reconnaissance personnel and light cargo.

GENERAL DATA

Crew..2; Passengers (including) crew 5
Weight (lb)..Net 2,450
   Payload.......................off highway 800; on highway 1,200
   Gross.....................off highway 3,250; on highway 3,650
Live-axle gear ratio...4.88 : 1
Axle load (lb):
   Empty.............................front 1,240; rear 1,210
   Loaded:
      Off highway.......................front 1,390; rear 1,860
      On highway........................front 1,465; rear 2,185
Tires.........................Ply 6; Size 6.00 x 16; Pressure (psi) 30
   Tread, center-to-center, front....................(in.) 49
Shipping dimensions, uncrated...........(cu ft) 247; (sq ft) 57
Vehicle dimensions:
   Ground clearance.................................(in.) 8¾
   Pintle height, loaded...........................(in.) 21
Electrical system..(volts) 6
   No. of batteries...1
   Type of ground.............................negative
Fuel octane rating...68
Capacities:
   Fuel...(gal) 15
   Cooling system...................................(qt) 11
   Crankcase, refill................................(qt) 4
   Transfer..(qt) 1½
   Transmission....................................(qt) 3¾
   Axles (each).....................................(qt) 1¼
Brakes:
   Manufacturer; Bendix....................Type; hydraulic
   Parking brake, type..................................transmission
Transmission:
   Forward speeds..3
   Gear ratio.......................High 1:1; Low 2.665 :1
Transfer:
   Speeds..2
   Gear ratio.......................High 1:1; Low 1.97:1

PERFORMANCE

Computed grade ability in lowest gear, loaded...............(percent) 58
Turning radius (ft)...........................right 18; left 18½
Fording depth..(in.) 25
Fuel consumption, loaded....................................(mpg) 19
Cruising range, loaded......................................(mi) 285
Allowable speed, recommended.................................(mph) 65
Maximum recommended towed load:
   Off highway..............................gross-(lb) 1,000
   On highway...............................gross-(lb) 2,000

ENGINE

Manufacturer: Willys.....................................Model 442
Type.....................L-head, 4-cycle; No. of cylinders (in line) 4
Displacement.................................(cu in.) 134.2
Bore..(in.) 3¼
Stroke..(in.) 4⅜
Compression ratio..............................6.48 : 1
Governed speed.............................not governed
Brake horsepower (max w/std accessories)...........54 at (rpm) 4,000
Torque (max)..................105 lb-ft at (rpm) 2,000

ADDITIONAL DATA

Live axles, type.............................hypoid, full-floating
Transmission, type..synchromesh

TRUCK, STATION WAGON, ¼-TON, 4 x 4
(Willys, Models 4 X 463 and 4 X 473)

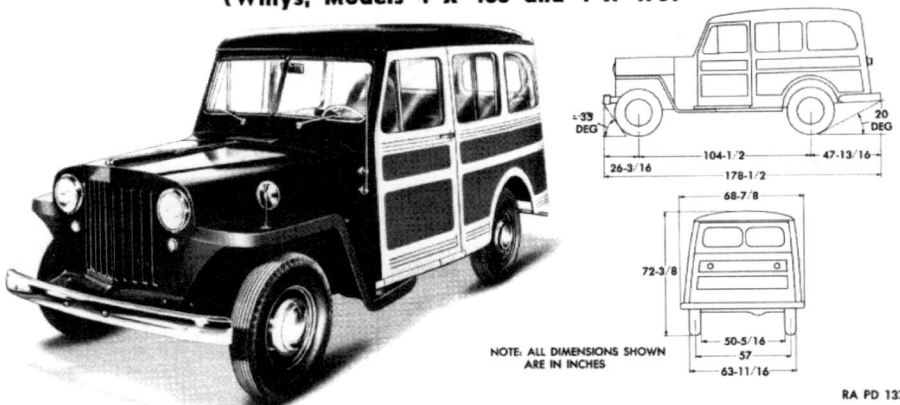

NOTE: ALL DIMENSIONS SHOWN
ARE IN INCHES

RA PD 137824

Technical Manuals: 9-804, 9-1804A, 9-1804B, 9-1825B, 9-1826A, 9-1827C, 9-1828A; Supply Catalog: SNL G-740.

Vehicle illustrated: Model 4 x 463.
Classification: Nonclassified.

Purpose: To transport personnel and light cargo.

GENERAL DATA

Crew..2; Passengers (including crew) 7
Weight (lb).......................Net 3,250; Payload 1,000; Gross 4,250
Live-axle gear ratio..5.38:1
Axle load (lb):
  Empty..front 1,452; rear 1,798
  Loaded...front 1,700; rear 2,550
Tires:
  Ply 4................Size 6.50 x 15; Pressure (psi) front 24; rear 28
  Tread, center-to-center, front...............................(in.) 57
Shipping dimensions, uncrated...............(cu ft) 515; (sq ft) 86
Vehicle dimensions (in.):
  Ground clearance...8⅝
  Loading height, empty.......................................22⅞
Electrical system.......................................(volts) 6
  No. of batteries..1
  Type of ground...negative
Fuel octane rating..68
Capacities:
  Fuel..(gal) 15
  Cooling system (qt)...........w/o heater 11; w/heater 12
  Crankcase, refill................................(qt) 4
  Transmission...................................(qt) 1½
  Transfer...(qt) 2
  Axles (each)....................................(qt) 1¼
Brakes:
  Manufacturer; Bendix......................Type; hydraulic
  Parking brake, type.............................rear-wheel
Transmission:
  Forward speeds...3
  Gear ratio......................High 1:1; Low 2.798:1
Transfer:
  Speeds...2
  Gear ratio......................High 1:1; Low 2.43:1

PERFORMANCE

Computed grade ability to lowest gear, loaded...........(percent) 57
Turning radius..(ft) 23
Fording depth..(in.) 18
Fuel consumption, loaded...................................(mpg) 20
Cruising range, loaded.......................................(mi) 300
Allowable speed, recommended...........................(mph) 60

ENGINE

Manufacturer: Willys...Model 4 x 463
Type.....................L-head, 4-cycle; No. of cylinders (in line) 4
Displacement...(cu in.) 134.2
Bore...(in.) 3⅛
Stroke..(in.) 4⅜
Compression ratio...6.48:1
Governed speed...not governed
Brake horsepower (max w/std accessories)..............54 at (rpm) 4,000
Torque (max).............................105 lb-ft at (rpm) 2,000

ADDITIONAL DATA

Live axles, type...hypoid, full-floating
Transmission, type..synchromesh
Above data given for Model 4 x 463.
Changes in data for model 4 x 473 are as follows:

ENGINE

Manufacturer: Willys...Model 4 x 473
Type.................F-head, 4-cycle; No. of cylinders (in line) 4
Displacement..(in.) 134.2
Compression ratio...7.4:1

152

TRUCK, UTILITY, ¼-TON, 4 x 4, W/WINCH

(Willys, Model CJ–3A)

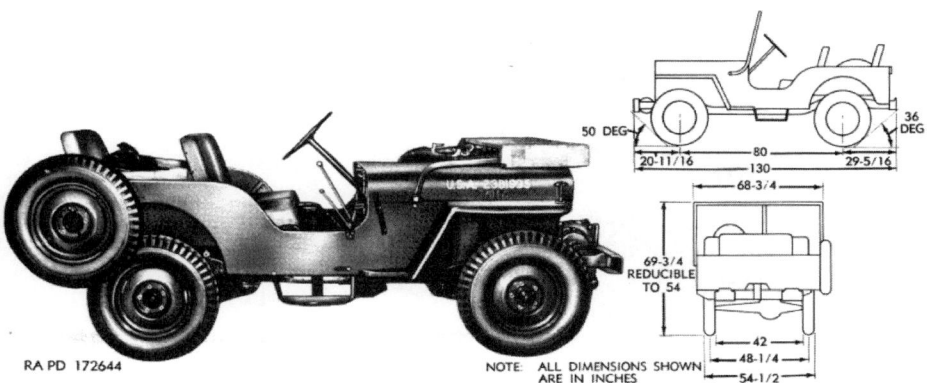

RA PD 172644

NOTE: ALL DIMENSIONS SHOWN ARE IN INCHES

Classification: Nonclassified.

Purpose: To transport command and reconnaissance personnel and light cargo.

GENERAL DATA

Crew....................................1; Passengers (including crew) 4
Weight (lb):
   Net..2,283
   Payload.........................off highway 800; on highway 1,200
   Gross.........................off highway 3,083; on highway 3,483
Live-axle gear ratio...5.38 : 1
Axle load (lb):
   Empty..................................front 1,305; rear 978
   Loaded:
     Off highway.........................front 1,449; rear 1,634
     On highway..........................front 1,521; rear 1,962
Tires:
   Ply 4....................Size 6.00 x 16; Pressure (psi) front 26; rear 28
   Tread, center-to-center, front.........................(in.) 48¾
Shipping dimensions, uncrated..............(cu ft) 276; (sq ft) 61½
Vehicle dimensions:
   Ground clearance......................................(in.) 8
   Pintle height, empty...............................(in.) 20¾
Electrical system...(volts) 6
   No. of batteries...1
   Type of ground.....................................negative
Fuel octane rating..68
Capacities:
   Fuel..(gal) 10½
   Cooling system.............(qt) w/o heater 11; w/heater 12
   Crankcase, refill..(qt) 4
   Transmission...(qt) 1½
   Transfer...(qt) 1¾
   Axles (each)...(qt) 1¼
   Winch...............Oil capacity (qt) ½; Load capacity (lb) 6,000
Brakes:
   Manufacturer: Bendix...........................Type; hydraulic
   Parking brake, type.................................transfer
Transmission:
   Forward speeds..3
   Gear ratio............................High 1:1; Low 2.80:1
Transfer:
   Speeds..2
   Gear ratio............................High 1:1; Low 2.43:1

PERFORMANCE

Computed grade ability in lowest gear, loaded...............(percent) 76
Turning radius...(ft) 18
Fuel consumption, loaded......................................(mpg) 17
Cruising range, loaded...(mi) 178
Allowable speed, governed.....................................(mph) 60
Maximum recommended towed load:
   Off highway, gross..(lb) 1,000
   On highway, gross...(lb) 2,000

ENGINE

Manufacturer: Willys...CJ–3A
Type......................L-head, 4 cycle; No. of cylinders (in line) 4
Displacement..(cu in.) 134.2
Bore...(in.) 3⅛
Stroke...(in.) 4⅜
Compression ratio..6.48:1
Governed speed...(rpm) 3,700
Brake horsepower (max w/std accessories).............51 at (rpm) 4,000
Torque (max)............................105 lb-ft at (rpm) 2,000

ADDITIONAL DATA

Live axles, type.......................................hypoid, full-floating
Transmission, type..synchromesh

TRUCK, UTILITY, ¼-TON, 4 x 4, M38

(Willys)

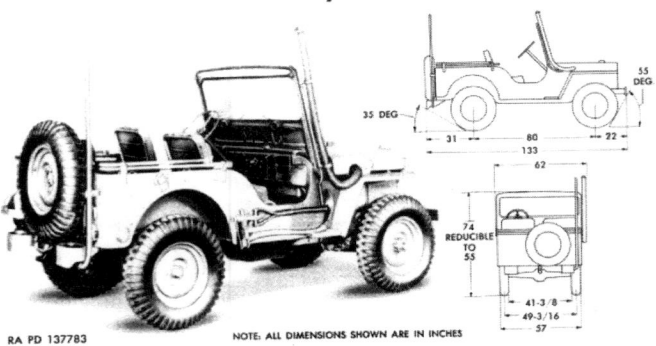

RA PD 137783   NOTE: ALL DIMENSIONS SHOWN ARE IN INCHES

Technical Manuals: 9-804, 9-1804A, 9-1804B, 9-1825B, 9-1826A, 9-1827C, 9-1828A; **Supply Catalog:** SNL G-740.

Classification: Standard.

Purpose: To transport command and reconnaissance personnel and light cargo.

GENERAL DATA

Crew..2; Passengers (including crew) 4
Weight (lb):
  Net..2,625
  Payload...........................off highway 800; on highway 1,200
  Gross.............................off highway 3,425; on highway 3,825
Live-axle gear ratio...5.38:1
Axle load (lb):
  Empty..front 1,363; rear 1,262
  Loaded:
    Off highway.........................front 1,475; rear 1,950
    On highway..........................front 1,475; rear 2,350
Tires:
  Ply 6; Size 7.00 x 16; Pressure (psi):
    Highway...28
    Off highway..22
    Mud, sand, or snow..15
  Tread, center-to-center, front.........................(in.) 49¾
Shipping dimensions, uncrated...(cu ft) 266; (sq ft) 57
Vehicle dimensions:
  Ground clearance...(in.) 9¼
  Pintle height, empty......................................(in.) 21½
Electrical system..(volts) 24
  No. of batteries...(12-volt) 2
  Type of ground..negative
Fuel octane rating..68
Capacities:
  Fuel...(gal) 13
  Cooling system..(qt) 11½
  Crankcase, refill..(qt) 4
  Transmission...(qt) 1½
  Transfer..(qt) 2
  Axles (qt)..front 1¼; rear 1¾
  Winch...............Oil capacity (qt) ½; load capacity (lb) 3,500
Brakes:
  Manufacturer; Bendix..............................Type: hydraulic
  Parking brake, type..................................transmission
Transmission:
  Forward speeds...3
  Gear ratio...........................High 1:1; Low 2.80:1
Transfer:
  Speeds..2
  Gear ratio...........................High 1:1; Low 2.43:1

PERFORMANCE

Computed grade ability in lowest gear, loaded...............(percent) 65
Turning radius (ft)...........................right 20; (left) 19
Fording depth..(in.) 70
Fuel consumption, loaded...................................(mpg) 17
Cruising range, loaded.......................................(mi) 220
Allowable speed, recommended............................(mph) 60
Maximum recommended towed load:
  Off highway, gross.....................................(lb) 1,500
  On highway, gross......................................(lb) 2,000

ENGINE

Manufacturer: Willys....................................Model MC
Type......................L-head, 4-cycle; No. of cylinders (in line) 4
Displacement..(cu in.) 134.2
Bore...(in.) 3¼
Stroke...(in.) 4⅜
Compression ratio..6.48:1
Governed speed......................................not governed
Brake horsepower (max w/std accessories).........51 at (rpm) 4,000
Torque (max).......................................97 lb-ft at (rpm) 2,000

ADDITIONAL DATA

Live axles, type.............hypoid, front full-floating; rear semi-floating
Transmission, type......................................synchromesh
  Weights and axle loads are given for vehicle w/o winch. For vehicle
w/winch, they are as follows:
Weight (lb):
  Net..2,750
  Payload...........................off highway 800; on highway 1,200
  Gross.............................off highway 3,550; on highway 3,950
Axle load (lb):
  Empty..front 1,482; rear 1,268
  Loaded:
    Off highway.........................front 1,595; rear 1,955
    On highway..........................front 1,595; rear 2,355

TRUCK, UTILITY, ¼-TON, 4 x 4 AND TRUCK, CARGO, ¼-TON, 4 x 4

(Willys, Model CJ–3A)

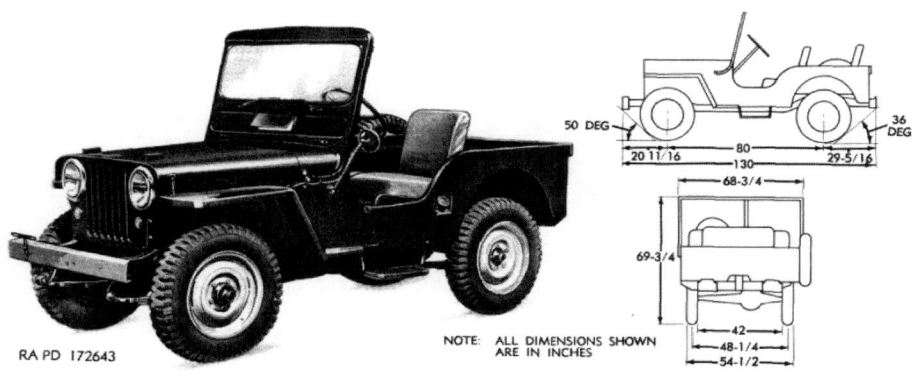

RA PD 172643

NOTE: ALL DIMENSIONS SHOWN ARE IN INCHES

Classification: Nonclassified.

Purpose: To transport command and reconnaissance personnel and light cargo.

GENERAL DATA

Crew................................1; Passengers (including crew) 4
Weight (lb):
  Net...2,203
  Payload.....................off highway 800; on highway 1,200
  Gross...................off highway 3,003; on highway 3,403
Live-axle gear ratio...5.38:1
Axle load (lb):
  Empty...............................front 1,215; rear 988
  Loaded:
    Off highway........................front 1,359; rear 1,644
    On highway.........................front 1,431; rear 1,972
Tires:
  Ply 4.....................Size 6.00 x 16; Pressure (psi) front 26; rear 28
  Tread, center-to-center, front......................(in.) 48¼
Shipping dimensions, uncrated...........(cu ft) 276; (sq ft) 61½
Vehicle dimensions:
  Ground clearance................................(in.) 8⅝
  Pintle height, empty............................(in.) 20¾
Electrical system.................................(volts) 6
  No. of batteries..1
  Type of ground..negative
Fuel octane rating...68
Capacities:
  Fuel...(gal) 10½
  Cooling system (qt)...........w/o heater 11; w/heater 12
  Crankcase, refill...............................(qt) 4
  Transmission, each.............................(qt) 1½
  Transfer.......................................(qt) 1¾
  Axles (each)...................................(qt) 1¼
Brakes:
  Manufacturer; Bendix.....................Type; hydraulic
  Parking brake, type..............................transfer
Transmission:
  Forward speeds..3
  Gear ratio....................High 1:1; Low 2.80:1
Transfer:
  Speeds..2
  Gear ratio....................High 1:1; Low 2.43:1

PERFORMANCE

Computed grade ability in lowest gear, loaded.............(percent) 76
Turning radius..(ft) 18
Fuel consumption, loaded.....................................(mpg) 17
Cruising range, loaded.......................................(mi) 178
Allowable speed, recommended................................(mph) 60
Maximum recommended towed load:
  Off highway, gross..(lb) 1,000
  On highway, gross...(lb) 2,000

ENGINE

Manufacturer: Willys..CJ-3A
Type..................L-head, 4-cycle; No. of cylinders (in line) 4
Displacement................................(cu in.) 134.2
Bore...(in.) 3⅛
Stroke.......................................(in.) 4⅜
Compression ratio.............................6.48:1
Governed speed.............................not governed
Brake horsepower, (max w/std accessories).........54 at (rpm) 4,000
Torque (max)........................105 lb-ft at (rpm) 2,000

ADDITIONAL DATA

Live axles, type...........................hypoid, full floating
Transmission...................................synchromesh

TRUCK, CARRYALL, ½-TON, 4 x 2

(Chevrolet, Model 3116, HP and JP, Suburban, 1950–51)

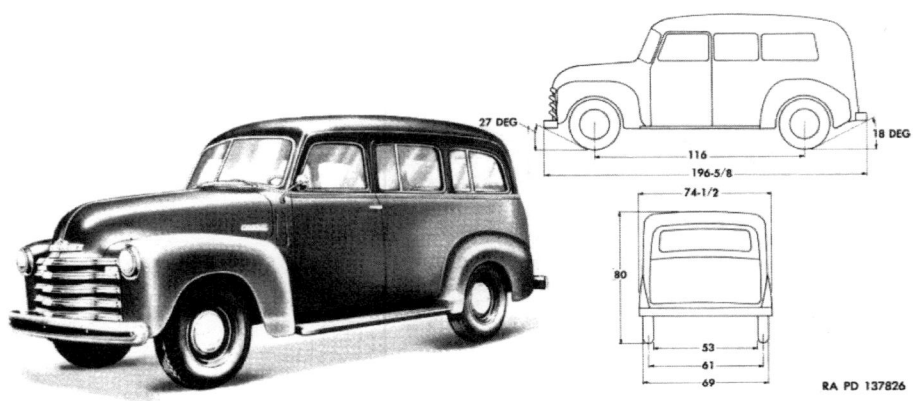

27 DEG · 116 · 196-5/8 · 18 DEG · 74-1/2 · 80 · 53 · 61 · 69

RA PD 137826

Classification: Standard.

Purpose: To transport light cargo and personnel.

GENERAL DATA

Crew..1; Passengers (including crew) 8
Weight (lb)...............Net 3,855; Payload 1,000; Gross 4,855
Rear-axle gear ratio...4.11:1
Axle load (lb):
  Empty..front 1,835; rear 2,020
  Loaded.......................................front 2,045; rear 2,810
Tires:
  Ply 6.....................Size 6.50 x 16; Pressure (psi) front 35; rear 45
  Tread, center-to-center, front.................................(in.) 56½
Shipping dimensions, uncrated.................(cu ft) 680; (sq ft) 102
Vehicle dimensions:
  Ground clearance...(in.) 8¾
  Loading height, empty.......................................(in.) 27½
  Body inside dimensions (in):
    Length 91½....................Width 61¹³⁄₁₆; Height 50¾
    Cargo space..(cu ft) 165
Electrical system...(volts) 6
  No. of batteries...1
  Type of ground...negative
Fuel octane rating...70
Capacities:
  Fuel...(gal) 16
  Cooling system..(qt) 15
  Crankcase, refill..(qt) 5
  Transmission..(qt) ¾
  Rear axle...(qt) 2¼
Brakes:
  Manufacturer; Chevrolet.......................Type; hydraulic
  Parking brake, type......................................rear-wheel
Transmission:
  Forward speeds...3
  Gear ratio.........................High 1:1; Low 2.94:1

PERFORMANCE

Computed grade ability in lowest gear, loaded.................(percent) 25
Turning radius (ft)...............................right 19¾; left 20
Fording depth..(in.) 18
Fuel consumption, loaded..(mpg) 13
Cruising range, loaded..(mi) 208
Allowable speed, recommended...................................(mph) 70

ENGINE

Manufacturer: Chevrolet.......................Model 1950-HB-1001 UP
                                Model 1951-JB-1001 UP
Type..................Valve-in-head, 4-cycle; No. of cylinders (in line) 6
Displacement..(cu in.) 216.5
Bore..(in.) 3½
Stroke..(in.) 3¾
Compression ratio...6.6:1
Governed speed..not governed
Brake horsepower (max w/std accessories)..............85 at (rpm) 3,300
Torque (max).............................170 lb-ft at (rpm) 1,500

ADDITIONAL DATA

Rear axle, type...hypoid, semifloating
Transmission, type..synchromesh

TRUCK, CARRYALL, ½-TON, 4 x 2

(Dodge, Models WC–36, T112; WC–48, T112)

34 DEG   18 DEG

116
196-5/8
74-1/2
80
54-3/8
61-1/4
68-1/8

NOTE: ALL DIMENSIONS SHOWN ARE IN INCHES

RA PD 172697

Technical Manual: 10-1378.

Classification: Standard.

Purpose: To transport light cargo and personnel.

GENERAL DATA

Crew..1; Passengers (including crew) 8
Weight (lb)...........Net 3,800; Payload 1,000 (on highway); Gross 4,800
Rear-axle gear ratio...4.1:1
Axle load (lb):
   Empty.....................................front 1,820; rear 1,980
   Loaded....................................front 2,030; rear 2,770
Tires:
   Ply 6.........................Size 6.50 x 16; Pressure (psi) 40
   Tread, center-to-center, front..........................(in.) 55¾
Shipping dimensions, uncrated...............(cu ft) 680; (sq ft) 102
Vehicle dimensions:
   Ground clearance..(in.) 8¹¹⁄₁₆
   Loading height, empty..................................(in.) 27½
Body inside dimensions (in.):
   Length...................91½; Width 61¾; Height 50¾
   Cargo space...(cu ft) 165
Electrical system..(volts) 6
   No. of batteries..1
   Type of ground.....................................positive
Fuel octane rating...72
Capacities:
   Fuel..(gal) 18
   Cooling system..(qt) 15½
   Crankcase, refill......................................(qt) 5
   Transmission...(qt) 1¾
   Rear axle..(qt) 1⅝
Brakes:
   Manufacturer; Dodge.........................Type; hydraulic
   Parking brake, type..............................transmission
Transmission:
   Forward speeds...3
   Gear ratio.............................High 1:1; Low 3.3:1

PERFORMANCE

Computed grade ability in lowest gear, loaded...........(percent) 37
Turning radius (ft)........................Right 20½; Left 23
Fording depth...(in.) 18
Fuel consumption, loaded................................(mpg) 10
Cruising range, loaded..................................(mi) 180
Allowable speed, governed...............................(mph) 60

ENGINE

Manufacturer: Dodge...............................Model T–112
Type.................L-head, 4-cycle; No. of cylinders (in line) 6
Displacement..(cu in.) 217.7
Bore...(in.) 3¼
Stroke...(in.) 4⅜
Compression ratio......................................6.8:1
Governed speed.....................................(rpm) 3,100
Brake horsepower (max w/std accessories)..........85 at (rpm) 3,000
Torque (max).......................170 lb-ft at (rpm) 1,200

ADDITIONAL DATA

Rear axle, type...........................hypoid, semifloating
Transmission, type.....................selective sliding-gear

TRUCK, PANEL, ½-TON, 4 x 2

(Chevrolet, Model 3105)

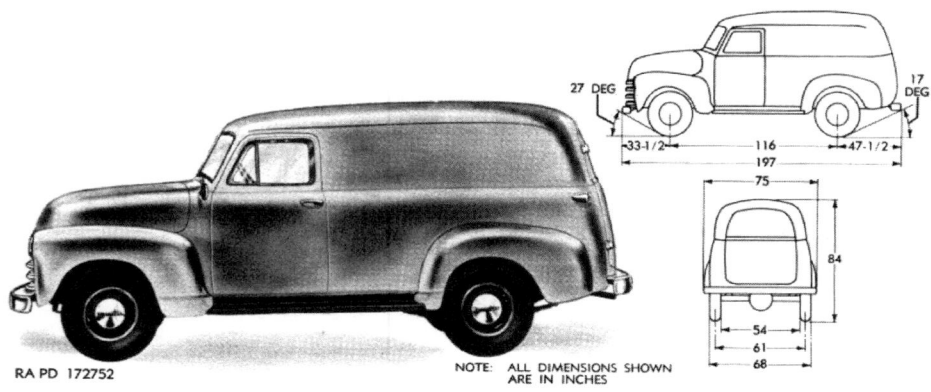

27 DEG 17 DEG
33-1/2 116 47-1/2
197
75
84
54
61
68

RA PD 172752

NOTE: ALL DIMENSIONS SHOWN ARE IN INCHES

Classification: Nonclassified.

Purpose: To transport light cargo.

GENERAL DATA

Crew...1; Passengers (including crew) 2
Weight (lb) ....Net 3,575
    Payload...1,175
    Gross...4,750
Rear-axle gear ratio...4. 11:1
Axle load (lb) :
    Empty..front 1,805; rear 1,770
    Loaded...front 2,000; rear 2,750
Tires:
    Ply 6....................Size 6.50 x 16; Pressure (psi) front 26; rear 36
    Tread, center-to-center, front.....................................(in.) 56½
Shipping dimensions, uncrated........................(cu ft) 723; (sq ft) 103
Vehicle dimensions:
    Ground clearance..(in.) 8¾
    Loading height, empty..(in.) 28½
    Body inside dimensions (in.):
        Length 77⅝........................Width 61¹³⁄₁₆; Height 51⅜
        Cargo space...(cu ft) 141
Electrical system...(volts) 6
    No, of batteries..1
    Type of ground...negative
Fuel octane rating 72
Capacities:
    Fuel...(gal) 16
    Cooling system (qt)..........................w/o heater 15; w/heater 16
    Crankcase, refill...(qt) 5
    Transmission...(qt) ¾
    Rear axle...(qt) 2¼
Brakes:
    Manufacturer; Chevrolet.............................Type; hydraulic
    Parking brake, type.......................................rear-wheel
Transmission:
    Forward speeds...3
    Gear ratio...High 1:1; Low 2.94:1

PERFORMANCE

Computed grade ability in lowest gear, loaded.................(percent) 30
Turning radius (ft).......................................right 19¾; left 20
Fording depth...(in.) 18
Fuel consumption, loaded...(mpg) 11
Cruising range, loaded...(mi) 176
Allowable speed, recommended.................................(mph) 60

ENGINE

Manufacturer; Chevrolet...........................Model HB or JB
Type.....................4-cycle, valve-in-head; No. of cylinders (in line) 6
Displacement...(cu in.) 216. 5
Bore...(in.) 3½
Stroke..(in.) 3¾
Compression ratio...6.6 :1
Governed speed (rpm)....................................not governed
Brake horsepower (max w/std accessories).................85 at (rpm) 3,300
Torque (max w/std accessories)..........170 lb-ft at (rpm) 1,000–2,000

ADDITIONAL DATA

Rear axle, type................................hypoid, semi-floating
Transmission, type..synchromesh

TRUCK, PANEL, ½-TON, 4 x 2

(Dodge, Model B1B108)

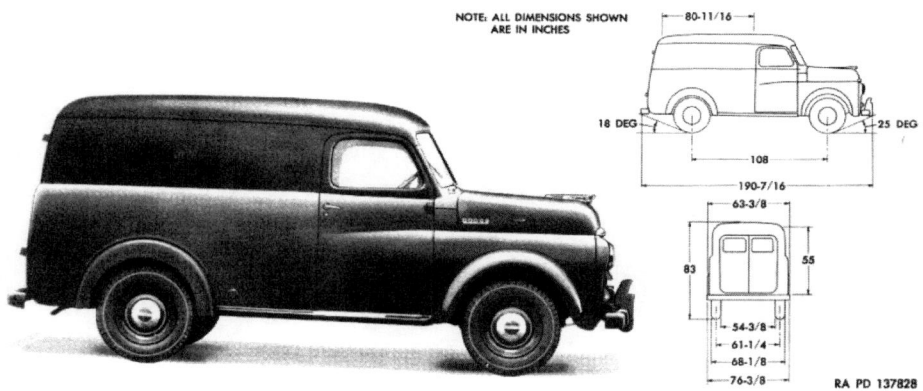

NOTE: ALL DIMENSIONS SHOWN ARE IN INCHES

RA PD 137828

Classification: Standard.

Purpose: To transport light cargo.

GENERAL DATA

Crew..2
Weight (lb)............Net 3,400; Payload 1,450; (on highway) Gross 4,850
Rear-axle gear ratio...4.1:1
Axle load (lb):
    Empty................................front 1,960; rear 1,440
    Loaded...............................front 2,000; rear 2,850
Tires:
    Ply 6............................Size 6.50 x 16; Pressure (psi) 36
    Tread, center-to-center, front............................(in.) 58⅝
Shipping dimensions, uncrated.......................(cu ft) 698; (sq ft) 101
Vehicle dimensions:
    Ground clearance..(in.) 8¹³⁄₁₆
    Loading height, empty.....................................(in.) 28¹¹⁄₁₆
Electrical system..(volts) 6
    No. of batteries...1
    Type of ground......................................positive
Fuel octane rating...70
Capacities:
    Fuel...(gal) 18
    Cooling system......................................(qt) 17½
    Crankcase, refill...................................(qt) 5
    Transmission..(qt) 1¾
    Rear axle...(qt) 1⅞
Brakes:
    Manufacturer; Dodge..........................Type; hydraulic
    Parking brake, type..........................transmission
Transmission:
    Forward speeds...3
    Gear ratio.........................High 1:1; Low 3.3:1

PERFORMANCE

Computed grade ability in lowest gear, loaded................(percent) 34
Turning radius...(ft) 19
Fording depth..(in.) 18
Fuel consumption, loaded.................................(mpg) 12
Cruising range, loaded...................................(mi) 216
Allowable speed, recommended.............................(mph) 60

ENGINE

Manufacturer: Dodge................................Model T-142
Type...................L-head, 4-cycle; No. of cylinders (in line) 6
Displacement...(cu in.) 218
Bore..(in.) 3¼
Stroke..(in.) 4⅜
Compression ratio.......................................6.6:1
Brake horsepower, (max w/std accessories)...............82 at (rpm) 3,200
Torque (max w/std accessories)................164 lb-ft at (rpm) 1,200

ADDITIONAL DATA

Rear axle, type...................................hypoid, semifloating
Transmission, type..............................selective sliding-gear

TRUCK, PICKUP, ½-TON, 4 x 2

(Chevrolet, Model 3104)

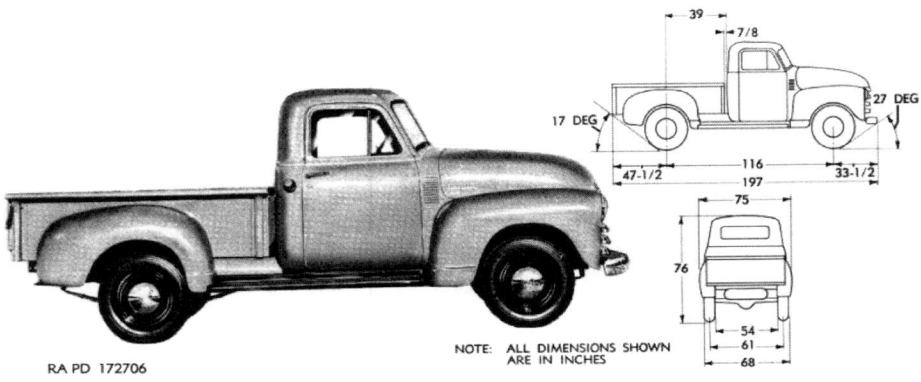

NOTE: ALL DIMENSIONS SHOWN ARE IN INCHES

RA PD 172706

Classification: Standard.

Purpose: To transport light cargo.

GENERAL DATA

Crew..1; No. Passengers (including crew) 3
Weight (lb):
    Net...3,330
    Payload..1,270
    Gross...4,600
Rear-axle gear ratio...4. 11:1
Axle load (lb):
    Empty...........................front 1,865; rear 1,465
    Loaded..........................front 1,950; rear 2,650
Tires:
    Ply 6...................Size 6.50 x 16; Pressure (psi) front 26; rear 36
    Tread, center-to-center, front.............................(in.) 56½
Shipping dimensions, uncrated...................(cu ft) 650; (sq ft) 103
Vehicle dimensions:
    Ground clearance.......................................(in.) 8¼
    Loading height, empty..................................(in.) 30
    Body inside dimensions (in.):
        Length 78......................Width 50; Height 16½
    Cargo space..(cu ft) 37
Electrical system..(volts) 6
    No. of batteries...1
    Type of ground......................................negative
Fuel octane rating...72
Capacities:
    Fuel...(gal) 17½
    Cooling system (qt)..............w/o heater 15; w/heater 16
    Crankcase, refill..(qt) 5
    Transmission..(qt) ¾
    Rear axle..(qt) 2¼
Brakes:
    Manufacturer; Chevrolet...................Type; hydraulic
    Parking brake, type...............................rear-wheel
Transmission:
    Forward speeds..3
    Gear ratio.......................High 1:1; Low 2.94:1

PERFORMANCE

Computed grade ability in lowest gear, loaded..................(percent) 31
Turning radius (ft)............................Right 19¾; Left 20
Fording depth...(in.) 18
Fuel consumption, loaded......................................(mpg) 11
Cruising range, loaded..(mi) 192
Allowable speed, recommended.................................(mph) 60

ENGINE

Manufacturer: Chevrolet.............................Model HB or JB
Type.....................4-cycle, valve-in-head; No. of cylinders (in line) 6
Displacement...(cu in.) 216.5
Bore...(in.) 3½
Stroke...(in.) 3¾
Compression ratio...6.6:1
Governed speed..not governed
Brake horsepower (max w/std accessories)..................85 at (rpm) 3,300
Torque (max w/std accessories)..........170 lb-ft at (rpm) 1,000–2,000

ADDITIONAL DATA

Rear axle, type..................................hypoid, semifloating
Transmission, type.................................synchromesh

TRUCK, PICKUP, ½-TON, 4 x 2

(Chevrolet, Models KC, 1940; AK, 3104, 1941; BK, 3104, 1942)

NOTE: ALL DIMENSIONS SHOWN ARE IN INCHES

RA PD 137760

Technical Manuals: 10–1251; 10–1305; **Supply Catalog:** SNL G–612.

Vehicle illustrated: 1941–42, AK, 3104 and BK, 3104.
Classification: Standard.

Purpose: To transport light cargo.

GENERAL DATA

Crew...2
Weight (lb)............................Net 3,385; Payload 1,000; Gross 4,385
Rear-axle gear ratio...4.11:1
Axle load (lb):
    Empty.......................................front 1,780; rear 1,605
    Loaded......................................front 1,855; rear 2,530
Tires:
    Ply 6............................Size 15 in; Pressure (psi) 36
    Tread, center-to-center, front.............................(in.) 57⅝
Shipping dimensions, uncrated...............(cu ft) 615; (sq ft) 101
Vehicle dimensions:
    Loading height, empty....................................(in.) 29
    Ground clearance.......................................(in.) 8½
    Body inside dimensions (in.):
        Length...78
        Width..48½
        Height:
            Under bows...56
            Over flares..16¼
    Body cargo space..............................(cu ft) 122
Electrical system...(volts) 6
    No. of batteries...1
    Type of ground.......................................negative
Fuel octane rating...70
Capacities:
    Fuel...(gal) 18
    Cooling system...(qt) 14
    Crankcase, refill...(qt) 5
    Transmission...(qt) 3¼
    Rear axle...(qt) 1¾
Brakes:
    Manufacturer; Chevrolet.......................Type; hydraulic
    Parking brake, type.................................rear-wheel
Transmission:
    Forward speeds..3
    Gear ratio...........................High 1:1; Low 2.94:1

PERFORMANCE

Computed grade ability in lowest gear, loaded.................(percent) 25
Turning radius (ft)...........................right 19½; left 20
Fording depth..(in.) 18
Allowable speed, governed.............................(mph) 60

ENGINE

Manufacturer: Chevrolet:
    1941.................................Model A D or AE-1001 up
    1942.................................Model BD 1001 up
Type..................Valve-in-head, 4 cycle; No. of cylinders (in line) 6
Displacement....................................(cu in.) 216.5
Bore...(in.) 3½
Stroke..(in.) 3¾
Compression ratio..................................6.5:1
Governed speed....................................(rpm) 3,100
Brake horsepower (max w/std accessories)........81.5 at (rpm) 3,100
Torque (max)..........................168 lb-ft at (rpm) 1,100

ADDITIONAL DATA

Rear axle, type........................hypoid, semi-floating
Transmission, type...........................synchromesh

TRUCK, PICKUP, ½-TON, 4 x 2

(Dodge, Model B1B108)

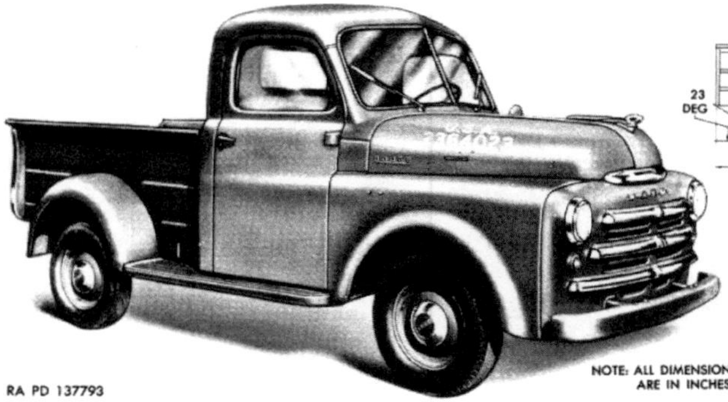

RA PD 137793

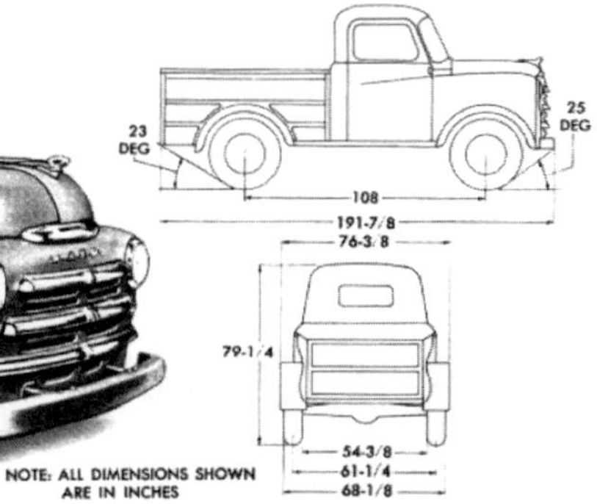

23 DEG
25 DEG
108
191-7/8
76-3/8
79-1/4
54-3/8
61-1/4
68-1/8
NOTE: ALL DIMENSIONS SHOWN ARE IN INCHES

Classification: Standard.

Purpose: To transport light cargo.

GENERAL DATA

Crew .... 2; Passengers (including crew) 3
Weight (lb):
- Net 3,325
- Payload .... off highway 1,000; on highway 1,275
- Gross .... off highway 4,325; on highway 4,600

Rear-axle gear ratio 4.1:1
Axle load (lb):
- Empty .... front 2,010; rear 1,315
- Loaded:
  - Off highway .... front 2,010; rear 2,315
  - On highway .... front 2,010; rear 2,590

Tires:
- Ply 6 .... Size 6.50 x 16; Pressure (psi) 45
- Tread, center-to-center, front .... (in.) 58⅝

Shipping dimensions, uncrated .... (cu ft) 672; (sq ft) 102
Vehicle dimensions (in.):
- Ground clearance 8⅞
- Loading height, empty 26
- Body inside dimensions (in.):
  - Length 78⅛
  - Width 49
  - Height:
    - Under bows 48
    - Side panel 22¼
- Cargo space .... (cu ft) 106

Electrical system .... (volts) 6
- No. of batteries 1
- Type of ground .... positive

Fuel octane rating 70
Capacities:
- Fuel .... (gal) 18
- Cooling system .... (qt) 17¼
- Crankcase, refill .... (qt) 5
- Transmission .... (qt) 1¾
- Rear axle .... (qt) 1⅜

Brakes:
- Manufacturer: Dodge .... Type, hydraulic
- Parking brake, type .... transmission

Transmission:
- Forward speeds 3
- Gear ratio .... High 1:1; Low 3.3:1

PERFORMANCE

Computed grade ability in lowest gear, loaded .... (percent) 33
Turning radius .... (ft) 19
Fording depth .... (in.) 18
Fuel consumption, loaded .... (mpg) 12
Cruising range, loaded .... (mi) 216
Allowable speed, recommended .... (mph) 61

ENGINE

Manufacturer: Dodge .... Model T-172
Type .... L-head, 4-cycle; No. of cylinders (in line) 6
Displacement .... (cu in.) 217.76
Bore .... (in.) 3¼
Stroke .... (in.) 4⅜
Compression ratio 6.6:1
Governed speed .... not governed
Brake horsepower (max w/std accessories) .... 82 at (rpm) 3,600
Torque (max w/std accessories) .... 165 lb-ft at (rpm) 1,200

ADDITIONAL DATA

Rear axle, type .... hypoid, semifloating
Transmission, type .... selective sliding-gear

TRUCK, PICKUP, ½-TON, 4 x 2

(Dodge, Model WC, 1947)

NOTE: ALL DIMENSIONS SHOWN
ARE IN INCHES

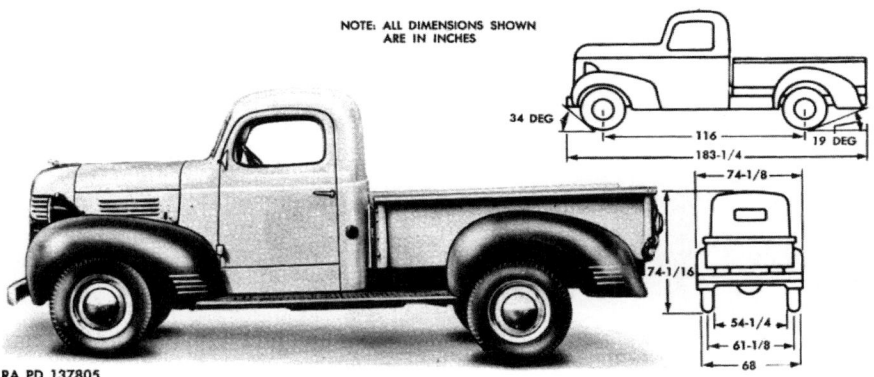

RA PD 137805

Classification: Standard.

Purpose: To transport light cargo and personnel.

GENERAL DATA

Crew..2
Weight (lb)......................Net 3,365; Payload 1,000; Gross 4,365
Rear-axle gear ratio...4.1:1
Axle load (lb):
  Empty......................................front 1,890; rear 1,475
  Loaded.....................................front 1,895; rear 2,470
Tires:
  Ply 6; Size 6.50 x 16; Pressure....................(psi) 36
  Tread, center-to-center, front....................(in.) 55¾
Shipping dimensions, uncrated.................(cu ft) 594; (sq ft) 96
Vehicle dimensions:
  Ground clearance...................................(in.) 8¹¹⁄₁₆
  Loading height, empty.............................(in.) 25⅜
  Body inside dimensions (in.):
    Length..78
    Width..48½
    Height:
      Over flares...............................16¼
      Under bows................................56
  Body cargo space.............................(cu ft) 122
Electrical system.......................................(volts) 6
Type of ground.......................................positive
No. of batteries...1
Fuel octane rating...72
Capacities:
  Fuel..(gal) 18
  Cooling system.................................(qt) 15½
  Crankcase, refill..............................(qt) 5
  Transmission...................................(qt) 1¾
  Rear axle......................................(qt) 1⅝
Brakes:
  Manufacturer: Dodge.......................Type: hydraulic
  Parking brake, type.........................transmission
Transmission:
  Forward speeds.......................................3
  Gear ratio.........................High 1:1; Low 3.3:1

PERFORMANCE

Computed grade ability in lowest gear, loaded.................(percent) 37
Turning radius (ft)...............................right 19; left 24
Fording depth...(in.) 32
Fuel consumption, loaded.............................(mpg) 12
Cruising range, loaded...............................(ml) 216
Allowable speed, governed............................(mph) 64

ENGINE

Manufacturer: Dodge...............................Model T-112
Type....................L-head, 4-cycle; No. of cylinders (in line) 6
Displacement...................................(cu in.) 217.7
Bore...(in.) 3¼
Stroke...(in.) 4⅜
Compression ratio.................................6.6:1
Governed speed................................(rpm) 3,200
Brake horsepower (max w/std accessories)...........85 at (rpm) 3,000
Torque (max)........................172 lb-ft at (rpm) 1,200

ADDITIONAL DATA

Rear axle, type...hypoid, semifloating
Transmission, type......................................selective sliding-gear

TRUCK, PICKUP, ½-TON, 4 x 2

(Ford, Model F–1)

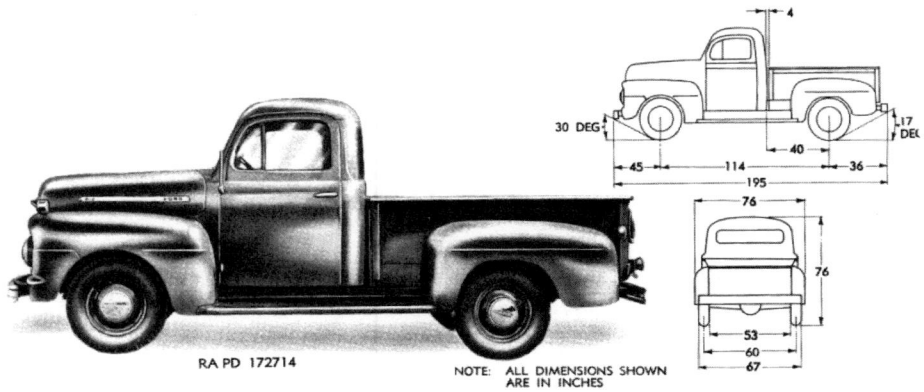

RA PD 172714

NOTE: ALL DIMENSIONS SHOWN ARE IN INCHES

Classification: Standard.

Purpose: To transport light cargo.

GENERAL DATA

Crew..2
Weight (lb)........................Net 3,305; Payload 1,295; Gross 4,600
Rear-axle gear ratio...3.92:1
Axle load (lb):
    Empty.......................................front 1,905; rear 1,400
    Loaded.......................................front 2,000; rear 2,600
Tires:
    Ply 6..............................Size 6.50 x 16; Pressure (psi) 36
    Tread, center-to-center, front.................................(in.) 58
Shipping dimensions, uncrated.....................(cu ft) 650; (sq ft) 103
Vehicle dimensions:
    Ground clearance.......................................(in.) 8⅝₆
    Loading height..(in.) 27
    Body inside dimensions (in.):
        Length 78....................Width 49; Height 20
    Cargo space...(cu ft) 44
Electrical system..(volts) 6
    No. of batteries...1
    Type of ground...positive
Fuel octane rating..72
Capacities:
    Fuel...(gal) 20
    Cooling system..(qt) 23
    Crankcase, refill...(qt) 5
    Transmission...(qt) 1½
    Rear axles...(qt) 1⅝
Brakes:
    Manufacturer; Ford.............................Type; hydraulic
    Parking brake, type.................................rear-wheel
Transmission:
    Forward speeds..3
    Gear ratio........................High 1:1; Low 2.819:1

PERFORMANCE

Computed grade ability in lowest gear, loaded.............(percent) 30
Turning radius...(ft) 21
Fording depth...(in.) 24
Fuel consumption, loaded..................................(mpg) 10
Cruising range, loaded....................................(mi) 200
Allowable speed, recommended..............................(mph) 55

ENGINE

Manufacturer: Ford.....................................Model R
Type....................4-cycle, L-head; No. of cylinders (90-deg V) 8
Displacement...(cu in.) 239
Bore...(in.) 3⅜₆
Stroke...(in.) 3¾
Compression ratio...6.8:1
Governed speed..not governed
Brake horsepower (max w/std accessories).........100 at (rpm) 3,800
Torque (max w/std accessories)..............176 lb-ft at (rpm) 2,000

ADDITIONAL DATA

Rear axle, type...........................hypoid, semi-floating
Transmission, type........................selective sliding-gear

TRUCK, PICKUP, ½-TON, 4 x 2

(Ford, Models 2GC, 6-cyl, 1942; 21C, 8-cyl, 1942)

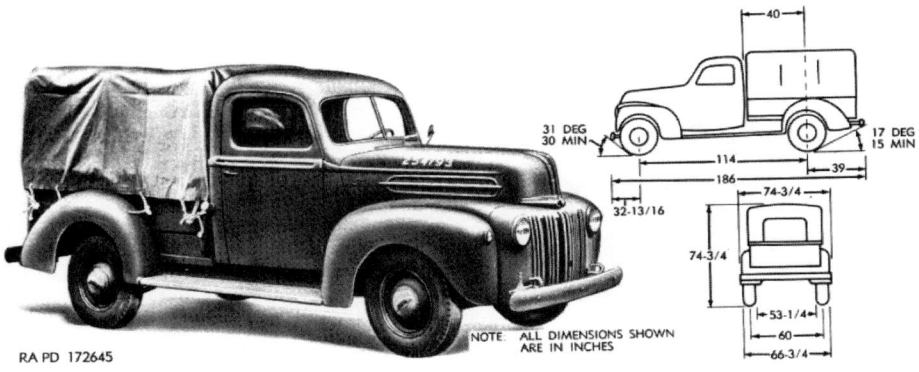

RA PD 172645

NOTE: ALL DIMENSIONS SHOWN ARE IN INCHES

Technical Manuals: 10-1436, 10-1437; **Supply Catalog:** SNL G-615.

Classification: Standard.

Purpose: To transport light cargo.

GENERAL DATA

Crew..2
Weight (lb): Net..3,290
    Payload....................off highway 1,000; on highway 1,310
    Gross......................off highway 4,290; on highway 4,600
Rear-axle gear ratio..3.78:1
Axle load (lb):
    Empty...............................front 1,700; rear 1,590
    Loaded:
      Off highway......................front 1,810; rear 2,480
      On highway.......................front 1,840; rear 2,760
Tires:
    Ply 6......................Size 6.50 x 16; Pressure (psi) 40
    Tread, center-to-center, front....................(in.) 58
Shipping dimensions, uncrated....................(cu ft) 626; (sq ft) 99
Vehicle dimensions:
    Ground clearance...............................(in.) 8⁵⁄₁₆
    Loading height, empty............................(in.) 27
    Body inside dimensions (in.):
      Length 78¾................Width 49; Height 50
    Cargo space....................................(cu ft) 112
Electrical system..(volts) 6
    No. of batteries...1
    Type of ground..positive
Fuel octane rating..72
Capacities:
    Fuel..(gal) 19
    Cooling system..(qt) 17½
    Crankcase, refill..(qt) 5
    Transmission..(pt) 2¾
    Differential...(pt) 2¾
Brakes:
    Manufacturer; Ford...........................type; hydraulic
    Parking brake, type.................................rear-wheel
Transmission:
    Forward speeds...3
    Gear ratio..........................High 1:1; Low 3.11:1

PERFORMANCE

Computed grade ability in lowest gear, loaded..............(percent) 38
Turning radius...(ft) 21
Fording depth...(in.) 24
Fuel consumption, loaded..(mpg) 10
Cruising range, loaded..(mi) 190
Allowable speed, recommended..................................(mph) 65

ENGINE

Manufacturer: Ford...Model 2GCS
Type.........................4-cycle, L-head; No. of cylinders (in line) 6
Displacement...(cu in.) 226
Bore...(in.) 3.3
Stroke...(in.) 4.4
Compression ratio..6.7:1
Governed speed..not governed
Brake horsepower (max w/std accessories)..............90 at (rpm) 3,300
Torque (max w/std accessories)...............180 lb-ft at (rpm) 1,200

ADDITIONAL DATA

Changes in data for Model 21C, 8 cyl, are as follows:
Capacity:
    Cooling system.......................................(qt) 21½
Engine:
    Manufacturer: Ford...................................Model 21A
    Type.................4-cycle, L-head; No. of cylinders (90-deg) V8
    Displacement.....................................(cu in.) 221
    Bore...3³⁄₁₆
    Stroke..3¾
    Compression ratio...................................6.2:1
    Governed speed.................................not governed
    Brake horsepower (max w/std accessories).........90 at (rpm) 3,800
    Torque (max w/std accessories)............156 lb-ft at (rpm) 2,000
Data for 4-speed transmission:
    Gear ratio.................High 1:1; Fourth 1.69:1; Low 6.4:1
Rear axle, type............................spiral-bevel, semifloating
Transmission, type.........................selective sliding-gear

TRUCK, PICKUP, ¾-TON, 4 x 2

(Chevrolet, Model 3604)

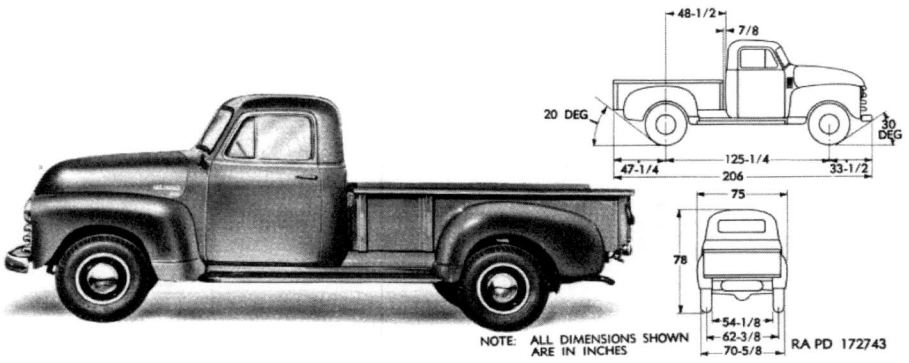

NOTE: ALL DIMENSIONS SHOWN ARE IN INCHES   RA PD 172743

Classification: Nonclassified.

Purpose: To transport light cargo.

GENERAL DATA

Crew..............................1; No. Passengers (including crew) 3
Weight (lb):
   Net...3,650
   Payload...1,750
   Gross..5,400
Rear-axle gear ratio...................................4.57:1
Axle load (lb):
   Empty.............................front 1,995; rear 1,655
   Loaded............................front 2,140; rear 3,260
Tires:
   Ply 6...............Size 15-in.; Pressure (psi) front 36; rear 40
   Tread, center-to-center, front........................(in.) 57⅛
Shipping dimensions, uncrated....................(cu ft) 698; (sq ft) 107
Vehicle dimensions:
   Ground clearance...................................(in.) 7⅝
   Loading height, empty...............................(in.) 32
   Body inside dimensions (in.):
     Length 87.....................Width 50; Height 16¼
   Cargo space.......................................(cu ft) 41
Electrical system.....................................(volts) 6
   No. of batteries...1
   Type of ground.....................................negative
Fuel octane rating..72
Capacities:
   Fuel..(gal) 17½
   Cooling system (qt)..................w/o heater 15; w/heater 16
   Crankcase, refill...................................(qt) 5
   Transmission (qt)....................3-speed, 3; 4-speed, 3¾
   Rear axle...(qt) 3
Brakes:
   Manufacturer; Chevrolet.....................Type; hydraulic
   Parking brake, type..............................rear-wheel
Transmission:
   Forward speeds....................................3 or 4
   Gear ratio.........................High 1:1; Low 2.94:1

PERFORMANCE

Computed grade ability in lowest gear loaded...............(percent) 24
Turning radius (ft)..........................Right 23¾; Left 24¾
Fording depth....................................,............(in.) 18
Fuel consumption, loaded.................................(mpg) 10
Cruising range, loaded......................................(mi) 175
Allowable speed, recommended............................(mph) 60

ENGINE

Manufacturer: Chevrolet........................Model HB or JB
Type.................4-cycle, valve-in-head; No. of cylinders (in line) 6
Displacement.......................................(cu in.) 216.5
Bore..(in.) 3½
Stroke...(in.) 3¾
Compression ratio....................................6.6:1
Governed speed................................not governed
Brake horsepower (max w/std accessories)...........85 at (rpm) 3,300
Torque (max w/std accessories)...........170 lb-ft at (rpm) 1,000-2,000

ADDITIONAL DATA

Rear axle, type..hypoid, full-floating
Transmission, type.......................................synchromesh
   This vehicle also comes equipped with 7.00 x 17 tires.

TRUCK, PICKUP, ¾-TON, 4 x 2
(Dodge, Model B1C116)

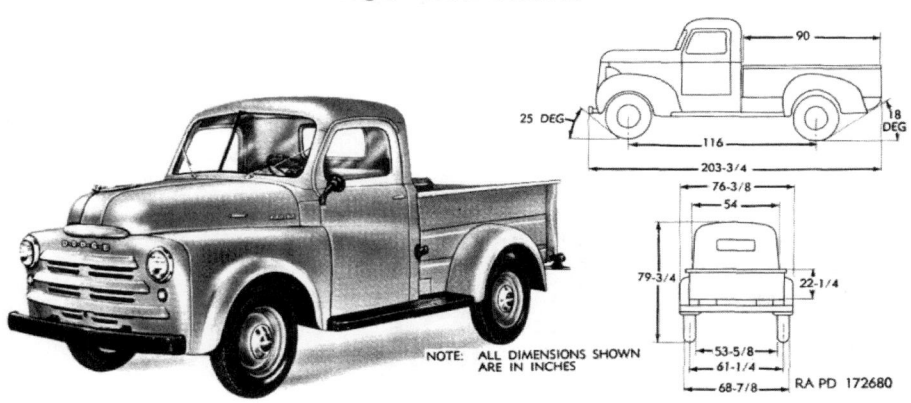

NOTE: ALL DIMENSIONS SHOWN ARE IN INCHES

RA PD 172680

Classification: Nonclassified.

Purpose: To transport light cargo.

GENERAL DATA

Crew..2; Passengers (including crew) 3
Weight (lb):
  Net...3,475
  Payload.........................off highway 1,500; on highway 1,500
  Gross.............................off highway 4,975; on highway 4,975
Rear-axle gear ratio...4.1:1
Axle load (lb):
  Empty...front 2,075; rear 1,400
  Loaded:
    Off highway...............................front 2,090; rear 2,885
    On highway...............................front 2,090; rear 2,885
Tires:
  Ply 6...........................Size 7.00 x 15; Pressure (psi) 40
  Tread, center-to-center, front..............................(in.) 58⁹⁄₁₆
Shipping dimensions, uncrated...............(cu ft) 718; (sq ft) 108
Vehicle dimensions:
  Ground clearance.......................................(in.) 8¾
  Loading height, empty..................................(in.) 30¾
  Body inside dimensions (in.):
    Length...90
    Width..54
    Height:
      Under bows...47
      Side panel...22¾
  Cargo space..(cu ft) 132
Electrical system...................................(volts) 6
  No. of batteries.......................................1
  Type of ground..................................positive
Fuel octane rating.....................................70
Capacities:
  Fuel...(gal) 18
  Cooling system....................................(qt) 17½
  Crankcase, refill...................................(qt) 5
  Transmission......................................(qt) 1¾
  Rear axle..(qt) 1⅝
Brakes:
  Manufacturer: Dodge...................Type; hydraulic
  Parking brake, type..........................transmission
Transmission:
  Forward speeds......................................3
  Gear ratio........................High 1:1; Low 3.3:1

PERFORMANCE

Computed grade ability in lowest gear, loaded..............(percent) 29
Turning radius..(ft) 20
Fording depth..(in.) 18
Fuel consumption, loaded......................................(mpg) 9
Cruising range..(mi) 162
Allowable speed, recommended...............................(mph) 62

ENGINE

Manufacturer: Dodge...Model T-144
Type........................L-head, 4 cycle; No. of cylinders (in line) 6
Displacement...(cu in.) 217.76
Bore..(in.) 3¼
Stroke..(in.) 4⅜
Compression ratio..6.6:1
Governed speed.....................................not governed
Brake horsepower (max w/std accessories)...........82 at (rpm) 3,200
Torque (max)...............................164 lb-ft at (rpm) 1,200

ADDITIONAL DATA

Rear axle, type...............................hypoid, semifloating
Transmission, type...........................selective sliding-gear

TRUCK, PICKUP, ¾-TON, 4 x 2

(Dodge, Model WD–15, 1947)

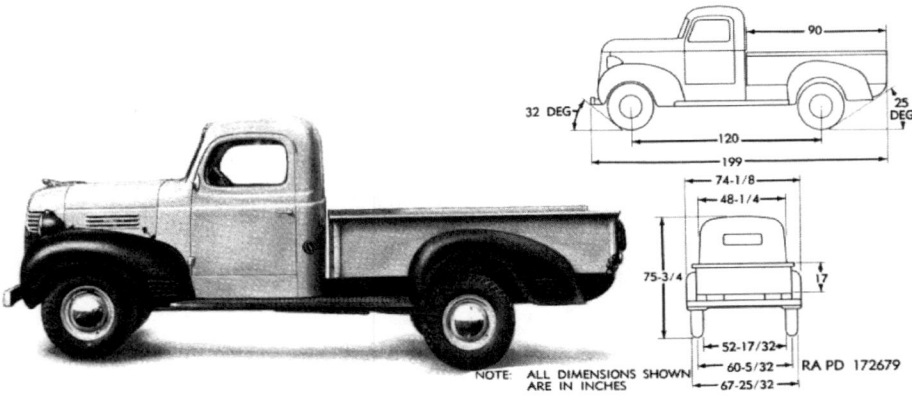

NOTE: ALL DIMENSIONS SHOWN ARE IN INCHES   RA PD 172679

Classification: Nonclassified.

Purpose: To transport light cargo.

GENERAL DATA

Crew..2; Passengers (including crew) 3
Weight (lb):
   Net..3,200
   Payload....................off highway 1,500; on highway 1,500
   Gross........................off highway 4,700; on highway 4,700
Rear-axle gear ratio..4.1:1
Axle load (lb):
   Empty...front 1,800; rear 1,400
   Loaded:
      Off highway..........................front 1,800; rear 2,900
      On highway..........................front 1,800; rear 2,900
Tires:
   Ply 6........................Size 7.00 x 15; Pressure (psi) 40
   Tread, center-to-center, front...................(in.) 55¹⁵⁄₁₆
Shipping dimensions, uncrated..........(cu ft) 647; (sq ft) 103
Vehicle dimensions:
   Ground clearance.......................................(in.) 8¾
   Loading height, empty................................(in.) 31⅛
   Body inside dimensions (in.):
      Length..90
      Width...48¾
      Height:
         Under bows...42½
         Side panel..17
   Cargo space..(cu ft) 107
Electrical system.......................................(volts) 6
   No. of batteries...1
   Type of ground..positive
Fuel octane rating..70
Capacities:
   Fuel..(gal) 18
   Cooling system...............................(qt) 17
   Crankcase, refill..............................(qt) 5
   Transmission....................................(qt) 1¾
   Rear axle...(qt) 1¾
Brakes:
   Manufacturer; Dodge....................Type; hydraulic
   Parking brake, type........................transmission
Transmission:
   Forward speeds..3
   Gear ratio.............................High 1:1; Low 3.3:1

PERFORMANCE

Computed grade ability in lowest gear, loaded...............(percent) 30
Turning radius (ft)...........................Right 21; Left 27
Fording depth...(in.) 18
Fuel consumption, loaded.....................................(mpg) 9
Cruising range, loaded...(mi) 162
Allowable speed, recommended...........................(mph) 62

ENGINE

Manufacturer; Dodge....................................Model T-114
Type.................L-head, 4-cycle; No. of cylinders (in line) 6
Displacement..................................(cu in.) 217.76
Bore..(in.) 3¼
Stroke...(in.) 4⅜
Compression ratio....................................6.6:1
Governed speed.................................not governed
Brake horsepower (max w/std accessories)..........80 at (rpm) 3,200
Torque (max).........................162 lb-ft at (rpm) 1,200

ADDITIONAL DATA

Rear axle, type...................................hypoid, semifloating
Transmission, type..........................selective sliding-gear

168

TRUCK, AMBULANCE, ¾-TON, 4 x 4, M43

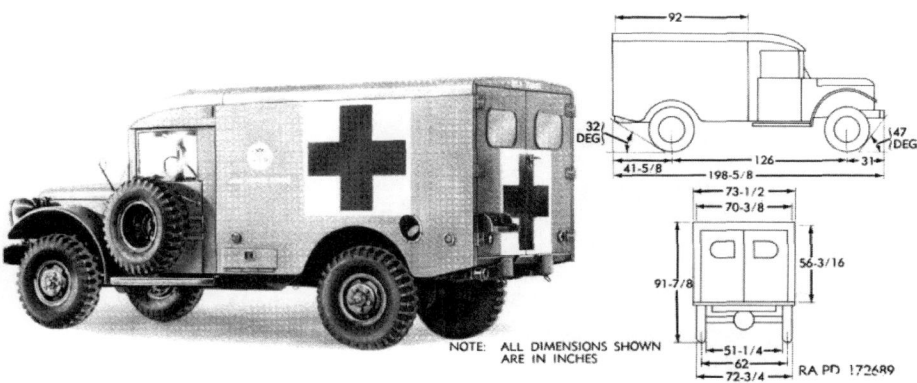

NOTE: ALL DIMENSIONS SHOWN ARE IN INCHES

RA PD 172689

Technical Manuals: 9–840, 9–1825A, 9–1825B, 9–1826A, 9–1828A, 9–1829A, 9–1840A, 9–1840B; **Supply Catalog:** SNL G–741.

Classification: Standard.

Purpose: To transport sick and wounded personnel.

GENERAL DATA

Crew..2
Weight (lb)...................................Net 7,150; Payload 1,400; Gross 8,550
Live-axle gear ratio...5. 83 : 1
Axle load (lb):
    Empty..front 3,300; rear 3,850
    Loaded...front 3,460; rear 5,090
Tires:
    Ply 8.................................Size 9.00 x 16; Pressure (psi) 40
    Tread, center-to-center, front............................(in.) 62
Shipping dimensions, uncrated...................(cu ft) 790; (sq ft) 103. 5
Vehicle dimensions:
    Ground clearance.......................................(in.) 10¾
    Loading height, empty..................................(in.) 34
Electrical system.......................................(volts) 24
    No. of batteries...2
    Type of ground.....................................negative
Fuel octane rating..72
Capacities:
    Fuel...(gal) 24
    Cooling system, w/o heater.............................(qt) 17
    Crankcase, refill...(qt) 5
    Transmission...(qt) 2½
    Transfer...(qt) 1½
    Axles..(each) (qt) 3
Brakes:
    Manufacturer; Dodge............................Type; hydraulic
    Parking brake, type..transfer
Transmission:
    Forward speeds...4
    Gear ratio..............................High 1:1; Low 6.4:1
Transfer:
    Speeds...2
    Gear ratio.............................High 1:1; Low 1.96:1

PERFORMANCE

Computed grade ability in lowest gear, loaded................(percent) 65
Turning radius..(ft) 27
Fuel consumption...(mpg) 9
Cruising range, loaded..(mi) 215
Allowable speed, governed.....................................(mph) 55

ENGINE

Manufacturer: Dodge..Model T–245
Type...........................4-cycle, L-head; No. of cylinders (in line) 6
Displacement..(cu in.) 230. 2
Bore...(in.) 3¼
Stroke..(in.) 4⅜
Compression ratio...6. 7 : 1
Governed speed...(rpm) 3,400
Brake horsepower (max w/std accessories)..............78 at (rpm) 3,200
Torque (max w/std accessories)...............177 lb-ft at (rpm) 1,200

ADDITIONAL DATA

4-litter, insulated body
Live axles, type.......................................hypoid, full-floating
Transmission, type...synchromesh

TRUCK, AMBULANCE, ¾-TON, 4 x 4
(Dodge, Model WC54, T214)

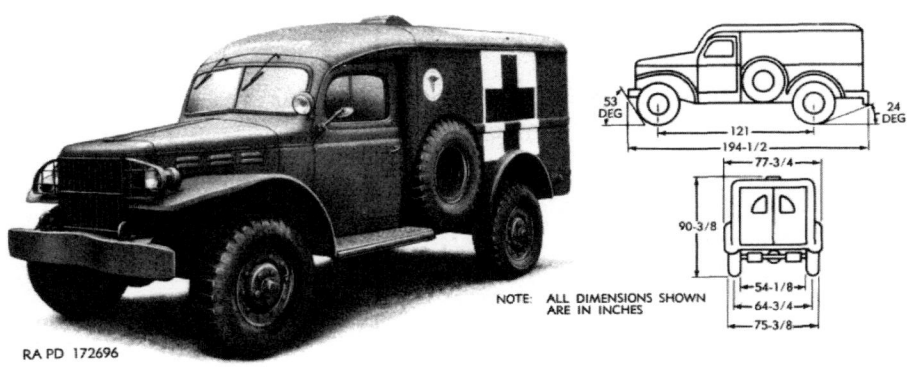

RA PD 172696

NOTE: ALL DIMENSIONS SHOWN ARE IN INCHES

Technical Manuals: 9-808; 9-1808A; 9-1808B; **Supply Catalog:** SNL G-502.

Classification: Limited Standard.

Purpose: To transport sick and wounded personnel.

GENERAL DATA

Crew...2
Passengers in addition to crew:
    Litter patients...4
    Or sitting patients..7
Weight (lb).........................Net 5,920; Payload 1,800; Gross 7,720
Live-axle gear ratio..5.83:1
Axle load (lb):
    Empty..front 2,740; rear 3,180
    Loaded..front 2,980; rear 4,740
Tires:
    Ply 8............................Size 9.00 x 16; Pressure (psi) 40
    Tread, center-to-center, front.................................(in.) 64¾
Shipping dimensions, uncrated....................(cu ft) 791; (sq ft) 105
Vehicle dimensions:
    Ground clearance..(in.) 10¾
    Loading height, empty..(in.) 30
    Pintle height (in.)...............................loaded 24; empty 28
Electrical system..(volts) 6
    No. of batteries...1
    Type of ground...negative
Fuel octane rating...72
Capacities:
    Fuel..(gal) 30
    Cooling system..(qt) 17
    Crankcase, refill...(qt) 5
    Transfer..(qt) 2
    Transmission...(qt) 3
    Axles (each)..(qt) 2½
Brakes:
    Manufacturer; Dodge................................Type; hydraulic
    Parking brake, type.....................................transmission
Transmission:
    Forward speeds...4
    Gear ratio.............................High 1:1; Low 6.40:1
Transfer:
    Speeds...1
    Gear ratio..1:1

PERFORMANCE

Computed grade ability in lowest gear, loaded.................(percent) 52
Turning radius...(ft) 26
Fording depth...(in.) 34
Fuel consumption, loaded..(mpg) 8
Cruising range, loaded..(mi) 240
Allowable speed, governed..(mph) 54
Maximum recommended towed load:
    Off highway, gross..(lb) 1,000
    On highway, gross..(lb) 4,000

ENGINE

Manufacturer: Dodge.......................................Model T-214
Type..................L-head, 4-cycle; No. of cylinders (in line) 6
Displacement...(cu in.) 230.2
Bore...(in.) 3¼
Stroke...(in.) 4⅜
Compression ratio...6.7:1
Governed speed...(rpm) 3,200
Brake horsepower (max w/std accessories)............76 at (rpm) 3,200
Torque (max)................................180 lb-ft at (rpm) 1,200

ADDITIONAL DATA

Live Axles, type.......................................hypoid, full-floating
Transmission, type.............................selective sliding-gear
S8 Body used on some World War II vehicles when rebuilt.

TRUCK, AMBULANCE, ¾-TON, 4 x 4, (KD)

(Dodge, Model WC 64, T214)

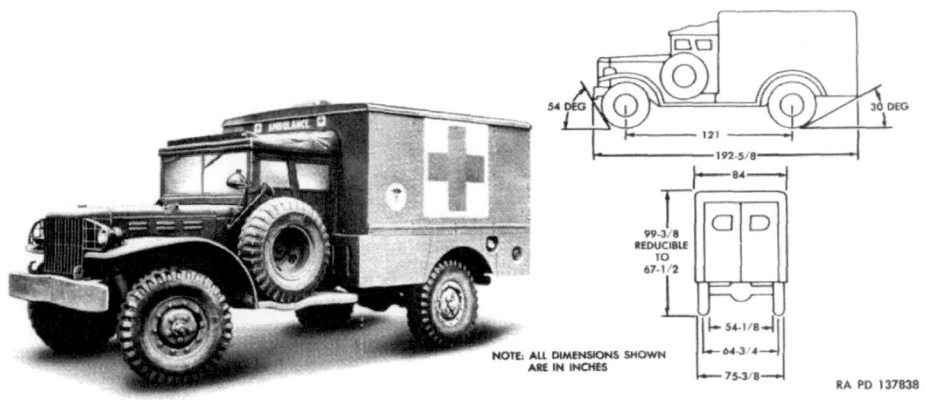

NOTE: ALL DIMENSIONS SHOWN ARE IN INCHES

RA PD 137838

Technical Manuals: 9–808; 9–1808A; 9–1808B; Supply Catalog: SNL G–502.

Classification: Limited Standard.

Purpose: To transport sick and wounded personnel.

GENERAL DATA

Crew..2; Passengers (including crew) 6
Weight (lb)...........................Net 7,000; Payload 1,500; Gross 8,500
Live-axle gear ratio...5.83:1
Axle load (lb):
    Empty.....................................front 2,895; rear 4,105
    Loaded.....................................front 2,935; rear 5,565
Tires:
    Ply 8......................Size 9.00 x 16; Pressure (psi) 40
    Tread, center-to-center, front......................(in.) 64¾
Shipping dimensions, uncrated................(cu ft) 917; (sq ft) 111
Vehicle dimensions:
    Ground clearance...............................(in.) 10½
    Pintle height, empty............................(in.) 28
Electrical system...............................(volts) 6
    No. of batteries....................................1
    Type of ground................................negative
Fuel octane rating.....................................72
Capacities:
    Fuel..(gal) 30
    Cooling system...............................(qt) 17
    Crankcase, refill.............................(qt) 5
    Transfer......................................(qt) 2
    Transmission.................................(qt) 3
    Axles (each).................................(qt) 2½
Brakes:
    Manufacturer: Dodge...................Type; hydraulic
    Parking brake, type......................transmission
Transmission:
    Forward speeds....................................4
    Gear ratio........................High 1:1; Low 6.40:1
Transfer:
    Speeds..1
    Gear ratio.......................................1:1

PERFORMANCE

Computed grade ability in lowest gear, loaded.............(percent) 46
Turning radius...(ft) 26
Fording depth...(in.) 34
Fuel consumption, loaded..............................(mpg) 8
Cruising range, loaded................................(mi) 240
Allowable speed, governed.............................(mph) 54
Maximum recommended towed load:
    Off highway, gross................................(lb) 1,000
    On highway, gross.................................(lb) 4,000

ENGINE

Manufacturer: Dodge............................Model T–214
Type.......................L-head, 4-cycle; No. of cylinders (in line) 6
Displacement..(cu in.) 230.2
Bore..(in.) 3¼
Stroke..(in.) 4⅜
Compression ratio......................................6.7:1
Governed speed....................................(rpm) 3,200
Brake horsepower (max w/std accessories)..........76 at (rpm) 3,200
Torque (max)........................180 lb-ft at (rpm) 1,200

ADDITIONAL DATA

Live Axles, type.........................hypoid, full-floating
Transmission, type.................selective sliding-gear
    S8 Body used on some World War II vehicles when rebuilt.

TRUCK, CARGO, ¾-TON, 4 x 4, M37, W/ AND W/O WINCH (Dodge)

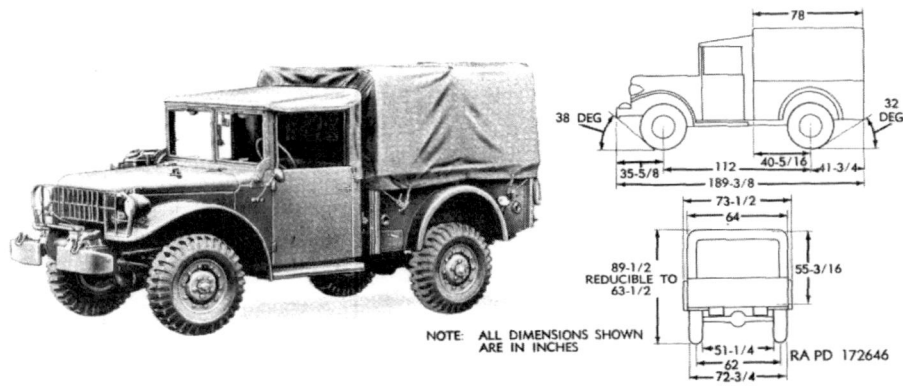

NOTE: ALL DIMENSIONS SHOWN ARE IN INCHES

RA PD 172646

Technical Manuals: 9-840, 9-1840A, 9-1480B; 9-1825A, 9-1825B, 9-1826A, 9-1828A, 9-1829A, Supply Catalog: SNL G-741.

Classification: Standard.

Purpose: To transport general cargo.

GENERAL DATA

Crew..2
Weight (lb):
  Net..5,917
  Payload w/crew................off highway 1,500; on highway 2,000
  Gross........................off highway 7,417; on highway 7,917
Live-axle gear ratio....................................5.83:1
Axle load (lb):
  Empty.................................front 3,251; rear 2,666
  Loaded:
    Off highway........................front 3,251; rear 4,166
    On highway.........................front 3,251; rear 4,666
Tires:
  Ply 8......................Size 9.00 x 16; Pressure (psi) 45
  Tread, center-to-center, front............................(in.) 62
Shipping dimensions, uncrated:
  W/winch.........................(cu ft) 515; (sq ft) 97
  W/o winch.......................(cu ft) 503; (sq ft) 95
Vehicle dimensions (in.):
  Ground clearance......................................10¾
  Pintle height, empty...................................25¼
  Loading height, empty..................................29¾
  Body inside dimensions:
    Length 78......................Width 64; Height 55³⁄₁₆
    Body cargo space..................................(cu ft) 160
Electrical system....................................(volts) 24
  No. of batteries.................................(12-volt) 2
  Type of ground...................................negative
Fuel octane rating..72
Capacities:
  Fuel...(gal) 24
  Cooling system..............................(qt) 25
  Crankcase, refill..............................(qt) 5
  Transmission (qt).................w/power take-off 5¼
                        w/o power take-off 4½
  Transfer....................................(qt) 2½
  Axles..................................(each) (qt) 3
  Winch..............Oil capacity (qt) 1; load capacity (lb) 7,500
Brakes:
  Manufacturer; Dodge.....................Type; hydraulic
  Parking brake, type...........................transfer

GENERAL DATA—Continued

Transmission:
  Forward speeds..4
  Gear ratio.........................High 1:1; Low 6.4:1
Transfer:
  Speeds...2
  Gear ratio........................High 1:1; Low 1.96:1

PERFORMANCE

Computed grade ability in lowest gear, loaded........(percent) 65
Turning radius...(ft) 25
Fording depth............................complete submergence
Fuel consumption, loaded............................(mpg) 9
Cruising range, loaded..............................(mi) 215
Allowable speed, governed...........................(mph) 55
Maximum recommended towed load.....................(lb) 4,000

ENGINE

Manufacturer: Dodge............................Model T-245
Type..................L-head, 4-cycle; No. of cylinders (in line) 6
Displacement...................................(cu in.) 230.2
Bore...(in.) 3¼
Stroke...(in.) 4⅝
Compression ratio..................................6.7:1
Governed speed.............................(rpm) 3,200
Brake horsepower (max w/std accessories).........78 at (rpm) 3,200
Torque (max w/std accessories)..........177 lb-ft at (rpm) 1,200

ADDITIONAL DATA

Live Axles, type...........................hypoid, full-floating
Transmission, type.................................synchromesh
  Data given for vehicle w/winch. Changes in data for vehicles w/o winch are as follows:
Length, over-all....................................(in.) 184¾
Weight (lb):
  Net..5,687
  Gross......................off highway 7,187; on highway 7,687
Axle load (lb):
  Empty.................................front 2,981; rear 2,706
  Loaded:
    Off highway........................front 2,981; rear 4,206
    On highway.........................front 2,981; rear 4,706

TRUCK, CARRYALL, ¾-TON, 4 x 4

(Dodge, Model WC53, T–214)

NOTE: ALL DIMENSIONS
SHOWN ARE IN INCHES   RA PD 137761

Technical Manuals: 9-808; 9-1808A; 9-1808B; 9-1829A; Supply Catalog: SNL G-502.

Classification: Limited Standard.

Purpose: To transport personnel and light cargo.

GENERAL DATA

Crew...2; Passengers (including crew) 7
Weight (lb)..............................Net 5,750; Payload 1,800; Gross 7,550
Live-axle gear ratio...5.83:1
Axle load (lb):
    Empty...front 2,875; rear 2,875
    Loaded..front 3,130; rear 4,420
Tires:
    Ply 8......................Size 9.00 x 16; Pressure (psi) front 40; rear 40
    Tread, center-to-center, front.............................(in.) 64¾
Shipping dimensions, uncrated....................(cu ft) 678; (sq ft) 102
Vehicle dimensions:
    Ground clearance...(in.) 10¾
    Loading height, empty..(in.) 29
Electrical system...(volts) 12
    No. of batteries...1
    Type of ground...negative
Fuel octane rating...72
Capacities:
    Fuel..(gal) 30
    Cooling system..(qt) 17
    Crankcase, refill..(qt) 5
    Transfer case..(qt) 2
    Transmission...(qt) 3
    Axles (each)...(qt) 2½
Brakes:
    Manufacturer; Dodge....................................Type; hydraulic
    Parking brake, type..transmission
Transmission:
    Forward speeds..4
    Gear ratio.............................High 1:1; Low 6.40:1
Transfer:
    Speeds..1
    Gear ratio...1:1

PERFORMANCE

Computed grade ability in lowest gear, loaded. ....(percent) 53
Turning radius (ft)..right 25; left 25
Fording depth..(in.) 34
Fuel consumption, loaded..(mpg) 8
Cruising range, loaded..(mi) 240
Allowable speed, governed..(mph) 54

ENGINE

Manufacturer:, Dodge...Model T-214
Type....................................L-head, 4-cycle; No. of cylinders (in line) 6
Displacement..(cu in.) 230.2
Bore..(in.) 3¼
Stroke...(in.) 4⅜
Compression ratio...6.7:1
Governed speed..(rpm) 3,200
Brake horsepower (max w/std accessories)................76 at (rpm) 3,200
Torque (max)............................180 lb-ft at (rpm) 1,200

ADDITIONAL DATA

Live axles, type..hypoid, full-floating
Transmission, type.................................selective sliding gear
Body inside dimensions (cargo space) (in.):
    Length 92.................................Width 58¾; Height 50½

TRUCK, COMMAND, ¾-TON, 4 x 4, M42

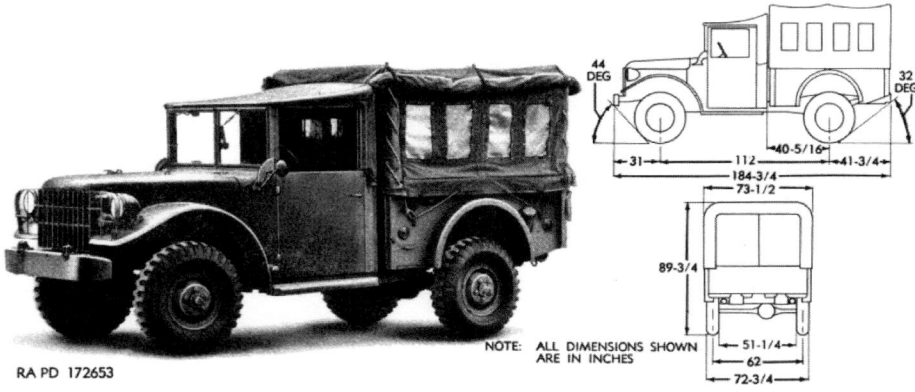

RA PD 172653

NOTE: ALL DIMENSIONS SHOWN ARE IN INCHES

Technical Manuals: 9-840, 9-1825A, 9-1825B, 9-1826A, 9-1828A, 9-1829A, 9-1840A, 9-1840B; Supply Catalog: SNL G-741.

Classification: Standard.

Purpose: To transport command and reconnaissance personnel and light cargo.

GENERAL DATA

Crew	2
Weight (lb)	Net 6,050; Payload 1,500; Gross 7,550
Live-axle gear ratio	5.83:1
Axle load (lb):	
Empty	front 3,000; rear 3,050
Loaded	front 3,175; rear 4,375
Tires:	
Ply 8	Size 9.00 x 16; Pressure (psi) 40
Tread, center-to-center, front	(in.) 62
Shipping dimensions, uncrated	(cu ft) 695; (sq ft) 93½
Vehicle dimensions:	
Ground clearance	(in.) 10¾
Pintle height, empty	(in.) 25⅛
Loading height, empty	(in.) 33
Body inside dimensions (in.):	
Length	78
Width	64
Height	53¾
Cargo space	(cu ft) 155
Electrical system	(volts) 24
No. of batteries	2
Type of ground	negative
Fuel octane rating	72
Capacities:	
Fuel	(gal) 24
Cooling system, w/o heater	(qt) 17
Crankcase, refill	(qt) 5
Transmission	(qt) 2½
Transfer	(qt) 1½
Axles (each)	(qt) 3
Brakes:	
Manufacturer: Dodge	Type; hydraulic
Parking brake, type	transfer
Transmission:	
Forward speeds	4
Gear ratio	High 1:1; Third 1.69:1; Low 6.4:1
Transfer:	
Speeds	2
Gear ratio	High 1:1; Low 1.96:1

PERFORMANCE

Computed grade ability in lowest gear, loaded	(percent) 65
Turning radius	(ft) 25
Fording depth	(in.) 84
Fuel consumption, loaded	(mpg) 9
Cruising range, loaded	(mi) 215
Allowable speed, governed	(mph) 55
Maximum recommended towed load	(lb) 4,000

ENGINE

Manufacturer: Dodge	Model T-245
Type	4-cycle, L-head; No. of cylinders (in line) 6
Displacement	(cu in.) 230.2
Bore	(in.) 3¼
Stroke	(in.) 4¾
Compression ratio	6.7:1
Governed speed	(rpm) 3,400
Brake horsepower (max w/std accessories)	78 at (rpm) 3,200
Torque (max w/std accessories)	177 lb-ft at (rpm) 1,200

ADDITIONAL DATA

Live Axles, type	hypoid, full-floating
Transmission, type	synchromesh

TRUCK, COMMAND RECONNAISSANCE, ¾-TON, 4 x 4

(Dodge, Model WC56, T214)

NOTE: ALL DIMENSIONS SHOWN ARE IN INCHES

RA PD 137862

Technical Manuals: 9-808; 9-1808A; 9-1808B; Supply Catalog: SNL G-502.

Classification: Limited Standard.

Purpose: To transport command and reconnaissance personnel in the field.

GENERAL DATA

Crew..2; Passengers (including crew) 5
Weight (lb).........................Net 5,375; Payload 1,800; Gross 7,175
Live-axle gear ratio 5. 83:1
Axle load (lb):
   Empty...front 2,635; rear 2,740
   Loaded...front 2,710; rear 4,465
Tires:
   Ply 8......................Size 9.00 x 16; Pressure (psi) 40
   Tread, center-to-center, front....................(in.) 64¾
Shipping dimensions, uncrated............(cu ft) 616; (sq ft) 91
Vehicle dimensions:
   Ground clearance................................(in.) 10¾
   Pintle height:
     Loaded..(in.) 25
     Empty..(in.) 27
Electrical system..................................(volts) 12
   No. of batteries..1
   Type of ground.....................................negative
Fuel octane rating......................................72
Capacities:
   Fuel..(gal) 30
   Cooling system....................................(qt) 17
   Crankcase, refill..................................(qt) 5
   Transfer..(qt) 2
   Transmission......................................(qt) 3
   Axles (each) ....(qt) 2½
Brakes:
   Manufacturer: Dodge.......................Type; hydraulic
   Parking brake, type...........................transmission
Transmission:
   Forward speeds...4
   Gear ratio.............................High 1:1; Low 6.40:1
Transfer:
   Speeds...1
   Gear ratio..1:1

PERFORMANCE

Computed grade ability in lowest gear, loaded................(percent) 56
Turning radius..(ft) 22
Fording depth..(in.) 34
Fuel consumption, loaded...............................(mpg) 8
Cruising range, loaded.................................(mi) 240
Allowable speed, governed.............................(mph) 54
Maximum recommended towed load:
   Off highway, gross..................................(lb) 1,000
   On highway, gross...................................(lb) 4,000

ENGINE

Manufacturer: Dodge.............................Model T214
Type....................L-head, 4-cycle; No. of cylinders (in line) 6
Displacement......................................(cu in.) 230. 2
Bore..(in.) 3¼
Stroke..(in.) 4⅝
Compression ratio....................................6. 7:1
Governed speed......................................(rpm) 3,200
Brake horsepower (max w/std accessories)..............76 at (rpm) 3,200
Torque (max)..........................180 lb-ft at (rpm) 1,200

ADDITIONAL DATA

Live axles, type............................hypoid, full-floating
Transmission, type.......................selective sliding-gear

TRUCK, COMMAND RECONNAISSANCE, ¾-TON, 4 x 4, W/WINCH
(Dodge, Model WC57, T214)

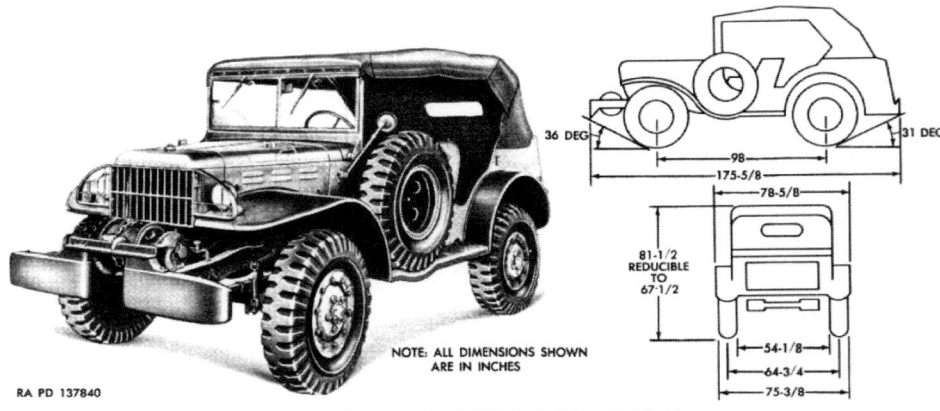

NOTE: ALL DIMENSIONS SHOWN
ARE IN INCHES

RA PD 137840

Technical Manuals: 9-808; 9-1808A; 9-1808B; Supply Catalog: SNL G-502.

Classification: Limited Standard.

Purpose: To transport command and reconnaissance personnel in the field.

GENERAL DATA

Crew..2; Passengers (including crew) 5
Weight (lb)..........................Net 5,675; Payload 1,800; Gross 7,475
Live-axle gear ratio..5.83:1
Axle load (lb):
    Empty...front 2,995; rear 2,680
    Loaded..front 3,075; rear 4,400
Tires:
    Ply 8...Size 9.00 x 16; Pressure (psi) 40
    Tread, center-to-center, front..........................(in.) 64¾
Shipping dimensions, uncrated....................(cu ft) 651; (sq ft) 96
Vehicle dimensions:
    Ground clearance..................................(in.) 10²³⁄₃₂
    Pintle height:
        Loaded..(in.) 24
        Empty...(in.) 27
Electrical system..(volts) 12
    No. of batteries..1
    Type of ground...negative
Fuel octane rating..72
Capacities:
    Fuel..(gal) 30
    Cooling system..(qt) 17
    Crankcase, refill...(qt) 5
    Transfer..(qt) 2
    Transmission w/power take-off............................(qt) 3¾
    Axles (each)...(qt) 2½
    Winch:
        Oil capacity...(qt) 1
        Load capacity..(lb) 5,000
Brakes:
    Manufacturer; Dodge...........................Type; hydraulic
    Parking brake, type..................................transmission
Transmission:
    Forward speeds..4
    Gear ratio..................................High 1:1; Low 6.40:1
Transfer:
    Speeds...1
    Gear ratio..1:1

PERFORMANCE

Computed grade ability in lowest gear, loaded...............(percent) 54
Turning radius...(ft) 22
Fording depth...(in.) 34
Fuel consumption, loaded....................................(mpg) 8
Cruising range, loaded......................................(mi) 240
Allowable speed, governed...................................(mph) 54
Maximum recommended towed load:
    Off highway, gross.......................................(lb) 1,000
    On highway, gross..(lb) 4,000

ENGINE

Manufacturer: Dodge.......................................Model T-214
Type............................L-head, 4-cycle; No. of cylinders (in line) 6
Displacement..(cu in.) 230.2
Bore...(in.) 3¼
Stroke...(in.) 4⅜
Compression ratio..6.7:1
Governed speed...(rpm) 3,200
Brake horsepower (max w/std accessories)............76 at (rpm) 3,200
Torque (max).............................180 lb-ft at (rpm) 1,200

ADDITIONAL DATA

Live axles, type....................................hypoid, full-floating
Transmission, type...............................selective sliding-gear

TRUCK, COMMAND RECONNAISSANCE, ¾-TON, 4 x 4, W/RADIO

(Dodge, Model WC58, T214)

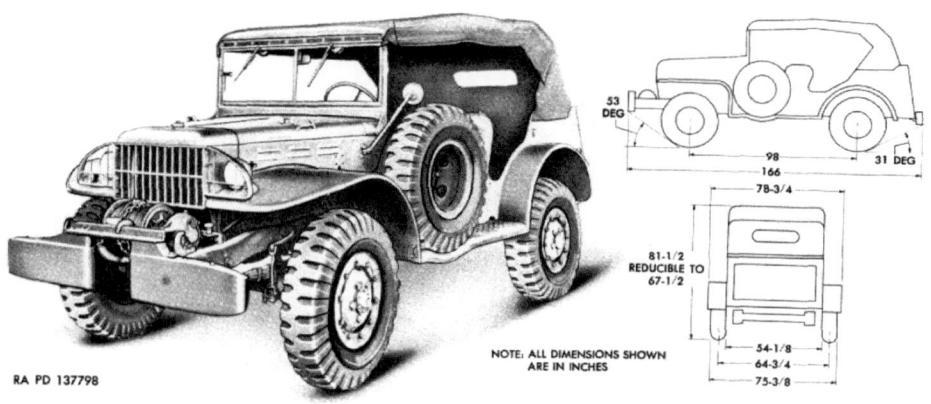

NOTE: ALL DIMENSIONS SHOWN ARE IN INCHES

RA PD 137798

Technical Manuals: 9-808, 9-1808A, 9-1808B; Supply Catalog: SNL G-502.

Classification: Limited Standard.

Purpose: To transport command and reconnaissance personnel.

GENERAL DATA

Crew...2; Passengers (including crew) 5
Weight (lb).....................Net 5,375; Payload 1,800; Gross 7,175
Live-axle gear ratio...5.83:1
Axle load (lb):
  Empty.......................................front, 2,635; rear 2,740
  Loaded.....................................front, 2,710; rear 4,465
Tires:
  Ply 8.....................Size 9.00 x 16; Pressure (psi) 40
  Tread, center-to-center, front.............................(in.) 64¾
Shipping dimensions, uncrated..............(cu ft) 616; (sq ft) 91
Vehicle dimensions:
  Ground clearance......................................(in.) 10¾
  Pintle height, empty..................................(in.) 27
Electrical system...(volts) 12
  No. of batteries...1
  Type of ground..negative
Fuel octane rating...72
Capacities:
  Fuel...(gal) 30
  Cooling system.......................................(qt) 17
  Crankcase, refill.......................................(qt) 5
  Transmission...(qt) 3
  Transfer..(qt) 2
  Axles (each)..(qt) 2½
Brakes:
  Manufacturer; Dodge...........................Type; hydraulic
  Parking brake, type..............................transmission
Transmission:
  Forward speeds..4
  Gear ratio............................High 1:1; Low 6.4:1
Transfer:
  Speeds...1
  Gear ratio...1:1

PERFORMANCE

Computed grade ability in lowest gear, loaded.............(percent) 56
Turning radius..(ft) 22
Fording depth..(in.) 34
Fuel consumption, loaded..................................(mpg) 8
Cruising range, loaded...................................(mi) 240
Allowable speed, governed................................(mph) 54
Maximum recommended towed load:
  Off highway, gross....................................(lb) 1,000
  On highway, gross.....................................(lb) 4,000

ENGINE

Manufacturer: Dodge.................................Model T-214
Type..................L-head, 4-cycle; No. of cylinders (in line) 6
Displacement...(cu in.) 230.2
Bore...(in.) 3¼
Stroke..(in.) 4⅜
Compression ratio.......................................6.7:1
Governed speed.......................................(rpm) 3,200
Brake horsepower (max w/std accessories)...........76 at (rpm) 3,200
Torque (max)................................180 lb-ft at (rpm) 1,200

ADDITIONAL DATA

Live axles, type............................hypoid, full-floating
Transmission, type........................selective sliding gear

TRUCK, WEAPONS CARRIER, ¾-TON, 4 x 4 (6-VOLT) AND (12-VOLT)

(Dodge, Model WC51, T214)

RA PD 137804

NOTE: ALL DIMENSIONS SHOWN ARE IN INCHES

Technical Manuals: 9-808; 9-1808A; 9-1808B; **Supply Catalog:** SNL G-502.

Classification: Limited Standard.

Purpose: To transport weapons, tools, equipment, and personnel.

GENERAL DATA

Crew	2; Passengers (including crew) 10
Weight (lb)	Net 5,645; Payload 1,800; Gross 7,445
Live-axle gear ratio	5.83:1

Axle load (lb):
Empty	front 2,785; rear 2,860
Loaded	front 2,825; rear 4,620

Tires:
Ply 8	Size 9.00 x 16; Pressure (psi) 40
Tread, center-to-center, front	(in.) 64¾
Shipping dimensions, uncrated	(cu ft) 684; (sq ft) 96

Vehicle dimensions:
Loading height, empty	(in.) 33⅞
Ground clearance	(in.) 10¾
Pintle height (in.)	loaded 24; empty 26

Body inside dimensions (in.):
Length 72	Width 48¼; Height, under bows 49½
Cargo space	(cu ft) 100
Electrical system	(volts) 6 or 12
No. of batteries	1
Type of ground	negative
Fuel octane rating	72

Capacities:
Fuel	(gal) 30
Cooling system	(qt) 17
Crankcase, refill	(qt) 5
Transfer	(qt) 2
Transmission	(qt) 3
Axles (each)	(qt) 2½

Brakes:
Manufacturer; Dodge	Type; hydraulic
Parking brake, type	transmission

Transmission:
Forward speeds	4
Gear ratio	High 1:1; Low 6.40:1
Transfer speeds	1
Gear ratio	1:1

PERFORMANCE

Computed grade ability in lowest gear, loaded	(percent) 56
Turning radius	(ft) 22
Fording depth	(in.) 34
Fuel consumption, loaded	(mpg) 8
Cruising range, loaded	(mi) 240
Allowable speed, governed	(mph) 54

Maximum recommended towed load:
Off highway, gross	(lb) 1,000
On highway, gross	(lb) 4,000

ENGINE

Manufacturer: Dodge	Model T214
Type	L-head, 4-cycle; No. of cylinders (in line) 6
Displacement	(cu in.) 230.2
Bore	(in.) 3¼
Stroke	(in.) 4⅝
Compression ratio	6.7:1
Governed speed	(rpm) 3,200
Brake horsepower (max w/std accessories)	76 at (rpm) 3,200
Torque (max)	180 lb-ft at (rpm) 1,200

ADDITIONAL DATA

Live axles, type	hypoid, full-floating
Transmission, type	selective sliding-gear

TRUCK, WEAPONS CARRIER, ¾-TON, 4 x 4, (6-VOLT) AND (12-VOLT) W/WINCH

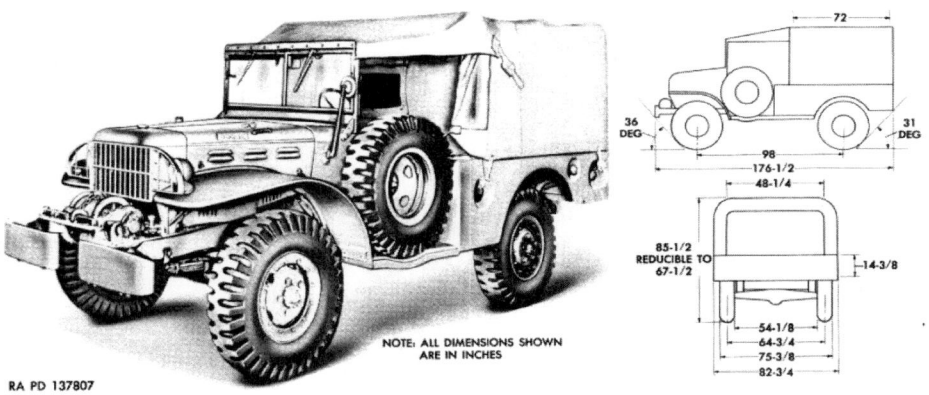

NOTE: ALL DIMENSIONS SHOWN ARE IN INCHES

RA PD 137807

Technical Manuals: 9–808; 9–1808A; 9–1808B; Supply Catalog: SNL G-502.

Classification: Limited Standard.

Purpose: To transport weapons, tools, equipment, and personnel.

GENERAL DATA

Crew..........................2; Passengers (including crew) 10
Weight (lb)..........................Net 5,940; Payload 1,800; Gross 7,740
Live-axle gear ratio..........................5.83:1
Axle load (lb):
    Empty..........................front 3,145; rear 2,795
    Loaded..........................front 3,185; rear 4,555
Tires:
    Ply 8..........................Size 9.00 x 16; Pressure (psi) 40
    Tread, center-to-center, front..........................(in.) 64¾
Shipping dimensions, uncrated..........................(cu ft) 723; (sq ft) 102
Vehicle dimensions:
    Ground clearance..........................(in.) 10¾
    Loading height, empty..........................(in.) 34
    Pintle height (in.)..........................loaded 24; empty 26
    Body inside dimensions (in.)
        Length 72..........................Width 48¼; Height, under bows 49½
        Body cargo space..........................(cu ft) 1,000
Electrical system..........................(volts) 6 or 12
    No. of batteries..........................1
    Type of ground..........................negative
Fuel octane rating..........................72
Capacities:
    Fuel..........................(gal) 30
    Cooling system..........................(qt) 17
    Crankcase, refill..........................(qt) 5
    Transfer..........................(qt) 2
    Transmission w/power take-off..........................(qt) 3½
    Winch..........................Oil capacity (qt) 1; Load capacity (lb) 5,000*
Brakes:
    Manufacturer: Dodge..........................Type: hydraulic
    Parking brake, type..........................transmission
Transmission:
    Forward speeds..........................4
    Gear ratio..........................High 1:1; Low 6.40:1
Transfer:
    Speeds..........................1
    Gear ratio..........................1:1

PERFORMANCE

Computed grade ability in lowest gear, loaded..........................(percent) 54
Turning radius (ft)..........................Right 22; Left 22
Fording depth..........................(in.) 34
Fuel consumption, loaded..........................(mpg) 8
Cruising range, loaded..........................(mi) 240
Allowable speed, governed..........................(mph) 54
Maximum recommended towed load:
    Off highway, gross..........................(lb) 1,000
    On highway, gross..........................(lb) 4,000

ENGINE

Manufacturer: Dodge..........................Model T214
Type..........................L-head, 4-cycle; No. of cylinders (in line) 6
Displacement..........................(cu in.) 230.2
Bore..........................(in.) 3¼
Stroke..........................(in.) 4⅝
Compression ratio..........................6.7:1
Maximum governed speed..........................(rpm) 3,200
Brake horsepower (max w/std accessories)..........................76 at (rpm) 3,200
Torque (max)..........................180 lb-ft at (rpm) 1,200

ADDITIONAL DATA

Live axles, type..........................hypoid, full-floating
Transmission..........................selective sliding-gear

---

*Last production equipped w/7,500-lb cap winch.

179

TRUCK, PANEL, 1-TON, 4 x 2
(Chevrolet, Model 3805)

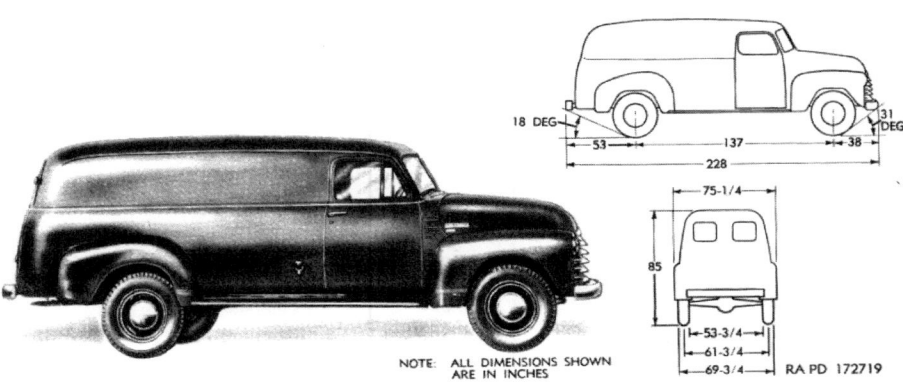

18 DEG — 53 — 137 — 38 — 31 DEG
228

75-1/4
85
53-3/4
61-3/4
69-3/4

RA PD 172719

NOTE: ALL DIMENSIONS SHOWN ARE IN INCHES

Classification: Nonclassified.

Purpose: To transport light cargo.

GENERAL DATA

Crew..2
Weight (lb)....................Net 4,505; Payload 2,495; Gross 7,000
Rear-axle gear ratio..5.14:1
Axle load (lb):
    Empty....................................front 2,155; rear 2,350
    Loaded...................................front 2,440; rear 4,560
Tires:
    Ply 8....................Size 7.50 x 17; Pressure—(psi) front 40; rear 60
    Tread, center-to-center, front.........................(in.) 56¼
Shipping dimensions, uncrated..................(cu ft) 845; (sq ft) 119
Vehicle dimensions:
    Ground clearance......................................(in.) 9¾
    Loading height, empty.................................(in.) 34
    Body inside dimensions (in.):
        Length.................108⅜; Width 62⅜; Height 51⅝
        Cargo space.......................................(cu ft) 203
Electrical system......................................(volts) 6
    No. of batteries...1
    Type of ground.......................................negative
Fuel octane rating.......................................72
Capacities:
    Fuel..(gal) 18
    Cooling system.......................................(qt) 15
    Crankcase, refill.....................................(qt) 5
    Transmission..(qt) 3
    Rear axle...(qt) 3
Brakes:
    Manufacturer; Chevrolet....................Type; hydraulic
    Parking brake, type...............................rear-wheel
Transmission:
    Forward speeds..4
    Gear ratio.............................High 1:1; Low 7.06:1

PERFORMANCE

Computed grade ability in lowest gear, loaded..............(percent) 57
Turning radius..(ft) 26
Fording depth..(in.) 21
Fuel consumption, loaded..................................(mpg) 10
Cruising range, loaded.....................................(mi) 180
Allowable speed, recommended..............................(mph) 55

ENGINE

Manufacturer: Chevrolet....................................Model AJC
Type....................4-cycle, valve-in-head; No. of cylinders (in line) 6
Displacement...(cu in.) 216.5
Bore..(in.) 3½
Stroke..(in.) 3¾
Compression ratio..6.6:1
Governed speed...not governed
Brake horsepower, gross.............................92 at (rpm) 3,400
Torque, maximum gross................176 lb-ft at (rpm) 1,000–2,000

ADDITIONAL DATA

Rear axle, type..................................hypoid, full-floating
Transmission..synchromesh

TRUCK, CARRYALL, 1-TON, 4 x 4
Dodge, Model B1PW26 w/Gerstenslager body

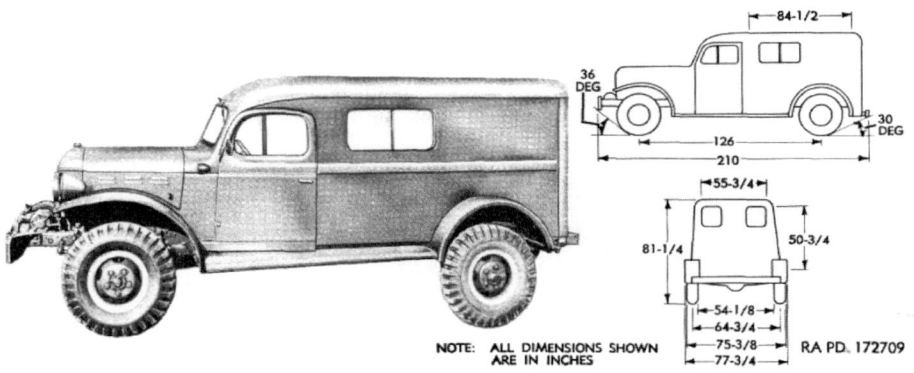

NOTE: ALL DIMENSIONS SHOWN ARE IN INCHES   RA PD. 172709

Classification: Nonclassified.

Purpose: To transport personnel and light cargo.

GENERAL DATA

Crew..2 Passengers (including crew) 8
Weight (lb)......................Net 5,500; Payload 1,775; Gross 7,275
Live-axle gear ratio..5.83:1
Axle load (lb):
    Empty..front 3,225; rear 2,275
    Loaded...front 3,375; rear 3,900
Tires:
    Ply 8....................................Size 9.00 x 16; Pressure (psi) 45
    Tread, center-to-center, front.............................(in.) 64¾
Shipping dimensions, uncrated....................(cu ft) 768; (sq ft) 114
Vehicle dimensions:
    Ground clearance...(in.) 10¾
    Pintle height, empty.......................................(in.) 27
    Loading height, empty.....................................(in.) 35
    Body inside dimensions (in.):
        Length 84½....................Width 55¾; Height 50¾
    Body cargo space..(cu ft) 138
Electrical system...(volts) 6
    No. of batteries..1
    Type of ground..positive
Fuel octane rating..72
Capacities:
    Fuel..(gal) 30
    Cooling system..(qt) 17
    Crankcase, refill..(qt) 5
    Transmission...(qt) 3
    Transfer...(qt) 1½
    Axles (each)...(qt) 3
Brakes:
    Manufacturer; Dodge...............................Type; hydraulic
    Parking brake, type...............................transmission
Transmission:
    Forward speeds..4
    Gear ratio.................................High 1:1; Low 6.40:1
Transfer:
    Speeds...2
    Gear ratio.................................High 1:1; Low 1.96:1

PERFORMANCE

Computed grade ability in lowest gear, loaded....................(percent) 65
Turning radius...(ft) 27½
Fording depth..(in.) 34
Fuel consumption, loaded......................................(mpg) 9
Cruising range, loaded..(mi) 240
Allowable speed (governed).....................................(mph) 54
Maximum recommended towed load:
    Off highway, gross......................................(lb) 1,000
    On highway, gross.......................................(lb) 4,000

ENGINE

Manufacturer: Dodge....................................Model T-137
Type.....................L-head, 4-cycle; No. of cylinders (in line) 6
Displacement..(cu in.) 230.2
Bore...(in.) 3¼
Stroke..(in.) 4⅜
Compression ratio...6.7:1
Governed speed...(rpm) 3,200
Brake horsepower (max w/std accessories)...............76 at (rpm) 3,200
Torque (max)........................180 lb-ft at (rpm) 1,200

ADDITIONAL DATA

Live axles, type.................................hypoid, full-floating
Transmission, type.........................selective sliding-gear

TRUCK, PICKUP, 1-TON, 4 x 4, W/WINCH
(Dodge, Model B2PW126, 1950)

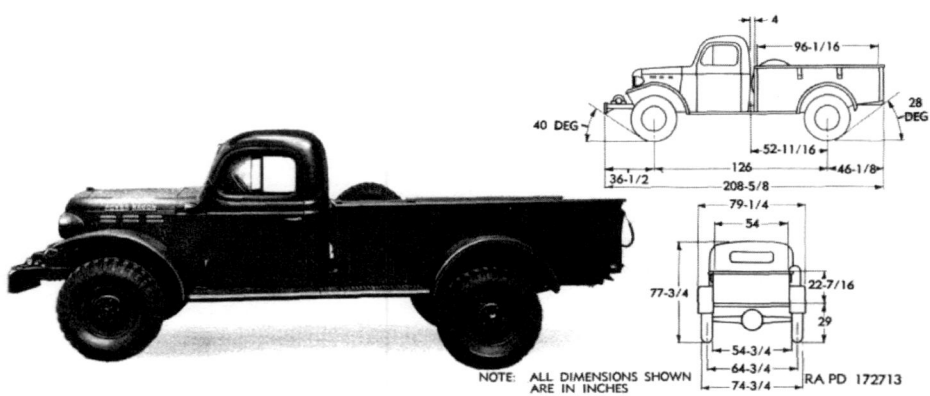

NOTE: ALL DIMENSIONS SHOWN ARE IN INCHES

RA PD 172713

Classification: Nonclassified.

Purpose: To transport light cargo.

GENERAL DATA

Crew..2
Weight (lb) Net...5,295
    Payload.......................off highway 2,000; on highway 3,405
    Gross.........................off highway 7,295; on highway 8,700
Live-axle gear ratio..5.83:1
Axle load (lb):
    Empty..front 3,155; rear 2,150
    Loaded:
        Off highway...............................front 3,215; rear 4,080
        On highway................................front 3,255; rear 5,445
Tires:
    Ply 8......................Size 9.00 x 16; Pressure (psi) 55
    Tread, center-to-center, front.........................(in.) 64¾
Shipping dimensions, uncrated...............(cu ft) 745; (sq ft) 115
Vehicle dimensions:
    Ground clearance..(in.) 10¾
    Loading height, empty....................................(in.) 29
    Body inside dimensions (in.): Length 96⅛.....Width 54; Height 22¾
    Cargo space...(cu ft) 68
Electrical system..(volts) 6
    No. of batteries..1
    Type of ground..positive
Fuel octane rating..72
Capacities:
    Fuel..(gal) 18
    Cooling system...(qt) 17
    Crankcase, refill..(qt) 5
    Transmission w/PTO......................................(qt) 3
    Transfer..(qt) 1½
    Axles (each)..(qt) 3
    Winch:
        Oil capacity...(qt) 1
        Load capacity.....................................(lb) 5,000
Brakes:
    Manufacturer; Dodge............................Type; hydraulic
    Parking brake, type....................................transfer
Transmission:
    Forward speeds...4
    Gear ratio..............................High 1:1; Low 6.4:1
Transfer:
    Speeds...2
    Gear ratio.............................High 1:1; Low 1.96:1

PERFORMANCE

Computed grade ability in lowest gear w/off-highway load......(percent) 65
Turning radius..(ft) 27½
Fording depth, loaded...(in.) 28
Fuel consumption, loaded...(mpg) 8
Cruising range, loaded...(mi) 144
Allowable speed, governed..(mph) 55

ENGINE

Manufacturer; Dodge..Model T-137
Type.......................4-cycle, L-head; No. of cylinders (in line) 6
Displacement...(cu in.) 230.2
Bore...(in.) 3¼
Stroke...(in.) 4⅜
Compression ratio..6.7:1
Governed speed..(rpm) 3,200
Brake horsepower (max w/std accessories)...............94 at (rpm) 3,200
Torque (max w/std accessories)...............186 lb-ft at (rpm) 1,200

ADDITIONAL DATA

Live axles, type...hypoid, full-floating
Transmission, type...syncromesh

TRUCK, PICKUP, 1-TON, 4 x 4
(Willys, Model 4–73–4WD, 1950)

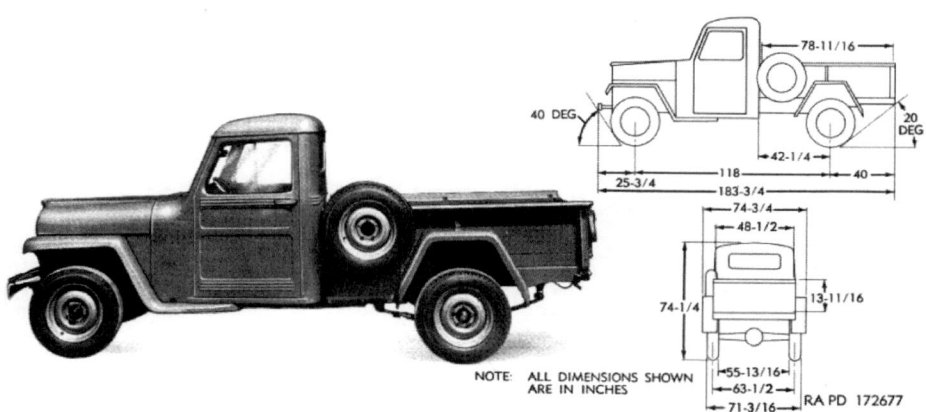

NOTE: ALL DIMENSIONS SHOWN ARE IN INCHES

RA PD 172677

Classification: Nonclassified.

Purpose: To transport light cargo.

GENERAL DATA

Crew..2; Passengers (including crew) 3
Weight (lb)..............Net 3,240; Payload (on highway) 2,060; Gross 5,300
Axle gear ratio...5.38:1
Axle load (lb):
    Empty.......................................front 1,655; rear 1,585
    Loaded.......................................front 1,700; rear 3,750
Tires:
    Ply 6................Size 7.00 x 16; Pressure (psi) front 30; rear 45
    Tread, center-to-center, front.......................................(in.) 57
Shipping dimensions, uncrated.......................(cu ft) 591; (sq ft) 96
Vehicle dimensions:
    Ground clearance...(in.) 9¾
    Loading height, empty...(in.) 28¾
    Pintle height, empty..(in.) 23½
    Body inside dimensions (in.):
        Length..78⅝
        Width...48½
        Height:
            Under bows...44½
            Side panel...13¾
    Cargo space..(cu ft) 98
Electrical system...(volts)6
    No. of batteries..1
    Type of ground..negative
Fuel octane rating...70
Capacities:
    Fuel..(gal) 15
    Cooling system (qt)...............w/o heater 11; w/heater 12
    Transmission..(qt) 1½
    Transfer...(qt) 1¾
    Axles (qt)..................................front 1¼; rear 1½
    Winch.................Oil capacity (qt) ½; Load capacity (lb) 6,000
Brakes:
    Manufacturer; Bendix..............................Type; hydraulic
    Parking brake, type.................................rear-wheel
Transmission:
    Forward speeds...3
    Gear ratio...............................High 1:1; Low 2.80:1
Transfer:
    Speeds...2
    Gear ratio...............................High 1:1; Low 2.43:1

PERFORMANCE

Computed grade ability in lowest gear, loaded.................(percent) 41
Turning radius...(ft) 25
Fording depth..(in.) 18
Fuel consumption, loaded.......................................(mpg) 17
Cruising range, loaded...(mi) 255
Allowable speed, governed......................................(mph) 60

ENGINE

Manufacturer: Willys..................................Model 473–4WD
Type........................F-head, 4-cycle; No. of cylinders (in line) 4
Displacement...(cu in.) 134.2
Bore...(in.) 3⅛
Stroke...(in.) 4⅜
Compression ratio..7.4:1
Governed speed..(rpm) 3,700
Brake horsepower (max w/std accessories).................64 at (rpm) 4,000
Torque (max).......................................114 lb-ft at (rpm) 2,000

ADDITIONAL DATA

Live axles, type................................hypoid, full-floating
Transmission, type.................................synchromesh

183

TRUCK, VAN, 1-TON, 4 x 4

(Willys, Model 4WD)

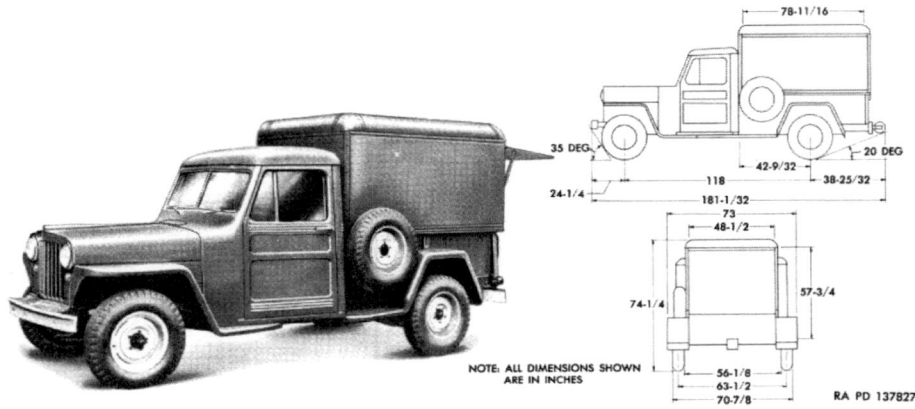

NOTE: ALL DIMENSIONS SHOWN
ARE IN INCHES

RA PD 137827

Classification: Nonclassified.

Purpose: To transport general cargo.

GENERAL DATA

Crew..2; Passengers (including crew) 3
Weight (lb).............Net 3,286; Payload (on highway) 2,014; Gross 5,300
Axle gear ratio..5.38:1
Axle load (lb):
  Empty..front 1,649; rear 1,637
  Loaded...front 1,806; rear 3,494
Tires:
  Ply 6...................Size 7.00 x 16; Pressure (psi) front 30; rear 45
  Tread, center-to-center, front..(in.) 57
Shipping dimensions, uncrated....................(cu ft) 570; (sq ft) 92
Vehicle dimensions:
  Ground clearance.......................................(in.) 9¾
  Loading height, empty.................................(in.) 28¾
  Pintle height, empty..................................(in.) 23½
  Body inside dimensions (in.):
    Length....................78¾; Width 48½; Height 57
    Cargo space..(cu ft) 126
Electrical system..(volts) 6
  No. of batteries..1
  Type of ground..negative
Fuel octane rating..68
Capacities:
  Fuel..(gal) 15
  Cooling system (qt)....................w/o heater 11; w/heater 12
  Crankcase, refill.......................................(qt) 4
  Transmission..(qt) 1½
  Transfer..(qt) 2
  Axles (qt)...................................front 1¼; rear 1½
Brakes:
  Manufacturer; Bendix...........................Type; hydraulic
  Parking brake, type............................rear-wheel
Transmission:
  Forward speeds..3
  Gear ratio.........................High 1:1; Low 2.798:1
Transfer:
  Speeds...2
  Gear ratio.........................High 1:1; Low 2.43:1

PERFORMANCE

Computed grade ability in lowest gear, loaded...................(percent) 48
Turning radius...(ft) 25
Fuel consumption, loaded..(mpg) 16
Cruising range, loaded...(mi) 240
Allowable speed, governed...(mph) 55
Maximum recommended towed load on highway, gross...........(lb) 1,500

ENGINE

Manufacturer: Willys...Model 4 WD
Type.........................L-head, 4-cycle; No. of cylinders (in line) 4
Displacement...(cu in.) 134.2
Bore...(in.) 3¼
Stroke..(in.) 4⅜
Compression ratio...6.48:1
Governed speed..(rpm) 3,700
Brake horsepower (max w/std accessories)...............51 at (rpm) 4,000
Torque (max)..............................105 lb-ft at (rpm) 2,000

ADDITIONAL DATA

Live axles, type...hypoid, full-floating
Transmission...synchromesh

TRUCK, CARGO, 1½-TON, 4 x 2
(Ford, Model 2G8T, 6-Cyl, 1942)

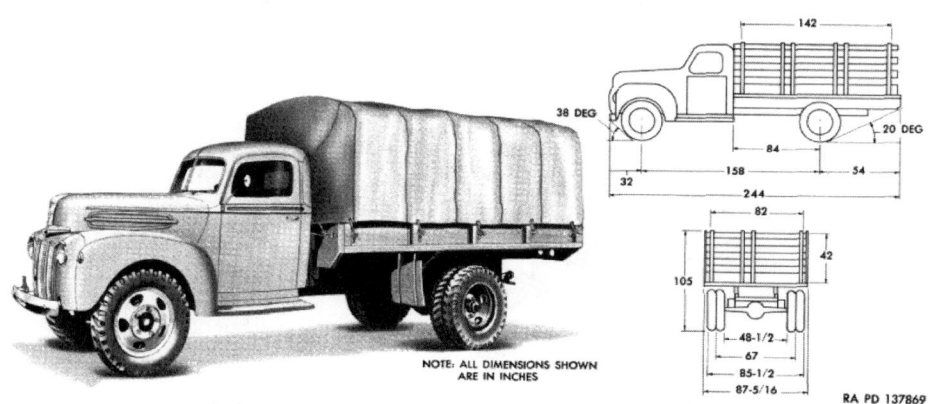

NOTE: ALL DIMENSIONS SHOWN
ARE IN INCHES

RA PD 137869

Technical Manuals: 9-806, 9-1806A, 9-1806B; Supply Catalog: SNL G-540.

Classification: Nonclassified.

Purpose: To transport general cargo.

GENERAL DATA

Crew..2
Weight (lb)..Net 5,138
    Payload.........................off highway 3,140; on highway 7,362
    Gross.........................off highway 8,278; on highway 12,500
Rear-axle gear ratio..6.67:1
Axle load (lb):
    Empty..front 2,338; rear 2,800
    Loaded:
        Off highway.............................front 2,448; rear 5,830
        On highway.............................front 2,600; rear 9,900
Tires:
    Ply 8......................Size 7.50 x 20; Pressure (psi) 55
    Tread, center-to-center, front........................(in.) 56¹³⁄₃₂
Shipping dimensions, uncrated....................(cu ft) 1,360; (sq ft) 155
Vehicle dimensions:
    Ground clearance.......................................(in.) 9¼
    Loading height, empty.................................(in.) 43⅞
    Pintle height, empty..................................(in.) 25⅜
    Body inside dimensions (in):
        Length...142
        Width..82
        Height:
            Under bows.............................57
            Side rack..............................42
        Cargo space...........................(cu ft) 385
Electrical system.......................................(volts) 6
    No. of batteries..1
    Type of ground....................................positive
Fuel octane rating...72
Capacities:
    Fuel......................................(gal) 49
    Cooling system..........................(qt) 17½
    Crankcase, refill.......................(qt) 5
    Transmission............................(qt) 2½
    Rear axle...............................(qt) 2½
Brakes:
    Manufacturer; Ford....................Type; hydraulic
    Parking brake, type........................transmission
Transmission:
    Forward speeds...4
    Gear ratio...................High 1:1; Low 6.4:1

PERFORMANCE

Computed grade ability in lowest gear, loaded..............(percent) 38
Turning radius...(ft) 29½
Fording depth...(in.) 25
Fuel consumption, loaded..................................(mpg) 9
Cruising range, loaded....................................(mi) 441
Allowable speed, governed.................................(mph) 45
Maximum recommended towed load:
    Off highway, gross....................................(lb) 3,000
    On highway, gross.....................................(lb) 6,000

ENGINE

Manufacturer: Ford................................Model 2GT
Type...............L-head, 4-cycle; No. of cylinders (in line) 6
Displacement..(cu in.) 226
Bore...(in.) 3.3
Stroke...(in.) 4.4
Compression ratio....................................6.7:1
Governed speed......................................(rpm) 3,400
Brake horsepower (max/std accessories).......81 at (rpm) 3,300
Torque (max)......................170 lb-ft at (rpm) 1,200

ADDITIONAL DATA

Rear axle, type........................spiral-bevel, full-floating
Transmission, type.....................selective sliding-gear

TRUCK, CARGO, 1½-TON, 4 x 2

(Ford, Model G8T, 6-Cyl, 1943)

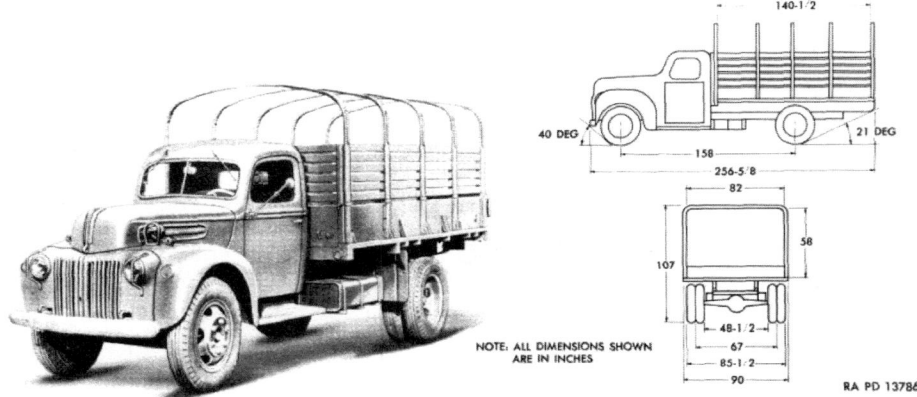

NOTE: ALL DIMENSIONS SHOWN ARE IN INCHES

RA PD 137868

Technical Manuals: 9-806; 9-1806A; 9-1806B; **Supply Catalog:** SNL G-540.

Classification: Nonclassified.

Purpose: To transport general cargo.

GENERAL DATA

Crew...2
Weight (lb): Net..6,500
    Payload.............................off highway 3,340; on highway * 6,000
    Gross...............................off highway 9,840; on highway 12,500
Rear-axle gear ratio...6. 67:1
Axle load (lb):
    Empty...front 2,630; rear 3,870
    Loaded:
      Off highway...........................front 2,981; rear 6,859
      On highway............................front 3,260; rear 9,240
Tires:
    Ply 8.............................Size 7.50 x 20; Pressure (psi) 55
    Tread, center-to-center, front..................................(in.) 59½
Shipping dimensions, uncrated......................(cu ft) 1,440; (sq ft) 161
Vehicle dimensions:
    Ground clearance..(in.) 10
    Loading height, empty..(in.) 46
    Pintle height, empty...(in.) 25⅜
    Body inside dimensions (in.):
      Length..140½
      Width..82
    Height:
      Under bows...58
      Side rack..42
    Body cargo space...(cu ft) 388
Electrical system..(volts) 6
    No. of batteries...1
    Type of ground..positive
Fuel octane rating..72
Capacities:
    Fuel...(gal) 49
    Cooling system..(qt) 16
    Crankcase..(qt) 5
    Transmission..(qt) 2½
    Rear axle...(qt) 2½

GENERAL DATA

Brakes:
    Manufacturer; Ford..............................Type; hydrovac
    Parking brake, type...............................transmission
Transmission:
    Forward speeds..4
    Gear ratio..........................High 1:1; Low 6. 4:1

PERFORMANCE

Computed grade ability in lowest gear, loaded...................(percent) 38
Turning radius...(ft) 31¾
Fording depth...(in.) 25
Fuel consumption, loaded......................................(mpg) 9
Cruising range, loaded.......................................(mi) 441
Allowable speed, governed....................................(mph) 45
Maximum recommended towed load:
    Off highway, gross.......................................(lb) 3,000
    On highway, gross..(lb) 6,000

ENGINE

Manufacturer: Ford..Model G8T
Type.....................L-head, 4-cycle; No. of cylinders (in line) 6
Displacement..(cu in.) 226
Bore...(in.) 3.3
Stroke...(in.) 4.4
Compression ratio..6. 7:1
Governed speed..(rpm) 3,400
Brake horsepower (max w/std accessories)..............81 at (rpm) 3,300
Torque (max)...............................170 lb-ft at (rpm) 1,200

ADDITIONAL DATA

Rear axle, type........................spiral-bevel, full-floating
Transmission, type.......................selective sliding-gear

* Truck must be equipped with helper springs for 3-ton payload.

TRUCK, CHASSIS, 1½-TON, 4 x 2

(Ford, Model G8T, 6-Cyl 1943, 1945)

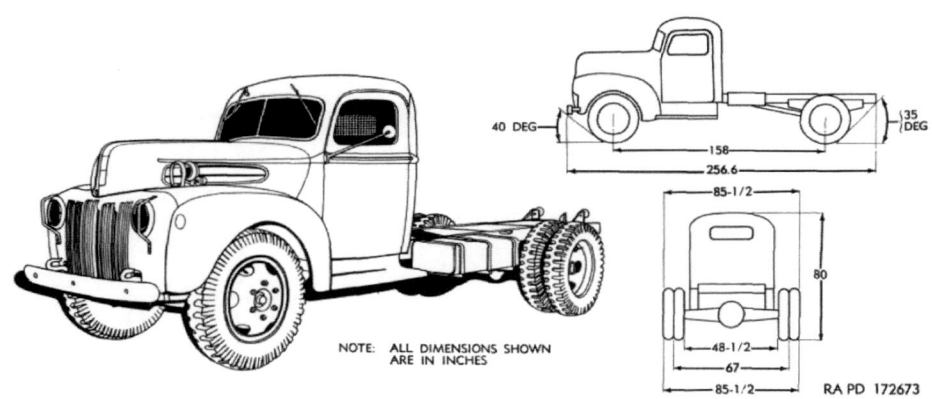

40 DEG

35 DEG

—158—

—256.6—

—85-1/2—

80

48-1/2
67
—85-1/2—

NOTE: ALL DIMENSIONS SHOWN
ARE IN INCHES

RA PD 172673

Technical Manuals: 9-806, 9-1806A, 9-1806B, 9-1828A, 9-1829A; Supply Catalog: SNL G-540.

Classification: Standard.

Purpose: To be used as component of general-purpose or special-equipment vehicle.

GENERAL DATA

Crew	2
Weight (lb) Net	5,025
Rear-Axle gear ratio	6.666:1
Axle load (lb):	
Empty	front 1,950; rear 3,075
Tires:	
Ply 8	Size 7.50 x 20; Pressure (psi) 55
Tread, center-to-center, front	(in.) 57½
Shipping dimensions, uncrated	(cu ft) 1,025; (sq ft) 153
Vehicle dimensions:	
Ground clearance	(in.) 9¾
Pintle height, empty	(in.) 25⅜
Height of frame	(in.) 34
Electrical system	(volts) 6
No. of batteries	1
Type of ground	positive
Fuel octane rating	70
Capacities:	
Fuel	(gal) 49
Cooling system	(qt) 16
Crankcase, refill	(qt) 5
Transmission	(qt) 2½
Rear axle	(qt) 2½
Brakes:	
Manufacturer: Ford	Type: hydraulic
Parking brake, type	transmission
Transmission:	
Forward speeds	4
Gear ratio	High 1:1; Low 6.4:1

PERFORMANCE

Computed grade ability in lowest gear, loaded	(percent) 32
Turning radius	(ft) 32
Fording depth	(in.) 25
Fuel consumption, loaded	(mpg) 9
Cruising range, loaded	(mi) 440
Allowable speed, governed	(mph) 45
Maximum recommended towed load (lb):	
Off highway, gross	(lb) 3,000
On highway, gross	(lb) 6,000

ENGINE

Manufacturer: Ford	Model G8T
Type	L-head, 4-cycle; No. of cylinders (in line) 6
Displacement	(cu in.) 225
Bore	(in.) 3.3
Stroke	(in.) 4.4
Compression ratio	6.7:1
Governed speed	(rpm) 3,400
Brake horsepower (max w/std accessories)	81 at (rpm) 3,300
Torque (max w/std accessories)	170 lb-ft at (rpm) 1,200

ADDITIONAL DATA

Rear Axle, type	spiral-bevel, full-floating
Transmission, type	selective sliding-gear

TRUCK, DUMP, 1½-TON, 4 x 2

(Chevrolet, Model 4103)

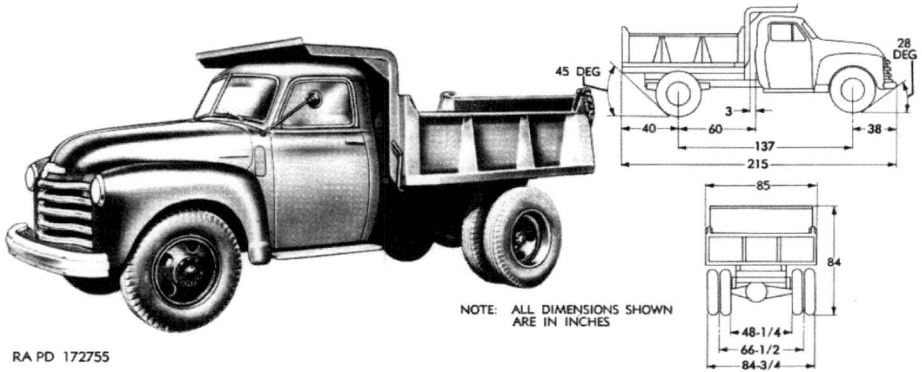

NOTE: ALL DIMENSIONS SHOWN ARE IN INCHES

RA PD 172755

Classification: Standard.

Purpose: To transport and dump earth, sand, gravel, etc., and transport general cargo.

GENERAL DATA

Crew.................................1; No. Passengers (including crew) 3
Weight (lb)..Net 6,415
    Payload...........................off highway 3,000; on highway 6,085
    Gross............................off highway 9,415; on highway 12,500
Rear-axle gear ratio...6.17:1
Axle load (lb):
    Empty....................................front 2,755; rear 3,660
    Loaded:
        Off highway......................front 2,995; rear 6,420
        On highway......................front 3,325; rear 9,175
Tires:
    Ply 8..............Size 7.50 x 20; Pressure (psi) front 40; rear 60
    Tread, center-to-center, front..............................(in.) 59¾
Shipping dimensions, uncrated..............(cu ft) 888; (sq ft) 127
Vehicle dimensions:
    Ground clearance....................................(in.) 10
    Body inside dimensions (in.):
        Length...................96; Width 72; Height 11
        Struck capacity....................(cu yds) 1½
Electrical system.......................................(volts) 6
    No. of batteries...1
    Type of ground.......................................negative
Fuel octane rating...72
Capacities:
    Fuel..(gal) 17½
    Cooling system (qt)................w/o heater 15; w/heater 16
    Crankcase, refill..................................(qt) 5
    Transmission w/PTO.................................(qt) 3½
    Rear axle...(qt) 5½
Brakes:
    Manufacturer; Chevrolet...................Type; hydrovac
    Parking brake, type..........................transmission
Transmission:
    Forward speeds...4
    Gear ratio.......................High 1:1; Low 7.06:1

PERFORMANCE

Computed grade ability in lowest gear w/off-highway load....(percent) 37
Turning radius (ft)..............................Right 24; Left 24¾
Fording depth......................................(in.) 22
Fuel consumption, loaded..............................(mpg) 8½
Cruising range, loaded................................. 150
Allowable speed, governed.............................(mph) 54

ENGINE

Manufacturer: Chevrolet.............................Model AJE
Type.............4-cycle, valve-in-head; No. of cylinders (in line) 6
Displacement.......................................(cu in.) 235.5
Bore..(in.) 3⅞
Stroke...(in.) 3¹⁵⁄₁₆
Compression ratio.......................................6.7:1
Governed speed......................................(rpm) 3,200
Brake horsepower (max w/std accessories)..............98 at (rpm) 3,500
Torque (max w/std accessories)...............186 lb-ft at (rpm) 2,000

ADDITIONAL DATA

Rear axle, type...........................hypoid, full-floating
Transmission, type..............................synchromesh

TRUCK, DUMP, 1½-TON, 4 x 2

(Dodge, Model WF–31, 1947)

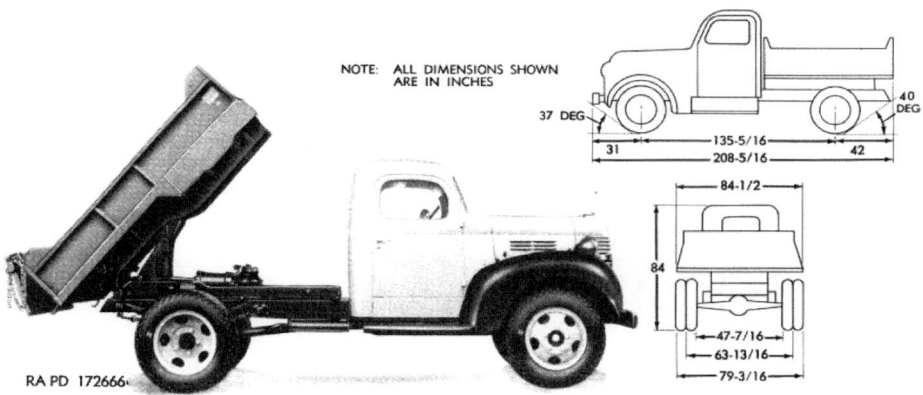

NOTE: ALL DIMENSIONS SHOWN ARE IN INCHES

37 DEG
40 DEG
135-5/16
31
42
208-5/16
84-1/2
84
47-7/16
63-13/16
79-3/16

RA PD 172666

Classification: Standard.

Purpose: To transport and dump stone, sand, gravel, etc., and to transport general cargo.

GENERAL DATA

Crew..3
Weight (lb)...........................Net 6,155; Payload 7,345; Gross 13,500
Rear-axle gear ratio...6.833:1
Axle load (lb):
    Empty...front 2,530; rear 3,625
    Loaded..front 3,020; rear 10,480
Tires:
    Ply 10.................................Size 7.00 x 20; Pressure (psi) 70
    Tread, center-to-center, front.............................(in.) 57¾
Shipping dimensions, uncrated.......................(cu ft) 965; (sq ft) 138
Vehicle dimensions:
    Ground clearance......................................(in.) 8¹³⁄₁₆
    Body inside dimensions (in.):
        Length.........................96; Width 72; Height 13½
        Struck capacity..............................(cu yd) 2
Electrical system......................................(volts) 6
    No. of batteries..1
    Type of ground.....................................positive
Fuel octane rating..70
Capacities:
    Fuel..(gal) 18
    Cooling system, w/o heater...........................(qt) 20½
    Crankcase, refill......................................(qt) 5
    Transmission (qt)......................w/power take-off 3½
    Rear-axle..(qt) 5½
Brakes:
    Manufacturer: Dodge...........................Type; hydraulic
    Parking brake, type..............................transmission
Transmission:
    Forward speeds..4
    Gear ratio.........................High 1:1; Low 6.4:1

PERFORMANCE

Computed grade ability in lowest gear, loaded.............(percent) 34
Turning radius (ft)...............................Right 22; Left 24
Allowable speed, recommended............................(mph) 45

ENGINE

Manufacturer: Dodge.......................................Model T–118
Type......................4-cycle, L-head: No. of cylinders (in line) 6
Displacement...(cu. in.) 236.6
Bore..(in.) 3⁷⁄₁₆
Stroke..(in.) 4¼
Compression ratio..6.6:1
Governed speed......................................not governed
Brake horsepower (max w/std accessories)...........87 at (rpm) 3,200
Torque (max w/std accessories)...........179 lb-ft at (rpm) 1,200

ADDITIONAL DATA

Rear Axle, type...............................hypoid, full-floating
Transmission, type...................................synchromesh

TRUCK, DUMP, 1½-TON, 4 x 2
(Dodge, Model B1F128, 1948)

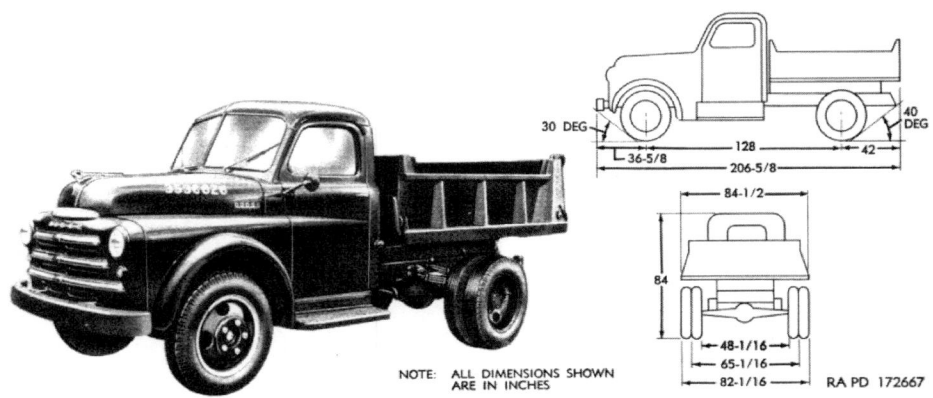

NOTE: ALL DIMENSIONS SHOWN ARE IN INCHES

RA PD 172667

Classification: Standard.

Purpose: To transport and dump stone, sand, gravel, etc, and transport general cargo.

GENERAL DATA

Crew..3
Weight (lb).........................Net 6,620; Payload 6,880; Gross 13,500
Rear-axle gear ratio..6.833:1
Axle load (lb):
    Empty...front 2,810; rear 3,810
    Loaded..front 3,295; rear 10,205
Tires:
    Ply 10..Size 7.00 x 20; Pressure (psi) 70
    Tread, center-to-center, front..(in.) 62
Shipping dimensions, uncrated....................(cu ft) 850; (sq ft) 121
Vehicle dimensions:
    Ground clearance..(in.) 8¹³⁄₁₆
    Body inside dimensions (in.)..........Length 96; Width 78; Height 16
    Struck capacity......................................(cu yd) 2½
Electrical system..(volts) 6
    No. of batteries...1
    Type of ground...positive
Fuel octane rating...70
Capacities:
    Fuel..(gal) 18
    Cooling system..(qt) 19¼
    Crankcase, refill..(qt) 5
    Transmission (qt)..............................w/power take off 3½
    Rear axle..(qt) 5½
Brakes:
    Manufacturer: Dodge.........................Type: hydraulic
    Parking brake, type....................................transmission
Transmission:
    Forward speeds..4
    Gear ratio.................................High 1:1; Low 6.4:1

PERFORMANCE

Computed grade ability in lowest gear, loaded...................(percent) 34
Turning radius..(ft) 22
Allowable speed, recommended.....................................(mph) 45

ENGINE

Manufacturer: Dodge..Model T-148
Type..................................4-cycle, L-head; No. of cylinders (in line) 6
Displacement...(cu in.) 236.6
Bore..(in.) 3⁷⁄₁₆
Stroke...(in.) 4¼
Compression ratio...6.6:1
Governed speed...not governed
Brake horsepower (max w/std accessories)................91 at (rpm) 3,200
Torque (max w/std accessories)..................180 lb-ft at (rpm) 1,200

ADDITIONAL DATA

Rear axle, type...hypoid, full-floating
Transmission, type...synchromesh

TRUCK, DUMP, 1½-TON, 4 x 2

(Dodge, Model B1FA128, w/Garwood Model G12 body, 1948)

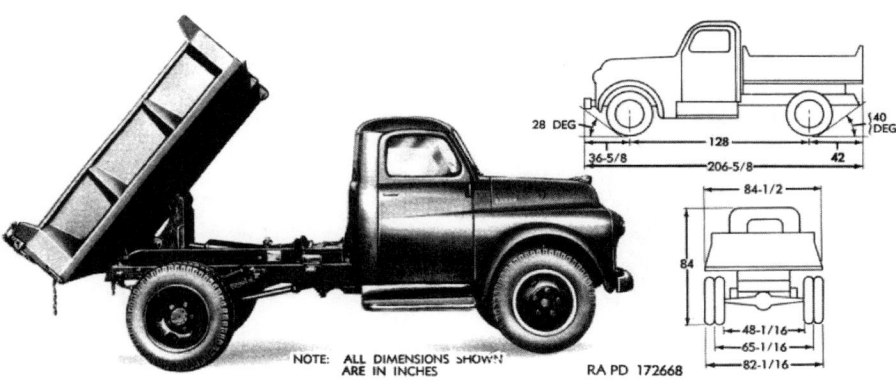

NOTE: ALL DIMENSIONS SHOWN ARE IN INCHES

RA PD 172668

Classification: Standard.

Purpose: To transport and dump stone, sand, gravel, etc., and to transport general cargo.

GENERAL DATA

Crew	3
Weight (lb)	Net 6,405; Payload 7,095; Gross 13,500
Rear-axle gear ratios (2-speed):	
High	5.83:1
Low	8.11:1
Axle load (lb):	
Empty	front 2,830; rear 3,575
Loaded	front 3,225; rear 10,275
Tires:	
Ply 8	Size 7.50 x 20; Pressure (psi) 60
Tread, center-to-center, front	(in.) 62
Shipping dimensions, uncrated	(cu ft) 965; (sq ft) 138
Vehicle dimensions:	
Ground clearance	(in.) 9
Body inside dimensions (in.):	
Length	96; Width 72; Height 13½
Struck capacity	(cu yds) 2
Electrical system	(volts) 6
No. of batteries	1
Type of ground	positive
Fuel octane rating	70
Capacities:	
Fuel	(gal) 18
Cooling system	(qt) 19¼
Crankcase	(qt) 5
Transmission (qt)	w/power take off 3½
Rear axle	(qt) 6½
Brakes:	
Manufacturer; Dodge	Type; vacuum-hydraulic
Parking brake, type	transmission
Transmission:	
Forward speeds	4
Gear ratio	High 1:1; Low 6.40:1

PERFORMANCE

Computed grade ability in lowest gear, loaded	(percent) 42
Turning radius	(ft) 22
Allowable speed, recommended	(mph) 50

ENGINE

Manufacturer: Dodge	Model T-178
Type	4-cycle, L-head; No. of cylinders (in line) 6
Displacement	(cu in.) 236.6
Bore	(in.) 3⅜
Stroke	(in.) 4¼
Compression ratio	6.6:1
Governed speed	not governed
Brake horsepower (max w/std accessories)	91 at (rpm) 3,200
Torque (max w/std accessories)	180 lb-ft at (rpm) 1,200

ADDITIONAL DATA

Rear axle, type	hypoid, full-floating
Transmission, type	synchromesh

TRUCK, DUMP, 1½-TON, 4 x 2

(International Harvester, Model KB 5, 1949)

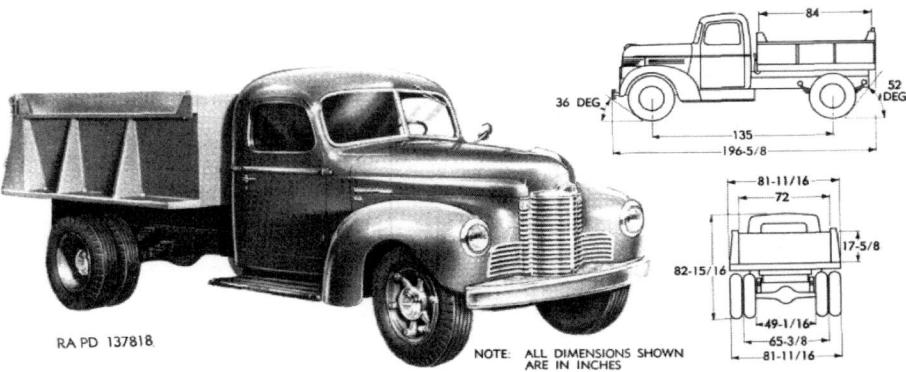

RA PD 137818

NOTE: ALL DIMENSIONS SHOWN ARE IN INCHES

Classification: Standard.

Purpose: To haul and dump earth, sand, gravel, coal, etc., and transport general cargo.

GENERAL DATA

Crew	2
Weight (lb)	Net 5,800
Payload:	
Off highway	3,000; Gross 8,800
On highway	5,900; Gross 11,700
Rear-axle gear ratio	6.166:1
Axle load (lb):	
Empty	front 2,500; rear 3,300
Loaded:	
Off highway	front 2,860; rear 5,940
On highway	front 3,208; rear 8,492
Tires:	
Ply 8	Size 7.00 x 20; Pressure (psi) 55
Tread, center-to-center, front	(in.) 58½
Shipping dimensions, uncrated	(cu ft) 771; (sq ft) 112
Vehicle dimensions:	
Ground clearance	(in.) 9¾
Body inside dimensions (in.):	
Length	84; Width 72; Height 17⅝
Struck capacity	(cu yd) 2⅜
Electrical system	(volts) 6
No. of batteries	1
Type of ground	positive
Fuel octane rating	75
Capacities:	
Fuel	(gal) 18
Cooling system	(qt) 14
Crankcase, refill	(qt) 5
Transmission w/power take-off	(qt) 2¾
Rear axle	(qt) 3½
Brakes:	
Manufacturer; Wagner	Type; hydraulic
Parking brake, type	transmission
Transmission:	
Forward speeds	4
Gear ratio	High 1:1; Low 6.4:1

PERFORMANCE

Computed grade ability in lowest gear, loaded	(percent) 46
Turning radius	(ft) 24
Fording depth	(in.) 28¾
Fuel consumption, loaded	(mpg) 10
Cruising range, loaded	(mi) 180
Allowable speed, governed	(mph) 56

ENGINE

Manufacturer: International Harvester	Model GRD–233
Type	L-head, 4-cycle; No. of cylinders (in line) 6
Displacement	(cu in.) 233
Bore	(in.) 3⁵⁄₁₆
Stroke	(in.) 4¼
Compression ratio	6.3:1
Governed speed	(rpm) 3,500
Brake horsepower (max w/std accessories)	93 at (rpm) 3,400
Torque (max)	181 lb-ft at (rpm) 1,000

ADDITIONAL DATA

Rear axle, type	spiral-bevel, full-floating
Transmission, type	synchromesh

TRUCK, STAKE AND PLATFORM, 1½-TON, 4 x 2

(Chevrolet, Model 4409)

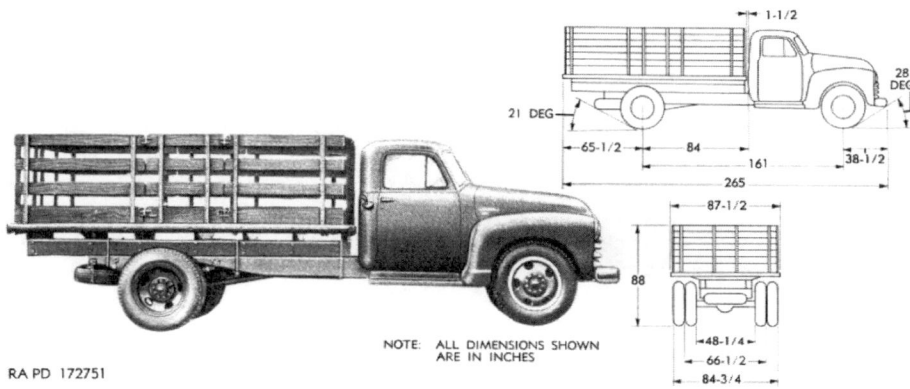

NOTE: ALL DIMENSIONS SHOWN ARE IN INCHES

RA PD 172751

Classification: Standard.

Purpose: To transport general cargo.

GENERAL DATA

Crew..................................1; No. Passengers (including crew) 3
Weight (lb)..Net 5,675
  Payload........................off highway 3,000; on highway 6,825
  Gross.......................off highway 8,675; on highway 12,500
Rear-axle gear ratio..6.17:1
Axle load (lb):
  Empty......................................front 2,650; rear 3,025
  Loaded:
    Off highway...........................front 2,830; rear 5,845
    On highway............................front 3,100; rear 9,400
Tires:
  Ply 8....................Size 7.50 x 20; Pressure (psi) front 40; rear 60
  Tread, center-to-center, front...........................(in.) 59¾
Shipping dimensions, uncrated...............(cu ft) 1,181; (sq ft) 161
Vehicle dimensions:
  Ground clearance..(in.) 10
  Loading height, empty...................................(in.) 49
  Body inside dimensions (in.):
    Length...141½
    Width..80¾
    Height...38½
  Cargo space...(cu ft) 254
Electrical system...(volts) 6
  No. of batteries..1
  Type of ground......................................negative
Fuel octane rating..72
Capacities:
  Fuel...(gal) 17½
  Cooling system (qt)....................w/o heater 15; w/heater 16
  Crankcase, refill....................................(qt) 5
  Transmission.......................................(qt) 3
  Rear axle..(qt) 5½
Brakes:
  Manufacturer: Chevrolet......................Type; hydrovac
  Parking brake, type...............................transmission
Transmission:
  Forward speeds..4
  Gear ratio..............................High 1:1; Low 7.06:1

PERFORMANCE

Computed grade ability in lowest gear w/off-highway load.....(percent) 37
Turning radius..(ft) 28
Fording depth..(in.) 22
Fuel consumption, loaded..................................(mpg) 8½
Cruising range, loaded.....................................(mi) 150
Allowable speed, governed.................................(mph) 54

ENGINE

Manufacturer: Chevrolet.............................Model AJE
Type....................4-cycle, valve-in-head; No. of cylinders (in line) 6
Displacement..(cu in.) 235.5
Bore..(in.) 3⁹⁄₁₆
Stroke..(in.) 3¹³⁄₁₆
Compression ratio.......................................6.7:1
Governed speed.......................................(rpm) 3,200
Brake horsepower (max w/std accessories)............98 at (rpm) 3,500
Torque (max w/std accessories)........186 lb-ft at (rpm) 2,000

ADDITIONAL DATA

Rear axle, type.............................hypoid, full floating
Transmission, type..................................synchromesh

TRUCK, STAKE AND PLATFORM, 1½-TON, 4 x 2

(Ford, Model F–5)

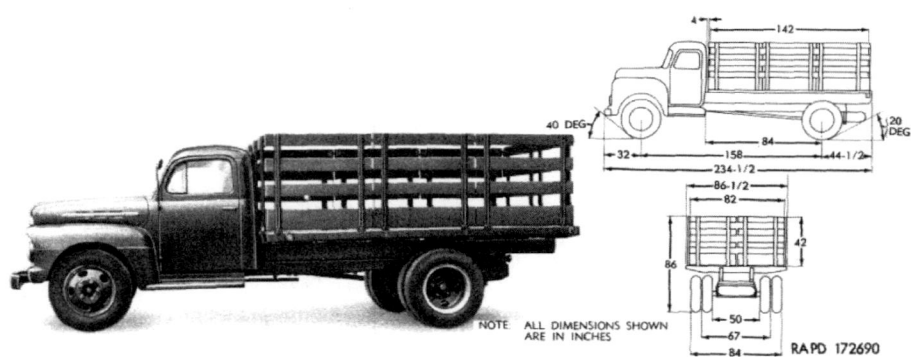

NOTE: ALL DIMENSIONS SHOWN ARE IN INCHES

RAPD 172690

Classification: Standard.

Purpose: To transport general cargo.

GENERAL DATA

Crew..2
Weight (lb): Net...5,885
   Payload...............................off highway 3,000; on highway 6,615
   Gross.................................off highway 8,885; on highway 12,500
Rear-axle gear ratio...6.67:1
Axle load (lb):
   Empty..front 2,600; rear 3,285
   Loaded:
     Off highway................................front 2,840; rear 6,045
     On highway.................................front 3,125; rear 9,375
Tires:
   Ply 8................................Size 7.50 x 20; Pressure (psi) 60
   Tread, center-to-center, front...........................(in.) 58½
Shipping dimensions, uncrated............(cu ft) 1,030; (sq ft) 141
Vehicle dimensions:
   Ground clearance......................................(in.) 9⅞
   Loading height, empty.................................(in.) 44
   Body inside dimensions (in.):
     Length.............................Width 82; Height 42
   Cargo space..(cu ft) 288
Electrical system..(volts) 6
   No. of batteries..1
   Type of ground.....................................positive
Fuel octane rating...72
Capacities:
   Fuel..(gal) 20
   Cooling system.....................................(qt) 23
   Crankcase, refill...................................(qt) 5
   Transmission.......................................(qt) 2½
   Transfer...(qt) 1½
   Rear axle..(qt) 2½

GENERAL DATA—Continued

Brakes:
   Manufacturer; Ford...........................Type; hydraulic
   Parking brake, type.............................transmission
Transmission:
   Forward speeds...4
   Gear ratio................................High 1:1; Low 6.4:1

PERFORMANCE

Computed grade ability in lowest gear w/off-highway load.....(percent) 65
Turning radius..(ft) 28
Fording depth..(in.) 24
Fuel consumption, loaded.................................(mpg) 9
Cruising range, loaded...................................(mi) 180
Allowable speed, governed................................(mph) 60

ENGINE

Manufacturer: Ford.................................Model 8RT
Type...................4-cycle, L-head; No. of cylinders (90-deg F) 8
Displacement.......................................(cu. in.) 239
Bore..(in.) 3⅟₁₆
Stroke..(in.) 3¾
Compression ratio...6.8:1
Governed speed....................................(rpm) 3,800
Brake horsepower, gross....................100 at (rpm) 3,800
Torque, gross.......................185 lb-ft at (rpm) 1,600

ADDITIONAL DATA

Rear axle, type..........................spiral-bevel, full-floating
Transmission, type..........................selective sliding gear

194

TRUCK, STAKE AND PLATFORM, 1½-TON, 4 x 2
(Ford, Model G8T)

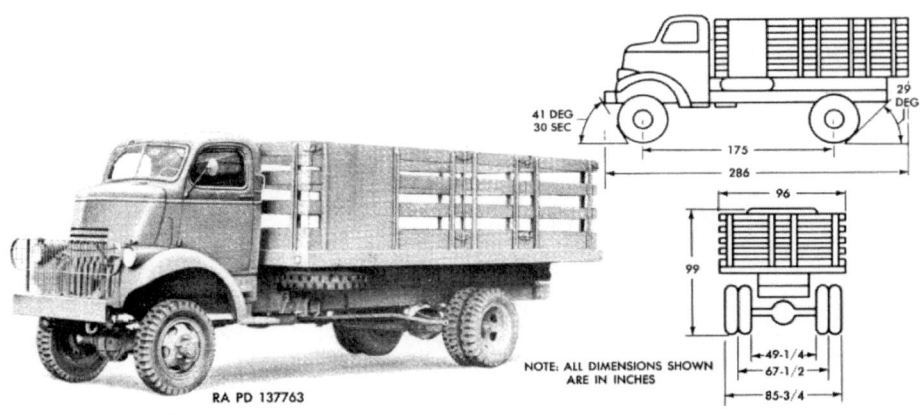

41 DEG
30 SEC

29 DEG

175

286

96

99

NOTE: ALL DIMENSIONS SHOWN
ARE IN INCHES

49-1/4
67-1/2
85-3/4

RA PD 137763

Technical Manuals: 9–806, 9–1806A, 9–1806B; Supply Catalog: SNL G–540.

Classification: Standard.

Purpose: To transport general cargo.

GENERAL DATA

Crew..2
Weight (lb) Net..6,500
    Payload.........................off highway 3,350; on highway 6,000
    Gross.........................off highway 9,850; on highway 12,500
Rear-axle gear ratio..6.67:1
Axle load (lb):
    Empty..front 2,630; rear 3,870
    Loaded:
        Off highway.........................front 3,006; rear 6,844
        On highway.........................front 3,290; rear 9,210
Tires:
    Ply 8........................Size 7.50 x 20; Pressure (psi) 55
    Tread, center-to-center, front..........................(in.) 59½
Shipping dimensions, uncrated...........(cu ft) 1,173; (sq ft) 167.4
Vehicle dimensions:
    Loading height, empty..(in.) 46
    Ground clearance...(in.) 10
    Pintle height, empty.......................................(in.) 25⅜
    Body inside dimensions (in.):
        Length..140½
        Width...82
        Height:
            Under bows......................................57
            Side rack.......................................42
    Body cargo space................................(cu ft) 370
Electrical system...(volts) 6
    No. of batteries...1
    Type of ground...positive
Fuel octane rating..70
Capacities:
    Fuel..(gal) 49
    Cooling system..(qt) 16
    Crankcase...(qt) 5
    Transmission..(qt) 2½
    Rear axle...(qt) 2½

GENERAL DATA—Continued

Brakes:
    Manufacturer; Ford...........................Type; hydraulic
    Parking brake, type...........................transmission
Transmission:
    Forward speeds..4
    Gear ratio..........................High 1:1; Low 6.4:1

PERFORMANCE

Computed grade ability in lowest gear, loaded..................(percent) 32
Turning radius..(ft) 29
Fording depth...(in.) 25
Fuel consumption, loaded..(mpg) 9
Cruising range, loaded..(mi) 440
Allowable speed, governed...(mph) 45
Maximum recommended towed load:
    Off highway, gross...(lb) 3,000
    On highway, gross..(lb) 6,000

ENGINE

Manufacturer: Ford...Model G8T
Type....................L-head, 4-cycle; No. of cylinders (in line) 6
Displacement..(cu in.) 225
Bore...(in.) 3.3
Stroke...(in.) 4.4
Compression ratio..6.7:1
Governed speed...(rpm) 3,400
Brake horsepower (max w/std accessories)..............81 at (rpm) 3,300
Torque (max)...........................170 lb-ft at (rpm) 1,200

ADDITIONAL DATA

Rear axle, type.....................spiral-bevel, full-floating
Transmission, type..................selective sliding-gear

195

TRUCK, STAKE AND PLATFORM, 1½-TON, 4 x 2

(Ford, Models 2GT, 1942; 2GT, 6-cyl, 1942; 2GT, 1943)

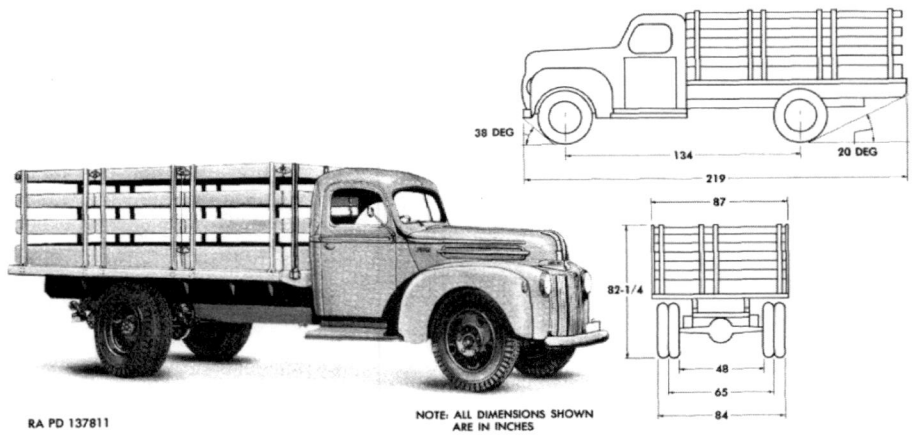

RA PD 137811

NOTE: ALL DIMENSIONS SHOWN
ARE IN INCHES

Technical Manuals: 9–806, 9–1806A, 9–1806B; Supply Catalog: SNL G–540.

Classification: Standard.

Purpose: To transport general cargo.

GENERAL DATA

Crew	2
Weight (lb): Net	4,680
Payload	off highway 3,000; on highway *7,820
Gross	off highway 7,680; on highway 12,500
Rear-axle gear ratio	6.67:1
Axle load (lb):	
Empty	front 2,010; rear 2,670
Loaded:	
Off highway	front 2,235; rear 5,445
On highway	front 2,590; rear 9,910
Tires:	
Ply 8	Size 7.50 x 20; Pressure (psi) 55
Tread, center-to-center, front	(in.) 56.66
Shipping dimensions, uncrated	(cu ft) 910; (sq ft) 133
Vehicle dimensions:	
Ground clearance	(in.) 9¼
Loading height, empty	(in.) 43⅝
Body inside dimensions (in.):	
Length	106
Width	82¹¹⁄₁₆
Height:	
Under bows	57
Side rack	42
Body cargo space	(cu ft) 284
Electrical system	(volts) 6
No. of batteries	1
Type of ground	positive
Fuel octane rating	72
Capacities:	
Fuel	(gal) 19
Cooling system	(qt) 17½
Crankcase, refill	(qt) 5
Transmission	(qt) 2½
Rear axle	(qt) 2½

GENERAL DATA—Continued

Brakes:	
Manufacturer; Ford	Type; hydraulic
Parking brake, type	transmission
Transmission:	
Forward speeds	4
Gear ratio	High 1:1; Low 6.4:1

PERFORMANCE

Computed grade ability in lowest gear, loaded	(percent) 38
Turning radius	(ft) 25
Fording depth	(in.) 25
Fuel consumption, loaded	(mpg) 9
Cruising range, loaded	(mi) 171
Allowable speed, governed	(mph) 45

ENGINE

Manufacturer: Ford	Model 2GT
Type	L-head, 4-cycle; No. of cylinders (in line) 6
Displacement	(cu in.) 226
Bore	(in.) 3.3
Stroke	(in.) 4.4
Compression ratio	6.7:1
Governed speed	(rpm) 3,400
Brake horsepower (max w/std accessories)	81 at (rpm) 3,300
Torque (max)	170 lb-ft at (rpm) 1,200

ADDITIONAL DATA

Rear axle, type	spiral-bevel, full-floating
Transmission, type	selective sliding-gear

*Truck must be equipped with helper springs for this payload.

196

TRUCK, STAKE AND PLATFORM, 1½-TON, 4 x 2

(Ford, Models 2G8T and 2GT86, 6-cyl, 1942)

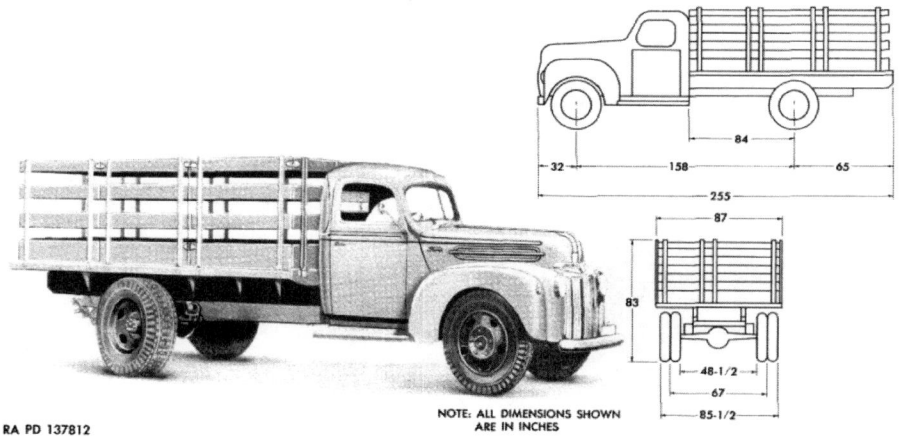

RA PD 137812

NOTE: ALL DIMENSIONS SHOWN
ARE IN INCHES

Technical Manuals: 9-806, 9-1806A, 9-1806B; Supply Catalog: SNL G-540.

Classification: Standard.

Purpose: To transport general cargo.

GENERAL DATA

Crew..2
Weight (lb)..Net 5,138
   Payload.........................off highway 3,140; on highway 7,362
   Gross.........................off highway 8,278; on highway 12,500
Rear axle-gear ratio...6.67:1
Axle load (lb):
   Empty:.................................front 2,338; rear 2,800
   Loaded:
      Off highway...........................front 2,448; rear 5,830
      On highway...........................front 2,600; rear 9,900
Tires:
   Ply 8.....................Size 7.50 x 20; Pressure (psi) 55
   Tread, center-to-center, front..........................(in.) 56²¹⁄₃₂
Shipping dimensions, uncrated...........(cu ft) 1,360; (sq ft) 155
Vehicle dimensions:
   Ground clearance............................(in.) 9¼
   Loading height, empty.......................(in.) 43⅜
   Pintle height, empty........................(in.) 25¾
   Body inside dimensions (in.):
      Length..142
      Width..82
      Height:
         Under bows...................................57
         Side rack....................................42
   Body cargo space.........................(cu ft) 385
Electrical system...........................(volts) 6
   No. of batteries..............................1
   Type of ground.........................positive
Fuel octane rating..72
Capacities:
   Fuel.......................................(gal) 49
   Cooling system............................(qt) 17½
   Crankcase, refill..........................(qt) 5
   Transmission...............................(qt) 2½
   Rear axle..................................(qt) 2½

GENERAL DATA—Continued

Brakes:
   Manufacturer: Ford.........................Type: hydraulic
   Parking brake, type.......................transmission
Transmission:
   Forward speeds...4
   Gear ratio........................High 1:1; Low 6.4:1

PERFORMANCE

Computed grade ability in lowest gear, loaded.............(percent) 38
Turning radius...(ft) 29½
Fording depth..(in.) 25
Fuel consumption, loaded.......................................(mpg) 9
Cruising range, loaded..(mi) 441
Allowable speed, governed.....................................(mph) 45
Maximum recommended towed load:
   Off highway, gross...(lb) 3,000
   On highway, gross..(lb) 6,000

ENGINE

Manufacturer: Ford..Model 2GT
Type....................L-head, 4-cycle; No. of cylinders (in line) 6
Displacement..(cu in.) 226
Bore..(in.) 3.3
Stroke..(in.) 4.4
Compression ratio..6.7:1
Governed speed..(rpm) 3,400
Brake horsepower (max w/std accessories).............81 at (rpm) 3,300
Torque (max)...........................170 lb-ft at (rpm) 1,200

ADDITIONAL DATA

Rear axle, type...........................spiral-bevel, full-floating
Transmission, type.......................selective sliding-gear

TRUCK, STAKE AND PLATFORM, 1½-TON, 4 x 2

(International Harvester, Model L–152)

NOTE: ALL DIMENSIONS SHOWN
ARE IN INCHES

RA PD 137803

Classification: Standard.

Purpose: To transport general cargo.

GENERAL DATA

Crew..2
Weight (lb): Net...5,505
   Payload.........................off highway 3,000; on highway 6,995
   Gross...........................off highway 8,505; on highway 12,500
Rear-axle gear ratio..6.166:1
Axle load (lb):
   Empty...front 2,830; rear 2,675
   Loaded:
      Off highway...............................front 3,010; rear 5,495
      On highway................................front 3,250; rear 9,250
Tires:
   Ply 8.........................Size 7.50 x 20; Pressure (psi) 60
   Tread, center-to-center, front......................(in.) 62¾₆
Shipping dimensions, uncrated...........(cu ft) 1,130; (sq ft) 150
Vehicle dimensions:
   Ground clearance....................................(in.) 10½
   Loading height, empty...............................(in.) 46⅝₆
   Body inside dimensions (in.):
      Length.......................140; Width 80; Height 42
      Cargo space.....................................(cu ft) 272
Electrical system......................................(volts) 6
   No. of batteries..1
   Type of ground.....................................positive
Fuel octane rating..72
Capacities:
   Fuel..(gal) 21
   Cooling system.....................................(qt) 17¾
   Crankcase refill.....................................(qt) 7
   Transmission......................................(qt) 2½
   Rear axle...(qt) 2¾
Brakes:
   Manufacturer; Bendix......................Type; hydraulic
   Parking brake, type..............................transmission
Transmission:
   Forward speeds..4
   Gear ratio............................High 1:1; Low 6.4:1

PERFORMANCE

Computed grade ability in lowest gear, loaded.............(percent) 33
Turning radius...(ft) 27
Fording depth...(in.) 24¼
Fuel consumption, loaded....................................(mpg) 6
Cruising range, loaded......................................(mi) 126
Allowable speed, governed...................................(mph) 57

ENGINE

Manufacturer: International Harvester...............Model SD–240
Type.................Valve-in-head, 4-cycle; No. of cylinders (in line) 6
Displacement...(cu. in.) 240.3
Bore..(in.) 3⅝₆
Stroke..(in.) 4⅛₆
Compression ratio...6.5:1
Governed speed...(rpm) 3,400
Brake horsepower (max w/std accessories)...........93 at (rpm) 3,400
Torque (max).........................186 lb-ft at (rpm) 1,100

ADDITIONAL DATA

Rear axle, type..................................hypoid, full-floating
Transmission, type....................................synchromesh

TRUCK, TRACTOR, 1½-TON, 4 x 2

(Ford, Models 2G8TA, 2GT, 1942; 2GT, 6-cyl, 1942; 2GT86, 6-cyl, 1942; 2G8T, 6-cyl, 1942; 2GT, 1943)

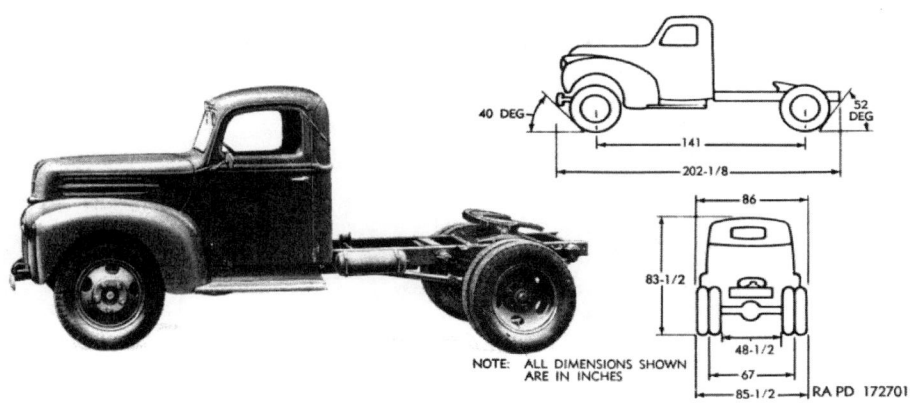

NOTE: ALL DIMENSIONS SHOWN ARE IN INCHES

RA PD 172701

Technical Manuals: 9-806, 9-1806A, 9-1806B, 9-1825B, 9-1827C, 9-1828A, 9-1829A; Supply Catalog: SNL G-540.

Classification: Standard.

Purpose: To tow semitrailers.

GENERAL DATA

Crew..2
Weight (lb):
  Net..5,800
  Payload.........................off highway 4,320; on highway 6,760
  Gross........................off highway 10,120; on highway 12,560
Rear-axle gear ratio...6.67:1
Axle load (lb):
  Empty.................................front 2,760; rear 3,040
  Loaded:
    Off highway..........................front 2,950; rear 7,170
    On highway..........................front 3,060; rear 9,500
Tires:
  Ply 8......................Size 7.50 x 20; Pressure (psi) 55
  Tread, center-to-center, front................................(in.) 65
Shipping dimensions, uncrated..............(cu ft) 840; (sq ft) 121
Vehicle dimensions:
  Ground clearance..(in.) 9¾
  Height to center of fifth wheel.........................(in.) 40
  Fifth-wheel center to center of rear axle....................(in.) 3
Electrical system...(volts) 6
  No. of batteries..1
  Type of ground...positive
Fuel octane rating...68
Capacities:
  Fuel...(gal) 19
  Cooling system...(qt) 16
  Crankcase...(qt) 5
  Transmission..(qt) 2½
  Rear axle...(qt) 2½
Brakes:
  Manufacturer...........Ford; Type: hydraulic w/vacuum booster
  Parking brake, type.................................transmission
Transmission:
  Forward speeds...4
  Gear ratio.........................High 1:1; Low 6.4:1

PERFORMANCE

Computed grade ability in lowest gear, loaded.............(percent) 24
Turning radius...(ft) 29
Fording depth..(in.) 25
Fuel consumption, loaded.....................................(mpg) 7
Cruising range, loaded......................................(mph) 130
Allowable speed, governed...................................(mph) 45
Maximum semitrailer, gross................................(lb) 12,000

ENGINE

Manufacturer: Ford...Model G8TA
Type..................4-cycle, L-head; No. of cylinders (in line) 6
Displacement...(cu in.) 225
Bore...(in.) 3¼
Stroke...(in.) 4¾
Compression ratio..6.7:1
Governed speed...(rpm) 3,400
Brake horsepower (max w/std accessories)............90 at (rpm) 3,400
Torque (max w/std accessories)............180 lb-ft at (rpm) 1,200

ADDITIONAL DATA

Equipped with controls for semitrailer electric brakes.
Rear axle, type...spiral-bevel, full-floating
Transmission, type....................................selective sliding gear

199

TRUCK, BOMB SERVICE, 1½-TON, 4 x 4, M6
(Chevrolet, Model NQ, G7128)

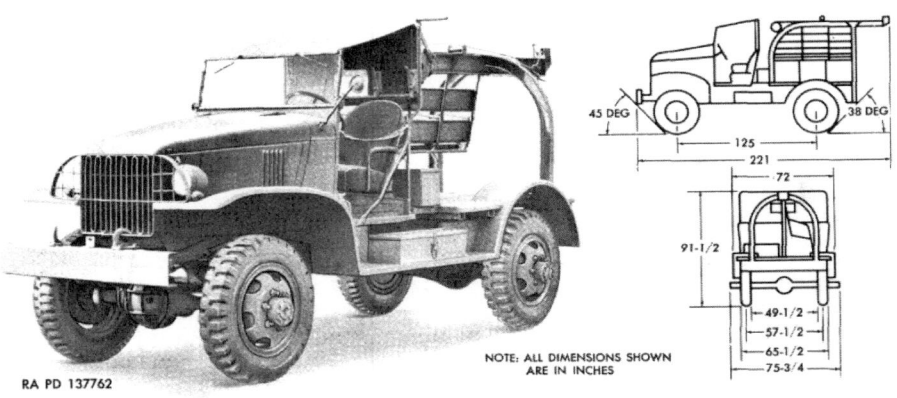

45 DEG   38 DEG

125
221

91-1/2

72

49-1/2
57-1/2
65-1/2
75-3/4

NOTE: ALL DIMENSIONS SHOWN
ARE IN INCHES

RA PD 137762

Technical Manuals: 9-765, 9-805, 9-1765A, 9-1765B, 9-1825A, 9-1827B; **Supply Catalog:** SNL G-85, Vol. 4.

Classification: Limited Standard.

Purpose: To tow bomb trailers and lift bombs on and off trailers.

GENERAL DATA

Crew	2; Passengers (including crew) 5
Weight (lb)	Net 6,325; Payload 2,000; Gross 8,325
Live-axle gear ratio	6.67:1
Axle load (lb):	
Empty	front 3,180; rear 3,145
Loaded	front 3,405; rear 4,920
Tires:	
Ply 8	Size 7.50 x 20; Pressure (psi) 55
Tread, center-to-center, front	(in.) 60½
Shipping dimensions, uncrated	(cu ft) 887; (sq ft) 116
Vehicle dimensions:	
Ground clearance	(in.) 9¾
Pintle height, loaded	(in.) 25½
Electrical system	(volts) 6
No. of batteries	1
Type of ground	negative
Fuel octane rating	70
Capacities:	
Fuel	(gal) 48
Cooling system	(qt) 17¼
Crankcase, refill	(qt) 5
Transfer	(qt) 2
Transmission	(qt) 2¾
Axles (each)	(qt) 7
Brakes:	
Manufacturer	Chevrolet; Type; hydrovac
Parking brake, type	transfer
Transmission:	
Forward speeds	4
Gear ratio	High 1:1; Low 7.06:1
Transfer:	
Speeds	2
Gear ratio	High 1:1; Low 1.941:1

PERFORMANCE

Computed grade ability in lowest gear, loaded	(percent) 65
Turning radius	(ft) 27½
Fording depth	(in.) 29
Fuel consumption, loaded:	
W/towed load	(mpg) 5
W/o towed load	(mpg) 9
Cruising range, loaded:	
W/towed load	(mi) 240
W/o towed load	(mi) 432
Allowable speed, governed	(mph) 50
Maximum recommended towed load, gross	(lb) 8,000

ENGINE

Manufacturer: Chevrolet	Model BV-1001 up
Type	Valve-in-head, 4-cycle; No. of cylinders (in line) 6
Displacement	(cu in.) 235.5
Bore	(in.) 3⁹⁄₁₆
Stroke	(in.) 3¹³⁄₁₆
Compression ratio	6.62:1
Governed speed (when governor is furnished)	(rpm) 3,100
Brake horsepower (max w/std accessories)	83 at (rpm) 3,100
Torque (max)	184 lb-ft at (rpm) 1,000

ADDITIONAL DATA

Hoist hand-operated. Capacity 1 ton.

Live axle, type	hypoid, full-floating
Transmission, type	selective sliding-gear

TRUCK, CARGO, 1½-TON, 4 x 4

(Chevrolet, Models YP, G4112, 1941; NJ, G7107, 1942)

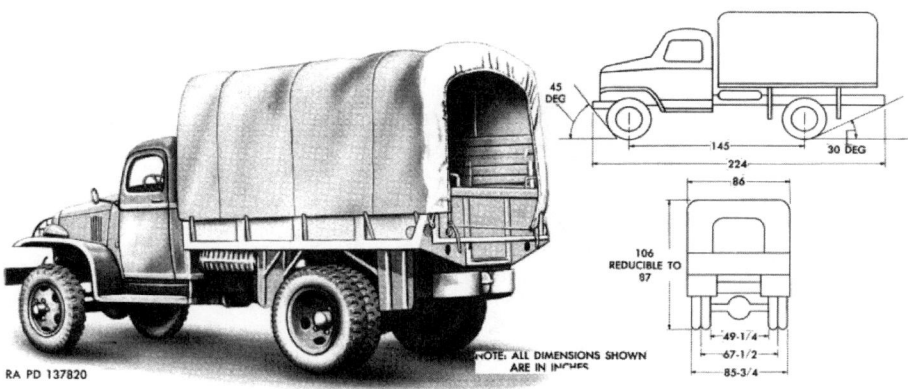

RA PD 137820

Technical Manuals: 9-805, 9-1765A, 9-1765B, 9-1825A, 9-1827B; Supply Catalog: SNL G-506.

Classification: Standard.

GENERAL DATA

Crew..2
Weight (lb) ....Net 7,545
  Payload:
    Off highway.....................3,350; Gross 10,895
    On highway......................5,400; Gross 12,945
Live-axle gear ratio....................................6.67:1
Axle load (lb):
  Empty...............................front 3,200; rear 4,345
  Loaded:
    Off highway....................front 3,610; rear 7,285
    On highway....................front 3,860; rear 9,085
Tires:
  Ply 8.............Size 7.50 x 20; Pressure (psi); front 55, rear 40
  Tread, center-to-center, front.......................(in.) 60½
Shipping dimensions, uncrated.................(cu ft) 970; (sq ft) 134
Vehicle dimensions:
  Ground clearance....................................(in.) 9¾
  Loading height, empty...............................(in.) 46
  Pintle height, loaded.................................(in.) 29
  Body inside dimensions (in.):
    Length...108
    Width..70
    Height:
      Under bows...............................59
      Side panel................................14
      Side rack.................................36½
  Body cargo space............................(cu ft) 258
Electrical system...................................(volts) 6
  No. of batteries....................................1
  Type of ground...............................negative
Fuel octane rating......................................70
Capacities:
  Fuel...(gal) 30
  Cooling system................................(qt) 17¾
  Crankcase, refill..................................(qt) 5
  Transmission......................................(qt) 2¾
  Transfer...(qt) 2
  Axles (each).......................................(qt) 7

Purpose: To transport general cargo and personnel.

GENERAL DATA—Continued

Brakes:
  Manufacturer..........................Chevrolet; Type; hydraulic
  Parking brake, type.................................transfer
Transmission:
  Forward speeds......................................4
  Gear ratio...............High 1:1; Low 7.06:1; on early YP 7.23:1
Transfer:
  Speeds..2
  Gear ratio...........................High 1:1; Low 1.94:1

PERFORMANCE

Computed grade ability in lowest gear, loaded..............(percent) 65
Turning radius...(ft) 31
Fording depth...(in.) 29
Fuel consumption, loaded:
  W/towed load...................................(mpg) 6½
  W/o towed load..................................(mpg) 9
Cruising range, loaded:
  W/towed load....................................(mi) 195
  W/o towed load..................................(mi) 270
Allowable speed.......................................(mph) 48
Maximum recommended towed load, gross...............(lb) 8,000

ENGINE

Manufacturer: Chevrolet.......................Model BV 1001 up
Type....................Valve-in-head, 4-cycle; No. of cylinders (in line) 6
Displacement.....................................(cu in.) 235.5
Bore..(in.) 3¾₆
Stroke...(in.) 3¹⁵⁄₁₆
Compression ratio...................................6.62:1
Governed speed..................................(rpm) 3,100
Brake horsepower (max w/std accessories)..........83 at (rpm) 3,100
Torque (max)...........................184 lb-ft at (rpm) 1,000

ADDITIONAL DATA

Live axle, type..........................hypoid, full-floating
Transmission, type........................selective sliding-gear

201

TRUCK, CARGO, 1½-TON, 4 x 4

(Chevrolet, Models YQ, G4112, 1941; ZQ, G4174, 1941; NP, G7127, 1942, LWB)

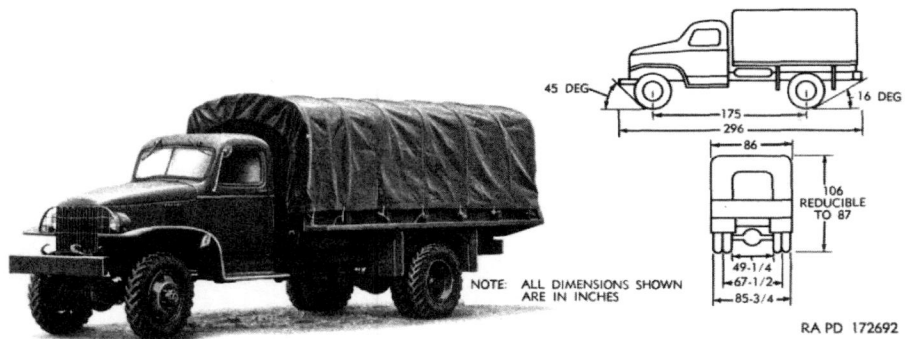

NOTE: ALL DIMENSIONS SHOWN ARE IN INCHES

RA PD 172692

Technical Manuals: 9-805, 9-1765A, 9-1765B, 9-1825A, 9-1827B; Supply Catalog: SNL G-506.

Classification: Limited Standard.

Purpose: To transport general cargo and personnel.

GENERAL DATA

Crew	2
Weight (lb)	Net 8,150
Payload:	
Off highway	3,350; Gross 11,500
On highway	4,800; Gross 12,950
Live-axle gear ratio	6.67:1
Axle load (lb):	
Empty	front 3,120; rear 5,030
Loaded:	
Off highway	front 3,415; rear 8,085
On highway	front 3,540; rear 9,410
Tires:	
Ply 8	Size 7.50 x 20; Pressure (psi) front 55; rear 45
Tread, center-to-center, front	(in.) 60½
Shipping dimensions, uncrated	(cu ft) 1,282; (sq ft) 177
Vehicle dimensions:	
Loading height, empty	(in.) 47
Ground clearance	(in.) 90⅞
Pintle height, loaded	(in.) 29
Body inside dimensions (in.):	
Length	180
Width	70
Height under bows	59
Body cargo space	(cu ft) 430
Electrical system	(volts) 6
No. of batteries	1
Type of ground	negative
Fuel octane rating	70
Capacities:	
Fuel	(gal) 30
Cooling system	(qt) 17¼
Crankcase, refill	(qt) 5
Transfer	(qt) 2
Transmission	(qt) 2¾
Axles (each)	(qt) 7
Brakes:	
Manufacturer: Chevrolet	Type: hydrovac
Parking brake, type	transfer on ZQ & NP; rear-wheel on YQ

GENERAL DATA—Continued

Transmission:	
Forward speeds	4
Gear ratio	High 1:1; Low 7.06:1; on early YQ 7.23:1
Transfer:	
Speeds	2
Gear ratio	High 1:1; Low 1.94:1

PERFORMANCE

Computed grade ability in lowest gear, loaded	(percent) 65
Turning radius	(ft) 36½
Fording depth	(in.) 29
Fuel consumption, loaded:	
W/towed load	(mpg) 6½
W/o towed load	(mpg) 9
Cruising range, loaded:	
W/towed load	(mi) 195
W/o towed load	(mi) 270
Allowable speed, governed	(mph) 48
Maximum recommended towed load, gross	(lb) 8,000

ENGINE

Manufacturer: Chevrolet	Model BV-1001 up
Type	Valve-in-head, 4-cycle; No. of cylinders (in line) 6
Displacement	(cu in.) 235.5
Bore	(in.) 3⅝
Stroke	(in.) 3¹⁵⁄₁₆
Compression ratio	6.62:1
Governed speed	(rpm) 3,100
Brake horsepower (max w/std accessories)	83 at (rpm) 3,100
Torque (max)	184 lb-ft at (rpm) 1,000

ADDITIONAL DATA

Live Axles, type	hypoid, full-floating
Transmission, type	selective sliding-gear

202

TRUCK, CARGO, 1½-TON, 4 x 4 W/WINCH

(Chevrolet, Models ZP, G4163, 1941; NM, G7117, (1942)

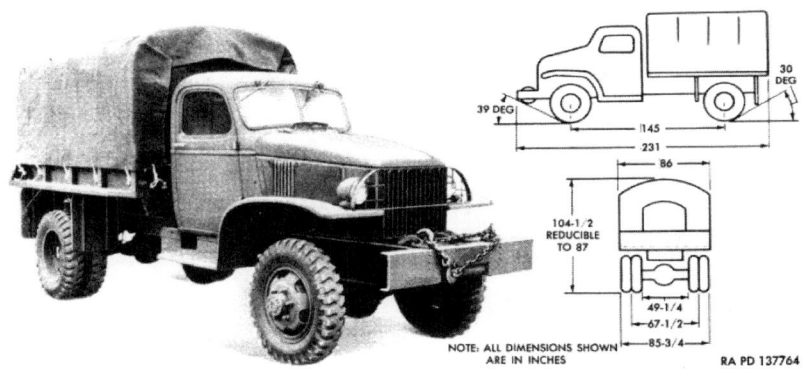

NOTE: ALL DIMENSIONS SHOWN ARE IN INCHES

RA PD 137764

Technical Manuals: 9-805; 9-1765A; 9-1765B; 9-1825A; 9-1827B; Supply Catalog: SNL G-506.

Classification: Standard.

Purpose: To transport general cargo and personnel.

GENERAL DATA

Crew..2
Weight (lb)..Net 8,215
  Payload:
    Off highway...................................3,350; Gross 11,565
    On highway....................................4,700; Gross 12,915
Live-axle gear ratio...6.67:1
Axle load (lb):
  Empty...front 3,825; rear 4,390
  Loaded:
    Off highway...................................front 4,235; rear 7,330
    On highway...................................front 4,395; rear 8,520
Tires:
  Ply 8..................Size 7.50 x 20; Pressure (psi) front 55; rear 40
  Tread, center-to-center, front...........................(in.) 60½
Shipping dimensions, uncrated..............(cu ft) 1,000; (sq ft) 138
Vehicle dimensions:
  Ground clearance.......................................(in.) 9⅞
  Loading height, empty.................................(in.) 47
  Pintle height, loaded..................................(in.) 29
  Body inside dimensions (in.):
    Length 108...Width 70
    Height........To roof bows 59; Side rack 36¼; Side panels 14
  Body cargo space..(cu ft) 258
Electrical system...(volts) 6
  No. of batteries..1
  Type of ground....................................negative
Fuel octane rating..70
Capacities:
  Fuel...(gal) 30
  Cooling system...(qt) 17¼
  Crankcase, refill......................................(qt) 5
  Transfer...(qt) 2
  Transmission w/power take-off...........................(qt) 5
  Axles (each)...(qt) 7
  Winch:
    Oil capacity.......................................(qt) 1¾
    Load capacity......................................(lb) 10,000

GENERAL DATA—Continued

Brakes:
  Manufacturer.....................Chevrolet; Type; hydrovac
  Parking brake, type....................................transfer
Transmission:
  Forward speeds...4
  Gear ratio..............................High 1:1; Low 7.06:1
Transfer:
  Speeds...2
  Gear ratio..............................High 1:1; Low 1.941:1

PERFORMANCE

Computed grade ability in lowest gear, loaded...............(percent) 65
Turning radius...(ft) 31
Fording depth..(in.) 29
Fuel consumption, loaded:
  W/towed load...(mpg) 6½
  W/o towed load...(mpg) 9
Cruising range, loaded:
  W/towed load...(mi) 195
  W/o towed load...(mi) 270
Allowable speed, governed..................................(mph) 48
Maximum recommended towed load, gross......................(lb) 8,000

ENGINE

Manufacturer: Chevrolet.........................Model BV-1001 up
Type...............Valve-in-head, 4-cycle; No. of cylinders (in line) 6
Displacement...(cu in.) 235.5
Bore...(in.) 3⅝
Stroke...(in.) 3¹⁵⁄₁₆
Compression ratio..6.62:1
Governed speed...(rpm) 3,100
Brake horsepower (max w/std accessories).............83 at (rpm) 3,100
Torque (max)...............................184 lb-ft at (rpm) 1,000

ADDITIONAL DATA

Live Axles, type...............................hypoid, full-floating
Transmission, type............................selective sliding-gear

203

TRUCK, CHASSIS, 1½-TON, 4 x 4

(Chevrolet, Models NJ, G7107, 1942; NE, G7103, 1942–43)

NOTE: ALL DIMENSIONS SHOWN
ARE IN INCHES

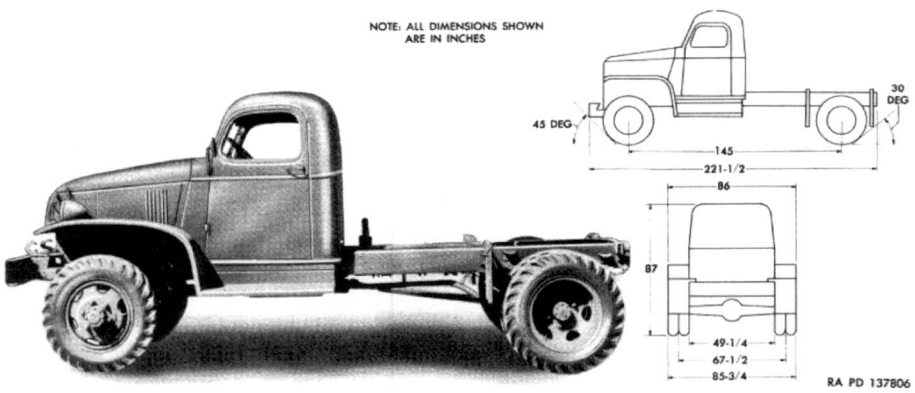

RA PD 137806

Technical Manuals: 9-805, 9-1765A, 9-1765B, 9-1825A, 9-1827B; Supply Catalog: SNL G-506.

Classification: Nonclassified.

Purpose: For use as component of cargo or special-equipment truck.

GENERAL DATA

Crew...2
Weight (lb)........................Net 5,935; Maximum gross 11,500
Live-axle gear ratio..6.67:1
Axle load (lb)................................front 3,265; rear 2,670
Tires:
  Ply 8.............Size 7.50 x 20; Pressure (psi) front 55; rear 40
  Tread, center-to-center, front..........................(in.) 60½
Shipping dimensions, uncrated................(cu ft) 960; (sq ft) 132
Vehicle dimensions:
  Ground clearance......................................(in.) 9¾
  Pintle height, empty..................................(in.) 30½
Electrical system....................................(volts) 6
  No. of batteries..1
  Type of ground....................................negative
Fuel octane rating....................................70
Capacities:
  Fuel.......................................(gal) 30
  Cooling system.............................(qt) 17¾
  Crankcase, refill..........................(qt) 5
  Transmission...............................(qt) 2¾
  Transfer...................................(qt) 2
  Axles (each)...............................(qt) 7
Brakes:
  Manufacturer; Chevrolet....................Type; hydraulic
  Parking brake, type................................transfer
Transmission:
  Forward speeds...................................4
  Gear ratio...................High 1:1; Low 7.06:1
Transfer:
  Speeds..2
  Gear ratio..................High 1:1; Low 1.94:1

PERFORMANCE

Computed grade ability in lowest gear, loaded..............(percent) 65
Turning radius....................................(ft) 31
Fording depth.....................................(in.) 29
Fuel consumption, loaded:
  W/towed load...................................(mpg) 6½
  W/o towed load.................................(mpg) 9
Cruising range, loaded:
  w/towed load...................................(mi) 195
  W/o towed load.................................(mi) 270
Allowable speed, governed.........................(mph) 48
Maximum recommended towed load, gross.............(lb) 8,000

ENGINE

Manufacturer: Chevrolet...........................Model BV 1001 up
Type....................Valve-in-head, 4-cycle; No. of cylinders (in line) 6
Displacement......................................(cu in.) 235.5
Bore..(in.) 3⁹⁄₁₆
Stroke..(in.) 3¹⁵⁄₁₆
Compression ratio.................................6.62:1
Governed speed....................................(rpm) 3,100
Brake horsepower (max w/std accessories).....83 at (rpm) 3,100
Torque (max)...................184 lb.ft at (rpm) 1,000

ADDITIONAL DATA

Live axles, type.............................hypoid, full-floating
Transmission, type...........................selective sliding-gear

TRUCK, DUMP, 1½-TON, 4 x 4

(Chevrolet, Models YP, G4112, 1941; ZP, G4152, 1941; NH, G7106, 1942)

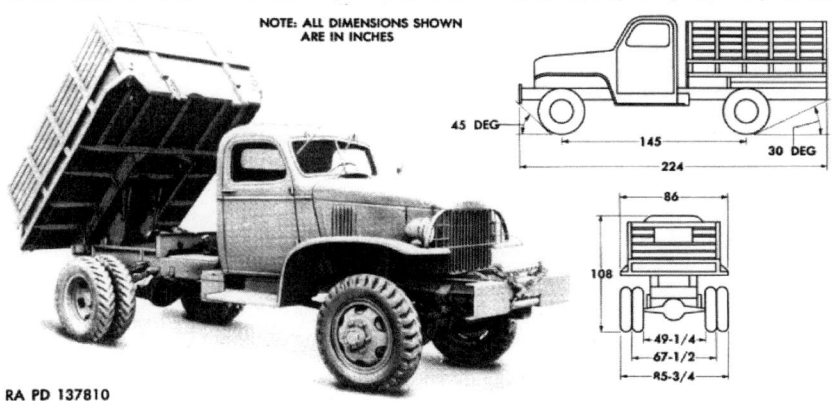

NOTE: ALL DIMENSIONS SHOWN
ARE IN INCHES

RA PD 137810

Classification: Substitute Standard.

Purpose: To haul and dump earth, sand, gravel, coal, etc, and transport general cargo.

GENERAL DATA

Crew..2
Weight (lb)..Net 8,365
Payload:
  Off highway..............................3,350; gross 11,715
  On highway..............................4,600; gross 12,965
Axle load (lb):
  Empty..........................front 3,425; rear 4,940
  Loaded:
    Off highway.......................front 3,835; rear 7,880
    On highway........................front 3,985; rear 8,980
Live-axle gear ratio...6.67:1
Tires:
  Ply 8....................Size 7.50 x 20; Pressure (psi) front 55; rear 40
  Tread, center-to-center, front..........................(in.) 60½
Shipping dimensions, uncrated................(cu ft) 970; (sq ft) 134
Vehicle dimensions:
  Ground clearance..................................(in.) 9¾
  Loading height, empty.............................(in.) 48
  Pintle height, loaded.............................(in.) 29
  Body inside dimensions (in.):
    Length..108
    Width..70
    Height:
      Under bows...............................59
      Side panel...............................14
      Side rack................................36½
  Body cargo space..............................(cu ft) 258
Electrical system.....................................(volts) 6
  No. of batteries...................................1
  Type of ground..............................negative
Fuel octane rating...70
Capacities:
  Fuel...(gal) 30
  Cooling system..................................(qt) 17¾
  Crankcase, refill..................................(qt) 5
  Transmission w/power take-off....................(qt) 3¾
  Transfer..(qt) 2
  Axles, each......................................(qt) 7

GENERAL DATA—Continued

Brakes:
  Manufacturer........................Chevrolet; Type; hydraulic
  Parking brake........type; transfer on ZP and NH; rear-wheel on YP
Transmission:
  Forward speeds......................................4
  Gear ratio....................High 1:1; Low 7.06:1; on early YP 7.23:1
Transfer:
  Speeds..2
  Gear ratio............................High 1:1; Low 1.94:1

PERFORMANCE

Computed grade ability in lowest gear, loaded.................(percent) 65
Turning radius..(ft) 31
Fording depth...(in.)29
Fuel consumption, loaded:
  W/towed load....................................(mpg) 6½
  W/o towed load....................................(mpg) 9
Cruising range, loaded:
  W/towed load.....................................(mi) 195
  W/o towed load...................................(mi) 270
Allowable speed, governed...............................(mph) 48
Maximum recommended towed load, gross................(lb) 8,000

ENGINE

Manufacturer: Chevrolet........................Model BV 1001 up
Type....................Valve-in-head, 4-cycle; No. of cylinders (in line) 6
Displacement..(cu. in.) 235.5
Bore...(in.) 3⁹⁄₁₆
Stroke...(in.) 3¹³⁄₁₆
Compression ratio...6.62:1
Governed speed..(rpm) 3,100
Brake horsepower (max w/std accessories).............83 at (rpm) 3,100
Torque (max)......................184 lb-ft at (rpm) 1,000

ADDITIONAL DATA

Live axles, type.............................hypoid, full-floating
Transmission, type.........................selective sliding gear

TRUCK, DUMP, 1½-TON, 4 x 4, W/WINCH
(Chevrolet, Models ZP, G4162, 1941; NL, G7116, 1942)

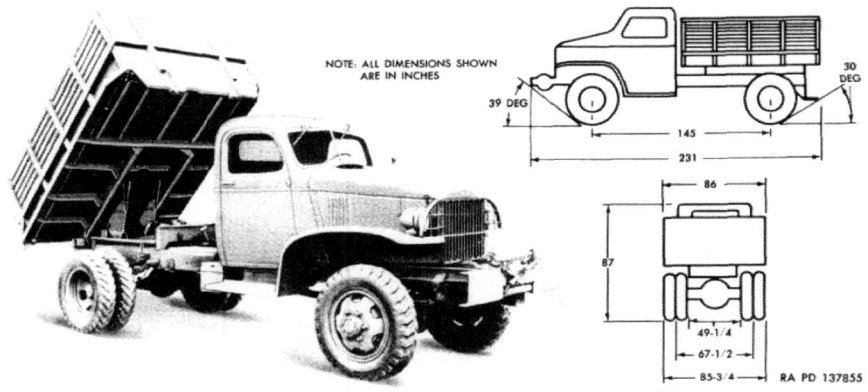

NOTE: ALL DIMENSIONS SHOWN ARE IN INCHES

RA PD 137855

Technical Manuals: 9-805, 9-1765A, 9-1765B, 9-1825A; 9-1827B, 9-1829A; **Supply Catalog:** SNL G-506.

Classification: Substitute Standard.

Purpose: To transport and dump earth, sand, gravel, coal, etc., and to carry general cargo.

GENERAL DATA

Crew	2
Weight (lb)	Net 9,010
Payload:	
Off highway	3,350; gross 12,360
On highway	3,900; gross 12,910
Live-axle gear ratio	6.67:1
Axle load (lb):	
Empty	front 4,040; rear 4,970
Loaded:	
Off highway	front 4,450; rear 7,910
On highway	front 4,520; rear 8,390
Tires:	
Ply 8	Size 7.50 x 20; Pressure (psi) front 55; rear 40
Tread, center-to-center, front	(in.) 60½
Shipping dimensions, uncrated	(cu ft) 1,000; (sq ft) 138
Vehicle dimensions:	
Ground clearance	(in.) 9⅞
Loading height, empty	(in.) 48
Pintle height, loaded	(in.) 29
Body inside dimensions (in.):	
Length	108
Width	70
Height:	
To roof bows	59
Side panels	14
Side rack	36½
Body cargo space	(cu ft) 258
Electrical system	(volts) 6
No. of batteries	1
Type of ground	negative
Fuel octane rating	70
Capacities:	
Fuel	(gal) 30
Cooling system	(qt) 17¼
Crankcase, refill	(qt) 5
Transmission w/power take-off	(qt) 5¼
Axles (each)	(qt) 7
Winch:	
Oil capacity	(qt) 1¾
Load capacity	(lb) 10,000

GENERAL DATA—Continued

Brakes:	
Manufacturer	Chevrolet; Type; hydrovac
Parking brake, type	transfer
Transmission:	
Forward speeds	4
Gear ratio	High 1:1; Low 7.06:1
Transfer:	
Speeds	2
Gear ratio	High 1:1; Low 1.941:1

PERFORMANCE

Computed grade ability in lowest gear, loaded	(percent) 65
Turning radius	(ft) 31
Fording depth	(in.) 29
Fuel consumption, loaded:	
W/towed load	(mpg) 6½
W/o towed load	(mpg) 9
Cruising range, loaded:	
W/towed load	(mi) 195
W/o towed load	(mi) 270
Allowable speed, governed	(mph) 48
Maximum recommended towed load, gross	(lb) 8,000

ENGINE

Manufacturer: Chevrolet	Model BV-1001 up
Type	Valve-in-head, 4-cycle; No. of cylinders (in line) 6
Displacement	(cu in.) 235.5
Bore	(in.) 3⁹⁄₁₆
Stroke	(in.) 3¹⁵⁄₁₆
Compression ratio	6.62:1
Governed speed	(rpm) 3,100
Brake horsepower (max w/std accessories)	83 at (rpm) 3,100
Torque (max)	184 lb-ft at (rpm) 1,000

ADDITIONAL DATA

Live axles, type	hypoid, full-floating
Transmission, type	selective sliding-gear

TRUCK, STAKE AND PLATFORM, 1½-TON, 4 x 4

(Chevrolet, Models YX, G4103, 1941; NN, G-7123, 1942-43, COE)

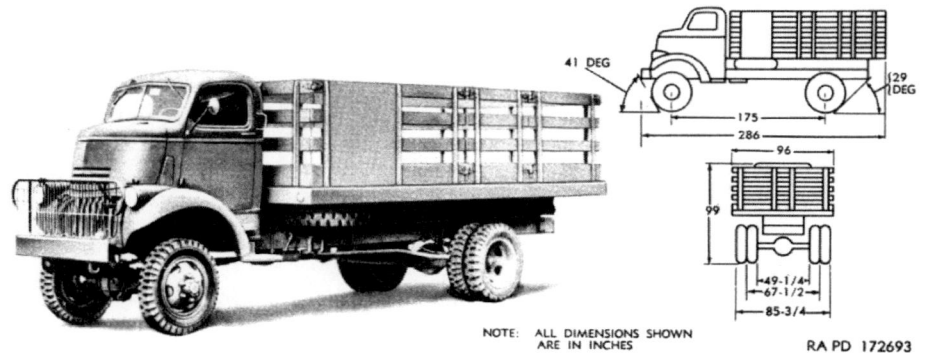

NOTE: ALL DIMENSIONS SHOWN ARE IN INCHES

RA PD 172693

Technical Manuals: 9-805, 9-1765A, 9-1765B, 9-1825A, 9-1827B; Supply Catalog: SNL G-506.

Classification: Limited Standard.

Purpose: To transport general cargo.

GENERAL DATA

Crew..2
Weight (lb)...Net 8,570
Payload:
    Off highway.........................3,350; gross 11,920
    On highway..........................4,400; gross 12,970
Live-axle gear ratio....................................6.67:1
Axle load (lb):
    Empty.........................front 4,070; rear 4,500
    Loaded:
        Off highway..................front 4,775; rear 7,145
        On highway...................front 4,995; rear 7,975
Tires:
    Ply 8................Size 7.50 x 20; Pressure (psi) front 55; rear 40
    Tread, center-to-center, front....................(in.) 60½
Shipping dimensions, uncrated.............(cu ft) 1,631; (sq ft) 198
Vehicle dimensions:
    Ground clearance.................................(in.) 9¾
    Pintle height, loaded.............................(in.) 28½
    Loading height...................................(in.) 52
    Body inside dimensions (in.):
        Length...................193; Width 89½; Height 42
    Body cargo space..............................(cu ft) 416
Electrical system...................................(volts) 6
    No. of batteries....................................1
    Type of ground................................negative
Fuel octane rating......................................70
Capacities:
    Fuel...(gal) 30
    Cooling system...................................(qt) 16
    Crankcase, refill..................................(qt) 5
    Transfer...(qt) 2
    Transmission....................................(qt) 2¾
    Axles (each)......................................(qt) 7
Brakes:
    Manufacturer: Chevrolet.................Type; hydrovac
    Parking brake, type: transfer on NN......rear-wheel on YX

GENERAL DATA—Continued

Transmission:
    Forward speeds....................................4
    Gear ratio.............................High 1:1; Low 7.06:1
Transfer:
    Speeds...2
    Gear ratio.............................High 1:1; Low 1.94:1

PERFORMANCE

Computed grade ability in lowest gear, loaded...............(percent) 65
Turning radius.......................................(ft) 36½
Fuel consumption, loaded:
    W/towed load...................................(mpg) 5½
    W/o towed load...................................(mpg) 8
Cruising range, loaded:
    W/towed load....................................(mi) 165
    W/o towed load..................................(mi) 240
Fording depth.......................................(in.) 29
Allowable speed, governed..........................(mph) 43
Maximum recommended towed load, gross.............(lb) 8,000

ENGINE

Manufacturer: Chevrolet...........................Model BVA-1001 up
Type...............Valve-in-head, 4-cycle; No. of cylinders (in line) 6
Displacement.....................................(cu in.) 235.5
Bore..(in.) 3⁹⁄₁₆
Stroke..(in.) 3¹⁵⁄₁₆
Compression ratio....................................6.62:1
Governed speed...................................(rpm) 2,850
Brake horsepower (max w/std accessories).........82 at (rpm) 3,000
Torque (max).........................183 lb-ft at (rpm) 1,000

ADDITIONAL DATA

Gas-tank filler neck extends 3½ in. beyond over-all width.
Live axles, type..........................hypoid, full-floating
Transmission, type.......................selective sliding-gear

TRUCK, TRACTOR, 1½-TON, 4 x 4
(Chevrolet, Model NK, G7113, 1942)

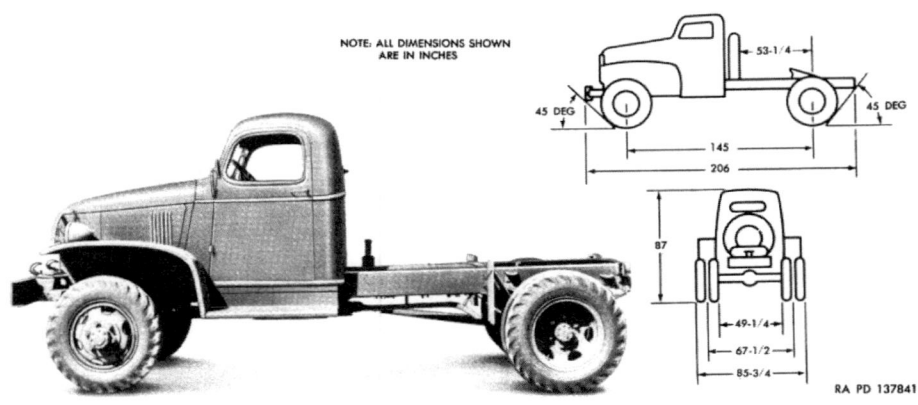

NOTE: ALL DIMENSIONS SHOWN
ARE IN INCHES

RA PD 137841

Technical Manuals: 9-805, 9-1765A, 9-1765B, 9-1825A, 9-1827B; **Supply Catalog:** SNL G-506.

Classification: Standard.

Purpose: To tow semitrailers.

GENERAL DATA

Crew...2
Weight (lb)...Net 6,140
  Payload........................off highway 4,830; on highway 6,845
  Gross.....................off highway 10,970; on highway 12,985
Live-axle gear ratio......................................6.67:1
Axle load (lb):
  Empty..front 3,255; rear 2,905
  Loaded:
    Off highway.............................front 3,510; rear 7,480
    On highway.............................front 3,605; rear 9,400
Tires:
  Ply 8................Size 7.50 x 20; Pressure (psi) front 55; rear 40
  Tread, center-to-center, front.......................(in.) 60½
Shipping dimensions, uncrated.................(cu ft) 890; (sq ft) 123
Vehicle dimensions:
  Ground clearance...................................(in.) 9⅝
  Pintle height, empty...............................(in.) 30
  Center of fifth wheel to center of rear axle............(in.) 3⅞
  Height to center of fifth wheel.....................(in.) 42
  Height to rear of fifth wheel........................(in.) 35
Electrical system....................................(volts) 6
  No. of batteries.......................................1
  Type of ground...................................negative
Fuel octane rating..70
Capacities:
  Fuel..(gal) 30
  Cooling system.....................................(qt) 17¾
  Crankcase, refill....................................(qt) 5
  Transfer...(qt) 2
  Transmission......................................(qt) 2¾
  Axles (each)..(qt) 7
Brakes:
  Manufacturer...................Chevrolet; Type; hydrovac
  Parking brake, type...............................transfer

GENERAL DATA—Continued

Transmission:
  Forward speeds...4
  Gear ratio.............................High 1:1; Low 7.06:1
Transfer:
  Speeds..2
  Gear ratio...........................High 1:1; Low 1.941:1

PERFORMANCE

Computed grade ability in lowest gear, loaded.............(percent) 65
Turning radius..(ft) 31
Fuel consumption:
  W/towed load...(mpg) 6
  W/o towed load......................................(mpg) 9
Cruising range:
  W/towed load...(mi) 180
  W/o towed load......................................(mi) 270
Fording depth..(in.) 29
Allowable speed, governed.............................(mph) 48
Maximum semitrailer, gross..........................(lb) 12,000

ENGINE

Manufacturer.........................Chevrolet; Model BV-1001 up
Type.................Valve-in-head, 4-cycle; No. of cylinders (in line) 6
Displacement..(cu in.) 235.5
Bore..(in.) 3⁹⁄₁₆
Stroke..(in.) 3¹³⁄₁₆
Compression ratio...6.62:1
Governed speed.......................................(rpm) 3,100
Brake horsepower (max w/std accessories).........83 at (rpm) 3,100
Torque (max)............................184 lb-ft at (rpm) 1,000

ADDITIONAL DATA

Live Axles, type..............................hypoid, full-floating
Transmission, type..........................selective sliding-gear

208

TRUCK, PERSONNEL AND CARGO, 1½-TON, 6 x 6
(Dodge, Models WC62 and WC63, T223, 1943)

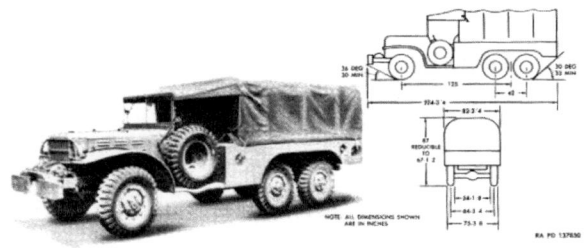

Technical Manuals: 9-810, 9-1808A, 9-1808B, 9-1825A, 9-1826A, 9-1826C; **Supply Catalog:** SNL G-507.

Vehicle illustrated: Model WC63, T223, 1943.
Classification: Standard.

Purpose: To transport personnel and general cargo.

GENERAL DATA

Crew..2; Passengers (including crew) 17
Weight (lb) ....Net 7,550
Payload:
  Off highway...............................gross 10,850
  On highway................................gross 12,450
Live-axle gear ratio.......................................5.83:1
Axle load (lb):
  Empty....................................front 3,314; rear (each) 2,118
  Loaded:
    Off highway......................front 3,414; rear (each) 3,718
    On highway.......................front 3,460; rear (each) 4,495
Tires:
  Ply 8.............................Size 9.00 x 16; Pressure (psi) 40
  Tread, center-to-center, front...................(in.) 64¾
Shipping dimensions, uncrated:
  W/winch..........................(cu ft) 937; (sq ft) 130
  W/o winch........................(cu ft) 895; (sq ft) 124
Vehicle dimensions:
  Ground clearance........................(in.) 10½
  Loading height, empty...................(in.) 31
  Pintle height:
    Loaded.............................(in.) 27
    Empty..............................(in.) 28
  Body inside dimensions (in.):
    Length.............................120
    Width..............................48½
    Height, under bows.................54
  Body cargo space.......................(cu ft) 181
Electrical system..........................(volts) 6
  No. of batteries..........................1
  Type of ground.......................negative
Fuel octane rating...70
Capacities:
  Fuel....................................(gal) 30
  Cooling system..........................(qt) 17
  Crankcase, refill.......................(qt) 5
  Transfer................................(qt) 2½
  Transmission (qt):
    W/power take-off...................3½
    W/o power take-off.................2¾
  Axles (each)............................(qt) 2½
  Winch:
    Oil capacity.......................(qt) 1
    Load capacity......................(lb) 7,500
Brakes:
  Manufacturer: Dodge....................Type: hydraulic
  Parking brake, type....................transfer

GENERAL DATA—Continued

Transmission:
  Forward speeds...4
  Gear ratio...........................High 1:1; Low 6.40:1
Transfer:
  Speeds...2
  Gear ratio.......................High 1:1; [a] Low 1.50:1

PERFORMANCE

Computed grade ability in lowest gear, loaded.............(percent) [b] 55
Turning radius.......................................(ft) 27
Fording depth.......................................(in.) 24
Fuel consumption, loaded............................(mpg) 8
Cruising range, loaded..............................(mi) 240
Allowable speed, governed...........................(mph) 50
Maximum recommended towed load, gross...............(lb) 8,000

ENGINE

Manufacturer: Dodge..............................Model T-223
Type....................L-head, 4-cycle; No. of cylinders (in line) 6
Displacement.....................................(cu in.) 230.2
Bore...(in.) 3¼
Stroke...(in.) 4¾
Compression ratio.................................6.7:1
Governed speed....................................(rpm) 3,200
Brake horsepower (max w/std accessories)........76 at (rpm) 3,200
Torque (max w/std accessories).........180 lb-ft at (rpm) 1,200

ADDITIONAL DATA

Data given for Model WC63 w/winch; for Model WC62 w/o winch changes in data are as follows:
Over-all length......................................(in.) 215
Weight (lb):
  Net..7,250
  Gross:
    Off highway.................................10,550
    On highway..................................12,450
Axle load (lb):
  Empty.............................front 2,970; rear (each) 2,140
  Loaded:
    Off highway...................front 3,070; rear (each) 3,740
    On highway....................front 3,130; rear (each) 4,660
Live Axles, type......................hypoid, full-floating
Transmission, type....................selective sliding-gear

[a] 1.96:1 on last production.
[b] 57 percent w/1.96:1 ratio in transfer.

209

TRUCK, CHASSIS, 2½-TON, 4 x 2
(International Harvester, Model L–171)

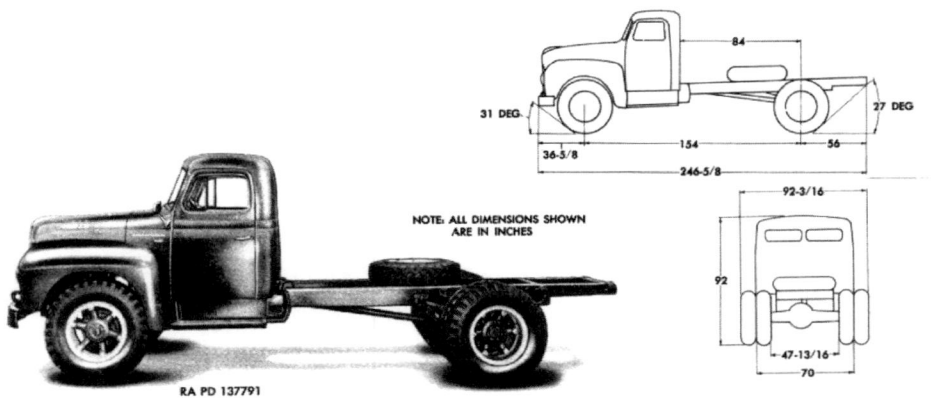

NOTE: ALL DIMENSIONS SHOWN
ARE IN INCHES

RA PD 137791

Classification: Standard.

Purpose: To be used as component of general-purpose or special-equipment truck.

GENERAL DATA

Crew..1
Weight (lb)....................................Net 6,080; Maximum gross 17,500
Rear-axle gear ratio (two-speed)....................High 6.33:1; Low 8.81:1
Axle load (lb)..................................Front 3,445; Rear 2,635
Tires:
  Ply 10........................Size 9.00 x 20; Pressure (psi) 65
  Tread, center-to-center, front..........................(in.) 64¹⁵⁄₁₆
Shipping dimensions uncrated......................(cu ft) 1,210; (sq ft) 157
Ground clearance...(in.) 10¾
Electrical system..(volts) 6
  No. of batteries...1
  Type of ground..negative
Fuel octane rating...72
Capacities:
  Fuel..(gal) 20
  Cooling system...(qt) 21
  Crankcase, refill...(qt) 7
  Transmission..(qt) 5¾
  Rear axle..(qt) 5½
Brakes:
  Manufacturer......................Wagner; Type; hydraulic
  Parking brake, type...............................transmission
Transmission:
  Forward speeds...5
  Gear ratio..................High 1:1; Fourth 1.42:1; Low 7.35:1

PERFORMANCE

Computed grade ability in lowest gear, loaded....................(percent) 42
Turning radius..(ft) 27½
Fording depth...(in.) 25
Fuel consumption, loaded.....................................(mpg) 5½
Cruising range, loaded......................................(mi) 110
Allowable speed, governed...................................(mph) 55

ENGINE

Manufacturer: International Harvester.......................Model BD–269
Type....................Valve-in-head, 4-cycle; No. of cylinders (in line) 6
Displacement..(cu in.) 269.1
Bore...(in.) 3⅞
Stroke...(in.) 4½
Compression ratio...6.3:1
Governed speed..(rpm) 3,000
Brake horsepower (max w/std accessories)............88 at (rpm) 2,800
Torque (max).............................216 lb-ft at (rpm) 1,000

ADDITIONAL DATA

Rear Axle, type.........................two-speed spiral-bevel, full-floating
Transmission, type...synchromesh

TRUCK, CHASSIS, 2½-TON, 4 x 2 AND
TRUCK, TRACTOR, 2½-TON, 4 x 2
(Federal, Model 25M2)

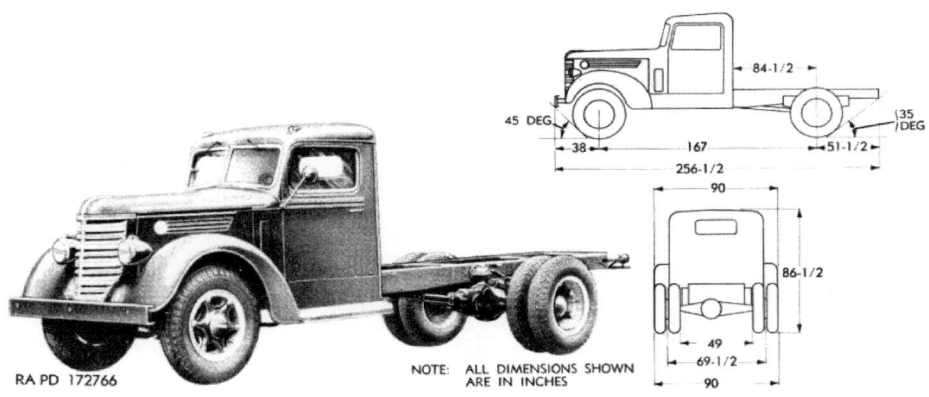

RA PD 172766

NOTE: ALL DIMENSIONS SHOWN ARE IN INCHES

Vehicle illustrated: Chassis.
Classification: Standard.

Purpose: Chassis; to be used as component of general-purpose or special equipment-vehicle. Tractor; to tow semitrailers.

GENERAL DATA

Crew..2
Weight (lb)..Net 5,745
Maximum gross..(lb) 16,500
Rear-axle gear ratio..8.15:1
Axle load (lb):
    Empty..front 3,050; rear 2,695
    Loaded.......................................front 4,000; rear 12,500
Tires:
    Ply 12.......................Size 9.00 x 20; Pressure (psi) 65
    Tread, center-to-center, front....................(in.) 63¹³⁄₁₆
Shipping dimensions, uncrated.............(cu ft) 1,150; (sq ft) 159
Vehicle dimensions:
    Ground clearance...(in.) 10½
    Frame height..(in.) 32
Electrical system...(volts) 6
    No. of batteries...1
    Type of ground..positive
Fuel octane rating...72
Capacities:
    Fuel...(gal) 26
    Cooling system..(qt) 23
    Crankcase, refill...(qt) 9
    Transmission..(qt) 6½
    Rear axle...(qt) 10
Brakes:
    Manufacturer:
        Front...............................Lockheed; Type; hydrovac
        Rear...Timken
    Parking brake, type..................................transmission
Transmission:
    Forward speeds..5
    Gear ratio...............High 1:1; Fourth 1.48:1; Low 7.58:1

PERFORMANCE

Computed grade ability in lowest gear w/maximum load........(percent) 34
Turning radius..(ft) 31
Fuel consumption, loaded...................................(mpg) 6
Cruising range, loaded.....................................(mi) 156
Allowable speed, governed................................(mph) 50

ENGINE

Manufacturer: Hercules..Model 5XCF
Type....................4-cycle, L-head; No. of cylinders (in line) 6
Displacement..(cu in.) 282
Bore..(in.) 3¾
Stroke..(in.) 4¼
Compression ratio..6.5:1
Governed speed..(rpm) 3,000
Brake horsepower (max w/std accessories)...............102 at (rpm) 3,000
Torque (max w/std accessories)................212 lb-ft at (rpm) 1,400

ADDITIONAL DATA

Rear axle, type..hypoid, full-floating
Transmission, type..constant-mesh
    Data given for chassis; changes in data for tractor truck are as follows:
Over-all length...(in.) 200
Shipping dimensions, uncrated...............(cu ft) 900; (sq ft) 125
Brakes:
    Service: Manufacturer; Bendix-Westinghouse.............Type; air
Maximum semitrailer, gross.............................(lb) 25,000
Maximum computed grade ability in lowest gear w/loaded semitrailer
                                         (percent) 14
Wheel base...(in.) 139
Chassis overhang, rear.....................................(in.) 23
Distance from rear of cab to center of rear axle...............(in.) 60½
Height to center of fifth wheel, empty.......................(in.) 39
Height to rear of fifth wheel, empty..........................(in.) 33
Fifth wheel mounted forward of rear axle......................(in.) 3

TRUCK, DUMP, 2½-TON, 4 x 2

(Federal, Model 2G)

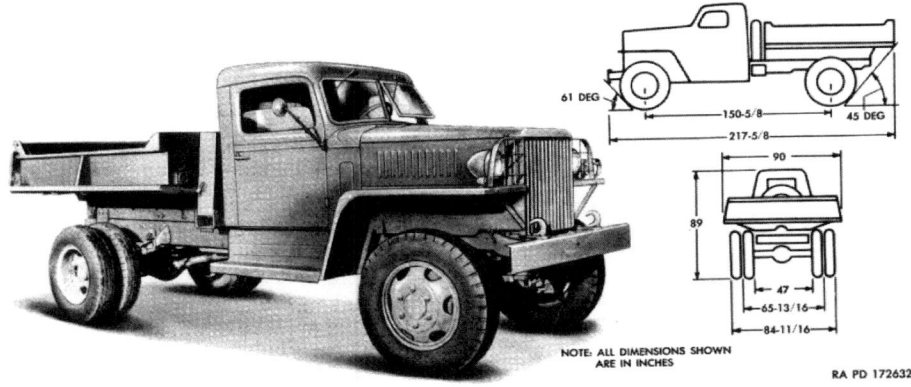

NOTE: ALL DIMENSIONS SHOWN
ARE IN INCHES

RA PD 172632

Technical Manuals: 9-821, 9-1821, 9-1825B, 9-1826A, 9-1827B, 9-1827C, 9-1828A, 9-1829A, 9-1832A; Supply Catalog: SNL G-539

Classification: Standard.

Purpose: To transport and dump earth, sand, gravel, etc, and to transport general cargo.

GENERAL DATA

Crew...2
Weight (lb):
  Net...7,975
  Payload.................Off highway 5,000; on highway 7,525
  Gross................Off highway 12,975; on highway 15,500
Rear-axle gear ratio...7.4:1
Axle load (lb):
  Empty.................................front 3,425; rear 4,550
  Loaded:
    Off highway.........................front 3,830; rear 9,145
    On highway.........................front 4,130; rear 11,370
Tires:
  Ply 10...................Size 8.25 x 20; Pressure (psi) 60
  Tread, center-to-center, front....................(in.) 63⅝₆
Shipping dimensions, uncrated.........(cu ft) 1,010; (sq ft) 137
Vehicle dimensions:
  Ground clearance....................................(in.) 9¾
  Pintle height, loaded...............................(in.) 31
  Body inside dimensions (in.):
    Length...96
  Struck capacity.................................(cu yd) 2
Electrical system................................(volts) 6
  No. of batteries.................................1
Fuel octane rating.................................72
Capacities:
  Fuel..(gal) 40
  Cooling system.................................(qt) 22
  Crankcase, refill..............................(qt) 6
  Transmission...................................(qt) 7
  Rear axle......................................(qt) 7½
Brakes:
  Manufacturer.............Timken-Bendix; Type; hydraulic
  Parking brake, type........................transmission
Transmission:
  Speeds...5
  Gear ratio............High 0.790:1; Fourth 1:1; Low 6.06:1

PERFORMANCE

Computed grade ability in lowest gear, loaded..........(percent) 43
Turning radius.....................................(ft) 25
Fording depth......................................(in.) 24
Fuel consumption, loaded...........................(mpg) 6¼
Cruising range, loaded.............................(mi) 250
Allowable speed, governed..........................(mph) 51
Maximum recommended towed load:
  Off highway, gross.............................(lb) 4,500
  On highway, gross..............................(lb) 7,500

ENGINE

Manufacturer: Hercules...............................Model JXD
Type....................4-cycle, L-head; No. of cylinders (in line) 6
Displacement..(cu in.) 320
Bore..(in.) 4
Stroke..(in.) 4¼
Compression ratio....................................5.9:1
Governed speed......................................(rpm) 2,800
Brake horsepower (max w/std accessories)...........86 at (rpm) 2,400
Torque (max w/std accessories).............228 lb-ft at (rpm) 1,200

ADDITIONAL DATA

Rear Axle, type.........................spiral-bevel, full-floating
Transmission, type.........................selective sliding-gear

TRUCK, DUMP, 2½-TON, 4 x 2

(GMC, Model HC–451)

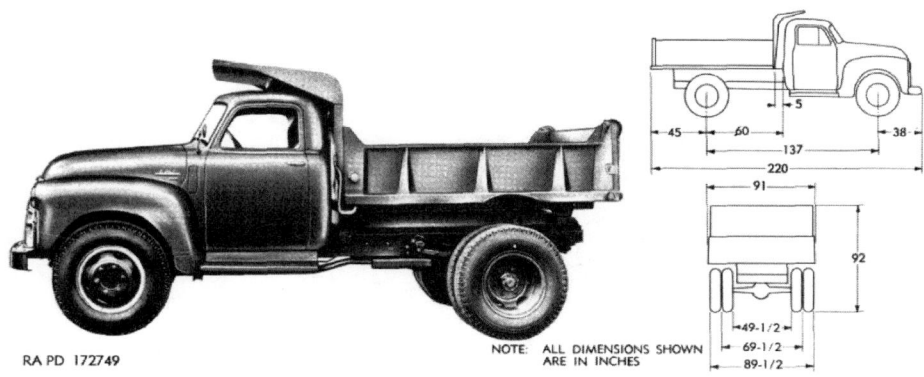

RA PD 172749

NOTE: ALL DIMENSIONS SHOWN
ARE IN INCHES

Classification: Standard.

Purpose: To transport and dump earth, sand, gravel, etc, and to transport general cargo.

GENERAL DATA

Crew	2
Weight (lb)	Net 8,135
Payload	Off highway 5,000; on highway 9,865
Gross	Off highway 13,135; on highway 18,000
Rear-axle gear ratio (two-speed)	High 6.50:1; Low 9.04:1
Axle load (lb):	
Empty	front 3,170; rear 4,965
Loaded:	
Off highway	front 3,445; rear 9,690
On highway	front 3,720; rear 14,280
Tires:	
Ply 10	Size 9.00 x 20; Pressure (psi) 65
Tread, center-to-center, front	(in.) 61⅜
Shipping dimensions, uncrated	(cu ft) 1,070; (sq ft) 139
Vehicle dimensions:	
Ground clearance	(in.) 9
Body inside dimensions (in.):	
Length	96; Width 78; Height 17
Struck capacity	(cu yds) 2½
Electrical system	(volts) 6
No. of batteries	1
Type of ground	negative
Fuel octane rating	72
Capacities:	
Fuel	(gal) 17½
Cooling system	(qt) 18
Crankcase, refill	(qt) 10½
Transmission	(qt) 6
Rear axle	(qt) 10
Brakes:	
Manufacturer	GMC; Type; hydrovac
Parking brake, type	transmission
Transmission:	
Forward speeds	5
Gear ratio	High 1:1; Fourth 1.72:1; Low 7.58:1

PERFORMANCE

Computed grade ability in lowest gear w/off-highway load	(percent) 45
Turning radius	(ft) 25
Fording depth	(in.) 26
Fuel consumption, loaded	(mpg) 7½
Cruising range, loaded	(mi) 130
Allowable speed, governed	(mph) 55

ENGINE

Manufacturer: GMC	Model 270
Type	4-cycle, valve-in-head; No. of cylinders (in line) 6
Displacement	(cu. in.) 269.5
Bore	(in.) 3²⁵⁄₃₂
Stroke	(in.) 4
Compression ratio	7.2:1
Governed speed	(rpm) 3,200
Brake horsepower (max w/std accessories)	115 at (rpm) 3,200
Torque (max w/std accessories)	226 lb-ft at (rpm) 2,000

ADDITIONAL DATA

Rear axle, type	two-speed, full-floating
Transmission, type	constant-mesh

TRUCK, DUMP, 2½-TON, 4 x 2

(GMC, Model HC–452, 1950)

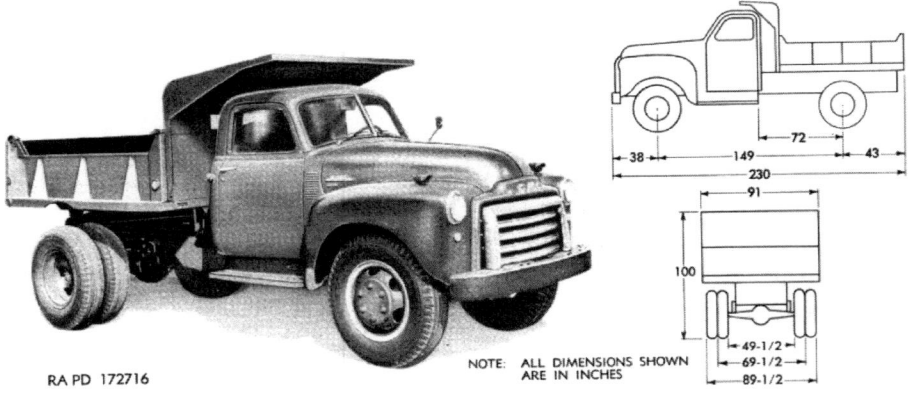

NOTE: ALL DIMENSIONS SHOWN ARE IN INCHES

RA PD 172716

Classification: Standard.

Purpose: To transport and dump earth, sand, gravel, coal, etc., and to carry general cargo.

GENERAL DATA

Crew	2
Weight (lb)	Net 8,371
Payload	Off highway 5,000; on highway 9,629
Gross	Off highway 13,371; on highway 18,000
Rear-axle gear ratios (2-speed)	High 6.50:1; Low 9.04:1
Axle load (lb):	
Empty	front 3,298; rear 5,073
Loaded:	
Off highway	front 3,618; rear 9,753
On highway	front 4,000; rear 14,000
Tires:	
Ply 10	Size 9.00 x 20; Pressure (psi) 65
Tread, center-to-center, front	(in.) 61⅞
Shipping dimensions, uncrated	(cu ft) 1,210; (sq ft) 145
Vehicle dimensions:	
Ground clearance	(in.) (
Pintle height, empty	(in.) 27
Body inside dimensions:	
Length	96; Width 72; Height 17
Cargo space	(cu ft) 68
Struck capacity	(cu yds) 2½
Electrical system	(volts) 6
No. of batteries	1
Type of ground	negative
Fuel octane rating	72
Capacities:	
Fuel	(gal) 17½
Cooling system	(qt) 18
Crankcase, refill	(qt) 10½
Transmission	(qt) 6
Rear axle	(qt) 10
Brakes:	
Manufacturer	GMC; Type; hydrovac
Parking brake, type	transmission
Transmission:	
Forward speeds	5
Gear ratio	High 1:1; Fourth 1.72:1; Low 7.58:1

PERFORMANCE

Computed grade ability in lowest gear w/off highway load	(percent) 58
Turning radius	(ft) 25
Fording depth	(in.) 26
Fuel consumption, loaded	(mpg) 7½
Cruising range, loaded	(mi) 130
Allowable speed, governed	(mph) 55
Maximum pintle tow:	
Off highway gross (lb)	10,000
On highway gross (lb)	5,000

ENGINE

Manufacturer: GMC	Model 270
Type	4-cycle, valve-in-head; No. of cylinders (in line) 6
Displacement	(cu in.) 270
Bore	(in.) 3¹⁵⁄₃₂
Stroke	(in.) 4
Compression ratio	7.2:1
Governed speed	(rpm) 3,200
Brake horsepower (max w/std accessories)	115 at (rpm) 3,200
Torque (max w/std accessories)	226 lb-ft at (rpm) 2,000

ADDITIONAL DATA

Rear Axle, type	two-speed, spiral-bevel, full-floating
Transmission type	synchromesh

TRUCK, DUMP, 2½-TON, 4 x 2

(International Harvester, Model K7, 1942–43)

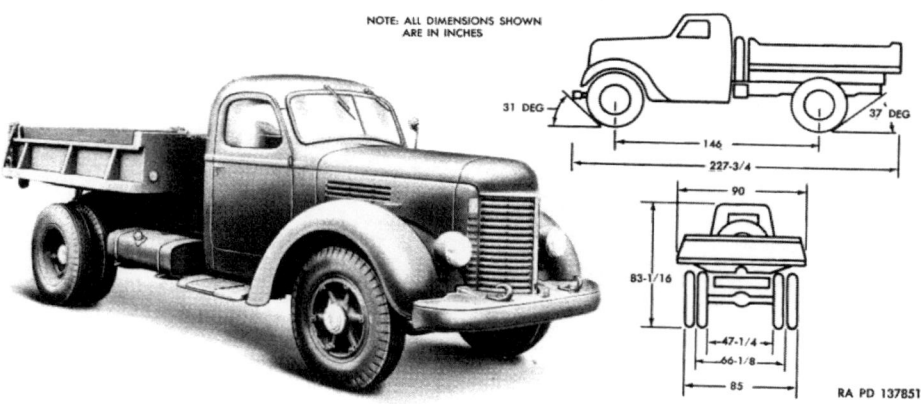

NOTE: ALL DIMENSIONS SHOWN ARE IN INCHES

31 DEG

37 DEG

146

227-3/4

90

83-1/16

47-1/4

66-1/8

85

RA PD 137851

Technical Manuals: 9-822, 9-1822, 9-1825A, 9-1827B, 9-1827C, 9-1828A; Supply Catalog: SNL G-541.

Classification: Standard.

Purpose: To haul and dump earth, sand, gravel, etc., and to transport general cargo.

GENERAL DATA

Crew..2
Weight (lb)...Net 7,850
  Payload:
    Off highway.............................5,000; gross 12,850
    On highway............................7,600; gross 15,450
Rear-axle gear ratio...7.16:1
Axle load (lb):
  Empty...........................front 3,565; rear 4,285
  Loaded:
    Off highway....................front 3,600; rear 9,250
    On highway...................front 3,620; rear 11,830
Tires:
  Ply 10...............Size 8.25 x 20; Pressure (psi) 60
  Tread, center-to-center, front.....................(in.) 65½
Shipping dimensions, uncrated............(cu ft) 989; (sq ft) 143
Vehicle dimensions:
  Ground clearance.................................(in.) 10¾
  Loading height, empty...........................(in.) 45½
  Pintle height, loaded............................(in.) 27⅞
  Body inside dimensions (in.):
    Length................96; Width 78; Height 12
  Struck capacity.................................(cu yd) 1.93
Electrical system:..................................(volts) 6
  No. of batteries....................................1
  Type of ground................................negative
Fuel octane rating..................................72
Capacities:
  Fuel...(gal) 31
  Cooling system..................................(qt) 23½
  Crankcase.......................................(qt) 6½
  Transmission, w/power take-off..................(qt) 6
  Rear axle.......................................(qt) 3½
Brakes:
  Manufacturer; Wagner.............Type; hydraulic-vacuum
  Parking brake, type.........................transmission
Transmission:
  Forward speeds....................................5
  Gear ratio...........High 0.823:1; Fourth 1:1; Low 6.525:1

PERFORMANCE

Computed grade ability in lowest gear, loaded............(percent) 43
Turning radius...(ft) 25¾
Fording depth...(in.) 30¼
Fuel consumption, loaded.................................(mpg) 9½
Cruising range, loaded....................................(mi) 290
Allowable speed, governed................................(mph) 55
Maximum recommended towed load, gross....................(lb) 10,000

ENGINE

Manufacturer: IHC..................................Model, BLD–269
Type...............Valve-in-head, 4-cycle; No. of cylinders (in line) 6
Displacement...(cu in.) 269.1
Bore...(in.) 3⁹⁄₁₆
Stroke..(in.) 4½
Compression ratio...6.3:1
Governed speed...(rpm) 3,000
Brake horsepower (max w/std accessories)..............88 at (rpm) 2,800
Torque (max)...........................216 lb-ft at (rpm) 1,000

ADDITIONAL DATA

Rear Axle, type.........................spiral-bevel, full-floating
Transmission, type.........................selective sliding-gear

TRUCK, DUMP, 2½-TON, 4 x 2

(International Harvester, Model L–171)

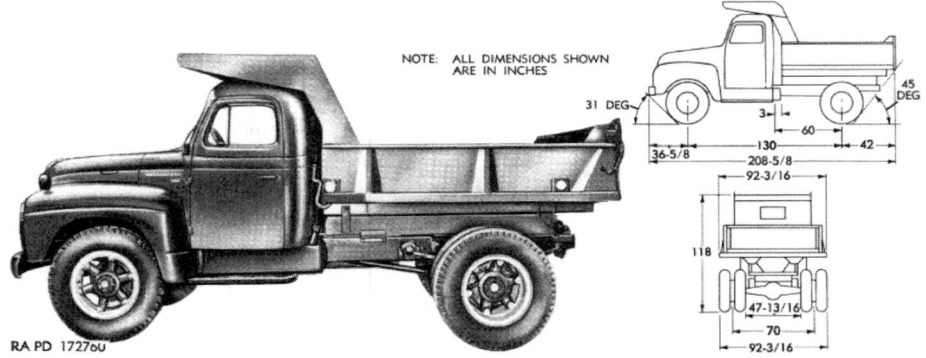

NOTE: ALL DIMENSIONS SHOWN ARE IN INCHES

31 DEG

45 DEG

3—

60

130

42

36-5/8

208-5/8

92-3/16

118

47-13/16

70

92-3/16

RA PD 17276U

Classification: Standard.

Purpose: To haul and dump earth, sand, gravel, coal, etc, and to transport general cargo.

GENERAL DATA

Crew..2
Weight (lb) ....Net 8,630
   Payload....................Off highway 5,000; on highway 9,070
   Gross....................Off highway 13,630; on highway 17,700
Rear-axle gear ratio (2-speed)....................High 6. 166:1; Low 8. 577:1
Axle load (lb):
   Empty...front 3,755; rear 4,875
   Loaded:
      Off highway.......................front 4,205; rear 9,425
      On highway.......................front 4,575; rear 13,125
Tires:
   Ply 10.........................Size 9.00 x 20; Pressure (psi) 65
   Tread, center-to-center, front......................(in.) 64¹³⁄₁₆
Shipping dimensions, uncrated....................(cu ft) 1,320; (sq ft) 134
Vehicle dimensions:
   Ground clearance....................................(in.) 10
   Body inside dimensions (in.):
      Length....................96; Width 78; Height 17
   Struck capacity..................................(cu yds) 2¼
Electrical system....................................(volts) 6
   No. of batteries......................................1
   Type of ground...................................positive
Fuel octane rating......................................72
Capacities:
   Fuel..(gal) 21
   Cooling system...............................(qt) 21½
   Crankcase, refill.................................(qt) 7
   Transmission.....................................(qt) 6
   Rear axle.......................................(qt) 7¾
Brakes:
   Manufacturer.....................Bendix-Wagner; Type; hydrovac
   Parking brake, type...........................transmission
Transmission:
   Forward speeds.......................................5
   Gear ratio....................High 1:1; Fourth 1. 42:1; Low 7. 35:1

PERFORMANCE

Computed grade ability in lowest gear w/off-highway load.....(percent) 52
Turning radius.......................................(ft) 24
Fording depth......................................(in.) 25
Fuel consumption, loaded...........................(mpg) 5½
Cruising range, loaded...............................(mi) 115
Allowable speed, governed...........................(mph) 50

ENGINE

Manufacturer: IHC....................................Model BD–269
Type....................4-cycle, valve-in-head; No. of cylinders (in line) 6
Displacement....................................(cu in.) 269
Bore...(in.) 3⅞
Stroke...(in.) 4½
Compression ratio....................................6. 3:1
Governed speed...................................(rpm) 2,800
Brake horsepower (max w/std accessories)...............89 at (rpm) 2,800
Torque (max w/std accessories)..................217 lb-ft at (rpm) 1,000

ADDITIONAL DATA

Rear axle, type...............................2-speed, full-floating
Transmission, type...................................synchromesh
   Dump bodies as follows: Daybrook, Model A54 w/model 7-DLH hoist; Anthony Model D-6 w/model 620-7 in hoist; Galion Model 12 w/model GS–567-A hoist.

TRUCK, DUMP, 2½-TON, 4 x 2

(Mack, Model EES, 1940)

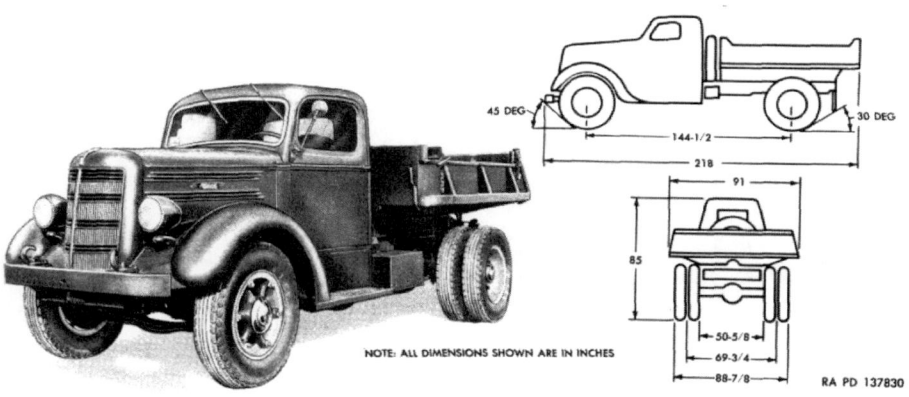

NOTE: ALL DIMENSIONS SHOWN ARE IN INCHES

RA PD 137830

Supply Catalog: SNL G–624.

Classification: Nonclassified.

Purpose: To haul and dump earth, sand, gravel, coal, etc.

GENERAL DATA

Crew...2
Weight (lb)...Net 8,450
Payload:
   Off highway......................................5,000; gross 13,450
   On highway.......................................7,000; gross 15,450
Axle load (lb):
   Empty......................................front 3,585; rear 4,865
   Loaded:
      Off highway.............................front 4,120; rear 9,330
      On highway..............................front 4,335; rear 11,115
Tires:
   Ply 10; Size 8.25 x 20; Pressure.....................(psi) 60
   Tread, center-to-center, front.......................(in.) 63
Shipping dimensions, uncrated.................(cu ft) 978; (sq ft) 138
Vehicle dimensions:
   Loading height, empty...............................(in.) 32½
   Ground clearance....................................(in.) 9
   Pintle height, loaded...............................(in.) 25
   Body inside dimensions (in.):
      Length.......................................96
      Width..78
      Height.......................................12
   Struck capacity....................................(cu yd) 1.93
Electrical system..(volts) 6
   No. of batteries....................................1
   Type of ground...................................positive
Fuel octane rating..70
Capacities:
   Fuel...(gal) 24
   Cooling system...................................(qt) 28
   Crankcase, refill................................(qt) 13
   Transmission w/PTO..............................(qt) 6
   Rear axle..(qt) 13

GENERAL DATA—Continued

Brakes:
   Manufacturer: Wagner................................Type: hydraulic
   Parking brake, type...............................transmission
Transmission:
   Forward speeds..5
   Gear ratio.......................High 1:1; Fourth 1.41:1; Low 7.53:1

PERFORMANCE

Computed grade ability in lowest gear, loaded.............(percent) 45
Turning radius (ft)...........................Right 27½; Left 29
Fording depth......................................(in.) 38½
Fuel consumption, loaded..............................(mpg) 7
Cruising range, loaded...............................(mi) 168
Allowable speed, governed............................(mph) 45
Maximum recommended towed load, gross................(lb) 10,000

ENGINE

Manufacturer: Mack....................................Model FK
Type....................L-head, 4-cycle; No. of cylinders (in line) 6
Displacement..(cu in.) 290
Bore..(in.) 3¾
Stroke..(in.) 4¾
Compression ratio.....................................6.00:1
Governed speed......................................(rpm) 2,750
Brake horsepower (max w/std accessories)...........91 at (rpm) 2,750
Torque (max).............................200 lb-ft at (rpm) 1,000

ADDITIONAL DATA

Rear axle, type...........................spiral-bevel, full-floating
Transmission, type...................................constant-mesh

TRUCK, STAKE AND PLATFORM, 2½-TON, 4 x 2
(International Harvester, Model K7, 1941)

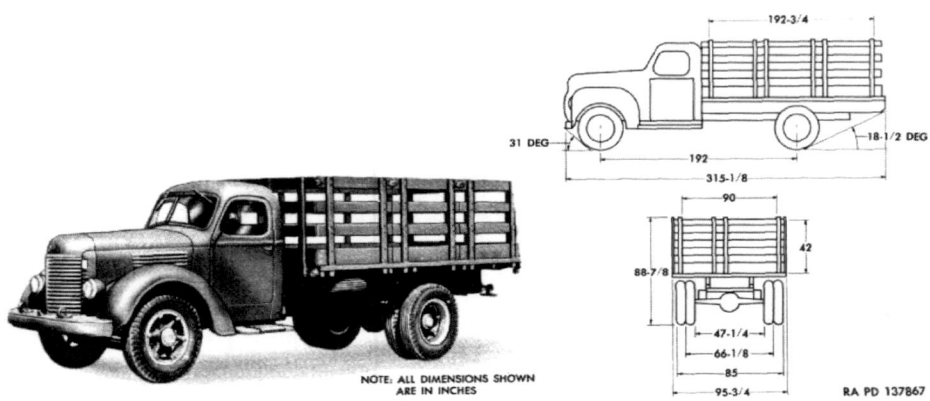

NOTE: ALL DIMENSIONS SHOWN
ARE IN INCHES

RA PD 137867

Technical Manuals: 9–822, 9–1822, 9–1825A, 9–1827B, 9–1827C, 9–1828A; Supply Catalog: SNL G–541.

Classification: Standard.

Purpose: To transport general cargo.

GENERAL DATA

Crew	2
Weight (lb)	Net 8,337
Payload:	
Off highway	5,000; gross 13,337
On highway	7,000; gross 15,337
Rear-axle gear ratio	7.16:1
Axle load (lb):	
Empty	front 3,739; rear 4,598
Loaded:	
Off highway	front 4,219; rear 9,118
On highway	front 4,409; rear 10,928
Tires:	
Ply 10	Size 8.25 x 20; Pressure (psi) 60
Tread, center-to-center, front	(in.) 65½
Shipping dimensions, uncrated	(cu ft) 1,552; (sq ft) 210
Vehicle dimensions:	
Ground clearance	(in.) 10⅝
Loading height, empty	(in.) 46⅞
Body inside dimensions (in.):	
Length	192¾; Width 90; Height 42
Body cargo space	(cu ft) 420
Electrical system	(volts) 6
No. of batteries	1
Type of ground	positive
Fuel octane rating	70
Capacities:	
Fuel	(gal) 31
Cooling system	(qt) 18½
Crankcase, refill	(qt) 6½
Transmission	(qt) 5½
Rear axle	(qt) 5
Brakes:	
Manufacturer	Wagner; Type; hydraulic-vacuum
Parking brake, type	transmission
Transmission:	
Forward speeds	5
Gear ratio	High 0.823:1; Fourth 1:1; Low 6.525:1

PERFORMANCE

Computed grade ability in lowest gear, loaded	(percent) 39
Turning radius	(ft) 27½
Fording depth	(in.) 26
Fuel consumption, loaded	(mpg) 9
Cruising range, loaded	(mi) 279
Allowable speed, governed	(mph) 45
Maximum recommended towed load, gross	(lb) 10,000

ENGINE

Manufacturer: International Harvester	Model FAC–269
Type	Valve-in-head, 4-cycle; No. of cylinders (in line) 6
Displacement	(cu in.) 269.1
Bore	(in.) 3⅞
Stroke	(in.) 4½
Compression ratio	6.2:1
Governed speed	(rpm) 3,000
Brake horsepower (max w/std accessories)	101 at (rpm) 3,200
Torque (max)	212 lb-ft at (rpm) 800

ADDITIONAL DATA

Rear axle, type	spiral-bevel, full-floating
Transmission, type	selective sliding-gear

TRUCK, STAKE AND PLATFORM, 2½-TON, 4 x 2
(International Harvester, Model L-172)

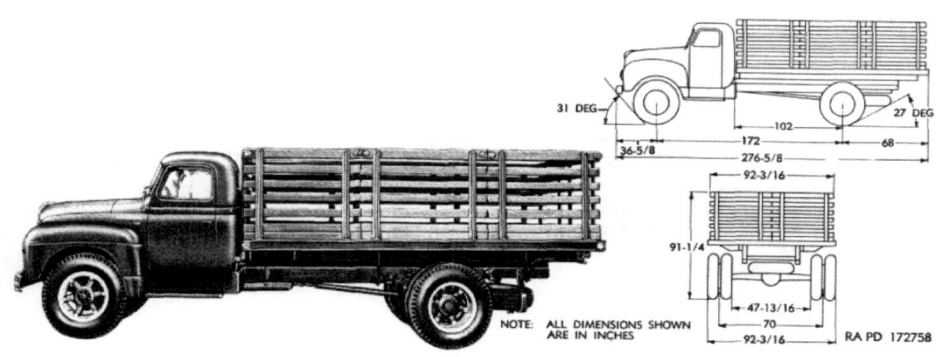

NOTE: ALL DIMENSIONS SHOWN ARE IN INCHES
RA PD 172758

Classification: Standard.

Purpose: To transport general cargo.

GENERAL DATA

Crew..2
Weight (lb)...Net 7,110
  Payload.............................Off highway 5,000; on highway 11,890
  Gross...........................Off highway 12,110; on highway 19,000
Rear-axle gear ratio (2 speed)....................High 6.33:1; Low 8.81:1
Axle load (lb):
  Empty...front 3,320; rear 3,790
  Loaded:
    Off highway..................................front 3,770; rear 8,340
    On highway...................................front 4,435; rear 14,565
Tires:
  Ply 10...............................Size 9.00 x 20; Pressure (psi) 65
  Tread, center-to-center, front........................(in.) 64¹⁵⁄₁₆
Shipping dimensions, uncrated............(cu ft) 1,350; (sq ft) 178
Vehicle dimensions:
  Ground clearance.....................................(in.) 10⅝
  Loading height..(in.) 45½
  Body inside dimensions (in.):
    Length...........................168; Width 84; Height 42
  Cargo space..(cu ft) 343
Electrical system...(volts) 6
  No. of batteries..1
  Type of ground...positive
Fuel octane rating..72
Capacities:
  Fuel..(gal) 21
  Cooling system...(qt) 21
  Crankcase, refill..(qt) 7
  Transmission..(qt) 6
  Rear axle..(qt) 4
Brakes:
  Manufacturer.......................Wagner; Type, hydraulic
  Parking brake, type...............................transmission
Transmission:
  Forward speeds..5
  Gear ratio...................High 1:1; Fourth 1.42:1; Low 7.35:1

PERFORMANCE

Computed grade ability in lowest gear w/off-highway load.....(percent) 61
Turning radius...(ft) 30
Fording depth...(in.) 25
Fuel consumption, loaded.....................................(mpg) 5½
Cruising range, loaded..(mi) 115
Allowable speed, governed....................................(mph) 50

ENGINE

Manufacturer: IHC...............................Model BD-269
Type.................4-cycle, valve-in-head; No. of cylinders (in line) 6
Displacement...(cu in.) 269
Bore...(in.) 3⁹⁄₁₆
Stroke..(in.) 4½
Compression ratio...6.3:1
Governed speed......................................(rpm) 2,800
Brake horsepower (max w/std accessories).............89 at (rpm) 2,800
Torque (max w/std accessories).............217 lb-ft at (rpm) 1,000

ADDITIONAL DATA

Rear axle, type..............................two-speed, full-floating
Transmission, type.................................synchromesh

TRUCK, TRACTOR, 2½-TON, 4 x 2

(GMC, Model HC–452, 1950)

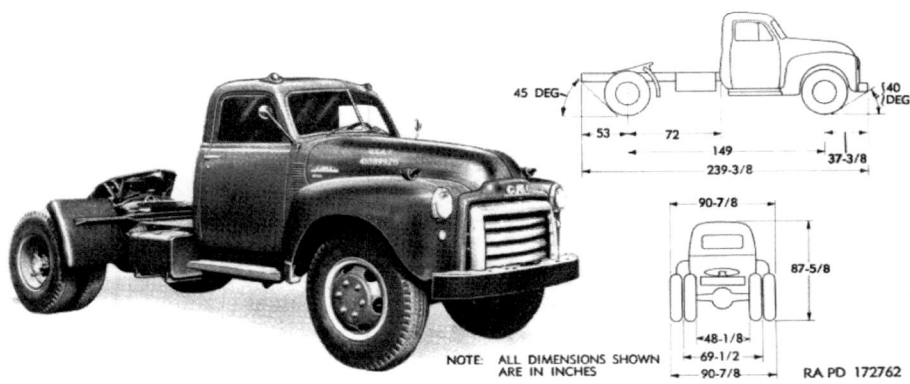

45 DEG

40 DEG

← 53 → ← 72 →

149

239-3/8

37-3/8

90-7/8

87-5/8

48-1/8

69-1/2

90-7/8

NOTE: ALL DIMENSIONS SHOWN ARE IN INCHES

RA PD 172762

Classification: Standard.

Purpose: To tow semitrailers.

GENERAL DATA

Crew	2
Weight (lb)	Net 7,470
Payload	11,530
Gross	19,000
Rear-axle gear ratio (two speed)	High 6.67:1 Low 8.85:1
Axle load (lb):	
Empty	front 3,810; rear 3,660
Loaded	front 5,000; rear 14,000
Tires:	
Ply 10	Size 9.00 x 20; Pressure (psi) 65
Tread, center-to-center, front	(in.) 61¾
Shipping dimensions, uncrated	(cu ft) 1,100; (sq ft) 151
Vehicle dimensions:	
Ground clearance	(in.) 10⅞
Frame height	(in.) 35¼
Height to center of fifth wheel, empty	(in.) 43⅞
Height to rear of fifth wheel, empty	(in.) 36⅞
Fifth wheel mounted forward of rear axle	(in.) 4
Electrical system	(volts) 6
No. of batteries	1
Type of ground	positive
Fuel octane rating	72
Capacities:	
Fuel	(gal) 50
Cooling system	(qt) 18
Crankcase, refill	(qt) 8
Transmission	(qt) 6
Rear axle	(qt) 6½
Brakes:	
Manufacturer	GMC; Type: air-hydraulic
Parking brake, type	transmission
Transmission:	
Forward speeds	5
Gear ratio	High 1:1; Fourth 1.72:1; Low 7.58:1

PERFORMANCE

Computed grade ability in lowest gear, loaded	(percent) 43
Turning radius	(ft) 26
Fording depth	(in.) 26
Fuel consumption, loaded	(mpg) 7½
Cruising range, loaded	(mi) 375
Allowable speed, governed	(mph) 55
Maximum semitrailer, gross	(lb) 20,000

ENGINE

Manufacturer: GMC	Model 270
Type	4-cycle, valve-in-head, No. of cylinders (in line) 6
Displacement	(cu in.) 269.5
Bore	(in.) 3²³⁄₃₂
Stroke	(in.) 4
Compression ratio	6.75:1
Governed speed	(rpm) 3,200
Brake horsepower (max w/std accessories)	106 at (rpm) 3,200
Torque (max w/std accessories)	216 lb-ft at (rpm) 1,000–1,200

ADDITIONAL DATA

Rear axle, type	two-speed, spiral-bevel, full-floating
Transmission, type	synchromesh

TRUCK, TRACTOR, 2½-TON, 4 x 2
(International Harvester, Model KR8R, 1942)

NOTE: ALL DIMENSIONS SHOWN
ARE IN INCHES

RA PD 137819

Technical Manuals: 9–822: 9–1822; 9–1825A; 9–1827B; 9–1827C; 9–1828A; Supply Catalog: SNL G–541.

Classification: Standard.

GENERAL DATA

Crew..2
Weight (lb)...................................Net 9,247; Payload 8,500; Gross 17,747
Rear-axle gear ratio..8.49:1
Axle load (lb.):
  Empty...front 4,480; rear 4,767
  Loaded...front 4,822; rear 12,925
Tires:
  Ply 12..............................Size 9.00 x 20; Pressure (psi) 80
  Tread, center-to-center, front.............................(in.) 68 13/16
Shipping dimensions, uncrated...................(cu ft) 1,023; (sq ft) 144
Vehicle dimensions:
  Ground clearance..(in.) 9¾
  Pintle height, empty....................................(in.) 34
  Center of fifth wheel to center of rear axle...........(in.) 6
  Height to center of fifth wheel, loaded................(in.) 44
  Height to rear of fifth wheel..........................(in.) 38
Electrical system...(volts) 6
  No. of batteries...1
  Type of ground...positive
Fuel octane rating..70
Capacities:
  Fuel...(gal) 21
  Cooling system.....................................(qt) 25½
  Crankcase, refill....................................(qt) 9
  Transmission, w/power take-off.......................(qt) 9
  Rear axle...(qt) 10
  Winch:
    Oil capacity.....................................(qt) 2
    Load capacity.................................(lb) 25,000
Brakes:
  Manufacturer.........................Wagner; Type; hydraulic
  Parking brake, type...........................transmission
Transmission:
  Forward speeds...5
  Gear ratio............High 0.823:1; Fourth 1:1; Low 6.525:1

Purpose: To tow semitrailers.

PERFORMANCE

Computed grade ability in lowest gear, loaded...............(percent) 37
Turning radius...(ft) 25
Fording depth...(in.) 30
Fuel consumption:
  W/towed load...(mpg) 5½
  W/o towed load..(mpg) 6
Cruising range:
  W/towed load...(mi) 115
  W/o towed load.......................................(mi) 126
Allowable speed, governed..................................(mph) 43
Maximum semitrailer, gross..............................(lb) 25,000

ENGINE

Manufacturer: International Harvester...............Model FBC-318
Type.....................4-cycle, valve-in-head; No. of cylinders (in line) 6
Displacement...(cu in.) 318.41
Bore..(in.) 3⅞
Stroke..(in.) 4½
Compression ratio.......................................5.45:1
Governed speed..(rpm) 2,700
Brake horsepower (max w/std accessories)............85 at (rpm) 2,600
Torque (max w/std accessories)................229 lb-ft at (rpm) 800

ADDITIONAL DATA

Rear-axle, type...........................spiral-bevel, full-floating
Transmission, type.........................selective sliding-gear

TRUCK, CARGO, 2½-TON, 6 x 4
(GMC, Model CCW353, 1941–42)

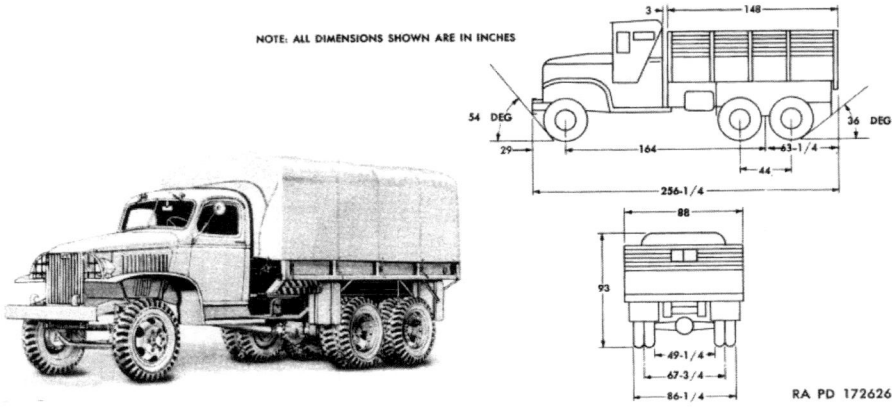

NOTE: ALL DIMENSIONS SHOWN ARE IN INCHES

RA PD 172626

Technical Manuals: 9–801, 9–1801, 9–1802A, 9–1825A, 9–1826C, 9–1827B, 9–1827C, 9–1828A; **Supply Catalog:** SNL G–508

Classification: Not classified.

Purpose: To transport general cargo.

GENERAL DATA

Crew..2
Weight (lb)..Net 10,050
   Payload:
      Off highway...................5,350; gross 15,400
      On highway....................6,550; gross 20,450
Live-axle gear ratio....................................6.6:1
Axle load (lb):
   Empty.........................front 3,120; rear (each) 3,465
   Loaded:
      Off highway............front 3,720; rear (each) 5,840
      On highway.............front 4,150; rear (each) 7,550
Tires:
   Ply 8...................Size 7.50 x 20; Pressure (psi) 55
   Tread, center-to-center, front.................(in.) 62¾
Shipping dimensions, uncrated........(cu ft) 1,216; (sq ft) 157
Vehicle dimensions:
   Ground clearance.............................(in.) 9⅝
   Pintle height, loaded.......................(in.) 31½
   Loading height, empty.......................(in.) 48½
   Body inside dimensions (in.):
      Length......................................144
      Width.....................................81½
      Height.....................................64
   Cargo space..............................(cu ft) 430
   Rear of cab to center of bogie axle..........(in.) 90
Electrical system.............................(volts) 6
   No. of batteries..............................1
   Type of ground...........................negative
Fuel octane rating.................................70
Capacities:
   Fuel.......................................(gal) 40
   Cooling system.............................(qt) 19
   Crankcase, refill (qt)......1-pc oil pan 10; 2-pc oil pan 7½
   Transmission...............................(qt) 4½
   Transfer...................................(qt) 2¾
   Live-axles (qt)................forward 6½; rear 5¼
Brakes:
   Manufacturer, GMC-Bendix............Type; hydrovac
   Parking brake, type.......................transfer

GENERAL DATA—Continued

Transmission:
   Forward speeds.................................5
   Gear ratio............High 0.799:1; Fourth 1:1; Low 6.06:1
Transfer:
   Speeds..2
   Gear ratio....................High 1.16:1; (blocked out) Low 2.63:1

PERFORMANCE

Computed grade ability in lowest gear, loaded...........(percent) 65
Turning radius.......................................(ft) 35
Fording depth.......................................(in.) 30
Fuel consumption, loaded..........................(mpg) 7½
Cruising range, loaded.............................(mi) 309
Allowable speed, governed.........................(mph) 45
Maximum recommended towed load:
   Off highway..........................gross (lb) 4,500
   On highway...........................gross (lb) 7,500

ENGINE

Manufacturer: GMC................................Model 270
Type................4-cycle, valve-in-head; No. of cylinders (in line) 6
Displacement....................................(cu in.) 269.5
Bore...(in.) 3²⁵⁄₃₂
Stroke...(in.) 4
Compression ratio................................6.75:1
Governed speed.............................(rpm) 2,750
Brake horsepower (max w/std accessories)......91.5 at (rpm) 2,750
Torque (max w/std accessories).........216 lb-ft at (rpm) 1,400

ADDITIONAL DATA

Live axles, type....................spiral-bevel, full-floating
Transmission, type...........................constant-mesh

TRUCK, GASOLINE TANK, 2½-TON, 6 x 4, 1,350-GAL

GMC; Body { Heil, single-compartment or
Gar Wood, single-compartment or
Gar Wood, double-compartment

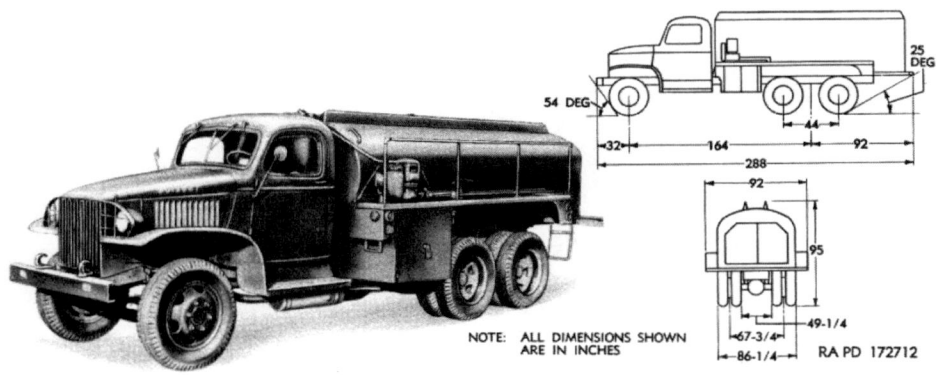

NOTE: ALL DIMENSIONS SHOWN ARE IN INCHES

RA PD 172712

Technical Manuals: 9-801, 9-1801, 9-1802A, 9-1825A, 9-1826C, 9-1827B, 9-1827C, 9-1828A; Supply Catalog: SNL G-718 (See G-508 for chassis parts).

Classification: Nonclassified.

Purpose: To transport and dispense gasoline.

GENERAL DATA

Crew..2
Weight (lb)....................Net 11,100; Payload 8,370; Gross, 19,470
Live-axle gear ratio..6.6:1
Axle load (lb):
    Empty.....................................front 4,590; rear (each) 3,255
    Loaded....................................front 5,362; rear (each) 7,054
Tires:
    Ply-8..............................Size 7.50 x 20; Pressure (psi) 55
    Tread, center-to-center, front....................(in.) 62¼
Shipping dimensions, uncrated.............(cu ft) 1,460; (sq ft) 184
Ground clearance.....................................(in.) 9¾
Electrical system...(volts) 6
    No. of batteries..1
    Type of ground...negative
Fuel octane rating..70
Capacities:
    Fuel...(gal) 40
    Cooling system..(qt) 19
    Crankcase, refill (qt)...............1-pc oil pan 10; 2-pc oil pan 7½
    Transmission..(qt) 4½
    Transfer...(qt) 2¾
    Live axles (qt).............................front 6½; rear 5¼
Brakes:
    Manufacturer...................GMC-Bendix; Type; hydrovac
    Parking brake, type..transfer
Transmission:
    Forward speeds..5
    Gear ratio..............High 0.799:1; Fourth 1:1; Low 6.06:1
Transfer:
    Speeds...2
    Gear ratio.............................High 1.16:1; Low 2.63:1

PERFORMANCE

Computed grade ability in lowest gear, loaded.............(percent) 59
Turning radius.....................................(ft) 35
Fording depth......................................(in.) 30
Fuel consumption, loaded..........................(mpg) 7½
Cruising range, loaded.............................(mi) 300
Allowable speed, governed..........................(mph) 45

ENGINE

Manufacturer: GMC..Model 270
Type.................Valve-in-head, 4-cycle; No. of cylinders (in line)
Displacement.....................................(cu in.) 269.5
Bore..(in.) 3²⁵⁄₃₂
Stroke...(in.) 4
Compression ratio...................................6.75:1
Governed speed.....................................(rpm) 2,750
Brake horsepower (max w/std accessories)...........91.5 at (rpm) 2,750
Torque (max)...........................216 lb-ft at (rpm) 1,400

ADDITIONAL DATA

Live axles, type.................................spiral-bevel, full-floating
Transmission, type......................................constant-mesh

223

TRUCK, AMPHIBIAN, 2½-TON, 6 x 6
(GMC, Model DUKW353)

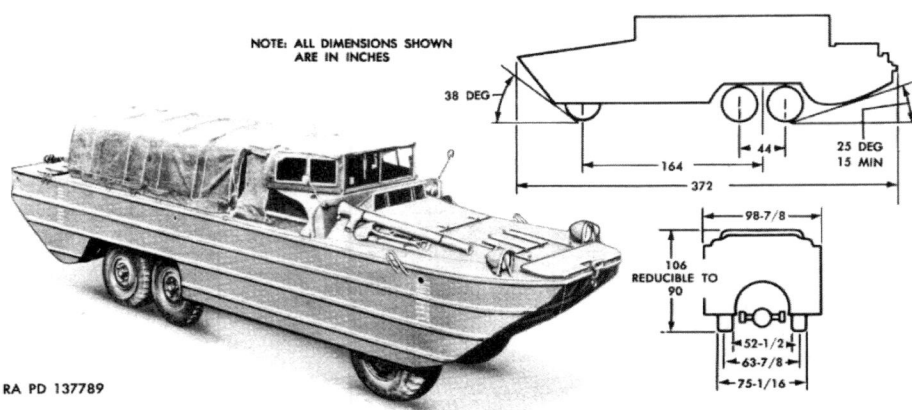

NOTE: ALL DIMENSIONS SHOWN ARE IN INCHES

RA PD 137789

Technical Manuals: 9–802, 9–1802A, 9–1802B, 9–1802C, 9–1825A, 9–1826C, 9–1827B, 9–1827C, 9–1828A; **Supply Catalog:** SNL G–501.

Classification: Standard.

Purpose: To transport cargo or personnel on land or water-

GENERAL DATA

Crew...2
Weight (lb)..........................Net 14,880; Payload 5,175; Gross 20,055
Live-axle gear ratio..6. 6:1
Tires:
  Ply 10..Size 11.00 x 18
  Pressure (psi) for paved roads.........................front 40; rear 40
  Tread, center-to-center, front..............................(in.) 63⅝
Shipping dimensions, uncrated...................(cu ft) 2,260; (sq ft) 256
Vehicle dimensions (in.):
  Water line length, loaded...344
  Loaded freeboard:
    At coaming...front 28; rear 28
    At deck...front 24; rear 16
  Loaded draft......................................front 42; rear 51
  Ground clearance...(in.) 11½
  Pintle height, loaded...................................(in.) 49⅜
  Cargo-space inside dimensions (in.):
    Length..................96; Width 72; Height, under bows 96
  Cargo capacity..(cu ft) 384
Electrical system.......................................(volts) 6
  No. of batteries...1
  Type of ground...negative
Fuel octane rating..70
Capacities:
  Fuel...(gal) 40
  Cooling system...(qt) 20
  Crankcase, refill.....................................(qt) 11½
  Transmission w/power take-off.........................(qt) 5½
  Axles (qt):...front 6½
    Bogie..........................front 6½; rear 5¾
  Transfer..(qt) 2¾
  Water-propeller transfer..............................(qt) ½
  Tire pump..(qt) ½
  Winch:
    Oil capacity.......................................(qt) ¾
    Load capacity...................................(lb) 10,000
Brakes:
  Manufacturer....................GMC-Bendix; Type; hydrovac
  Parking brake, type...................................transfer

GENERAL DATA—Continued

Transmission:
  Forward speeds...5
  Gear ratio...............High 0.799:1; Fourth 1:1; Low 6.06:1
Water-propeller-transfer:
  Speeds...2
  Gear ratio......................Reverse 0.38:1; Forward 0.743:1

PERFORMANCE

Computed grade ability in lowest gear, loaded...........(percent) 55
Turning radius:
  Right (ft).......................................land 35; water 20
  Left (ft)..land 36; water 20
Fuel consumption, loaded:
  Land..(mpg) 6
  Water..(mpg) 0.9
Cruising range, loaded: land...........................(mi) 240
  On water: at top speed, 2nd gear (mi) 30...........3rd gear (mi) 50
Allowable speed:
  Land, governed.....................................(mph) 50
  Water..(mph) 6
Maximum recommended towed load:
  Off highway.....................................gross (lb) 4,500
  On highway......................................gross (lb) 7,500

ENGINE

Manufacturer: GMC..Model 270
Type....................Valve-in-head, 4-cycle; No. of cylinders (in line) 6
Displacement..(cu in.) 269. 5
Bore..(in.) 3²⁵⁄₃₂
Stroke...(in.) 4
Compression ratio...6. 75:1
Governed speed.....................................(rpm) 2,750
Brake horsepower (max w/std accessories)...........91. 5 at (rpm) 2,750
Torque (max)...............................216 lb-ft at (rpm) 1,400

ADDITIONAL DATA

Live-axles, type..............................spiral-bevel, full-floating
Transmission, type..................................constant-mesh

TRUCK, BOMB SERVICE, 2½-TON, 6 x 6, M27 AND M27B1
(GMC, Model CCKW353, LWB)

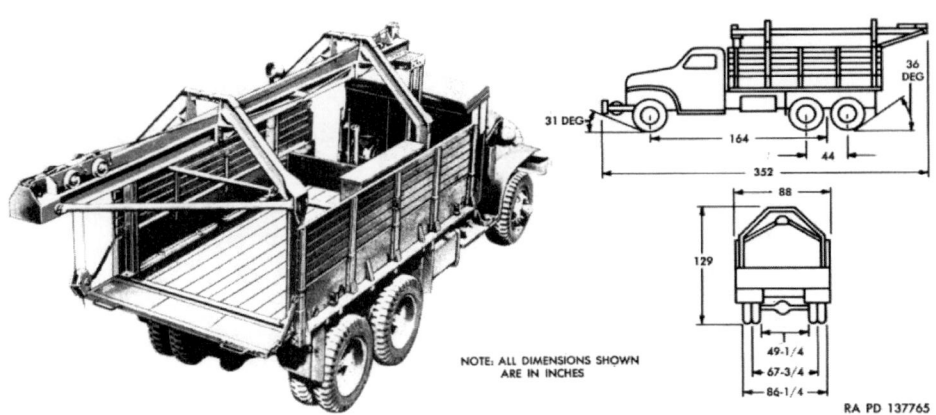

NOTE: ALL DIMENSIONS SHOWN
ARE IN INCHES

RA PD 137765

Technical Manuals: 9–766, 9–801, 9–1801, 9–1802A, 9–1825A, 9–1826C, 9–1827B, 9–1827C, 9–1828A; **Supply Catalog:** SNL G–508.

Classification: M27B1 standard; M27 substitute standard.

Purpose: To lift and transport bombs from depots to planes and airfields.

GENERAL DATA

```
Crew..............................................................................2
Weight (lb)......................Net 14,115; Payload 5,158; Gross 19,273
Live-axle gear ratio...............................................6.6:1
Axle load (lb):
    Empty.................................front 5,081; rear (each) 4,517
    Loaded................................front 5,649; rear (each) 6,812
Tires:
    Ply 8..........................Size 7.50 x 20; Pressure (psi) 55
    Tread, center-to-center, front...........................(in.) 62¼
Shipping dimensions, uncrated...............(cu ft) 2,312; (sq ft) 215
Vehicle dimensions:
    Loading height, empty................................(in.) 48½
    Ground clearance.......................................(in.) 9⅝
    Pintle height, loaded..................................(in.) 31½
Electrical system...........................................(volts) 6
    No. of batteries..........................................1
    Type of ground......................................negative
Fuel octane rating............................................70
Capacities:
    Fuel....................................................(gal) 40
    Cooling system.........................................(qt) 19
    Crankcase, refill (qt)..............1-pc oil pan 10; 2-pc oil pan 7½
    Tranfer................................................(qt) 3
    Transmission w/power take-off..........................(qt) 6¼
    Axles (qt).............................................front 3
        Bogie.........................................front 3; rear 2½
    Winch:
        Oil capacity......................................(qt) 1½
        Load capacity...................................(lb) 10,000
Brakes:
    Manufacturer....................GMC-Bendix; Type; hydrovac
    Parking brake, type.................................transfer
Transmission:
    Forward speeds...........................................5
    Gear ratio..................High 0.799:1; Fourth 1:1; Low 6.06:1
Transfer:
    Speeds...................................................2
    Gear ratio...................................High 1.16:1; Low 2.63:1
```

PERFORMANCE

```
Computed grade ability in lowest gear, loaded...............(percent) 65
Turning radius...............................................(ft) 35
Fording depth................................................(in.) 30
Fuel consumption, loaded....................................(mpg) 7½
Cruising range, loaded......................................(mi) 300
Allowable speed, governed...................................(mph) 45
Maximum recommended towed load:
    Off highway gross (lb)...................................4,500
    On highway gross (lb)....................................7,500
```

ENGINE

```
Manufacturer: GMC...................................Model 270
Type...................Valve-in-head, 4-cycle; No. of cylinders (in line) 6
Displacement..........................................(cu in.) 269.5
Bore......................................................(in.) 3³³⁄₃₂
Stroke......................................................(in.) 4
Governed speed..........................................(rpm) 2,750
Brake horsepower (max w/std accessories)...............91.5 at (rpm) 2,750
Torque (max).......................................216 lb-ft at (rpm) 1,400
```

ADDITIONAL DATA

```
Live-axles, type.............................spiral-bevel, full-floating
Transmission, type.................................constant-mesh
    Data given for vehicle with split-type axle.   For banjo-type axle, changes
in data are as follows:
Tread:
    Center-to-center (in.)..........................front 60; rear 67½
    Outside to outside (in.)..............86; Inside to inside (in.) 49
Capacities:
    Transfer..............................................(qt) 2¾
    Axles (qt)............................................front 6½
        Bogie.........................................front 6½; rear 5¼
```

225

TRUCK, CARGO, 2½-TON, 6 x 6
(GMC, Model AFKWX353, COE, 15-ft. body)

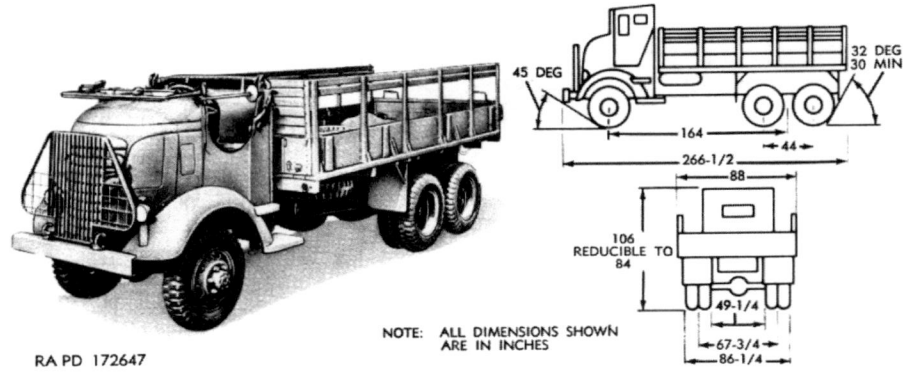

RA PD 172647

NOTE: ALL DIMENSIONS SHOWN ARE IN INCHES

Technical Manuals: 9–809, 9–1801, 9–1802A, 9–1825A, 9–1826C, 9–1827B, 9–1827C, 9–1828A, 9–1829A; **Supply Catalog:** SNL G–508.

Classification: Limited Standard.

GENERAL DATA

Crew...2
Weight (lb)......................................Net 10,800; Payload 5,350; Gross 16,150
Live-axle gear ratio...6.6:1
Axle load (lb):
    Empty...front 4,439; rear (each) 3,180
    Loaded*..front 5,148; rear (each) 5,501
Tires:
    Ply 8.........................Size 7.50 x 20; Pressure (psi); front 55; rear 55
    Tread, center-to-center, front.......................................(in.) 62¼
Shipping dimensions, uncrated.....................(cu ft) 1,440; (sq ft) 163
Vehicle dimensions:
    Loading height, empty..(in.) 49½
    Ground clearance...(in.) 9⅝
    Pintle height, loaded..(in.) 31½
    Body inside dimensions (in.):
        Length....................176; Width 80; Height, under bows 59
    Cargo space...(cu ft) 475
Electrical system...(volts) 6
    No. of batteries..1
    Type of ground..negative
Fuel octane rating..70
Capacities:
    Fuel...(gal) 40
    Cooling system..(qt) 21
    Crankcase, refill (qt).............1-pc oil pan 10; 2-pc oil pan 7½
    Transmission..(qt) 4½
    Transfer...(qt) 3
    Axles (qt)...front 3
    Bogie...front 3; rear 2½
Brakes:
    Manufacturer.......................GMC-Bendix; Type; hydrovac
    Parking brake, type..transfer
Transmission:
    Forward speeds...5
    Gear ratio..................High 0.799:1; Fourth 1:1; Low 6.06:1
Transfer:
    Speeds...2
    Gear ratio..High 1.16:1; Low 2.63:1

Purpose: To transport general cargo.

PERFORMANCE

Computed grade ability in lowest gear, loaded...................(percent) 65
Turning radius (ft)....................................Right 35; Left 35
Fording depth...(in.) 30
Fuel consumption, loaded..(mpg) 7½
Cruising range, loaded...(mi) 300
Allowable speed, governed..(mph) 45
Maximum recommended towed load, gross.....................(lb) 4,500

ENGINE

Manufacturer: GMC...................................Model 270
Type................Valve-in-head, 4-cycle; No. of cylinders (in line) 6
Displacement...(cu in.) 269.5
Bore..(in.) 3²⁵⁄₃₂
Stroke...(in.) 4
Compression ratio..6.75:1
Governed speed...(rpm) 2,750
Brake horsepower (max w/std accessories)............91.5 at (rpm) 2,750
Torque (max w/std accessories)..................216 lb-ft at (rpm) 1,400

ADDITIONAL DATA

Live axles, type...spiral-bevel, full-floating
Transmission, type...constant-mesh
    Data given for vehicle with split-type axle. For banjo-type axle, changes in data are as follows:
Tread dimensions (in.):
    Front...60
    Rear...67½
        Outside to outside..86
        Inside to inside...49
Capacities:
    Transfer...(qt) 2¾
    Axles (qt)..front 6½
    Bogie...front 6½; rear 5¼

* Increased loading of this vehicle on highway not permitted.

TRUCK, CARGO, 2½-TON, 6 x 6, W/ AND W/O WINCH

(GMC, Model CCKW352, SWB, 1941–42–43)

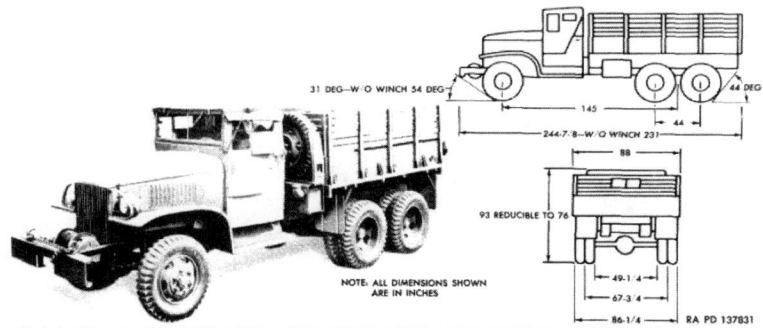

NOTE: ALL DIMENSIONS SHOWN ARE IN INCHES

RA PD 137831

Technical Manuals: 9-801, 9-1801, 9-1802A, 9-1825A, 9-1826C, 9-1827B, 9-1827C, 9-1828A; **Supply Catalog:** SNL G–508.

Classification: Limited Standard.

Purpose: To transport general cargo and personnel.

GENERAL DATA

```
Crew..................................................................2
Weight (lb)..................................................Net 10,350
  Payload:
    Off highway..............................5,350; Gross 15,700
    On highway...............................10,000; Gross 20,350
Live-axle gear ratio...........................................6.6:1
Axle load (lb):
  Empty.......................................front 3,792; rear (each) 3,279
  Loaded:
    Off highway...............................front 3,992; rear (each) 5,854
    On highway................................front 4,170; rear (each) 8,090
Tires:
  Ply 8.........................Size 7.50 x 20; Pressure (psi) 55
  Tread, center-to-center, front....................(in.) 62¼
Shipping dimensions, uncrated:
  W/winch..............................(cu ft) 1,160; (sq ft) 150
  W/o winch............................(cu ft) 1,136; (sq ft) 147
Vehicle dimensions:
  Loading height, empty............................(in.) 48½
  Ground clearance.................................(in.) 9⅝
  Pintle height, loaded............................(in.) 31½
  Body inside dimensions (in.):
    Length......................120; Width 81½; Height 64
  Body cargo space..................................(cu ft) 340
Electrical system................................(volts) 6
  No. of batteries.................................1
  Type of ground..................................negative
Fuel octane rating.................................70
Capacities:
  Fuel.............................................(gal) 40
  Cooling system..................................(qt) 19
  Crankcase, refill (qt).........1-pc oil pan 10; 2-pc oil pan 7½
  Transfer.........................................(qt) 3
  Transmission (qt).................w/PTO 6½; w/o PTO 4½
  Axles (qt)......................................front 3
    Bogie.....................................front 3; rear 2½
  Winch:
    Oil capacity.................................(qt) 1½
    Load capacity...............................(lb) 10,000
Brakes:
  Manufacturer................GMC-Bendix; Type; hydrovac
  Parking brake, type.............................transfer
Transmission:
  Forward speeds...................................5
  Gear ratio..........High 0.799:1; Fourth 1:1; Low 6.06:1
```

GENERAL DATA—Continued

```
Transfer:
  Speeds...........................................2
  Gear ratio.........................High 1.16:1; Low 2.63:1
```

PERFORMANCE

```
Computed grade ability in lowest gear, loaded.........(percent) 65
Turning radius....................................(ft) 34
Fording depth.....................................(in.) 30
Fuel consumption, loaded..........................(mpg) 7½
Cruising range, loaded............................(mi) 300
Allowable speed, governed.........................(mph) 45
Maximum recommended towed load:
  Off highway.....................................4,500
  On highway......................................7,500
```

ENGINE

```
Manufacturer: GMC.................................Model 270
Type.................Valve-in-head, 4-cycle; No. of cylinders (in line) 6
Displacement......................................(cu in.) 269.5
Bore..............................................(in.) 32½⁄₃₂
Stroke............................................(in.) 4
Compression ratio.................................6.75:1
Governed speed....................................(rpm) 2,750
Brake horsepower (max w/std accessories)...........91.5 at (rpm) 2,750
Torque (max)...............................216 lb-ft at (rpm) 1,400
```

ADDITIONAL DATA

Weights and axle loads given for vehicle w/o winch, Weight of winch 700 lb.

```
Live axles, type...........................spiral-bevel, full-floating
Transmission, type..............................constant-mesh
```

Data given for vehicle with split-type axle. For banjo-type axle, changes in data are as follows:

```
Tread dimensions (in.):
  Front...........................................60
  Rear............................................67½
    Outside to outside............................86
    Inside to inside..............................49
Capacities:
  Transfer........................................(qt) 2¼
  Axles (qt)......................................front 6½
    Bogie......................................front 6½; rear 5¼
```

TRUCK, CARGO, 2½-TON, 6 x 6, W/ AND W/O WINCH

(GMC, Models CCKW353, LWB, 1941–42–43 and CCKWX353, LWB, 1941)

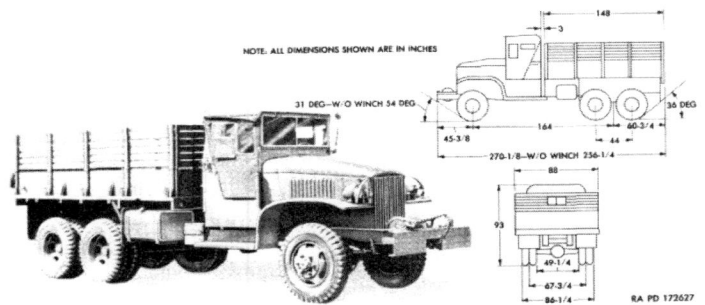

NOTE: ALL DIMENSIONS SHOWN ARE IN INCHES

RA PD 172627

Technical Manuals: 9–801, 9–1801, 9–1802A, 9–1825A, 9–1826C, 9–1827B, 9–1827C, 9–1828A; **Supply Catalog:** SNL G–508.

Classification: Limited standard.

Purpose: To transport general cargo and personnel.

GENERAL DATA

Crew..2
Weight (lb)..Net 11,250
  Payload:
    Off highway...............................5,350; Gross 16,600
    On highway.................................9,200; Gross 20,450
Live-axle gear ratio..6.6 : 1
Axle load (lb):
  Empty.....................................front 4,120; rear (each) 3,565
  Loaded:
    Off highway...................front 4,270; rear (each) 5,940
    On highway....................front 5,150; rear (each) 7,650
Tires:
  Ply 8; Size 7.50 x 20; Pressure.........................(psi) 55
  Tread, center-to-center, front........................(in.) 62¼
Shipping dimensions, uncrated:
  W/winch...........................(cu ft) 1,280; (sq ft) 165
  W/o winch........................(cu ft) 1,216; (sq ft) 157
Vehicle dimensions:
  Loading height, empty................................(in.) 48½
  Ground clearance.....................................(in.) 9⅞
  Pintle height, loaded................................(in.) 31½
  Body inside dimensions (in.):
    Length...144
    Width...81½
    Height...64
  Body cargo space...................................(cu ft) 430
  Rear of cab to center of bogie axle...................(in.) 90
Electrical system...(volts) 6
  No. of batteries...1
  Type of ground..negative
Fuel octane rating..70
Capacities:
  Fuel..(gal) 40
  Cooling system..(qt) 19
  Crankcase, refill (qt)..........1-pc oil pan 10; 2-pc oil pan 7½
  Transfer..(qt) 3
  Transmission (qt)..............w/PTO 6¾; w/o PTO; (qt) 4½
  Axles (qt)..front 3
  Bogie..front 3; rear 2½
  Winch:
    Oil capacity...(qt) 1½
    Load capacity.....................................(lb) 10,000
Brakes:
  Manufacturer: GMC-Bendix....................Type; hydrovac
  Parking brake, type.....................................transfer

GENERAL DATA—Continued

Transmission:
  Forward speeds...5
  Gear ratio..........High 0.799 : 1; Fourth 1 : 1; Low 6.06 : 1
Transfer:
  Speeds..2
  Gear ratio.......................High 1.16 : 1; Low 2.63 : 1

PERFORMANCE

Computed grade ability in lowest gear, loaded.............(percent) 65
Turning radius..(ft) 35
Fording depth...(in.) 30
Fuel consumption, loaded...(mpg) 7½
Cruising range, loaded..(mi) 300
Allowable speed, governed..(mph) 45
Maximum recommended towed load:
  Off highway; gross (lb)....................................4,500
  On highway; gross (lb)....................................7,500

ENGINE

Manufacturer: GMC...Model 270
Type......................Valve-in-head, 4-cycle; No. of cylinders (in line) 6
Displacement.....................................(cu in.) 269.5
Bore..(in.) 3²³⁄₃₂
Stroke...(in.) 4
Compression ratio...6.75 : 1
Governed speed...(rpm) 2,750
Brake horsepower (max w/std accessories)......91.5 at (rpm) 2,750
Torque (max)...........................216 lb-ft at (rpm) 1,400

ADDITIONAL DATA

Weight and axle loads given for vehicle w/winch. Weight of winch 700 lb.
Live-axles, type............................spiral-bevel, full-floating
Transmission, type.............................constant-mesh
Data given for vehicle with split-type axle. For banjo-type axle, changes in data are as follows:
Tread dimensions (in.):
  Front...60
  Rear...67½
    Outside to outside..86
    Inside to inside..49
Capacities:
  Transfer..(qt) 2¼
  Axles (qt)...front 6½
  Bogie...front 6½; rear 5¼

TRUCK, CARGO, 2½-TON, 6 x 6, 17 FT, M427

(GMC, Model AFKWX353, COE, 1942)

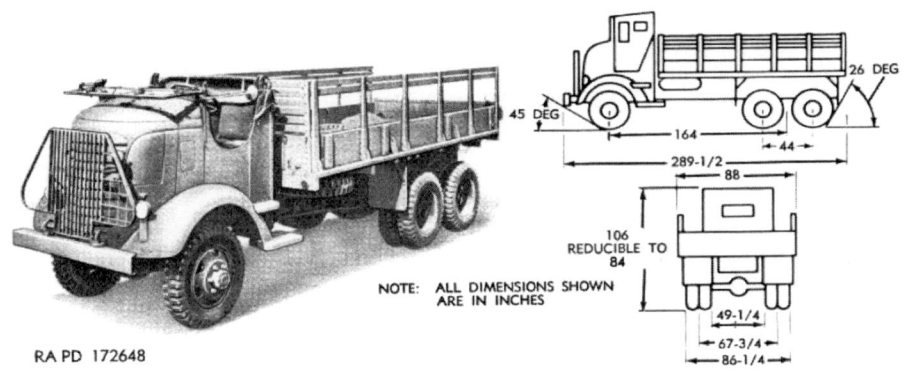

NOTE: ALL DIMENSIONS SHOWN ARE IN INCHES

RA PD 172648

Technical Manuals: 9-809, 9-1801, 9-1802A, 9-1825A, 9-1826C, 9-1827B, 9-1827C, 9-1828A; Supply Catalog: SNL G-508.

Classification: Standard.

Purpose: To transport general cargo and personnel.

GENERAL DATA

Crew..2
Weight (lb.):.........................Net 11,950; Payload 5,350; Gross 17,300
Live-axle gear ratio...6.6:1
Axle load (lb.):
  Empty...front 4,439; rear (each) 3,755
  Loaded*..front 5,148; rear (each) 6,076
Tires:
  Ply 8...Size 7.50 x 20; Pressure (psi) 55
  Tread, center-to-center, front...(in.) 62¾
Shipping dimensions, uncrated......................(cu ft) 1,788; (sq ft) 193
Vehicle dimensions:
  Loading height, empty...(in.) 49½
  Ground clearance...(in.) 9⅞
  Pintle height, loaded...(in.) 31½
  Body inside dimensions (in.):
    Length.......................200; Width 80; Height, under bows 59
  Body cargo space...(cu ft) 540
Electrical system...(volts) 6
  No. of batteries..1
  Type of ground...negative
Fuel octane rating...70
Capacities:
  Fuel..(gal) 40
  Cooling system..(qt) 21
  Crankcase, refill (qt).................1-pc oil pan 10; 2-pc oil pan 7½
  Transfer...(qt) 3
  Transmission...(qt) 4½
  Axles (qt)..front 3
  Bogie..front 3; rear 2½
Brakes:
  Manufacturer................GMC-Bendix; Type; hydrovac
  Parking brake, type...transfer
Transmission:
  Forward speeds...5
  Gear ratio.............High 0.799:1; Fourth 1:1; Low 6.06:1
Transfer:
  Speeds...2
  Gear ratio.........................High 1.16:1; Low 2.63:1

*Increased loading of this vehicle on highways not permitted.

PERFORMANCE

Computed grade ability in lowest gear, loaded...............(percent) 65
Turning radius...(ft) 35
Fording depth...(in.) 30
Fuel consumption, loaded..(mpg) 7½
Cruising range, loaded..(mi) 300
Allowable speed, governed...(mph) 45
Maximum recommended towed load, gross.................................(lb) 4,500

ENGINE

Manufacturer: GMC..Model 270
Type......................Valve-in-head, 4-cycle; No. of cylinders (in line) 6
Displacement..(cu in.) 269.5
Bore..(in.) 3²⁵⁄₃₂
Stroke..(in.) 4
Compression ratio...6.75:1
Governed speed..(rpm) 2,750
Brake horsepower (max w/std accessories).............91.5 at (rpm) 2,750
Torque (max w/std accessories)......................216 lb-ft at (rpm) 1,400

ADDITIONAL DATA

Live-axles, type.......................................spiral-bevel, full-floating
Transmission, type...constant-mesh
  Data given for vehicle with split-type axles. For banjo-type axles, changes in data are as follows:
Tread dimensions (in.):
  Front...60
  Rear..67½
    Outside to outside..86
    Inside to inside..49
Capacities:
  Transfer...(qt) 2½
  Axles (qt)...front 6½
  Bogie...front 6½; rear 5¼

229

TRUCK, CARGO, 2½-TON, 6 x 6, M34, W/ AND W/O WINCH

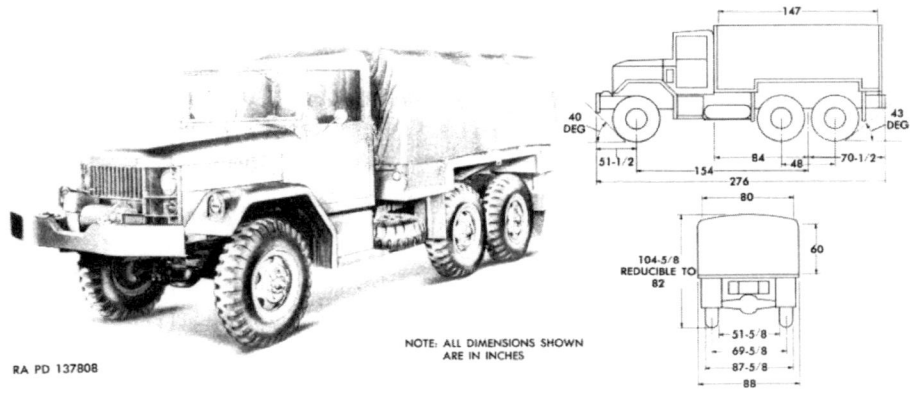

NOTE: ALL DIMENSIONS SHOWN
ARE IN INCHES

RA PD 137808

Technical Manual: 9-819; Supply Catalog: SNL G-742.

Classification: Standard.

GENERAL DATA

Crew..2
Weight (lb)..Net 2,190¼
   Payload w/crew...............off highway 5,350; on highway 10,350
   Gross......................off highway 17,540; on highway 22,540
Live-axle gear ratio..6.72:1
Axle load (lb):
   Empty.........................front 5,900; rear (each) 3,145
   Loaded:
      Off highway...............front 6,325; rear (each) 5,607
      On highway................front 6,525; rear (each) 8,007
Tires:
   Ply 12.........................Size 11.00 x 20; Pressure (psi) 50
   Tread, center-to-center, front...........................(in.) 69⅜
Shipping dimensions, uncrated:
   W/winch....................................(cu ft) 1,150; (sq ft) 169
   W/o winch.................................(cu ft) 1,094; (sq ft) 160
Vehicle dimensions:
   Ground clearance..(in.) 19½
   Loading height, empty......................................(in.) 43½
   Pintle height, empty..(in.) 35⅝
   Body inside dimensions (in.): Length......147; Width 80; Height 60
   Cargo space...(cu ft) 408
Electrical system...(volts) 24
   No. of batteries (12-volt)..2
   Type of ground...negative
Fuel octane rating..75
Capacities:
   Fuel..(gal) 50
   Cooling system (qt)..........w/o heater 22; w/heater 24
   Crankcase, refill..(qt) 9
   Transmission (qt):
      W/o power take-off..4¾
      W/power take-off...5
   Transfer..(qt) 7
   Axles, each...(qt) 7
   Winch:
      Oil capacity..(qt) 2
      Load capacity..(lb) 10,000
Brakes:
   Manufacturer; Timken.............Type: air-actuated hydraulic
   Parking brake, type...................................transfer

Purpose: To transport general cargo.

GENERAL DATA—Continued

Transmission:
   Forward speeds...5
   Gear ratio................High 1:1; Fourth 1.45:1; Low 7.55:1
Transfer:
   Speeds..2
   Gear ratio....................................High 1:1; Low 1.98:1

PERFORMANCE

Computed grade ability in lowest gear, w/5,350-lb payload....(percent) 64
Turning radius (ft)...................w/winch 36; w/o winch 35
Fording depth...(in.) 72
Fuel consumption, loaded.................................(mpg) 7
Cruising range, loaded....................................(mi) 350
Allowable speed, governed................................(mph) 62
Maximum recommended towed load:
   Off highway, gross.....................................(lb) 6,000
   On highway, gross.....................................(lb) 10,000

ENGINE

Manufacturer: Reo Motors, Inc.....................Model OA-331
Type...............Valve-in-head, 4-cycle; No. of cylinders (in line) 6
Displacement...(cu in.) 331
Bore..(in.) 4⅛
Stroke..(in.) 4⅛
Compression ratio...6.73:1
Governed speed.......................................(rpm) 3,400
Brake horsepower (max w/std accessories)......127 at (rpm) 3,200
Torque (max).............................248 lb-ft at (rpm) 1,400

ADDITIONAL DATA

Live axles, type............spiral-bevel, double-reduction, full-floating
Transmission, type......................................synchromesh
   Weights and axle loads given are for vehicle w/winch; for vehicle w/o
   winch, they are as follows:
Weight (lb):
   Net..11,775
   Gross.................off highway 17,125; on highway 22,125
Axle load (lb):
   Empty.........................front 5,405; rear (each) 3,185
   Loaded:
      Off highway...............front 5,830; rear (each) 5,647
      On highway................front 6,030; rear (each) 8,047

TRUCK, CARGO, 2½-TON, 6 x 6, M35, W/ AND W/O WINCH

NOTE: ALL DIMENSIONS SHOWN ARE IN INCHES

RA PD 172780

Technical Manuals: 9-819, 9-1819A, 9-1819B, 9-1825A, 9-1826D, 9-1827A, 9-1827C, 9-1828A; **Supply Catalog:** SNL G-742.

GENERAL DATA

Crew..2

Weight (lb):
  Net..w/o winch 12,465; w/winch 12,880
  Payload:
    Off highway...5,000
    On highway...10,000
  Gross:
    Off highway....................w/o winch 17,465; w/winch 17,880
    On highway....................w/o winch 22,465; w/winch 23,380
Axle gear ratio..6.722 : 1
Axle load (lb):
  Empty:
    Front:
      W/o winch..............5,315; rear (each) w/o winch 3,575
      W/winch...............................5,810; w/winch 3,535
  Loaded, off highway:
    Front:
      W/o winch..............5,511; rear (each) w/o winch 5,977
      W/winch...............................6,006; w/winch 5,937
  Loaded on highway:
    Front:
      W/o winch..............5,705; rear (each) w/o winch 8,380
      W/winch...............................6,700; w/winch 8,340
Tires:
  Ply 8.................................Size 9.00 x 20; Pressure (psi) 45
  Tread, center-to-center, front...........................(in.) 67⅞
Shipping dimensions, uncrated:
  W/o winch....................................(cu ft) 1,610; (sq ft) 174
  W/winch.......................................(cu ft) 1,690; (sq ft) 183
Vehicle dimensions:
  Ground clearance...(in.) 12¹³⁄₁₆
  Pintle height, empty..(in.) 34¾
  Loading height, empty...(in.) 51
  Body inside dimensions (in.):
    Length......................147; Width 88; Height 60
  Cargo space...(cu ft) 456
Electrical system..(volts) 24
  No. of batteries...2
  Type of ground...negative
Fuel octane rating..80
Capacities:
  Fuel...(gal) 50
  Cooling system...(qt) 22
  Crankcase, refill..(qt) 9

Purpose: To transport general cargo and personnel and tow 105-mm howitzer.

GENERAL DATA—Continued

Capacities:
  Transmission (qt).....................w/o PTO 4¼; w/PTO 5¼
  Transfer...(qt) 7
  Axle...(qt) 7
  Winch:
    Oil capacity...(qt) 1
    Load capacity...(lb) 10,000
Brakes:
  Manfacturer....................Timken-Detroit; Type: air-hydraulic
  Parking brake, type..transfer
Transmission:
  Forward speeds...5
  Gear ratio...........High 1:1; Fourth 1.45:1; Low 7.55:1
Transfer:
  Speeds...2
  Gear ratio.................................High 1:1; Low 1.98:1

PERFORMANCE

Computed grade ability in lowest gear, w/off-highway load......(percent) 65
Turning radius...(ft) 36
Fording depth..(in.) 72
Fuel consumption, loaded..(mpg) 6
Cruising range, loaded...(mi) 300
Allowable speed, governed......................................(mph) 58
Maximum pintle tow:
  Off highway, gross...6,000
  On highway, gross...10,000

ENGINE

Manufacturer: Reo..Model 331 OA
Type.................4-cycle, valve-in-head; No. of cylinders (in line) 6
Displacement...(cu in.) 331
Bore..(in.) 4⅜
Stroke...(in.) 4⅜
Compression ratio..6.73:1
Governed speed...(rpm) 3,400
Brake horsepower (max w/std accessories)..........127 at (rpm) 3,400
Torque (max w/std accessories)..............248 lb-ft at (rpm) 1,400

ADDITIONAL DATA

Axles, type...........................double-reduction, full floating
Transmission, type..synchromesh

TRUCK, CARGO, 2½-TON, 6 x 6, M36, W AND W/O WINCH

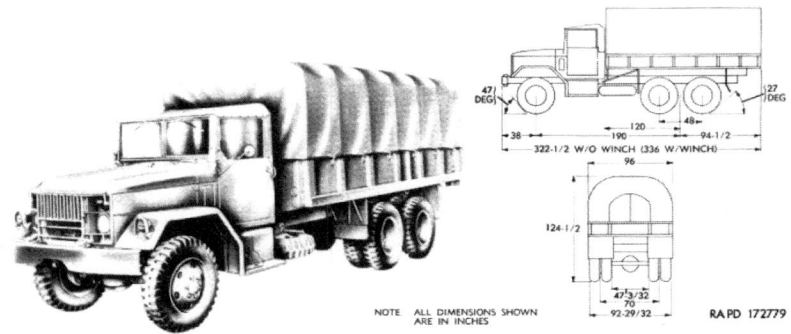

NOTE ALL DIMENSIONS SHOWN ARE IN INCHES

RAPD 172779

Technical Manuals: 9-819, 9-1819A, 9-1819B, 9-1825A, 9-1826D, 9-1827A, 9-1827C, 9-1828A; **Supply Catalog:** SNL G-742.

Purpose: To transport general cargo and personnel.

GENERAL DATA

Crew...2

Weight (lb).......................Net w/o winch 13,500; w/winch 13,915
  Payload:
    Off highway..5,000
    On highway..10,000
  Gross:
    Off highway................w/o winch 18,500; w/winch 18,915
    On highway................w/o winch 23,500; w/winch 23,915

Axle gear ratio...6.722:1

Axle load (lb):
  Empty:
    Front:
      W/o winch.............5,580; rear (each) w/o winch 3,960
      W/winch........................6,085; w/winch 3,915
  Loaded:
    Off highway:
      Front:
        W/o winch.............5,850; rear (each) w/o winch 6,325
        W/winch........................6,355; w/winch 6,280
    On highway:
      Front:
        W/o winch.............6,120; rear (each) w/o winch 8,690
        W/winch........................6,625; w/winch 8,645

Tires:
  Ply 8.........................Size 9.00 x 20; Pressure (psi) 45
  Tread, center-to-center, front............................(in.) 67⅜

Shipping dimensions, uncrated:
  W/o winch...........................(cu ft) 2,240; (sq ft) 217
  W/winch.............................(cu ft) 2,320; (sq ft) 223

Vehicle dimensions:
  Ground clearance......................................(in.) 12¹¹⁄₁₆
  Pintle height, empty...................................(in.) 34¾
  Loading height, empty..................................(in.) 51⅛
  Body inside dimensions (in.):
    Length..204
    Width..88
    Height...60
  Cargo space...(cu ft) 630

Electrical system.....................................(volts) 24
  No. of batteries..2
  Type of ground....................................negative

Fuel octane rating...80

GENERAL DATA—Continued

Capacities:
  Fuel...(gal) 50
  Cooling system......................................(qt) 22
  Crankcase, refill......................................(qt) 9
  Transmission (qt)..............w/o PTO 4¾; w/PTO 5¼
  Transfer..(qt) 7
  Axle...(each) (qt) 7
  Winch:
    Oil capacity.......................................(qt) 1
    Load capacity..................................(lb) 10,000

Brakes:
  Manufacturer..............Timken-Detroit; Type; air-hydraulic
  Parking brake, type..................................transfer

Transmission:
  Forward speeds...5
  Gear ratio........High 1:1; Fourth 1.45:1; Low 7.55:1

Transfer:
  Speeds...2
  Gear ratio........................High 1:1; Low 1.98:1

PERFORMANCE

Computed grade ability in lowest gear w/off-highway load.....(percent) 65
Turning radius..(ft) 45
Fording depth..(in.) 72
Fuel consumption, loaded.............................(mpg) 6
Cruising range, loaded...............................(mi) 300
Allowable speed, governed............................(mph) 58
Maximum pintle tow:
  Off highway..................................gross (lb) 6,000
  On highway..................................gross (lb) 10,000

ENGINE

Manufacturer: Reo.......................................Model 331 OA
Type.............4-cycle, valve-in-head; No. of cylinders (in line) 6
Displacement..(cu in.) 331
Bore...(in.) 4⅛
Stroke...(in.) 4⅛
Compression ratio....................................6.73:1
Governed speed......................................(rpm) 3,400
Brake horsepower (max w/std accessories)........127 at (rpm) 3,400
Torque (max w/std accessories)........248 lb-ft at (rpm) 1,400

ADDITIONAL DATA

Axles, type..........................double-reduction, full-floating
Transmission, type....................................synchromesh

TRUCK, CARGO, 2½-TON, 6 x 6, M135 W/ AND W/O WINCH

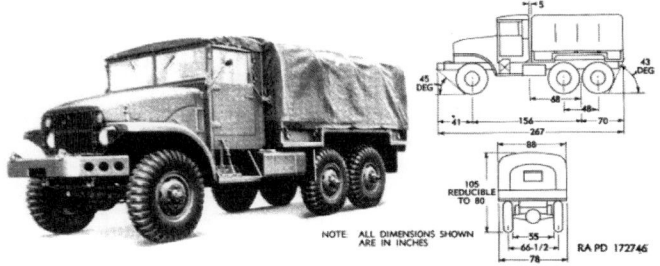

NOTE: ALL DIMENSIONS SHOWN ARE IN INCHES

RA PD 172746

Technical Manual: 9-819A; Supply Catalog: SNL G-749.

Purpose: To transport general cargo and personnel and tow 105-mm howitzer.

GENERAL DATA

Crew..2
Weight (lb):
  Net..w/o winch 12,330; w/winch 12,740
  Payload.........................off highway 5,000; on highway 10,000
  Gross:
    Off highway:
      W/o winch.......................................17,680
      W/winch...18,090
    On highway:
      W/o winch.......................................22,680
      W/winch...23,090
Live-axle gear ratio......................................6.17:1
Axle load (lb):
  Empty:
    Front:
      W/o winch..5,360
      W/winch...5,540
    Rear (each):
      W/o winch..3,485
      W/winch...3,600
  Loaded:
    Off highway:
      Front:
        W/o winch......................................5,780
        W/winch.......................................6,270
      Rear (each):
        W/o winch......................................5,950
        W/winch.......................................5,910
    On highway:
      Front:
        W/o winch......................................7,430
        W/winch.......................................7,970
      Rear (each):
        W/o winch......................................7,625
        W/winch.......................................7,560
Tires:
  Ply 12......................................Size 11.00 x 20
  Pressure (psi)..................On highway 70; off highway 35
  Tread, center-to-center, front.......................(in.) 71
Shipping dimensions, uncrated...............(cu ft) 1,425; (sq ft) 163
Vehicle dimensions:
  Ground clearance.................................(in.) 12½
  Pintle height, empty.............................(in.) 37½
  Loading height, empty...............................(in.) 45
  Body inside dimensions (in.):
    Length..................147; Width 80; Height 60
  Cargo space......................................(cu ft) 408
Electrical system..(volts) 24
  No. of batteries...2
  Type of ground.......................................negative

GENERAL DATA—Continued

Fuel octane rating..72
Capacities:
  Fuel...(gal) 56
  Cooling system.....................................(qt) 22
  Crankcase, refill...................................(qt) 11
  Transmission.......................................(qt) 15
  Transfer (qt)..........................w/PTO 3¾; w/o PTO 3¼
  Axles (qt)..............front 7¾; intermediate 6¾; rear 5¾
  Winch:
    Oil capacity.....................................(pt) 1¼
    Load capacity.................................(lb) 10,000
Brakes:
  Manufacturer....................Bendix; Type; air-hydraulic
  Parking brake, type...............................transfer
Transmission:
  Forward speeds..8
  High range................High 1:1; Third 1.55:1; Low 4.07:1
  Low range............High 3.82:1; Third 5.92:1; Low 15.55:1
Transfer:
  Speeds..1
  Gear ratio..1.16:1

PERFORMANCE

Computed grade ability in lowest gear w/off-highway load......(percent) 60
Turning radius...(ft) 35
Fording depth, w/o fording kit...........................(in.) 60
Fuel consumption, loaded..................................(mpg) 4
Cruising range, loaded...................................(mi) 224
Allowable speed, governed...............................(mph) 58
Maximum pintle tow:
  Off highway...............................gross (lb) 6,000
  On highway...............................gross (lb) 10,000

ENGINE

Manufacturer: GMC.................................Model 302
Type.................4-cycle, valve-in-head; No. of cylinders (in line) 6
Displacement..(cu in.) 302
Bore..(in.) 4
Stroke..(in.) 4
Compression ratio....................................7.2:1
Governed speed...................................(rpm) 3,400
Brake horsepower (max w/std accessories).........130 at (rpm) 3,200
Torque, maximum, gross...................262 lb-ft at (rpm) 1,200

ADDITIONAL DATA

Live axles, type.........................hypoid, full-floating
Transmission, type................................hydramatic

TRUCK, CARGO AND DUMP, 2½-TON, 6 x 6, W/ AND W/O WINCH

(GMC, Model CCKW353, LWB, 1941–42–43)

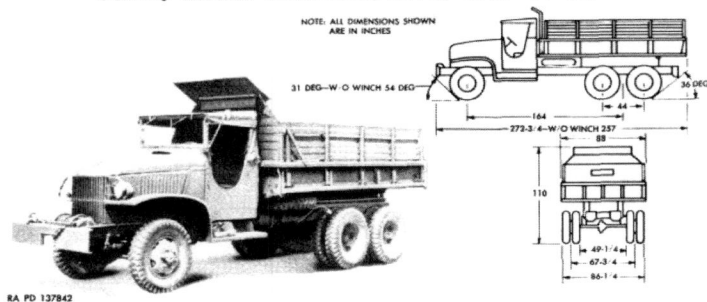

NOTE: ALL DIMENSIONS SHOWN ARE IN INCHES

RA PD 137842

Technical Manuals: 9-801; 9-1801; 9-1802A; 9-1825A; 9-1826C; 9-1827C; 9-1828A; **Supply Catalog:** SNL G-508.

Classification: Standard.

Purpose: To transport and dump earth, sand, gravel, coal, etc., and to carry general cargo.

GENERAL DATA

Crew..2
Weight (lb)...Net 11,950
   Payload:
      Off highway..............................5,350; Gross 17,300
      On highway..............................8,500; Gross 20,450
Live-axle gear ratio...6.6:1
Axle load (lb):
   Empty......................front 4,900; rear (each) 3,525
   Loaded:
      Off highway.............front 6,180; rear (each) 5,560
      On highway.............front 6,940; rear (each) 6,755
Tires:
   Ply 8.......................Size 7.50 x 20; Pressure (psi) 55
   Tread, center-to-center, front.................(in.) 62¼
Shipping dimensions, uncrated:
   W/winch..............................(cu ft) 1,530; (sq ft) 167
   W/o winch...........................(cu ft) 1,440; (sq ft) 157
Vehicle dimensions:
   Loading height, empty..........................(in.) 49½
   Ground clearance...................................(in.) 9⅞
   Pintle height, loaded.............................(in.) 31½
   Body inside dimensions (in.):
      Length 120....................Width 81½; Height 64
      Body cargo space.........................(cu ft) 340
Electrical system...................................(volts) 6
   No. of batteries...1
   Type of ground..................................negative
Fuel octane rating......................................70
Capacities:
   Fuel..(gal) 40
   Cooling system...............................(qt) 19
   Crankcase, refill (qt)....1-pc oil pan 10; 2-pc oil pan 7½
   Transfer......................................(qt) 3
   Transmission (qt)..........w/PTO 6¼; w/o PTO 4½
   Axles (qt).................................front 3
      Bogie.............................front 3; rear 2½
   Winch:
      Oil capacity..........................(qt) 1½
      Load capacity.......................(lb) 10,000
Brakes:
   Manufacturer...............GMC-Bendix; Type; hydrovac
   Parking brake, type..........................transfer
Transmission:
   Forward speeds.....................................5
   Gear ratio.........High 0.799:1; Fourth 1:1; Low 6.06:1

GENERAL DATA—Continued

Transfer:
   Speeds..2
   Gear ratio...........................High 1.16:1; Low 2.63:1

PERFORMANCE

Computed grade ability in lowest gear, loaded (percent).................65
Turning radius.......................................(ft) 35
Fording depth.......................................(in.) 30
Fuel consumption, loaded.......................(mpg) 7½
Cruising range, loaded..........................(mi) 300
Allowable speed, governed.....................(mph) 45
Maximum recommended towed load:, gross (lb):
   Off highway.......................................4,500
   On highway..7,500

ENGINE

Manufacturer: GMC..............................Model 270
Type.............Valve-in-head, 4-cycle; No. of cylinders (in line) 6
Displacement...............................(cu in.) 269.5
Bore...................................(in.) 3²⁵⁄₃₂
Stroke...(in.) 4
Compression ratio...........................6.75:1
Governed speed...........................(rpm) 2,750
Brake horsepower (max w/std accessories).............91.5 at (rpm) 2,750
Torque (max)...............216 lb-ft at (rpm) 1,400

ADDITIONAL DATA

   Weights and axle loads given for vehicle w/winch. Weight of winch 700 lb.
Live Axles, type..................spiral-bevel, full-floating
Transmission, type.........................constant-mesh
   Above data given for vehicles w/split-type axle. For vehicles w/banjo-type axle changes in data are as follows:
Tread dimensions (in.):
   Front...60
   Rear..67½
      Outside to outside..........................86
      Inside to inside.............................49
Capacities:
   Transfer......................................(qt) 2¼
   Axles (qt)...................................front 6½
      Bogie.......................front 6½; rear 4¼

TRUCK, CHASSIS, 2½-TON, 6 x 6

(GMC, Models CCKWX353, 1941; CCKW353, 1941–42–43, LWB)

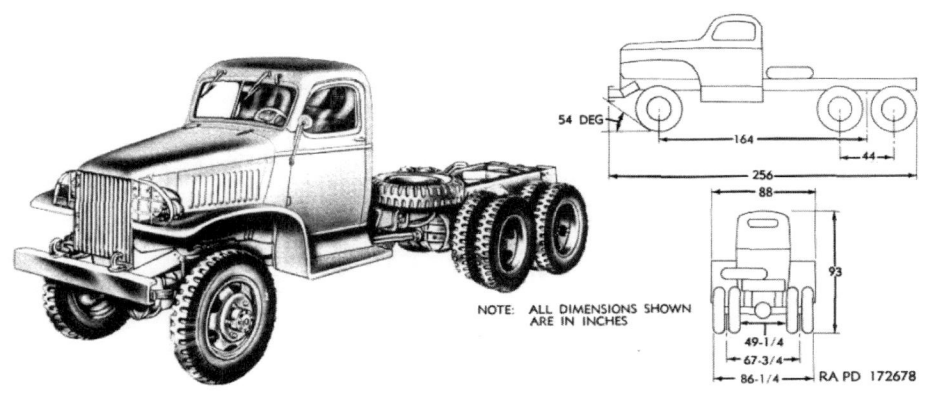

NOTE: ALL DIMENSIONS SHOWN ARE IN INCHES

RA PD 172678

Technical Manuals: 9-801, 9-1801, 9-1802A, 9-1825A, 9-1826C, 9-1827C, 9-1828A; Supply Catalog: SNL G-508.

Vehicle illustrated: Model CCKW353.
Classification: Standard.

Purpose: For use as component of cargo or special-equipment vehicle.

GENERAL DATA

Crew..1
Weight (lb)..Net 8,100
Live-axle gear ratio...6.6:1
Axle load (lb).............................front 4,290; rear (each) 1,905
Tires:
  Ply 8.................................Size 7.50 x 20; Pressure (psi) 55
  Tread, center-to-center, front................................(in.) 62¼
Shipping dimensions, uncrated....................(cu ft) 1,220; (sq ft) 157
Vehicle dimensions:
  Ground clearance...(in.) 9⅜
  Pintle height, loaded....................................(in.) 31½
Electrical system...(volts) 6
  No. of batteries...1
  Type of ground...................................negative
Fuel octane rating..70
Capacities:
  Fuel..(gal) 40
  Cooling system.......................................(qt) 19
  Crankcase, refill (qt)............1-pc oil pan 10; 2-pc oil pan 7½
  Transmission...(qt) 4½
  Transfer...(qt) 3
  Axles (qt)..front 3
    Bogie.....................................front 3; rear 2½
Brakes:
  Manufacturer............GMC-Bendix; Type, hydrovac
  Parking brake, type.............................transfer
Transmission:
  Forward speeds..5
  Gear ratio........High 0.799:1; Fourth 1:1; Low 6.06:1
Transfer:
  Speeds..2
  Gear ratio........................High 1.16:1; Low 2.63:1

PERFORMANCE

Computed grade ability in lowest gear, loaded..............(percent) 65
Turning radius...(ft) 35
Fording depth...(in.) 30
Fuel consumption..(mpg) 9
Cruising range..(mi) 360
Allowable speed, governed...................................(mph) 45
Maximum recommended towed load:
  Off highway..gross (lb) 4,500
  On highway...gross (lb) 7,500

ENGINE

Manufacturer: GMC.....................................Model 270
Type..................Valve-in-head, 4-cycle; No. of cylinders (in line) 6
Displacement..(cu in.) 269.5
Bore..(in.) 3²⁵⁄₃₂
Stroke..(in.) 4
Compression ratio...6.75:1
Governed speed..(rpm) 2,750
Brake horsepower (max w/std accessories)..............91.5 at (rpm) 2,750
Torque (max)..............................216 lb-ft at (rpm) 1,400

ADDITIONAL DATA

Live axles, type.............................spiral-bevel, full-floating
Transmission, type.................................constant-mesh
  Data given for vehicle with split-type axle. For banjo-type axle, changes in data are as follows:
Tread dimensions:
  Front..(in.) 60
  Rear...(in.) 67½
    Outside to outside.................................(in.) 86
    Inside to inside...................................(in.) 49
Capacities:
  Transfer...(qt) 2¼
  Axles (qt)..front 6½
    Bogie...front 6½; rear 5¼

TRUCK, CHASSIS, 2½-TON, 6 x 6, W/WINCH
(GMC, Model CCKWX353, LWB, 1941)

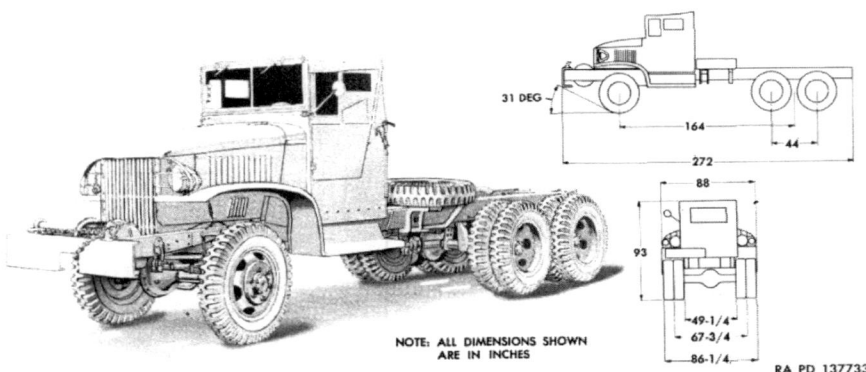

NOTE: ALL DIMENSIONS SHOWN
ARE IN INCHES

31 DEG

164

44

272

88

93

49-1/4
67-3/4
86-1/4

RA PD 137733

Technical Manuals: 9–801; 9–1801; 9–1802A; 9–1825A; 9–1826C; 9–1828A; Supply Catalog: SNL G–508.

Classification: Standard.

Purpose: For use as component of cargo or special equipment vehicle.

GENERAL DATA

Crew..1
Weight (lb)...Net 8,800
Live-axle gear ratio..6.6:1
Axle load (lb)....................front 4,990; rear (each) 1,905
Tires:
  Ply 8; Size 7.50 x 20; Pressure.....................(psi) 55
  Tread, center-to-center, front........................(in.) 62¼
Shipping dimensions, uncrated....................(cu ft) 1,290; (sq ft) 166
Vehicle dimensions:
  Ground clearance...(in.) 9¾
  Pintle height, loaded...................................(in.) 31½
Electrical system..(volts) 6
  No. of batteries...1
  Type of ground.......................................negative
Fuel octane rating...70
Capacities:
  Fuel..(gal) 40
  Cooling system...(qt) 19
  Crankcase, refill (qt.)..........1-pc oil pan 10; 2-pc oil pan 7½
  Transmission...(qt) 6¼
  Transfer...(qt) 3
  Axles (qt)..front 3
  Bogie.................................front 3; rear 2½
  Winch:
    Oil capacity..(qt) 1½
    Load capacity....................................(lb) 10,000
Brakes:
  Manufacturer: GMC-Bendix.....................Type: hydrovac
  Parking brake, type................................transfer
Transmission:
  Forward speeds..5
  Gear ratio..........High 0.799:1; Fourth 1:1; Low 6.06:1
Transfer:
  Speeds...2
  Gear ratio.........................High 1.16:1; Low 2.63:1

PERFORMANCE

Computed grade ability in lowest gear, loaded.............(percent) 65
Turning radius...(ft) 35
Fording depth...(in.) 30
Fuel consumption..(mpg) 9
Cruising range..(mi) 360
Allowable speed, governed..............................(mph) 45
Maximum recommended towed load, gross.............(lb) 10,000

ENGINE

Manufacturer: GMC..................................Model 270
Type..................Valve-in-head, 4-cycle; No. of cylinders (in line) 6
Displacement..(cu in.) 269.5
Bore..(in.) 3²⁵⁄₃₂
Stroke..(in.) 4
Compression ratio.......................................6.75:1
Governed speed.......................................(rpm) 2,750
Brake horsepower (max w/std accessories)..........91.5 at (rpm) 2,750
Torque (max)...........................216 lb-ft at (rpm) 1,400

ADDITIONAL DATA

Live axles, type.......................spiral-bevel, full-floating
Transmission, type..................................constant-mesh
  Data given for vehicle with split-type axle. For banjo-type axle, changes in data are as follows:
Tread dimensions:
  Front..(in.) 60
  Rear..(in.) 67½
    Outside to outside...............................(in.) 86
    Inside to inside...................................(in.) 49
Capacities:
  Transfer...(qt) 2¼
  Axles (qt)...front 6½
    Bogie.............................front 6½; rear 5¼

TRUCK, DUMP, 2½-TON, 6 x 6, M47, W/ AND W/O WINCH

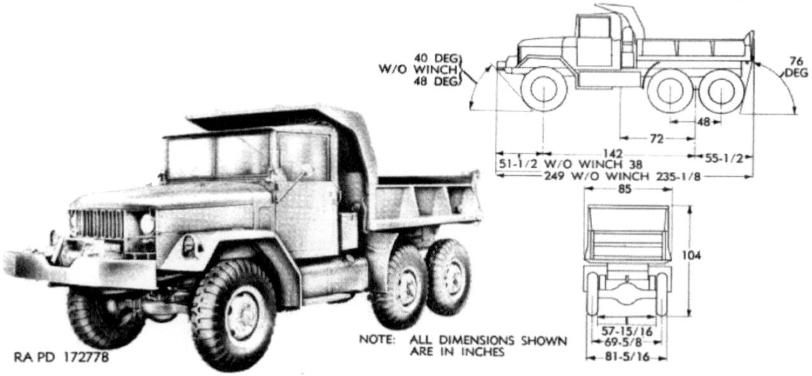

40 DEG
W/O WINCH
48 DEG
76 DEG
48
72
142
55-1/2
51-1/2 W/O WINCH 38
249 W/O WINCH 235-1/8
85
104
57-15/16
69-5/8
81-5/16
NOTE: ALL DIMENSIONS SHOWN ARE IN INCHES
RA PD 172778

Technical Manuals: 9-819, 9-1819A, 9-1819B, 9-1825A, 9-1826D, 9-1827A, 9-1827C, 9-1828A; **Supply Catalog:** SNL G-742.

Purpose: To haul and dump earth, sand, gravel, coal, etc., and to transport general cargo.

GENERAL DATA

Crew ... 2

Weight (lb):
- Net ... w/o winch 13,540; w/winch 13,860
- Payload:
  - Off highway ... 5,000
  - On highway ... 10,000
- Gross:
  - Off highway ... w/o winch 18,450; w/winch 18,860
  - On highway ... w/o winch 23,450; w/winch 23,860

Axle gear ratio ... 6.722:1

Axle load (lb):
- Empty:
  - Front:
    - W/o winch ... 5,580; rear (each) w/o winch 3,935
    - W/winch ... 6,110; w/o winch 3,875
- Loaded:
  - Off highway:
    - Front:
      - W/o winch ... 5,630; rear (each) w/o winch 6,410
      - W/winch ... 6,110: w/o winch 6,350
  - On highway:
    - Front:
      - W/o winch ... 5,680: rear (each) w/o winch 8,885
      - W/winch ... 6,210: w/o winch 8,825

Tires:
- Ply 12 ... Size 11.00 x 20; Pressure (psi) 50
- Tread, center-to-center, front ... (in.) 69⅝

Shipping dimensions, uncrated:
- W/o winch ... (cu ft) 1,200; (sq ft) 139
- W/winch ... (cu ft) 1,270; (sq ft) 147

Vehicle dimensions:
- Ground clearance ... (in.) 13¾
- Pintle height, empty ... (in.) 34⅞
- Body inside dimensions (in.):
  - Length ... 108; Width 70; Height 15
- Struck capacity ... (cu yds) 2½

Electrical system ... (volts) 24
- No. of batteries ... 2
- Type of ground ... negative

Fuel octane rating ... 80

Brakes:
- Manufacturer ... Timken-Detroit; Type; air-hydraulic
- Parking brake, type ... transfer

GENERAL DATA—Continued

Capacities:
- Fuel ... (gal) 50
- Cooling system ... (qt) 22
- Crankcase, refill ... (qt) 9
- Transmission (qt) ... w/o PTO 4¼; w/PTO 5¼
- Transfer ... (qt) 7
- Axles (each) ... (qt) 7
- Winch:
  - Oil capacity ... (qt) 1
  - Load capacity ... (lb) 10,000

Transmission:
- Forward speeds ... 5
- Gear ratio ... High 1:1; Fourth 1.45:1; Low 7.55:1

Transfer:
- Speeds ... 2
- Gear ratio ... High 1:1; Low 1.98:1

PERFORMANCE

Computed grade ability in lowest gear, w/off-highway load ... (percent) 65

Turning radius ... (ft) 35

Fording depth ... (in.) 72

Fuel consumption, loaded ... (mpg) 6

Cruising range, loaded ... (mi) 300

Allowable speed, governed ... (mph) 62

Maximum pintle tow:
- Off highway ... gross (lb) 6,000
- On highway ... gross (lb) 10,000

ENGINE

Manufacturer: Reo ... Model 331 OA

Type ... 4-cycle, valve-in-head; No. of cylinders (in line) 6

Displacement ... (cu in.) 331

Bore ... (in.) 4⅛

Stroke ... (in.) 4⅛

Compression ratio ... 6.73:1

Governed speed ... (rpm) 3,400

Brake horsepower (max w/std accessories) ... 127 at (rpm) 3,400

Torque (max w/std accessories) ... 248 lb-ft at (rpm) 1,400

ADDITIONAL DATA

Axles, type ... double-reduction, full-floating

Transmission, type ... synchromesh

TRUCK, GASOLINE TANK, 2½-TON, 6 x 6, 750-GAL

(GMC, Models CCKW353, 1941–42–43; CCKWX353, 1941, LWB)

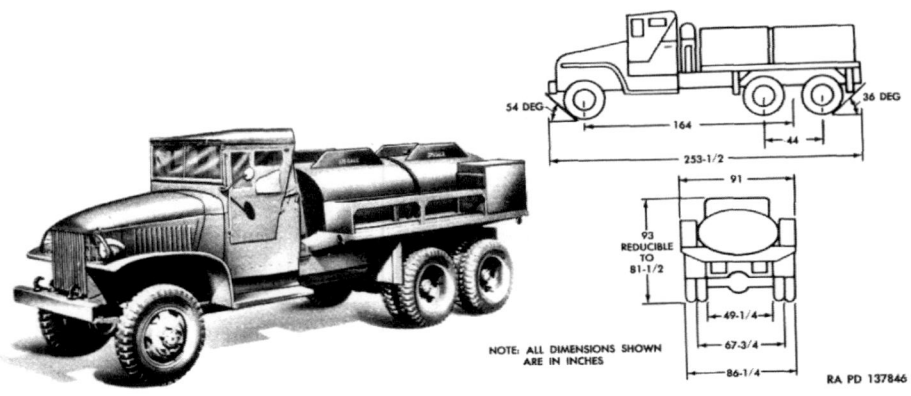

54 DEG
36 DEG
164
44
253-1/2
91
93 REDUCIBLE TO 81-1/2
49-1/4
67-3/4
86-1/4

NOTE: ALL DIMENSIONS SHOWN ARE IN INCHES

RA PD 137846

Technical Manuals: 9-801, 9-1801, 9-1802A, 9-1825A, 9-1826C, 9-1827B, 9-1827C, 9-1828A; **Supply Catalog:** SNL G-508.

Classification: Standard.

Purpose: To transport and dispense gasoline.

GENERAL DATA

Crew...2
Weight (lb)......................Net 10,750; Payload 5,350; Gross 16,100
Live-axle gear ratio..6.6:1
Axle load (lb):
    Empty...................................front 4,126; rear (each) 3,312
    Loaded.................................front 4,480; rear (each) 5,810
Tires:
    Ply 8........................Size 7.50 x 20; Pressure (psi) 55
    Tread, center-to-center, front.........................(in.) 62¾
Shipping dimensions, uncrated................(cu ft) 1,242; (sq ft) 160
Ground clearance...(in.) 9⅝
Electrical system...(volts) 6
    No. of batteries..1
    Type of ground.......................................negative
Fuel octane rating..70
Capacities:
    Fuel...(gal) 40
    Cooling system...(qt) 19
    Crankcase, refill (qt)...........1-pc oil pan 10; 2-pc oil pan 7½
    Transfer..(qt) 3
    Transmission...(qt) 4½
    Axles (qt)...front 3
    Bogie..front 3; rear 2½
Brakes:
    Manufacturer................GMC-Bendix; Type; hydrovac
    Parking brake, type.................................transfer
Transmission:
    Forward speeds..5
    Gear ratio.........High 0.799:1; Fourth 1:1; Low 6.06:1
Transfer:
    Speeds..2
    Gear ratio......................High 1.16:1; Low 2.63:1

PERFORMANCE

Computed grade ability in lowest gear, loaded................(percent) 65
Turning radius...(ft) 35
Fording depth...(in.) 30
Fuel consumption, loaded....................................(mpg) 7½
Cruising range, loaded......................................(mi) 300
Allowable speed, governed...................................(mph) 45

ENGINE

Manufacturer: GMC..Model 270
Type.................Valve-in-head, 4-cycle; No. of cylinders (in line) 6
Displacement...(cu in.) 269.5
Bore...(in.) 3¹³⁄₃₂
Stroke...(in.) 4
Compression ratio...6.75:1
Governed speed..(rpm) 2,750
Brake horsepower (max w/std accessories)............91.5 at (rpm) 2,750
Torque (max)..........................216 lb-ft at (rpm) 1,400

ADDITIONAL DATA

Live axles, type.............................spiral-bevel, full-floating
Transmission, type..................................constant-mesh
Data given for vehicle with split-type axle. For banjo-type axle, changes
in data are as follows:
Tread dimensions:
    Front...(in.) 60
    Rear...(in.) 67½
        Outside to outside...............................(in.) 86
        Inside to inside.................................(in.) 49
Capacities:
    Transfer..(qt) 2¾
    Axles (qt)...front 6½
    Bogie................................front 6½; rear 5¼

TRUCK, SHOP VAN, 2½-TON, 6 x 6

GMC, Model CCKW353, w/ST5 Non-Collapsible Body)

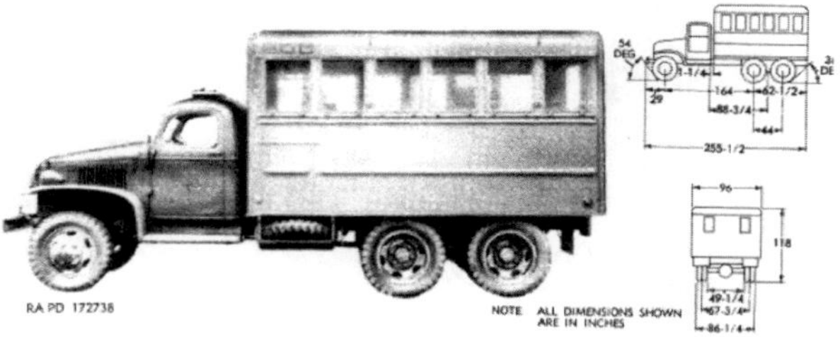
RA PD 172738
54 DEG
29
164
62-1/2
88-3/4
44
255-1/2
96
118
49-1/4
67-3/4
86-1/4
NOTE ALL DIMENSIONS SHOWN ARE IN INCHES

Technical Manuals: 9-801, 9-1801, 9-1802A, 9-1825A, 9-1826C, 9-1827B, 9-1827C, 9-1828A, 9-1829A; **Supply Catalogs:** SNL G-138, 139, 140, 141, 142, 146, 229, 508

GENERAL DATA

Crew	2
Weight (lb)	Net 10,100; Payload 5,000; Gross 15,100
Axle gear ratio	6.66:1
Axle load (lb):	
Empty	front 3,366; rear (each) 3,367
Loaded	front 3,856; rear (each) 5,622
Tires:	
Ply 8	Size 7.50 x 20; Pressure (psi) 55
Tread, center-to-center, front	(in.) 62¼
Shipping dimensions, uncrated	(cu ft) 1,690; (sq ft) 171
Vehicle dimensions:	
Ground clearance	(in.) 9⅞
Pintle height, empty	(in.) 31½
Loading height, empty	(in.) 40½
Body inside dimensions (in.):	
Length	144
Width	90
Height	75½
Cargo space	(cu ft) 565
Electrical system	(volts) 6
No. of batteries	1
Type of ground	negative
Fuel octane rating	70
Capacities:	
Fuel	(gal) 40
Cooling system	(qt) 19
Crankcase, refill (qt)	1-pc oil pan 10; 2-pc oil pan 7½
Transmission	(qt) 4½
Transfer	(qt) 3
Axles (qt)	front 3
Bogie	front 3; rear 2½
Brakes:	
Manufacturer	GMC-Bendix; Type; hydrovac
Parking brake, type	transfer
Transmission:	
Forward speeds	5
Gear ratio	High 0.799:1; Fourth 1:1; Low 6.06:1
Transfer:	
Speeds	2
Gear ratio	High 1.16:1; Low 2.63:1

PERFORMANCE

Computed grade ability in lowest gear, loaded	(percent) 65
Turning radius (ft)	Right 35; Left 36
Fording depth	(in.) 30
Fuel consumption, loaded	(mpg) 7½
Cruising range, loaded	(mi) 300
Allowable speed, governed	(mph) 45
Maximum pintle tow:	
Off highway	gross (lb) 4,500
On highway	gross (lb) 7,500

Classification: Nonclassified.

Purpose: To provide mobile facilities for maintenance and repair for various services.

ENGINE

Manufacturer: GMC	Model 270
Type	4-cycle, valve-in-head; No. of cylinders (in line) 6
Displacement	(cu in.) 270
Bore	(in.) 3 25/32
Stroke	(in.) 4
Compression ratio	6.75:1
Governed speed	(rpm) 2,750
Brake horsepower (max w/std accessories)	92 at (rpm) 2,750
Torque (max w/std accessories)	216 lb-ft at (rpm) 1,400

ADDITIONAL DATA

Axles, type	spiral-bevel, full-floating
Transmission, type	constant-mesh

Insulated body and personnel heater.

Above data given for vehicles with split axle; for banjo axle, changes in data are as follows:

Tread dimensions:	
Front	(in.) 60
Rear	(in.) 67½
Outside to outside	(in.) 86
Inside to inside	(in.) 49
Capacities:	
Transfer	(qt) 2¾
Axles (qt)	front 6½
Bogie	front 6½; rear 5½

The same chassis and body is also used in the following vehicles:

Truck, 2½-ton, 6 x 6, Artillery Repair, M9	(L Std)
Truck, 2½-ton, 6 x 6, Artillery Repair, M9A1	(Std)
Truck, 2½-ton, 6 x 6, Automotive Repair, Load A, M8	(L Std)
Truck, 2½-ton, 6 x 6, Automotive Repair, Load B, M8	(L Std)
Truck, 2½-ton, 6 x 6, Electrical Repair, M18	(L Std)
Truck, 2½-ton, 6 x 6, Instrument Repair, Load A, M10	(L Std)
Truck, 2½-ton, 6 x 6, Instrument Repair, Load B, M10	(L Std)
Truck, 2½-ton, 6 x 6, Instrument Repair, Load A, M10A1	(Std)
Truck, 2½-ton, 6 x 6, Instrument Repair, Load B, M10A1	(Std)
Truck, 2½-ton, 6 x 6, Machine Shop, Load A, M16	(L Std)
Truck, 2½-ton, 6 x 6, Machine Shop, Load B, M16	(L Std)
Truck, 2½-ton, 6 x 6, Machine Shop, Load B1, M16	(L Std)
Truck, 2½-ton, 6 x 6, Machine Shop, Load B2, M16	(L Std)
Truck, 2½-ton, 6 x 6, Machine Shop, Load C, M16	(L Std)
Truck, 2½-ton, 6 x 6, Machine Shop, Load D, M16	(L Std)
Truck, 2½-ton, 6 x 6, Machine Shop, Load F, M16	(L Std)
Truck, 2½-ton, 6 x 6, Small Arms Repair, M7	(L Std)
Truck, 2½-ton, 6 x 6, Small Arms Repair (Signal Corps), M7	(L Std)
Truck, 2½-ton, 6 x 6, Spare Parts, Load A, M14	(L Std)
Truck, 2½-ton, 6 x 6, Spare Parts, Load B, M14	(L Std)
Truck, 2½-ton, 6 x 6, Welding, M12	(L Std)

TRUCK, SHOP VAN, 2½-TON, 6 x 6, M535

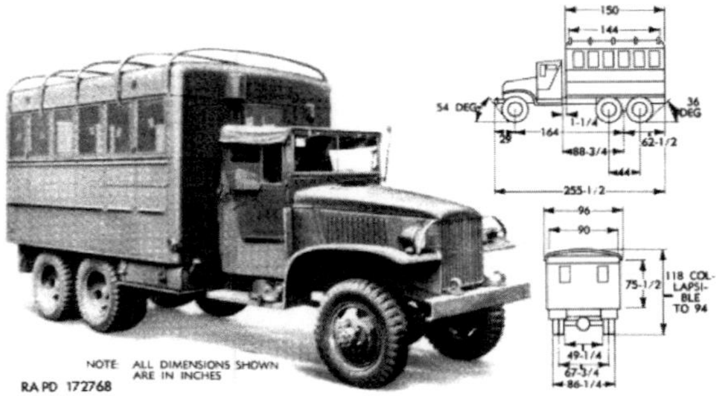

150
144
54 DEG
36 DEG
1-1/4
29
164
62-1/2
88-3/4
44
255-1/2
96
90
75-1/2
118 COL-LAPSI-BLE TO 94
49-1/4
67-3/4
86-1/4
NOTE: ALL DIMENSIONS SHOWN ARE IN INCHES
RA PD 172768

Technical Manuals: 9-801, 9-1801, 9-1802A, 9-1825A, 9-1826C, 9-1827B, 9-1827C, 9-1828A, 9-1829A; **Supply Catalogs:** SNL G-138, 139, 142, 146, 149, 178, 229, 234, 235, 508

Classification: Standard.

GENERAL DATA

Crew	2
Weight (lb)	Net 10,100; Payload 5,000; Gross 15,100
Axle gear ratio	6.66:1
Axle load (lb):	
Empty	front 3,366; rear (each) 3,367
Loaded	front 3,856; rear (each) 5,622
Tires:	
Ply 8	Size 7.50 x 20; Pressure (psi) 55
Tread, center-to-center, front	(in.) 62¼
Shipping dimensions, uncrated	(cu ft) 1,340; (sq ft) 171
Vehicle dimensions:	
Ground clearance	(in.) 9⅞
Pintle height, empty	(in.) 31½
Loading height, empty	(in.) 40½
Electrical system	(volts) 6
No. of batteries	1
Type of ground	negative
Fuel octane rating	70
Capacities:	
Fuel	(gal) 40
Cooling system	(qt) 19
Crankcase, refill (qt)	1-pc oil pan 10; 2-pc oil pan 7½
Transmission	(qt) 4½
Transfer	(qt) 3
Axles (qt)	front 3
Bogie	front 3; rear 2½
Brakes:	
Manufacturer	GMC-Bendix; Type; hydrovac
Parking brake, type	transfer
Transmission:	
Forward speeds	5
Gear ratio	High 0.799:1; Fourth 1:1; Low 6.06:1
Transfer:	
Speeds	2
Gear ratio	High 1.16:1; Low 2.63:1

PERFORMANCE

Computed grade ability in lowest gear, loaded	(percent) 65
Turning radius (ft)	Right 35; Left 36
Fording depth	(in.) 30
Fuel consumption, loaded	(mpg) 7½
Cruising range, loaded	(mi) 300
Allowable speed, governed	(mpg) 45
Maximum pintle tow:	
Off highway	gross (lb) 4,500
On highway	gross (lb) 7,500

Purpose: To provide mobile facilites for maintenance and repair for various services.

ENGINE

Manufacturer: GMC	Model 270
Type	4-cycle, valve-in-head; No. of cylinders (in line) 6
Displacement	(cu in.) 270
Bore	(in.) $3\frac{25}{32}$
Stroke	(in.) 4
Compression ratio	6.75:1
Governed speed	(rpm) 2,750
Brake horsepower (max w/std accessories)	92 at (rpm) 2,750
Torque (max w/std accessories)	216 lb-ft at (rpm) 1,400

ADDITIONAL DATA

Axles, type	spiral-bevel, full-floating
Transmission, type	constant-mesh

Insulated body and personnel heater.

Above data given for vehicles with split axle; for banjo axle, changes in data are as follows:

Tread dimensions:	
Front	(in.) 60
Rear	(in.) 67½
Outside to outside	(in.) 86
Inside to inside	(in.) 49
Capacities:	
Transfer	(qt) 2¼
Axles (qt)	Front 6½
Bogie	front 6½; rear 5½

The same chassis and body is also used in the following vehicles:

Truck, 2½-ton, 6 x 6, Automotive Repair, Load A, M8A1	(L Std)
Truck, 2½-ton, 6 x 6, Automotive Repair, Load B, M8A1	(L Std)
Truck, 2½-ton, 6 x 6, Electrical Repair, M18A1	(L Std)
Truck, 2½-ton, 6 x 6, Electrical Repair, M18A2	(Std)
Truck, 2½-ton, 6 x 6, Instrument Bench, M23	(Std)
Truck, 2½-ton, 6 x 6, Machine Shop, Load A, M16A1	(L Std)
Truck, 2½-ton, 6 x 6, Machine Shop, Load B, M16A1	(L Std)
Truck, 2½-ton, 6 x 6, Machine Shop, Load B1, M16A1	(L Std)
Truck, 2½-ton, 6 x 6, Machine Shop, Load B2, M16A1	(L Std)
Truck, 2½-ton, 6 x 6, Machine Shop, Load C, M16A1	(Std)
Truck, 2½-ton, 6 x 6, Machine Shop, Load D, M16A1	(Std)
Truck, 2½-ton, 6 x 6, Machine Shop, Load F, M16A1	(Std)
Truck, 2½-ton, 6 x 6, Machine Shop, Load A, M16A2	(Std)
Truck, 2½-ton, 6 x 6, Machine Shop, Load B, M16A2	(Std)
Truck, 2½-ton, 6 x 6, Signal Corps General Repair, M30	(Std)
Truck, 2½-ton, 6 x 6, Signal Corps General Repair, M31	(Std)
Truck, 2½-ton, 6 x 6, Small Arms Repair, M7A1	(L Std)
Truck, 2½-ton, 6 x 6, Small Arms Repair, M7A2	(Std)
Truck, 2½-ton, 6 x 6, Tire Repair, Load A, M32	(Std)
Truck, 2½-ton, 6 x 6, Tire Repair, Load B, M32	(Std)
Truck, 2½-ton, 6 x 6, Welding, M12A1	(L Std)

TRUCK, TRACTOR, 2½-TON, 6 x 6, M48, W/ AND W/O WINCH

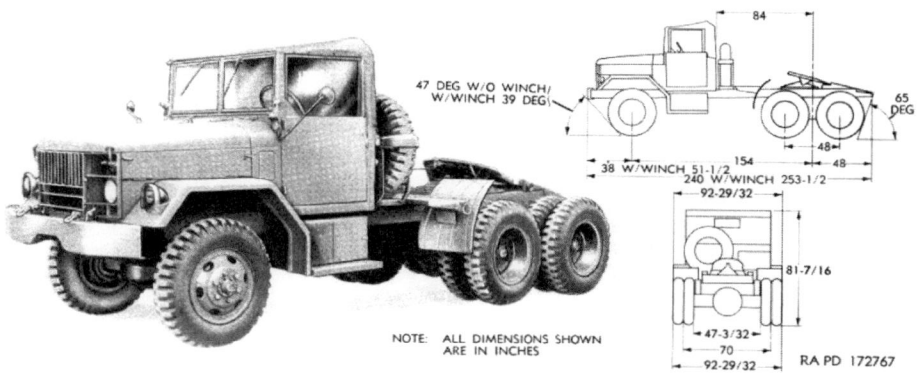

47 DEG W/O WINCH/
W/WINCH 39 DEG

84

65 DEG

48

38 W/WINCH 51-1/2
240 W/WINCH 253-1/2
154
48

92-29/32

81-7/16

NOTE: ALL DIMENSIONS SHOWN
ARE IN INCHES

47-3/32
70
92-29/32

RA PD 172767

Technical Manuals: 9–819, 9–1819A, 9–1819B, 9–1825A, 9–1826D, 9–1827A, 9–1827C, 9–1828A; Supply Catalog: SNL G–742.

GENERAL DATA

Crew..2
Weight (lb):
  Net....................................w/o winch 11,430; w/winch 11,841
  Payload:
    Off highway..7,000
    On highway..12,000
  Gross:
    Off highway...............w/o winch 18,430; w/winch 18,841
    On highway...............w/o winch 23,430; w/winch 23,841
Axle gear ratio.......................................6.722:1
Axle load (lb):
  Empty:
    Front:
      W/o winch...........5,420; rear (each) w/o winch 3,005
      W/winch....................5,915; w/winch 2,963
  Loaded:
    Off highway:
      Front:
        W/o winch...........5,600; rear (each) w/o winch 6,415
        W/winch....................6,097; w/winch 6,372
    On highway:
      Front:
        W/o winch...........5,227; rear (each) w/o winch 8,850
        W/winch....................5,730; w/winch 8,807
Tires:
  Ply 8....................Size 9.00 x 20; Pressure (psi) 45
  Tread, center-to-center, front...............(in.) 67¾
Shipping dimensions, uncrated:
  W/o winch..........................(cu ft) 1,058; (sq ft) 155
  W/winch............................(cu ft) 1,118; (sq ft) 164
Vehicle dimensions:
  Ground clearance....................................(in.) 12¾
  Pintle height, empty...............................(in.) 34⅜₆
  Height to center of fifth wheel, empty.............(in.) 51½
  Height to rear of fifth wheel, empty..............(in.) 39⅛₆
  Fifth wheel mounted forward of bogie axle..........(in.) 4
Electrical system...................................(volts) 24
  No. of batteries................................(12-volts) 2
  Type of ground....................................negative
Fuel octane rating.....................................80
Brakes:
  Manufacturer.............Timken-Detroit; Type; air hydraulic
  Parking brake, type..................................transfer

Purpose: To tow semitrailers.

GENERAL DATA—Continued

Capacities:
  Fuel..(gal) 50
  Cooling system....................................(qt) 22
  Crankcase, refill..................................(qt) 9
  Transmission (qt)................w/o PTO 4¾; w/PTO 5¾
  Transfer..(qt) 7
  Axles......................................(each) (qt) 7
  Winch:
    Oil capacity......................................(qt) 1
    Load capacity................................(lb) 10,000
Transmission:
  Forward speeds..5
  Gear ratio...........High 1:1; Fourth 1.45:1; Low 7.55:1
Transfer:
  Speeds..2
  Gear ratio...........................High 1:1; Low 1.98:1

PERFORMANCE

Computed grade ability in lowest gear, w/off-highway load.....(percent) 40
Turning radius..(ft) 36
Fording depth...(in.) 72
Fuel consumption, loaded..............................(mpg) 6
Cruising range, loaded................................(mi) 300
Allowable speed, governed.............................(mph) 58
Maximum pintle tow:
  Off highway...................................gross (lb) 6,000
  On highway...................................gross (lb) 10,000
Maximum semitrailer, gross............................(lb) 25,000

ENGINE

Manufacturer: Reo...........................Model 331 OA
Type..............4-cycle, valve-in-head; No. of cylinders (in line) 6
Displacement..(cu in.) 331
Bore..(in.) 4⅛
Stroke..(in.) 4⅜
Compression ratio.....................................6.73:1
Governed speed..(rpm) 3,400
Brake horsepower (max w/std accessories)........127 at (rpm) 3,400
Torque (max w/std accessories).............248 lb-ft at (rpm) 1,400

ADDITIONAL DATA

Axles, type......................double-reduction, full-floating
Transmission, type...................................synchromesh

241

TRUCK, WATER TANK, 2½-TON, 6 x 6, 700-GAL

(GMC, Model CCKW353, LWB, 1941–42–43)

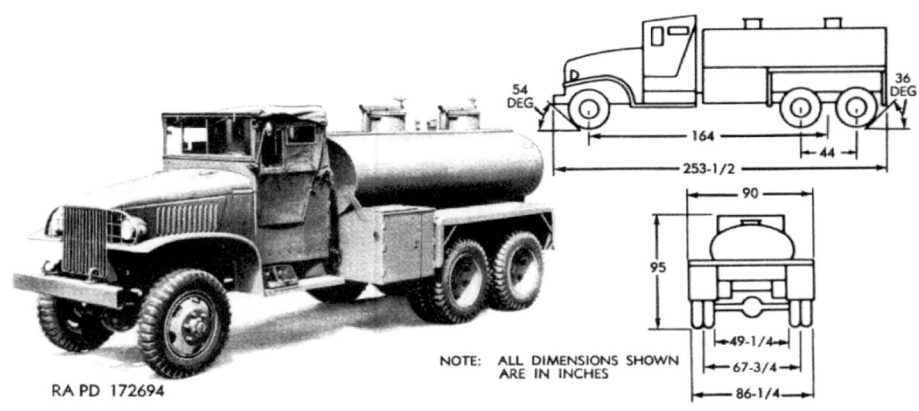

NOTE: ALL DIMENSIONS SHOWN ARE IN INCHES

RA PD 172694

Technical Manuals: 9-801, 9-1801, 9-1802A, 9-1825A, 9-1826C, 9-1827B, 9-1828A; Supply Catalog: SNL G-508.

Classification: Standard.

Purpose: To transport drinking water.

GENERAL DATA

Crew...2
Weight (lb)....................Net 11,913; Payload 5,350; Gross 17,263
Live-axle gear ratio...6.6:1
Axle load (lb,):
    Empty...front 4,261; rear (each) 3,826
    Loaded...front 6,151; rear (each) 5,556
Tires:
    Ply 8.....................................Size 7.50 x 20; Pressure (psi) 55
    Tread, center-to-center, front.............................(in.) 62¼
Shipping dimensions, uncrated.........(cu ft) 1,260; (sq ft) 159
Ground clearance...(in.) 9⅞
Electrical system...(volts) 6
    No. of batteries...1
    Type of ground...negative
Fuel octane rating..70
Capacities:
    Fuel..(gal) 40
    Cooling system.......................................(qt) 19
    Crankcase, refill (qt)..............1-pc oil pan 10; 2-pc oil pan 7½
    Transfer...(qt) 3
    Transmission..(qt) 4½
    Axles (qt)..front 3
    Bogie...front 3; rear 2½
Brakes:
    Manufacturer.......................GMC-Bendix; Type; hydrovac
    Parking brake, type...transfer
Transmission:
    Forward speeds..5
    Gear ratio.................High 0.799:1; Fourth 1:1; Low 6.06:1
Transfer:
    Speeds..2
    Gear ratio...............................High 1.16:1; Low 2.63:1

PERFORMANCE

Computed grade ability in lowest gear, loaded.................(percent) 65
Turning radius...(ft) 33
Fording depth...(in.) 30
Fuel consumption, loaded..(mpg) 7½
Cruising range, loaded...(mi) 300
Allowable speed, governed.......................................(mph) 45

ENGINE

Manufacturer: GMC..Model 270
Type....................Valve-in-head, 4-cycle; No. of cylinders (in line) 6
Displacement..(cu in.) 269.5
Bore...(in.) 32⁵⁄₃₂
Stroke...(in.) 4
Compression ratio...6.75:1
Governed speed..(rpm) 2,750
Brake horsepower (max w/std accessories)...............91.5 at (rpm) 2,750
Torque (max)..................................216 lb-ft at (rpm) 1,400

ADDITIONAL DATA

Live axles, type...........................spiral-bevel, full-floating
Transmission, type....................................constant-mesh
    Data given for vehicle with split-type axle. For banjo-type, changes in
data are as follows:
    Tread, center-to-center, front 60 in.; rear 67½ in., outside to outside
86 in., inside to inside 49 in.
Capacities:
    Transfer...(qt) 2¾
    Axles (qt)..front 6½
    Bogie...front 6½; rear 5¾

TRUCK, CARGO, 4-TON, 6 x 6

(Diamond T, Model 968A, SWB, 1942)

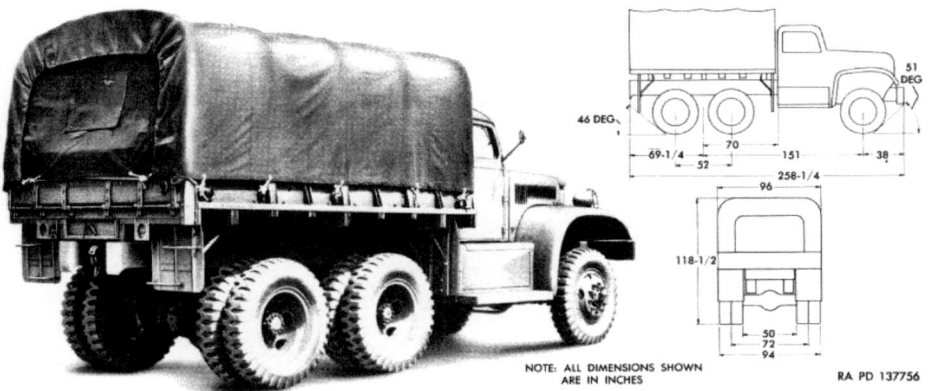

NOTE: ALL DIMENSIONS SHOWN ARE IN INCHES

RA PD 137756

Technical Manuals: 9-811, 9-1811, 9-1825B, 9-1826C, 9-1827A, 9-1828A, 9-1832A; Supply Catalog: SNL G-509.

Classification: Standard.

Purpose: To transport general cargo and tow 155-mm howitzer.

GENERAL DATA

Crew...2
Weight (lb)...Net 17,200
   Payload w/crew...................off highway 8,350; on highway 17,300
   Gross...........................off highway 25,550; on highway 34,500
Live-axle gear ratio...8.435:1
Axle load (lb):
   Empty.............................front 6,620; rear each 5,290
   Loaded:
      Off highway....................front 6,870; rear each 9,340
      On highway....................front 6,870; rear each 13,815
Tires:
   Ply 10; Size 9.00 x 20; Pressure............................(psi) 65
   Tread, center-to-center, front..........................(in.) 73¾
Shipping dimensions, uncrated..............(cu ft) 1,700; (sq ft) 172
Vehicle dimensions:
   Ground clearance...(in.) 11
   Pintle height, loaded...............................(in.) 36¹³⁄₁₆
   Loading height, empty...............................(in.) 58⁵⁄₁₆
   Body inside dimensions (in.):
      Length...132
      Width..88
      Height...59
   Cargo space (cu ft)....................................397
Electrical system (12-volt starting)....................(volts) 6
   No. of batteries..................................(6-volt)2
   Type of ground.....................................positive
Fuel octane rating...72
Capacities:
   Fuel...(gal) 60
   Cooling system....................................(qt) 48
   Crankcase, refill..................................(qt) 16
   Transmission......................................(qt) 10½
   Transfer..(qt) 1½
   Axles (qt)..........................front 7½; rear (each) 3¾
   Winch:
      Oil capacity....................................(qt) 1¾
      Load capacity...............................(lb) 15,000

GENERAL DATA—Continued

Brakes:
   Manufacturer: Bendix-Westinghouse....................Type: air
   Parking brake, type...............................transmission
Transmission:
   Forward speeds...5
   Gear ratio....................High 0.768:1; Fourth 1:1; Low 7.08:1
Transfer:
   Speeds...2
   Gear ratio.............................High 1:1; Low 1.72:1

PERFORMANCE

Computed grade ability in lowest gear, loaded.............(percent) 65
Turning radius (ft)..............................Right 32½; Left 34
Fording depth..(in.) 24
Fuel consumption, loaded.....................................(mpg) 3
Cruising range, loaded.......................................(mi) 180
Allowable speed, governed....................................(mph) 40
Maximum recommended towed load:
   Off highway, gross...............................(lb) 11,000
   On highway, gross...............................(lb) 25,000

ENGINE

Manufacturer: Hercules.....................................Model RXC
Type........................L-head, 4-cycle; No. of cylinders (in line) 6
Displacement...(cu in.) 529
Bore...(in.) 4¾
Stroke...(in.) 5¼
Compression ratio..5.4:1
Governed speed...(rpm) 2,300
Brake horsepower (max w/std accessories)........106 at (rpm) 2,300
Torque (max w/std accessories)................342 lb-ft at (rpm) 900

ADDITIONAL DATA

Over-all height with gun mount..........................(in.) 127¼
   This model supplied w/both open and closed cabs.
Live axles, type......................double-reduction, full-floating
Transmission, type.....................................constant-mesh

TRUCK, CARGO, 4-TON, 6 x 6, W/WINCH
(Diamond T, Model 967, SWB, 1941)

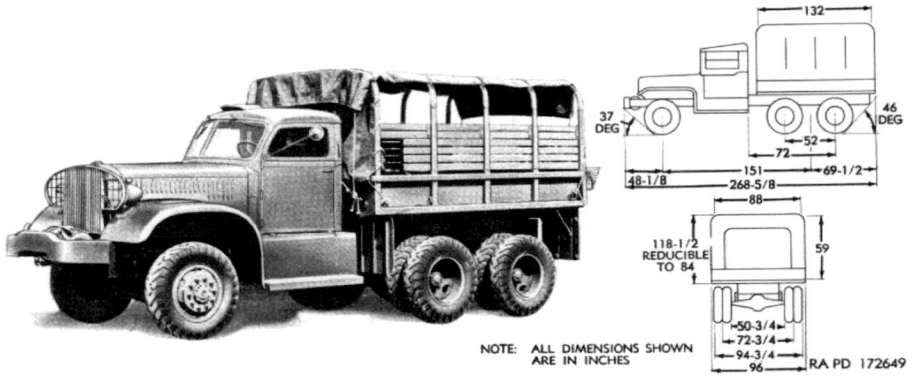

NOTE: ALL DIMENSIONS SHOWN ARE IN INCHES

RA PD 172649

Technical Manuals: 9–811, 9–1811, 9–1825B, 9–1826C, 9–1827A, 9–1828A, 9–1832A; Supply Catalog: SNL G–509.

Classification: Standard.

Purpose: To transport general cargo and tow 155-mm howitzer.

GENERAL DATA

Crew..2
Weight (lb): Net...18,050
  Payload w/crew..................off highway 8,350; on highway 16,450
  Gross..........................off highway 26,400; on highway 34,500
Live-axle gear ratio..8.435:1
Axle load (lb):
  Empty..............................front 7,600; rear (each) 5,225
  Loaded:
    Off highway.................front 7,850; rear (each) 9,275
    On highway................front 8,100; rear (each) 13,200
Tires:
  Ply 10..........................Size 9.00 x 20; Pressure (psi) 65
  Tread, center-to-center, front....................(in.) 73¾
Shipping dimensions, uncrated.............(cu ft) 1,760; (sq ft) 179
Vehicle dimensions:
  Ground clearance....................................(in.) 11
  Pintle height, loaded...........................(in.) 36¹³⁄₁₆
  Loading height, empty..........................(in.) 58⁹⁄₁₆
  Body inside dimensions (in.):
    Length...................132; Width 88; Height 59
    Cargo space..................................(cu ft) 397
Electrical system (12-volt starting)................(volts) 6
  No. of batteries...........................(6-volt) 2
  Type of ground...................................positive
Fuel octane rating....................................68
Capacities:
  Fuel..(gal) 60
  Cooling system.................................(qt) 36
  Crankcase......................................(qt) 16
  Transfer..(qt) 5
  Transmission, w/power take-off.................(qt) 12
  Axles (qt).........................front 6; rear (each) 3
  Winch:
    Oil capacity...............................(qt) 1¾
    Load capacity.............................(lb) 15,000
Brakes:
  Manufacturer..............Bendix-Westinghouse; Type: air
  Parking brake, type.........................transmission

GENERAL DATA—Continued

Transmission:
  Forward speeds......................................5
  Gear ratio.............High 0.768:1; Fourth 1:1; Low 7.08:1
Transfer:
  Speeds..2
  Gear ratio..........................High 1:1; Low 2.05:1

PERFORMANCE

Computed grade ability in lowest gear, loaded..............(percent) 68
Turning radius (ft)....................right 32½; left 34
Fording depth..................................(in.) 24
Fuel consumption, loaded........................(mpg) 3
Cruising range, loaded.........................(mi) 180
Allowable speed, governed.......................(mph) 40
Maximum recommended towed load:
  Off highway, gross..........................(lb) 11,000
  On highway, gross...........................(lb) 25,000

ENGINE

Manufacturer: Hercules............................Model RXB
Type..................L-head, 4-cycle; No. of cylinders (in line) 6
Displacement..................................(cu in.) 501
Bore..(in.) 4½
Stroke..(in.) 5¾
Compression ratio................................5.4:1
Governed speed...............................(rpm) 2,300
Brake horsepower (max w/std accessories)........98 at (rpm) 2,200
Torque (max w/std accessories)........311 lb-ft at (rpm) 1,000

ADDITIONAL DATA

Live axles, type....................double-reduction, full-floating
Transmission, type........................constant-mesh

TRUCK, CARGO, 4-TON, 6 x 6, W/WINCH

(Diamond T, Models 968, SWB, 1941; 968A, SWB, 1942; and 968B, SWB)

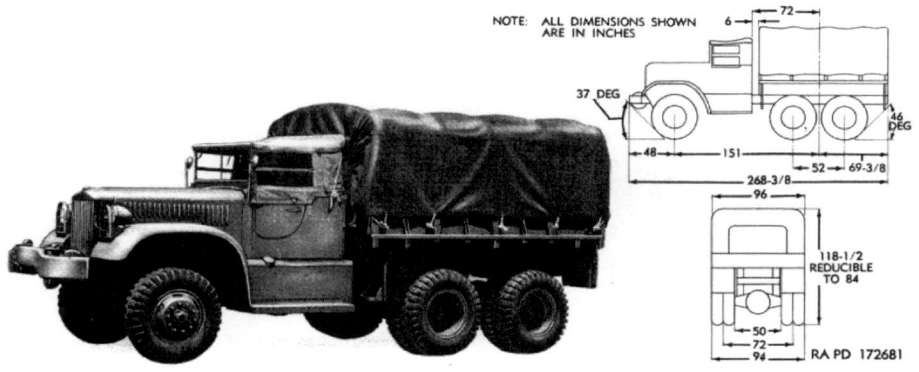

NOTE: ALL DIMENSIONS SHOWN ARE IN INCHES

RA PD 172681

Technical Manuals: 9-811, 9-1811, 9-1825B, 9-1826C, 9-1827A, 9-1828A, 9-1832A; Supply Catalog: SNL G-509.

Vehicle illustrated: Model 968B, SWB.
Classification: Standard.

Purpose: To transport general cargo and tow 155-mm howitzer.

GENERAL DATA

Crew	2
Weight (lb)	Net 18,050
Payload w/crew	off highway 8,350; on highway 16,450
Gross	off highway 26,400; on highway 34,500
Live-axle gear ratio	8.435 : 1
Axle load (lb):	
Empty	front 6,620; rear (each) 5,290
Loaded:	
Off highway	front 6,870; rear (each) 9,340
On highway	front 6,870; rear (each) 13,815
Tires:	
Ply 10	Size 9.00 x 20; Pressure (psi) 65
Tread, center-to-center, front	(in.) 73¾
Shipping dimensions, uncrated	(cu ft) 1,246; (sq ft) 178
Vehicle dimensions (in.):	
Ground clearance	11
Pintle height, loaded	36¹³⁄₁₆
Loading height, empty	58³⁄₁₆
Body inside dimensions (in.):	
Length	132; Width 88; Height 59
Cargo space	(cu ft) 397
Electrical system (12-volt starting)	(volts) 6
No. of batteries	(6-volt) 2
Type of ground	positive
Fuel octane rating	72
Capacities:	
Fuel	(gal) 60
Cooling system	(qt) 48
Crankcase, refill	(qt) 16
Transmission	(qt) 10½
Transfer	(qt) 1½
Axles (qt)	front 7½; rear (each) 3¾
Winch:	
Oil capacity	(qt) 1¾
Load capacity	(lb) 15,000
Brakes:	
Manufacturer	Bendix-Westinghouse; Type; air
Parking brake, type	transmission

GENERAL DATA—Continued

Transmission:	
Forward speeds	5
Gear ratio	High 0.768 :1; Fourth 1:1; Low 7.08 :1
Transfer:	
Speeds	2
Gear ratio	High 1:1; Low 1.72 :1

PERFORMANCE

Computed grade ability in lowest gear, loaded	(percent) 65
Turning radius (ft)	Right 32½; Left 34
Fording depth	(in.) 24
Fuel consumption, loaded	(mpg) 3
Cruising range, loaded	(mi) 180
Allowable speed, governed	(mph) 40
Maximum recommended towed load:	
Off highway, gross	(lb) 11,000
On highway, gross	(lb) 25,000

ENGINE

Manufacturer: Hercules	Model RXC
Type	L-head, 4-cycle; No. of cylinders (in line) 6
Displacement	(cu in.) 529
Bore	(in.) 4⅝
Stroke	(in.) 5¼
Compression ratio	5.4:1
Governed speed	(rpm) 2,300
Brake horsepower (max w/std accessories)	106 at (rpm) 2,300
Torque (max w/std accessories)	342 lb-ft at (rpm) 900

ADDITIONAL DATA

Over-all height with gun mount (in.)	127¼

Models 968 and 968B supplied with closed cab; model 968A with open and closed cabs.

Live axles, type	double-reduction, full-floating
Transmission, type	constant-mesh

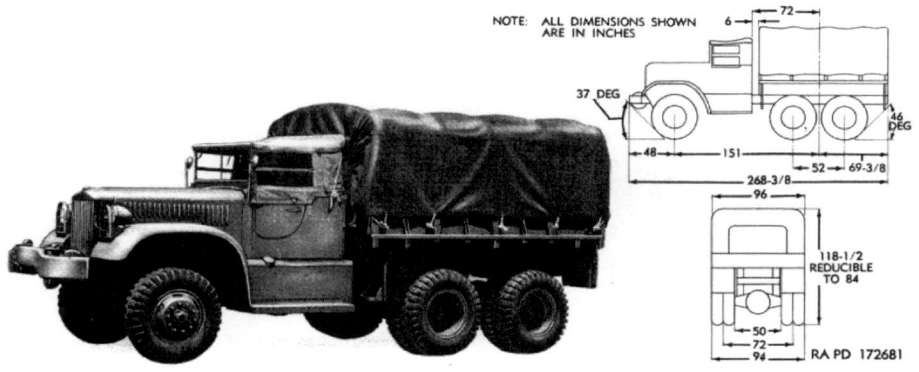

TRUCK, CARGO, 4-TON, 6 x 6, W/WINCH

(Diamond T, Model 970A, LWB, 1942)

RA PD 172650

NOTE: ALL DIMENSIONS SHOWN ARE IN INCHES

Technical Manuals: 9-811, 9-1811, 9-1825B, 9-1826C, 9-1827A, 9-1828A, 9-1832A; Supply Catalog: SNL G-509.

Classification: Standard.

Purpose: To transport general cargo and tow 155-mm howitzer.

GENERAL DATA

Crew..2
Weight (lb)..Net 18,450
   Payload w/crew...............off highway 8,350; on highway 16,050
   Gross.........................off highway 26,800; on highway 34,500
Live-axle gear ratio...8.435:1
Axle load (lb):
   Empty.....................front 7,745; rear (each) 5,353
   Loaded:
      Off highway.............front 7,850; rear (each) 9,475
      On highway.............front 7,965; rear (each) 13,268
Tires:
   Ply 10....................Size 9.00 x 20; Pressure (psi) 65
   Tread, center-to-center, front......................(in.) 73¾
Shipping dimensions, uncrated................(cu ft) 1,970; (sq ft) 199
Vehicle dimensions (in.):
   Ground clearance.......................................11
   Pintle height, loaded..............................36¹³⁄₁₆
   Loading height, empty.............................58½
   Body inside dimensions (in.):
      Length...............147; Width 88; Height 59
      Cargo space........................(cu ft) 44
Electrical system (12-volt starting)....................(volts) 12
   No. of batteries............................(6-volt) 2
   Type of ground...................................positive
Fuel octane rating...72
Capacities:
   Fuel...(gal) 60
   Cooling system..............................(qt) 48
   Crankcase, refill............................(qt) 16
   Transmission................................(qt) 12
   Transfer....................................(qt) 1½
   Axles (qt)..................front 7½; rear (each) 3¾
   Winch:
      Oil capacity.........................(qt) 1¾
      Load capacity.....................(lb) 15,000
Brakes:
   Manufacturer..............Bendix-Westinghouse; Type; air
   Parking brake, type..........................transmission

GENERAL DATA—Continued

Transmission:
   Forward speeds...5
   Gear ratio.............High 0.768:1; Fourth 1:1; Low 7.08:1
Transfer:
   Speeds..2
   Gear ratio........................High 1:1; Low 1.72:1

PERFORMANCE

Computed grade ability in lowest gear, loaded...........(percent) 65
Turning radius (ft).......................right 37½; left 39
Fording depth..(in.) 24
Fuel consumption, loaded..................................(mpg) 3
Cruising range, loaded...................................(mi) 180
Allowable speed, governed...............................(mph) 40
Maximum recommended towed load:
   Off highway, gross..............................(lb) 11,000
   On highway, gross..............................(lb) 25,000

ENGINE

Manufacturer: Hercules.............................Model RXC
Type....................L-head, 4-cycle; No. of cylinders (in line) 6
Displacement...(cu in.) 529
Bore...(in.) 4⅝
Stroke...(in.) 5¼
Compression ratio..5.4:1
Governed speed.......................................(rpm) 2,300
Brake horsepower (max w/std accessories)...........106 at (rpm) 2,300
Torque (max w/std accessories)...........342 lb-ft at (rpm) 900

ADDITIONAL DATA

Supplied w/open and closed cabs.
Live axles, type..........................double-reduction, full-floating
Transmission, type..constant-mesh

246

TRUCK, CHASSIS, 4-TON, 6 x 6, W/ AND W/O WINCH

(Diamond T, Model 968A, SWB, 1942)

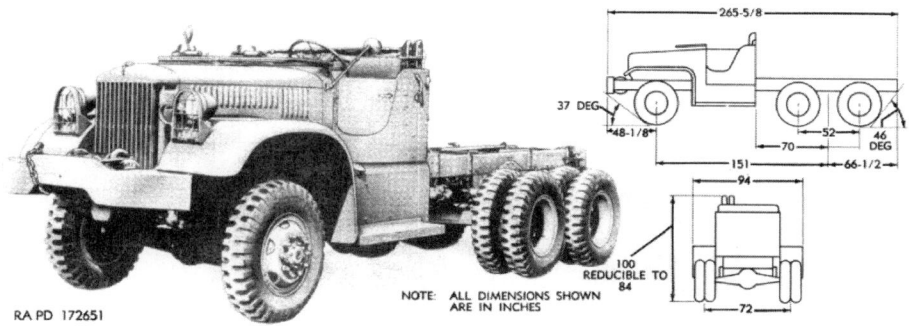

RA PD 172651

NOTE: ALL DIMENSIONS SHOWN ARE IN INCHES

Technical Manuals: 9-811, 9-1811, 9-1825B, 9-1826C, 9-1827A, 9-1828A, 9-1832A; **Supply Catalog:** SNL G-509.

Classification: Nonclassified.

Purpose: To be used as component of general-purpose or special-equipment truck.

GENERAL DATA

Crew	2
Weight (lb)	Net 14,800; Max gross 34,500
Live-axle gear ratio	8.435:1
Axle load, empty (lb)	front 7,600; rear (each) 3,600
Tires:	
Ply 10	Size 9.00 x 20; Pressure (psi) 65
Tread, center-to-center, front	(in.) 73¾
Shipping dimensions, uncrated	(cu ft) 1,440; (sq ft) 173
Vehicle dimensions:	
Ground clearance	(in.) 11
Pintle height, loaded	(in.) 36¹³⁄₁₆
Electrical system	(12-volt starting) (volts) 6
No. of batteries	(6-volt) 2
Type of ground	positive
Fuel octane rating	72
Capacities:	
Fuel	(gal) 60
Cooling system	(qt) 48
Crankcase, refill	(qt) 16
Transmission	(qt) 12
Transfer	(qt) 1½
Axles (qt)	front 7½; rear (each) 3¾
Winch:	
Oil capacity	(qt) 1¾
Load capacity	(lb) 15,000
Brakes:	
Manufacturer	Bendix-Westinghouse; Type; air
Parking brake, type	transmission
Transmission:	
Forward speeds	5
Gear ratio	High 0.768:1; Fourth 1:1; Low 7.08:1
Transfer:	
Speeds	2
Gear ratio	High 1:1; Low 1.72:1

PERFORMANCE

Computed grade ability in lowest gear, loaded	(percent) 68
Turning radius (ft)	Right 32½; Left 34
Fording depth	(in.) 24
Fuel consumption, loaded	(mpg) 3
Cruising range, loaded	(mi) 180
Allowable speed, governed	(mph) 40
Maximum recommended towed load:	
Off highway, gross	(lb) 11,000
On highway, gross	(lb) 25,000

ENGINE

Manufacturer: Hercules	Model RXC
Type	L-head, 4-cycle; No. of cylinders (in line) 6
Displacement	(cu in.) 529
Bore	(in.) 4⅜
Stroke	(in.) 5¼
Compression ratio	5.4:1
Governed speed	(rpm) 2,300
Brake horsepower (max w/std accessories)	106 at (rpm) 2,300
Torque (max w/std accessories)	342 lb-ft at (rpm) 900

ADDITIONAL DATA

Over-all height with gun mount (empty)	(in.) 127¼

Weights and dimensions given for chassis w/winch; for chassis w/o winch they are as follows:

Weight, net	(lb) 13,950
Axle loads (lb)	front 6,620; rear (each) 3,665
Over-all length	(in.) 250½
Shipping dimensions, uncrated	(cu ft) 1,390; (sq ft) 166

Supplied w/open and closed cabs.

Live Axles, type	double-reduction, full-floating
Transmission, type	constant-mesh

TRUCK, DUMP, 4-TON, 6 x 6

(Diamond T, Model 972, SWB)

NOTE: ALL DIMENSIONS SHOWN
ARE IN INCHES

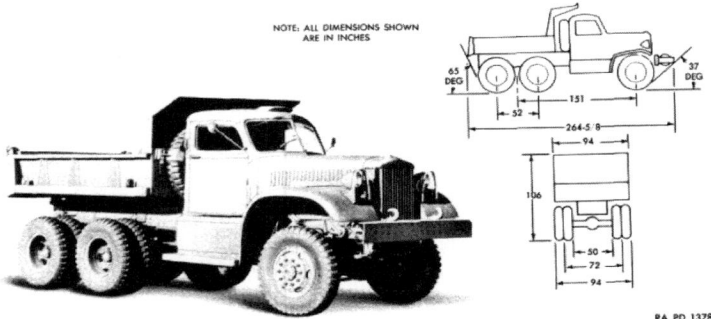

RA PD 137844

Technical Manuals: 9–811, 9–1811, 9–1825B, 9–1826C, 9–1827A, 9–1828A, 9–1832A; Supply Catalog: SNL G–509.

Classification: Standard.

GENERAL DATA

Crew..2
Weight (lb):
  Net......................................w/o winch 17,200; w/winch 18,050
  Payload:
    W/crew:
      W/o winch...............off highway 9,200; on highway 17,300
      W/winch................off highway 8,350; on highway 16,450
  Gross:
    W/o winch..................off highway 26,400; on highway 34,500
    W/winch...................off highway 26,400; on highway 34,500
Live-axle gear ratio...8.435:1
Axle load (lb):
  Empty:
    W/o winch.......................front 6,620; rear (each) 5,290
    W/winch........................front 7,600; rear (each) 5,225
  Loaded:
    W/o winch:
      Off highway.....................front 6,660; rear (each) 9,870
      On highway.....................front 7,140; rear (each) 13,680
    W/winch:
      Off highway.....................front 7,850; rear (each) 9,275
      On highway.....................front 8,100; rear (each) 13,200
Tires:
  Ply 10..........................Size 9.00 x 20; Pressure (psi) 65
  Tread, center-to-center, front....................... (in.) 73¾
Shipping dimensions:
  Uncrated:
    W/winch.......................(cu ft) 1,520; (sq ft) 173
    W/o winch......................(cu ft) 1,465; (sq ft) 166
Vehicle dimensions:
  Ground clearance................................... (in.) 11
  Loading height, empty.............................(in.) 58⁵⁄₁₆
  Pintle height, loaded..............................(in.) 36¾
  Body inside dimensions (in.):
    Length.....................120; Width 80; Height 17
  Struck capacity...................................(cu yd) 3½
Electrical system (12-volt starting)......................(volts) 6
  No. of batteries..................................(6-volt) 2
  Type of ground.....................................positive
Fuel octane rating..72
Brakes:
  Manufacturer.....................Bendix-Westinghouse; Type; air
  Parking brake, type.................................transfer

Purpose: To haul and dump earth, sand, gravel, etc.

GENERAL DATA—Continued

Capacities:
  Fuel...(gal) 60
  Cooling system.................................(qt) 48
  Crankcase, refill...............................(qt) 16
  Transfer, w/PTO................................(qt) 1½
  Transmission.................w/o PTO (qt) 10½; w/PTO (qt) 12
  Axles (qt)........................front 7½; rear (each) 3¾
  Winch..........Oil capacity (qt) 2; load capcity (lb) 15,000
Transmission:
  Forward speeds....................................5
  Gear ratio................High 0.768:1; Fourth 1:1; Low 7.08:1
Transfer:
  Speeds..2
  Gear ratio..............................High 1:1; Low 1.72:1

PERFORMANCE

Computed grade ability in lowest gear, loaded................(percent) 68
Turning radius (ft) ....Right 32½; Left 34
Fording depth....................................(in.) 24
Fuel consumption, loaded...........................(mpg) 3
Cruising range, loaded.............................(mi) 180
Allowable speed, governed..........................(mph) 40
Maximum recommended towed load:
  Off highway, gross............................(lb) 11,000
  On highway, gross.............................(lb) 25,000

ENGINE

Manufacturer: Hercules...........................Model RXC
Type.................L-head, 4-cycle; No. of cylinders (in line) 6
Displacement..................................(cu in.) 529
Bore..(in.) 4⅜
Stroke..(in.) 5¼
Compression ratio.................................5.4:1
Governed speed.................................(rpm) 2,300
Brake horsepower (max w/std accessories)..............106 at (rpm) 2,300
Torque (max w/std accessories)...............342 lb-ft at (rpm) 900

ADDITIONAL DATA

Over-all length w/o winch (in.) 254½.
Live Axles, type.......................double-reduction, full-floating
Transmission, type................................constant-mesh

248

TRUCK, PONTON, 4-TON, 6 x 6, W/WINCH

(Diamond T, Models 970, LWB, 1941 and 970A, LWB, 1942–43)

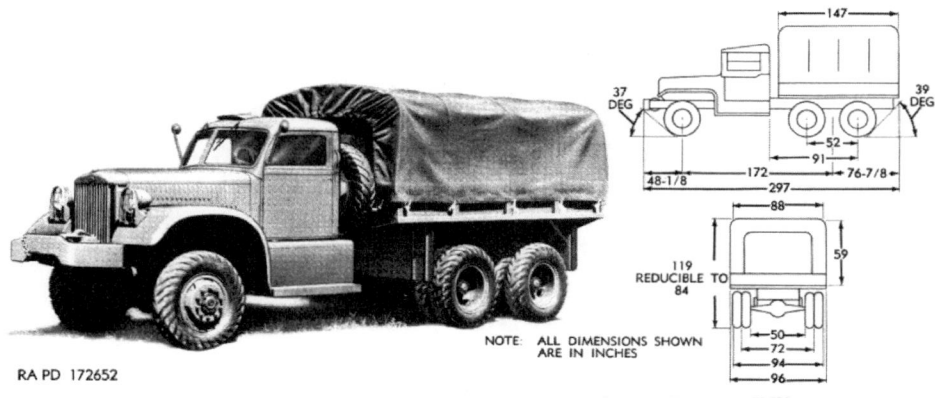

RA PD 172652

NOTE: ALL DIMENSIONS SHOWN ARE IN INCHES

Technical Manuals: 9-811, 9-1811, 9-1825B, 9-1826C, 9-1827A, 9-1828A, 9-1832A; Supply Catalog: SNL G-509.

Vehicle illustrated: Model 970.
Classification: Standard.

GENERAL DATA

Crew	2
Weight (lb) Net	18,450
Payload w/crew	off highway 8,350; on highway 16,050
Gross	off highway 26,800; on highway 34,500
Live-axle gear ratio	8.435:1
Axle load (lb):	
Empty	front 7,745; rear (each) 5,353
Loaded:	
Off highway	front 7,850; rear (each) 9,475
On highway	front 7,965; rear (each) 13,268
Tires:	
Ply 10	Size 9.00 x 20; Pressure (psi) 65
Tread, center-to-center, front	(in.) 73¾
Shipping dimensions, uncrated	(cu ft) 1,970; (sq ft) 199
Vehicle dimensions (in.):	
Ground clearance	11
Pintle height, loaded	36¹³⁄₁₆
Loading height, empty	58½
Body inside dimensions (in.):	
Length	147; Width 88; Height 59
Cargo space	(cu ft) 441
Electrical system (12-volt starting)	(volts) 6
No. of batteries	(6-volt) 2
Type of ground	positive
Fuel octane rating	72
Capacities:	
Fuel	(gal) 60
Cooling system	(qt) 48
Crankcase, refill	(qt) 16
Transmission	(qt) 12
Transfer	(qt) 1½
Axles (qt)	front 7½; rear (each) 3¾
Winch:	
Oil capacity	(qt) 1¾
Load capacity	(lb) 15,000
Brakes:	
Manufacturer	Bendix-Westinghouse; Type; air
Parking brake, type	transmission

Purpose: Used by Corps of Engineers to transport pontons or cargo.

GENERAL DATA—Continued

Transmission:	
Forward speeds	5
Gear ratio	High 0.768:1; Fourth 1:1; Low 7.08:1
Transfer:	
Speeds	2
Gear ratio	High 1:1; Low 1.72:1

PERFORMANCE

Computed grade ability in lowest gear, loaded	(percent) 67
Turning radius (ft)	Right 37½; Left 39
Fording depth	(in.) 24
Fuel consumption, loaded	(mpg) 3
Cruising range, loaded	(mi) 180
Allowable speed, governed	(mph) 40
Maximum recommended towed load:	
Off highway, gross	(lb) 11,000
On highway, gross	(lb) 25,000

ENGINE

Manufacturer: Hercules	Model RXC
Type	L-head, 4-cycle; No. of cylinders (in line) 6
Displacement	(cu in.) 529
Bore	(in.) 4¾
Stroke	(in.) 5¼
Compression ratio	5.4:1
Governed speed	(rpm) 2,300
Brake horsepower (max w/std accessories)	106 at (rpm) 2,300
Torque (max w/std accessories)	342 lb-ft at (rpm) 900

ADDITIONAL DATA

Model 970 supplied w/closed cab; Model 970A w/open and closed cabs.

Live Axles, type	double-reduction, full-floating
Transmission, type	constant-mesh

TRUCK, WRECKER, 4-TON, 6 x 6, W/WINCH

(Diamond T, Models 969, SWB, 1941; 969A, SWB 1942; and 969B, SWB)

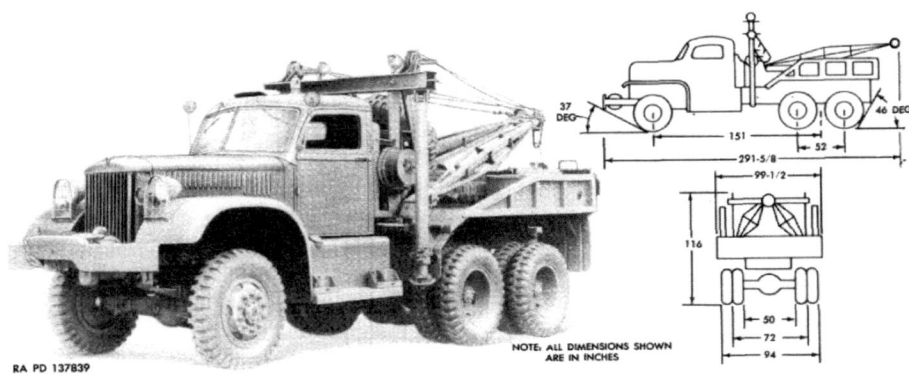

RA PD 137839

NOTE: ALL DIMENSIONS SHOWN ARE IN INCHES

Technical Manuals: 9–811, 9–1811, 9–1825B, 9–1826C, 9–1827A, 9–1828A, 9–1832A; Supply Catalog: SNL G–509.

Vehicle illustrated: Model 969A or 969B, SWB.
Classification: Standard.

Purpose: To lift and tow disabled vehicles.

GENERAL DATA

Crew	2
Weight (lb)	Net 21,350; w/crew (350 lb) 21,700
Live-axle gear ratio	8.435:1
Axle load w/equipment and crew (lb):	
Front	8,000; rear (each) 6,850
Tires	Ply 10; Size 9.00 x 20; Pressure (psi) 65
Tread, center-to-center, front	(in.) 73¾
Shipping dimensions, uncrated	(cu ft) 1,950; (sq ft) 202
Vehicle dimensions:	
Ground clearance	(in.) 11
Pintle height, loaded	(in.) 36¾
Electrical system (12-volt starting)	(volts) 6
No. of batteries	(6-volt) 2
Type of ground	positive
Fuel octane rating	72
Capacities:	
Fuel	(gal) 60
Cooling system	(qt) 48
Crankcase, refill	(qt) 16
Transfer w/power take-off	(qt) 1½
Transmission w/power take-off	(qt) 12
Axles (qt)	front 7½; rear (each) 3¾
Winch: Oil capacity	(qt) 2; Load capacity (lb) 15,000
Brakes:	
Manufacturer	Bendix-Westinghouse; Type; air
Parking brake, type	transfer
Transmission:	
Forward speeds	5
Gear ratio	High 0.768:1; Fourth 1:1; Low 7.08:1
Transfer:	
Speeds	2
Gear ratio	High 1:1; Low 1.72:1

PERFORMANCE

Computed grade ability in lowest gear, w/o towed load	(percent) 65
Turning radius (ft)	Right 32½; Left 34
Fording depth	(in.) 24
Fuel consumption, loaded	(mpg) 3
Cruising range, loaded	(mi) 180
Allowable speed, governed	(mph) 40
Maximum recommended towed load:	
Off highway, gross	(lb) 11,000
On highway, gross	(lb) 25,000

ENGINE

Manufacturer: Hercules	Model RXC
Type	L-head, 4-cycle; No. of cylinders (in line) 6
Displacement	(cu in.) 529
Bore	(in.) 4⅝
Stroke	(in.) 5¼
Compression ratio	5.4:1
Governed speed	(rpm) 2,300
Brake horsepower (max w/std accessories)	106 at (rpm) 2,300
Torque (max)	342 lb-ft at (rpm) 900

ADDITIONAL DATA

Live-axles, type	double-reduction, full-floating
Transmission, type	constant-mesh
Crane lifting capacity:	
Per boom, while standing	(lb) 10,000
Max boom load when towed	(lb) 6,000

Model 969 supplied with closed cab; models 969A and 969B with open and closed cabs.

TRUCK, TRACTOR, 4- TO 5-TON, 4 x 4

(Autocar, Model U7144T, COE)

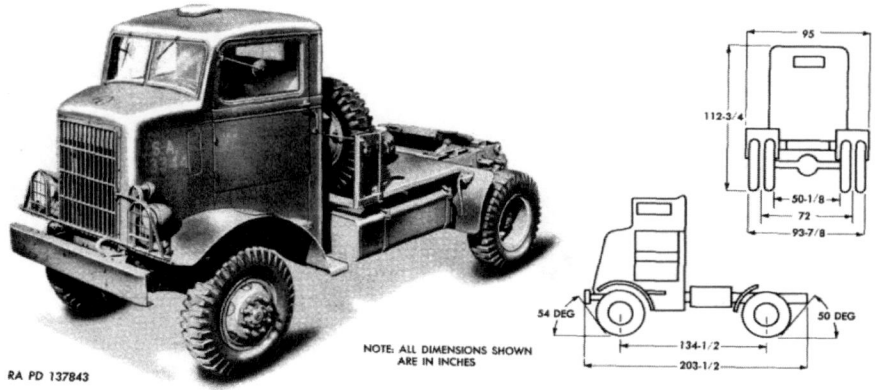

RA PD 137843

NOTE: ALL DIMENSIONS SHOWN ARE IN INCHES

Technical Manuals: 9-816, 9-1816, 9-1825B, 9-1826C, 9-1827A, 9-1828A, 9-1832A; **Supply Catalog:** SNL G-510.

Classification: Standard.

Purpose: To tow semitrailers.

GENERAL DATA

Crew	2
Weight (lb)	Net 12,360; Payload 8,650; Gross 21,010
Live-axle, gear ratio	8.43:1
Axle load (lb):	
Empty	front 7,020; rear 5,340
Loaded	front 7,120; rear 13,890
Tires:	
Ply 10; Size 9.00 x 20; Pressure	(psi) 65
Tread, center-to-center, front	(in.) 73¾
Shipping dimensions, uncrated	(cu ft) 1,260; (sq ft) 135
Vehicle dimensions:	
Ground clearance	(in.) 11⅞
Pintle height, loaded	(in.) 32½
Center of fifth wheel to rear of cab	(in.) 87
Center of fifth wheel to center of rear axle	(in.) 3
Height to center of fifth wheel	(in.) 48
Height to rear of fifth wheel	(in.) 42
Electrical system	(volts) 12
No. of batteries	(6-volt) 2
Type of ground	positive
Fuel octane rating	68
Capacities:	
Fuel	(gal) 60
Cooling system	(qt) 40
Crankcase	dryfill (qt) 14; refill (qt) 12
Transfer	(qt) 2
Transmission	summer (qt) 7; winter (qt) 10
Axles	front (qt) 8; rear (qt) 10
Brakes:	
Manufacturer: Bendix-Westinghouse	Type; air
Parking brake, type	transmission
Transmission:	
Forward speeds	5
Gear ratio	High 0.75:1; Fourth 1:1; Low 5.9:1
Transfer:	
Speeds	2
Gear ratio	High 1:1; Low 1.72:1

PERFORMANCE

Computed grade ability in lowest gear, w/semitrailer	(percent) 48
Turning radius	(ft) 30
Fording depth	(in.) 24½
Fuel consumption (empty)	(mpg) 9
With maximum allowable towed load	(mpg) 3.3
Cruising range (empty)	(mi) 540
With maximum allowable towed load	(mi) 198
Allowable speed, governed	(mph) 41
Maximum recommended semitrailer, gross	(lb) 20,000

ENGINE

Manufacturer: Hercules	Model RXC
Type	L-head, 4-cycle; No. of cylinders (in line) 6
Displacement	(cu in.) 529
Bore	(in.) 4⅝
Stroke	(in.) 5¼
Compression ratio	5.4:1
Governed speed	(rpm) 2,300
Brake horsepower (max w/std accessories)	112 at (rpm) 2,200
Torque (max)	368 lb-ft at (rpm) 1,000

ADDITIONAL DATA

Height with closed cab 108½ in.

Live-axles, type	double-reduction, full-floating
Transmission, type	constant-mesh

TRUCK, TRACTOR, 4- TO 5-TON, 4 x 4

(Federal, Model 94X43A, 94X43B, 94X43C)

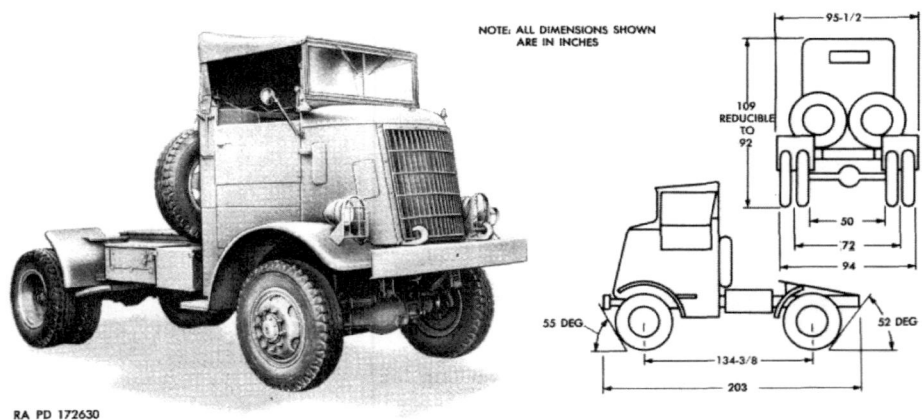

NOTE: ALL DIMENSIONS SHOWN ARE IN INCHES

RA PD 172630

Technical Manuals: 9–820, 9–1816, 9–1825A, 9–1825B, 9–1826C, 9–1827A, 9–1828A, 9–1829A, 9–1832A; **Supply Catalog:** SNL G–513.

Vehicle Illustrated: Model 94X43C.
Classification: Standard.

Purpose: To tow semitrailers.

GENERAL DATA

Crew..2
Weight (lb)........................Net 11,950; Payload 8,270; Gross 20,220
Live-axle gear ratio...8.43:1
Axle load (lb):
  Empty....................................front 6,650; rear 5,300
  Loaded................................front 6,650; rear 13,570
Tires:
  Ply 10...........................Size 9.00 x 20; Pressure (psi) 65
  Tread, center-to-center, front........................(in.) 73¾
Shipping dimensions, uncrated.............(cu ft) 1,035; (sq ft) 135
Vehicle dimensions:
  Ground clearance...................................(in.) 11½
  Pintle height, empty..................................(in.) 38
  Fifth wheel center to center of rear axle.............(in.) 3
  Height to center of fifth wheel........................(in.) 48
Electrical system (12-volt starting)....................(volts) 6
  No. of batteries...................................(6-volt) 2
Fuel octane rating...72
Capacities:
  Fuel...(gal) 62
  Cooling system......................................(qt) 40
  Crankcase, refill...................................(qt) 14
  Transmission..(qt) 10
  Transfer...(qt) 2
  Axles (each)...(qt) 6
Brakes:
  Manufacturer; Bendix-Westinghouse...............Type; air
  Parking brake, type........................propeller-shaft
Transmission:
  Forward speeds..5
  Gear ratio.............High 0.768:1; Fourth 1:1; Low 7.08:1
Transfer:
  Speeds..2
  Gear ratio...........................High 1:1; Low 1.72:1

PERFORMANCE

Computed grade ability w/loaded semitrailer.............(percent) 50
Turning radius...(ft) 27
Fording depth...(in.) 26
Fuel consumption w/loaded semitrailer..................(mpg) 4½
Cruising range w/loaded semitrailer......................(mi) 280
Allowable speed, governed...............................(mph) 40
Maximum semitrailer, gross...............................(lb) 30,000

ENGINE

Manufacturer: Hercules............................Model RXC
Type...................L-head, 4-cycle; No. of cylinders (in line) 6
Displacement..(cu in.) 529
Bore...(in.) 4⅝
Stroke...(in.) 5¼
Compression ratio.....................................5.4:1
Governed speed......................................(rpm) 2,300
Brake horsepower (max w/std accessories).............112 at (rpm) 2,200
Torque (max w/std accessories)..............368 lb-ft at (rpm) 1,000

ADDITIONAL DATA

These models equipped with either hard or soft cab.
Live axles, type.....................double-reduction, full-floating
Transmission, type..........................selective sliding-gear

TRUCK, TRACTOR, 4- TO 5-TON, 4 x 4

(White, Model 444T, COE)

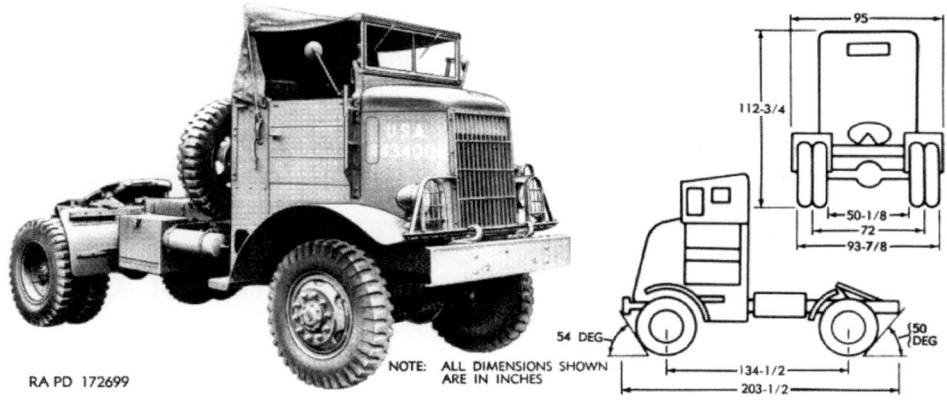

RA PD 172699

NOTE: ALL DIMENSIONS SHOWN ARE IN INCHES

Technical Manuals: 9-816, 9-1816, 9-1825B, 9-1826C, 9-1827A, 9-1828A, 9-1829A, 9-1832A; Supply Catalog: SNL G-691.

Classification: Standard.

Purpose: To tow semitrailers.

GENERAL DATA

Crew 2
Weight (lb) .... Net 11,660; Payload 9,350; Gross 21,010
Live-axle gear ratio 8.43:1
Axle load (lb):
    Empty .... front 7,020; rear 4,640
    Loaded .... front 7,120; rear 13,890
Tires:
    Ply 10 .... Size 9.00 x 20; Pressure (psi) 65
    Tread, center-to-center, front .... (in.) 73¾
Shipping dimensions, uncrated .... (cu ft) 1,260; (sq ft) 135
Vehicle dimensions:
    Ground clearance .... (in.) 11⅝
    Pintle height, empty .... (in.) 38
    Center of fifth wheel to center of rear axle .... (in.) 3
    Height to center of fifth wheel .... (in.) 48½
Electrical system .... (volts) 12
    No. of batteries .... (6-volt) 2
Fuel octane rating 72
Capacities:
    Fuel .... (gal) 60
    Cooling system .... (qt) 40
    Crankcase, refill .... (qt) 12
    Transfer .... (qt) 2
    Transmission .... (qt) 7
    Axles (qt) .... front 8; rear 10
Brakes:
    Manufacturer .... Bendix-Westinghouse; Type; air
    Parking brake, type .... transfer
Transmission:
    Forward speeds 5
    Gear ratio .... High 0.75:1; Fourth 1:1; Low 5.9:1
Transfer:
    Speeds 2
    Gear ratio .... High 1:1; Low 1.72:1

PERFORMANCE

Computed grade ability in lowest gear w/semitrailer .... (percent) 52
Turning radius .... (ft) 30
Fording depth .... (in.) 24½
Fuel consumption: w/max allowable towed load .... (mpg) 3
Cruising range: w/max allowable towed load .... (mi) 198
Maximum allowable speed, governed .... (mph) 41
Maximum semitrailer, gross .... (lb) 30,000

ENGINE

Manufacturer: Hercules .... Model RXC
Type .... 4-cycle, L-head; No. of cylinders (in line) 6
Displacement .... (cu in.) 529
Bore .... (in.) 4¾
Stroke .... (in.) 5¼
Compression ratio .... 5.4 : 1
Governed speed .... (rpm) 2,300
Brake horsepower (max w/std accessories) .... 112 at (rpm) 2,200
Torque (max w/std accessories) .... 368 lb-ft at (rpm) 1,000

ADDITIONAL DATA

This model equipped with either hard or soft cab.
Live axles, type .... double reduction, full-floating
Transmission, type .... constant-mesh

TRUCK, CHASSIS, 5-TON, 4 x 2

(Federal, Model 45M2, 167-in WB and 179-in WB)

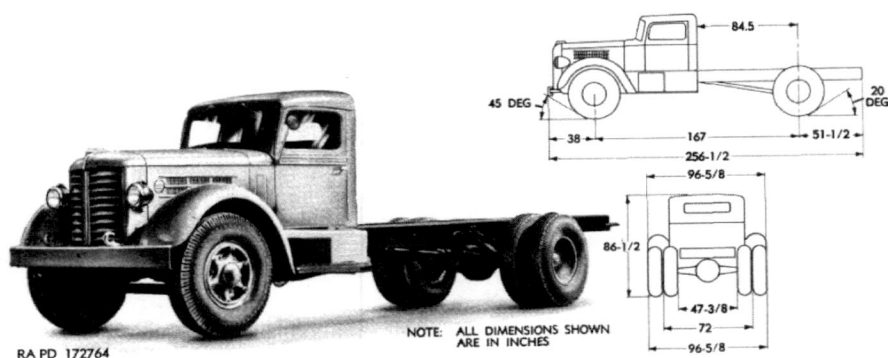

RA PD 172764

NOTE: ALL DIMENSIONS SHOWN ARE IN INCHES

Vehicle illustrated: 167-in. WB.
Classification: Standard.

Purpose: To be used as component of general-purpose or special-equipment vehicle.

GENERAL DATA

Crew..2
Weight (lb):
  Net:
    167-in. WB...9,475
    179-in. WB...9,785
    Maximum gross..15,350
  Rear-axle gear ratio (two-speed).................High 6.53:1; Low 8.53:1
Axle load (lb):
  Empty:
    167-in. WB....................................front 5,100; rear 4,375
    179-in. WB....................................front 4,900; rear 4,885
Tires:
  Ply 12.................................Size 11.00 x 20; Pressure (psi) 70
  Tread, center-to-center, front.................................(in.) 70⅜
Shipping dimensions, uncrated:
  167-in. WB.................................(cu ft) 1,230; (sq ft) 171
  179-in. WB.................................(cu ft) 1,380; (sq ft) 192
Ground clearance..(in.) 10
Electrical system...(volts) 6
  No. of batteries...1
  Type of ground...positive
Fuel octane rating...72
Capacities:
  Fuel...(gal) 60
  Cooling system..(qt) 29
  Crankcase, refill..(qt) 8
  Transmission...(qt) 10
  Rear axle..(qt) 15½
Brakes:
  Manufacturer; Bendix-Westinghouse.....................Type; air
  Parking brake, type.....................................transmission
Transmission:
  Forward speeds..5
  Gear ratio.....................High 1:1; Fourth 1.48:1; Low 7.88:1

PERFORMANCE

Computed grade ability in lowest gear, loaded.................(percent) 65
Turning radius (ft):
  167-in. WB...30
  179-in. WB...36
Fuel consumption, loaded................................(mpg) 4½
Cruising range, loaded.....................................(mi) 270
Allowable speed, governed...............................(mph) 48

ENGINE

Manufacturer: Continental...........................Model T-6427F
Type......................4-cycle, valve-in-head; No. of cylinders (in line) 6
Displacement..(cu in.) 427
Bore..(in.) 4⁵⁄₁₆
Stroke...(in.) 4⅝
Compression ratio..6.4:1
Governed speed..(rpm) 2,600
Brake horsepower (max w/std accessories).........158 at (rpm) 2,600
Torque (max w/std accessories)..............325 lb-ft at (rpm) 1,400

ADDITIONAL DATA

Rear axle, type...............................2-speed, full-floating
Transmission, type...synchromesh

TRUCK, CHASSIS, 5-TON, 4 x 2

(International Harvester, Model L–207, 175-in and 193-in WB)

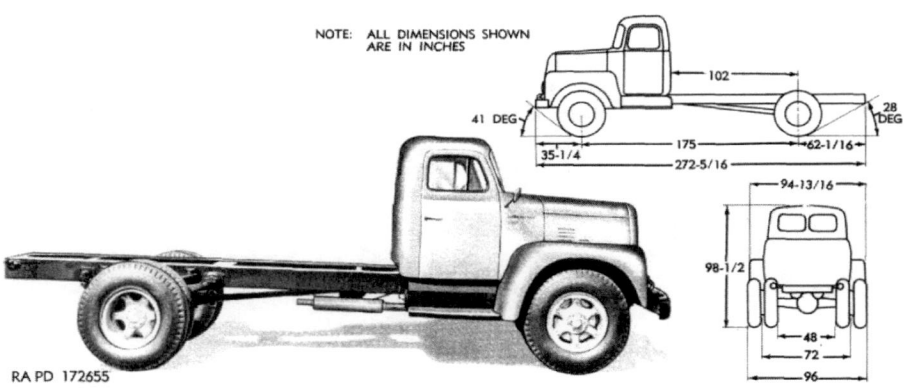

NOTE: ALL DIMENSIONS SHOWN ARE IN INCHES

102

41 DEG

28 DEG

175

35-1/4

62-1/16

272-5/16

94-13/16

98-1/2

48

72

96

RA PD 172655

Vehicle Illustrated: 175-in. WB.
Classification: Standard.

Purpose: To be used as component of general-purpose or special-equipment truck.

GENERAL DATA

Crew...1
Weight (lb)...Net 8,820; Max gross 27,000
Rear-axle gear ratio.....................................High 6.53:1; Low 8.54:1
Axle load (lb):
  Empty...front 4,795; rear 4,070
Tires:
  Ply 12..................................Size 11.00 x 20; Pressure (psi) 70
  Tread, center-to-center, front...........................(in.) 70¼
Shipping dimensions, uncrated....................(cu ft) 1,457; (sq ft) 179
Ground clearance..(in.) 10⁵⁄₁₆
Electrical system...(volts) 6
  No. of batteries...1
  Type of ground...negative
Fuel octane rating..72
Capacities:
  Fuel...(gal) 31
  Cooling system...(qt) 28
  Crankcase, refill...(qt) 9
  Transmission..(qt) 9½
  Rear axle...(qt) 8
Brakes:
  Manufacturer......................Bendix-Westinghouse; Type; air
  Parking brake, type...................................transmission
Transmission:
  Forward speeds..5
  Gear ratio.......................High 1:1; Fourth 1.41:1; Low 8.03:1

PERFORMANCE

Computed grade ability in lowest gear, loaded................(percent) 40
Turning radius..(ft) 31
Fording depth..(in.) 29½
Fuel consumption, loaded....................................(mpg) 3½
Cruising range, loaded.......................................(mi) 108
Allowable speed, governed...................................(mph) 50

ENGINE

Manufacturer......................International Harvester; Model RD–406
Type.....................Valve-in-head, 4-cycle; No. of cylinders (in line) 6
Displacement...(cu in.) 405.9
Bore..(in.) 4⅜
Stroke..(in.) 4½
Compression ratio...6.3:1
Governed speed...(rpm) 2,750
Brake horsepower (max w/std accessories)...............138 at (rpm) 2,750
Torque (max)...313 lb-ft at (rpm) 1,000

ADDITIONAL DATA

Rear axle, type.....................two-speed, spiral-bevel, full-floating
Transmission, type....................................synchromesh
  Data given for chassis with 175-in. wheelbase. Changes in data for
chassis with 193-in. wheelbase are as follows:
Net weight (lb)...8,865
Axle load (lb)........................Empty; front 4,885; rear 3,935
Shipping dimensions, uncrated...................(cu ft) 1,586; (sq ft) 195
Turning radius (ft)..34
Overall length...(in.) 296¾
Distance from rear of cab to center of rear axle.............(in.) 120
Rear overhang...(in.) 68½
Angle of departure..(deg) 25

TRUCK, CHASSIS, W/CAB, 5-TON, 4 x 2
(White, Model WC22)

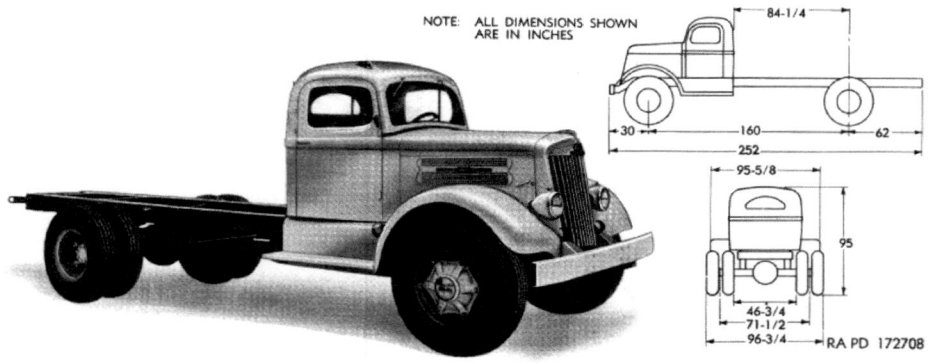

NOTE: ALL DIMENSIONS SHOWN ARE IN INCHES

RA PD 172708

Classification: Standard.

Purpose: To be used as component of general-purpose or special-equipment vehicle.

GENERAL DATA

Crew..2
Weight (lb): Net...15,360
Rear-axle gear ratio (two-speed)...............High 6.5 : 1; Low 8.87 : 1
Axle load (lb):
  Empty...front 4,840; rear 10,520
Tires:
  Ply 12...Size 11.00 x 20; Pressure (psi) 70
  Tread, center-to-center, front.................................(in.) 70¾
Shipping dimensions, uncrated.......................(cu ft) 1,320; (sq ft) 167
Vehicle dimensions:
  Ground clearance..(in.) 17¼
  Frame height...(in.) 47
Electrical system..(volts) 6
  No. of batteries..1
  Type of ground..positive
Fuel octane rating..72
Capacities:
  Fuel..(gal) 32
  Cooling system...(qt) 30
  Crankcase, refill..(qt) 12
  Transmission...(qt) 8
  Rear axle..(qt) 9
Brakes:
  Manufacturer; Bendix-Westinghouse......................Type; air
  Parking brake, type....................................transmission
Transmission:
  Forward speeds...5
  Gear ratio...................High 1 : 1; Fourth 1.48 : 1; Low 7.88 : 1

PERFORMANCE

Computed grade ability in lowest gear, loaded.................(percent) 43
Turning radius..(ft) 29
Fording depth..(in.) 30
Fuel consumption, loaded..(mpg) 3
Cruising range, loaded...(mi) 95
Allowable speed, governed.......................................(mph) 55

ENGINE

Manufacturer: White.......................................Model 150A
Type.....................4-cycle, L-head; No. of cylinders (in line) 6
Displacement..(cu in.) 386
Bore...(in.) 4
Stroke..(in.) 5¾
Compression ratio...6.40 : 1
Governed speed..(rpm) 3,000
Brake horsepower (max w/std accessories)...............735 at (rpm) 3,000
Torque (max w/std accessories)...............315 lb-ft at (rpm) 1,300

ADDITIONAL DATA

Rear axle, type...........................two-speed, spiral-bevel, full-floating
Transmission, type...synchromesh

TRUCK, DUMP, 5-TON, 4 x 2

(International Harvester, Model KR11)

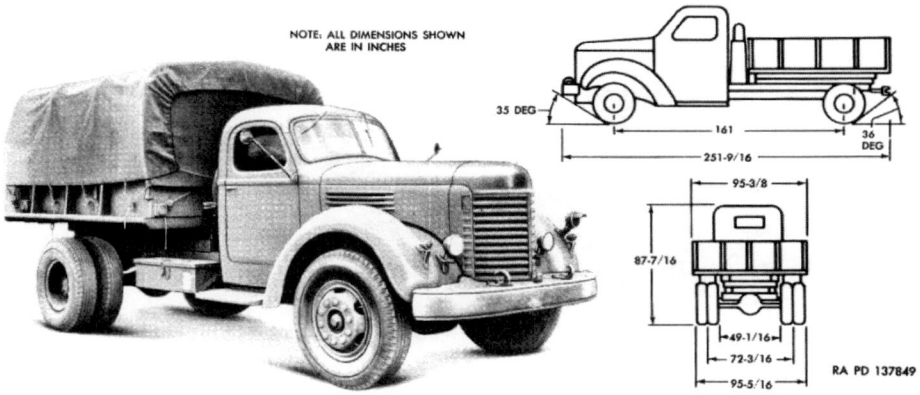

NOTE: ALL DIMENSIONS SHOWN
ARE IN INCHES

35 DEG

161

251-9/16

36 DEG

95-3/8

87-7/16

49-1/16

72-3/16

95-5/16

RA PD 137849

Technical Manuals: 9–823, 9–1823, 9–1825A, 9–1826C, 9–1827A, 9–1828A; **Supply Catalog:** SNL G–542.

Classification: Standard.

Purpose: To haul and dump earth, sand, gravel, etc., and to transport general cargo.

GENERAL DATA

Crew	2
Weight (lb)	Net 12,815
Payload	10,000
Gross	22,815
Rear-axle gear ratio	8.05:1
Axle load (lb):	
Empty	front 5,285; rear 7,530
Loaded	front 5,845; rear 16,970
Tires:	
Ply 12	Size 10.00 x 20; Pressure (psi) 70
Tread, center-to-center, front	(in.) 71¾
Shipping dimensions, uncrated	(cu ft) 1,215; (sq ft) 167
Vehicle dimensions:	
Ground clearance	(in.) 11¼
Pintle height, loaded	(in.) 32¾
Loading height, empty	(in.) 48⅞₁₆
Body inside dimensions (in.):	
Length....114; Width 84; Height under bows 59, side panels 31	
Cargo space	(cu ft) 172
Electrical systems	(volts) 12
No. of batteries (6-volt)	2
Type of ground	positive
Fuel octane rating	72
Capacities:	
Fuel	(gal) 31
Cooling system	(qt) 27
Crankcase, refill	(qt) 8
Transmission w/power take-off	(qt) 13
Rear axle	(qt) 8½
Brakes:	
Manufacturer	Bendix-Westinghouse; Type; air
Parking brake, type	transmission
Transmission:	
Forward speeds	5
Gear ratio	High 1:1; Fourth 1.38:1; Low 8.08:1

PERFORMANCE

Computed grade ability in lowest gear, loaded	(percent) 50
Turning radius	(ft) 29
Fording depth	(in.) 32¾
Fuel consumption, loaded	(mpg) 5¼
Cruising range, loaded	(mi) 162
Allowable speed, governed	(mph) 36
Maximum recommended towed load	(lb) 15,000

ENGINE

Manufacturer: I.H.C.	Model REO 450–D
Type	Valve-in-head, 4-cycle; No. of cylinders (in line) 6
Displacement	(cu in.) 450.99
Bore	(in.) 4⅜
Stroke	(in.) 5
Compression ratio	6.3:1
Governed speed	(rpm) 2,600
Brake horsepower (max w/std accessories)	133 at (rpm) 2,600
Torque (max)	300 lb-ft at (rpm) 1,000

ADDITIONAL DATA

Overall height w/top	(in.) 109⅞₁₆
Rear axle, type	double-reduction, full-floating
Transmission, type	constant-mesh

TRUCK, DUMP, 5-TON, 4 x 2
(International Harvester, Model L–201)

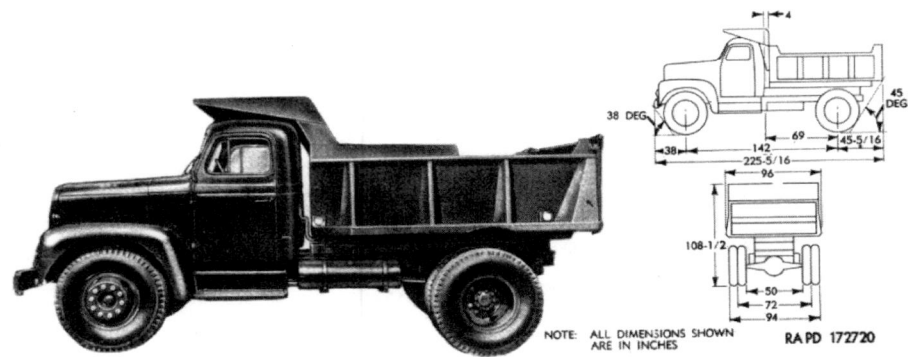

NOTE: ALL DIMENSIONS SHOWN ARE IN INCHES   RA PD 172720

Classification: Standard.

Purpose: To transport and dump earth, sand, gravel, coal, etc, and to carry general cargo.

GENERAL DATA

Crew..2
Weight (lb)...Net 12,435
    Payload...........................off highway 10,000; on highway 11,500
    Gross..............................off highway 22,435; on highway 23,935
Rear-axle gear ratio (2 speed)....................High 6.5:1; Low 8.866:1
Axle load (lb):
    Empty..front 4,995; rear 7,440
    Loaded:
        Off highway...........................front 5,845; rear 16,590
        On highway............................front 5,935; rear 18,000
Tires:
    Ply 12....................................Size 11.00 x 20; Pressure (psi) 70
    Tread, center-to-center, front...................................(in.) 70¼
Shipping dimensions, uncrated......................(cu ft) 1,360; (sq ft) 151
Vehicle dimensions:
    Ground clearance...(in.) 10⅞
    Body inside dimensions (in.):
        Length...............108; Width 84; Height 25¾
    Struck capacity...(cu yds) 5
Electrical system..(volts) 6
    No. of batteries..1
    Type of ground..positive
Fuel octane rating...72
Capacities:
    Fuel...(gal) 31
    Cooling system...(qt) 28
    Crankcase, refill...(qt) 9
    Transmission...(qt) 6
    Rear axle...(qt) 8
Brakes:
    Manufacturer....................Bendix-Westinghouse; Type; air
    Parking brake, type..................................transmission
Transmission:
    Forward speeds...5
    Gear ratio...............High 1:1; Fourth 1.45:1; Low 7.4:1

PERFORMANCE

Computed grade ability in lowest gear w/off-highway load....(percent) 45
Turning radius...(ft) 29
Fuel consumption, loaded....... ....(mpg) 4½
Cruising range, loaded.......................................(mi) 140
Allowable speed, governed..(mph) 50

ENGINE

Manufacturer: International...............................Model RD-406
Type................4-cycle, valve-in-head; No. of cylinders (in line) 6
Displacement...(cu in.) 406
Bore..(in.) 4⅜
Stroke..(in.) 4½
Compression ratio..6.3:1
Governed speed...(rpm) 2,800
Brake horsepower (max w/std accessories).............138 at (rpm) 2,750
Torque (max w/std accessories)....................314 lb-ft at (rpm) 1,000

ADDITIONAL DATA

Rear axle, type....................two-speed, spiral-bevel, full-floating
Transmission, type...synchromesh

TRUCK, TRACTOR, 5-TON, 4 x 2

(Diamond T, Model 720)

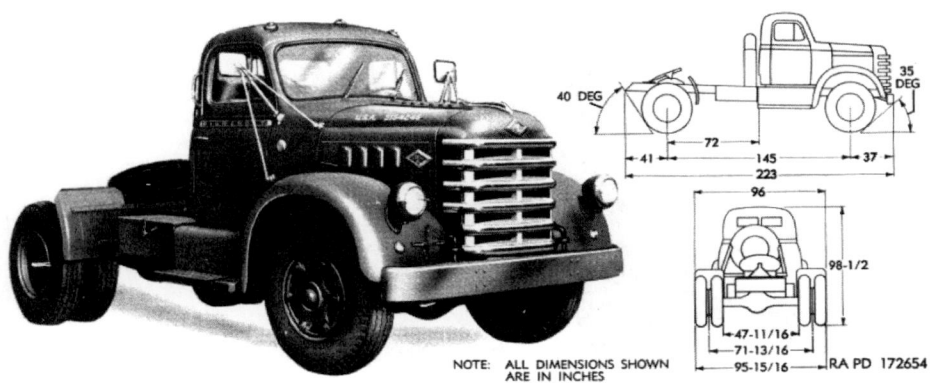

NOTE: ALL DIMENSIONS SHOWN ARE IN INCHES

RA PD 172654

Purpose: To tow semitrailers.

GENERAL DATA

Crew..2
Weight (lb)..Net 10,260
    Payload..14,740
    Gross..25,000
Rear-axle gear ratio (two speed)......................High 6.5:1; Low 8.86:1
Axle load (lb):
    Empty.......................................front 5,320; rear 4,940
    Loaded:
        On highway.............................front 6,000; rear 19,000
Tires:
    Ply 12..................................Size 11.00 x 20; Pressure (psi) 80
    Tread, center-to-center, front.............................(in.) 71¹⁵⁄₁₆
Shipping dimensions, uncrated..................(cu ft) 1,220; (sq ft) 149
Vehicle dimensions:
    Ground clearance...(in.) 10¼
    Frame height...(in.) 38½
    Height to center of fifth wheel, empty.......................(in.) 47½
    Height to rear of fifth wheel, empty.........................(in.) 39½
    Fifth wheel mounted forward of rear axle......................(in.) 6
Electrical system...(volts) 6
    No. of batteries...1
    Type of ground...positive
Fuel octane rating...72
Capacities:
    Fuel...(gal) 86
    Cooling system (qt).............w/o heater 36; w/heater 37
    Crankcase, refill...(qt) 10
    Transmission..(qt) 9
    Rear axle..(qt) 10
Brakes:
    Manufacturer.....................Bendix; Type, air-hydraulic
    Parking brake, type...................................transmission
Transmission:
    Forward speeds..5
    Gear ratio...................High 1:1; Fourth 1.48:1; Low 7.88:1

PERFORMANCE

Computed grade ability in lowest gear, loaded...................(percent) 26
Turning radius (ft)...............................Right 47; Left 50
Fording depth...(in.) 23
Fuel consumption, loaded......................................(mpg) 4½
Cruising range, loaded..(mi) 390
Allowable speed, governed.....................................(mph) 50
Maximum semitrailer, gross?..................................(lb) 39,750

ENGINE

Manufacturer.........................Continental; Model T6427
Type..................4-cycle, valve-in-head; No. of cylinders (in line) 6
Displacement...(cu in.) 427
Bore...(in.) 4⁵⁄₁₆
Stroke..(in.) 4¾
Compression ratio..6.44:1
Governed speed..(rpm) 2,700
Brake horsepower (max w/std accessories)..............148 at (rpm) 2,700
Torque (max w/std accessories)..............328 lb-ft at (rpm) 1,500

ADDITIONAL DATA

Rear axle, type.................................2-speed, full-floating
Transmission, type..synchromesh

TRUCK, TRACTOR, 5-TON, 4 x 2
(Federal, Model 45M2)

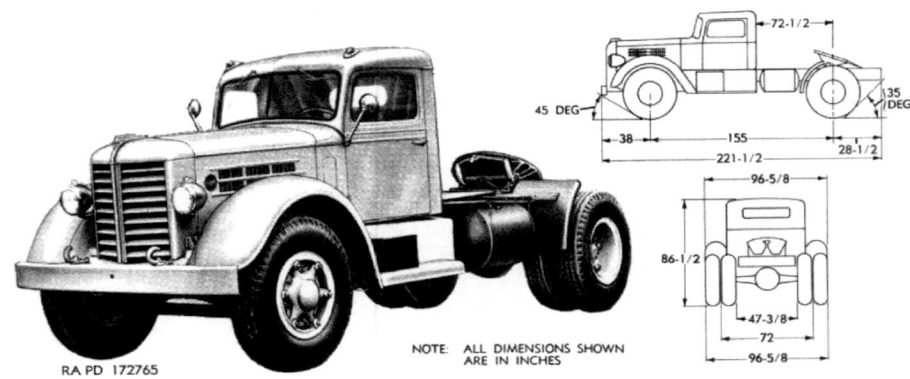

RA PD 172765

NOTE: ALL DIMENSIONS SHOWN ARE IN INCHES

Classification: Nonclassified.

Purpose: To tow semitrailers.

GENERAL DATA

Crew	2
Weight (lb)	Net 9,800
Payload	14,700
Gross	24,500
Rear-axle gear ratio (two-speed)	High 6.53:1; Low 8.53:1
Axle load (lb):	
Empty	front 5,040; rear 4,760
Loaded	front 6,000; rear 18,500
Tires:	
Ply 12	Size 11.00 x 20; Pressure (psi) 70
Tread, center-to-center, front	(in.) 70¾
Shipping dimensions, uncrated	(cu ft) 1,070; (sq ft) 149
Vehicle dimensions:	
Ground clearance	(in.) 10
Frame height	(in.) 45
Height to center of fifth wheel, empty	(in.) 52
Height to rear of fifth wheel, empty	(in.) 46
Fifth wheel mounted forward of rear axle	(in.) 4
Electrical system	(volts) 6
No. of batteries	1
Type of ground	positive
Fuel octane rating	72
Capacities:	
Fuel	(gal) 60
Cooling system	(qt) 29
Crankcase, refill	(qt) 8
Transmission	(qt) 10
Rear axle	(qt) 15½
Brakes:	
Manufacturer	Bendix-Westinghouse; Type, air
Parking brake, type	transmission
Transmission:	
Forward speeds	5
Gear ratio	High 1:1; Fourth 1.48:1; Low 7.88:1

PERFORMANCE

Computed grade ability in lowest gear, loaded	(percent) 23
Turning radius	(ft) 28
Fuel consumption, loaded	(mpg) 4½
Cruising range, loaded	(mi) 270
Allowable speed, governed	(mph) 48
Maximum semitrailer, gross	(lb) 25,000

ENGINE

Manufacturer: Continental	Model T-6427F
Type	4-cycle, valve-in-head; No. of cylinders 6
Displacement	(cu in.) 427
Bore	(in.) 11⅝₆
Stroke	(in.) 4¾
Compression ratio	6.4:1
Governed speed	(rpm) 2,600
Brake horsepower (max w/std accessories)	158 at (rpm) 2,600
Torque (max w/std accessories)	325 lb-ft at (rpm) 1,400

ADDITIONAL DATA

Rear axle, type	two-speed, full-floating
Transmission, type	synchromesh

TRUCK, TRACTOR, 5-TON, 4 x 2

(International Harvester, Model KR11, 1943)

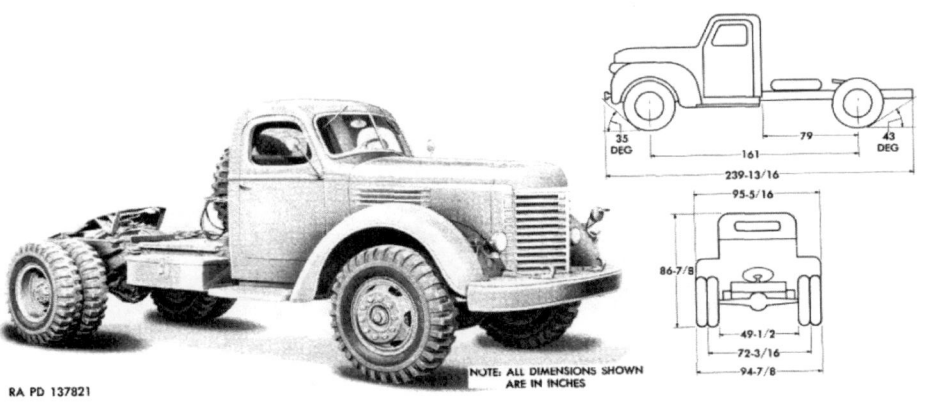

35 DEG   79   43 DEG

161

239-13/16

95-5/16

86-7/8

49-1/2

72-3/16

94-7/8

RA PD 137821

NOTE: ALL DIMENSIONS SHOWN ARE IN INCHES

Technical Manuals: 9–823, 9–1823, 9–1825A, 9–1826C, 9–1827A, 9–1828A; Supply Catalog: SNL G–542.

Classification: Nonclassified.

Purpose: To tow semitrailers.

GENERAL DATA

Crew..2
Weight (lb)................Net 9,801; Payload 13,000; Gross 22,801
Rear-axle gear ratio...8. 05:1
Axle load (lb):
    Empty..front 4,798; rear 5,003
    Loaded..front 5,201; rear 17,600
Tires:
    Ply 12............................Size 10.00 x 20; Pressure (psi) 70
    Tread, center-to-center, front............................(in.) 72⅜
Shipping dimensions, uncrated............(cu ft) 1,149; (sq ft) 159
Vehicle dimensions:
    Ground clearance..(in.) 10¾
    Pintle height, empty......................................(in.) 34¾
    Center of fifth wheel to center of rear axle............(in.) 5
    Height to center of fifth wheel, empty..............(in.) 48⅜
    Height to rear of fifth wheel............................(in.) 42
Electrical system..(volts) 6
    N of batteries..2
    Type of ground..positive
Fuel octane rating..70
Capacities:
    Fuel..(gal) 40
    Cooling system..(qt) 26½
    Crankcase, refill..(qt) 8
    Transmission..(qt) 13
    Rear axle..(qt) 8½
Brakes:
    Manufacturer............Bendix-Westinghouse; Type; air
    Parking brake, type..............................transmission
Transmission:
    Forward speeds..5
    Gear ratio............High 0.776:1; Fourth 1:1; Low 7.07:1

PERFORMANCE

Computed grade ability in lowest gear, loaded...........(percent) 25
Turning radius...(ft) 29
Fording depth..(in.) 32½
Fuel consumption:
    W/max towed load......................................(mpg) 3.5
    W/o towed load..(mpg) 4.5
Cruising range:
    W/max towed load......................................(mi) 140
    W/o towed load..(mi) 180
Allowable speed, governed................................(mph) 50
Maximum semitrailer, gross..........................(lb) 30,000

ENGINE

Manufacturer..................International Harvester; Model RED–450
Type..............4-cycle, valve-in-head; No. of cylinders (in line) 6
Displacement......................................(cu in.) 450.99
Bore..(in.) 4⅜
Stroke..(in.) 5
Compression ratio.....................................6.3:1
Governed speed......................................(rpm) 2,700
Brake horsepower (max w/std accessories)........130 at (rpm) 2,600
Torque (max)................................354 lb-ft at (rpm) 900

ADDITIONAL DATA

Rear Axle, type..........................double-reduction, full-floating
Transmission, type..................................constant-mesh

261

TRUCK, TRACTOR, 5-TON, 4 x 2
(International Harvester Model L–201)

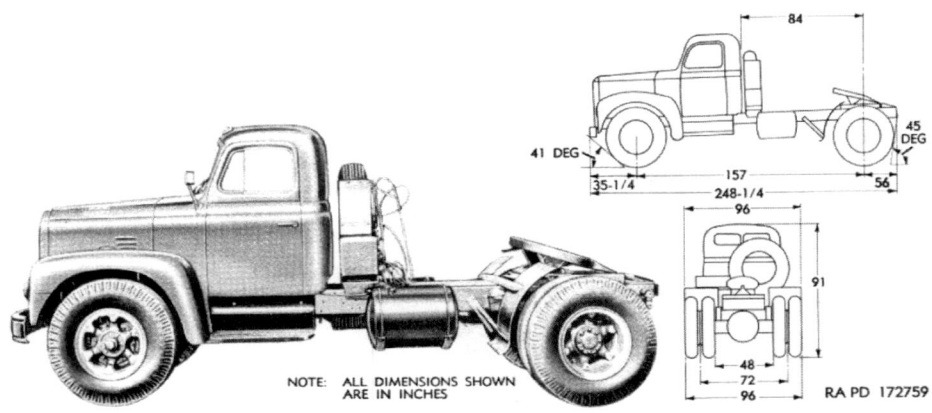

NOTE: ALL DIMENSIONS SHOWN ARE IN INCHES

RA PD 172759

Classification: Nonclassified.

Purpose: To tow semitrailers.

GENERAL DATA

Crew..2
Weight (lb)......................Net 10,220; Payload 13,500; Gross 23,720
Rear-axle gear ratio (2-speed).........................High 6.5:1; Low 8.866:1
Axle load (lb):
  Empty...front 5,180; rear 5,040
  Loaded..front 5,720; rear 18,000
Tires:
  Ply 12.............................Size 11.00 x 20; Pressure (psi) 70
  Tread, center-to-center, front...............................(in.) 70¼
Shipping dimensions, uncrated......................(cu ft) 1,250; (sq ft) 165
Vehicle dimensions:
  Ground clearance...(in.) 10⅜
  Frame height...(in.) 38¾
  Height to center of fifth wheel, empty.......................(in.) 52
  Height to rear of fifth wheel, empty.........................(in.) 45
  Fifth wheel mounted forward of rear axle.....................(in.) 6
Electrical system...(volts) 6
  No. of batteries...1
  Type of ground..positive
Fuel octane rating...72
Capacities:
  Fuel..(gal) 68
  Cooling system...(qt) 28
  Crankcase, refill..(qt) 9
  Transmission...(qt) 9½
  Rear axle..(qt) 11
Brakes:
  Manufacturer: Bendix-Westinghouse.......................Type, air
  Parking brake, type....................................transmission
Transmission:
  Forward speeds..5
  Gear ratio..................High 1:1; Fourth 1.41:1; Low 8.03:1

PERFORMANCE

Computed grade ability in lowest gear, loaded.................(percent) 28
Turning radius...(ft) 28½
Fording depth...(in.) 29½
Fuel consumption, loaded.......................................(mpg) 3.4
Cruising range, loaded...(mi) 232
Allowable speed, governed......................................(mph) 50
Maximum semitrailer, gross.....................................(lb) 25,000

ENGINE

Manufacturer.....................................IHC; Model RD-406
Type................4-cycle, valve-in-head; No. of cylinders (in line) 6
Displacement...(cu in.) 406
Bore..(in.) 4⅜
Stroke..(in.) 4½
Compression ratio...6.3:1
Governed speed..(rpm) 2,750
Brake horsepower (max w/std accessories).............138 at (rpm) 2,750
Torque (max w/std accessories)..................314 lb-ft at (rpm) 1,000

ADDITIONAL DATA

Rear axle, type.................................two-speed, full-floating
Transmission, type...constant-mesh

TRUCK, TRACTOR, 5-TON, 4 x 2

(White, Model WC 22 PLT)

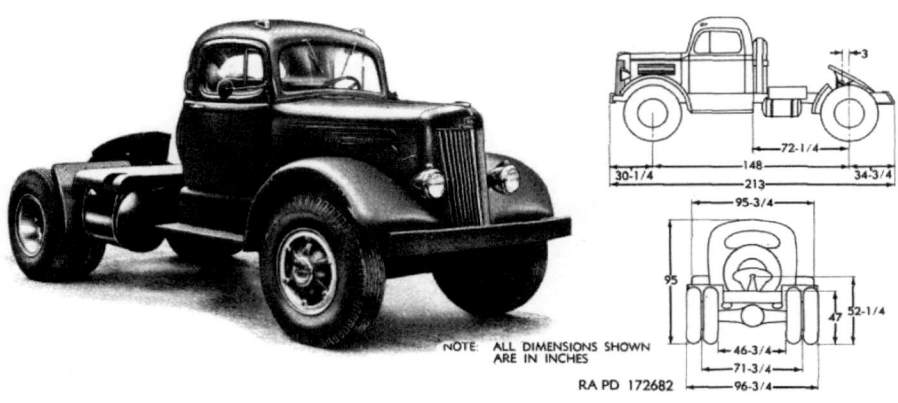

NOTE: ALL DIMENSIONS SHOWN ARE IN INCHES

RA PD 172682

Classification: Nonclassified.

Purpose: To tow semitrailers.

GENERAL DATA

Crew..2
Weight (lb).........................Net 9,840; Payload 14,530; Gross 24,370
Rear-axle gear ratio (two-speed)...................High 6.5:1; Low 8.87:1
Axle load (lb):
    Empty..front 4,570; rear 5,270
    Loaded...............................on highway 6,370; rear 18,000
Tires:
    Ply 12......................Size 11.00 x 20; Pressure (psi) 70
    Tread, center-to-center, front..........................(in.) $70\frac{11}{16}$
Shipping dimensions, uncrated...............(cu ft) 1,120; (sq ft) 142
Vehicle dimensions:
    Ground clearance..................................(in.) $17\frac{1}{4}$
    Frame height...(in.) 47
Electrical system.......................................(volts) 6
    No. of batteries...1
    Type of ground..................................positive
Fuel octane rating..72
Capacities:
    Fuel...(gal) 68
    Cooling system...................................(qt) 30
    Crankcase, refill.................................(qt) 12
    Transmission.......................................(qt) 8
    Rear axle...(qt) $11\frac{1}{2}$
Brakes:
    Manufacturer....................Bendix-Westinghouse; Type; air
    Parking brake, type................................transmission
Transmission:
    Forward speeds...5
    Gear ratio.................High 1:1; Fourth 1.48:1; Low 7.88:1

PERFORMANCE

Computed grade ability in lowest gear, loaded..................(percent) 43
Turning radius...(ft) 28
Fording depth..(in.) 30
Fuel consumption, loaded.......................................(mpg) 3
Cruising range, loaded...(mi) 200
Allowable speed, governed.....................................(mph) 55
Maximum semitrailer, gross...................................(lb) 30,000

ENGINE

Manufacturer: White...Model 150A
Type........................4-cycle, L-head; No. of cylinders (in line) 6
Displacement..(cu in.) 386
Bore...(in.) 4
Stroke..(in.) $5\frac{1}{8}$
Compression ratio...6.45:1
Governed speed...(rpm) 3,000
Brake horsepower (max w/std accessories)..............135 at (rpm) 3,000
Torque (max w/std accessories)....................315 lb-ft at (rpm) 1,300

ADDITIONAL DATA

Rear-axle, type.....................two-speed, spiral-bevel, full-floating
Transmission, type.............................selective sliding-gear

TRUCK, TRACTOR, 5-TON, 4 x 2, M425

(International Harvester, Model H542–9, COE)

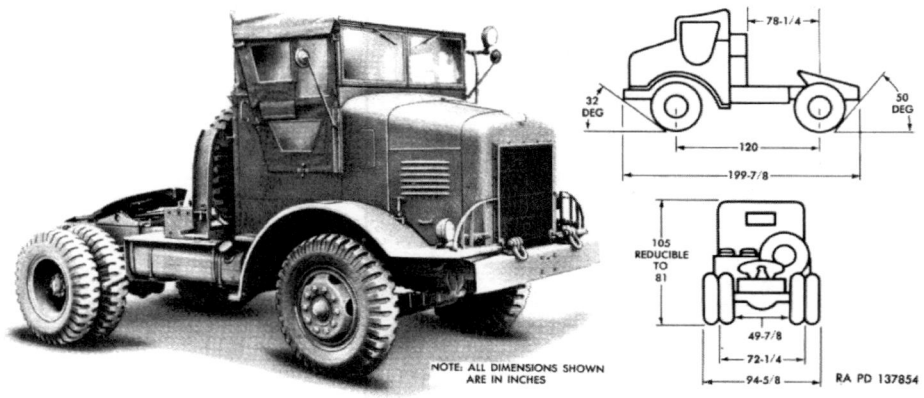

NOTE: ALL DIMENSIONS SHOWN ARE IN INCHES

RA PD 137854

Technical Manuals: 9–812, 9–1812, 9–1825A, 9–1826C, 9–1827A, 9–1828A; **Supply Catalog:** SNL G–671.

Classification: Limited Standard.

Purpose: To tow semitrailers.

GENERAL DATA

```
Crew................................................................................2
Weight (lb)........................Net 11,400; Payload 13,000; Gross 24,400
Rear-axle gear ratio..............................................8.14:1
Axle load (lb):
    Empty...............................................front  6,617; rear  4,783
    Loaded..............................................front  7,717; rear 16,683
Tires:
    Ply 10...............................Size 9.00 x 20; Pressure (psi) 65
    Tread, center-to-center, front.....................................(in.) 69⅜
Shipping dimensions, uncrated..................(cu ft) 1,122; (sq ft) 132
Vehicle dimensions:
    Ground clearance....................................................(in.) 9
    Pintle height (in.)......................Loaded 30¾; Empty 33¾
    Center of fifth wheel to center of rear axle......................(in.) 3
    Height to center of fifth wheel, empty.........................(in.) 53½
    Height to rear of fifth wheel..................................(in.) 47½
Electrical system.....................................................(volts) 6
    No. of batteries....................................................1
    Type of ground..................................................negative
Fuel octane rating...................................................72
Capacities:
    Fuel.............................................................(gal) 80
    Cooling system..................................................(qt) 36
    Crankcase, refill...............................................(qt) 15
    Transmission....................................................(qt) 12¼
    Rear axle.......................................................(qt) 10
Brakes:
    Manufacturer;  Bendix-Westinghouse................Type;  air
    Parking brake, type.......................................transmission
Transmission:
    Forward speeds......................................................5
    Gear ratio................High 1:1; Fourth 1.5:1; Low 8.08:1
```

PERFORMANCE

```
Computed grade ability in lowest gear, loaded..............(percent) 41
Turning radius..................................................(ft) 23½
Fording depth....................................................(in.) 32⅜
Fuel consumption, empty........................................(mpg) 4
    W/max towed load.............................................(mpg) 3½
Cruising range, empty..........................................(mi) 320
    W/max towed load............................................(mi) 280
Allowable speed, governed.....................................(mph) 35
Maximum semitrailer, gross....................................(lb) 30,000
```

ENGINE

```
Manufacturer.............................................IHC; Model REO 450–D
Type..................Valve-in-head, 4-cycle; No. of cylinders (in line) 6
Displacement..............................................(cu in.) 450.99
Bore........................................................(in.) 4¾
Stroke......................................................(in.) 5
Compression ratio..........................................6.3:1
Governed speed.........................................(rpm) 2,600
Brake horsepower (max w/std accessories)..........124.5 at (rpm) 2,600
Torque (max)........................................348 lb-ft at (rpm) 800
```

ADDITIONAL DATA

All vehicles equipped with truck mount M36 for antiaircraft machine gun.

```
Rear axle, type.............................double-reduction, full-floating
Transmission, type..................................constant-mesh
```

TRUCK, TRACTOR, 5-TON, 4 x 2, M426

(International Harvester, Marmon Herrington, Kenworth, Model H542–11, COE)

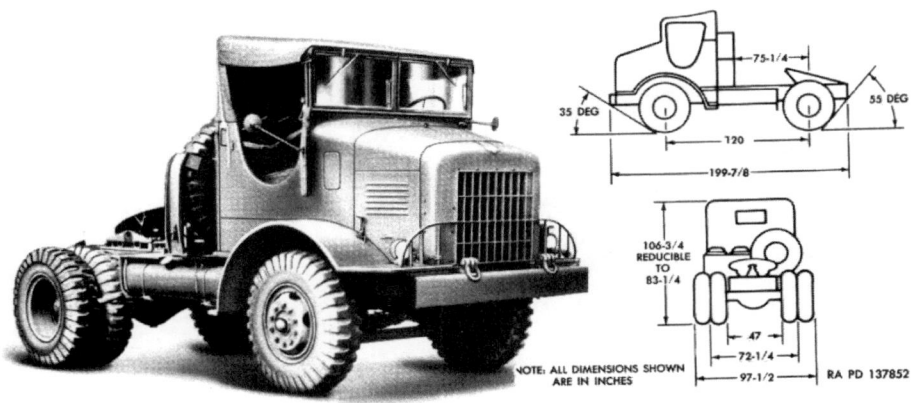

NOTE: ALL DIMENSIONS SHOWN ARE IN INCHES   RA PD 137852

Technical Manuals: 9-812, 9-1812, 9-1825A, 9-1826C, 9-1827A, 9-1828A; Supply Catalog: SNL G-671.

Vehicle illustrated: International Harvester.
Classification: Standard.

Purpose: To tow semitrailers.

GENERAL DATA

Crew	2
Weight (lb)	Payload 13,000; Gross 25,100; Net 12,100
Payload	off highway 13,000; on highway 15,400
Gross	off highway 25,100; on highway 27,500
Rear-axle gear ratio	8.14:1
Axle load (lb)	front 6,800; rear 5,300
Loaded:	
Off highway	front 7,900; rear 17,200
On highway	front 8,100; rear 19,400
Tires:	
Ply 14	Size 11.00 x 20; Pressure (psi) 70
Tread, center-to-center, front	(in.) 69¾
Shipping dimensions, uncrated	(cu ft) 1,182; (sq ft) 136
Vehicle dimensions:	
Ground clearance	(in.) 10⅞₆
Pintle height (in.)	Loaded 34; Empty 37
Center of fifth wheel to center of rear axle	(in.) 6
Height to center of fifth wheel, empty	(in.) 53½
Height to rear of fifth wheel, empty	(in.) 47½
Electrical system	(volts) 6
No. of batteries	1
Type of ground	negative
Fuel octane rating	72
Capacities:	
Fuel	(gal) 80
Cooling system	(qt) 36
Crankcase refill	(qt) 15
Transmission	(qt) 12¼
Rear axle	(qt) 10
Brakes:	
Manufacturer	Bendix-Westinghouse; Type: air
Parking brake, type	transmission
Transmission:	
Forward speeds	5
Gear ratio	High 1:1; Fourth 1.5:1; Low 8.08:1

PERFORMANCE

Computed grade ability in lowest gear, loaded	(percent) 25
Turning radius (ft)	Right 25½; Left 25¼
Fording depth	(in.) 35¼
Fuel consumption:	
Empty	(mpg) 4
W/towed load	(mpg) 3
Cruising range:	
Empty	(mi) 320
W/towed load	(mi) 240
Allowable speed, governed	(mph) 38
Maximum semitrailer, gross	(lb) 30,000

ENGINE

Manufacturer	International Harvester; Model Red-450-D
Type	Valve-in-head, 4-cycle; No. of cylinders (in line) 6
Displacement	(cu in.) 450.99
Bore	(in.) 4¾
Stroke	(in.) 5
Compression ratio	6.3:1
Governed speed	(rpm) 2,600
Brake horsepower (max w/std accessories)	124.5 at (rpm) 2,600
Torque (max)	348 lb-ft at (rpm) 800

ADDITIONAL DATA

All vehicles equipped with truck mount M36 for antiaircraft machine gun.

Rear axle, type	double-reduction, full-floating
Transmission, type	constant-mesh

TRUCK, CARGO, 5-TON, 6 x 6, M41

NOTE: ALL DIMENSIONS SHOWN
ARE IN INCHES

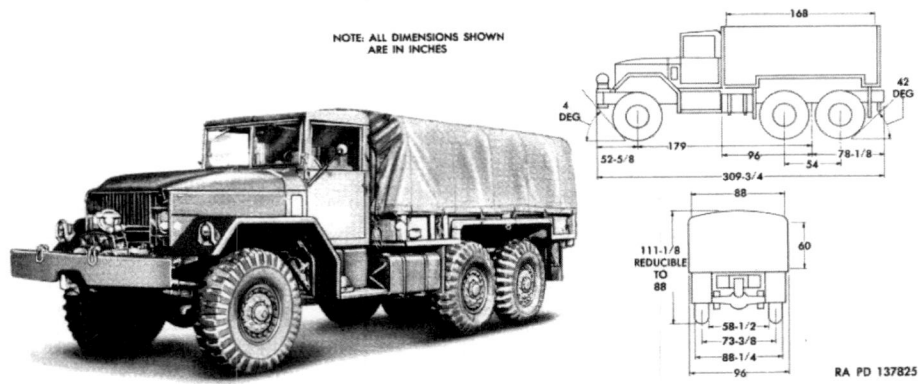

RA PD 137825

Technical Manuals: 9-837, 9-1837A, 9-1837B; Supply Catalog: SNL G-744.

Classification: Standard.

Purpose: To transport general cargo and tow 155-mm howitzer.

GENERAL DATA

Crew..2
Weight (lb):
  Net.............................w/o winch 19,119; w/winch 19,835
  Payload w/crew..............off highway 10,350; on highway 15,350
  Gross:
    W/o winch...............off highway 29,469; on highway 34,469
    W/winch.................off highway 30,185; on highway 35,185
Live-axle gear ratio..6.443:1
Axle load (lb):
  Empty:
    W/o winch......................front 8,331; rear (each) 5,394
    W/winch........................front 9,185; rear (each) 5,325
  Loaded:
    W/o winch:
      Off highway...............front 8,811; rear (each) 10,329
      On highway...............front 8,941; rear (each) 12,764
    W/winch:
      Off highway...............front 9,663; rear (each) 10,261
      On highway...............front 9,793; rear (each) 12,696
Tires:
  Ply 12..............................Size 14 x 20; Pressure (psi) 45
  Tread, center-to-center, front..........................(in.) 76¾
Shipping dimensions:
  Uncrated:
    W/winch........................(cu ft) 1,912; (sq ft) 206
    W/o winch......................(cu ft) 1,817; (sq ft) 196
Vehicle dimensions:
  Ground clearance...(in.) 13
  Pintle height, empty.......................................(in.) 32¾
  Loading height, empty......................................(in.) 48¾
Electrical system..(volts) 24
  No. of batteries......................................(12-volt) 2
  Type of ground...negative
Brakes:
  Manufacturer.............Timken; Type, air-actuated hydraulic
  Parking brake, type......................................transfer
Transmission:
  Forward speeds..5
  Gear ratio.................High 1:1; Fourth 1.43:1; Low 7.31:1
Transfer:
  Speeds...2
  Gear ratio................................High 1:1; Low 2.024:1

GENERAL DATA—Continued

Fuel octane rating..80
Capacities:
  Fuel...(gal) 70
  Cooling system..(qt) 44
  Crankcase, refill.....................................(qt) 18
  Transmission.....................w/o PTO (qt) 13; w/PTO (qt) 14
  Transfer...(qt) 5
  Axles (each)..(qt) 12
  Winch:
    Oil capacity.....................................(qt) 1
    Load capacity................................(lb) 20,000

PERFORMANCE

Computed grade ability in lowest gear, loaded.........(percent) 65
Turning radius..(ft) 41
Fording depth..(in.) 78
Fuel consumption, loaded.....................................(mpg) 4
Cruising range, loaded.......................................(mi) 280
Allowable speed, governed...................................(mph) 59
Maximum recommended towed load:
  Off highway, gross (lb)...............................15,000
  On highway, gross (lb)................................30,000

ENGINE

Manufacturer.....................Continental; Model R-680[2]
Type.................Valve-in-head, 4-cycle, No. of cylinders (in line) 6
Displacement...(cu in.) 602
Bore..(in.) 4⅜
Stroke..(in.) 5⅜
Compression ratio..6.4:1
Governed speed..(rpm) 2,800
Brake horsepower (max w/std accessories)............196 at (rpm) 2,800
Torque (max w/std accessories)..................480 lb-ft at (rpm) 1,200

ADDITIONAL DATA

Dimensions w/o winch: over-all length (in.) 294¼; chassis overhang, front (in.) 37¼; angle of approach (deg) 57.
Live-axles, type...........................double-reduction, full-floating
Transmission, type...synchromesh
Equipped with hydraulic power steering gear.

TRUCK, CHASSIS, 5-TON, 6 x 6, M139

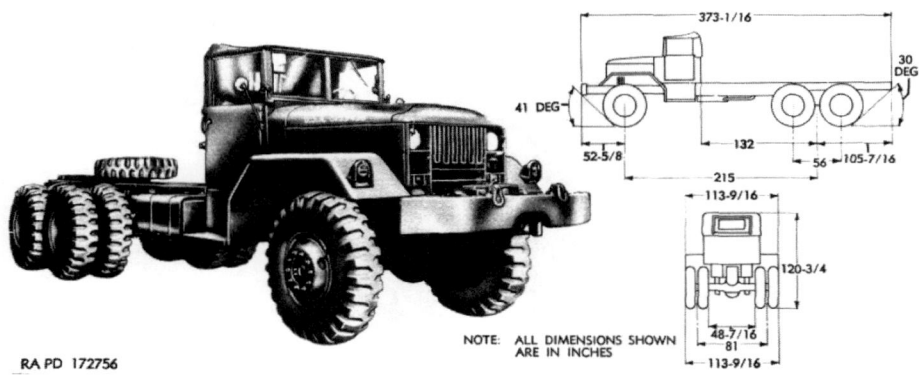

NOTE: ALL DIMENSIONS SHOWN ARE IN INCHES

RA PD 172756

Technical Manual: 9-837.

Purpose: To be used as component of general-purpose or special-equipment vehicle.

GENERAL DATA

Crew..2
Weight (lb)..Net 19,590
Maximum gross...(lb) 42,000
Axle gear ratio...6. 443:1
Axle load (lb):
   Empty..............................front 9,070; rear (each) 10,520
Tires:
   Ply...........................Size 14.00 x 20; Pressure (psi) 45
   Tread, center-to-center, front........................(in.) 76¾
Shipping dimensions, uncrated.............(cu ft) 2,950; (sq ft) 293
Vehicle dimensions:
   Ground clearance...(in.) 13
   Pintle height, empty.......................................(in.) 33
   Frame height...(in.) 45¾
Electrical system...(volts) 24
   No. of batteries...2
   Type of ground...negative
Fuel octane rating...80
Capacities:
   Fuel...(gal) 70
   Cooling system...(qt) 44
   Crankcase, refill.......................................(qt) 22
   Transmission w/PTO...................................(qt) 11
   Transfer...(qt) 5
   Axles, each...(qt) 12
   Winch:
      Oil capacity....................................(qt) 1½
      Load capacity.............................(lb) 20,000
Brakes:
   Serivce:
      Manufacturer................Timken-Bendix-Westinghouse
      Type...air-hydraulic
   Parking brake, type....................................transfer
Transmission:
   Forward speeds..5
   Gear ratio...............High 1:1; Fourth 1.43:1; Low 7.31:1
Transfer:
   Speeds..2
   Gear ratio...........................High 1:1; Low 2.024:1

PERFORMANCE

Computed grade ability in lowest gear w/off-highway load.....(percent) 43
Turning radius...(ft) 47
Fording depth..(in.) 78
Fuel consumption, loaded..................................(mpg) 3. 2
Cruising range, loaded....................................(mi) 224
Allowable speed, governed.................................(mph) 59
Maximum pintle tow:
   Off highway.....................................gross (lb) 15,000
   On highway......................................gross (lb) 30,000

ENGINE

Manufacturer: Continental..............................Model R6602
Type..................4-cycle, valve-in-head; No. of cylinders (in line) 6
Displacement..(cu in.) 602
Bore..(in.) 4¾
Stroke..(in.) 5¾
Compression ratio..6.4 : 1
Governed speed..(rpm) 2,800
Brake horsepower (max w/std accessories)............196 at (rpm) 2,800
Torque (max w/std accessories)..................480 lb-ft at (rpm) 1,200

ADDITIONAL DATA

Axles, type...............................double-reduction, full-floating
Transmission, type..synchromesh
   Equipped with hydraulic power steering gear.

267

TRUCK, DUMP, 5-TON, 6 x 6, M51

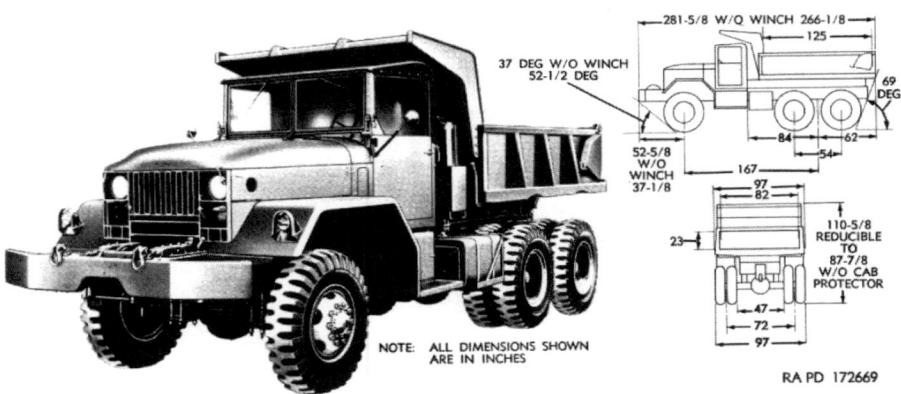

NOTE: ALL DIMENSIONS SHOWN ARE IN INCHES

RA PD 172669

Technical Manuals: 9-837, 9-1837A, 9-1837B; Supply Catalog: SNL G-744.

Classification: Standard.

Purpose: To haul and dump earth, sand, gravel, etc.

GENERAL DATA

Crew..2
Weight (lb): Net.................................w/o winch 21,981; w/winch 22,664
    Payload, w/crew...............off highway 10,350; on highway 20,350
    Gross:
        W/o winch...........off highway 32,331; on highway 42,331
        W/winch.............off highway 33,014; on highway 43,014
Live-axle gear ratio..6.443:1
Axle load (lb):
    Empty:
        W/o winch.....................front 8,459; rear (each) 6,761
        W/winch.......................front 9,304; rear (each) 6,680
    Loaded:
        W/o winch:
            Off highway..............front 8,867; rear (each) 11,732
            On highway...............front 9,067; rear (each) 16,632
        W/winch:
            Off highway..............front 9,712; rear (each) 11,651
            On highway...............front 9,912; rear (each) 16,551
Tires:
    Ply 12........................Size 11.00 x 20; Pressure (psi) 50
    Tread, center-to-center, front.........................(in.) 73¾
Shipping dimensions:
    Uncrated:
        W/winch.................(cu ft) 1,753; (sq ft) 190
        W/o winch...............(cu ft) 1,657; (sq ft) 179
Vehicle dimensions:
    Ground clearance.......................................(in.) 10½
    Pintle height, empty...................................(in.) 30¾
    Loading height, empty...................................(in.) 58
    Struck capacity..(cu yd) 5
Electrical system:..(volts) 24
    No. of batteries...(12-volt) 2
    Type of ground..negative
Brakes:
    Manufacturer.................Timken; Type, air-actuated hydraulic
    Parking brake, type...transfer
Transmission:
    Forward speeds...5
    Gear ratio.................High 1:1; Fourth 1.43:1; Low 7.31:1
Transfer:
    Speeds...2
    Gear ratio..........................High 1:1; Low 2.024:1

GENERAL DATA—Continued

Fuel octane rating..80
Capacities:
    Fuel...(gal) 110
    Cooling system...(qt) 44
    Crankcase, refill...(qt) 18
    Transmission, w/PTO.......................................(qt) 13
    Transfer...(qt) 5
    Axles...(qt) 12
    Winch:
        Oil capacity..(qt) 1
        Load capacity.......................................(lb) 20,000

PERFORMANCE

Computed grade ability in lowest gear, loaded...............(percent) 65
Turning radius...(ft) 39½
Fording depth..(in.) 78
Fuel consumption, loaded..(mpg) 4
Cruising range, loaded..(mi) 440
Allowable speed, governed..(mph) 52
Maximum recommended towed load:
    Off highway...gross (lb) 15,000
    On highway...gross (lb) 30,000

ENGINE

Manufacturer................................Continental Motors; Model; R-6602
Type......................Valve-in-head, 4-cycle; No. of cylinders (in line) 6
Displacement..(cu in.) 602
Bore...(in.) 4⅞
Stroke...(in.) 5⅜
Compression ratio..6.4:1
Governed speed..(rpm) 2,800
Brake horsepower (max w/std accessories).................196 at (rpm) 2,800
Torque (max w/std accessories)....................480 lb-ft at (rpm) 1,200

ADDITIONAL DATA

Dimensions w/o winch: over-all length (in.) 266⅛; chassis overhang, front (in.) 37⅛; angle of approach (deg) 52.
Live-axles, type..........................double-reduction, full-floating
Transmission, type..synchromesh
Equipped with hydraulic power steering gear.

268

TRUCK, TRACTOR, 5-TON, 6 x 6, M52, W/ AND W/O WINCH

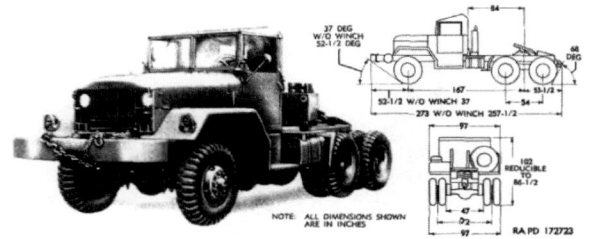

Technical Manual: 9-837; Supply Catalog: SNL G-744.

Classification: Standard.

Purpose: To tow semitrailers.

GENERAL DATA

Crew 2
Weight (lb):
  Net:
    W/winch 18,313
    W/o winch 18,996
  Payload .... off highway 15,000; on highway 25,000
  Gross:
    Off highway:
      W/winch 33,996
      W/o winch 33,313
    On highway:
      W/winch 43,996
      W/o winch 43,313
Rear-axle gear ratio 6.443:1
Axle load (lb):
  Empty:
    Front:
      W/winch 9,008
      W/o winch 8,163
    Rear:
      W/winch .... (each) 4,994
      W/o winch .... (each) 5,075
  Loaded:
    Off highway:
      Front:
        W/winch 9,618
        W/o winch 8,773
      Rear:
        W/winch .... (each) 12,189
        W/o winch .... (each) 12,270
    On highway:
      Front:
        W/winch 9,868
        W/o winch 9,023
      Rear:
        W/winch .... (each) 17,064
        W/o winch .... (each) 17,145
Tires:
  Ply 12 .... Size 11.00 x 20; Pressure (psi) 70
  Tread, center-to-center, front .... (in.) 73¾
Shipping dimensions, uncrated:
  W/winch .... (cu ft) 1,580; (sq ft) 184
  W/o winch .... (cu ft) 1,500; (sq ft) 174
Vehicle dimensions:
  Ground clearance .... (in.) 11¾
  Pintle height, empty .... (in.) 31½
  Frame height .... (in.) 44⅝
  Height to center of fifth wheel, empty .... (in.) 56¹¹⁄₁₆
  Height to rear of fifth wheel, empty .... (in.) 45¾
  Center of fifth wheel forward of rear axle ..... (in.) 4⅝
Electrical system .... (volts) 24
  No. of batteries 2
  Type of ground .... negative

GENERAL DATA—Continued

Fuel octane rating 80
Capacities:
  Fuel .... (gal) 110
  Cooling system .... (qt) 44
  Crankcase, refill .... (qt) 18
  Transmission (qt) .... w/o power take-off 6; w/power take-off 8
  Transfer .... (qt) 5
  Rear axle .... (qt) 12
  Winch:
    Oil capacity .... (qt) 3
    Load capacity .... (lb) 20,000
Brakes:
  Manufacturer .... Bendix; Type, air-hydraulic
  Parking brake, type .... transfer
Transmission:
  Forward speeds 5
  Gear ratio .... High 1:1; Fourth 1.43:1; Low 7.31:1
Transfer:
  Speeds 2
  Gear ratio .... High 1:1; Low 2.024:1

PERFORMANCE

Computed grade ability in lowest gear w/off highway load .... (percent) 65
Turning radius (ft):
  W/o winch 38
  W/winch 38½
Fording depth .... (in.) 30
Fuel consumption, loaded .... (mpg) 2.7
Cruising range, loaded .... (mi) 300
Allowable speed, governed .... (mph) 52
Maximum pintle tow:
  Off highway .... gross (lb) 15,000
  On highway .... gross (lb) 30,000
Maximum semitrailer, gross .... (lb) 30,000

ENGINE

Manufacturer: Continental .... Model R6602-69
Type .... 4-cycle, valve-in-head; No. of cylinders (in line) 6
Displacement .... (cu in.) 602
Bore .... (in.) 4¾
Stroke .... (in.) 5⅜
Compression ratio 6.4:1
Governed speed .... (rpm) 2,800
Brake horsepower (max w/std accessories) ...... 196 at (rpm) 2,800
Torque (max w/std accessories) .... 480 lb-ft at (rpm) 1,200

ADDITIONAL DATA

Live axles, type .... double-reduction, full-floating
Transmission, type .... synchromesh
  Equipped with hydraulic power steering gear.

TRUCK, PONTON TRACTOR, 5- TO 6-TON, 4 x 4

(Autocar, Model U8144T, COE)

NOTE: ALL DIMENSIONS SHOWN
ARE IN INCHES

RA PD 137847

Technical Manuals: 9-817, 9-1817, 9-1825B, 9-1826C, 9-1827A, 9-1828A, 9-1832A; **Supply Catalog:** SNL G-511.

Classification: Standard.

GENERAL DATA

Crew...2
Weight (lb)...................... Net 16,660; Payload, 10,460; Gross, 27,120
Live-axle gear ratio..8.148:1
Axle load (lb):
    Empty...front 9,490; rear 7,170
    Loaded..front 11,020; rear 16,100
Tires:
    Ply 14........................Size 12.00 x 20; Pressure (psi) 80
    Tread, center-to-center, front............................(in.) 71¾
Shipping dimensions, uncrated.................(cu ft) 1,605; (sq ft) 168
Vehicle dimensions:
    Ground clearance..(in.) 10⅜
    Pintle height (in.)..........................Loaded 34½; empty 38
    Center of fifth wheel to center of rear axle...............(in.) 3
    Height to center of fifth wheel...........................(in.) 48½
    Height to rear of fifth wheel.............................(in.) 42½
Electrical system...(volts) 12
    No. of batteries.......................................(6-volt) 2
    Type of ground...positive
Fuel octane rating...68
Capacities:
    Fuel..(gal) 90
    Cooling system..(qt) 40
    Crankcase (qt)...........................dryfill 14; refill 12
    Transfer...(qt) 2
    Transmission w/PTO (qt)................winter 10; summer 8
    Axles (qt)......................................front 8; rear 10
    Winch:
        Oil capacity...(qt) 2
        Load capacity.....................................(lb) 15,000
Brakes:
    Manufacturer....................Bendix-Westinghouse; Type, air
    Parking brake, type..............................transmission
Transmission:
    Forward speeds...5
    Gear ratio..........High 0.75:1; Fourth 1:1; Low 5.9:1
Transfer:
    Speeds...2
    Gear ratio........................High 1:1; Low 1.72:1

Purpose: Used by Corps of Engineers to tow semi-trailers with ponton equipment.

PERFORMANCE

Computed grade ability in lowest gear, loaded...........(percent) 36.2
Turning radius..(ft) 35
Fording depth...(in.) 25
Fuel consumption, empty...............................(mpg) 7
    With maximum allowable towed load.................(mpg) 3
Cruising range, empty.................................(mi) 630
    With maximum allowable towed load.................(mi) 270
Allowable speed, governed............................(mph) 45
Maximum semitrailer, gross.........................(lb) 30,000

ENGINE

Manufacturer.........................Hercules; Model RXC
Type.....................4-cycle, L-head; No. of cylinders (in line) 6
Displacement...(cu in.) 529
Bore..(in.) 4⅝
Stroke..(in.) 5¼
Compression ratio.....................................5.4:1
Governed speed.....................................(rpm) 2,300
Brake horsepower (max w/std accessories)...........112 at (rpm) 2,200
Torque (max).........................368 lb-ft at (rpm) 1,000

ADDITIONAL DATA

Over-all height w/closed cab.........................(in.) 110
Live axles, type.....................double-reduction, full-floating
Transmission, type..............................constant-mesh

TRUCK, CARGO, 6-TON, 6 x 6, W/WINCH

(Mack, Models NM1, NM3 NM5, NM6)

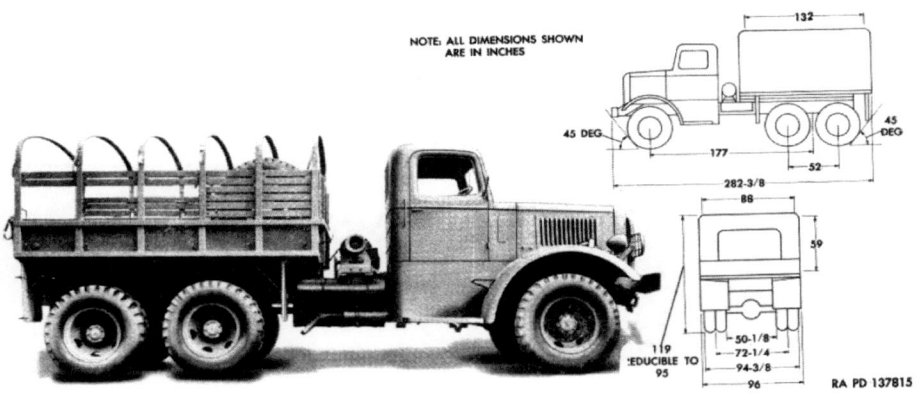

NOTE: ALL DIMENSIONS SHOWN ARE IN INCHES

RA PD 137815

Technical Manual: 10-1477; Supply Catalog: SNL G-535.

Classification: Nonclassified.

Purpose: To transport general cargo, and prime mover for field artillery.

GENERAL DATA

Crew..2
Weight (lb) Net..22,659
  Payload:
    Off highway..............................12,350; Gross 35,009
    On highway...............................19,300; Gross 41,959
Live-axle gear ratio..7.33:1
Axle load (lb):
  Empty.................................front 9,687; rear (each) 6,486
  Loaded:
    Off highway.......................front 10,337; rear (each) 12,336
    On highway........................front 10,703; rear (each) 15,628
Tires:
  Ply 12......................Size 10.00 x 22; Pressure (psi) 70
  Tread, center-to-center, front.....................(in.) 73½
Shipping dimensions, uncrated.............(cu ft) 1,870; (sq ft) 188
Vehicle dimensions:
  Ground clearance..................................(in.) 10¾
  Pintle height, empty..............................(in.) 32
  Loading height, empty.............................(in.) 58
  Body inside dimensions (in.):
    Length...132
    Width...88
    Height..59
  Body cargo space............................(cu ft) 396
Electrical system (12-volt starting)...................(volts) 6
  No. of batteries (6-volt).............................2
  Type of ground...................................positive
Fuel octane rating....................................70
Brakes:
  Manufacturer..............Bendix-Westinghouse; Type: air
  Parking brake, type..............................transfer
Transmission:
  Forward speeds..5
  Gear ratio.............High 1:1; Fourth 1.45:1; Low 8.05:1
Transfer:
  Speeds..2
  Gear ratio...................High 1:1; Low 2.55:1

GENERAL DATA—Continued

Capacities:
  Fuel..(gal) 80
  Cooling system....................................(qt) 54
  Crankcase, refill.................................(qt) 19
  Transmission...∤................................(qt) 10
  Transfer..(qt) 4
  Axles (qt)......................................front 6
    Bogie (each)......................................10
  Winch:
    Oil capacity...................................(qt) 2¾
    Load capacity...............................(lb) 30,000

PERFORMANCE

Computed grade ability in lowest gear, loaded.............(percent) 65
Turning radius (ft)........................Right 37; Left 36
Fording depth...(in.) 44
Fuel consumption, loaded................................(mpg) 3½
Cruising range, loaded..................................(mi) 280
Allowable speed, governed...............................(mph) 34
Maximum recommended towed load:
  Off highway gross (lb)..............................15,000
  On highway gross (lb)...............................30,000

ENGINE

Manufacturer.................................Mack; Model EY
Type...............Valve-in-head, 4-cycle; No. of cylinders (in line) 6
Displacement..(cu in.) 707
Bore..(in.) 5
Stroke..(in.) 6
Compression ratio....................................5.35:1
Governed speed......................................(rpm) 2,100
Brake horsepower (max w/std accessories).........159 at (rpm) 2,100
Torque (max)...........................530 lb-ft at (rpm) 1,000

ADDITIONAL DATA

Live axles, type....................double-reduction, full-floating
Transmission, type...............................constant-mesh

TRUCK, CRANE CHASSIS, 6-TON, 6 x 6

(Corbitt, Model C666)

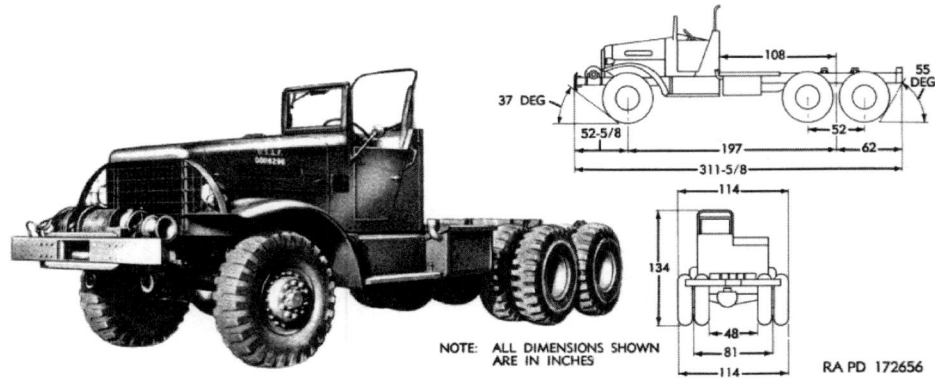

NOTE: ALL DIMENSIONS SHOWN ARE IN INCHES

RA PD 172656

Technical Manuals: 9–813, 9–1813, 9–1825A, 9–1826C, 9–1827A, 9–1828A, 9–1829A, 9–1832A; **Supply Catalog:** SNL G–514.

Classification: Nonclassified.

Purpose: Used by Corps of Engineers for mounting crane.

GENERAL DATA

Crew..1
Weight (lb):
  Net......................22,400; Payload (crane) 10,450; Gross 32,850
Live-axle gear ratio...7.33:1
Axle load (lb):
  Loaded...........................front 11,600; rear (each) 10,675
Tires:
  Ply 18.............................Size 14.00 x 20; Pressure (psi) 40
  Tread, center-to-center, front..........................(in.) 74
Shipping dimensions, uncrated..................(cu ft) 4,390; (sq ft) 251
Vehicle dimensions:
  Ground clearance...(in.) 13
  Pintle height, empty.....................................(in.) 41
Electrical system (12-volt starting)..........................(volts) 6
  No. of batteries......................................(6-volt) 2
  Type of ground...positive
Fuel octane rating..72
Capacities:
  Fuel..(gal) 118
  Cooling system...(qt) 58
  Crankcase, refill......................................(qt) 14
  Transmission...(qt) 10
  Transfer...(qt) 3½
  Axles.........................(qt) front 8; rear (each) 6
  Winch:
    Oil capacity..(qt) 1
    Load capacity.....................................(lb) 25,000
Brakes:
  Manufacturer..................Bendix-Westinghouse; Type; air
  Parking brake, type....................................transfer
Transmission:
  Forward speeds..4
  Gear ratio.......................High 1:1; Low 6.54:1
Transfer:
  Speeds...2
  Gear ratio.......................High 1:1; Low 2.55:1

PERFORMANCE

Computed grade ability in lowest gear, loaded.............(percent) 65
Turning radius (ft)...............................(Right) 44; (Left) 43
Fording depth...(in.) 35
Fuel consumption, loaded................................(mpg) 2.6
Cruising range, loaded....................................(mi) 306
Allowable speed, governed................................(mph) 37

ENGINE

Manufacturer: Hercules...................................Model HXD
Type....................4-cycle, L-head; No. of cylinders (in line) 6
Displacement...(cu in.) 855
Bore...(in.) 5½
Stroke...(in.) 6
Compression ratio.......................................5.5:1
Governed speed.......................................(rpm) 2,150
Brake horsepower (max w/std accessories)..............202 at (rpm) 2,150
Torque (max w/std accessories)..................642 lb-ft at (rpm) 900

ADDITIONAL DATA

Live axles, type............................double-reduction, full-floating
Transmission, type.................................constant-mesh

TRUCK, GASOLINE TANK, 6-TON, 6 x 6, 2,000-GAL

(White, Model 666, 1942–43–44)

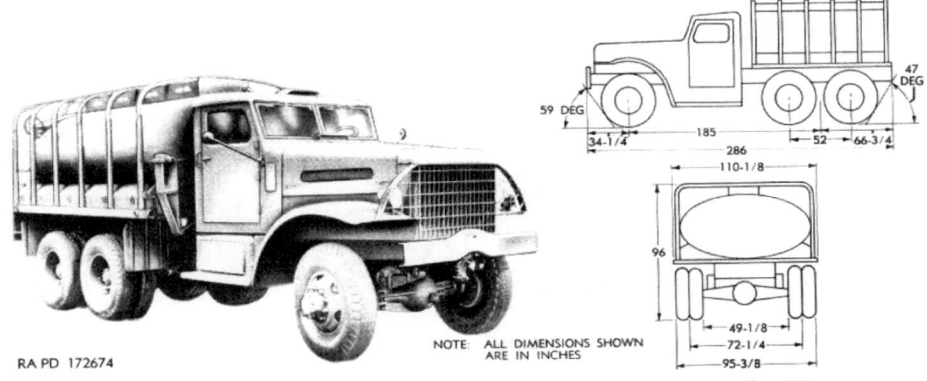

RA PD 172674

NOTE: ALL DIMENSIONS SHOWN
ARE IN INCHES

Technical Manuals: 9–813, 9–1813, 9–1825A, 9–1826C, 9–1827A, 9–1828A, 9–1829A, 9–1832A; **Supply Catalog:** SNL G–514.

Classification: Nonclassified.

Purpose: To transport and dispense gasoline.

GENERAL DATA

Crew..2
Weight (lb).....................Net 23,820; Payload 12,000; Gross 35,820
Live-axle gear ratio...7.33:1
Axle load (lb):
    Empty..............................front 8,580; rear (each) 7,620
    Loaded............................front 8,780; rear (each) 13,520
Tires:
    Ply 12..............................Size 10.00 x 22; Pressure (psi) 70
    Tread, center-to-center, front..........................(in.) 73¼
Shipping dimensions, uncrated...................(cu ft) 1,760; (sq ft) 220
Vehicle dimensions:
    Ground clearance...(in.) 10¾
    Distance from rear of cab to center of rear suspension..........(in.) 96
    Distance from rear of cab to front of body.....................(in.) 18
Electrical system (12-volt starting)..............................(volts) 6
    No. of batteries...(6-volt) 2
    Type of ground..positive
Fuel octane rating..72
Capacities:
    Fuel..(gal) 80
    Cooling system..(qt) 58
    Crankcase, refill...(qt) 16
    Transmission..(qt) 9
    Transfer...(qt) 3½
    Live axles, each (qt)...........................front 8; rear 6
Brakes:
    Manufacturer................Bendix-Westinghouse; Type; air
    Parking brake, type...................................transfer
Transmission:
    Forward speeds..4
    Gear ratio...........................High 1:1; Low 6.54:1
Transfer:
    Speeds..2
    Gear ratio...........................High 1:1; Low 2.55:1

PERFORMANCE

Computed grade ability in lowest gear, loaded.................(percent) 65
Turning radius..(ft) 41
Fording depth...(in.) 24
Fuel consumption, loaded..(mpg) 3¾
Cruising range, loaded..(mi) 300
Allowable speed, governed...(mph) 35

ENGINE

Manufacturer...Hercules; Model HXD
Type.....................4-cycle, L-head; No. of cylinders (in line) 6
Displacement...(cu in.) 855
Bore...(in.) 5½
Stroke...(in.) 6
Compression ratio...5.49:1
Governed speed..(rpm) 2,150
Brake horsepower (max w/std accessories)...............202 at (rpm) 2,150
Torque (max w/std accessories).......................642 lb-ft at (rpm) 900

·ADDITIONAL DATA

Live axles, type.........................double-reduction, full-floating
Transmission, type..constant-mesh

TRUCK, HEAVY WRECKER, 6-TON, 6 x 6, M1

(Ward La France, Model 1000, Series 1, 2, 3, and 4; Kenworth, Models 570, 571, and 572)

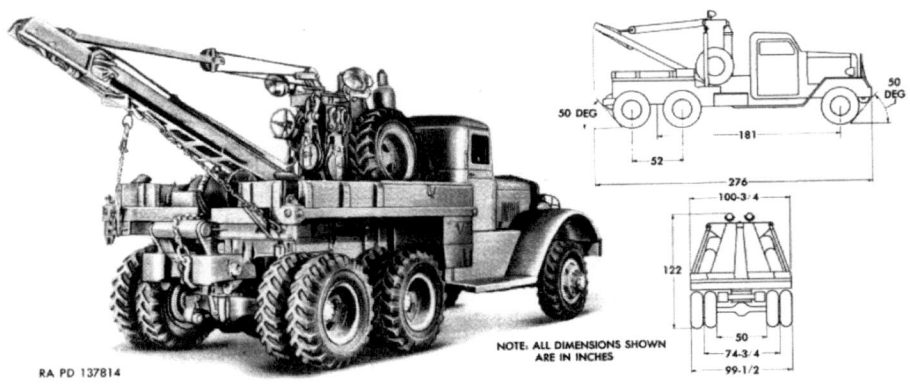

RA PD 137814

NOTE: ALL DIMENSIONS SHOWN
ARE IN INCHES

Technical Manual: 9-796; Supply Catalog: SNL G-116.

Classification: Limited Standard.

Purpose: To tow, salvage, and recover disabled heavy vehicles and equipment and for numerous repair operations where heavy hoist and winch equipment is needed.

GENERAL DATA

Crew	2
Weight (lb)	Net 27,330; Payload 8,000; Gross 35,330
Live-axle gear ratio	8.27:1
Axle load (lb):	
Empty	front 7,652; rear (each) 9,839
Loaded	front 9,892; rear (each) 12,719
Tires:	
Ply 12	Size 11 x 20; Pressure (psi) 70
Tread, center-to-center, front	(in.) 72
Shipping dimensions, uncrated	(cu ft) 1,900; (sq ft) 194
Vehicle dimensions (in.):	
Ground clearance	11
Loading height, empty	56
Pintle height, loaded	36
Electrical system	(volts) 12
No. of batteries	1
Type of ground	positive
Fuel octane rating	68
Capacities:	
Fuel	(gal) 100
Cooling system	(qt) 40
Crankcase, refill	(qt) 10
Transmission	(qt) 12
Transfer	(qt) 2½
Axles (qt)	front 8; rear (each) 7
Winch	
Oil capacity (qt)	front 2; rear 4½
Load capacity (lb)	front 20,000; rear 47,500
Boom winch gear case	(qt) 2
Crane winch gear case	(qt) 2
Pivot gear case	(qt) 4
Crane lift capacity (max)	(lb) 20,000
Brakes:	
Manufacturer	Bendix-Westinghouse; Type; air
Parking brake, type	transfer

GENERAL DATA—Continued

Transmission:	
Forward speeds	5
Gear ratio	High 0.776:1; Fourth 1:1; Low 7.07:1
Transfer:	
Speeds	2
Gear ratio	High 1:1; Low 2.55:1

PERFORMANCE

Computed grade ability in lowest gear, loaded	(percent) 54
Turning radius	(ft) 44
Fording depth	(in.) 40
Fuel consumption, loaded	(mpg) 2½
Cruising range, loaded	(mi) 250
Allowable speed, governed	(mph) 45
Maximum recommended towed load, gross	(lb) 60,000

ENGINE

Manufacturer	Continental; Model 22R
Type	Valve-in-head, 4-cycle; No. of cylinders (in line) 6
Displacement	(cu in.) 4½
Bore	(in.) 4½
Stroke	(in.) 5¼
Compression ratio	5.23:1
Governed speed	(rpm) 2,400
Brake horsepower (max w/std accessories)	145 at (rpm) 2,400
Torque (max)	372 lb-ft at (rpm) 1,200

ADDITIONAL DATA

Live axles, type	double-reduction, full-floating
Transmission, type	constant-mesh

TRUCK, HEAVY WRECKER, 6-TON, 6 x 6, M1A1

(Ward La France, Model 1000, Series 5; Kenworth, Model 573)

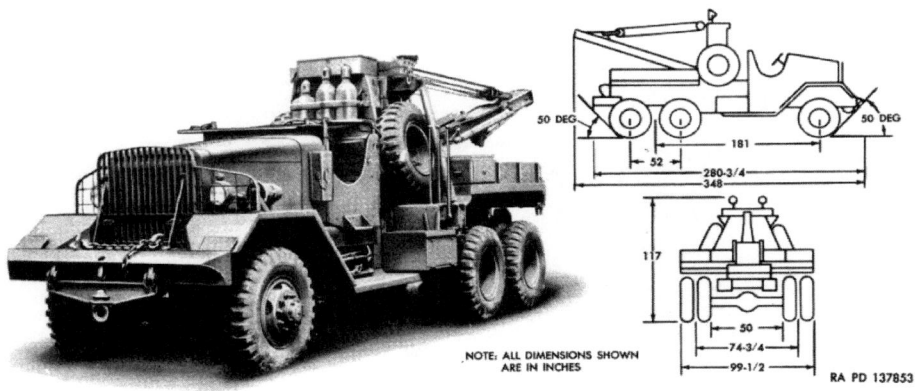

NOTE: ALL DIMENSIONS SHOWN
ARE IN INCHES

RA PD 137853

Technical Manual: 9-796; Supply Catalog: SNL G-116.

Vehicle illustrated: Ward La France.
Classification: Standard.

Purpose: To tow, salvage, and recover disabled heavy vehicles and equipment and for numerous repair operations where heavy hoist and winch equipment is needed.

GENERAL DATA

Crew..2
Weight (lb)......................Net 30,000; Payload 8,000; Gross 38,000
Live-axle gear ratio...8.27:1
Axle load (lb):
  Empty.......................................front 8,400; rear (each) 10,800
  Loaded......................................front 10,640; rear (each) 13,680
Tires:
  Ply 12......................................Size 11.00 x 20; Pressure (psi) 70
  Tread, center-to-center, front...........................(in.) 73
Shipping dimensions, uncrated.................(cu ft) 1,900; (sq ft) 195
Vehicle dimensions:
  Ground clearance.......................................(in.) 11
  Loading height..(in.) 56
  Pintle height, loaded...................................(in.) 36
Electrical system..(volts) 12
  No. of batteries..1
  Type of ground.......................................positive
Fuel octane rating...68
Capacities:
  Fuel...(gal) 100
  Cooling system..(qt) 35
  Crankcase, refill.......................................(qt) 10
  Transmission..(qt) 12

  Transfer..(qt) 2½
  Axles (qt)......................................front 8; rear (each) 7
  Winch:
    Oil capacity (qt)................................front 1½; rear 4
    Load capacity (lb)..................front 20,000; rear 47,500
  Rear-winch transmission................................(qt) 3
  Crane:
    Oil capacity.......................................(qt) 3½
    Lift capacity (max).............................(lb) 16,000
Brakes:
  Manufacturer........................Bendix-Westinghouse; Type; air
  Parking brake, type.....................................transfer

GENERAL DATA—Continued

Transmission:
  Forward speeds...5
  Gear ratio.....................High 0.776:1; Fourth 1:1; Low 7.07:1
Transfer:
  Speeds...2
  Gear ratio.............................High 1:1; Low 2.55:1

PERFORMANCE

Computed grade ability in lowest gear, loaded................(percent) 54
Turning radius..(ft) 35
Fording depth...(in.) 40
Fuel consumption, loaded....................................(mpg) 2½
Cruising range, loaded......................................(mi) 250
Allowable speed, governed...................................(mph) 45
Maximum recommended toward load, gross......................(lb) 60,000

ENGINE

Manufacturer.....................................Continental; Model 22R
Type...................Valve-in-head, 4-cycle; No. of cylinders (in line) 6
Displacement..(cu in.) 501
Bore..(in.) 4½
Stroke..(in.) 5¼
Compression ratio...5.23:1
Governed speed..(rpm) 2,400
Brake horsepower (max w/std accessories)............145 at (rpm) 2,400
Torque (max)..372 lb-ft at (rpm) 1,200

ADDITIONAL DATA

Height with gun mount.......................................(in.) 119½
Live axles, type..........................double-reduction, full-floating
Transmission, type..constant-mesh

TRUCK, PRIME MOVER, 6-TON, 6 x 6, W/WINCH
(Corbitt Model 50SD6)

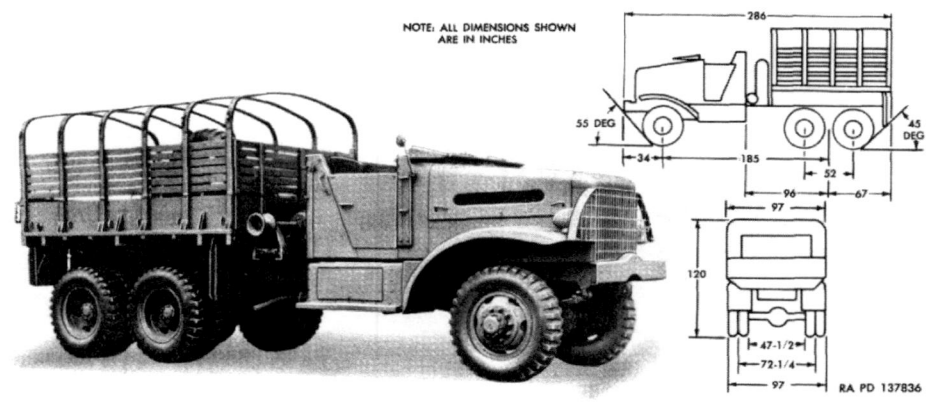

NOTE: ALL DIMENSIONS SHOWN ARE IN INCHES

RA PD 137836

Technical Manuals: 9-813, 9-1813, 9-1825A, 9-1826C, 9-1827A, 9-1828A, 9-1832A; Supply Catalog: SNL G-512.

Classification: Standard.

Purpose: To tow heavy artillery and transport personnel and cargo.

GENERAL DATA

Crew...2
Weight (lb)...Net 22,070
  Payload:
    Off highway...........................12,350*; gross 34,420
    On highway..............................20,000; gross 42,070
Live-axle gear ratio..7.33:1
Axle load (lb):
  Empty................................front 8,650; rear (each) 6,710
  Loaded:
    Off highway....................front 8,820; rear (each) 12,800
    On highway.....................front 8,900; rear (each) 16,585
Tires:
  Ply 12........................Size 10.00 x 22; Pressure (psi) 70
  Tread, center-to-center, front.........................(in.) 73¼
Shipping dimensions, uncrated...........(cu ft) 1,450; (sq ft) 193
Vehicle dimensions:
  Ground clearance.......................................(in.) 10
  Loading height, empty.................................(in.) 57½
  Pintle height, loaded..................................(in.) 32
  Body inside dimensions (in.):
    ʹ Length..................132; Width 93; Height 60
  Body cargo space.....................................(cu ft) 427
Electrical system (12-volt starting)....................(volts) 6
  No. of batteries......................................(6-volt) 2
  Type of ground...positive
Fuel octane rating..70
Capacities:
  Fuel..(gal) 80
  Cooling system...(qt) 65
  Crankcase, refill......................................(qt) 14
  Transfer...(qt) 3½
  Transmission...(qt) 9
  Axles (qt).....................................front 8; rear (each) 6
  Winch:
    Oil capacity..(qt) 1
    Load capacity...................................(lb) 15,000

*With maximum trailed load, the payload should be reduced to 10,350 lb.

GENERAL DATA—Continued

Brakes:
  Manufacturer...........................Westinghouse; Type; air
  Parking brake, type..................................transfer
Transmission:
  Forward speeds...4
  Gear ratio.........................High 1:1; Low 6.51:1
Transfer:
  Speeds..2
  Gear ratio.........................High 1:1; Low 2.55:1

PERFORMANCE

Computed grade ability in lowest gear, loaded...........(percent) 65
Turning radius (ft)....................Right 41; Left 42
Fording depth..(in.) 24
Fuel consumption, loaded..............................(mpg) 2½
Cruising range, loaded................................(mi) 200
Allowable speed, governed.............................(mph) 37½
Maximum recommended towed load:
  Off highway, gross..................................(lb) 16,500
  On highway, gross...................................(lb) 40,000

ENGINE

Manufacturer: Hercules..............................Model HXD
Type.................L-head, 4-cycle; No. of cylinders (in line) 6
Displacement..(cu in.) 855
Bore..(in.) 5½
Stroke..(in.) 6
Compression ratio....................................5.49:1
Governed speed.......................................(rpm) 2,150
Brake horsepower (max w/std accessories)........202 at (rpm) 2,150
Torque (max w/std accessories)..............642 lb-ft at (rpm) 900

ADDITIONAL DATA

Equipped with controls for electric trailer brakes.
Live axles, type....................double-reduction, full-floating
Transmission, type.................................constant-mesh

TRUCK, PRIME MOVER AND CARGO, 6-TON, 6 x 6, W/WINCH

(White, Model 666, 1942–43–44)

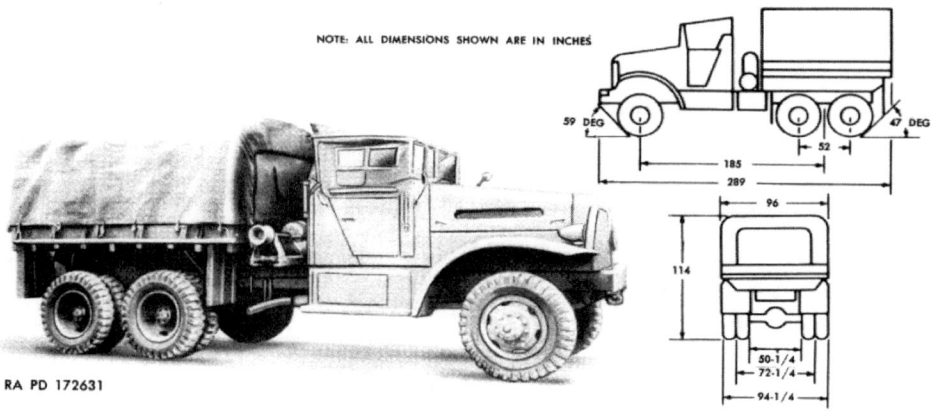

NOTE: ALL DIMENSIONS SHOWN ARE IN INCHES

RA PD 172631

Technical Manuals: 9-813, 9-1813, 9-1825A, 9-1826C, 9-1827A, 9-1828A, 9-1829A, 9-1832A; Supply Catalog: SNL G-514.

Classification: Standard.

Purpose: To tow heavy artillery and transport personnel and cargo.

GENERAL DATA

Crew..2
Weight (lb): Net..22,900
    Payload.........................off highway 12,000; on highway 19,100
    Gross...........................off highway 34,900; on highway 42,000
Live-axle gear ratio...7:33:1
Axle load (lb):
    Empty...front 8,580; rear (each) 7,160
    Loaded:
      Off highway....................front 8,780; rear (each) 13,060
      On highway.....................front 8,980; rear (each) 16,540
Tires:
    Ply..................12; Size 10.00 x 22; Pressure (psi) 70
    Tread, center-to-center, front.........................(in.) 73¼
Shipping dimensions, uncrated..............(cu ft) 1,840; (sq ft) 193
Vehicle dimensions:
    Ground clearance....................................(in.) 18¾
    Loading height, empty...............................(in.) 58¾
    Pintle height, loaded................................(in.) 29¼
    Body inside dimensions (in.):
      Length...............90; Width 92; Height 43¼
    Body cargo space..................................(cu ft) 208
Electrical system (12-volt starting)......................(volts) 6
    No. of batteries....................................(6-volt) 2
    Type of ground.....................................positive
Fuel octane rating..72
Capacities:
    Fuel..(gal) 80
    Cooling system.....................................(qt) 58
    Crankcase, refill...................................(qt) 14
    Transmission.......................................(qt) 9
    Transfer...(qt) 3½
    Axles (qt)...........................front 11; rear (each) 12
Winch..................Oil capacity (qt) 3; Load capacity (lb) 25,000
Brakes:
    Manufacturer.................Bendix-Westinghouse; Type; air
    Parking brake, type................................propeller-shaft

GENERAL DATA—Continued

Transmission:
    Forward speeds...4
    Gear ratio............................High 1:1; Low 6.54:1
Transfer:
    Speeds..2
    Gear ratio............................High 1:1; Low 2.55:1

PERFORMANCE

Computed grade ability in lowest gear, loaded..............(percent) 65
Turning radius..(ft 41)
Fording depth...(in.) 24
Fuel consumption, loaded.......................................(mpg) 3¾
Cruising range, loaded..(mi) 300
Allowable speed, governed......................................(mph) 35
Maximum recommended towed load:
    Off highway...................................gross (lb) 20,000
    On highway....................................gross (lb) 40,000

ENGINE

Manufacturer..............................Hercules; Model HXD
Type..................4-cycle, L-head; No. of cylinders (in line) 6
Displacement.................................(cu in.) 855
Bore...(in.) 5½
Stroke.......................................(in.) 6
Compression ratio.............................5.5:1
Governed speed...............................(rpm) 2,150
Brake horsepower (max w/std accessories).........202 at (rpm) 2,150
Torque (max w/std accessories).............642 lb-ft at (rpm) 900

ADDITIONAL DATA

Live axles, type...............double reduction, full-floating
Transmission, type............................constant-mesh

TRUCK, TRACTOR, 6-TON, 6 x 6

(White, Model 666, 1942–43–44)

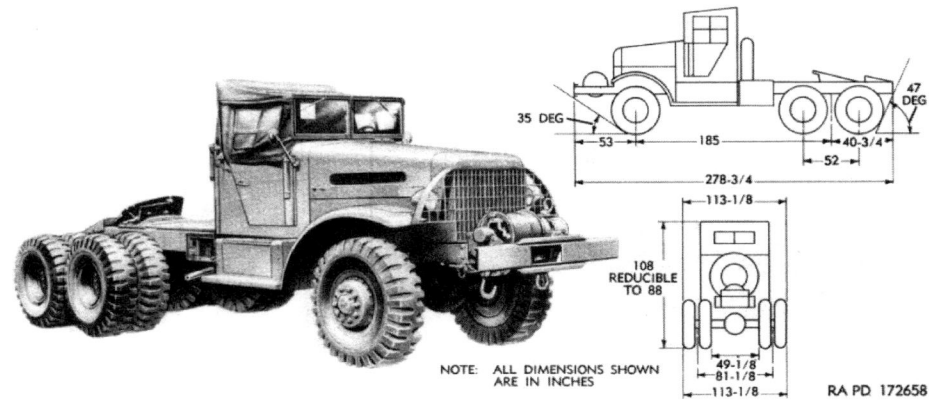

NOTE: ALL DIMENSIONS SHOWN ARE IN INCHES

RA PD 172658

Technical Manuals: 9–813, 9–1813, 9–1825A, 9–1826C, 9–1827A, 9–1828A, 9–1829A, 9–1832A; **Supply Catalog:** SNL G–514.

Classification: Standard.

Purpose: To tow semitrailers.

GENERAL DATA

Crew..2
Weight (lb)...Net 21,530
  Payload........................off highway 12,000; on highway 20,000
  Gross............................off highway 33,530; on highway 41,530
Live-axle gear ratio...7.33:1
Axle load (lb):
  Empty.....................................front 9,080; rear (each) 6,225
  Loaded:
    Off highway.......................front 9,480; rear (each) 12,025
    On highway.......................front 9,580; rear (each) 15,975
Tires:
  Ply 12........................Size 14.00 x 20; Pressure: (psi) 70
  Tread, center-to-center, front............................(in.) 75½
Shipping dimensions, uncrated, w/winch:
  (cu ft) 1,970..(sq ft) 218
Vehicle dimensions:
  Ground clearance.......................................(in.) 13¾
  Pintle height, empty...................................(in.) 33½
  Height of frame...(in.) 48½
  Height of fifth wheel...................................(in.) 59⅝
  Horizontal center-to-center distance between fifth wheel and axle
    (in.) 3¼
Electrical system (12-volt starting)...................(volts) 6
  No. of batteries..2
  Type of ground..positive
Fuel octane rating...72
Capacities:
  Fuel...(gal) 80
  Cooling system...(qt) 58
  Crankcase, refill...(qt) 16
  Transmission..(qt) 9
  Transfer..(qt) 3½
  Live axles, each (qt).........................front 8; rear 6
  Winch:
    Oil capacity..(qt) 3
    Load capacity.....................................(lb) 25,000

GENERAL DATA—Continued

Brakes:
  Manufacturer: Bendix-Westinghouse.............Type: air
  Parking brake, type...transfer
Transmission:
  Forward speeds...4
  Gear ratio...............................High 1:1; Low 6.54:1
Transfer:
  Speeds..2
  Gear ratio...............................High 1:1; Low 2.55:1

PERFORMANCE

Computed grade ability in lowest gear, loaded.................(percent) 65
Turning radius...(ft) 41
Fording depth...(in.) 24
Fuel consumption, loaded..............................(mpg) 3¾
Cruising range, loaded..................................(mi) 300
Allowable speed, governed...........................(mph) 35
Maximum semitrailer, gross........................(lb) 30,000

ENGINE

Manufacturer: Hercules.........................Model HXD
Type.......................4-cycle, L-head; No. of cylinders (in line) 6
Displacement..(cu in.) 855
Bore...(in.) 5½
Stroke..(in.) 6
Compression ratio......................................5.49:1
Governed speed..(rpm) 2,150
Brake horsepower (max w/std accessories)...............202 at (rpm) 2,150
Torque (max w/std accessories).....................642 lb-ft at (rpm) 900

ADDITIONAL DATA

Equipped with controls for trailer electric brakes.
Live axles, type...............................double-reduction, full-floating
Transmission, type..constant-mesh

TRUCK, PRIME MOVER, 7½-TON, 6 x 6, W/WINCH
(Mack, Models N02, N03, N06, N07)

NOTE: ALL DIMENSIONS SHOWN ARE IN INCHES

RA PD 172675

Technical Manuals: 10-1679, 9-1826C, 9-1828A, 9-1829A; Supply Catalog: SNL G-532.

Classification: Standard.

GENERAL DATA

Crew..2
Weight (lb) ....Net 29,103
  Payload.............................off highway 15,350;* on highway 20,897
  Gross.............................off highway 44,453; on highway 50,000
Live-axle gear ratio..9.02:1
Axle load (lb):
  Empty.................................front 12,634; rear (each) 8,235
  Loaded:
    Off highway.....................front 13,363; rear (each) 15,545
    On highway.....................front 13,581; rear (each) 18,209
Tires:
  Ply 14..............Size 12.00 x 24; Pressure (psi) front 80; rear 65
  Tread, center-to-center, front.......................(in.) 76½
Shipping dimensions, uncrated..........(cu ft) 2,200; (sq ft) 212
Vehicle dimensions:
  Ground clearance............................(in.) 12⁹⁄₁₆
  Loading height, empty......................(in.) 63¼
  Pintle height, loaded......................(in.) 42⅝
  Body inside dimensions (in.):
    Length.................................132
    Width....................................96
    Height...................................58
  Body cargo space..........................(cu ft) 425
Electrical system (volts)..................6; starting 12
  No. of batteries..........................(6-volt) 2
  Type of ground...........................positive
Brakes:
  Manufacturer; Bendix-Westinghouse................Type, air
  Parking brake, type......................propeller-shaft
Transmission:
  Forward speeds.............................5
  Gear ratio.......................High 1:1; Low 8.05:1
Transfer:
  Speeds....................................2
  Gear ratio.......................High 1:1; Low 2.55:1

*With maximum towed load, the payload should be reduced to 10,350 lb.

Purpose: To tow heavy artillery (155-mm gun and 8-in. howitzer) and transport general cargo and personnel.

GENERAL DATA—Continued

Fuel octane rating...70
Capacities:
  Fuel....................................(gal) 160
  Cooling system..........................(qt) 54
  Crankcase, refill.......................(qt) 19
  Transmission............................(qt) 14
  Transfer (w/PTO)........................(qt) 15
  Axles (qt)...................front 7½; rear (each) 11¼
  Winch:
    Oil capacity (qt)..................3
    Load capacity (lb)............40,000

PERFORMANCE

Computed grade ability in lowest gear, loaded............(percent) 65
Turning radius..(ft) 36
Fording depth..(in.) 48
Fuel consumption, loaded.................................(mpg) 2½
Cruising range, loaded...................................(mi) 400
Allowable speed, governed................................(mph) 32
Maximum recommended towed load:
  Off highway..........................gross (lb) 32,000
  On highway...........................gross (lb) 50,000

ENGINE

Manufacturer: Mack....................................Model EY
Type.................4-cycle, valve-in-head; No. of cylinders (in line) 6
Displacement...(cu in.) 707
Bore...(in.) 5
Stroke...(in.) 6
Compression ratio.......................................5.35:1
Governed speed.....................................(rpm) 2,100
Brake horsepower (max w/std accessories).........159 at (rpm) 2,100
Torque (max w/std accessories).............534 lb-ft at (rpm) 800

ADDITIONAL DATA

Live axles, type......................double-reduction, full-floating
Transmission, type..............................constant-mesh

TRUCK, PRIME MOVER, 12-TON, 6 x 4, M20

(Diamond T, Models 980 and 981)

Used w/TRAILER, 45-ton, 12-wheel, Transporter, M9, as component of TRUCK-TRAILER, 45-Ton, Tank Transporter, M19

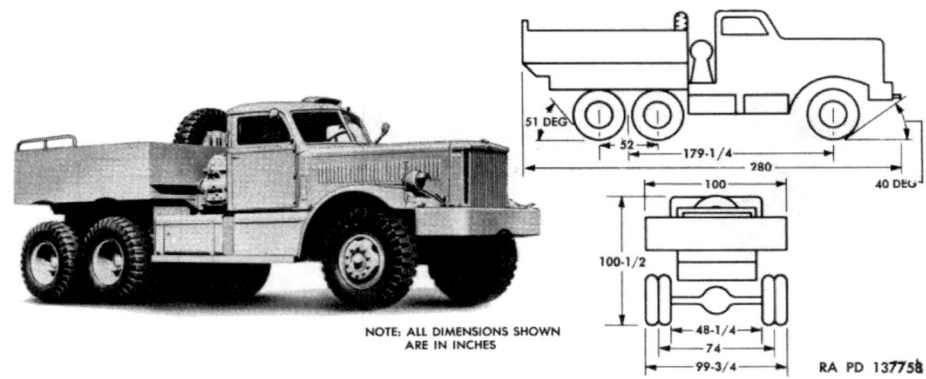

NOTE: ALL DIMENSIONS SHOWN ARE IN INCHES

RA PD 137758

Technical Manuals: 9-768, 9-1768A, 9-1768B, 9-1768C, 9-1825A, 9-1827A, 9-1829A; Supply Catalog: SNL G-159.

Classification: Substitute Standard.

GENERAL DATA

Crew..2
Weight (lb)......................Net 26,950; Payload 18,050; Gross 45,000
Live-axle gear ratio...11.66:1
Axle load (lb):
    Empty...........................front 10,950; rear (each) 8,000
    Loaded.......................front 11,300; rear (each) 16,850
Tires: Ply 14..............................Size 12.00 x 20; Pressure (psi) 80
Shipping dimensions, uncrated...............(cu ft) 1,630; (sq ft) 194
Vehicle dimensions:
    Ground clearance.....................................(in.) 11¼
    Loading height, empty................................(in.) 57¾
    Pintle height, loaded................................(in.) 30
    Ballast body inside dimensions (in.):
      Length 102..................Width 94; Height 24
Electrical system.......................................(volts) 24
    No. of batteries.....................................(6-volt) 4
    Type of ground...................................positive
Fuel octane rating...45
Capacities:
    Fuel (diesel fuel oil)................................(gal) 150
    Cooling system......................................(qt) 61
    Crankcase, refill...................................(qt) 26
    Transmission (qt)..............Main 9; Auxiliary w/PTO 8½
Live axles (each).........................Oil capacity (qt) 10
Winch..............Oil capacity (qt) 4; Load capacity (lb) 40,000
Brakes:
    Manufacturer.................Bendix-Westinghouse; Type, Air
    Parking brake, type.............................transmission
Transmission:
    Forward speeds.....................................4
    Gear ratio........................High 1:1; Low 5.55:1
Auxiliary transmission:
    Speeds...3
    Gear ratio........High 0.754:1; Second 1:1; Low 2.09:1

Purpose: To recover and transport damaged tanks and matériel weighing up to 90,000 pounds in connection with trailer, 45-ton, M9, component of 45-ton tank transporter truck-trailer, M19.

PERFORMANCE

Computed grade ability in lowest gear w/towed load...........(percent) 27
Turning radius (ft)...........................right 32½; left 36
Fording depth.....................................(in.) 22
Fuel consumption, loaded............................(mpg) 2
Cruising range, loaded..............................(mi) 300
Allowable speed, governed...........................(mph) 23
Maximum recommended towed load, gross..............(lb) 115,000

ENGINE

Manufacturer...........................Hercules; Model DXFE
Type............Valve-in-head, 4-cycle diesel, No. of cylinders (in line) 6
Displacement.....................................(cu in.) 895
Bore...(in.) 5¼
Stroke...(in.) 6
Compression ratio................................14.8:1
Governed speed...................................(rpm) 1,600
Brake horsepower (max w/std accessories)...........185 at (rpm) 1,600
Torque (max)........................665 lb-ft at (rpm) 1,200

ADDITIONAL DATA

Live axles, type.................double-reduction, full-floating
Transmission, type...............................constant-mesh

TRUCK, TRACTOR, 12-TON, 6 x 6, M26 AND M26A1

(Pacific Car and Foundry Co)

Used w/SEMITRAILER, 45-ton, 8-wheel, transporter, M15 and SEMITRAILER, 45-ton, 8-wheel, transporter, M15A1 as component of TRUCK-TRAILER, 40-ton, tank recovery, M25

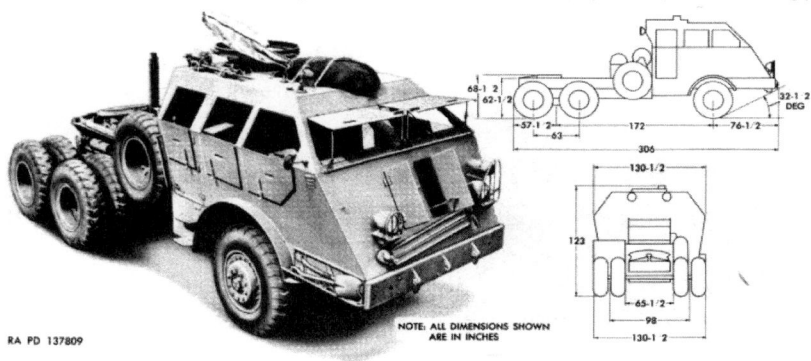

RA PD 137809

NOTE: ALL DIMENSIONS SHOWN ARE IN INCHES

Technical Manuals: 9-767, 9-1767A, 9-1767B, 9-1767C; **Supply Catalog:** SNL G-160.

Classification: Limited Standard.

Purpose: To tow 40-ton semitrailers M15 and M15A1 in recovery and transportation of damaged tanks, and matériel weighing up to 80,000 lb.

GENERAL DATA

Crew	7
Weight (lb)	Net 48,895
Payload	On fifth wheel 60,000; Gross 108,895
Live-axle gear ratio	7.69:1
Axle load (lb):	
Empty	front 22,950; rear 25,945
Loaded	front 22,950; rear 85,945
Tires:	
Ply 20	Size 14 x 24; Pressure (psi) 90
Tread, center-to-center, front	(in.) 82
Shipping dimensions, uncrated	(cu ft) 2,957; (sq ft) 278
Vehicle dimensions:	
Ground clearance	(in.) 15
Pintle height, loaded	(in.) 39
Center of fifth wheel to center of jackshaft	(in.) 4
Height to center of fifth wheel	(in.) 68½
Height to rear of fifth wheel	(in.) 62½
Electrical system	(volts) 12
No. of batteries	(6-volt) 2
Type of ground	negative
Fuel octane rating	72
Capacities:	
Fuel	(gal) 120
Cooling system	(qt) 56
Crankcase, refill	(qt) 28
Transmission (qt)	main 8½; auxiliary 10
Transfer	(qt) 2½
Axles (qt)	front 20; rear 14
Steering gear	(qt) 8½
Winch:	
Oil capacity, each	(qt) 4
Load capacity (lb)	front 35,000; rear (2) (ea) 60,000
Chain oilers	(qt) 20
Hydraulic steering	(qt) 10
Brakes:	
Manufacturer	Bendix-Westinghouse; Type; air
Parking brake, type	transfer

GENERAL DATA—Continued

Transmission:	
Forward speeds	4
Gear ratio	High 1:1; Low 5.55:1
Auxiliary transmission:	
Speeds	3
Transfer:	
Speeds	1
Gear ratio	1.91:1

PERFORMANCE

Computed grade ability in lowest gear, loaded	(percent) 30
Turning radius	(ft) 40
Fording depth	(in.) 56
Fuel consumption, w/towed load	(mpg) 4
Cruising range, w/towed load	(mi) 120
Allowable speed, governed	(mph) 28
Maximum semitrailer, gross	(lb) 117,500

ENGINE

Manufacturer	Hall Scott; Model 440
Type	Valve-in-head, 4-cycle; No. of cylinders (in line) 6
Displacement	(cu in.) 1,090
Bore	(in.) 5¾
Stroke	(in.) 7
Compression ratio	5.7:1
Governed speed	(rpm) 2,100
Brake horsepower (max w/std accessories)	240 at (rpm) 2,000
Torque (max w/std accessories)	810 lb-ft at (rpm) 1,200

ADDITIONAL DATA

Winch, front 300 ft ¾-in. cable.
Winches, rear (2) 300 ft ⅞-in. cable (each).

Live axles, type	double-reduction, full-floating
Transmission, type	constant-mesh

VEHICLE, ARMORED INFANTRY, FULL-TRACK, T18E1

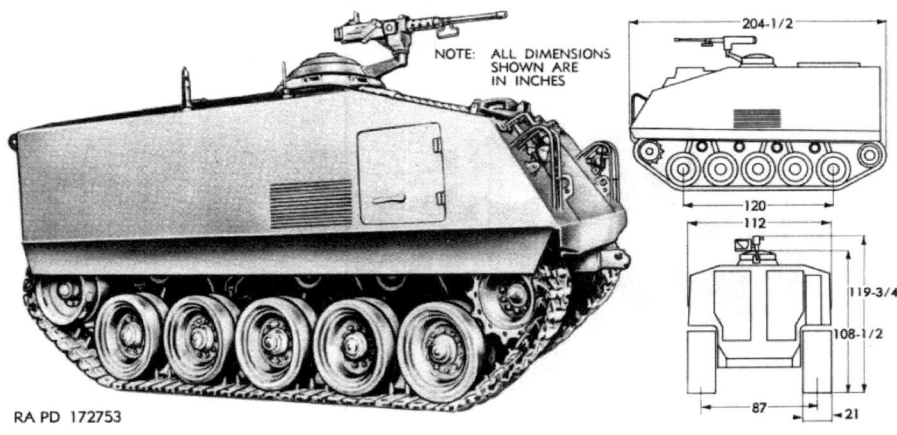

NOTE: ALL DIMENSIONS SHOWN ARE IN INCHES

RA PD 172753

Technical Manuals: 9-755B, 9-1730B, 9-1730F, 9-1825C, 9-1825E, 9-1826B, 9-1828A, 9-1829A; Supply Catalog: SNL G-260.

Armament: 1 gun, machine, cal. .50, Browning, M2, heavy barrel (flexible) mounted on revolving ring at top of vehicle.

Ammunition: 1,800 rounds, cal. .50; 10 rockets; 180 rounds, cal. .30 carbine.

Fire Control and Vision Devices: Periscope, M17 (vision).

GENERAL DATA

Crew	1; Passengers (including crew) 12
Weight, fighting	(lb) 42,000
Shipping dimensions, uncrated	(cu ft) 1,438; (sq ft) 159
Ground pressure	(psi) 8.3
Ground clearance	(in.) 17¾
Pintle height, loaded	(in.) 29¾₆
Electrical system	(volts) 24
No. of batteries	(12-volt) 2
Type of ground	negative
Fuel octane rating	80
Capacities:	
Fuel	(gal) 150
Crankcase, refill	(qt) 48
Auxiliary-engine crankcase, refill	(qt) 4
Transmission, cross-drive (including cooler)	(qt) 64
Final drive	(each) (qt) 2

Brakes: Hand-lever-controlled, hydraulic, multiple-disk steering brakes. Pedal operates them as service brakes.

Parking brake, type	pedal for locking service brakes
No. of ranges (High, Low, and Reverse)	3
Ratio from engine output to torque-converter input	0.769:1
Torque-converter stall ratio	4:1
Ratio from torque converter output shaft to final-drive flange:	
High range	1.4:1; Low range 5.34:1
Final-drive gear ratio	4:1
Hull construction	welded steel plate

Purpose: To transport, and furnish protection for troops with full equipment.

Communications: Location No. 1: (SCR–508) or (SCR–528) or (SCR–608B) or (AN/VRC–7) or (BC–667); or (SCR–510 or SCR–610 or SCR 619) and (BC–667); or (SCR–510 or SCR–610 or SCR–619) and (AN/VRC–7). Location No. 2: (SCR–506) or (SCR–694C) or (AN/GRC–9) or (AN/ARC–3) or (AN/GRC–5).

PERFORMANCE

Maximum grade ability	(percent) 60
Fording depth:	
W/o kit	(in.) 48
W/kit	(in.) 80
Maximum width of ditch vehicle can cross	(in.) 66
Maximum vertical obstacle vehicle can climb	(in.) 18
Fuel consumption (average conditions)	(mpg) 0.8
Cruising range (average conditions)	(mi) 115
Maximum speed	(mph) 43
Maximum recommended towed load, gross	(lb) 14,000

ENGINE

Manufacturer	Continental; Model: AO–895–4
Type	4-cycle, valve-in-head; air cooled
No. of cylinders (horizontal opposed)	6
Displacement	(cu in.) 896
Bore	(in.) 5¾
Stroke	(in.) 5¾
Compression ratio	6.5:1
Governed speed	(rpm) 2,800
Brake horsepower (max w/std accessories)	295 at (rpm) 2,660
Torque (max w/std accessories)	672 lb-ft at (rpm) 1,850
Type of ignition	magneto

ADDITIONAL DATA

Data given for vehicle equipped w/track, rubber-backed-steel, T–91E3 w/detachable rubber grousers.

Auxiliary generator set: Engine, GMC Model A41–1; Generator, Delco Model GM-A-8585.

VEHICLE, TANK RECOVERY, M32 SERIES

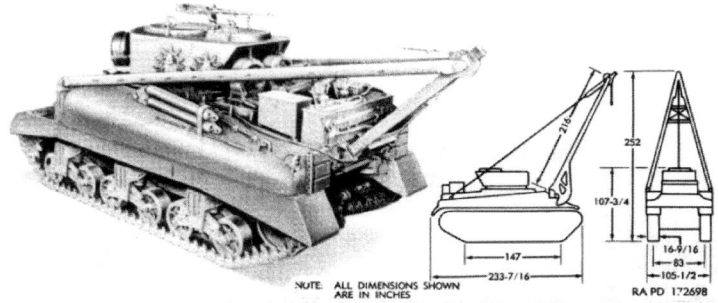

NOTE: ALL DIMENSIONS SHOWN ARE IN INCHES

RA PD 172698

Technical Manuals: 9–738, 9–1725, 9–1731D, 9–1750A, 9–1750B, 9–1750C, 9–1750D, 9–1750K, 9–1825B, 9–1826B, 9–1828A, 9–1829A; **Supply Catalogs:** SNL G–185 and G–187.

Vehicle illustrated: M32A1.

Classification: See additional data.

Purpose: To recover disabled tanks and mechanized equipment.

Armament: 1 gun, machine, cal. .50, M2, heavy barrel (flexible) ring mounted in turret; 1 gun, machine, cal. .30, M1919A4 (flexible) ball mounted at right front of hull.

Ammunition: 2,000 rounds, cal. .30, machine gun; 600 rounds, cal. .45, sub-machine-gun; 315 rounds, cal. .50; 20 hand grenades; 6 smoke pots.

GENERAL DATA

Crew	5
Weight, fighting (all models)	(lb) 61,700
Shipping dimensions, uncrated:	
M32 and M32A1	(cu ft) 1,880; (sq ft) 195
M32A1B1, M32A1B3, M32B1, and M32B3	(cu ft) 2,090; (sq ft) 218
Ground pressure	(psi) 8.9
Ground clearance	(in.) 18
Pintle height, loaded	(in.) 28
Boom:	
Height above ground in traveling position	(in.) 115½
Height above ground in lifting position	(in.) 252
Length of boom	(in.) 216
Electrical system	(volts) 24
No. of batteries	(12-volt) 2
Type of ground	negative
Fuel octane rating	80
Capacities:	
Fuel	(gal) 172
Oil tank	(qt) 36
Winch transmission	(qt) 2
Winch oil capacity	(qt) 3
Winch load capacity	(lb) 60,000
Winch and boom lifting capacity	(lb) 30,000
Winch and boom lifting and moving capacity	(lb) 20,000
Winch and boom lifting and moving capacity w/o stabilizer plates	(lb) 10,000
Transmission, differential and final drives:	
Three-piece, round-nose	(qt) 152
One-piece, sharp-nose	(qt) 164
Brakes	mechanical, controlled-differential
Parking brake, type	pedal for locking steering brakes
Transmission forward speeds	5
Gear ratio	High 0.73:1; Fourth 1:1; Low 7.56:1
Differential-drive gear ratio	3.53:1
Final-drive gear ratio	2.84:1
Hull construction	welded homogeneous armor plate
Turret	cast homogeneous armor

Fire-Control and Vision Devices: Periscope, M13, M13B1, or M6 (vision).

Communications: (SCR–619 or SCR–610) and (RC–99); or (RC–99) and (AN/VRC–3); or (SCR–528); or (AN/GRC–3, –4, –5, –6, –7, or –8); or (AN/VRC–13, –14, or –15).

PERFORMANCE

Maximum grade ability	(percent) 60
Turning radius	(ft) 31
Fording depth	(in.) 42
Maximum width of ditch vehicle can cross	(in.) 90
Maximum vertical obstacle vehicle can climb	(in.) 24
Fuel consumption (average conditions)	(mpg) 0.6
Cruising range (average conditions)	(mi) 100
Allowable speed, governed	(mph) 26
Maximum allowable towed load, gross	(lb) 20,000

ENGINE

Manufacturer	Continental; Model R975–C1
Type	4-cycle, radial, air-cooled; No. of cylinders 9
Displacement	(cu in.) 973
Bore	(in.) 5
Stroke	(in.) 5½
Compression ratio	5.7:1
Governed speed	(rpm) 2,400
Brake horsepower (max w/std accessories)	350 at (rpm) 2,400
Torque (max w/std accessories)	840 lb-ft at (rpm) 1,800
Type of ignition	magneto

ADDITIONAL DATA

Tank recovery vehicle, M32 is manufactured from the medium tank M4 chassis. Classification: Limited Standard.

Tank recovery vehicle, M32A1 is manufactured from the medium tank M4 chassis. Classification: Standard.

Tank recovery vehicle, M32A1B1 is manufactured from the medium tank M4A1 chassis. Classification: Standard.

Tank recovery vehicle, M32A1B3 is manufactured from the medium tank M4A3 chassis. Classification: Standard.

Tank recovery vehicle, M32B1 is manufactured from the medium tank M4A1 chassis. Classification: Limited Standard.

Tank recovery vehicle, M32B3 is manufactured from the medium tank M4A3 chassis. Classification: Limited Standard.

The M32 and M32B series are earlier models, and have tracks 16⅞₆ in. wide. Applicable tracks are T48, T49, T54E1, and T74. The M32A1 series are later models, and have a track 23 in. wide. Applicable tracks are T66, T80, and T84. All the recovery vehicles have fixed turrets.

VEHICLE, ARMORED, UTILITY, M39

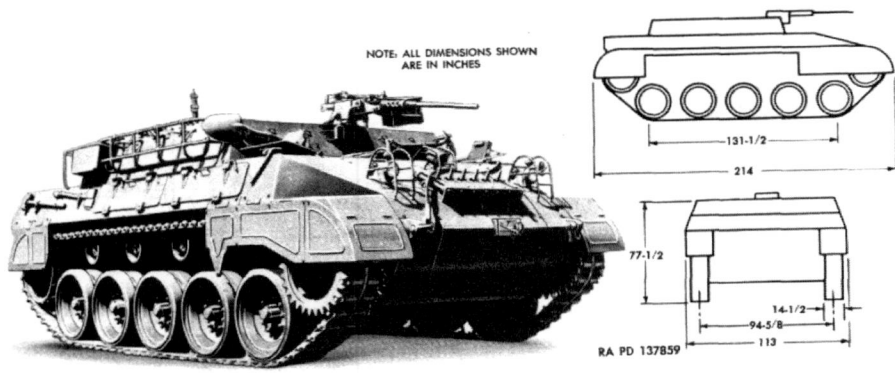

NOTE: ALL DIMENSIONS SHOWN
ARE IN INCHES

131-1/2

214

77-1/2

14-1/2

94-5/8

113

RA PD 137859

Technical Manuals: 9-755, 9-1725, 9-1731K, 9-1750D, 9-1755A, 9-1755B, 9-1826B, 9-1828A, 9-1829A; **Supply Catalog:** SNL G-163.

Classification: Standard.

GENERAL DATA

Crew	10
Weight, fighting	(lb) 35,500
Shipping dimensions, uncrated	(cu ft) 1,127; (sq ft) 168
Ground clearance	(in.) 14¾
Pintle height, loaded	(in.) 25¾
Ground pressure	(psi) 9.6
Electrical system	(volts) 24
No. of batteries	(12-volt) 2
Type of ground	negative
Fuel octane rating	80
Capacities:	
Fuel	(gal) 165
Auxiliary-generator fuel tank	(gal) 5
Transmission (and cooler)	(qt) 48
Differential and transfer (including cooler)	(qt) 20
Final drive	(each) (qt) 5
Engine oil tank	(qt) 44
Brakes	mechanical, controlled-differential
Parking brake, type	lever locks on steering brakes
Transmission forward speeds	3
Gear ratio	High 1:1; Low 2.286:1
Transfer speeds	1
Gear ratio	1:1
Differential-drive gear ratio	3.133:1
Final-drive gear ratio	2.176:1
Hull construction	welded homogeneous armor plate

PERFORMANCE

Maximum grade ability	(percent) 60
Turning radius	(ft) 33
Fording depth	(in.) 48
Maximum width of ditch vehicle can cross	(in.) 74
Maximum vertical obstacle vehicle can climb	(in.) 36
Fuel consumption (average conditions)	(mpg) 0.9
Cruising range (average conditions)	(mi) 155
Allowable speed, governed	(mph) 60
Maximum allowable towed load, gross	(lb) 10,000

ADDITIONAL DATA

Data given for vehicle w/track, steel, T69. Track, rubber, T85E1 applicable w/changed sprocket and hub assembly.

Auxiliary generator: Homelite model HRUH-28.

Purpose: To transport cargo and personnel in combat zone and use as a prime mover for artillery.

Armament: 1 gun, machine, cal. .50, Browning, heavy barrel, M2 (flexible) mounted on revolving ring in machine-gun turret.

Ammunition: 945 rounds, cal. .50; 1,620 rounds, cal. .30, carbine; 12 hand grenades; 4 smoke pots; 10 signals, aircraft, pyrotechnic.

Communications: (SCR-506) and (SCR-608B); or (SCR-619 or SCR-610) and (RC-99); or (SCR-506 or AN/GRC-9 or SCR-694C or AN/VRC-3) and (SCR-508 or SCR-510 or SCR-528); or (SCR-506) and (SCR-510) or (SCR-619) and (RC-99); or (SCR-506 or SCR-510 or SCR-619) and (RC-99); or (SCR-506) and (SCR-508) and (SCR-593 or SCR-499); or (SCR-508) and (SCR-593) and (AN/GRC-9 or SCR-694C); or (SCR-506 or SCR-508) and (VRC-3); or (SCR-508) and (SCR-510 or SCR-619 or SCR-610); or (SCR-499 or SCR-628 or AN/ARC-3); or (AN/GRC-3, -4, -5, -6, -7, or -8); or (AN/GRC-3, -4, -5, -6, -7, or -8) and (SCR-506 or AN/GRC-9 or SCR-694C); or (AN/VRQ-1, -2, or -3) and (AN/V1C-1); or (AN/VRQ-1, -2, or -3) and (SCR-506) and (AN/V1C-1, or AN/VRC-13, -14, or -15) and (SCR-593 or AN/GRR-5); or (AN/GRC-3, -4, -5, -6, -7, or -8) and (SCR-506) and (AN/ARC-3).

ENGINE

Manufacturer: Continental	Model R975C4
Type	4-cycle, radial, air-cooled; No. of cylinders 9
Displacement	(cu in.) 973
Bore	(in.) 5
Stroke	(in.) 5⅛
Governed speed	(rpm) 2,400
Brake horsepower (max w/std accessories)	400 at (rpm) 2,400
Torque (max w/std accessories)	940 lb-ft at (rpm) 1,700
Type of ignition	magneto

APPENDIX
REFERENCES

1. Publication Indexes

The following publication indexes and lists of current issue should be consulted frequently for latest changes or revisions of references given in this appendix and for new publications relating to matériel covered in this manual:

2. Supply Catalogs

The following catalog of the Department of the Army Supply Catalog pertains to this matériel:

3. Other Publications

The following explanatory publications contain information pertinent to this matériel and associated equipment:

a. General.

b. Preventive Maintenance.

INDEX

Semitrailers

Tractor Trucks—Continued

Trailers (See also Amphibious Vehicles)

Trucks—Continued

U. S. GOVERNMENT PRINTING OFFICE: O—1953